WILLIAM SHAKESPEARE

TRAGEDIES
VOLUME 2

We read Shakespeare line by line for his supernatural mastery of all the poetic resources of the English language, and play by play for his utterly human, utterly intimate feeling for our condition as individuals and as social beings. Through these works, which deal with the transcendence and the corruption of love, the exigencies of power, the domination of fate, and the algebra of human need, an entire civilization has come to understand its character and its destiny.

EVERYMAN'S LIBRARY

EVERYMAN,
I WILL GO WITH THEE,
AND BE THY GUIDE,
IN THY MOST NEED
TO GO BY THY SIDE

WILLIAM SHAKESPEARE

Tragedies

with an Introduction by Tony Tanner
General Editor – Sylvan Barnet

VOLUME 2

EVERYMAN'S LIBRARY

Alfred A. Knopf New York Toronto

164

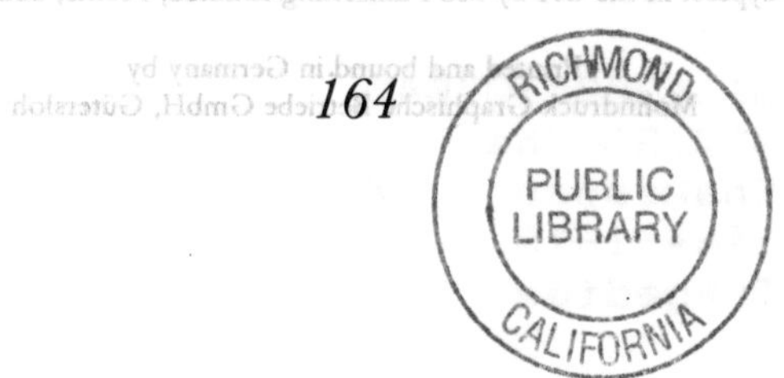

THIS IS A BORZOI BOOK
PUBLISHED BY ALFRED A. KNOPF, INC.

First included in Everyman's Library, 1906

These plays are published by arrangement with New American Library, a division of Penguin Books USA, Inc.

Typography by Peter B. Willberg

ISBN 0-679-42306-0
LC 92-52907

Library of Congress Cataloging-in-Publication Data
Shakespeare, William, 1564–1616.
Tragedies.
(Everyman's library)
ISBN 0-679-41742-1 (v. 1)
ISBN 0-679-42306-0 (v. 2)
I. Title. II. Series.

PR2763 1992 92-52907
822.3'3 CIP

Book Design by Barbara de Wilde and Carol Devine Carson

TRAGEDIES

CONTENTS

SHAKESPEARE: THE GREEK AND ROMAN PLAYS

Thou art a Roman, be not barbarous ...
(*Titus Andronicus*, I, i, 379)

dost thou not perceive
That Rome is but a wilderness of tigers?
(ibid., III, i, 53–4)

When Shakespeare perused North's translation of Plutarch's *Lives* (1579) – which he did most carefully; the main source for the last four plays in this volume is North's translation – he would have read this:

> To be short, it may be truly sayd, that the reading of histories, is the schole of wisedome, to facion mens understanding, by considering advisedly the state of the world that is past, and by marking diligently by what lawes, maners and discipline, Empires, Kingdomes and dominions, have in old time bene stablished and afterward maintayned and increased: or contrariwise changed, diminished and overthrown.

Just why the history of Rome was so important to the Elizabethans, and how and to what ends Shakespeare imaginatively deployed that history, will, I hope, be made a little clearer in the course of this introduction. But, from the outset, it is important to remember that although the following six plays are conventionally, and correctly, classified as tragedies, they are also histories. Indeed, to describe them, we can scarcely do better than avail ourselves of one of Polonius' felicitous, and too often wrongly mocked, compounds. These plays are 'tragical-historical'.

*

TITUS ANDRONICUS (1592–4)

Rome, Roman, Romans – the name of the imperial city echoes and re-echoes throughout the long opening scene (in varying forms, it occurs at least sixty times by my count). The play is certainly 'The most Lamentable Romaine Tragedie of Titus Andronicus', as the quarto has it, but it is also, and inextricably, a play about Rome itself. More will emerge concerning this Elizabethan preoccupation with Rome, but at this point it will be helpful to have an authoritative statement from T. J. B. Spencer, who made a special study of the Roman plays.

> Roman history was used as the material for political lessons, because it was one of the few bodies of consistent and continuous historical material available. English national history, in spite of patriotic sentiment, was much more limited in scope and interest, and the historians were not nearly so good as the ancient Latin writers . . . When Shakespeare turned from English history to Roman history as the subject of plays, he was touching upon grave and provocative problems of political morality . . . Rome loomed much larger in the history of the world than it does to modern historians and writers; and the Roman Empire was much more important than the Roman Republic. The potentates elected as heads of the Holy Roman Empire were still numbered from Julius Caesar by Shakespeare's contemporaries. There were very few republics in sixteenth-century Europe, but there were plenty of aspiring Roman emperors; and it was therefore from the history of the growth of monarchical rule in Rome (the political events which allowed the rise and led to the fall of Julius Caesar and the conflict between Octavian and Mark Antony) that the most useful and relevant lessons could be learnt.
>
> (*Shakespeare: The Roman Plays*, p.9)

The Rome of the opening scene displays all the panoply and adjuncts of a proud, imperial city. In the first speech we hear of 'noble patricians', 'the justice of my cause', 'the imperial diadem', 'my father's honors'. We hear of 'the gods of Rome', there are vows to heaven, priests with holy water, sacrificial rites, sacred monuments to the dead. There is a triumphal entry of the returning victorious general (Titus) along with his prisoners and spoils. We seem to be witnessing the confident ceremonies of the – very patriarchal – power of invincible Rome. But the scene starts with ferocious dispute about the imperial succession, and moves on to a brutal human sacrifice. This is followed by a disastrous mistake when Titus rejects election as Emperor and, being a believer in hereditary monarchy, bestows the title on the manifestly unscrupulous and ignoble Saturninus. Worse is to come when Titus kills one of his own sons who is courageously, and correctly, defending the rights of his sister; then the new Emperor Saturninus impulsively – and one infers lustfully – marries the captive Gothic Queen, Tamora. It was her son whom Titus had sacrificed, so when she murmurs in an aside to her new husband – 'I'll find a day to massacre them all' (I, i, 451) – meaning Titus and his family – it is clear that there is trouble ahead. Almost her last words in this scene are

> Titus, I am incorporate in Rome,
> A Roman now adopted happily . . .
>
> (I, i, 463–4)

The Goth, the vengeful woman, is now '*incorporate*' in patriarchal Rome. Whatever condition the 'body' of the state of Rome was in – and despite the litany of 'just', 'noble', 'virtue', etc., it seems far from stable – that body is now going to be threatened from within by an alien, savage, female agent.

'Kind Rome' (I, i, 165) says Titus at one point. But this Rome is visibly far from 'kind'. The matter of the human sacrifice is particularly pertinent here:

> Give us the proudest prisoner of the Goths,
> That we may hew his limbs, and on a pile
> *Ad manes fratrum* sacrifice his flesh . . .
>
> (I, i, 96–8)

Rome was a singularly brutal state, but it did *not* practise human sacrifice. Spencer makes the point that, although Shakespeare's depiction of Rome can be rather confused (at times it seems to be 'a free commonwealth, with the characteristic mixture of patrician and plebeian institutions'), he does seem to be trying to get Roman history 'right'. But then he deliberately inserts this archaic barbarity. As the 'barbarian' Goths note – 'Was never Scythia half so barbarous' (I, i, 131). It is as if, *from the very beginning*, Shakespeare wants to suggest that the conventional opposition of Rome–Barbarian simply will not hold. And we may note the words of Tamora, mother of the sacrificed Goth, as she pleads that her son be spared:

O, if to fight for king and commonweal
Were piety in thine, it is in these.
Andronicus, stain not thy tomb with blood.
Wilt thou draw near the nature of the gods?
Draw near them then in being merciful;
Sweet mercy is nobility's true badge.

(I, i, 114–19)

We may recall what Portia says of mercy in *The Merchant of Venice* – 'it becomes/The throned monarch better than his crown' (IV, i, 189) – and feel that from every conceivable perspective Tamora is, here, humanly in the right of it. And Titus in the wrong. Tamora's comment, as the sacrifice is taking place – 'O cruel, irreligious piety!' (I, i, 130) – inevitably becomes a comment on all the 'pieties' which noble, just, kind Rome regards as the distinguishing mark of its civilized state.

Titus is surely as equally in the wrong when he stabs his son Mutius who is honourably defending his sister Lavinia. As his brother Marcus – one of the few wise and temperate figures in the play – says to Titus, he has 'In a bad quarrel slain a virtuous son' (I, 1, 343). The insensate rage of Titus at this point, his fury at any sign of filial insubordination, his willingness to destroy his own child, have suggested to a number of critics, rightly I think, that we can already detect here the early signs of a King Lear – a proleptic similarity enhanced when, as he is buffeted with grief after grief and atrocity after atrocity, it seems he must go mad ('my heart all mad with misery', 'no man should be mad but I' – III, ii, 9, 24). Like Lear, in this opening scene, Titus gets everything – the succession, the sacrifice, the treatment of his children – terribly, and as it will prove disastrously, wrong. (It might be added that some have also seen adumbrations of the figure of Othello in Titus – the great soldier living by a naive, martial code, who proves to be hopelessly vulnerable to the machinations of evil plotters when he moves from the battlefield to the city. In fact, in his courage, almost maniacal bravery, stubbornness, hardness, intemperate anger, and – yes – stupidity, the old warrior, an almost archaic pre-political figure, looks straight forward to Shakespeare's last Roman tragic hero,

Coriolanus – whose desire to be revenged on Rome is referred to in this play – IV, iv, 69.)

Titus kills his son because he claims he has 'dishonored all our family' (I, i, 346). When his other sons plead that, since Mutius 'died in honor', he should be allowed a place in the family tomb, Titus most grudgingly allows it, but comments 'To be dishonored by my sons in Rome!' (I, i, 386). When the decent Bassianus attempts to defend Titus to the evil Saturninus, Titus stops him:

> leave to plead my deeds;
> 'Tis thou and those that have dishonored me.
> Rome and the righteous heavens be my judge,
> How I have loved and honored Saturnine!
>
> (I, i, 425–8)

Saturninus, hypocritically pretending that he has been robbed of Lavinia, has the gall to protest to Tamora:

> What, madam! Be dishonored openly,
> And basely put it up without revenge?

These Romans are everywhere and continuously invoking 'honor' (the word occurs at least seventeen times), not least when they are committing some cruel and ruthless deed. Contrariwise, any attempt at a decent or just deed is said by one man or other to 'dishonor' him. Clearly something has gone hopelessly wrong with the very concept of 'honor'; not only has it been devalued and emptied out of any positive value or meaning – it has been perverted, indeed at times inverted. It will not be long before Falstaff is famously asking 'what is this honor?' and we will be hearing much about 'honor' in later plays by Shakespeare. But, from the start, Roman honour is made to seem a twisted, deviant thing.

Act II starts with a shock – the black Aaron standing alone in front of the palace in Rome. We have seen the northern barbarian – the Goth – made 'incorporate' in Rome, and now here is the southern barbarian – the Moor – in the same city. He immediately announces his determination to 'wanton' with Tamora, the new queen of Rome, and cause the 'shipwrack' of the whole state. Aaron, of course, is *the* villain –

lustful, infinitely sadistic, delighting in the cruellest tricks and stratagems (for example, persuading Titus to cut off his hand in the deluded belief it will save the life of his son), incapable of remorse and completely committed to evil. Characteristically, he says such things as 'Aaron will have his soul black like his face' (III, i, 205) and:

> But, I have done a thousand dreadful things
> As willingly as one would kill a fly,
> And nothing grieves me heartily indeed,
> But that I cannot do ten thousand more.
>
> (V, i, 141–4)

and

> If one good deed in all my life I did,
> I do repent it from my very soul . . .
>
> (V, iii, 189–90)

We may find the racist implications disturbing, but Aaron's soul is meant to seem of the same 'hue' as his body – 'Spotted, detested, and abominable' (II, iii, 74). He takes such a ghoulish pleasure in committing or arranging atrocities that some people have claimed to find him a comic figure – and indeed, faced with the horrors he contrives, that may be the more comfortable strategy. But I doubt that was how it struck the Elizabethan audience, and I'm not sure it should us. Certainly, he is an extreme and in some ways crudely outlined figure (probably owing something to Marlowe's Barabas), but as Titus is an early Lear, so Aaron foreshadows Iago (there is a premonitory hint of this when on one occasion he threatens 'I'll speak no more but "Vengeance rot you all!"' – V, i, 58). He is an embodiment of that phenomenon, awesome to Shakespeare, of almost motiveless and utterly uncontainable evil, though Shakespeare does add one rather surprising touch – Aaron's devotion to his illegitimate child by Tamora. There is no such blurring of the figure of Iago.

After the solo appearance of Aaron at the start of Act II, we move to 'A forest near Rome'. Shakespeare was to make much of the juxtaposition of the different realms of court and forest (or city and country), and in this play, where Rome was undoubtedly dominated by men and 'law' and ceremony, the forest offers the release of the barbarous – it is dominated by Tamora and Aaron, the woman and the savage, and is the place of lustful sexuality and the hunting of animals, literal and metaphorical. The occasion is a supposedly celebratory panther hunt. And here again, Shakespeare seems to be adding a deliberate anachronism, or non-historical incongruity, for his own purposes – there was no panther-hunting in ancient Rome. But it enables him to relate the literal pursuit of animals to all the sexual pursuit going on ('as if a double hunt were heard at once,' as Tamora says), and have them converge horribly on the 'doe', Lavinia, who is first ravished, then hideously mutilated. The forest is the ideal realm for Aaron's operations. As he says:

> The Emperor's court is like the House of Fame,
> The palace full of tongues, of eyes, and ears:
> The woods are ruthless, dreadful, deaf, and dull …
> (II, I, 126–8)

It is there he can 'wanton' with Tamora, and it is there he digs the pit which will fatally trap Quintus and Marcus. That pit itself becomes the image of frightening female sexuality, as is made tolerably explicit:

> What subtle hole is this,
> Whose mouth is covered with rude-growing briers,
> Upon whose leaves are drops of new-shed blood …
> (II, iii, 198–200)

It is also described as 'this detested, dark, blood-drinking pit' and 'this fell devouring receptacle' (II, III, 224, 235); and while one part of the forest is full of animal life, in the dark part where there is the 'abhorred pit', as sexual and fecund Tamora says – 'here nothing breeds' (II, iii, 96). That Shakespeare felt a nausea, a fear, at certain aspects of female sexuality becomes clear in later plays. But here, thus early, he identifies or equates this kind of ravenous, negative female sexuality – it 'devours' rather then 'breeds' – with treachery, murder, death.

Thus the forest is made to appear the complete opposite of

the city. And yet, perhaps not quite so, either. The Capitol has its murders, and the palace has its 'wantonness' and irrational cruelties, as we have seen. Limbs are 'lopped' in Rome as they are, less 'ceremoniously', in the 'ruthless, vast, and gloomy woods', as Titus describes the forest (IV, i, 53). Confronted with the appalling spectacle of the tongueless, handless Lavinia, ravished and maimed in the dark part of the forest, the good Marcus asks:

> O, why should nature build so foul a den,
> Unless the gods delight in tragedies?
>
> (IV, i, 59–60)

But you cannot blame tragedy on terrain, and, as in *King Lear*, the invoked 'gods' are not remotely in evidence. It is *men* who 'foul' the den.

The remainder of the play takes in Rome, mainly in or near the house of Titus – though there is a scene on 'a plain near Rome'. We watch the intensification and acceleration of the horrors visited on Titus and his family (through the devices of Aaron and Tamora and the willing participation of Saturninus). We witness the apparent madness of Titus as the multiplication of atrocities passes way beyond the bearable. When he is confronted with his mutilated daughter, Lavinia, he reacts with powerful tropes:

> What fool hath added water to the sea,
> Or brought a faggot to bright-burning Troy?
> My grief was at the height before thou cam'st,
> And now like Nilus it disdaineth bounds.
>
> (III, i, 68–71)

It is all, simply and literally, *too much* – Titus' grief is as uncontainable as Aaron's evil. Shakespeare was always drawn to the study of what 'disdaineth bounds' – excess of all kinds – and with the image of the rampant, overflowing Nile, we already have an adumbration of his greatest drama of excess – *Antony and Cleopatra*. Marcus, the balanced humane Marcus, laments that 'These miseries are more than may be borne!' (III, i, 243), and Titus' son Lucius refers to his father as 'The woefull'st man that ever lived in Rome!' (III, i, 289). Here again, this is where the tragedy prefigures *King Lear*. But another play, too, when Titus seems to go mad. He shoots arrows to the gods with letters attached, asking for justice and revenge ('There's not a god left unsolicited'). But there is method in his madness for, of course, the arrows and letters fall in Rome, as Saturninus recognizes, 'blazoning our unjustice everywhere ... As who would say, in Rome no justice were' (IV, iv, 18–20). That is exactly what Titus is saying – he has already called Rome 'a wilderness of lions', definitively confounding the conventional culture–nature distinctions. But if he is mad – deranged with grief – he is also steely sane. During Tamora's final, grotesque, attempt to trick him (pretending she is 'Revenge, sent from below'), in an aside Titus says:

> I knew them all, though they supposed me mad;
> And will o'erreach them in their own devices ...
>
> (V, ii, 142–3)

This anticipates Shakespeare's most famous character. *Titus Andronicus* is a 'revenge' play and shows some of the crudities of that genre, but by the time Shakespeare has finished transforming that genre, we will have *Hamlet*.

The final Act depicts Titus' revenge, as, in the last ghoulish incident in the play, he serves up to Tamora her sons baked in a pie ('Eating the flesh that she herself hath bred' – V, iii, 62) – a feast, incidentally, described by the unwitting Marcus as 'ordained to an honorable end,/For peace, for love, for league, and good to Rome' (V, iii, 22–3). Honorific terms are by now taking a hiding. The play ends in a rout of deaths and killings (but so does *Hamlet* – 'This quarry cries on havoc,' exclaims Fortinbras). More interesting, perhaps, is the spectacle of what we may call the radical shift, or inversion, of allegiance. The great defender and saviour of Rome becomes its most implacable enemy as Titus' son, Lucius, goes off to raise an army of Goths to attack Rome. This, of course, is to be the great theme of Shakespeare's last Roman play, *Coriolanus*. But here it is, from the start. When Lucius is banished, Titus says:

> How happy art thou then,
> From these devourers to be banished!
>
> (III, i, 57)

Lucius himself has some rather Coriolanus-like lines:

> Lastly, myself unkindly banished,
> The gates shut on me, and turned weeping out,
> To beg relief among Rome's enemies ...
> I am the turned-forth ...
>
> (V, iii, 104–9)

What does it mean, what does it portend, when Rome 'turns-forth' its bravest and most illustrious defender-heroes? When a Goth can say:

> the great Andronicus,
> Whose name was once our terror, now our comfort,
> Whose high exploits and honorable deeds
> Ingrateful Rome requites with foul contempt ...
>
> (V, i, 9–12)

Where is the authoritative voice now? With the Goths rather than the Romans? Can a 'terror' so quickly become a 'comfort' – and, presumably, *vice versa*? Here are problems of inversion, reversibility, even inter-changeability, to which Shakespeare was clearly extraordinarily well attuned. Now a Roman, now a Goth – handy-dandy, which is which?

This is not to say that Shakespeare erases all differences between the Romans and Goths, between the city and the forest. There is always the possibility – in patriarchal, cruel, and – yes – 'barbarous' Rome – of law, order, stability, degree. Though if Saturninus is Emperor, one feels that Romans might as well head for the forest. But the forest offers *no* possibility of law. The emergence of the ravished and mutilated Lavinia from the forest is an apt image of what the realm encourages and permits. The continuous presence of Marcus – just, rational, decent, humane – is a reminder of what Rome can produce and what it might stand for. If – *if* – it can get the words right, it can, could, be the place and source of honour, virtue, nobility. *If*. At the end, Lucius is the new Emperor of Rome and seems to bespeak or promise a restoration of true justice and order:

may I govern so,
To heal Rome's harms and wipe away her woe!
(V, iii, 147–8)

But the actual, and dramatic, ending has Rome disgorging itself of the body of the female Goth, Tamora, which had been so disastrously 'incorporated' into the city. Rome's ceremony ends here – there are to be no commemorative, funereal rites:

But throw her forth to beasts and birds of prey.
Her life was beastly and devoid of pity,
And being dead, let birds on her take pity.
(V, iii, 198–200)

But Rome has been shown to be 'devoid of pity' – where was 'mercy' in scene one? The issues are not clear cut, and Shakespeare makes very sure that we see that.

So what of the play as a whole? Famously, Edward Ravenscroft in 1687 described it as 'a heap of rubbish'. It has been described as black comedy, Grand Guignol, and melodrama (by H. B. Charlton, who found in the play no 'inner world' of the characters). Because the particularly horrifying episodes are quite explicitly 'quotations', as it were, from Ovid (Lavinia's mutilation repeats the story of Tereus and Philomena) and Seneca (the children in the pie comes from *Thyestes* out of Aeschylus), Muriel Bradbrook offered the opinion that '*Titus Andronicus* is a Senecal exercise; the horrors are all classical and quite unfelt, so that the violent tragedy is contradicted by the decorous imagery. The tone is cool and cultured in its effect.' I can understand this response, but do not share it. Modern readers will, of course, make up their own minds; but, while the play is marked by harsh oratory rather than the sinuous and subtle speech of psychological revelation, it seems to me to touch on issues of great moment – for the Elizabethans and for us. Not least – what does our Roman heritage – and we in the West are all inheritors of Rome – really comprise and stand for? And – is it possible, ever, to delimit and demarcate the 'barbarous'?

*

TROILUS AND CRESSIDA (1601–2)

In *Titus Andronicus* 'our Troy, our Rome', are elided; Titus himself is referred to as the 'Roman Hector'. It was easy for Shakespeare to move from Rome to Troy as the two great cities – and their fates – were closely linked in the European imagination. Troy had a particular significance for western Europe since it traced its ancestry back to the Trojans, through Aeneas and Ascanius. According to the legend as recounted by Geoffrey of Monmouth, Brute, the great-grandson of Aeneas, founded London, which was New Troy. The legend of Troy was well known to Elizabethans: eight translations of Homer were available; there was plenty of Trojan material in Ovid's *Metamorphoses*, Chaucer's epic poem *Troilus and Criseyde* was well known, and Shakespeare would also almost certainly have known Henryson's *The Testament of Cresseid*, which offers itself as a sequel to Chaucer and traces out her pitiful life – and death – as a whore after Diomed has tired of her. Before considering the kind of drama Shakespeare made out of this familiar legend, it is important to bear in mind that the many medieval re-tellings of the legend of the Trojan war invariably debased it and degraded the participants. As Phillips puts it: 'the history of Troy in the middle ages is a history of degeneration and debasement' (*The State in Shakespeare*, p. 114). The Greeks in particular were invariably shown in a bad light – 'merry Greek' was a pejorative, disparaging term. It is what Helen is called in Shakespeare's play. So it is perhaps not surprising that Shakespeare should choose to dramatize a moment in the war when demoralization and social disintegration – not to say corruption and rottenness – are heavy in the air. There are 'heroes', but heroism degenerates into squalid thuggery. There are 'lovers', but love deliquesces into lubricious promiscuity. The positive graces should be valour and devotion – but 'war and lechery confound all!' (II, iii, 77). Values are everywhere degraded – 'soiled' in the language of the play. The root cause of the war is 'the soil of [Helen's] fair rape' (II, ii, 148), and this early oxymoron discolours the whole play, in which what seems fair invariably turns out to be soiled. The 'soilure' (IV, i, 56) of Helen permeates the play, so that even when Troilus maintains that it is a matter of honour for Troy to keep Helen, his metaphor partakes of the general contamination. 'We turn not back the silks upon the merchant/When we have soiled them' (II, ii, 69–70).

The play starts, rather unusually, with an 'armed Prologue'. His last words are distinctly casual, nonchalant to the point of indifference:

> Like or find fault; do as your pleasures are;
> Now good or bad, 'tis but the chance of war.

In a way, this sets the tone of the play. In the first Act, Pandarus and Cressida are discussing whether or not Troilus has a 'brown' – dark – complexion:

> *Pandarus.* Faith, to say truth, brown and not brown.
> *Cressida.* To say the truth, true and not true.
>
> (I, ii, 97–8)

What it is to 'say the truth', and whether it is still possible, become matters of some moment. We seem to be tending, sliding, towards a situation, a world, in which things are indifferently 'good or bad', 'true and not true'. When Cressida asks Pandarus if Helenus can fight, his answer perfectly expresses this mood. 'No. Yes, he'll fight indifferent well' (I, ii, 228). A positive compounded with a negative producing – indifference. Good, bad; true, not true; yes, no. 'Tis but the chance of war.

The first scene in the Greek camp opens with Agamemnon summarizing and describing the current state of the army:

> Checks and disasters
> Grow in the veins of actions highest reared,
> As knots, by the conflux of meeting sap,
> Infects the sound pine and diverts his grain
> Tortive and errant from his course of growth.
>
> (I, iii, 5–9)

I will simply note that 'knots' is a word which occurs quite frequently – things, people, are constantly being blocked from following what might seem their natural course; but 'tortive and errant' – twisted and wandering in wrong directions – is a phrase that might fairly be said to apply to the whole play. When, shortly after, in his 'Degree' speech, Ulysses depicts the chaos that follows 'when the planets/In evil mixture to disorder wander', he says that the resultant 'commotion' serves to 'deracinate/The unity and married calm of states/Quite from their fixture' (I, iii, 94–5, 99–101). Troilus thinks that 'Never did young man fancy/With so eternal and so fixed a soul' (V, ii, 163). But there is no 'married calm' in the vortex, or wasteland, stemming from Helen's 'soilure', and nothing is 'fixed' any more in this world. At the very start of the play, we hear this. 'Hector, whose patience/Is as a virtue fixed, today was moved' (I, ii, 4–5). Even Hector. All are 'deracinated' in one way or another – Cressida most visibly, as she is brutally shifted from the Trojan to the Greek camp; but Hector as notably, as he suddenly shifts from one side to the other in the vital debate concerning the keeping or giving up of Helen. Too much of the movement (and thinking and feeling) in this play is 'tortive and errant'.

To return to Agamemnon's opening speech. He says that things have gone wrong ('bias and thwart') since the start of the siege, but that we should regard all these failures as:

> But the protractive trials of great Jove
> To find persistive constancy in men ...
>
> (I, iii, 21–2)

Here indeed is a question raised by the play – is it possible to find any 'persistive constancy' in men? A constancy that would help to create and ensure stability and continuity – 'unity and married calm' – both in individual relationships and the state? It is not to be found in this play, in which there is more discontinuity and instability of character than anywhere else in Shakespeare. Inconstancy is the norm. The one character who shows 'persistive constancy' is Thersites, and it is the constancy of virulent and scabrous negation. Agamemnon likens true constancy to a fine, rare metal. You will not find it if you leave it to Fortune – Fortune, he says, conflates and confounds all values. You need – it is an unusual personification – Distinction.

> Distinction, with a broad and powerful fan,
> Puffing at all, winnows the light away,
> And what hath mass or matter by itself
> Lies rich in virtue and unmingled.
>
> (I, iii, 27–30)

Winnowing and straining or distilling are processes referred to more than once, and are connected to one of the great motivating questions of the play. If, in the name of 'Distinction', all the 'light' stuff, the chaff, the rubbish, is blown and winnowed away, will you be left with something solid and of unquestionable value – 'rich in virtue and unmingled'? The question applies particularly to people, and one of the disquieting or dismaying – or displeasing – features of this play is the sense one has at the end of the main characters having been winnowed away to nothingness, as though none of them had the requisite 'mass or matter' to persist as on-goingly authentic, reliable human beings throughout the wasting and debilitating travails of the war. Thersites and Pandarus alone retain their original shape, remain what they were – 'unmingled' perhaps, but hardly 'rich in virtue'.

Distinction – 'distinguishableness', if I may gloss with an ugly but useful word – is visibly, audibly being lost. In his 'Degree' speech, Ulysses maintains:

> Take but degree away, untune that string,
> And hark what discord follows. Each thing meets
> In mere oppugnancy.
>
> (I, iii, 109–11)

In the Quarto, 'meets' reads as 'melts' (to be a crucial word in *Antony and Cleopatra*) – I have no wish, and certainly no competence, to adjudicate between the readings. Indeed, ideally one would hear both words, for there is a sense in this play in which 'meeting' in oppugnancy becomes tantamount to 'melting' – it becomes hard to tell one thing from the other. Ulysses continues his vision of a world bereft of degree:

Force should be right, or rather right and wrong –
Between whose endless jar justice resides –
Should lose their names, and so should justice too.
Then everything include itself in power,
Power into will, will into appetite,
And appetite, an universal wolf,
So doubly seconded with will and power,
Must make perforce an universal prey
And last eat up himself.

(I, iii, 116–24)

Right and wrong and justice should lose their names ('Now good or bad, 'tis but the chance of war'), and everything be resolved, dissolved (melted) into the single matter of force, power, will, and self-devouring appetite. And not only ethical categories – most of the main characters effectively 'lose their names' as well, winnowed away by the long attritions of the war. Hector makes a comparable point in the Trojan camp when he answers the impetuous arguments offered by Troilus and Paris for continuing the war:

The reasons you allege do more conduce
To the hot passion of distempered blood
Than to make up a free determination
'Twixt right and wrong; for pleasure and revenge
Have ears more deaf than adders to the voice
Of any true decision.

(II, ii, 168–73)

In the atmosphere of this war, it no longer seems possible to make a true decision – 'a free determination' – between right and wrong. And if this 'distinction' is gone, then clearly all distinctions are at risk.

Of course, differences remain. The Trojans – Hector certainly – seem to retain a vestige of the old heroic code and traces and shreds of a chivalric ideal; they are more courtly and courteous than their adversaries. As Thersites says – 'the Grecians begin to proclaim barbarism, and policy grows into an ill opinion' (V, iv, 16–18). When Achilles calls on his gang of Myrmidons to fall on the unarmed Hector, we witness the ultimate debasement, or rather abandonment, of any and every code of conduct – martial or otherwise. Achilles' relish in the foulness of his act is sickening:

> Look, Hector, how the sun begins to set,
> How ugly night comes breathing at his heels.
> Even with the vail and dark'ning of the sun,
> To close the day up, Hector's life is done . . .
> The dragon wing of night o'erspreads the earth . . .
>
> (V, viii, 5–8, 17)

It is as though night is falling – the curtain coming down (the play is nearly over) – on whatever values might have operated – in war, in love, in politics and government – in the pre-Christian classical world. Although Hector's magnanimity in sparing Greeks at his mercy – including Achilles – seems like the cherishable remnant of an older and better code, in the current atmosphere it is disparaged as a foolish anachronism. ' 'Tis fair play,' he says to his brother Troilus, who replies – 'Fool's play, by heaven, Hector'. Fair is soiled, fair is foolish – it has come to this.

In this great melt-down of distinctions and values, which the play both portends and enacts, questions of value and valuation become of paramount importance. What is this worth? How do you esteem that? What are your grounds for attributing this value, this worth, this price? Is it intrinsic, or in the eye of the beholder, the appraiser, the attributor, the reflector? Here, of course, the debate among the Trojans as to whether to send Helen back to the Greeks is central. Hector is very clear in his own mind – 'Let Helen go'. He gives his reasons, and unanswerably good reasons they are. But Troilus invokes 'honor' and pours metaphoric contempt on 'reason'.

> You fur your gloves with reason . . .
> . . . Nay, if we talk of reason,
> Let's shut our gates and sleep! Manhood and honor
> Should have hare-hearts, would they but fat their thoughts
> With this crammed reason.
>
> (II, ii, 38, 46–9)

Hector is too intelligent to be rebuffed and beclouded by metaphors, and simply, cogently replies:

Brother, she is not worth what she doth cost
The keeping.

(II, ii, 51–2)

At which point, Troilus articulates the central question of the play: 'What's aught but as 'tis valued?' The question implies an extreme relativism in the realm of values (and we may remember that in *Hamlet*, written perhaps one year earlier, Hamlet had delivered himself of the opinion that 'There is nothing good or bad but thinking makes it so'). Troilus is saying, or implying, that there are no intrinsic values, only attributed ones. Coming from a young man who regards himself as exemplifying, as incorporating, an absolute standard of fidelity, this is somewhat inconsistent – but inconsistency prevails in this play. However, at this point, Hector deals firmly with his younger brother's casuistry:

But value dwells not in particular will.
It holds his estimate and dignity
As well wherein 'tis precious of itself
As in the prizer. 'Tis mad idolatry
To make the service greater than the god;
And the will dotes that is attributive
To what infectiously itself affects,
Without some image of th' affected merit.

(II, ii, 53–60)

Difficult words (as so often in this tortive and errant play), but Hector is saying that many Trojans, like Troilus, have made 'the service' (of keeping Helen) 'greater than the god' (Helen's own worth). There is, he says, a lot of doting 'attributive' will around, which ascribes value without any objective sense of the thing or person thus evaluated. Mainly Hector wants to assert that something, someone, can be 'precious of itself/As in the prizer'. Simply, there are intrinsic, non-contingent values – values not dependent on the eye of the 'prizer' or appraiser. Things are *not* simply as they are valued. Hector is still capable of making a 'free determination' between right and wrong. Of course Helen should be given back to the Greeks:

> There is a law in each well-ordered nation
> To curb those raging appetites that are
> Most disobedient and refractory.
> If Helen, then, be wife to Sparta's king,
> As it is known she is, these moral laws
> Of nature and of nations speak aloud
> To have her back returned. Thus to persist
> In doing wrong extenuates not wrong,
> But makes it much more heavy. Hector's opinion
> Is this in way of truth.
>
> (II, ii, 180–89)

In way of truth. This is the absolutely crucial moment in the play – is it still possible to think, and speak, and winnow your way down and along to 'truth'? Or is everything now merely a matter of 'opinion'? This is a word which keeps occurring in the play, as if to mock the unitary pretensions of 'truth', until we realize the aptness and accuracy of Thersites' outburst – 'A plague of opinion! A man may wear it on both sides like a leather jerkin' (III, iii, 265–6). There is opinion – lots of it – but so far from leading to the 'way of truth', it seems to lead, scatteringly, away from it. You can turn it this way and that way, inside and out; good–bad; right–wrong; true–false – either way, a reversible leather jerkin. Hector is still speaking out for the stabilities of truth against the unpredictable sways and surges of the errant tides of 'opinion'. But if we think we now have a 'fixed' point, we are about to be monumentally disappointed. Hector is about to reverse himself.

Following his statement that 'Hector's opinion/Is this in way of truth' – where for just one moment in the play opinion and truth are at one, identical – he announces:

> Yet ne'ertheless,
> My spritely brethren, I propend to you
> In resolution to keep Helen still ...
>
> (II, ii, 189–91)

Having clearly perceived and delineated the 'way of truth', Hector suddenly abandons it, swerves away – he 'propends' to the others, a strange word meaning leans or inclines, a tortive and errant movement and moment indeed. Cressida's rapid metamorphosis from chaste lover to one of the 'daughters of the game' – under gruesome Grecian mass male pressure, be it said – is not more swift or surprising than Hector's defection from the 'way of truth'. Of course, Shakespeare had made things impossibly difficult for himself. He can write against the grain of history, as he often, dazzlingly, does. But even he could not rewrite history. Helen was not given back, and Troy fell. No way round that. Hector's arguments cannot prevail if the play is to remain within the plausible limits of the legend. What Shakespeare can show in this extraordinary moment in which, for one last time, truth is unanswerably articulated and asserted, and then haplessly abandoned, is that truth, and a free determination of right and wrong, are prime casualties of the war.

After this putting aside of 'truth' it is perhaps not surprising that things and people are no longer regarded as 'precious of themselves' but only in the eye of the 'prizer' or appraiser. There is much discussion – centred on Achilles who hopes to keep his fame while refusing to fight – as to the extent to which fame and value are essentially reflective. A man, says Ulysses:

> Cannot make boast to have that which he hath
> Nor feels not what he owes but by reflection . . .
>
> (III, iii, 98–9)

Achilles takes the point:

> What the declined is
> He shall as soon read in the eyes of others
> As feel in his own fall . . .
>
> (III, iii, 76–8)

This means, of course, a complete externalization of value – it is completely in the eye of the beholder, and for that eye to confer or withhold. And, indeed, an ephemeralization of value – 'The present eye praises the present object' (III, iii, 179). It is as if nothing (no one) can any longer be something (someone) in and for itself. Through time. No wonder they are all winnowed away. Ulysses comments to Achilles:

> Nature, what things there are
> Most abject in regard and dear in use!

> What things again most dear in the esteem
> And poor in worth ...
> (III, iii, 127–30)

Abject, poor, dear – worth, esteem, use: this is the shifting value-lexicon of the play. At one end of the spectrum there is a lot of merchant talk (particularly among the Greeks) using terms concerned with prices, weights, measures – scruples, little characters, ounces, counters, spans, inches, fractions, orts, etc. At the other end, there is a more metaphysical language of truth and honour, but that language is as terribly under siege as Troy itself, and even sooner to be undermined. When Cressida is handed over to the Greeks, Troilus urges and warns Diomedes to value her in absolute, soaring terms. Diomedes replies: 'I'll answer to my lust ... To her own worth/ She shall be prized' (IV, iv, 133–4). Once she is surrounded and serially kissed by the merchant-macho Greek 'prizers' (hints of a gang rape there), we can imagine what that 'worth' will be, and how it will be esteemed. Diomedes will answer to his lust. Ominous.

Troy–Greece; chivalry–barbarism; it looks, at the beginning, as if some such simple dualism and polarity is to be envisaged – and to an extent something of that remains. The Greeks, certainly, are the real bastards of the play. But there is, throughout, too much 'commixtion' to sustain any sense of simple divisions and oppositions. When, as the result of the rather foolish challenge to single combat, Hector is to confront Ajax, Trojan Aeneas says:

> This Ajax is half made of Hector's blood,
> In love whereof half Hector stays at home;
> Half heart, half hand, half Hector comes to seek
> This blended knight, half Troyan, and half Greek ...
> (IV, v, 83–6)

– blended, melted, it is difficult to sort things out into stable oppositional – Troy–Greece – categories. As Hector himself recognizes (speaking to Ajax):

> The obligation of our blood forbids
> A gory emulation 'twixt us twain.
> Were thy commixtion Greek and Troyan so

That thou couldst say, 'This hand is Grecian all,
And this is Troyan; the sinews of this leg
All Greek, and this all Troy; my mother's blood
Runs on the dexter cheek, and this sinister
Bounds in my father's,' by Jove multipotent,
Thou shouldst not bear from me a Greekish member
Wherein my sword had not impressure made
Of our rank feud.

(IV, v, 121–31)

But it cannot be done. You cannot say of a person's body – or temperament, or being – that's the Trojan bit and that's the Greek bit. I'll reject this, save that. We are all, put it this way, Trojan–Greek compounds or 'commixtions', and, going by this play, not the much better off for it.

All of this makes the question of 'identity' a troubling matter (you may be as much of a Trojan as a Greek, but you have to take sides). People seem endlessly uncertain as to other people's identities. Who are you? Who is that? Is that so-and-so? Are you so-and so? Such questions are asked more in this play than in any other of Shakespeare's works. Even self-identity is in doubt. An early exchange:

Pandarus. Well, I say Troilus is Troilus
Cressida. Then you say as I say, for I am sure he is not Hector.
Pandarus. No, nor Hector is not Troilus in some degrees.
Cressida. 'Tis just to each of them; he is himself.
Pandarus. Himself? Alas, poor Troilus, I would he were.
Cressida. So he is.
Pandarus. Condition, I had gone barefoot to India.
Cressida. He is not Hector.
Pandarus. Himself? No, he's not himself. Would 'a were himself.

(I, ii, 66–78)

There is a good deal of splitting of the self in the play – these days we would, of course, refer to the divided self. A simple example is provided by warriors meeting during a truce. Aeneas greets Diomedes very courteously, but says – when we meet on the field, I will inflict all possible damage on you. That is absolutely all right by Diomedes:

The one and other Diomed embraces.
Our bloods are now in calm, and, so long, health!

But when contention and occasion meet,
By Jove, I'll play the hunter for thy life
With all my force, pursuit, and policy.

(IV, i, 14–18)

Which encounter prompts Paris to comment:

This is the most despiteful gentle greeting,
The noblest hateful love, that e'er I heard of.

(IV, i, 32–4)

These are the oxymorons of war, and in the event it is the gentleness and nobleness that go under, while spite and hate triumph. But it is the splitting occasioned by this war – 'the one and other' – I want briefly to stay with. And while all the main characters are split – divided, fractured, fragmented – in various ways, the crucial figure is Cressida.

This play is one of three by Shakespeare which has for its title the names of a pair of lovers (*Romeo and Juliet* and *Antony and Cleopatra* are the others). In fact, by the most generous estimate, barely one third of the play directly concerns the doomed lovers – and perhaps Shakespeare has not quite managed to make the private erotic affair fruitfully and illuminatingly coalesce with the public matters of the war – though clearly he wants to show love and war, or the erotic and martial, as inseparably intertwined. This is a play about the Trojan war, but still, the tragically split Cressida is central to the play, and she is aware of latent instabilities and divisions within herself, almost from the start:

I have a kind of self resides with you;
But an unkind self, that itself will leave
To be another's fool. I would be gone.
Where is my wit? I know not what I speak.

(III, ii, 149–52)

There is a kind of hapless honesty about Cressida. Secure in Troy, there is no reason to doubt that she would have been sincerely faithful to Troilus; but in a new, alien, context, with new pressures, fears, needs, importunities, other aspects of her self, or other selves, emerge (for which of us would that not be the case?). Troilus seems to have some intimation of possible danger ahead:

> But something may be done that we will not;
> And sometimes we are devils to ourselves
> When we will tempt the frailty of our powers,
> Presuming on their changeful potency.
>
> (IV, iv, 94–7)

All this leads up to the crucial speech by Troilus when he actually witnesses Cressida being unfaithful with Diomedes:

> This she? No, this is Diomed's Cressida.
> If beauty have a soul, this is not she;
> If souls guide vows, if vows be sanctimonies . . .
> If there be rule in unity itself,
> This was not she. O madness of discourse,
> That cause sets up with and against itself:
> Bifold authority, where reason can revolt
> Without perdition, and loss assume all reason
> Without revolt. This is, and is not, Cressid.
> Within my soul there doth conduce a fight
> Of this strange nature that a thing inseparate
> Divides more wider than the sky and earth;
> And yet the spacious breadth of this division
> Admits no orifex for a point as subtle
> As Ariachne's broken woof to enter.
> Instance, O instance, strong as Pluto's gates;
> Cressid is mine, tied with the bonds of heaven.
> Instance, O instance, strong as heaven itself;
> The bonds of heaven are slipped, dissolved, and loosed,
> And with another knot, five-finger-tied,
> The fractions of her faith, orts of her love,
> The fragments, scraps, the bits, and greasy relics
> Of her o'ereaten faith, are given to Diomed.
>
> (V, ii, 134–57)

There should be one Cressida – 'a thing inseparate' – but she seems to have 'divided' into Troilus' Cressida and Diomedes' Cressida. There should be 'rule in unity' (i.e. one cannot equal two) but in the case of Cressida one has become two. Hence Troilus finds himself pushed to the ontologically impossible conclusion – 'This is, and is not, Cressid.' As he experiences it, there is a madness seeping into language itself: 'O madness of discourse,/That cause sets up with and against itself: Bifold authority'. Language seems to be going in opposite directions at the same time – with and against itself; bifold authority – an authority which upholds and refutes at the same time. Such is the double, self-contradictory, authority operative in this play.

It is particularly horrifying and unacceptable to Troilus that the bonds which tied Cressida to him and which should be absolute – 'strong as heaven itself' – 'are slipped, dissolved, and loosed'. Bonds were holy things for Shakespeare, too 'intrince t'unloose' (*Lear* II, ii, 77). If they do not hold, nothing else holds. And in this play, nothing else does. It is notable that Troilus, in his understandable nausea, thinks of Cressida's 'love' with Diomedes in terms of unpleasant left-overs – 'greasy relics of her o'ereaten faith'. In a play in which rampant appetite is allowed free rein, it is hardly surprising that so many of the activities and processes are likened to eating, with taste constantly sickening over into distaste. From the start, love, or rather sex, is made a kitchen matter – 'He that will have a cake out of the wheat must tarry the grinding' (I, i, 15). Reputation in war is, likewise, a table matter: 'For here the Troyans taste our dear'st repute/With their fin'st palate' (I, iii, 337–8). War is a ravenous glutton – 'what else dear that is consumed/In hot digestion of this cormorant war' (II, ii, 5–6). So is Time – 'A great-sized monster of ingratitudes./Those scraps are good deeds past, which are devoured/As fast as they are made' (III, iii, 147–9). (In this play, time is only and always 'injurious' – in other plays, 'mature' or 'ripe' time can be an agent of restoration, regeneration, renewed continuities. It is what always defeats evil when it seems that nothing else can. But in this play – it is part of its bleakness – time is only a gobbler-up, a destroyer. 'What's past and what's to come is strewed with husks/And formless ruin of oblivion;/But in this extant moment ...' (IV, v, 165–7). These Trojans and Greeks live only in the 'extant moment' – and it is desolating.) Agamemnon tells Achilles that virtues left unused 'like fair fruit in an unwholesome dish,/Are like to rot untasted' (II, iii, 122–3). But perhaps the most important food is honey, associated from the first with Helen, and by implication with the lubricious pleasures of sex. There is one scene in Priam's palace in which Helen ('honey-sweet'), Paris and Pandarus bandy innuendoes and the word 'sweet' is used seven times (II, i). By which time it has come to sound, and feel, distinctly sickly, sickening. One rather sympathizes with a later, spitting comment from Thersites – '"Sweet," quoth 'a! Sweet sink, sweet sewer' (V, i, 79). In the epilogue by Pandarus, added later, he refers to the time when a bee loses 'his honey and his sting' and 'Sweet honey and sweet notes together fail' (V, x, 45). As they have failed in this play. The play was to have ended with Troilus' line – 'Hector is dead; there is no more to say' (V, x, 22). But Shakespeare decided there was just a little more to say, and he lets Pandarus say it. It is a speech about brothels, prostitution, venereal disease, and his own imminent death. No other play ends with such an unpleasant gesture to the audience:

> Till then I'll sweat and seek about for eases,
> And at that time bequeath you my diseases.
>
> (V, x, 55–6)

*

It is a strange play, and in many ways a sour and abrasive one. Any intimations of grace and a return to normal human life are ruthlessly excluded. It is easy to agree with Brockbank that there is 'no sense of betrayal of an heroic and chivalric tradition, for of that there were no glimpses', and his summing up seems apt: 'Love's infinity, heroic glory, and universal harmonies of state have only a transient visionary and verbal validity in a world that has lost touch with the values by which it pretends to live' (*On Shakespeare*, p. 10). There is little physical action in the play – Cressida goes to bed with Troilus, Hector is murdered. Most of the time, in both camps, is taken up with debate. Some scholars see this as supporting the theory that it was written for the Inns of Court, with its forensically sophisticated audience in mind. Certainly a lot of the rhetoric is strangely formal, intricate, hyperbolic. At the height of his anguish, Troilus uses words like 'recordation', 'esperance', 'deceptious' (V, ii, 113–21); wooing Cressida intensely he says things like – 'What makes this pretty abruption? What too curious dreg espies my sweet lady in the fountain of our love?' (III, ii, 65–7) – which is oddly elaborate, to say the least. The language usage ranges from the smooth political orations of Ulysses (often founded on banalities, clichés, and tautologies), to the snarling, splenetic invective of Thersites – 'all the argument is a whore and a cuckold' (II, iii, 75); ' – nothing but lechery! All incontinent varlets!' (V, i, 103). We must allow Thersites the validity and consistency of his perspective, but he is too biliously predictable to merge as the reliable voice of the play. There is no such voice. Interestingly, Thersites and Ulysses never meet and confront each other. Perhaps these are two discourses which can just run on, uninterruptedly, forever. Perhaps too there is a sense in which the play is an experiment in language and its possibilities – certainly, the characters seem to stand a long way from us, and hardly engage us as characters in Shakespeare's other plays do. Nevertheless it is a disturbing and disconsolating experience as Shakespeare shows us, as only Shakespeare could, how war devours everything.

*

JULIUS CAESAR (1599)

Plutarch's *Parallel Lives* of twenty-three Romans and twenty-three Greeks (as translated by North in 1579 from Amyot's French) was probably the most important book Shakespeare read from the point of view of his play-writing. (Terence Spencer reminds us that it was no easy undertaking – he would have had to pore over more than a thousand pages in a very large and heavy folio volume.) No play owes as much to Plutarch's *Lives* (*Life of Caesar*, *Life of Brutus*, *Life of Antonius*) as *Julius Caesar* – all the matters of substance, most of the events, many of the details, and indeed quite a number of lines, are transcribed directly from Plutarch. Of course, Shakespeare made additions, modifications, amplifications, and crucial shifts in interpretative emphasis, and in the event this play is one of his most searching dramatic explorations of the nature and processes of politics and power. But so close does the play seem to Plutarch that I want to start by quoting a number of passages from his work, as a prelude, perhaps, to appreciating what Shakespeare did with his source material.

Plutarch was a Greek philosopher, writing in the latter half of the first century AD. His preference was for republican ideals. In Spencer's words: 'The triumph of the monarchical principle was something that Plutarch, a Greek philosopher who looked back on the past of his own country and its brilliant small city-states with admiration and a kind of sentimental regret, detested although he saw its inevitability.' He regarded Caesar as the cause of the downfall of the Roman republic. And yet, many positive features emerge from his account of Caesar:

> the Romans, inclining to Caesar's prosperity and taking the bit in the mouth, supposing that to be ruled by one man alone, it would be a good mean for them *to take breath a little, after so many troubles and miseries as they had abidden in these civil wars, they chose him perpetual dictator* ... And now for himself, after he had ended his civil wars, he did so honorably behave himself, that there was no fault to be found in him ...

The italicized words apply exactly to the Elizabethans, worn out after the Wars of the Roses and the power-struggles of Catholics and Protestants under Edward VI and Mary, and glad to be 'ruled by one *woman* alone'. And we should remember that Brutus finds no actual fault with Caesar. Furthermore, Caesar treated the people with paternalistic fondness and respect:

> Now Caesar immediately won many men's good wills at Rome, through his eloquence in pleading of their causes, and the people loved him marvellously also, because of the courteous manner he had to speak to every man, and to use them gently, being more *ceremonius* therein than was looked for in one of his years. Furthermore, he ever kept a good board ...

Almost Caesar's first words are 'Set on, and leave no ceremony out' (I, ii, 11) and I shall be returning to the word I have italicized. We shall also catch a very significant glimpse of Caesar keeping that 'good board'.

So wherein did he offend? Well, there was the nature of his

last 'triumph into Rome' (with which the play begins). A reminder of a little actual history might help here. Caesar had defeated Pompey at Pharsalus in 48 BC, and now he has returned from his final triumph over Pompey's sons in Spain in 45 BC. This made him sole dictator; more beneficially, it ended the factional strife which had marred and disturbed civil life under the Republic. But is it true that, with this victory and consolidation of Caesar as dictator, the citizens lost all their power and the Senatorial party lost much of its? Plutarch sees this as a bad moment. 'But the triumph he made into Rome for the same did as much offend the Romans, and more, than any thing that ever he had done before: because he had not overcome captains that were strangers, nor barbarous kings, but had destroyed the sons of the noblest man of Rome, whom fortune had overthrown.' But – for Plutarch – there was worse. 'But the chiefest cause that made him mortally hated was the covetous desire he had to be called king: which first gave the people just cause, and next his secret enemies honest colour, to bear him ill will . . . they could not abide the name of a king, detesting it as the utter destruction of their liberty.' Given his republican sympathies, Plutarch seems more on the side of Brutus, to whom he gives all the Roman virtues – he was noble minded, lowly, virtuous, valiant, and so on. He ascribes to him only the purest and highest of motives for killing Caesar. Yet Plutarch also gives us a troubled Brutus: 'when he was out of his house, he did so frame and *fashion* his countenance and looks that no man could discern he had anything to trouble his mind. But when night came that he was in his own house, then he was clean changed: for either care did wake him against his will when he would have slept, or else oftentimes of himself he fell into such deep thoughts of his enterprise, casting in his mind all the dangers that might happen: that his wife, lying by him, found that there was some marvellous great matter that troubled his mind . . .' (my italics). This is all Shakespeare needs to dramatize a crucial split in Brutus between the public and the private man – between the noble, idealistic, Roman, performer; and the tormented, introspecting, insomniac, individual. And he will make devastating use of that word 'fashion'. Plutarch certainly lends no nobility to the actual killing of Caesar – quite the reverse: 'Caesar ... was hacked and mangled among them, as a wild beast taken of hunters.' In the play Brutus tries to make a 'sacrifice' out of the deed, but Plutarch's description is definitive. And after the assassination, in Plutarch's description, Caesar's 'great prosperity and good fortune that favoured him all his lifetime, did continue afterwards in the revenge of his death, pursuing the murtherers both by sea and land, till they had not left a man more to be executed, all of them that were actors or counsellers in the conspiracy of his death'. Only, in Shakespeare, it is not Caesar's 'good fortune' which 'did continue afterward' – but his 'spirit'.

It has also to be remembered that, by Shakespeare's time, Caesar and Brutus had acquired symbolic identities in the popular imagination; they were seen as representative world-historical figures who embodied respectively – I simplify – the monarchical (and imperial) principle, and the republican ideal. It is undeniable that the numerous references to Caesar in Shakespeare's other plays treat him almost without exception with admiration, if not with something more. We may take one example, from *Hamlet* which refers to

the most high and palmy state of Rome,
A little ere the mightiest Julius fell ...

(I, i, 113–14)

– as if the time of Julius Caesar was regarded as the high point of Roman history. According to Spencer, 'Shakespeare's audience seem to have regarded Caesar's death as one of the great crimes of history' (idem, p. 20). This is in line with Ernest Schanzer's contention in his essay on the play that 'a large part of the audience were in sympathy with the mediaeval apotheosis of Caesar'. (And, of course, Dante put Brutus at the bottom of his Inferno.) In the same article however, Schanzer reminds us that during the Renaissance there were also divided and ambivalent readings of the two men – Caesar as boastful tyrant, Brutus as liberator and patriot. As we have seen, there are detectable ambivalences in Plutarch himself. It is certainly true that by the sixteenth century a number of writers openly admired Brutus, and his reputation seems to have increased after Shakespeare's time – understandable, perhaps, as the monarchical principle faded and waned. The period of Roman history from Julius Caesar to Augustus was of particular importance for a number of Elizabethan and Renaissance political thinkers to confirm the argument in favour of monarchy. As Phillips puts it: 'In the stability which Caesar achieved under his dictatorship, in the civil strife which followed his assassination, and in the peace which returned under the imperial rule of Augustus, Tudor theorists found proof that under monarchy states flourish, under divided authority they decline' (op. cit., pp. 172–3). I hope all this gives some slight idea of the wealth and weight of material, and contradictoriness of opinion and interpretation, which Shakespeare could draw on when he turned to write the play he decided to call *Julius Caesar*.

I put it that way because, over the years, some commentators have questioned the appropriateness of naming a play after a character who has such a small part (some 130 lines out of 2,500), and who dies in the middle of the action. We may start from a consideration of this – quite accurate – point. Visibly, audibly, Caesar appears on stage for a shorter period than any other major Shakespearian protagonist. Yet his *name* occurs, re-echoes, throughout the play on *more* occasions than that of any other major protagonist: 211 times to Brutus' 130. This is a non-trivial point. The body goes: the name lives on. Caesar and Brutus both refer to themselves in the third person, as though it were possible to distinguish between, and separate, the self and the name (e.g. Caesar: 'I fear him not./Yet if my name were liable to fear . . .' – I, ii, 198–9). In the final battle at Philippi, for the defeated allies of Brutus it seems as though their names are all that remain to them – Cato: 'I will proclaim my name about the field' (V, iv, 4). Lucilius, to protect his leader, announces to the enemy soldiers – 'And I am Brutus, Marcus Brutus, I;/Brutus, my country's friend; know me for Brutus!' (V, iv, 8–9). And, imprisoning the 'name', they think they have caught the man. Perhaps the most important speech in this connection comes from Cassius early on, when he is trying to 'seduce' Brutus to his murderous cause:

Brutus and Caesar: what should be in that 'Caesar'?
Why should that name be sounded more than yours?
Write them together, yours is as fair a name;
Sound them, it doth become the mouth as well;
Weigh them, it is as heavy; conjure with 'em,
'Brutus' will start a spirit as soon as 'Caesar'.

(I, ii, 142–7)

Cassius is a materialist (at this point) – there is nothing in a name. But the mistake articulated in that last line is absolutely central to the play. 'Brutus' does *not* 'start' (raise) 'a spirit' – 'Caesar' does. The possible divorce and discrepancy between the 'name' (the concept, the ideal, the image) and the actual thing (person, behaviour, event) is constantly coming to the fore. How lethal this divorce can be is vividly brought out in the short scene in which the plebeians kill Cinna the poet:

Cinna. I am not Cinna the conspirator.
Fourth Plebeian. It is no matter, his name's Cinna; pluck but his name out of his heart, and turn him going.

(III, iii, 32–5)

Can you pluck out the name without plucking out the heart? No – says the play. The name of 'Rome' and 'Romans' are as constantly heard (seventy-two times) as in *Titus Andronicus*, and I will not try to better the comment of Foakes: 'There is a contrast between the Roman ideal and Romans in action, as is seen in the behaviour of the conspirators and the plebeians, similar to that between the ideal and the living person represented in Caesar and Brutus.' Perhaps the most telling and central dramatized illustration of this split between the bodily self and name (reputation, image) is provided by Antony's vivid evocation of the death of Caesar – of Caesar the man, that is:

Then burst his mighty heart;
And, in his mantle muffling up his face,
Even at the base of Pompey's statue
(Which all the while ran blood) great Caesar fell.
O, what a fall was there, my countrymen!
Then I, and you, and all of us fell down,
Whilst bloody treason flourished over us.

(III, ii, 188–94)

The bodily Caesar can fall – we have already had intimations of this in his 'falling sickness'. But while the body falls, the statues of previous great men (here Pompey the Great) stand erect after the death of those they commemorate. Monument, reputation, image, name – spirit – these are phenomena which can outlast corporeal terminations.

What do we gather of the living, speaking Caesar of the first two Acts and from his last speeches before the Capitol? Hazlitt – always a commentator to attend to – found the depiction disappointing. 'We do not much admire the representation here given of Julius Caesar, nor do we think it answers to the portrait given of him in his Commentaries. He makes several vapouring and rather pedantic speeches, and does nothing.' There is some vapour and pedantry in his speeches, but whether he 'does nothing' depends on your sense of action and agency. From one point of view, Caesar, or rather 'Caesar', does almost everything. The play opens with a street festival – Lupercal, a fertility festival which Shakespeare conflates with Caesar's triumph (which actually took place some five months earlier – there are numerous compressions and compactions in this play, a lot of history sometimes being dramatically squeezed into a single day). Apart from giving us our first glimpse of the people or 'commoners' – here quite effervescent and holiday-merry (later to turn mutinous and murderous) – this first scene is most important for the behaviour of the tribunes (representatives of the people and thus on guard against the Senate, never mind 'kings') – Flavius and Marullus. The people have festooned the images of Caesar in the city with 'trophies' (i.e. ornaments in honour of Caesar, not – here – spoils of war), and the tribunes go around stripping them:

> Disrobe the images,
> If you do find them decked with ceremonies.
> ... let no images
> Be hung with Caesar's trophies.
>
> (I, i, 67–8, 71–2)

I have mentioned that almost Caesar's first words are 'leave no ceremony out', and after his death Brutus says 'we are contented Caesar shall/Have all true rites and lawful ceremonies' (III, i, 240–1). In these three uses of the word, it means, variously and not mutually exclusively, symbols of state and ritual observances. But the word is used on two other occasions with a different meaning. (The original Latin word – *caeromonia* – means reverence or dread, and in the plural form came to refer to the rituals by which people express or cope with these feelings; also it came to refer to the respect felt for dread-ful portents.) When Cassius expresses his doubt as to whether Caesar will go to the Capitol he says:

> For he is superstitious grown of late,
> Quite from the main opinion he held once
> Of fantasy, of dreams, and ceremonies.

Here the word means portents or omens. It is used in this sense in the next scene when Caesar's wife, Calphurnia, tries to persuade Caesar to remain at home because of her ominous dreams and the terrible prodigies seen in the city the previous night. 'Caesar, I never stood on ceremonies,/Yet now they fright me' (II, ii, 13–14). It is an important part of the movement and atmosphere of the play that Cassius himself, an extreme materialist in the Epicurus line, grows 'superstitious' as his end approaches:

> You know that I held Epicurus strong,
> And his opinion; now I change my mind,
> And partly credit things that do presage.
>
> (V, i, 76–8)

The play is full of superstition of all kinds – soothsayers, prophets or fortune-tellers, augurers, omens and portents and 'things that do presage' – the 'prodigies' seen during the storm on the night preceding the assassination which seem to show 'a civil strife in heaven', presaging, indeed, a civil strife on earth (most of the prodigies are from Plutarch, be it said), and of course the ghost of Caesar. In respect of this atmosphere of gathering portentousness, one may adopt the sharp, dismissive sanity of Cicero:

> Indeed, it is a strange-disposed time:
> But men may construe things after their fashion,
> Clean from the purpose of the things themselves.
>
> (I, iii, 33–5)

Or one may hover, awed and respectful, between belief and unbelief. After all, if Caesar had not defied augury and overcome his superstition with some rather bombastic self-grandiloquizing ('Danger knows full well/That Caesar is more dangerous than he . . . Caesar shall go forth' – II, ii, 45, 48) he might well have lived to fight – *and* be crowned – another day. Whether or not Shakespeare believed in ghosts, auguries, prodigies and so on, is nothing to the point. What he unerringly understood was that at a time when some crisis or catastrophic breakdown of the known social order seems or feels imminent, superstition floods the streets. We have seen it in our era in times of war, and it can be seen in California (in suitably ersatz form) any day of the week. That there *are* 'things that do presage' – straws in the wind, hints in the air, signs of things to come – Shakespeare, of course, knew was simply true.

From the start, then, Caesar is associated with 'ceremony' – rituals (with the troubling shadow-meaning of portents), images, symbols, trophies. These, indeed, can all be part of the panoply and mystique of power and hierarchy, but they can also help to maintain and reinforce order, civic regularity, peace – 'after so many troubles and miseries as they had abidden in these civil wars'. Caesar is, in the exact Plutarch–North word – 'ceremonious'. All these adornments and appurtenances can serve to make Caesar seem almost god-like, and there is no question but that Caesar is approaching this status at the start of the play. The ambiguous cheers of the crowd (reported in scene two) as Caesar is both offered and refuses the crown (*three* times is too loaded to pass unnoticed in a Christian culture), reveals something of Shakespeare's insight into mob psychology. It likes to create heroes, or kings, or gods – but, as we later see, it is as equally willing to tear them down.

The tribunes want to do away with ceremony, symbol, image, and strip Caesar down to the poor, forked, fallible, physical body he undoubtedly is. This is the republican–reductive drive at its crudest – no great men, please. (For their pains, they are 'put to silence' – in view of the brutal eliminations to come, it is worth noting that this may simply mean they lost their jobs as spokesmen for the people.) But we cannot – or at least should not – take the tribunes' view of Caesar. If you strip away *all* the 'ceremonies', it is not clear what might be left to hold the city – the state – together and in order. That Caesar is physically vulnerable even when he is at his most masterful – god-like and imperial – Shakespeare brings out in a little touch which, for once, he did not find in Plutarch. At the end of his wonderfully penetrating and acutely accurate analysis of Cassius, there is a sudden lapse into intimations of mortality:

> Such men as he be never at heart's ease
> Whiles they behold a greater than themselves,
> And therefore are they very dangerous.
> I rather tell thee what is to be feared
> Than what I fear; for always I am Caesar.
> Come on my right hand, for this ear is deaf …
>
> (I, ii, 208–13)

The deafness is provided by Shakespeare – at our most potent and resplendent, we are already beginning to deteriorate and decay (as the Sonnets everywhere insist). But this is not a matter for contempt – the sort of contempt which Cassius expresses when he describes Caesar shaking like 'a sick girl' when he had a fever in Spain. It is hardly to Caesar's discredit that, whatever else he may be, he is unavoidably corporal and human. Just *what* Caesar is remains, perhaps, something of an enigma. There are various versions of Caesar, ranging from that of the mean and envious Cassius ('he doth bestride the narrow world/Like a Colossus' – I, ii, 135–6) to that of the loyal and loving Antony ('Thou art the ruins of the noblest man/That ever lived in the tide of times' – III, i, 256–7). And there is Caesar's version of himself, not to mention the crowd's Caesar. We only see him as he is constructed – *fashioned*, but I'll come back to that – by others, and by himself. In this connection, it is pertinent to acknowledge that a good deal of his speech (little enough though we hear of it), is self-aggrandizing and self-inflating, somewhat thrasonical and given to self-hyperbolizing. But to suggest that the arrogance of his last speech –

> Yet in the number I do know but one
> That unassailable holds on his rank,
> Unshaked of motion; and that I am he ...
> (III, i, 68–70)

is sufficient justification for his assassination, as some critics have, seems to me to submit to conspiratorial homicidal intoxication, and identification with Cassius, that 'hot, choleric, and cruel man' (Plutarch). There is one little scene in Caesar's house on the morning of the murder which seems to me crucial – and here we come to what Plutarch called Caesar's 'good board'. Caesar is surrounded with, supposedly his good friends, actually those who will kill him. Before they set out for the Capitol, Caesar says:

> Good friends, go in and taste some wine with me,
> And we (like friends) will straightway go together.

To which, Brutus adds a concluding aside:

> That every like is not the same, O Caesar,
> The heart of Brutus earns to think upon.
> (II, ii, 126–9)

Shortly afterwards, in front of the Capitol, Brutus who, as these lines reveal, knows he is only a dissembling friend, says to Caesar – 'I kiss thy hand, but not in flattery, Caesar' (III, i, 52). No, not in flattery – in betrayal. After the ceremonial communal wine of the Last Supper, the Judas kiss. At this point, the Elizabethans would surely have known what they were witnessing.

Brutus is a more complex figure. One reading sees him as a noble, idealistic, exemplary Roman who is 'seduced' into the conspiracy by the envious and bloody-minded Cassius (who knows very well that the 'work' he has 'in hand' is 'Most bloody, fiery, and most terrible' – I, iii, 130). Certainly he hopes that 'the great opinion/That Rome holds of his name' (I, ii, 319–20) will give honour and respectability to their enterprise. Just as Casca hopes that:

> that which would appear offense in us,
> His countenance, like richest alchemy,
> Will change to virtue and to worthiness ...
>
> (I, iii, 158–60)

(In the event, Brutus proves to be a failed alchemist – he cannot transform 'butchery' into 'sacrifice', betrayal into virtue, murder into worthiness.) This view of Brutus was fostered by Plutarch, and Shakespeare is happy enough to take a Plutarchian line for Antony's panegyric over the dead Brutus:

> All the conspirators save only he
> Did that they did in envy of great Caesar;
> He, only in a general honest thought
> And common good to all, made one of them.
>
> (V, v, 69–71)

Did he, now? All Romans seemingly become 'noble' at their death. Brutus calls the vicious Cassius 'the last of all the Romans'; Antony dubs betrayer-murderer Brutus 'the noblest Roman of them all'; Octavius Caesar, in a later play, casts around for some appropriately respectful things to say about Antony whom he always regarded as a hopelessly debauched defector, but, as we shall see, he cannot even be bothered to finish. These encomiastic elegies are formulaic, Roman prescriptions which are, to all intents and purposes, interchangeable. Death can certainly bring dignity in Shakespeare, and it is appropriate at such a moment to let remembered virtues shine while flaws fade. But do not look for the truth of a man – and that includes Brutus – in these conventional orations and exequies.

From the very start, Brutus, by his own account, is 'with himself at war' (I, ii, 46). Cassius offers to be his 'glass', a mirror which:

> Will modestly discover to yourself
> That of yourself which you yet know not of.
>
> (I, ii, 69–70)

He *does* know it, as we shall see, but he does not want to know that he knows it. Shakespeare is nowhere more brilliant in this play than in showing the operations and stratagems of self-deception. At the end of the scene, Cassius is content with his work:

> Well Brutus, thou art noble; yet I see
> Thy honorable *mettle* may be *wrought*
> From that it is disposed . . .
> For who so firm that cannot be seduced?
>
> (I, ii, 308–10, 312: my italics)

There are a number of references to 'mettle' in the play (the people, not surprisingly, are regarded as 'the basest mettle') and there is always an implicit play on 'mettle' (disposition) and 'metal' (a material which can be 'wrought'). In this play, people can be sharp or blunt or dull, but, more importantly, they can be 'wrought'. The dictionary glosses that as meaning 'fashioned or formed'. It is the past participle of 'work' – another important word in the play. Crowds, of course, can be 'wrought' – now this shape, now that. And so can individuals, as when Brutus says of Caius Ligarius – 'Send him but hither, and I'll fashion him' (II, i, 220). The vocabulary bespeaks a manipulative and instrumental – not to say materialistic – view of people, at the least. Perhaps Shakespeare thought this was very 'Roman' – though what price 'honour' and 'nobility' in such metallic people? But there is an even more insidious form of 'fashioning', as emerges in Brutus' first soliloquy. His first words to himself are – 'It must be by his death'. That is, deep inside him the decision has been taken – Caesar, his best friend, is to be killed. Make no mistake, this Brutus is a murderer, though not the usual ambitious regicide of other Tudor plays. Now he has to find some reasons for the deed – political imperatives to mask the personal compulsion. Has to find them because – 'for my part/I know no personal cause to spurn at him' and 'to speak truth of Caesar,/I have not known when his affections swayed/More than his reason' (II, I, 10–11, 19–21). So he moves from the indicative tense – Caesar as he *is* – to the subjunctive and conditional, drawing hypothetical scenarios. *If* Caesar is crowned, he '*may* do danger' – 'So Caesar *may*' (my italics). Always 'may' is allowed to supplant 'is'. Then this, which is decisive:

And, since the quarrel
Will bear no color for the thing he *is*,
Fashion it thus: that what he is, augmented,
Would run to these and these extremities;
And therefore *think him as* a serpent's egg
Which hatched, *would* as his kind grow mischievous,
And kill him in the shell.
(II, i, 28–34: my italics)

Fashion it thus – words and arguments are like people, as far as Brutus is concerned; you can mould and shape them to suit, and justify, any ulterior intention. But this perverse substitution of the possible for the actual, is a step into anarchy – of self, and then of state. His own internal anarchy is revealed in a following soliloquy which starts: 'Since Cassius first did whet me against Caesar,/I have not slept' (II, i, 61–2). Note 'whet' – by which Brutus depicts himself as a tool which has been sharpened. He goes on – in a speech which anticipates Macbeth – to describe the 'phantasma' and nightmare inner world he is living in:

The genius and the mortal instruments
Are then in council, and the state of a man,
Like to a little kingdom, suffers then
The nature of an insurrection.
(II, i, 66–9)

Brutus has been 'at war' with himself since the beginning, and what he effectively does is to extend that inner 'insurrection' to the state at large.

As the conspirators come in with their heads cloaked and concealed – as Portia says, they 'hide their faces/Even from darkness' (II, i, 277–8) – Brutus reveals, by his words, that he is well aware of the evil nature of the deed they are premeditating:

O conspiracy
Sham'st thou to show thy dang'rous brow by night,
When evils are most free? O, then by day
Where wilt thou find a cavern dark enough
To mask thy monstrous visage? Seek none, conspiracy;
Hide it in smiles and affability . . .
(II, i, 77–82)

'Monstrous' is an important word for Shakespeare, indicating something which is in nature, since it is undeniably *there*, but also horribly *un*natural as well. Nature against itself. Brutus could hardly have chosen a more self-incriminating, self-damning, word. He also reveals a Machiavellian streak as he indicates the need for concealment, simulation and dissembling:

> And let our hearts, as subtle masters do,
> Stir up their servants to an act of rage,
> And after seem to chide 'em.
>
> (II, i, 175–7)

Calculated self-manipulation and strategic self-deception – let our hearts goad our hands to the act of murder, then afterwards, 'seem' to reproach them for doing it. What a splitting of the self! No wonder he can't sleep. But perhaps the key metaphor comes from the stage. As the conspirators are dispersing, Cassius says 'show yourselves true Romans', immediately followed by this exhortation from Brutus:

> Good gentlemen, look fresh and merrily.
> Let not our looks put on our purposes,
> But bear it as our Roman actors do,
> With untired spirits and formal constancy.
>
> (II, i, 224–7)

'False face must hide what the false heart doth know,' as Macbeth will say. We have had the stage mentioned before – while Caesar was dallying with the crown, the people, according to Casca, did 'clap him and hiss him, according as he pleased and displeased them, as they use to do the players in the theater' (I, ii, 259–60). After the assassination, in a strange self-conscious moment, Cassius says:

> How many ages hence
> Shall this our lofty scene be acted over
> In states unborn and accents yet unknown ...

and Brutus: 'How many times shall Caesar bleed in sport' (III, i, 111–14). It seems as if 'true Romans' have to be 'Roman actors' and that public Rome – street, Capitol,

Forum – is akin to theatre (Brutus, indeed, refers to 'our performance').

At this moment, in the theatre of Rome, Caesar is bleeding in dead earnest (although of course in the Globe Theatre he is even now bleeding 'in sport'). As the blood 'streams forth' from Caesar's 'wounds' – 'rushing out of doors, to be resolved/ If Brutus so unkindly knocked, or no,' as Antony remarkably puts it, stirring up the people (III, ii, 181–2) – we seem to have entered a blood storm: 'bloody men' with 'bloody hands' at their 'bleeding business', reducing Caesar to a 'bleeding piece of earth':

> Pardon me, Julius! Here wast thou bayed, brave hart;
> Here didst thou fall, and here thy hunters stand,
> Signed in thy spoil and crimsoned in thy lethe ...
>
> (III, i, 204–6)

and 'all the while' Pompey's statue 'ran blood'.

In the 'play' as Brutus plans it he will act the role of high priest and doctor of the republic – 'Let's be sacrificers, but not butchers ... purgers, not murderers' (II, i, 166, 180) – but Shakespeare knew that Plutarch's hunting image was the right one. Hunters and butchers. In the event, the conspirators fall on Caesar and 'hew him as a carcass fit for hounds' (II, i, 174). There will be blood everywhere – as if still streaming from Caesar's wounds – until the end of the ensuing civil war. As foretold by Antony:

> Over thy wounds now do I prophesy ...
> Domestic fury and fierce civil strife
> Shall cumber all the parts of Italy;
> Blood and destruction shall be so in use ...
> And Caesar's spirit, ranging for revenge,
> With Ate by his side come hot from hell,
> Shall in these confines with a monarch's voice
> Cry 'Havoc,' and let slip the dogs of war,
> That this foul deed shall smell above the earth
> With carrion men, groaning for burial.
>
> (III, i, 259–75)

This pretty exactly describes the rest of the play, which will be dominated by Caesar's 'spirit', and in which Antony will prove to be one of the fiercest of the 'dogs of war' (his opening words in Act IV – 'These many then shall die' – are as, if not more, ominous as Brutus' 'It must be by his death'. By the end, Brutus is more than justified in his comment – 'Slaying is the word;/It is a deed in fashion' (V, v, 4–5).

Naively (to be generous), Brutus seems to think that after the assassination, it will be enough if they go into the streets and 'cry "Peace, freedom, and liberty!"' (III, i, 110), as if the republic would somehow run itself, without any structured authority. (However idealistic he may be, Brutus is a disastrously bad practical politician: he does not dispatch Antony; he lets Antony address the people; he insists on the wrong military tactics at Philippi – in all these matters, from a purely political point of view, Cassius is right. That they should quarrel after the assassination, and thus weaken their cause, seems almost inevitable – a case, as I see it, of rogues falling out.) Caesar kept, and represented, a central control of power. In killing him – as a 'tyrant' – Brutus merely releases chaos, anarchy, and civil war as different factions struggle for the masterless power let loose. Brutus has not purged the republic, but destroyed *all* government, and helped to usher in the new tyranny of the triumvirate, which will prove to be far more cruel, oppressive, and terrible than anything associated with the rule (if not reign) of Caesar. (The triumvirate, at first dominated by Antony, kill one hundred senators, including Cicero, and deliberately – nastily – including a number of each others' relatives – thus eliminating the senatorial party. Antony also tries to fiddle Caesar's will. Before Caesar's death, Antony appeared headstrong and passionately loyal – though Cassius knows him for a 'shrewd contriver'. Afterwards he becomes both greedy and barbarous. A dog of war indeed.)

Before the assassination, Brutus says to his fellow conspirators:

> We all stand up against the spirit of Caesar,
> And in the spirit of men there is no blood.
> O, that we then could come by Caesar's spirit,
> And not dismember Caesar! But, alas,
> Caesar must bleed for it.
>
> (II, i, 167–71)

They do dismember Caesar, and he certainly bleeds: but they do not 'come by' his spirit, which escapes and returns to haunt and hunt them – 'ranging for revenge' as Antony predicts. Caesar seems to have a terrible posthumous power. Cassius and Brutus both commit suicide with his name on their lips, and Brutus comes to recognize that, indeed, they never did 'come by' his spirit:

> O Julius Caesar, thou art mighty yet!
> Thy spirit walks abroad, and turns our swords
> In our own proper entrails.
>
> (V, iii, 94–6)

'Spirit' is closely associated with 'fire' in this play:

> You are dull, Casca, and those sparks of life
> That should be in a Roman you do want ...
>
> (I, iii, 57–8)

Cicero, on the other hand, has 'fiery eyes'. Cassius is glad 'That my weak words have struck but thus much show/Of fire from Brutus' (I, ii, 176–7).

During the night of prodigies there is 'a tempest dropping fire' and 'Men, all in fire, walk up and down the streets' (I, iii, 10, 25). It seems as if there is fire, flickering or flaming, all over the place. There are fires of portent; there is literal fire – the plebeians, incited by Antony, go for 'firebrands' crying 'Burn all', while Portia, who eats coals in Plutarch, here simply 'swallowed fire' (IV, iii, 155); and there is inner fire – 'new-fired' hearts, the 'hasty spark' of anger, fiery spirits. Clearly, it is preferable to be 'fiery' with Cicero than 'dull' with Casca. But fire is the most dangerous element, spreading rapidly in unpredictable directions, and in this play there is a sense that it has become lethally out of control. And this loss of control is associated with the death of Caesar. After that, the fire rages and 'ranges' along with Caesar's spirit.

The source of fire is, ultimately the sun. There is an odd moment during the night-time meeting of the conspirators when three of them argue just where the sun is rising – 'doth not the day break here?' No, there; both wrong, over there is where he 'first presents his fire' (II, i, 101, 110). It is as if they sense that they are standing on the threshold of a new dawn in Roman history, but are not quite sure, as it were, where the fire will be coming from. Nor, by the same token, the direction it will take. At the end, Titinius laments over dead Cassius:

> O setting sun,
> As in thy red rays thou dost sink to night,
> So in his red blood Cassius' day is set.
> The sun of Rome is set. Our day is gone ...
> (V, iii, 60–63)

The bloody, fiery day of Roman history initiated by Brutus and his followers is over. But another sun is rising.

Octavius Caesar has very few lines in the play – about forty – and comes across as passionless, cold, detached. (It might be mentioned that much of the language in this play is cool, sparing of images, formal – perhaps because the play is dominated by Roman males.) But it is extraordinary how he makes his presence felt. Shakespeare did something very interesting here. In Plutarch, Octavius is sick and does not take part in the battle of Philippi. In Shakespeare, of course, he does; and there is this curiously telling exchange:

> *Antony.* Octavius, lead your battle softly on
> Upon the left hand of the even field.
> *Octavius.* Upon the right hand I; keep thou the left.
> *Antony.* Why do you cross me in this exigent?
> *Octavius.* I do not cross you; but I will do so.
> (V, i, 16–20)

This calm assertive confidence, at once emotionless and assured, is rather chilling. You begin to realize, as perhaps Antony does – this man is going to run *everything!* Not for nothing does he, literally, have the last word of the play. Shakespeare will show Octavius' sun reach its zenith in his next Roman play. But the atmosphere in that play will be very different. For there we will have Egypt – and Cleopatra.

*

ANTONY AND CLEOPATRA (1607)

This, from North's translation of Plutarch's *Life of Antonius*: 'For they [Antony and Cleopatra] made an order between them, which they called AMIMETOBION (as much as to say, no life comparable and matcheable with it). Later, they invented another word – SYNAPOTHANUMENON (signifying the order and agreement of those that will die together).' They invented words. That is, from what was available they put together special terms which would apply to them alone – using language as a repository of possibilities, trying to transcend the limitations of the available formulations, rehearsing reality by stretching language in new directions and combinations. Shakespeare gloriously takes the hint. His Antony and Cleopatra seem intent on pre-empting language to establish new words to describe their love. New words, new worlds – this is the linguistic atmosphere of the play; ordinary language must be 'melted' (a key word) and reconstituted, so that new propositions and descriptions can be articulated to project and express their emotions. In their speech, everything tends towards hyperbole – i.e. 'excess, exaggeration'. Rhetorically this is related to *Superlatio*, which a dictionary of rhetorical terms glosses as 'exaggerated or extravagant terms used for emphasis and not intended to be understood literally'. Of course, Antony and Cleopatra do not want to be understood 'literally' – they do not work, or play, or love, or live, by the 'letter'. It is precisely the 'letter', and all fixed alphabetical restrictions, that they talk, and love, to dissolve, so that, as it were, they can live and speak in a 'higher' language of their own inventing. For Antony, to burst his armour and his alphabet are, alike, related modes of energy moving towards transcendence.

In his introductory *Lectures on Philosophy*, Hegel wrote that 'alphabetic writing is in itself and for itself the most intelligent'; he also wrote 'everything oriental must be excluded from the history of philosophy'. Alphabetic writing is transparent, an instrument of clarity, it maintains the unity of consciousness; the oriental thus becomes an opaque script, another, more iconic, language altogether, another mode of writing and thus of being-in-the-world, which threatens to disturb and disrupt, even destroy, the alphabetic clarity of consciousness. We can apply this opposition to the play. Caesar is nothing if not 'alphabetic'. He instructs Taurus and his army as he hands out his written orders before the battle of Actium – 'Do not exceed/The prescript of this scroll' (III, viii, 4–5). He never deviates from exact 'pre-scriptions' – the already written – and lives by and from within the orderings of his 'scroll'. Cleopatra, on the other hand, is quintessentially oriental – in Hegel's terms: her actions, like her temperament, are impossible to 'read' in any alphabetic way. She is, from Caesar's point of view, illegible; hardly to be 'read' in his Roman language. She is an ultimate opacity – from Rome's point of view – confounding all customary alphabetic descriptions and decodings. She is in no way 'prescribed' or prescribable, and can no more be held within Caesar's 'scroll' than she can be trapped by his plots and policies.

But first, let me turn to the question of armour, the steel second skin of the man, the soldier, the Roman. As so often in Shakespeare, the opening lines set up terms and problems which will reverberate throughout the play. Philo, a Roman soldier with Antony in Egypt, opens:

> Nay, but this dotage of our general's
> O'erflows the measure.
>
> (I, i, 1–2)

The play, unlike any other by Shakespeare, opens with a negative. It thus implies the denial of a previous assertion – perhaps more affirmative – and his speech goes on to negate, or attempt to degrade and belittle, Antony's behaviour since he has been in Egypt. 'Overflowing the measure' immediately opposes the flooding Nile of Egypt to the concept of 'measure' – control, constraint, containment – which is the very language of Rome. The contest of the play is to be between overflow (excess) and measure (boundaries). Philo goes on to describe the transformation – or rather, in his terms, the deformation – of Antony the soldier into Antony the 'strumpet's fool', the victim of 'lust'. Philo always chooses the diminishing, pejorative word when referring to anything to do with Cleopatra and Egypt, anything which is not connected with Rome, Mars, and the 'office and devotion' of the warrior's code. Thus it is that he goes on to recall the great *soldier* Antony, to contrast him with the man who now serves Eros and Venus–Cleopatra. Again, his terms anticipate much that is to follow:

> His captain's heart
> Which in the scuffles of great fights hath burst
> The buckles on his breast, reneges all temper
> And is become the bellows and the fan
> To cool a gypsy's lust.
>
> (I, i, 6–10)

In battle, then, Antony could not be confined within his own armour; such was his force and energy that it broke out of his soldier's attire – it burst the buckles. Now his great heart 'reneges all temper' – renounces all restraint – but it is clear that it is not finally possible for Antony to be held within any 'temper', any restraints, or, indeed, any bonds. To be sure, he occasionally tries to stay within Roman rules; but in whatever he does – in war, in love – he is driven to burst whatever is 'buckling' him.

In Act IV, Antony is preparing for battle and calls for his armour. The aptly named Eros (as in Plutarch) brings it; but Cleopatra wants to help. She thus becomes, in Antony's words, 'the armourer of my heart' as she fastens the buckles and asks – 'Is this not buckled well?' Antony:

> Rarely, rarely:
> He that unbuckles this, till we do please
> To daff't for our repose, shall hear a storm.
> Thou fumblest, Eros, and my queen's a squire
> More tight at this than thou.
>
> (IV, iv, 11–15)

Armour – amour: there is no etymological connection, but phonetically the words are close. And what we see here, with Cleopatra buckling Antony's armour, almost while they are still in bed, is an overlaying of amour onto armour, so that the armour is eroticized and sensualized – the *business* of war (often referred to) here subsumed into the more all-embracing game of love. (By contrast, we may say that any sensuality and physicality of love and play is 'armoured' by Caesar and

Rome: there the policy of war tries to subsume love's body, making marriage and mating into mere instruments of policy.) Antony's armour, erotically saturated by the hands of Cleopatra, will not be taken off, he says, 'till we do please to daff't for our repose'. This anticipates his death.

As he moves towards that death, Antony says to Eros:

> Sometime we see a cloud that's dragonish,
> A vapor sometime like a bear or lion ...
> ... Thou hast seen these signs:
> They are black vesper's pageants ...
> That which is now a horse, even with a thought
> The rack dislimns, and makes it indistinct
> As water is in water.
>
> (IV, xiv, 2–11)

'Dis-limn' – that is, un-paint, efface – is Shakespeare's own invention; it is part of the 'reversal' which is happening to Antony, whose role in the 'pageant' (which also meant a mobile play or stage) is nearly over. He is moving towards 'indistinctness' – he, the man of the greatest 'distinction' in the world: he is being physically 'dis-limned' (which sounds the homophone 'dislim*b*ed'), effaced by Caesar, by nature, by himself. (Cleopatra will 'paint' him again after his death, but we will come to that dazzling act of retrieval and recuperation.) Antony continues:

> My good knave Eros, now thy captain is
> Even such a body: here I am Antony,
> Yet cannot hold this visible shape ...
>
> (IV, xiv, 12–14)

He is in fact moving towards physical invisibility, because Antony, the name, the individual, the specific and world-famous identity, can no longer 'hold' onto his bodily shape. He is moving out, moving through, moving beyond; melting, but also transcending the final barrier – the body itself. And so *he* takes his armour off, since he is indeed ready for 'repose':

> Unarm Eros. The long day's task is done,
> And we must sleep ...

> Off, pluck off:
> The sevenfold shield of Ajax cannot keep
> The battery from my heart. O, cleave, my sides!
> Heart, once be stronger than thy continent,
> Crack thy frail case! Apace, Eros, apace.
> No more a soldier. Bruised pieces, go;
> You have been nobly borne . . .
>
> (IV, xiv, 35–43)

The armour is not broken or burst, but discarded; it is almost as though he is taking his body to pieces and throwing it away – 'Bruised pieces, go' does seem almost to refer to the body as well, for it is that 'frail case' which he now wishes to burst free from. The body is the final boundary.

Boundary; bounty; bound; bond; band – these are words of varying importance in the play, but they all serve to set up a crucial series of echoes, half-echoes, indeed anti-echoes, if one can imagine such a thing. Rome is the place of bonds (Caesar: 'I know it for my bond'); and bounds ('He's bound unto Octavia,' the luckless messenger tells Cleopatra); and bands (Caesar says to Octavia – 'prove such a wife . . . as my farthest band/Shall pass on thy aproof'). It is also the place of 'hoops' and 'knots' (in relation to the problem of what can bind Caesar and Antony together), and of 'squares', 'rules', and 'measures'. Antony tries to make a return to this Roman world, but no matter what 'bonds' he enters into, no matter how much he intends to try to live 'by the rule', it is, for him, finally not possible. This is not because he is a traitorous man, making and breaking promises for devious purposes. He simply cannot, as we say, be held 'within bounds'. When he is in Rome, in Caesar's house – in the heart of the heart of Rome, as it were – he seems to lose his natural strength and spirit and fortune. As his soothsayer tells him: 'If thou dost play with him at any game,/Thou art sure to lose; and of that natural luck/He beats thee 'gainst the odds' (II, iii, 26–8). And Antony recalls that this is indeed true; whatever game they play, with dice, cocks, quail etc., Caesar always wins. These details are all in Plutarch, but note the word that Shakespeare gives to Antony – 'and his quails ever/Beat mine, inhooped, at odds' (II, iii, 38–9). 'Inhooped' refers to the game of putting the quails within a hoop so that they could not avoid fighting (apparently a very ancient sport, going back to China). But of course it is really Antony who is 'inhooped' in Rome, and within the hoop he cannot be himself, rendered almost impotent within the 'bounds' of Caesar's domain. Antony is most remarkable for his 'bounty', with all that that word suggests of generosity, an endless spending and giving of a superabundant nature. In North's Plutarch, this 'liberality' is often referred to – and with admiration, even when Plutarch is criticizing Antony for his riotous feasting and wasteful negligence. Antony, whatever else, is an example of '*magnanimitas*'.

In the play, this 'bounty' is constantly referred to and made manifest. I shall single out three notable occasions. On the night before the critical battle of Actium, Antony reasserts himself as 'Antony'. 'Come,/Let's have one other gaudy night: call to me/All my sad captains; fill our bowls once more', and Cleopatra joins in the spirit of the occasion, reasserting the *role* which in this case is the *reality*, of both of them: 'But since my lord/Is Antony again, I will be Cleopatra' (III, xiii, 182–7). They are most themselves when playing themselves. They are out-playing history, as I shall suggest later. But we then immediately go over to Caesar's camp and hear Caesar give *his* instructions on this important night: 'And feast the army; we have store to do't,/And they have earned the waste. Poor Antony!' (IV, i, 15–16). Then we are back in Cleopatra's palace, and hear Antony saying – 'Be bounteous at our meal . . .' (IV, ii, 10). In the context and frame of Antony's 'bounty', Caesar's arid, quantifying speech seems like the utterance of a very small soul indeed – the epitome of cynical parsimony, so that 'feast' is translated into 'store', and then further degraded into 'waste'. Here is another absolutely basic opposition in the play, a confrontation and contestation of vocabularies so that what is 'feast' in one, is regarded as 'waste' in the other. Antony gives from bounty; Caesar works from inventories. 'Poor Antony!' – yes, from one point of view; from another he is rich Antony, since he gives unthinkingly from his spirit, while Caesar – poor Caesar – distributes carefully from his 'store'. 'Feast' celebrates excess: 'waste' defers to boundaries.

In North's Plutarch (and Shakespeare took almost as much

from Plutarch for this play as he did for *Julius Caesar*) there is a little incident during the battle of Actium recorded thus:

Furthermore, he dealt very friendly and courteously with Domitius, and against Cleopatra's mind. For, he being sick of an ague when he went and took a little boat to go to Caesar's camp, Antonius was very sorry for it, but yet he sent after him all his carriage, train, and men; and the same Domitius, as though he gave him to understand that he repented his open treason, he died immediately after.

Shakespeare amplifies this in his account of the defection and death of Enobarbus. Enobarbus, a good though cynical soldier, begins to feel that it is foolish to remain loyal to Antony in his visible decline:

Mine honesty and I begin to square.
The loyalty well held to fools does make
Our faith mere folly: yet he that can endure
To follow with allegiance a fall'n lord
Does conquer him that did his master conquer,
And earns a place 'i th' story.

(III, xiii, 41–6)

But shortly thereafter he leaves Antony and goes over to Caesar. Antony's reaction is immediate. He sends 'gentle adieus, and greetings', and soon a Roman soldier is telling Enobarbas:

Antony
Hath after thee sent all thy treasure, with
His bounty overplus.

(IV, vi, 20–23: my italics)

Bounty *overplus* – superabundant abundance, excessive excess. This is the mark of Antony. Enobarbus has no ague; but this act of bounty effectively kills him. His reaction:

I am alone the villain of the earth,
And feel I am so most. O Antony,
Thou mine of bounty, how wouldst thou have paid
My better service, when my turpitude
Thou dost so crown with gold! This blows my heart . . .
I fight against thee! No, I will go seek

Some ditch wherein to die: the foul'st best fits
My latter part of life.

(IV, vi, 30–39)

His last words are:

O, Antony,
Nobler than my revolt is infamous,
Forgive me in thine own particular,
But let the world rank me in register
A master-leaver and a fugitive.
O, Antony! O, Antony!

(IV, ix, 18–23)

Thus Enobarbus dies in a ditch – the lowest earth– untranscended; unlike Antony and Cleopatra, who move towards fire and air from the mud of the Nile. To be 'politic' with Caesar after being loyal to Antony, is a degenerative deformation which cannot be endured. And Enobarbus effectively 'loses his place in the story' – he cancels himself, writes himself out of the poetic termination of Antony's life, annihilates himself in a ditch. And his parting word is – not 'Poor Antony!'; but the far more expressive 'O, Antony!' This Antony is the measureless measure of all that Enobarbus has deserted. After such bounty – what forgiveness?

My third reference is to Cleopatra's imaginative re-creation and recuperation of Antony after his death. It takes place in the presence of Dolabella, and leads to one of the most crucial exchanges in the play. Cleopatra has her own oriental bounty, and she now speaks with an overflowing super-abundance of language which makes her final speeches perhaps the most poetically powerful and coruscating in the whole of Shakespeare. Her re-creation of Antony concludes:

For his bounty,
There was no winter in't: an autumn 'twas
That grew the more by reaping. His delights
Were dolphinlike, they show'd his back above
The element they lived in. In his livery
Walked crowns and crownets: realms and islands were
As plates dropped from his pocket.

(V, ii, 86–93)

Such a way of speaking, which goes beyond hyperbole into

another realm of 'truth', is too much for the Roman-practical-empirical Dolabella, who interrupts her – 'Cleopatra –'. To which she says:

> Think you there was or might be such a man
> As this I dreamt of?

Dolabella is sure – 'Gentle madam, no.'

> You lie, up to the hearing of the gods.
> But if there be nor ever were one such,
> It's past the size of dreaming; nature wants stuff
> To vie strange forms with fancy, yet t'imagine
> An Antony were nature's piece 'gainst fancy,
> Condemning shadows quite.
>
> (V, ii, 93–100)

Cleopatra's image of Antony out-imagines the imagination, out-dreams dream. If you agree with Dolabella's Roman negative, the Roman deflationary perspective – the 'nay' which starts the play, then you deny Cleopatra's poetry and its power; deny Antony's bounty and *its* power. And you are well in danger of 'losing a place in the story'. But that is hardly possible; for by this stage, the soaring bounty of the imagination has passed beyond the boundaries and circumscriptions of nature itself. This is the awesome, magical excess which makes the world itself but a place of limits and limitations. Recall Antony and Cleopatra's opening words:

> *Cleopatra.* If it be love indeed, tell me how much.
> *Antony.* There's beggary in the love that can be reckoned.
> *Cleopatra.* I'll set a bourn how far to be beloved.
> *Antony.* Then must thou needs find out new heaven, new earth.
>
> (I, i, 14–17)

Philo's 'lust' is immediately rephrased as 'love'. Cleopatra, playing, speaks temporarily in Roman terms – how much? (quantifying), and wanting to set a 'bourn' (boundary) on being loved. But Antony already points out the direction in which the play will move. For they do have to find out 'new heaven, new earth', a whole new world beyond quantifications and boundaries, until the 'truth' engendered by their love, their imagination, their dreaming, goes far beyond the restricted and impoverished realism of the Roman eye. By which point it simply *is* 'paltry to be Caesar'.

There is a great stress on 'time' in *Julius Caesar*, and it is well to remember that this is a history play. The outcome of the events it dramatized was the so-called 'Augustan peace', during which Christ was born and the pagan Empire – which Virgil called the Empire without end – was established, according to later writers, as a divine preparation for the Christian Empire. Octavius Caesar, himself a pagan, unknowingly laid the way for the True City, so in Christian terms the struggles and battles in the play affect, not merely his society, but all human society, the *orbis terrae* of Augustine. The events of the play are indeed of 'world' importance – world-shattering, world-remaking (the word 'world' occurs at least forty-five times in the play). By the same token, an earlier pagan world is being silenced, extinguished, and history – as the audience would know – is on Caesar's side. He is in time with Time. Antony and Cleopatra are out of time, in more than one sense. Thus, at the beginning, when Antony decides that he must return to Rome, Cleopatra silences his apologies, referring to the time-out-of-time when they were together – 'Eternity was in our lips and eyes' – while Antony, thinking Romanly for the moment, refers to 'the strong necessity of time'. Egypt, in this play, is a timeless present, which is to say an Eternity.

It can hardly escape our attention that the play is full of messengers from the start – two in the first scene, some thirty-five in all, with nearly every scene having a messenger of some kind. The play itself is extremely episodic, with some forty-two scenes (no scene breaks at all in the Folio), which makes for a very rapid sequence of change of place. There are nearly two hundred entrances and exits, all contributing to what Dr Johnson called the 'continual hurry' and 'quick succession' of events, which 'call the mind forward without intermission'. This can all be interpreted in different ways, but it certainly depicts a world in constant movement, in which time and place move and change so quickly that the whole world seems in a 'hurry' and in a state of flux – fluid, melting, re-forming. Messengers and messages bring information from the outside –

they are interruptions, irruptions, precipitants of change. History is going on, and on, and at an ever accelerating pace. Yet the remarkable thing is that time seems somehow to stand still in Egypt – both within and without the reach of 'messages'; both vulnerable to history yet outside it. When Antony is away, Cleopatra simply wants to 'sleep out this great gap of time' (I, v, 6). (When she first approaches Antony in her 'barge', the city goes out to see her, leaving Antony alone 'Whistling to th' air; which, but for vacancy,/Had gone to gaze on Cleopatra too,/And made a gap in nature' – II, ii, 222–4. It is as if Cleopatra creates 'gaps' – gaps of time, gaps of nature.) For Rome, Egypt represents a great waste of time while the 'business' of history is going on. The word 'business', more often than not, carries pejorative connotations in Shakespeare. It is notable that Caesar interrupts his formulaic (as I hear it), elegiac 'praise' of the dead Antony because of – a messenger: 'The *business* of this man looks out of him;/We'll hear him what he says' (V, i, 50: my italics). He never completes the speech. Conversely, Cleopatra interrupts history to complete her poetic re-creation of Antony – from which no 'business' can distract her. From the Egyptian perspective, history itself is a 'gap of time', and Cleopatra, though growing physically older ('wrinkled deep in time'), seems to linger in Eternity, waiting for Antony to return from the trivial – though world-shattering – distractions of history.

As well as being a history play, *Antony and Cleopatra* contains within it traces of the outlines of a morality play – for by the early Renaissance the 'moral' of the story of the illustrious lovers was well established. We can find it in Spenser's *Fairie Queene*, Book V, Canto VIII:

> Nought under heaven so strongly doth allure
> The sence of man, and all his minde possesse,
> As beauties lovely baite, that doth procure,
> Great warriours oft their rigour to represse,
> And mighty hands forget their manlinesse . . .
> So also did that great Oetean Knight
> For his loves sake his Lions skin undight:

and

so did warlike Antony neglect
The worlds whole rule for Cleopatra's sight.
Such wondrous powre hath womens fair aspect,
To captive men, and make them all the world reject.

This 'moral' reading is there in Plutarch's version, in which Antony becomes 'effeminate' and made 'subject to a woman's will'. He is particularly critical of Antony's behaviour at the battle of Actium (when he followed the fleeing Cleopatra). 'There Antonius showed plainly, that he had not only lost the courage and heart of an Emperor, but also of a valiant man, and that he was not his own man ... he has so carried away with the vain love of this woman, as if he had been glued unto her, and that she could not have removed without moving of him also.' In Spenser's terms, Antony 'rejected' the world for the mere love of a woman. Whether he found or made a better world is not, of course, considered. But, while Shakespeare's play does include these historical–morality elements (unquestionably, his glue-like relationship with Cleopatra ruins him as a politician and spoils him as a soldier, and, in worldly terms, she does – as he recognizes – lead him 'to the very heart of loss' – IV, xii, 29) – it complicates any ethical 'reading' of the story, so there can be no question of seeing it simply as another version of a good soldier losing his empire because of a bad woman. To understand this more clearly, we have to take into account another figure. For, if Octavius Caesar is related to the onward and inexorable movement of History, Antony is related to a god, Hercules.

This relationship is suggested in Plutarch who, however, relates Antony more closely to Bacchus. Shakespeare strengthens the association with Hercules. Hercules was famous for his anger, and so is Antony. As his anger begins to rise, Cleopatra says: 'Look, prithee, Charmian,/How this Herculean Roman does become/The carriage of his chafe' (I, iii, 84–5). Reacting in fury to Cleopatra's flight from the battle and what ensues, he cries out:

The shirt of Nessus is upon me; teach me,
Alcides, thou mine ancestor, thy rage.

(IV, xii, 44–5)

Plutarch refers to Antony being deserted by a god: 'it is said that suddenly they heard a marvellous sweet harmony of sundry sorts of instruments of music ... as they use in Bacchus feasts ... Now, such as in reason sought the depth of the interpretation of this wonder, thought it was the god unto whom Antonius bare singular devotion to counterfeit and resemble him, that did forsake them.' Shakespeare takes the scene, and the interpretation, but makes one telling change. Late in the play, some soldiers hear 'Music i' th' air' and decide ''Tis the god Hercules, whom Antony loved,/Now leaves him' (IV, iii, 15–16). Where his Antony is concerned – despite his manifest taste for wine – Shakespeare wants us to think more of Hercules, less of Bacchus. Hercules was of course *the* hero – hero turned god – *par excellence*. There were many allegories concerning Hercules current by the Middle Ages. One (apparently from the Sophist, Prodicus), has Hercules as a young man arriving at a place where the road branches into two paths, one leading up a steep hill, the other into a pleasant glade. At the dividing point, two fair women meet him: one, modest and sober, urges him to take the steep path; the other, seductive if meretricious, uses her arts in an attempt to attract him into the glade. The hero, of course chooses the steep hill of Virtue over the beckoning glades of Pleasure. There were many medieval and Renaissance depictions of this struggle of Virtue and Pleasure over Hercules (there is a famous Dürer engraving of it – *Der Hercules*), with Pleasure, *hedone*, *voluptas*, sometimes associated with Venus. The implications, for us, are quite clear: if Antony is related to Hercules, Cleopatra is related to Venus. The key difference, of course, is that Hercules–Antony chooses Pleasure, pays heed to the solicitations of Venus – thus inverting the traditional moral of this allegory. According then to the accumulated traditional lore which had grown up around the much metamorphosed and allegorized figure of Hercules, Antony is indeed a version of Hercules, but one who, as it were, decided to take the wrong road – not up the steep hill of (Roman) virtue, but off the track into the (oriental) glades of pleasure.

There are other divinities in the play, and if Hercules deserts Antony, he in turn goes on to play Osiris to Cleopatra's Isis.

The union of these divinities assures the fertility of Egypt: in Plutarch's study of the myth (well known in Shakespeare's time), Osiris is the Nile which floods and makes fertile the land – he is form, the seminal principle, and Isis is matter. From their union are bred not only crops, but animals, such as the serpents of the Nile. Typhon the crocodile, born of Nile mud, represents for Plutarch the irrational, bestial part of the soul by which Osiris is deceived and torn to pieces. There are, of course, numerous references to the Nile, its floods, its serpents, and so on, in the play, and Shakespeare clearly has this myth actively in mind. But it is not a stable or fixed incorporation. Cleopatra is Isis but also Antony's 'serpent of old Nile', and by a serpent of Nile will she die – a serpent by a serpent 'valiantly vanquished', as Antony–Osiris is 'a Roman by a Roman valiantly vanquished' (the second Roman is more Antony than Caesar – as Cleopatra says: 'Not Caesar's valor hath o'erthrown Antony,/But Antony's hath triumphed on itself' – IV, xv, 14–15). The monster-crocodile who destroys Antony is, in this play, Octavius Caesar – though he is hardly seen in those terms. He is a disguised Typhon for Antony and Cleopatra, who are playing at being Osiris and Isis – but, really, he is not in their self-mythologizing act, not in their 'play' at all. I use the word 'play' advisedly and deliberately. Cleopatra is, of course, above all a great actress. She can play with Antony to beguile him; she can play at being Isis, thus anticipating her own move towards transcendence; and she can 'play' at her death, easily outplaying Caesar's crafty political deviousness. In this way, she completely transforms her desolate state, not submitting to the downward turn of Fortune, but inverting it into the occasion of her own triumph of the imagination:

> My desolation does begin to make
> A better life. 'Tis paltry to be Caesar:
> Not being Fortune, he's but Fortune's knave,
> A minister of her will . . .
>
> (V, ii, 1–4)

Cleopatra will be her *own* Fortune – a triumph of the 'will'.

She is aware that Caesar will display her in Rome, and that

her life with Antony will be 'staged' in a degraded form, in keeping with that tendency of Roman rhetoric to devalue and translate downwards the life associated with Egypt:

> The quick comedians
> Extemporally will stage us, and present
> Our Alexandrian revels: Antony
> Shall be brought drunken forth, and I shall see
> Some squeaking Cleopatra boy my greatness
> I' th' posture of a whore.
>
> (V, ii, 216–21)

(Which, of course, exactly describes what is going on in the Elizabethan theatre at that moment, with some boy 'squeaking' Cleopatra. This is not Nabokovian self-reflexivity. Rather, it is effectively as if the drama is so incandescent that it is scorning its own resources, shedding the very medium which has served to put its poetry into flight. It is as though 'representation' is scorching itself away to reveal the thing itself – an electrifying moment of astonishing histrionic audacity and magic.) So – Cleopatra puts on her own play, on her own stage, with her own costume, speeches, and gestures:

> Now, Charmian!
> Show me, my women, like a queen: go fetch
> My best attires. I am again for Cydnus,
> To meet Mark Antony. Sirrah Iras, go ...
> And when thou hast done this chare, I'll give thee leave
> To play till doomsday. – Bring our crown and all.
>
> (V, ii, 227–32)

> My resolution's placed, and I have nothing
> Of woman in me: now from head to foot
> I am marble-constant: now the fleeting moon
> No planet is of mine.
>
> (V, ii, 238–41)

She is moving beyond the body, beyond time, beyond the whole world of transcience and decay, beyond her own planet the moon, with all that it implies of tidal periodicity. The clown enters with his figs, which contain the serpent she will use for her suicide (at the beginning, Charmian says 'I love long life better than figs' – I, ii, 32 – by the end this, like so much else, is reversed: Cleopatra likes figs better than long life). We move to her final self-apotheosis, played with great dignity and ceremony, at which Cleopatra is at once her own directress and her own priestess:

> Give me my robe, put on my crown, I have
> Immortal longings in me . . .
> . . . Husband, I come:
> Now to that name my courage prove my title!
> I am fire, and air; my other elements
> I give to baser life . . .
>
> (V, ii, 280–90)

Out of the earth, mud, dung, water associated with the Nile and its fertility, she has distilled an essence composed only of the higher elements, air and fire. She is 'marble' for the duration of the performance; she is also, like Antony, 'melting', dissolving, but melting into a higher atmosphere. She gives a farewell kiss to Iras who falls down dead – perhaps from poison, perhaps from grief – and Cleopatra comments:

> Dost thou lie still?
> If thus thou vanishest, thou tell'st the world
> It is not worth leave-taking.
>
> (V, ii, 296–8)

To the snake she says:

> O, couldst thou speak,
> That I might hear thee call great Caesar ass
> Unpolicied!
>
> (V, ii, 306–8)

She has seen through Caesar's tricks and stratagems – 'He words me, girls, he words me, that I should not/Be noble to myself' (V, ii, 191–2); she knows, too, that he uses language instrumentally, merely for devious political ends. And when Proculeus refers to Caesar's 'bounty', she knows that it is but a pitiful and transparent travesty of the real bounty of Antony. In her superbly performed death, we see the triumph of the 'oriental' imagination over the 'alphabetic' utilitarianism of Caesar. The world will indeed be his, and another kind of Empire inaugurated; but from the perspective of Cleopatra, and *just for the duration of the play*, it seems a world 'not worth leave-taking'. So her last words are an incomplete question: 'What should I stay – ' as she passes out of language, body, world, altogether. There is no *staying* her now. Charmian completes her question with her own final speech:

> In this wild world? So, fare thee well.
> Now boast thee, death, in thy possession lies
> A lass unparalleled. Downy windows, close;
> And golden Phoebus never be beheld
> Of eyes again so royal! Your crown's awry;
> I'll mend it, and then play –
>
> (V, ii, 314–19)

Thus Cleopatra, and her girls, play their way out of the reach of history, with an intensity of self-sustaining, self-validating poetry which does indeed eclipse the policies and purposes of Caesar. (There are some recent readings which see Antony and Cleopatra as failed politicians who turn to aesthetics to gloss over their mistakes and cheer themselves up with poetry. I can imagine such a play, but this one is not it.) Cleopatra was 'confined' in her monument, a prisoner of Caesar's force – apparently secure within the boundaries of his soldiers and his 'scroll'. It is by the unforgettable excess and bounty/beauty of her last 'Act' that she triumphs over all that would confine her, and turns death into 'play', *the* play that will take her into Eternity.

Let me return to the opposition between feast and waste. Feast derives from *festa* – holiday – and in one sense, Antony and Cleopatra turn life in Egypt into a perpetual holiday. 'Waste' is more interesting. Just as 'dirt' has been defined as 'matter out of place', so the idea of 'waste' presupposes a boundary or classification mark which enables one to draw a distinction between what is necessary, valuable, usable in some way, and what lies outside these categories – 'waste'. Antony, we may say, recognizes no such boundary. Indeed, he 'wastes' himself, in the sense that he is endlessly prodigal of all he has and does not count the cost. From Antony's point of view, all life in Egypt can be seen as a feast; in Caesar's eyes – the Roman perspective – it is all 'waste'. From the etymology of the word (*uacare*, to be empty or vacant; *uanus*, hollow, vain; *uastus*, desolated, desert, vast; up to Old English *weste* – see Eric Partridge's *Origins*), we can say that there is a connection between vastness, vacancy, vanity, and waste. Antony is inhabiting a realm of vastness, vanity, vacancy – the 'great gap' named by Cleopatra (Caesar, indeed, refers to Antony's 'vacancy'). From Caesar's point of view, and those who see with the Roman eye, Antony is indeed 'empty' while Caesar is referred to as 'the fullest man'. Thus Enobarbus, commenting on Antony's challenge to Caesar to meet him in single battle: 'that he should dream,/Knowing all measures, the full Caesar will/Answer his emptiness!' Caesar is, from one point of view, *full* – full of history, of Fortune, of time. Antony is 'empty' – committed to vacancy, vanity, waste. The question implicitly posed is whether he and Cleopatra, and their way of life, are not 'full' of something quite outside of Caesar's discourse and his measurements, something which makes *him* the empty man. Caesar is full of politics, empty of poetry: Antony and Cleopatra reach a point where they are empty of politics, but full of poetry. Which is the real 'vacancy'? It depends where you are standing, how you are looking. But there is nothing 'vast' about Caesar: even if he conquers the whole world, everything is done with 'measure' and 'temper' (temperance). If Antony and Cleopatra melt and dissolve, it is into a 'vastness' which is the necessary space for their exceeding, their excess – 'beyond the size of dreaming'. In this play, Shakespeare compels a complete revaluation of 'waste'. Historically, it was *not* paltry to be Caesar, certainly not this Caesar, who is insured of, and will ensure, a 'temperate' imperial future, during which time Christ would be born. This Caesar certainly has his place in the story of history. But in this play, his conquest is registered as a gradual diminishment as he – alphabetically – takes over the Orient, but in doing so merely imposes Roman 'prescriptions' on a vast world of pagan fecundity, spilled plenty, and an oriental magnificence which transforms 'waste' into 'bounty', and makes Caesar seem like the 'merchant' he is, a calculating Machiavel – an ass unpolicied.

Boundaries are, of course, of central importance for civilization. For Vico, in *The New Science*, civilized man is precisely one who creates and guards 'confines' – 'for it was necessary to set up boundaries to the field in order to put a stop to the infamous promiscuity of things in the bestial state. On these boundaries were to be fixed the confines first of families, then of gentes or houses, later of peoples, and finally of nations.' There is much in Shakespeare which honours and defends the importance of recognizing the need for boundaries. But in this play, writing against the recorded, inexorable grain and movement of history, Shakespeare makes us re-value what might have been lost in the triumph of Caesar:

O, see, my women,
The crown o' th' earth doth melt. My lord!
O, withered is the garland of the war,
The soldier's pole is fall'n: young boys and girls
Are level now with men. The odds is gone,
And there is nothing left remarkable
Beneath the visiting moon.

(IV, xv, 62–8)

This is 'waste'? Rather, the fecundity, plenitude and bounty associated with Egypt, and Antony in Egypt, have fed into and nourished Cleopatra's speech, until she is speaking a kind of language of pure poetry about which alphabetic man can have nothing to say. A whole pagan age is over; the future belongs to Caesar – and Christ. But confronted with this kind of transcendent poetry, which is indeed all 'excess', that future seems merely trivial, temporal, temperate. 'The road of excess leads to the Palace of Wisdom,' wrote Blake. In this play, the poetry of excess leads to the unbounded, unboundaried, spaces of infinity. Saving leads to earthly empire: squandering opens an avenue to Eternity. All air and fire – and poetry. Bounty overplus.

*

TIMON OF ATHENS (1607–8?)

'Bounty' figures prominently and plays a large role in what may, or may not, be Shakespeare's next play – *Timon of Athens*. (It first finds print in the Folio of 1623 where it occupies the place intended for *Troilus and Cressida*, which had to be withdrawn because of copyright difficulties. On internal evidence, it belongs to the 1605–9 period of Shakespeare's plays. But it seems unfinished and could conceivably have been written later. I give the conventionally agreed-on date.) Bounty, bounteous, bounteousness – the words occur at least seventeen times by my count. But something has taken a turn. This is the wrong kind of bounty, bounty gone wrong. We hear, in the opening lines as the Poet, Painter, Jeweler, and Merchant enter Timon's house (bent on hypocritical sycophancy and cynical exploitation): 'See,/Magic of bounty, all these spirits thy power/Hath conjured to attend' (I, i, 5–7). But the 'magic' is irresponsible, discreative, ruinous, and all the 'spirits' it 'conjures to attend' turn out to be venal, heartless, 'monstrous'. As well as the continuous acclaiming of Timon's 'bounty', there are some warning lines:

> 'Tis pity bounty had not eyes behind,
> That man might ne'er be wretched for his mind.
>
> (I, ii, 166–7)

'for his mind' – on account of his inclinations: this from Flavius, the loyal and honest steward.

> No villainous bounty yet hath passed my heart;
> Unwisely, not ignobly, have I given.
>
> (II, ii, 183–4)

Thus Timon defends himself against the 'sermon' of his despairing steward. And it is the steward who, in response to Timon's expression of confidence that his friends will not let him 'sink', comments sadly:

> I would I could not think it; that thought is bounty's foe.
> Being free itself, it thinks all others so.
>
> (II, ii, 242–3)

Of course, Timon's friends are no friends at all – and first he 'sinks', and then he dives.

> Strange, unusual blood,
> When man's worst sin is, he does too much good.

Who then dares to be half so kind again?
For bounty, that makes gods, do still mar men.
(IV, ii, 38–41)

It is something of a question whether Timon is truly 'kind' – and how much *good* he actually does. Dr Johnson maintained that the play 'is a warning against that ostentatious liberality which scatters bounty but confers no benefits and buys flattery but no friendship'. Another eighteenth-century writer, William Richardson, also judges Timon adversely. In this play, he says, Shakespeare 'illustrates the consequences of that inconsiderate profusion which has the appearance of liberality and is supposed even by the inconsiderate person himself to proceed from a generous principle, but which, in reality, has its chief origin in the love of distinction'. As Richardson trenchantly points out, Timon 'is not so solicitous of alleviating the distress of obscure affliction . . . He is not represented as visiting the cottage of the fatherless and widow, but is wonderfully generous to men of high rank and character.' It would only be a little overstating the case to say that Timon's idea of 'bounty' is to lay on drunken orgies for his posh acquaintances. Witness Flavius:

When all our offices have been oppressed
With riotous feeders, when our vaults have wept
With drunken spilth of wine, when every room
Hath blazed with lights and brayed with minstrelsy,
I have retired me to a wasteful cock,
And set mine eyes at flow.
(II, ii, 168–73)

('b*l*azed with lights and b*r*ayed with minstrelsy' – this is Shakespeare at his most powerful). Aristotle states; 'he is liberal who spends according to his substance *and on the right objects*; and he who exceeds is prodigal' (my italics). Timon is not liberal: he is prodigal, culpably prodigal.

But certainly, his flatterers treat him, and possibly he regards himself, as a god. One of them says of his 'bounty':

He pours it out. Plutus, the god of gold,
Is but his steward . . .
(I, i, 283–4)

We will come back to gods – and gold. Here it will serve to note that Timon's kind of 'bounty' – blind, indiscriminate, proud, self-deceiving, and terribly vulnerable – certainly 'mars the man'. Indeed, it could be said that Timon is never seen as a 'man' at all. When he can no longer go on playing 'god', he insists on being 'beast' – the two words recur, often in close proximity as if squeezing out, or foreclosing on, possible intermediate states. This is a play about extremes.

The main point about Timon's munificence is that it is as reckless, indiscriminate, and all-embracing, as his later invectives and denunciations are to be. All motives come mixed, but there is something distinctly impure in Timon's generosity. As the honest Flavius tells him:

> Great Timon, noble, worthy, royal Timon!
> Ah, when the means are gone that buy this praise,
> The breath is gone whereof this praise is made.
> Feast-won, fast-lost . . .
>
> (II, ii, 178–81)

Proud, ostentatious Timon has been buying praise and adulation – but, as Flavius well knows, all he purchases is empty words. He is indeed often called 'noble' and worthy', just as his 'bounty' is consistently referred to. But the words undergo what is sometimes referred to as devaluation through repetition (something similar happens to the word 'honourable' in Antony's famous speech over Caesar's body). When Flaminius goes to Lucullus to ask for money to help Timon, Lucullus, expecting another gift, asks him what he has under his cloak. 'Faith, nothing but an empty box, sir, which in my lord's behalf I come to entreat your honor to supply' (III, i, 16–19). But Lucullus has no 'honour' to 'supply' (fill) the box, so it remains empty. This is what happens to the honorific terms in the play. There is no longer anything to fill them; they are emptied out, and by the end, words like 'bounty' and 'noble' have a hollow ring. As with the key words, so with the main characters in this Athens – they are hollow, all 'outside', no inside. Timon commends painting because 'These penciled figures are/Even such as they give out' (I, i, 159–60). What you see is all there is. This is true of the characters who may, indeed, be said to be 'penciled' – outlined, sketched. They are just as hypocritical, mean, ungrateful as they appear. Most unusually for Shakespeare, they have no interiority (this very definitely includes Timon himself). Indeed, the play itself may be said to have no 'inside' and is, itself, something of an empty box.

Coleridge called this play an 'after vibration' of *King Lear*, and there are certainly distinctive echoes. These include the horror of ingratitude ('O see the monstrousness of man/When he looks out in an ungrateful shape' – III, ii, 77–8); Timon's denudation and reduction to an 'unhoused' condition in the wilderness outside the city walls; and the ominous reiteration of the word 'nothing' ('For these my present friends, as they are to me nothing, so in nothing bless them, and to nothing are they welcome' – III, vi, 82–5). But there is a very definite 'after vibration' of *Antony and Cleopatra* as well, an after-echo which has a distressing or displeasing tendency towards satire and even travesty, of a rather bleak kind. There is good reason to think that Shakespeare wrote the two plays closely together (but no point in speculating as to the possible explanations for such a drastic change of mood and tone). At times, Timon speaks lines reminiscent of Antony (e.g. 'Methinks I could deal kingdoms to my friends' – I, ii, 228), but it is somehow not the same. As in *Antony and Cleopatra* we have the regular use of the words 'bind', 'bond', 'bound'; but not only is 'bounty' revalued, or rather devalued, but 'feast' is rather horribly degraded, even, I shall suggest, to the point of sacrilegious parody. In *Antony and Cleopatra*, 'feast' was opposed to 'waste'; in *Timon of Athens* 'feast' *is* 'waste'. The first feast in the play is a veritable debauch, exemplifying Flavius' description of Timon's habitual prodigal entertainment – amply justifying the question to Timon, 'What needs these feasts, pomps, and vainglories?' (I, ii, 253–4). This is spoiled ceremony, hospitality vulgarized, wasteful bounty. As a Senator comments: 'Still in motion/Of raging waste? It cannot hold, it will not' (II, i, 3–4). Timon's bounty starts out as a flow of gold ('He pours it out' – I, i, 283); it manifests itself as a 'flow of riot' (II, ii, 3); and soon becomes a 'flow of debts' (II, ii, 152). Uncontrolled spillage. 'Feast-won, fast-lost,' as Flavius succinctly puts it.

Trying to 'win' people with this kind of feasting, ensures that you will lose them. Timon's second 'feast', at which he serves water to his ungrateful 'friends' ('Uncover, dogs, and lap'), is a sort of anti-feast, a complete negation at the opposite extreme from the earlier squandering. These are Timon's two, Timon's *only*, positions. 'One day he gives us diamonds, next day stones' (III, vi, 121), says one of the lords as they are driven away from the anti-feast. Diamonds or stones: nothing in between.

But something worse. At the first feast, there is the following exchange:

Timon. You had rather be at a breakfast of enemies than a dinner of friends.
Alcibiades. So they were bleeding new, my lord, there's no meat like 'em; I could wish my best friends at such a feast.

(I, ii, 76–80)

The exaggeration or jesting of a military man, perhaps. But there is more than a hint of cannibalism in this play in which flatterers are said to 'drink' men, and ladies to 'eat' lords. Timon, in his glory days, 'had the world as my confectionary' (IV, iii, 261), which suggests a too sickly-sweet meal, luxurious rather than nourishing. When, at the height of his hysterical revulsion, he scrabbles around in the wilds and finds a root, he says:

That the whole life of Athens were in this!
Thus would I eat it.

(IV, iii, 282–3)

Sweets, roots, Athenians – it is all 'eating'. This is a society in which, to the very edges of metaphor, people variously 'devour' each other. Feast as waste; feast as cannibalism. It is no wonder that, in this play, feasting leads to 'vomit' and what should be nourishment turns to 'poison'. And there is one more turn to this particular screw. Here is Apemantus, the scourge at the feast:

O you gods! What a number of men eats Timon, and he sees 'em not! It grieves me to see so many dip their meat in one man's blood, and all the madness is, he cheers them up too.

I wonder men dare trust themselves with men.
Methinks they should invite them without knives:
Good for their meat, and safer for their lives.
There's much example for't; the fellow that sits next him, now parts bread with him, pledges the breath of him in a divided draught, is the readiest man to kill him.

(I, ii, 38–49)

Much example indeed – Jesus and Judas providing the most famous example of all. And here is the First Stranger – from outside Athens and revealed to be both dispassionate and compassionate:

Who can call him his friend
That dips in the same dish?

(III, ii, 70–71)

Honest Flavius refers to the 'glutt'nous maws' of the 'false masters [who] ate of my lord's meat' (III, iv, 50). And when Timon is set upon by the servants of ruthless creditors, he cries out: 'Tell out my blood ... Tear me, take me, and the gods fall upon you' (III, iv, 94, 99). As you (his well-feasted 'friends') fall upon the god, taking and tearing his meat, his bread, his blood, his body. Of course, there are here deliberate echoes of the Last Supper, and Christian communion (and the eating of gods in general); it would be impossible to miss them. But to argue from this, as some have done (most famously Wilson Knight), that this makes of Timon something of a Christ figure, seems to me badly to misread, misapprehend, the tone and atmosphere of the play. Certainly, Timon disports himself as a god, and is willing to be treated (or addressed) as one by his flatterers, who readily comply as long as his 'grace' and beneficence is flowing their way. Tear, take, eat: this is my blood, this is my body. And so they do. But this is no *sparagmos* and *omophagia*, in the ancient sense; or, to the extent that it is, it has been sordidly translated into financial terms. Nor is it even analogous to the Christian communion. There is no hint of the sacred here; not a touch of ritual observance. What we *do* have is a blasphemous, empty, parody or travesty of sacrificial rites which have elsewhere and at other times been dignifying, meaningful, perhaps redeeming. But not here, not now – not in *this* Athens.

Timon of Athens is a very schematic play. It is composed of two starkly contrasting halves (the first half clearly more finished than the second). It is very static, the second half consisting of a series of interviews. Characterization is cursory, 'penciled', thin to the point of impersonality and abstraction. It seems more like an allegory or morality play (or even a folk tale – three false friends, loyal servant, etc.) than a fully developed drama. For the first ninety-four lines none of the speakers is named – they are types. (At line ninety-four, Timon enters and his first word is 'Imprisoned' – anticipating his own imprisonment, in his own house, his debts, but most of all in his temperament – for he, too, proves to be a fixed 'type'.) The play has been seen as more of a bitter satire than a tragedy, and certainly there is none of the dramatic conflict and sense of inexorable progress (or development and movement) that we experience in Shakespeare's great tragedies (just compare *Macbeth*). Perhaps more to the point, there is no development in the 'characters', particularly of Timon. There is no halting but growing self-awareness, no bruising stumbling to an initially resisted self-knowledge. In his soliloquies, Timon exhibits none of the meditative inwardness and deepening self-exploration of Hamlet. When he stops giving, he starts cursing. Having postured and dispensed like a god, he turns to crawling and snarling like a beast. Where Hamlet really thinks, Timon mainly rants. This is not to deny the undoubted power of some of his furious and nauseated outbursts (see, for example, the speech beginning 'O blessed breeding sun, draw from the earth/Rotten humidity' – IV, iii, 1 *et seq.*; or his address to the bandits starting 'I'll example you with thievery' – IV, iii, 442 *et seq.*; both worthy of Lear himself). But like his 'generosity', his hatred is indiscriminate, all-inclusive. At times, he is reduced – if that is the word – to lists:

Piety, and fear,
Religion to the gods, peace, justice, truth,
Domestic awe, night-rest, and neighborhood,

> Instruction, manners, mysteries, and trades,
> Degrees, observances, customs, and laws,
> Decline to your confounding contraries,
> And let confusion live.
>
> (IV, i, 15–21)

In other words, *everything* that makes human, civilized life possible – damn and confound the lot. Having instantly arrived at, jumped or inverted to, this state of terminal misanthropic nihilism, there is no way in which Timon can change or develop – he can only reiterate, and die. The dramatic possibilities of such a figure are strictly limited, and perhaps that is why Shakespeare left the play unfinished and moved on to more fruitful fields.

Apemantus, the Cynic (i.e. 'dog' – the word re-echoes through the play), has some cogent insights into Timon during their climactic exchange in Act IV:

> Thou'dst courtier be again
> Wert thou not beggar.
>
> (IV, iii, 242–3)

The middle of humanity thou never knewest, but the extremity of both ends.

(IV, iii, 301–2)

God, or beast – this extremism was familiar to the Elizabethans from the well-known saying of Aristotle that 'that man which cannot live in civil company either he is a god or a beast, seeing only God is sufficient of himself, and a solitary life agreeth with a beast' (this is, of course, very relevant for *Coriolanus* as well). Whatever we think of Apemantus, a descendant of Jacques and Thersites, we may take William Richardson's felicitous formulation – 'his invectives are bitter, but his remarks are true'.

The god who really *does* rule and dominate in the play is – gold:

> What a god's gold, that he is worshiped
> In a baser temple than where swine feed!
>
> (V, i, 49–50)

Thus Timon, as people come flocking to him in the wilderness, trying to ease, or flatter, out of him his new-found gold. As a 'god' himself, he had 'poured' out gold in Athens; now he distributes it freely again, with, of course, a directly opposite motive:

> Thou visible god,
> That sold'rest close impossibilities
> And mak'st them kiss; that speak'st with every tongue
> To every purpose. O thou touch of hearts,
> Think thy slave man rebels, and by thy virtue
> Set them into confounding odds, that beasts
> May have the world in empire.
>
> (IV, iii, 391–7)

May the god gold turn all humans to beasts (again, the words appear in close proximity as if to occlude intermediary possibilities). And if the announced position of the two prostitutes is anything to go by – 'we'll do anything for gold' (IV, iii, 151) – his hope may well be realized. Perhaps it has been realized already, given Apemantus' declaration – 'The commonwealth of Athens is become a forest of beasts.' (Incidentally, the Greek word *time* or *timos* means both honour and price, thus pointing to the equivocal nature of true 'value'. Timon's initial belief in the 'honour' of his friends, switches to an unshakable conviction that money rules all. He carries his fate in his name.)

But the Athenians are not, not quite, *all* beasts. Lowly figures often play a vital role in Shakespeare – for instance the unnamed servant who turns on his master, Cornwall, and kills him – refusing to stand and watch his cruelty – and it is a very important part of this play that Timon's steward, Flavius, also unnamed in the early part of the folio version, is truly loyal and loving to his master, Timon. (Flaminius and Timon's other servants are also loyal, and disgusted at the base and cruel rapacity of their so-called 'betters'.) In the first half of the play, Flavius agonizes over the irresponsible waste he is helpless to prevent – 'I bleed inwardly for my lord' (I, ii, 210). And when the impoverished Timon takes to the wilds, Flavius seeks him out, loyal as ever:

> O you gods!
> Is yond despised and ruinous man my lord?

> Full of decay and failing? ...
> ... I will present
> My honest grief unto him, and as my lord
> Still serve him with my life. My dearest master.
>
> (IV, iii, 467–9, 477–9)

In the face of Timon's suspicions as to his motives for seeking him out – having trusted everyone he will, of course, henceforth trust no one – Flavius protests:

> That which I show, heaven knows, is merely love,
> Duty and zeal to your unmatched mind ...
>
> (IV, iii, 524–5)

We may blink at that 'unmatched mind', of which we have seen precious little evidence (similarly it strains credulity when the Senators come and beg him to take over the captaincy of the city as being the only man who can save Athens from the threatened attack of Alcibiades – one senses Timon would be hardly a better strategist than he is an economist); but – 'only love'. With the crucial exception of Flavius' unwavering devotion, this non-commercial 'commodity' is *entirely* absent from the play. And this is, certainly, intimately connected to another absence – the absence of women, apart from two prostitutes (who, like the Athenian men, will 'do anything for gold') and the Amazons in the masque (hardly representative of 'the female'). When Flavius announces himself to the misanthrope Timon as 'an honest poor servant of yours', Timon feigns non-recognition:

> Then I know thee not.
> I never had honest man about me, I; *all*
> I kept were knaves ...
>
> (IV, iii, 485–7: my italics)

As he had cried out at the end of his 'anti-feast' – 'henceforth hated be/Of Timon man and *all* humanity' (III, vi, 105–6). Given Timon's particular mentality and temperament, it always has to be 'all' – or 'nothing', of course. But with 'humanity', you never can say 'all', whether in this direction or that. With tears, Flavius protests the genuineness of his honest compassion – 'Nev'r did poor steward wear a truer grief/For his undone lord than mine eyes for you' (IV, iii, 489–90). What follows is a key speech by Timon:

> What, dost thou weep? Come nearer. Then I love thee
> Because thou art a woman, and disclaim'st
> Flinty mankind, whose eyes do never give
> But thorough lust and laughter. Pity's sleeping.
>
> (IV, iii, 491–4)

No one who remembers Cordelia's tears will need reminding of the importance of weeping in Shakespeare. It is associated – certainly not exclusively, but predominantly – with women, and true compassion and devotion. Pity is certainly sleeping among the Athenian men in this play (Flavius and other servants apart). And it is a powerful reminder of the absence of 'true women' from this play that Timon should identify Flavius as 'a woman' simply on account of his manifesting 'pity' – as though that makes him an anomaly among men. Timon continues:

> Had I a steward
> So true, so just, and now so comfortable?
> It almost turns my dangerous nature mild.
> ...
> Forgive my general and exceptless rashness,
> You perpetual-sober gods. I do proclaim
> One honest man. Mistake me not, *but one*.
> No more I pray – and he's a steward.
> How fain would I have hated *all* mankind,
> And thou redeem'st thyself. But *all* save thee
> I fell with curses.
>
> (IV, iii, 499–510: my italics)

'and he's a steward' – so he *almost* doesn't count. But of course he does. Enormously. Because once an exception is admitted to a totalizing generalization, once absolutism is punctured, the protective shell of '*all*' is broken. One, two – who *knows* how many there may be? Potentially, Timon would not be able to staunch a leak of his own conceding.

Perhaps this is the point of including Alcibiades and his story in the play (a point that has been queried by some commentators). He, too, is most ungratefully treated by an

Athens which he has valiantly defended. The Senate is determined to execute a brave fellow-soldier who has been involved in some civic violence. In a speech reminiscent of the 'mercy' speeches of Portia (*The Merchant of Venice*), and Isabella (*Measure for Measure*), and, come to that, Tamora (*Titus Andronicus*), Alcibiades pleads for his friends:

> For pity is the virtue of the law,
> And none but tyrants use it cruelly.
>
> (III, v, 8–9)

The Senators abjure 'mercy' and, unmoved and unmovable, identify with the supreme rigour of the 'law'. 'We are for law. He dies' (III, v, 86). As the admirably humane 'First Stranger' comments: 'But I perceive/Men must learn now with pity to dispense,/For policy sits above conscience' (III, ii, 91–3). Alcibiades vows revenge against Athens (which is why, in Plutarch, Timon makes much of him; and why, in the play, he gives him gold). At the end of the play, he is indeed marching on Athens. Having failed to secure Timon's apparently indispensable help, the Senators can only plead with Alcibiades who is approaching their city 'like a boar too savage' (V, i, 166 – it would be otiose to point out how often men are referred to as animals in this 'beastly' play). And their case is, to a rational person, unassailable:

> We were not all unkind, nor all deserve
> The common stroke of war.
>
> (V, iv, 21–2)

> All have not offended.
> For those that were, it is not square to take
> On those that are, revenge.
>
> (V, iv, 35–7)

We were not *all* unkind ... *all* have not offended ... those that are, are not the same as those that were. Times change; one generation yields to another; it is not an absolute world. Unlike Timon, Alcibiades accepts this, and exchanges vengeance for that mercy which he himself had once pleaded for. In a rather perfunctory conclusion, he takes on the role of a

Richmond, a Malcolm, a Fortinbras, restoring peace and order to the city-state:

> And I will use the olive with my sword,
> Make war breed peace ...
>
> (V, iv, 82–3)

This is the sort of change or modification of attitude which is impossible for Timon, who can only live in, and by, extremes. The only 'action' he is capable of in the second half is negative speech, and when he gives that up – 'Lips, let four words go by and language end' (V, i, 221) – he can only die, under two – just to make sure – characteristically venomous and nihilistic epitaphs. Arguably, death has been his real aim:

> My long sickness
> Of health and living now begins to mend,
> And nothing brings me all things.
>
> (V, i, 187–9)

And all things bring him nothing. These lines offer a curious, distant echo of Cleopatra's 'My desolation does begin to make/A better life'; yet, as is fitting in a play in which, indeed, 'all's obliquy' – twisted, crooked, awry – they are utterly unlike them as well, Again, Shakespeare seems to be exploring, experimenting with, a completely negative version of some of the drives and values, and poetic achievements, of *Antony and Cleopatra.* In that play, I suggested, we could appreciate the meaning of Blake's assertion that 'the road of excess leads to the palace of wisdom'. In *Timon of Athens*, the road of excess leads to nothing – nothing at all. Shortly after writing his most glorious play, it seems that Shakespeare wrote his bitterest. Who knows why?

*

CORIOLANUS (1608)

Timon was *first* a god – or 'godded' by his sycophantic friends (to use an apt and striking noun-verb from *Coriolanus*) – and *then* a beast. Coriolanus, in what appears to be the last of Shakespeare's Roman plays (and thus, arguably, his last tragedy), seems to move inexorably towards becoming both at the same time. Both, and more besides. More and less. But here again, as, once more and for the last time, Shakespeare turns to Plutarch for the main outlines of his hero and the events of his play, it signally helps to have some of North's version of Plutarch before us:

Caius Martius, whose life we intend now to write, . . . was brought up under his mother a widow . . . This man also is a good proof to confirm men's opinions, that a rare and excellent wit, untaught, doth bring forth many good and evil things together . . . For this Martius' natural wit and great heart did marvelously stir up his courage to do and attempt notable acts. But on the other side, for lack of education, he was so choleric and impatient, that he would yield to no living creature, which made him churlish, uncivil, and altogether unfit for any man's conversation. Yet men marveling much at his constancy, that he was never overcome with pleasure nor money and how he would endure easily all manner of pains and travails, thereupon they well liked and commended his stoutness and temperancy. But for all that, they could not be acquainted with him, as one citizen useth to be with another in the city. His behaviour was so unpleasant to them by reason of a certain insolent and stern manner he had, which, because he was too lordly, was disliked. And to say truly, the greatest benefit that learning bringeth unto men is this: that it teachest men that be rude and rough of nature, by compass and rule of reason, to be civil and courteous, and to like better the mean state than the higher. Now in those days, valiantness was honored in Rome above all other virtues, which they call *virtus*, by the name of virtue itself, as including in that general name all other special virtues besides. So that *virtus* in the Latin was as much as valiantness. But Martius, being more inclined to the wars than any other gentleman of his time, began from his childhood to give himself to handle weapons . . .

As we shall see, 'handle weapons' is what Shakespeare's Coriolanus does from very first to very last. But first, one more amplification of his character from Plutarch:

For he was a man too full of passion and choler, and too much given over to self-will and opinion, as one of a high mind and great courage that lacked the gravity and affability that is gotten with judgment of learning and reason, which only is to be looked for in a *governor of state*: and that remembered not how willfulness is the thing of the world, which a *governor of a commonwealth*, for pleasing should shun, being that which Plato called 'solitariness,' as in the end, all men that are willfully given to a self-opinion and obstinate mind, and who will never yield to others' reason but to their own, remain without company and forsaken of all men.

(My italics)

During the Renaissance there was much discussion concerning the proper education, duties, and responsibilities of the good prince or governor – what qualified a person to exercise 'the speciality of rule'. As Plutarch stresses, it is precisely these qualifications which Coriolanus so signally lacks: he is a prime example of what Renaissance thinkers regarded as the ill-educated prince, a man from the governing classes who is, by nature, temperament, and upbringing, unfitted and unfit to rule. Magnificent as a soldier, he is disastrous as a politician. Shakespeare takes the latent tensions between martial and civic (and domestic) values, between the battlefield and the city, between – in the play's terms – the 'casque' (a helmet) and the 'cushion' (indicating a seat in the Senate), and screws these tensions up to breaking point, dramatically exposing, in the process, not just their perennially potential incompatibility, but – *in extremis* – their very actual and active explosive oppugnancy. The problem – a permanent one – baldly stated is as simple as this. You certainly could not found, much less renew and prolong, any form of civil society on such figures as Coriolanus. But it is debatable whether you could defend and thus preserve any such society *without* such men. (Having banished Coriolanus, the tribunes complacently say 'Rome/ sits safe and still without him' – IV, vi, 37. They could not be more wrong, nor was Rome ever more vulnerable.) Society cannot do *without* the sort of '*virtus*-valiantness' embodied in Coriolanus; but, given its uncontainable explosiveness, it cannot very well do *with* it either. Shakespeare never took hold of a more enduring and intractable social problem. This is one of the most violent of Shakespeare's plays, with tremendous and terrible powers released to do their 'mammocking' and 'mangling' work (two apt words – from the play – for the wrecking forces let loose). And, when Coriolanus is savagely cut down, we feel awed at what Bradley eloquently called 'the instantaneous cessation of enormous energy'.

The legendary history of Coriolanus dates from the fifth century BC, and refers to the creation of the tribunate of 494 BC and the corn riots three years later (Shakespeare, for more urgent impact, conflates these events). Phillips summarizes the importance of this period of Roman history for the Elizabethans. 'The consular government which had supplanted the earlier monarchy underwent further modification in the direction of popular rule when economic unrest forced the Senate to grant political representation to citizens of Rome. One result of this concession was conflict between the democratic and aristocratic elements within the republic. In the turbulent history of Rome in this period Tudor theorists who argued in defence of monarchy and the hierarchy of degrees found a convincing demonstration of the dangers of democratic government' (op. cit., p. 147). There was no previous play about Coriolanus, and his story was only occasionally referred to by political writers as illustrative of the dangers of popular riot, or of civic ingratitude. Shakespeare certainly uses Plutarch, but the play is all his own. He makes it a very 'Roman'-feeling play. Four of the early Roman kings are referred to (Numa, Tullus, Ancus Martius, and Tarquin), and there are references to political and religious customs and the Roman mythology and pantheon. Dryden thought that there was something in the play 'that is truly great and truly Roman' – though, as always in Shakespeare, Rome and the Romans appear in a far from unequivocal light. But there are also Greek, Homeric, echoes. Hector is twice named in connection with Coriolanus (and Virgilia is 'another Penelope'). Plutarch mentions Homer as well, and he also names Achilles. Curiously, that name is absent from Shakespeare's play; yet, given the well-known epic theme of the wrath of Achilles, this would seem a more appropriate name to invoke than that of the more moderate, temperate Hector – for Coriolanus is nothing if not 'choleric'. Perhaps, by withholding the obvious name, but reminding us of Greek heroes, Shakespeare is prompting us to see Coriolanus as an Achilles in a Roman context. (Achilles also had a mother, Thetis, who made him almost, but not quite, invulnerable – a point certainly not lost on Shakespeare.) Certainly, Coriolanus is another of Shakespeare's great warriors, embodying an almost archaic heroic code, who gets hopelessly, disastrously confused when he is removed from the relative simplicities of the battlefield, and forced to negotiate the more complicated political world of the *polis* (I am thinking of, in particular, Titus Andronicus and Othello). Coriolanus cannot, or will not, see that words and conduct which are most fitting and efficacious on the battlefield might be ruinously inappropriate in the city. The fearless and undefeatable soldier may, using the same code, sound politically like an intolerant and unacceptable tyrant. You can't, in this case, make a cushion out of a casque.

The god invoked by Coriolanus himself is, understandably enough, Mars – 'Now, Mars, I prithee, make us quick in work' (I, iv, 10). Then, effectively, he *becomes* Mars – 'thou Mars' (IV, v, 122) – thus Aufidius addresses him when he goes over to the Volscians. Indeed, as Cominius says, 'He is their god' (IV, vi, 91). But this is not a god of mercy ('there is no more mercy in him than there is milk in a male tiger' – V, iv, 28–30), but an angry god:

> You speak o' th' people,
> As if you were a god, to punish, not
> A man of their infirmity.
>
> (III, i, 80–82)

By the end, his harsh and uncompromising demeanour moves Menenius to declare: 'He wants nothing of a god but eternity and a heaven to throne in' (V, iv, 24–5). (A Volscian soldier gives the not very different opinion that 'He's the devil' – I, x, 17.) But, if a god, also a beast, and a very particular beast. He is once an eagle, once a tiger, once a horse, but three times a 'dragon'. First, by his own designation, after being banished – 'I go alone,/Like to a lonely dragon, that his fen/Makes feared and talked of more than seen' (IV, i, 29–31). For the Volscians, he fights 'dragon-like' (IV, vii, 23). After he has switched his allegiance, his old Roman friend Menenius comments:

> There is a differency between a grub and a butterfly; yet your butterfly was a grub. This Marcius is grown from man to dragon: he has wings; he's more than a creeping thing.
>
> (V, iv, 11–14)

In post St-George times, knights are obliged to kill dragons; this ancient pre-Christian, and decidedly *un*Christian, proto-knight is metamorphosing *into* a dragon. (This late reference to butterflies of course echoes the early account of Coriolanus' son's characteristic conduct: 'I saw him run after a gilded butterfly; and when he caught it, he let it go again . . . catched it again; or whether his fall enraged him, or how 'twas, he did so set his teeth, and tear it. O, I warrant, how he mammocked it!'. Volumnia's comment 'One on's father's moods' – I, iii, 63–70 – might well prepare us for Coriolanus' subsequent behaviour. Butterflies for boys: dragons, or dragonish behaviour, for men.)

God, and beast, he is also described as a 'planet' and an 'engine'. Always more or less than human. And perhaps the most decisive pointer to his inhumanity, non-humanity, is the number of times he is referred to simply as a 'thing':

from face to foot
He was a thing of blood, whose every motion
Was timed with dying cries.

(II, ii, 110–11)

He sits in his state as a thing made for Alexander.

(V, iv, 22)

He also becomes 'a kind of *nothing*' (V, i, 13: my italics). Talk of reification, or self-reification, is perhaps superegoratory; we all know, more or less, what it implies to call a person a 'thing'. Whether, and how, we can witness the 'tragedy' of a 'thing' – or a 'no-thing' – is a matter to which we will have to return.

More specifically, Coriolanus is closely identified with his sword. It is often referred to, usually 'smoking' with slaughter. One comes to feel that he is seldom happy, or quite at ease with himself, when it is out of his hand. Like his little son, he 'had rather see the swords and hear a drum than look upon his schoolmaster' (I, iii, 58–9). His ambitions are entirely military and not, indeed, remotely 'scholastic', nor even – in truth – political. He is happy with, and perhaps only with, the casque.

And the sword. One of his earliest interventions in the row precipitated by the 'mutinous citizens' is:

> And let me use my sword, I'd make a quarry
> With thousands of these quartered slaves ...
>
> (I, i, 199–200)

His very last words are 'To use my lawful sword' (V, vi, 129) – his sword is full of law, *is* the law as far as he is concerned. But civic society depends on having laws *instead* of swords. In his younger days he 'lurched all swords of the garland' (II, ii, 102), and at Corioles 'His sword, death's stamp,/Where it did mark, it took' (II, ii, 108–9). Lartius pays him a rather curious compliment:

> O noble fellow!
> Who sensibly outdares his senseless sword,
> And when it bows stand'st up!
>
> (I, iv, 53–5)

This seems to suggest that Coriolanus himself remains erect, even when his sword droops. I think there is an entirely appropriate phallic hint there. Effectively, *all* his energy and appetite and drive – in sum, a colossal force – have been directed (displaced, if you will) into his fearful, 'smoking', instrument of death – Eros 'bowing' to the stand-up work of Thanatos. When his soldiers lift him up in their arms (presumably carrying him on their shoulders), after his exploits at Corioles, Coriolanus cries out, not unhappily one feels – 'Make you a sword of me?' (I, vi, 76). He is, indeed, to all intents and purposes, *the* sword of the city. The deeper truth is that he has made a sword out of himself.

This engine, this thing, this sword, this man of steel (let us say) – it is hard to see what could break or bend, deflect or deter, him. Yet that, of course, is just what happens at the climax of the play. After his victory at Corioles, Marcius (soon to be named 'Coriolanus'), in a speech refusing praise and flattery, says:

> When steel grows soft as the parasite's silk,
> Let him be made a coverture for th' wars!
>
> (I, ix, 45–6)

This is a much disputed and debated passage, marked by that harsh, over-compacted meaning so characteristic of the play. Take one possible meaning as – when the army turns soft, use silk for armour. The power of the image lies, of course, in the idea of steel growing soft as silk. Impossible. Yet steel Coriolanus does turn, briefly, fatally, as soft as silk, when he capitulates to the intercessionary pleas to spare Rome. Aufidius picks up the image for us, after the capitulation:

> Breaking his oath and resolution, like
> A twist of rotten silk; never admitting
> Counsel o' th' war; but at his nurse's tears
> He whined and roared away your victory ...
>
> (V, vi, 95–8)

Man of steel to man of silk (rotten silk to the critical) – part of the tragic power of the play surely lies in this sudden transformation, and we must inquire a little as to how it comes about.

The crucial factor, or influence, is of course his mother, Volumnia. Plutarch–North has this to say concerning the relationship between Marcius (later Coriolanus) and his mother:

> the only thing that made him to love honor was the joy he saw his mother did take of him. For he thought nothing made him so happy and honorable, as that his mother might hear everybody praise and commend him, that she might always see him return with a crown upon his head ... thinking all due to his mother ... at her desire [he] took a wife also, by whom he had two young children, and yet *never left his mother's house therefore.*
>
> (My italics)

There is not much more concerning Volumnia in Plutarch, apart from the crucial intercessionary scene when she dissuades her son from sacking his native city, Rome. All the other scenes involving Volumnia in the play are Shakespeare's invention, and, with powerful dramatic economy, they serve to reveal how – psychologically and emotionally – Coriolanus, indeed, never leaves 'his mother's house'. Whatever else he is or becomes – sword, engine, dragon, planet, god – he remains, ineradicably, a *mother's-boy*. These two words are central and crucial to the play.

Volumnia embodies, and articulates, the martial values of Rome. In her first speech, she celebrates that shift of affect, and affection, from the cushion to the casque – or rather, from the bed to the battlefield – we have already noted as a 'Roman' predisposition:

If my son were my husband, I should freelier rejoice in that absence wherein he won honor than in the embracements of his bed where he would show most love.

(I, iii, 3–5)

Better an absent honour than a present embrace – that's Rome. Or, at least, Volumnia's Rome. Virgilia, the wife of Coriolanus, is given no words by Plutarch, though he makes nothing of the fact. Shakespeare's Virgilia is, as it were, audibly silent. 'My gracious silence, hail! (II, i, 181) is about as amorous as Coriolanus gets in exchanges with his wife – but though she is almost entirely effaced and displaced by the extremely vociferous Volumnia, there *is* grace in Virgilia's silence. Ruskin found her 'perhaps the loveliest of Shakespeare's female characters', and, while that doubtless tells us something about Ruskin, as always he has a point. Most of the speech in this play is, one way or another, pretty unpleasant. In the circumstances, there is, as it were, much to be said for not speaking. Such *very* few words as she does speak (Desdemona and Cordelia are loquacious by comparison), are either modestly decorous, or right against the Roman grain. For example, when Volumnia voluptuously wallows in the thought of her son's 'bloody brow' in battle, Virgilia's involuntary interjection is 'O Jupiter, no blood!' (I, iii, 41). Virgilia is, in Volumnia's terms, very distinctly *not* a 'Roman' woman – and more power to her!

*

Having made him what he is – 'Thy valiantness was mine, thou suck'st it from me' (III, ii, 129) – Volumnia, on two crucial occasions, uses her influence to persuade him, against his better judgement (or steely, intransigent resolve), to go right against the rigid martial inclinations and instincts which she herself nurtured in him. It is she who launches the idea that he should stand for consulship – 'There's one thing wanting, which I doubt not but/Our Rome will cast upon thee.' Knowing that that will involve having to ingratiate himself with the common people, whom he quite intemperately and viscerally loathes, Coriolanus, rightly, senses immediately that such a role is not for him – 'Know, good mother,/I had rather be their servant in my way/Than sway with them in theirs' (II, i, 207–10). In particular, he shrinks in aversion from the prospect of having to put off his armour and don the 'vesture of humility' and then going to stand in the market-place, showing his wounds and begging for votes. Such a parade of pseudo-humility ill becomes a man who is uncorruptibly a total soldier – a butcher-soldier perhaps, but with his martial integrity intact. Quite simply, he won't do it:

> I do beseech you
> Let me o'erleap that custom, for I cannot
> Put on the gown, stand naked, and entreat them,
> For my wounds' sake, to give their suffrage. Please you
> That I may pass this doing.
>
> (II, ii, 136–40)

More pertinently – 'It is a part/That I shall blush in acting' (II, ii, 145–6). Coriolanus is a soldier who can, emphatically, do *deeds* (there is much stress on this), but who cannot act parts. But Volumnia is a mother who always gets her way. So he tries, though not without some heavy irony concerning the self-falsification it involves. 'I will practice the insinuating nod, and be off to them most counterfeitly; that is, sir, I will counterfeit the bewitchment of some popular man' (II, iii, 103–6). Though his instinct is all the other way. 'Rather than fool it so,/Let the high office and the honor go' (II, iii, 126–7). After his session in the market-place, he cannot wait to 'change these garments' – thereby 'knowing myself again' (II, iii, 153). He seems to have the people's 'voice', but then the tribunes agitate the crowd and it turns against Coriolanus. Coriolanus lets the tribunes know what he thinks of 'the mutable, rank-scented meiny [crowd]' (III, i, 66), and as his anger mounts his words concerning the people (Hydra-headed mob etc.) become more bilious and choleric, until the tribunes can say he has 'spoken like a traitor' (III, i, 162) and urge his execution. Coriolanus draws his sword – knowing himself again – and the people are beaten back. He intends to be uncompromisingly defiant, uncompromisingly himself, come what may – 'yet will I still/Be thus to them' (III, ii, 5–6). But he has reckoned without his mother – and her maternal desires and ambitions. She wants to be able to say 'my son the consul' as well as 'my son the soldier'. Coriolanus is confused. His mother had taught him *always* to despise the people:

> I muse my mother
> Does not approve me further, who was wont
> To call them woolen vassals, things created
> To buy and sell with groats . . .
> [Volumnia enters]
> I talk of you:
> Why did you wish me milder – Would you have me
> False to my nature? Rather say I play
> The man I am.
>
> (III, ii, 7–16)

But she, with some clever if partly specious arguments, urges him to play the man he is *not*:

> You are too absolute;
> Though therein you can never be too noble
> But when extremities speak. I have heard you say,
> Honor and policy, like unsevered friends,
> I' th' war do grow together. Grant that, and tell me
> In peace what each of them by th' other lose
> That they combine not there.
>
> (III, ii, 39–45)

Coriolanus' response is a rather helpless 'Tush, tush!', as well it might be, since the point is a tricky one, though one that touches on the problem at the centre of the play. All's fair, certainly in war, and there it is not incompatible with 'honour' to outwit your enemy with 'politic' stratagems. So why not in peacetime? Why not trick the plebeians, for the honour of a consulship? Coriolanus knows, or rather *feels*, that there is an important difference, but he is quite unable to argue it through. No man is less a sophist than Coriolanus. Just what his 'nature' is, and what being true or false to it might entail, we must consider later. Here, his mother – 'I would dissemble with my nature ... I should do so in honor' – asserts herself as his instructor-director:

> speak
> To th' people, not by your own instruction,
> Nor by th' matter which your heart prompts you,
> But with such words that are but roted in
> Your tongue, though but bastards and syllables
> Of no allowance to your bosom's truth.
>
> (III, ii, 52–7)

We have only recently heard Coriolanus' old friend Menenius say of him – 'His heart's his mouth:/What his breast forges, that his tongue must vent' (III, i, 256–7), and we should recognize that, with their theatrical instructions – 'perform a part', 'come, we'll prompt you' (Cominius) – his mother and the supporting Roman nobles are making an impossible demand of Coriolanus. Cornered, the intellectually unresourceful Coriolanus can only capitulate, though not without a good deal of foot-dragging and something like a tantrum of protest at the self-division, self-dispersal, indeed self-dissolution, which is being asked of him:

> Well, I will do't ...
> You have put me now to such a part which never
> I shall discharge to th' life.
>
> (III, ii, 101–6)

Be like a harlot, eunuch, virgin, knave, schoolboy, beggar? – why can't I just be a soldier? Why should I make my mind and body play false to each other? No, damn it, I *won't* go through with it! At which, his mother turns from him, as if giving up on a child in a particularly fretful and tiresome mood. 'At thy choice then.' As much as to say – well, if you are going to be *that* difficult! And Coriolanus wilts back into her scolded, remorseful little boy.

> Pray, be content:
> Mother, I am going to the marketplace;
> Chide me no more ...
>
> (III, ii, 130–32)

And, though we do not know it yet, there will indeed be some 'boy's tears' to follow. This mother will be the death of him.

Coriolanus leaves for the market-place, attended by the hopeless injunction – 'mildly' (repeated five times). 'Well, mildly be it then – mildly' (III, ii, 145). 'Mildness' is certainly *not* in his nature, whatever that nature might be; and, as the tribunes well know, it will take little to make him 'play the man I am':

> Being once chafed, he cannot
> Be reined again to temperance; then he speaks
> What's in his heart, and that is there which looks
> With us to break his neck.
>
> (III, iii, 27–30)

Coriolanus is nothing if not honest, and once the tribunes have 'chafed' him by calling him 'traitor' (the word is not in Plutarch), he lets fly at the people with such vitriolic fury that by communal (or rather, mob) agreement, he is banished. His response is, we may say, predictable:

> You common cry of curs, whose breath I hate
> As reek o' th' rotten fens, whose loves I prize
> As the dead carcasses of unburied men
> That do corrupt my air, I banish you.
> ... Despising
> For you the city, thus I turn my back.
> There is a world elsewhere.
>
> (III, iii, 120–35)

Brave and powerful talk; and we can surely still respond to a something heroic in Coriolanus' 'absolute' and unyielding refusal of compromise, his furious and contemptuous rejection of the mass, the masses, the world *here*. The question the remainder of the play will explore is whether it is finally possible for Coriolanus to 'banish' Rome – his city, his class, his friends, his family, his *mother*. Or – put it another way – can there finally be, for a Roman, 'a world elsewhere'?

Coriolanus has always appeared as single, singular; sharply outlined and standing out against the rest. He is 'constant', 'absolute', *adamant* we might say. During the war against the Volscians, he is locked, trapped, within the enemy's gates on his own – as a soldier says: 'He is himself alone,/To answer all the city' (I, iv, 52–3). This description holds good whether the city is Corioli or Rome. 'O me alone!' he cries, after his one-man victory (I, vii, 76) – and the cry reverberates throughout the play. After his banishment from Rome, he goes – instantly – over to the enemy. As in the case of Timon, it seems that 'absolutists' are either rigidly 'constant', or must *totally* invert their commitments. As we have seen, Shakespeare is very interested in these sudden switches of allegiance whereby a passionate Roman becomes a virulent anti-Roman (I am thinking of Lucius in *Titus Andronicus* and Alcibiades in *Timon of Athens*) – on the spot, as it were. In what is arguably his only soliloquy (as with Timon, there is no inwardness in the depiction of Coriolanus, none of the wracked, intelligent, conscience-searching of a Macbeth: Coriolanus is all outside, all deed, all sword), Coriolanus says:

> O world, thy slippery turns! Friends now fast sworn . . .
> On a dissension of a doit, break out
> To bitterest enmity . . .
> . . . So with me:
> My birthplace hate I, and my love's upon
> This enemy town.
>
> (IV, iv, 12–24)

Well, it might be – and Shakespeare could be exploring the unstable and changeable foundations of what we fondly take to be our our most immovably fixed commitments, allegiances, and loyalties. But Coriolanus might not be so rid of his 'birthplace', so cleanly and hatefully disengaged from Rome, as he thinks. It is notable that, after his banishment, he is seen entering the enemy town of Actium 'in mean apparel, disguised and muffled'. This detail, unremarked, is in Plutarch.

But Shakespeare would surely have seen an added irony in Coriolanus having recourse to almost the same 'dissembling' strategies he had so furiously repudiated in Rome. Has he learnt theatricals in spite of himself? Is he going to 'play' the dragon, 'act' the vengeful god, 'counterfeit' the ireful anti-Roman? If so, he may well not prove as impregnable as he has hitherto seemed, for a time could come when the 'acting' has to stop. Not that he gives signs of dissembling. His determined disavowal and rejection of Rome seems absolutely resolute and total. His single imperative to his old friend, Menenius, who comes to plead with him on Rome's behalf, summarizes the stance of denial and dismissal he has adopted – 'Away!' He spells it out:

> Wife, mother, child, I know not. My affairs
> Are servanted to others ...
> Therefore be gone.
>
> (V, ii, 83–4, 88)

Away *every* Roman; away even his own Roman self. Cominius receives as much of a brush-off as Menenius:

> Coriolanus
> He would not answer to; forbad all names;
> He was a kind of nothing, titleless,
> Till he had forged himself a name o' th' fire
> Of burning Rome.
>
> (V, i, 11–15)

I will come to the importance of 'names' in the play. Here we may note his attempt entirely to erase and disown all traces of his Roman identity, rendering himself – certainly from the Roman point of view – 'a kind of nothing'. Just as swords are 'forged', so he will forge a new name in the fire of burning Rome.

To my knowledge, it was Bradley who first pointed out how references to fire and burning Rome (not mentioned in Plutarch), suddenly start and then proliferate in Acts IV and V, as the not-Coriolanus, the anonymous, titleless 'nothing', starts to move inexorably – all engine-beast-god now – against the city of his birth. This dragon is breathing fire. Territories are being 'consumed with fire'; there is terrified talk of burned temples and houses put to 'the brand'. Menenius gives his opinion:

> If he could burn us all into one coal,
> We have deserved it.
>
> (IV, vi, 138–9)

Volscian soldiers, talking to downcast Romans, refer gleefully to 'the intended fire your city is ready to flame in' (V, ii, 47), and Menenius, trying to get through to the alienated and no-longer Coriolanus, haplessly recognizes – 'Thou art preparing fire for us' (V, ii, 72). It is all summed up in Cominius' description of the oncoming avenger:

> I tell you he does sit in gold, his eye
> Red as 'twould burn Rome, and his injury
> The jailer to his pity.
>
> (V, i, 63–5)

Fire consumes everything and leaves, effectively, nothing. A total razing and cleansing. This is not so much revenge as an intended eradication, obliteration, annihilation. This unnamable and omnipotent figure is, indeed, absolute – 'too absolute'.

The nightmare prospect behind all this, is the destruction, the 'unbuilding', the 'unroofing', or the 'melting', of the city – THE city. Rome. When things come to crisis point between the plebeians and the tribunes, and Coriolanus and the nobles, Cominius cries out:

> That is the way to lay the city flat,
> To bring the roof to the foundation,
> And bury all which yet distinctly ranges,
> In heaps and piles of ruin.
>
> (III, i, 203–6)

For Rome, the 'city' simply *was* the available civilization (no matter what its internal impairments might be), and whatever was outside the city was uncontainable and unformulable (out of language, out of bounds), potentially 'monstrous' – dragons clawing their way towards the city walls. But there was a nightmare within the nightmare – pointed to when, in the internal crisis, Menenius beseechingly cries out:

> Proceed by process [i.e. by law, the cement of the city];
> Lest parties (as he is beloved) break out,
> *And sack great Rome with Romans.*
>
> (III, i, 312–14: my italics)

From the start of Shakespeare's Roman plays, we have seen that Rome could be 'barbarous', Romans barbarians (as in this play the plebeians are to Coriolanus – 'I would they were barbarians, as they are,/Though in Rome littered' – III, i, 237–8 – though no one, on his day, more 'barbaric' than Coriolanus). That could be handled, contained, perhaps worked out. The city would still stand. But if Rome should self-destructively turn on itself; not just a Roman by a Roman 'valiantly' vanquished, but *Rome* by Romans ... if the city tears *itself* to pieces, what price *any* hope for civilization and order then? We must be clear about this. Shakespeare is very far, *very* far, from being an uncritical admirer of the Roman world as he conceived it, or at least as he dramatized his version of it. It is a hard, brutal, militarized, legalistic, excessively male world, with women and domestic values and virtues – procreative eroticism, love, gentleness, mildness, pity – marginalized to the point of near-extinction. But Rome – arid, unimaginative, unbounteous, politic and cruel Rome – was the alternative to chaos, the (badly faulted) prototype of civilized (problematic, question-begging word, as Shakespeare well knew) societies in the western world. Shakespeare being Shakespeare, he lent some of his finest poetry to a final elegiac efflorescent flaring of an Egyptian world that was inevitably superseded. For good or bad, good *and* bad, Rome was the future, and the future was to be – *mutatis, mutandis* – Roman.

The Rome of *Coriolanus* is a noisy place; more specifically it is a city of 'voices'. Since most plays are comprised of speakers, I must attempt to avoid a fatuity here. But the word 'voice' (or 'voices') occurs over forty times, far more often than in any other Shakespeare play. And the voices are, pre-eminently, the voices of the people. In this play, the people (or mob, or rabble, or children, or slaves – according to their behaviour and your point of view) are, certainly, volatile, fickle, too – easily swayable, and, when pressed too hard or deprived too far, dangerously dissentious and mutinous. (They are probably 'stinking' too – the working classes are the sweating classes, and doubtless, their food is none of the best either.) But the play makes clear that many of their grievances are justified, while the behaviour of the supposedly responsible, 'paternalistic' patricians, leaves a lot to be desired. Coriolanus is only the *most* obscenely contemptuous of the common people among his class – it is a matter of degree, not kind. Menenius is as willing to call them 'rats' as Coriolanus is determined to call them 'curs'. The use by Menenius of the tired allegory of the body politic to placate the mob in the first scene, is really a piece of gross effrontery. Smugly and complacently, he allows the Belly (= the Senators) to explain to the 'mutinous members' (= the people) that they 'From me receive that natural competency/Whereby they live'. A 'natural competency' is just exactly what these famished citizens–plebeians lack, and, indeed, all they ask for. Later in the play, Menenius says how 'supple' we are 'when we have stuffed/These pipes and these conveyances of our blood/With wine and feeding' (V, i, 53–5). Clearly, he speaks from experience, and the earlier, hostile case against the Belly–Senate –

it did remain
I' th' midst o' th' body, idle and unactive,
Still cupboarding the viand, never bearing
Like labor with the rest ...

(I, i, 99–102)

– would seem to fit him, and who knows how many other Senators, perfectly. The voice and 'voices' of the people, then; to which we should add the unusually large number of references to mouth(s), tongue(s), breath(s). There is the heroic-martial Coriolanian world of swordly doings and deeds; and the people's world of voices, or mouthly deeds. Coriolanus is an 'engine', but the voice of the people is an instrument, too. Voices are votes (as in some Elizabethan elections, during this period in Rome the elected where chosen by vocal acclaim, or 'shouting'), and it is having to supplicate for the people's 'voices' in the market-place which is anathema to Coriolanus. But – 'the people/Must have their voices' (II, ii, 140–41), and if Coriolanus cannot finally bring himself to ask for them 'kindly', the voices will turn on him. In the event, he will be 'Whooped out of Rome' by, as he sees it, 'th' voice of slaves' (IV, v, 81–2). (For all his gnashing vituperations, Coriolanus is not really at ease using tongue, mouth, voice. When Cominius describes how Coriolanus dismissed him 'with his speechless hand' – V, i, 67 – we have the essential man in all his silent physicality.) But the voices which 'did hoot him out o' th' city' might well 'roar him in again' (IV, vi, 124–5). When it is learned that Coriolanus will spare Rome, a Senator exhorts the city, impossibly as it sounds, to 'Unshout the noise that banished Marcius' (V, v, 4). Shouting, whooping, hooting, roaring – this civic noise sounds ugly. And there is not much to redeem it in the rhetoric of the patrician, either. Gordon would seem to be justified in his pessimistic summing up of the play (in his essay 'Name to Fame'; see bibliography):

> It is a show of civil life. The city must stand and continue, for outside it there is the monstrous, or the nothing. But within the walls absolutes turn out to be instrumental; the words that identify and bind become words that debase and destroy: whoops, or hoots, curses, lies, flatteries, voices, stinking breath . . . In this city to speak is to be guilty.

No wonder Virgilia prefers to remain silent.

'Voices' are also intimately connected with 'fame' and 'name' – two more words which often recur. Gordon again: 'Name is Fame, is Honour, and is won by deeds – in Rome, by deeds in war' (ibid. p. 60). Fame depends on 'praise', 'renown', 'applause and clamor', 'good report' – all more or less dependent on 'voice'. Volumnia, explaining to Virgilia how she brought up her son, says: 'I, considering how honor would become such a person – that it was no better than picture-like to hang by th' wall, if *renown made it not stir* – was pleased to let him seek danger where he was like to find *fame*' (I, iii, 10–14: my italics). To acquire 'name' and 'fame', Coriolanus will need 'voices' in a more than electoral sense.

(In ancient Greece, the word for 'truth' – '*aletheia*' – meant, literally, *not* forgetting, or forgotten. The epic singers and reciters were so important just because they prevented the silent deeds of heroic warriors from falling into an eternal, soundless, oblivion. They preserved and perpetuated the 'renown', exactly by *re*knowing, *re*naming. This keeps the honour 'stirring'.) Caius Marcus of course wins fame and name after his exploits at Corioli:

from this time,
For what he did before Corioles, call him,
With all th' applause and clamor of the host,
Caius Marcius Coriolanus.
Bear th' addition nobly ever!

(I, ix, 62–6)

Or, as the Herald announces it:

he hath won,
With fame, a name to Caius Marcius; these
In honor follows Coriolanus.

(II, i, 169–71)

As his mother proudly says – he is 'By deed-achieving honor newly named' (II, i, 179).

But if name and fame depend upon voice, mouth, breath, their possible persistingness is always vulnerable, precarious. Voices can be withheld, or – just like that – shout the other way. (It is notable that only once does Coriolanus think of *writing* as possibly a proper preservative of fame – and I will come to that moment.) Of course, when Coriolanus leaves Rome to join the Volscians, he makes a point of trying to shed and disown all his previous names, both family-given and war-won ('forbad all names'). This attempt by Coriolanus to reject or leave behind his names is highlighted by Shakespeare (but not Plutarch) when the disguised and prevaricating Coriolanus first arrives in Antium, and Aufidius has to ask him *five times* – 'what is thy name?' At last, Coriolanus has to answer. His attempt at an act of willed dis-nomination proves finally to be impossible. And when Aufidius at the end refuses to call his Roman ally by 'thy stol'n name/Coriolanus' (V, vi, 89), it is, to be exact, the last but one straw. Perhaps the most poignant episode illustrating both the cardinal importance and the ephemeral forgettability of names, occurs after the first battle with the Volscians. Victorious Coriolanus asks a modest, and indeed honourable, favour of his commander Cominius:

> I sometimes lay here in Corioles
> At a poor man's house; he used me kindly.
> He cried to me; I saw him prisoner;
> . . . I request you
> To give my poor host freedom.
>
> (I, ix, 82–7)

Cominius is more than happy to comply. All they need is 'his name'.

> By Jupiter, forgot!
> I am weary; yea, my memory is tired.
> Have we no wine here?
>
> (I, ix, 90–92)

So easily can a 'name' be 'lost'. In Plutarch, the kindly 'enemy' host is wealthy, and there is no mention of his name having been forgotten by Coriolanus. You can decide what kind of a point Shakespeare was making with his changes. But, clearly, some amnesias are lethal, and the forgetting of a person's name may cost the forgotten one not less than everything. Coriolanus himself will effectively give up his life in one last desperate attempt to secure fitting and appropriate remembrance.

When his mother and family approach, to plead for Rome, he tries to stiffen his resolve:

> But out, affection!
> All bond and privilege of nature, break!
> Let it be virtuous to be obstinate.
>
> (V, iii, 24–6)

But, even at the sight of them (particularly his mother), he is beginning to crack (he is too brittle, too 'forged', to bend):

I melt, and am not
Of stronger earth than others. My mother bows,
... and my young boy
Hath an aspect of intercession which
Great Nature cries 'Deny not.' Let the Volsces
Plough Rome, and harrow Italy! I'll never
Be such a gosling to obey instinct, but stand
As if a man were author of himself
And knew no other kin.
(V, iii, 28–37)

He is trying to hold on to his inflexible intransigence, regain that unshakable, immovable erectness he so admires – 'Like a great sea-mark, standing every flaw' (V, iii, 74). But he is wobbling, 'melting' (he even speaks of kissing his wife), slipping from steel to silk. Coriolanus is discovering that he cannot 'stand' as if he were 'author of himself', some 'unnatural' parthenogenetic freak; discovering that there are some bonds of nature which cannot be broken, some imperatives of 'Great Nature' which cannot be refused. He *will* be a 'gosling' and 'obey instinct', before reasserting his lost identity as an 'eagle'. But, even as he is capitulating to nature, he feels he is also being untrue to his *own* nature. Coriolanus is being torn apart by contradictions in nature, contradictions *of* nature. We have heard much of his nature – he cannot help his nature, his nature is too noble for this world, 'his nature/In that's no changeling' (IV, vii, 10–11), and so on. Aufidius has the most searching speech about Coriolanus, when explaining to his lieutenant why Rome banished him:

Whether 'twas pride,
Which out of daily fortune ever taints
The happy man; whether defect of judgment,
To fail in the disposing of those chances
Which he was lord of; or whether *nature*,
Not to be other than one thing, not moving
From th' casque to th' cushion, but commanding peace
Even with the same austerity and garb
As he controlled the war; but one of these –
As he hath spices of them all ...
... made him feared,
So hated, and so banished.
(IV, vii, 37–48: my italics)

The tragedy which Coriolanus experiences and enacts is the discovered impossibility for a man 'not to be other than one thing'. He tries, more ferociously than any other of Shakespeare's heroes. He can certainly dispense with the 'cushion' – never wanted it, anyway. But he cannot defy or deny his mother. It is not, finally, in his 'nature'. Whatever that nature is. We hear and see quite a lot of his *un*nature, too, best summed up in Cominius' description of him as he marches on Rome with the Volscians:

he leads them like a thing
Made by some other deity than Nature,
That shapes men better ...

(IV, vi, 91–3)

To his mother, in the final scene, still trying to stave off her influence, he cries out:

Tell me not
Wherein I seem unnatural. Desire not
T' allay my rages and revenges with
Your colder reasons.

(V, iii, 83–6)

It is perhaps his truest nature to *be* unnatural? In which case, when he capitulates and obeys 'Great Nature', is he finally maturing into a new, recognized, and accepted humanity (as some have thought)? Or is he succumbing to an internal splitting which will destroy whatever integrity of identity he may have – helplessly regressing to the enfeebled status of 'mother's boy'? You can see it in either way; though I think it is better, somehow, to try to see it as both.

As he feels his resolve slipping in front of his family, he says:

Like a dull actor now,
I have forgot my part and I am out,
Even to a full disgrace.

(V, iii, 40–43)

When he was asked to stop being a soldier and at least pretend he was a politician, he discovered it just wasn't in him to act a part. But this speech seems to imply that he is being discomfited out of his 'part' of the adamantine warrior. Or does he just mean that being confronted with his mother again gives him the equivalent of stage-fright? Is he losing his grip on what, exactly, he is as a man? The arguments and appeals with which his mother works on him need not be summarized here. He is effectively lost when she kneels to him – 'What's this?/Your knees to me? To your corrected son?' (V, iii, 55–6); it horrifies him as if it were some chaotic inversion in nature. She inevitably has her way with her 'corrected son'. But there is a barb in the words that recognize her triumph:

O mother, mother!
What have you done? Behold, the heavens do ope,
The gods look down, and this unnatural scene
They laugh at. O my mother, mother! O!
You have won a happy victory to Rome;
But, for your son – believe it, O, believe it! –
Most dangerously you have with him prevailed,
If not most mortal to him. But let it come.
(V, iii, 182–9)

What *has* she done? She has saved Rome: but in the case of her son, she has both made and marred him; taught him immutability and made him change; 'manned' him and unmanned him. Made him steel, turned him silk. As Aufidius says:

He bowed his nature, never known before
But to be rough, unswayable, and free
(V, vi, 25–6)

For Plutarch, the moment when Coriolanus gives in is all 'nature'. 'And nature so wrought with him that the tears fell from his eyes and ... [he] yielded to the affection of his blood.' It is Shakespeare who makes Coriolanus deem it an '*unnatural* scene'. At the very least, we can say that one 'nature' has been undermined by another, and while that is undoubtedly good for Rome (and perhaps humanity), Coriolanus is clearly right in sensing that it will prove disastrous for him. Much of the rest of his speech is in Plutarch – but not those last four words. 'But let it come.' This, as Brockbank remarked, is directly reminiscent of Hamlet's 'Let be.' It is as if he recognizes that, by what had just happened, an inexorable process has been set in train, the outcome of which is at once unforeseeable and ineluctable. It amounts to a recognition and acceptance of the tragic workings of nature.

After this, it is easy for Aufidius to goad Coriolanus to a self-destructive fury. He calls him 'traitor' – as Rome did; denies him his 'stol'n' name; and, when Coriolanus invokes Mars, delivers the final taunt which he knows will drive him completely out of control: 'Name not the god, thou boy of tears!' (V, vi, 101). This makes Coriolanus explode:

> Measureless liar, thou hast made my heart
> Too great for what contains it.
>
> (V, vi, 103–4)

and he calls down the knives:

> Cut me to pieces, Volsces, men and lads,
> Stain all your edges on me. 'Boy'! False hound!
> If you have writ your annals true, 'tis there,
> That, like an eagle in a dovecote, I
> Fluttered your Volscians in Corioles.
> Alone I did it. 'Boy'?

In a sense, Aufidius is absolutely correct (sometimes, nothing wounds like the truth) – Coriolanus *did* regress to being a 'boy of tears' in front of his mother. (Though, of course, there could be a less denigrating, more generous way of describing his transformation.) But if he goes down as 'Boy', he wants once more to assert his old martial-eagle identity of the matchless warrior who could take a city 'alone'. And he wants to think of this identity and exploit set down and preserved in the immutability of writing (not trusting to the vagaries of voice). 'Annals' are the distinctively Roman form of history, primarily associated with Tacitus (it is the only time Shakespeare used the word). Having employed the heroized Coriolanus, banished and then besought him, Rome will continue without him, finding other soldiers for other wars. That is why Coriolanus wants what he has been and done to be written '*true*' and written '*there*'. So ends the last great tragedy written for the English stage.

King's College, Cambridge — Tony Tanner

SELECT BIBLIOGRAPHY

BIOGRAPHY

The standard biography is now Samuel Schoenbaum, *William Shakespeare: A Documentary Life*, Oxford University Press, Oxford, 1975. A shortened version of this excellent volume was published in 1977. For those interested in Shakespearian mythology, Schoenbaum has also produced *Shakespeare's Lives*, Clarendon Press, Oxford, 1970, a witty dissection of the myriad theories concerning the playwright's identity and the authorship of the plays. Rather in the same vein is Anthony Burgess, *Shakespeare*, Penguin, London, 1972, a lively introduction to the presumed facts of the poet's life, enhanced by novelistic licence.

BIBLIOGRAPHY

Among the vast quantity of Shakespeare criticism it is probably only useful to list texts which are both outstanding and easily available. This I do below. For further information the serious student may consult the bibliographies of works listed. There are also three major journals which record the flow of critical work: the *Shakespeare Quarterly*; and the *Shakespeare Survey* and *Shakespeare Studies* which are published annually.

CRITICISM

The two indispensable Shakespearian critics are Johnson and Coleridge. Their dispersed comments are collected in *Samuel Johnson on Shakespeare*, ed., H. R. Woodhuysen, Penguin, London, 1989, and S. T. Coleridge, *Shakespearian Criticism*, two vols., Everyman's Library, London, 1960.

Among distinguished older commentaries which still have a great deal to offer are A. C. Bradley, *Shakespearian Tragedy*, Macmillan, London, 1904; Lily B. Campbell, *Shakespeare's Tragic Heroes: Slaves of Passion*, Cambridge University Press, Cambridge, 1930; H. B. Charlton, *Shakespearian Tragedy*, Cambridge University Press, Cambridge, 1948; G. W. Knight, *The Wheel of Fire*, Methuen, London, 1930; and Harley Granville-Barker, *Prefaces to Shakespeare*, two vols., Batsford, London, 1958. All contain detailed commentary on individual plays and discussion of Shakespeare's theatrical art, though Bradley concentrates on character study and Barker on dramaturgy, while the others pay more attention to themes, imagery and structure. All five grapple in different ways with the perplexing question of whether Shakespeare can be said to have a consistent practice and an implicit theory of tragedy – issues also addressed by more recent commentators, including Kenneth Muir, *Shakespeare and the Tragic Pattern*, Longman, London, 1958, and *William Shakespeare: The Great Tragedies*, Longman, London, 1961; Ruth Nevgo, *Tragic Form in Shakespeare*, Princeton University Press, Princeton, N.J., 1972; J. V. Cunningham, *Woe or Wonder: The Emotional Effect of Shakespearian Tragedy*, University of Denver Press, Denver, 1951; Maynard Mack, *Killing the King: Three Studies in Shakespeare's Tragic Structure*, Yale University Press, New Haven, 1973; and Irving Ribner, *Patterns in Shakespearian Tragedy*, Methuen, London, 1960.

John Holloway, *The Story of the Night: Studies in Shakespearian Tragedy*, Routledge, London, 1967; and John Lawlor, *The Tragic Sense in Shakespeare*, Chatto & Windus, London, 1960, both comment on the plays severally and together. N. M. Proser, *The Heroic Image in Five Shakespearian Tragedies*, Princeton University Press, Princeton, N.J., 1965, pursues the evolution of a single crucial image; P. N. Siegel considers the political context in *Shakespearian Tragedy and the Elizabethan Compromise*, New York University Press, New York, 1957; while William Rosen, *Shakespeare and the Craft of Tragedy*, Harvard University Press, Cambridge, Mass., 1960, and V. K. Whitaker, *The Mirror Up To Nature: The Technique of Shakespeare's Tragedies*, Huntingdon Library, San Marino, California, 1965, offer detailed examinations of the playwright's artistry with reference to contemporary writers.

Three innovative views can be found in Northrop Frye, *Fools of Time: Studies in Shakespearian Tragedy*, University of Toronto Press, Toronto, 1967; Jonathon Dollimore, *Radical Tragedy*, Harvester, Brighton, 1984; and Stephen Greenblatt, *Shakespearian Negotiations*, Clarendon, Oxford, 1988. Dollimore is a Cultural Materialist who wants to situate Shakespeare in the economic and political circumstances of his time; Greenblatt is a New Historicist who weaves the plays into a complex tapestry of contemporary texts and events; while Frye writes against the background of his own theory of Archetypes.

As their titles indicate, the following commentaries all provide an overview of the Greek and Roman plays or discuss crucial aspects of their political, historical or literary context:

BROCKBANK, J. P., *On Shakespeare*, 1989.

SELECT BIBLIOGRAPHY

BROWER, REUBEN, *Shakespeare and the Graeco-Roman Heroic Tradition*, 1971.

CHARNEY, MAURICE, *Shakespeare's Roman Plays: The Function of Imagery in the Drama*, 1961.

CHARNEY, MAURICE, ed., *Discussions of Shakespeare's Roman Plays*, 1964.

HONIGMAN, E. A. J., *Shakespeare: Seven Tragedies*, 1976.

KNIGHT, G. W., *The Imperial Theme*, 1931.

MACCULLUM, M. W., *Shakespeare's Roman Plays and Their Background*, 1910.

MIOLA, ROBERT S., *Shakespeare's Rome*, 1983.

PALMER, JOHN, *Political Characters of Shakespeare*, 1945.

PHILLIPS, J. E., *The State in Shakespeare's Greek and Roman Plays*, 1940.

RICHMOND, HUGH M., *Shakespeare's Political Plays*, 1967.

SHAKESPEARE SURVEY (10), 1957 (mainly on the Roman plays).

SPENCER, T. J. B., *Shakespeare: The Roman Plays*, 1963.

STAMPFER, JUDITH, *The Tragic Engagement: A Study of Shakespeare's Classical Tragedies*, 1963.

TRAVERSI, DEREK, *Shakespeare: The Roman Plays*, 1963.

WAITH, EUGENE, *The Herculean Hero*, 1962.

WHITAKER, VIRGIL K., *Shakespeare's Use of Learning*, 1953.

On particular plays the following texts may be found useful:

Titus Andronicus

BAKER, HOWARD, *Induction to Tragedy*, 1939.

HAMILTON, A. C., '*Titus Andronicus*: The Form of Shakespearian Tragedy', *Shakespeare Survey* 10, 1963.

HUNTER, G. K., 'Sources and Meanings in *Titus Andronicus*' in *The Mirror Up To Nature*, ed. J. C. Gray, 1983.

ROBERTS, JEANNE ANDERSON, *The Shakespearian Wild*, 1991.

SOMMERS, ALAN, '"Wilderness of Tigers": Structure and Symbolism in *Titus Andronicus*', *Essays in Criticism* 10, 1960.

TRICOMI, ALBERT H., 'The Mutilated Garden in *Titus Andronicus*', *Shakespeare Studies* 9, 1976.

Troilus and Cressida

ADELMAN, JANET, '"This Is and Is Not Cressid": The Characterization of Cressida' in *The M(o)ther Tongue*, ed. Shirley Nelson Garner, 1985.

BAYLEY, JOHN, 'Time and the Trojans', *Essays in Criticism* 25, 1975.

BRADBROOK, MURIEL C., 'What Shakespeare Did to Chaucer's *Troilus and Criseyde*', *Shakespeare Quarterly* 9, 1958.

EMPSON, WILLIAM, *Some Versions of Pastoral*, 1935.

GIRARD, RENE, 'The Politics of Desire in *Troilus and Cressida*' in *Shakespeare and the Question of Theory*, ed. Patricia Parker and Geoffrey Hartman, 1985.

HUNTER, G. K., '*Troilus and Cressida:* A Tragic Satire', *Shakespeare Studies* 13, 1974–5.

KERMODE, FRANK, '"Opinion" in *Troilus and Cressida*' in *Teaching the Text*, ed. Susanne Kappeler and Norman Bryson, 1983.

KIMBROUGH, ROBERT, *Shakespeare's Troilus and Cressida and Its Setting*, 1964.

PRESSON, R. K., *Shakespeare's Troilus and Cressida and the Legends of Troy*, 1953.

RABKIN, NORMAN, '*Troilus and Cressida:* The Uses of the Double Plot', *Shakespeare Studies* 1, 1965.

SOUTHALL, RAYMOND, 'Troilus and Cressida and the Spirit of Capitalism' in *Shakespeare in the Changing World*, ed. Arnold Kettle, 1964.

STEIN, ARNOLD, '*Troilus and Cressida*: The Disjunctive Imagination', *ELH* 36, 1969.

Julius Caesar

BARTON, ANNE, '*Julius Caesar* and *Coriolanus*: Shakespeare's Roman World of Words' in *Shakespeare's Craft*, ed. Philip H. Highfill, 1982.

BONJOUR, ADRIEN, *The Structure of Julius Caesar*, 1958.

FOAKES, R. A., 'An Approach to *Julius Caesar*', *Shakespeare Quarterly* V, 1954.

HEILMAN, ROBERT, 'To Know Himself: An Aspect of Tragic Structure', *Review of English Literature* 4, 1964.

LEVITSKY, RUTH M., '"The Elements Were So Mix'd ..."', *PMLA* 88, 1973.

SCHANZER, ERNEST, 'The Problem of *Julius Caesar*', *Shakespeare Quarterly* VI, 1955.

SMITH, GORDON ROSS, 'Brutus, Virtue, and Will', *Shakespeare Quarterly* 10, 1959.

STEWART, J. I. M., *Character and Motive in Shakespeare*, 1949.

Antony and Cleopatra

ADELMAN, JANET, *The Common Liar: An Essay on Antony and Cleopatra*, 1973.

BARROLL, J. LEEDS, *Shakespearean Tragedy: Genre, Tradition, and Change in Antony and Cleopatra*, 1984.

BAYLEY, JOHN, *Shakespeare and Tragedy*, 1981.

COATES, JOHN, '"The Choice of Hercules" in *Antony and Cleopatra*', *Shakespeare Survey* 31, 1978.

DANBY, JOHN F., *Poets on Fortune's Hill*, 1952.
FARNHAM, WILLARD, *Shakespeare's Tragic Frontier*, 1950.
LEAVIS, F. R., '*Antony and Cleopatra* and *All For Love*: A Critical Exercise', *Scrutiny* 5, 1936–7.
LLOYD, MICHAEL, 'Cleopatra as Isis', *Shakespeare Survey* 12, 1959.
MARKELS, JULIAN, *The Pillar of the World: Antony and Cleopatra in Shakespeare's Development*, 1968.

Timon of Athens

BRILL, LESLEY W., 'Truth and *Timon of Athens*', *Modern Language Quarterly* 40, 1979.
BUTLER, FRANCILIA, *The Strange Critical Fortunes of Shakespeare's Timon of Athens*, 1966.
CAMPBELL, OSCAR JAMES, *Shakespeare's Satire*, 1943.
ELLIS-FERMOR, UNA, '*Timon of Athens*: An Unfinished Play', *Review of English Studies* 18, 1942.
HANDELMAN, SUSAN, 'The Rise of Disillusion', *American Image* 36, 1979.
HONIGMAN, E. A. J., '*Timon of Athens*', *Shakespeare Quarterly* 12, 1961.
KNIGHT, G. WILSON, *The Wheel of Fire*, 1930.
SLIGHTS, WILLIAM W. E., '*Genera mixta* and *Timon of Athens*', *Studies in Philology* 74, 1977.
SOELLNER, ROLF, *Timon of Athens: Shakespeare's Pessimistic Tragedy*, 1979.
SPENCER, T. J. B., 'Shakespeare Learns the Value of Money: The Dramatist at Work on *Timon of Athens*', *Shakespeare Survey* 6, 1953.

Coriolanus

BROCKBANK, J. P., *Coriolanus*, The Arden Edition, 1976.
BROWNING, I. R., 'Coriolanus – "Boy of Tears" ', *Essays in Criticism* 5, 1955.
FRYE, DEAN, 'Commentary in Shakespeare: The Case of Coriolanus', *Shakespeare Studies* 1, ed. J. Leeds Barroll, 1965.
GORDON, D. J., 'Name and Fame: Shakespeare's Coriolanus' in *Papers Mainly Shakespearian*, ed. G. L. Duthie, 1964.
HEUER, HERMAN, 'From Plutarch to Shakespeare: A Study of *Coriolanus*', *Shakespeare Survey* 10, 1957.
MAXWELL, J. C., 'Animal Imagery in *Coriolanus*', *Modern Language Review* 42, 1947.
RABKIN, NORMAN, '*Coriolanus*: The Tragedy of Politics', *Shakespeare Quarterly* 37, 1987.
SICHERMAN, CAROL, '*Coriolanus*: The Failure of Words', *ELH* 39, 1972.

VAN DYKE, JOYCE, 'Making a Scene: Language and Gesture in *Coriolanus*', *Shakespeare Survey* 30, 1977.

WATSON, ROBERT N., *Shakespeare and the Hazards of Ambition*, 1984.

BACKGROUND AND SOURCES

Shakespeare scholarship is massive and exhaustive, covering every imaginable aspect of the writer's work, life and times. Most editions of the text, including the Everyman Shakespeare, are now supplied with notes which are more than adequate for all normal purposes. However, those who wish to explore questions of Shakespearian language further may care to consult John Bartlett, *A New and Complete Concordance to Shakespeare*, Macmillan, New York, 1894, and C. T. Onions, *A Shakespeare Glossary*, Oxford University Press, London, 1911 (and frequently reprinted). Between them, these texts define and explain every single word Shakespeare uses, citing the places where they appear and exploring obsolete usages.

The thorny questions of textual transmission are covered in W. W. Greg's *The Shakespeare First Folio*, Oxford University Press, New York and London, 1955. This gives a detailed history of the first collected edition of the plays which appeared in 1623.

Finally, a word on sources. Most individual editions of the plays include a note on particular sources, together with extensive quotation. The most readily available and accessible general book on this matter is Kenneth Muir's *Shakespeare's Sources*, Methuen, London, 1957. Muir was one of the most distinguished scholar-critics of his time and his book throws fascinating light on the whole field of Shakespeare studies.

Even more comprehensive – though considerably more daunting – are the eight volumes of Geoffrey Bullough's *Narrative and Dramatic Sources of Shakespeare*, Routledge & Kegan Paul, London, and Columbia University Press, New York, 1957–75.

CHRONOLOGY

DATE	AUTHOR'S LIFE	LITERARY CONTEXT
1564	Born in Stratford, Warwickshire, the eldest surviving son of John Shakespeare, glover and occasional dealer in wool, and Mary Arden, daughter of a prosperous farmer.	Birth of Christopher Marlowe.
1565	John Shakespeare elected Alderman of Stratford.	Clinthio: *Hecatommithi*. Edwards: *Damon and Pythias*.
1566	Birth of Shakespeare's brother Gilbert.	Gascoigne: *Supposes*.
1567		Udall: *Roister Doister*. Golding: *The Stories of Venus and Adonis and of Hermaphroditus and Salamcis*.
1568	His father is elected bailiff.	Gascoigne: *Jocasta*. Wilmot: *Tancred and Gismunda*. Second Edition of Vasari's *Lives of the Artists*.
1569	Probably starts attending the petty school attached to the King's New School in Stratford. Birth of his sister Joan.	
1570	His father involved in money-lending.	
1571	John Shakespeare is elected Chief Alderman and deputy to the new bailiff.	
1572		Whitgift's *Answer* to the 'Admonition' receives Cartwright's *Reply*, beginning the first literary debate between Anglicans and Puritans.
1573		Tasso: *Aminta*.
1574	Probably enters the Upper School (where studies include rhetoric, logic, the Latin poets, and a little Greek). Birth of his brother Richard.	

HISTORICAL EVENTS

Death of Michelangelo. Birth of Galileo.

Rebellion against Spain in the Netherlands. Birth of the actor Edward Alleyn.

Birth of the actor Richard Burbage.

Mary Stuart flees to England from Scotland.

Northern Rebellion.

Excommunication of Elizabeth. *Baïf's* Academy founded in Paris to promote poetry, music and dance.

Ridolfi Plot. Puritan 'Admonition' to Parliament.

Dutch rebels conquer Holland and Zeeland. Massacre of St Bartholomew's Day in Paris.

Accession of Henry III and new outbreak of civil war in France. First Catholic missionaries arrive in England from Douai. Earl of Leicester's Men obtain licence to perform within the City of London.

DATE	AUTHOR'S LIFE	LITERARY CONTEXT
1575		*Gammer Gurton's Needle* is printed.
1576		Castiglione's *The Book of the Courtier* banned by the Spanish Inquisition. George Gascoigne: *The Steel Glass.*
1577		John Northbrooke's attack in *Treatise wherein Dicing, Dancing, Vain Plays etc are reproved.*
1578	Shakespeare family fortunes are in decline, and John is having to sell off property to pay off his increasing debts.	Sidney writes *The Lady of May* and begins the 'Old' *Arcadia.* George Whetstone: *Promos and Cassandra.* John Lyly: *Euphues, the Anatomy of Wit.* Pierre de Ronsard, leader of the Pléiade, publishes his *Sonnets pour Hélène.* He is said to have exercised a considerable influence on the English sonnet-writers of the sixteenth century.
1579		Spenser: *The Shepherd's Calendar.* North: translation of Plutarch. Gossen: *The School of Abuse, and Pleasant Invective against Poets, Pipers, Players etc.*
1580	Birth of Shakespeare's brother Edmund.	
1581		John Newton's translation of Seneca's *Ten Tragedies.* Barnaby Rich: *Apolonius and Silla.*
1582	Shakespeare marries Anne Hathaway, a local farmer's daughter, 7 or 8 years his senior, who is already pregnant with their first child.	Tasso: *Gerusalemme Liberata.* Watson: *Hekatompathia* (First sonnet sequence published in England). Whetstone: *Heptameron of Civil Discourses.* Sidney begins *Astrophel and Stella* and the 'New' *Arcadia.* Lope de Vega writing for the Corrals in Madrid.

HISTORICAL EVENTS

Kenilworth Revels.

Restricted by the City of London's order that no plays be performed within the City boundaries, James Burbage of The Earl of Leicester's Men builds The Theatre only just outside the boundaries in Shoreditch. The Blackfriars Theatre is built. End of civil war in France. Observatory of Uraniborg built for the Danish astronomer, Tycho Brahe. Death of Titian.

Drake's circumnavigation of the world. The Curtain Theatre built. Birth of Rubens.

First visit to England of the duc d'Alençon as a suitor to Elizabeth, provoking much opposition to a French match. The Corral de la Cruz built in Madrid.

Spanish conquest of Portugal. Jesuit mission arrives in England from Rome led by Edmund Campion and Parsons.

Stricter enforcement of treason laws and increased penalties on recusants. Campion captured and executed. Northern provinces of the Netherlands renounce their allegiance to Phillip II, and invite the duc d'Alençon to be their sovereign.

Sir Walter Ralegh established in the Queen's favour. The Corral del Principe built in Madrid.

DATE	AUTHOR'S LIFE	LITERARY CONTEXT
1583	Birth of their daughter Susanna.	
1583–4	The players' companies of the Earls of Essex, Oxford and Leicester perform in Stratford.	Giordarno Bruno visits England.
1584		Bruno publishes *La cena de le Ceneri* and *Spaccio della bestia trionfante*. Reginald Scott: *The Discovery of Witchcraft*.
1585	Birth of Shakespeare's twins Hamnet and Judith. The following years until 1592 are the 'Lost Years' for which no documentary records of his life survive, only legends such as the one of deer-stealing and flight from prosecution, and conjectures such as ones that he became a schoolmaster, travelled in Europe, or went to London to be an actor as early as the mid 1580s.	Death of Pierre de Ronsard. Bruno: *De gli eroici furori*, dedicated to Sidney.
1586		Timothy Bright: *A Treatise of Melancholy*.
1586–7	Five players' companies visit Stratford, including the Queen's, Essex's, Leicester's and Stafford's.	
1587		Holinshed: *Chronicles of England Scotland and Ireland*. Marlowe: First part of *Tamburlaine the Great* acted. New edition of *The Mirror for Magistrates*.
1588		Marlowe: Second part of *Tamburlaine*. Thomas Kyd: *The Spanish Tragedy*. Lope de Vega, serving with the Armada, writes some of *The Beauty of Angelica*.

CHRONOLOGY

HISTORICAL EVENTS

First meeting of the Durham House Set led by Ralegh, Northumberland and Harriot, to promote mathematics, astronomy and navigation. Archbishop Whitgift leads more extreme anti-Puritan policy. Throckmorton plot, involving the Spanish ambassador.

Death of d'Alençon. Assassination of William of Orange. The Teatro Olimpico, Vicenza, built by Palladio.

England sends military aid to the Dutch rebels under the command of Leicester. Ralegh organizes the colonization of Virginia.

Babington plot. Death of Sir Philip Sidney. Rise of the Earl of Essex. Colonization of Munster.

Execution of Mary Stuart. Drake's raid on Cadiz.

Defeat of the Armada. Death of the Earl of Leicester. The first of the Puritan Marprelate Tracts published.

DATE	AUTHOR'S LIFE	LITERARY CONTEXT
1589	The earliest likely date at which Shakespeare began composition of his first plays (1 *Henry VI*, *The Taming of the Shrew*) when he would have been working as an actor at The Theatre, with Burbage's company.	Marlowe: *The Jew of Malta.* Thomas Nashe: *The Anatomy of Absurdity.* Richard Hakluyt: *Principal Navigations, Voyages and Discoveries of the English nation.*
1590	2 *Henry VI*, 3 *Henry VI.*	Spenser: first 3 books of *The Faerie Queen.* Publication of Sidney's 'New' *Arcadia.* Nashe: *An Almond for a Parrot*, one of the Marprelate Tracts. Greene: *Menaphon.* Guarina: *The Faithful Shepherd.*
1590–91	*King John* written.	
1590–92	Performances of *Henry VI*, parts 2 and 3, *Titus* and *The Shrew* by the Earl of Pembroke's Men.	
1591	*Richard III* and *The Comedy of Errors* written.	Spenser's *Complaints* which includes his translation of fifteen of Joachim du Bellay's sonnets – du Bellay was a member of the Pléiade and responsible for its manifesto. Sir John Harington's translation of *Orlando Furioso.* Publication of Sidney's *Astrophel and Stella.*
1592	First recorded reference to Shakespeare as an actor and playwright in Greene's attack in *The Groatsworth of Wit* describing him as 'an upstart crow'.	Samuel Daniel: *Delia.* Marlowe's *Edward II* and *Doctor Faustus* performed. *Arden of Feversham* printed. Nashe: *Strange News.*
1592–4	*Titus Andronicus* written.	
1593	Publication of *Venus and Adonis*, dedicated to the Earl of Southampton. The *Sonnets* probably begun.	Marlowe: *Massacre of Paris. The Phoenix Nest*, miscellany of poems including ones by Ralegh, Lodge and Breton. Barnabe Barnes: *Parthenophil and Parthenope.* George Peele: *The Honour of the Garter.* Lodge: *Phillis.* Nashe: *Christ's Tears over Jerusalem.*

CHRONOLOGY

HISTORICAL EVENTS

Failure of the Portugal expedition. Henry III of France assassinated. English military aid sent to Henry of Navarre. Marlowe's tutor, Francis Ket, burned at the stake for atheism.

English government discovers and suppresses the Puritan printing press.

Earl of Essex given command of the English army in France. The last fight of the *Revenge* under Spanish attack.

Capture of Madre de Dios. Split in the main players' company. Shakespeare and Burbage's group remain at The Theatre, Alleyn's move to the Rose on Bankside. Plague in London: the theatres closed.

Marlowe arrested on blasphemy charges and murdered two weeks later. Kyd arrested for libel. Henry of Navarre converts to Catholicism in order to unite France.

DATE	AUTHOR'S LIFE	LITERARY CONTEXT
1593–4	*The Two Gentlemen of Verona.*	
1593–6		John Donne writing his early poems, the Satires and Elegies.
1594	*The Rape of Lucrece* dedicated to his patron Southampton. *The Comedy of Errors* and *Titus Andronicus* performed at the Rose. Shakespeare established as one of the shareholders in his company, The Chamberlain's Men, which performs before the Queen during the Christmas festivities.	Daniel: *Cleopatra.* Spenser: *Amoretti* and *Epithalamion.* Drayton: *Idea's Mirror.* Nashe: *The Terrors of the Night, The Unfortunate Traveller.* Greene: *Friar Bacon and Friar Bungay.*
1594–5	*Love's Labour's Lost* and *Romeo and Juliet* written.	
1595	*Richard II.*	Daniel: *The First Four Books of the Civil Wars between the two houses of Lancaster and York.* Sidney: *Defence of Poesy* published. Ralegh: *The Discovery of the Empire of Guiana.*
1595–6	*A Midsummer Night's Dream.*	
1596	Death of his son, Hamnet. *The Merchant of Venice.* Shakespeare living in Bishopsgate ward. His father, John, is granted a coat of arms.	Lodge: *Wits Miserle.* First complete edition of Spenser's *Faerie Queen.*
1597	*Henry IV* Part 1. First performance of *The Merry Wives of Windsor.* Shakespeare's company now under the patronage of the new Lord Chamberlain, Hunsdon. In Stratford, Shakespeare buys New Place, the second largest house in the town, with its own orchards and vines.	John Donne writes 'The Storme' and 'The Calme'. Francis Bacon: first edition of *Essays.* Jonson and Nashe imprisoned for writing *The Isle of Dogs.*
1597–8	*Henry IV* Part 2.	
1598	Shakespeare one of the 'principal comedians' with Richard Burbage, Heminge and Cordell in Jonson's *Every Man in his Humour.* For the second year, Shakespeare is listed as having failed to pay tax levied on all householders.	Publication of Sidney's *Works* and of Marlowe's *Hero and Leander* (together with Chapman's continuation). *Seven Books of the Iliads* (first of Chapman's Homeric translations). Meres: *Palladia Tamia.*

CHRONOLOGY

HISTORICAL EVENTS

Henry of Navarre accepted as King in Paris. Rebellion in Ireland. The London theatres re-open. The Swan Theatre is built. Ralegh accused of blasphemy.

France declares war on Spain. Failure of the Indies voyage and death of Hawkins. Ralegh's expedition to Guiana.

England joins France in the war against Spain. Death of Drake. Raid on Cadiz led by Essex. In long-standing power struggle with Essex, Robert Cecil is appointed Secretary of State.

Islands Voyage led by Essex and Ralegh. The government suppresses the *Isle of Dogs* at the Swan and closes the theatres. Despite the continued hostility of the City of London, they soon re-open. James Burbage builds the second Blackfriars Theatre. Death of James Burbage.

Peace between France and Spain. Death of Philip II. Tyrone defeats the English at Armagh. Essex appointed Lord Deputy of Ireland.

DATE	AUTHOR'S LIFE	LITERARY CONTEXT
1598 *cont.*		New edition of Lodge's *Rosalynde*. Lope de Vega: *La Arcadia*. James VI of Scotland: *The True Law of Free Monarchies*.
1598–9	*As You Like It*.	
1598–1600	*Much Ado About Nothing*.	
1599	*Henry V*, *Julius Caesar*. Shakespeare one of the shareholders in the Globe Theatre. He moves lodgings to Bankside. Publication of *The Passionate Pilgrim*, a miscellany of 20 poems, at least 5 by Shakespeare.	Jonson: *Every Man out of his Humour*. Dekker: *The Shoemaker's Holiday*. Sir John Hayward: *The First Part of the Life and Reign of King Henry IV*. Greene's translation of *Orlando Furioso*.
1600		'England's Helicon'.
1600–1	*Hamlet* (performed with Burbage as the Prince and Shakespeare as the Ghost).	
1601	*The Phoenix and the Turtle*. The Lord Chamberlain's Men paid by one of Essex's followers to perform *Richard II* on the day before the rebellion. Death of John Shakespeare.	
1601–2	*Troilus and Cressida*.	
1602	Shakespeare buys more property in Stratford.	
1602–4	*Alls Well That Ends Well*.	
1603	Shakespeare's company now under the patronage of King James. Shakespeare is one of the principal tragedians in Jonson's *Sejanus*.	Montaigne's *Essays* translated into English. Thomas Heywood: *A Woman Killed with Kindness*.
1604	Shakespeare known to be lodging in Silver Street with a Huguenot family called Mountjoy. *Othello*; first performance of *Measure for Measure*.	Chapman: *Bussy d'Ambois*. Marston: *The Malcontent*.
1604–5	Ten of his plays performed at court by the King's Men.	

CHRONOLOGY

HISTORICAL EVENTS

The Burbage brothers, Richard and Cuthbert, pull down The Theatre and, with its timbers, build the Globe on Bankside. Essex's campaign fails in Ireland, and after returning without permission to court he is arrested. The government suppresses satirical writings, and burns pamphlets by Nashe and Harvey.

Essex released but still in disgrace. The Fortune Theatre built by Alleyn and Henslowe. Bruno executed for heresy by the Inquisition in Rome.

Essex's Rebellion. Essex and Southampton arrested, and the former executed. Spanish invasion of Ireland. Monopolies debates in Parliament.

Spanish troops defeated in Ireland.

Death of Elizabeth, and accession of James I. Ralegh imprisoned in the Tower. Plague in London. Sir Thomas Bodley re-founds the library of Oxford University.

Peace with Spain. Hampton Court Conference.

DATE	AUTHOR'S LIFE	LITERARY CONTEXT
1605	First performance of *King Lear* at the Globe, with Burbage as the King, and Robert Armin as the Fool. Shakespeare makes further investments in Stratford, buying a half interest in a lease of tithes.	Cervantes: *Don Quixote* (part one). Bacon: *The Proficience and Advancement of Learning*. Jonson and Inigo Jones: *The Masque of Blackness*. Jonson and co-authors imprisoned for libellous references to the court in *Eastward Ho*.
1605–6		Jonson: *Volpone*.
1606	First performance of *Macbeth*.	John Ford's masque *Honour Triumphant*.
1607	*Antony and Cleopatra*. Susanna marries John Hall, a physician. Death of Shakespeare's brother Edmund, an actor.	Tourneur's *The Revenger's Tragedy* printed. Barnes: *The Devil's Charter*.
1607–8	*Timon of Athens*, *Coriolanus*, *Pericles*.	
1608	Shakespeare one of the shareholders in the Blackfriars Theatre. Death of his mother.	Lope de Vega: *Peribanez*. Beaumont and Fletcher: *Philaster*. Jonson and Jones: *The Masque of Beauty*. Donne writes *La Corona*. Twelve books of Homer's *Iliad* (Chapman's translation).
1609	Publication, probably unauthorized, of the quarto edition of the *Sonnets* and *A Lover's Complaint*.	Jonson and Jones: *The Masque of Queens*. Donne's 'The Expiration' printed; 'Liturgie' and 'On the Annunciation' written. Bacon: *De Sapientia Veterum*. Lope de Vega: *New Art of Writing Plays for the Theatre*.
1609–10	*Cymbeline*.	
1610		Donne: *Pseudo-Martyr* printed and *The First Anniversarie* written. Jonson: *The Alchemist*. Beaumont and Fletcher: *The Maid's Tragedy*.
1610–11	*The Winter's Tale*.	
1611	*The Tempest* performed in the Banqueting House, Whitehall. Simon Forman records seeing performances of *Macbeth*, *The Winter's Tale* and *Cymbeline*.	Beaumont and Fletcher: *A King and No King*, *The Knight of the Burning Pestle*. Tourneur: *The Atheist's Tragedy*.

CHRONOLOGY

HISTORICAL EVENTS

Gunpowder Plot.

Monteverdi: *Orfeo*.
Bacon appointed Solicitor General.

Galileo's experiments with the telescope confirm the Copernican theory. Kepler draws up 'Laws of Planetary Motion'. Twelve-year Truce between Spain and Netherlands.

Galileo: *The Starry Messenger*. Assassination of Henry IV of France. Parliament submits the Petition of Grievances.

The Inquisition of Rome begins investigating Galileo.

DATE	AUTHOR'S LIFE	LITERARY CONTEXT
1611 *cont.*		Jonson and Jones: *Masque of Oberon.* Authorized Version of the Bible. Sir John Davies: *The Scourge of Folly.* Donne writes the *The Second Anniversarie* and a 'A Valediction: forbidding mourning'.
1612	Shakespeare appears as a witness in a Court of Requests case involving a dispute over a dowry owed by his former landlord, Mountjoy, to his son-in-law, Belott. Death of his brother Gilbert.	Webster: *The White Devil* printed. Tourneur: *The Nobleman.* Lope de Vega: *Fuente Ovejuna.*
1613	At a performance of his last play, *Henry VIII*, the Globe Theatre catches fire and is destroyed. As part of the court celebrations for the marriage of Princess Elizabeth, The King's Men perform 14 plays, including *Much Ado*, *Othello*, *The Winter's Tale* and *The Tempest.* Death of his brother Richard.	Sir Thomas Overbury: *The Wife.* Donne: 'Good Friday' and 'Epithalamion' on Princess Elizabeth's marriage. Cervantes: *Novelas ejemplares* – a collection of short stories.
1614	In Stratford, Shakespeare protects his property interests during a controversy over a threat to enclose the common fields.	Jonson: *Bartholomew Fair.* Webster: *The Duchess of Malfi.* Ralegh: *The History of the World.*
1615	The Warwick Assizes issue an order to prevent enclosures, which ends the dispute in Stratford.	Cervantes publishes 8 plays and *Don Quixote* (part two).
1616	Marriage of his daughter Judith to Thomas Quincy, a vintner, who a month later is tried for fornication with another woman whom he had made pregnant. Death of Shakespeare (23 April).	Jonson: *The Devil is an Ass.* Jonson publishes his *Works.*
1623	The players Heminge and Condell publish the plays of the First Folio.	

HISTORICAL EVENTS

Death of Henry, Prince of Wales.

Marriage of Princess Elizabeth to Frederick, Elector Palatine. Bacon appointed Attorney-General.

The second Globe and the Hope Theatre built.

Inquiry into the murder of Sir Thomas Overbury in the Tower implicates the wife of the King's favourite, Somerset.

Ralegh released from the Tower to lead an expedition to Guiana; on his return he is executed.

WILLIAM SHAKESPEARE

THE MOST LAMENTABLE ROMAN TRAGEDY OF TITUS ANDRONICUS

Edited by Sylvan Barnet

[*Dramatis Personae*

SATURNINUS, son to the late Emperor of Rome, afterward Emperor
BASSIANUS, brother to Saturninus
TITUS ANDRONICUS, a noble Roman
MARCUS ANDRONICUS, Tribune, and brother to Titus
LUCIUS, QUINTUS, MARTIUS, MUTIUS — sons to Titus Andronicus
YOUNG LUCIUS, a boy, son to Lucius
PUBLIUS, son to Marcus Andronicus
SEMPRONIUS, CAIUS, VALENTINE — kinsmen to Titus Andronicus
AEMILIUS, a noble Roman
ALARBUS, DEMETRIUS, CHIRON — sons to Tamora
AARON, a Moor, beloved by Tamora
A CAPTAIN
A MESSENGER
A CLOWN
TAMORA, Queen of the Goths
LAVINIA, daughter to Titus Andronicus
NURSE, and a blackamoor Infant
ROMANS, GOTHS, SENATORS, TRIBUNES, OFFICERS, SOLDIERS, and ATTENDANTS

Scene: Rome, and the countryside near it]

THE MOST LAMENTABLE ROMAN TRAGEDY OF TITUS ANDRONICUS

[ACT I

Scene I. *Rome. Before the Capitol.*]

[*Flourish.*[1]] *Enter the Tribunes and Senators aloft; and then enter Saturninus and his followers at one door, and Bassianus and his followers* [*at the other,*] *with drums and trumpets.*

SATURNINUS Noble patricians, patrons of my right,
Defend the justice of my cause with arms;
And, countrymen, my loving followers,
Plead my successive title with your swords.
I am his first-born son that was the last
That ware the imperial diadem of Rome;
Then let my father's honors live in me,
Nor wrong mine age with this indignity.

BASSIANUS Romans, friends, followers, favorers of my right,
If ever Bassianus, Caesar's son,

1. Text references are printed in bold type; the annotation follows in roman type.
I.i.s.d. **Flourish** trumpet fanfare 4 **successive title** right to the succession
8 **age** i.e., seniority

Were gracious in the eyes of royal Rome,
Keep then this passage to the Capitol,
And suffer not dishonor to approach
The imperial seat, to virtue consecrate,
To justice, continence, and nobility;
But let desert in pure election shine,
And, Romans, fight for freedom in your choice.

MARCUS (*With the crown*) Princes, that strive by factions and by friends
Ambitiously for rule and empery,
Know that the people of Rome, for whom we stand
A special party, have by common voice,
In election for the Roman empery,
Chosen Andronicus, surnamèd Pius
For many good and great deserts to Rome.
A nobler man, a braver warrior,
Lives not this day within the city walls.
He by the senate is accited home
From weary wars against the barbarous Goths;
That with his sons, a terror to our foes,
Hath yoked a nation strong, trained up in arms.
Ten years are spent since first he undertook
This cause of Rome, and chastisèd with arms
Our enemies' pride: five times he hath returned
Bleeding to Rome, bearing his valiant sons
In coffins from the field.
And now at last, laden with honor's spoils,
Returns the good Andronicus to Rome,
Renownèd Titus, flourishing in arms.
Let us entreat, by honor of his name,
Whom worthily you would have now succeed,

11 **gracious** acceptable 12 **Keep** guard 15 **continence** restraint 19 **empery** dominion (but in line 22 **empery**=emperor) 27 **accited** summoned 30 **yoked** subjugated 35 **field** (this word is followed by: "and at this day/To the monument of that Andronici/Done sacrifice of expiation,/And slain the noblest prisoner of the Goths." These lines, omitted from the second and third quartos and from the Folio, are inconsistent with the ensuing action, in which Alarbus is sacrificed. Perhaps Shakespeare neglected to cancel them in the manuscript after deciding to make Alarbus' execution part of the action)

And in the Capitol and Senate's right,
Whom you pretend to honor and adore,
That you withdraw you and abate your strength,
Dismiss your followers, and, as suitors should,
Plead your deserts in peace and humbleness.

SATURNINUS How fair the tribune speaks to calm my thoughts!

BASSIANUS Marcus Andronicus, so I do affy
In thy uprightness and integrity,
And so I love and honor thee and thine,
Thy noble brother Titus and his sons,
And her to whom my thoughts are humbled all,
Gracious Lavinia, Rome's rich ornament,
That I will here dismiss my loving friends;
And to my fortunes and the people's favor
Commit my cause in balance to be weighed.

Exit [his] soldiers.

SATURNINUS Friends, that have been thus forward in my right,
I thank you all, and here dismiss you all,
And to the love and favor of my country
Commit myself, my person, and the cause.

[*Exeunt his followers.*]

Rome, be as just and gracious unto me
As I am confident and kind to thee.
Open the gates and let me in.

BASSIANUS Tribunes, and me, a poor competitor.

[*Flourish.*] *They go up into the Senate house.*

Enter a Captain.

CAPTAIN Romans, make way! The good Andronicus,
Patron of virtue, Rome's best champion,
Successful in the battles that he fights,
With honor and with fortune is returned
From where he circumscribèd with his sword

41 **the Capitol and Senate's right** the right of the Capitol and the Senate 42 **pretend** claim 46 **fair** courteously 47 **affy** trust 59 **cause** affair 61 **confident and kind** trusting and natural(ly devoted) 63 **competitor** candidate 65 **Patron** representative

And brought to yoke the enemies of Rome.

Sound drums and trumpets, and then enter two of Titus' sons, and then two men bearing a coffin covered with black, then two other sons, then Titus Andronicus, and then Tamora, the Queen of Goths, and her three sons, [*Alarbus*,] *Chiron, and Demetrius, with Aaron the Moor, and others as many as can be; then set down the coffin, and Titus speaks.*

TITUS Hail, Rome, victorious in thy mourning weeds!
Lo, as the bark that hath discharged his fraught
Returns with precious lading to the bay
From whence at first she weighed her anchorage,
Cometh Andronicus, bound with laurel boughs,
To re-salute his country with his tears,
Tears of true joy for his return to Rome.
Thou great defender of this Capitol,
Stand gracious to the rites that we intend!
Romans, of five and twenty valiant sons,
Half of the number that King Priam had,
Behold the poor remains, alive and dead!
These that survive let Rome reward with love;
These that I bring unto their latest home,
With burial amongst their ancestors.
Here Goths have given me leave to sheathe my
sword.
Titus, unkind and careless of thine own,
Why suffer'st thou thy sons, unburied yet,
To hover on the dreadful shore of Styx?
Make way to lay them by their brethren.
They open the tomb.
There greet in silence, as the dead are wont,
And sleep in peace, slain in your country's wars!
O sacred receptacle of my joys,
Sweet cell of virtue and nobility,

70 **weeds** apparel 71 **his fraught** its freight 73 **anchorage** anchors 77 **Thou** i.e., Jupiter 83 **latest** last 86 **unkind** unnatural 88 **Styx** river surrounding Hades 89 **brethren** (trisyllabic here and occasionally elsewhere: "breth-e-rin")

How many sons hast thou of mine in store,
That thou wilt never render to me more!

LUCIUS Give us the proudest prisoner of the Goths,
That we may hew his limbs, and on a pile
Ad manes fratrum sacrifice his flesh,
Before this earthy prison of their bones,
That so the shadows be not unappeased,
Nor we disturbed with prodigies on earth.

TITUS I give him you, the noblest that survives,
The eldest son of this distressèd queen.

TAMORA Stay, Roman brethren! Gracious conqueror,
Victorious Titus, rue the tears I shed,
A mother's tears in passion for her son:
And if thy sons were ever dear to thee,
O, think my son to be as dear to me!
Sufficeth not that we are brought to Rome,
To beautify thy triumphs and return,
Captive to thee and to thy Roman yoke,
But must my sons be slaughtered in the streets,
For valiant doings in their country's cause?
O, if to fight for king and commonweal
Were piety in thine, it is in these.
Andronicus, stain not thy tomb with blood.
Wilt thou draw near the nature of the gods?
Draw near them then in being merciful;
Sweet mercy is nobility's true badge.
Thrice-noble Titus, spare my first-born son.

TITUS Patient yourself, madam, and pardon me.
These are their brethren, whom your Goths beheld
Alive and dead, and for their brethren slain
Religiously they ask a sacrifice.
To this your son is marked, and die he must,
T' appease their groaning shadows that are gone.

LUCIUS Away with him! And make a fire straight,

98 **Ad manes fratrum** to the ghosts of our brothers (Latin) 101 **prodigies** ominous disturbances 106 **passion** violent emotion 110 **triumphs** triumphal processions 121 **Patient** calm

And with our swords, upon a pile of wood,
Let's hew his limbs till they be clean consumed.
Exit Titus' sons with Alarbus.

TAMORA O cruel, irreligious piety!

CHIRON Was never Scythia half so barbarous.

DEMETRIUS Oppose not Scythia to ambitious Rome.
Alarbus goes to rest, and we survive
To tremble under Titus' threat'ning look.
Then, madam, stand resolved, but hope withal
The selfsame gods that armed the Queen of Troy
With opportunity of sharp revenge
Upon the Thracian tyrant in his tent
May favor Tamora, the Queen of Goths,
(When Goths were Goths and Tamora was queen)
To quit the bloody wrongs upon her foes.

Enter the sons of Andronicus again.

LUCIUS See, lord and father, how we have performed
Our Roman rites! Alarbus' limbs are lopped,
And entrails feed the sacrificing fire,
Whose smoke like incense doth perfume the sky.
Remaineth naught but to inter our brethren,
And with loud 'larums welcome them to Rome.

TITUS Let it be so, and let Andronicus
Make this his latest farewell to their souls.
Sound trumpets, and lay the coffin in the tomb.
In peace and honor rest you here, my sons,
Rome's readiest champions, repose you here in rest,
Secure from worldly chances and mishaps!
Here lurks no treason, here no envy swells,
Here grow no damnèd drugs, here are no storms,

131 **Scythia** a region in southern Russia noted for its savage inhabitants 132 **Oppose** compare 135 **withal** with this 136 **Queen of Troy** Hecuba (who murdered the sons of Polymnestor—**the Thracian tyrant** of line 138—in revenge for his murder of her son) 141 **quit** requite, repay 147 **'larums** alarms, calls to arms 153 **envy** malice 154 **drugs** poisonous plants

No noise, but silence and eternal sleep:
In peace and honor rest you here, my sons!

Enter Lavinia.

LAVINIA In peace and honor live Lord Titus long,
My noble lord and father, live in fame!
Lo, at this tomb my tributary tears
I render for my brethren's obsequies,
And at thy feet I kneel, with tears of joy
Shed on this earth for thy return to Rome.
O, bless me here with thy victorious hand,
Whose fortunes Rome's best citizens applaud.

TITUS Kind Rome, that hast thus lovingly reserved
The cordial of mine age to glad my heart!
Lavinia, live, outlive thy father's days
And fame's eternal date, for virtue's praise!

[*Enter above Marcus Andronicus, Saturninus, Bassianus, and others.*]

MARCUS Long live Lord Titus, my belovèd brother,
Gracious triumpher in the eyes of Rome!

TITUS Thanks, gentle tribune, noble brother Marcus.

MARCUS And welcome, nephews, from successful wars,
You that survive, and you that sleep in fame!
Fair lords, your fortunes are alike in all,
That in your country's service drew your swords,
But safer triumph is this funeral pomp,
That hath aspired to Solon's happiness
And triumphs over chance in honor's bed.
Titus Andronicus, the people of Rome,
Whose friend in justice thou hast ever been,
Send thee by me, their tribune and their trust,
This palliament of white and spotless hue,
And name thee in election for the empire
With these our late-deceasèd emperor's sons:

159 **tributary** given as tribute 166 **cordial** comfort (literally: stimulant to the heart) 168 **date** duration 177 **aspired** risen 177 **Solon's happiness** (Solon said: "Call no man happy until he is dead") 182 **palliament** robe

Be *candidatus* then, and put it on,
And help to set a head on headless Rome.

TITUS A better head her glorious body fits
Than his that shakes for age and feebleness:
What should I don this robe and trouble you?
Be chosen with proclamations today,
Tomorrow yield up rule, resign my life,
And set abroad new business for you all?
Rome, I have been thy soldier forty years,
And led my country's strength successfully,
And buried one and twenty valiant sons,
Knighted in field, slain manfully in arms,
In right and service of their noble country:
Give me a staff of honor for mine age,
But not a scepter to control the world.
Upright he held it, lords, that held it last.

MARCUS Titus, thou shalt obtain and ask the empery.

SATURNINUS Proud and ambitious tribune, canst thou tell?

TITUS Patience, Prince Saturninus.

SATURNINUS Romans, do me right.
Patricians, draw your swords and sheathe them not
Till Saturninus be Rome's emperor.
Andronicus, would thou were shipped to hell
Rather than rob me of the people's hearts.

LUCIUS Proud Saturnine, interrupter of the good
That noble-minded Titus means to thee!

TITUS Content thee, Prince, I will restore to thee
The people's hearts, and wean them from themselves.

BASSIANUS Andronicus, I do not flatter thee,
But honor thee, and will do till I die.
My faction if thou strengthen with thy friends,

185 **candidatus** candidate (Latin; literally: clad in white) 189 **What** why
201 **obtain and ask** i.e., obtain if you ask for

I will most thankful be, and thanks to men
Of noble minds is honorable meed.

TITUS People of Rome, and people's tribunes here,
I ask your voices and your suffrages:
Will ye bestow them friendly on Andronicus?

TRIBUNES To gratify the good Andronicus,
And gratulate his safe return to Rome,
The people will accept whom he admits.

TITUS Tribunes, I thank you, and this suit I make,
That you create our emperor's eldest son,
Lord Saturnine; whose virtues will, I hope,
Reflect on Rome as Titan's rays on earth,
And ripen justice in this commonweal:
Then, if you will elect by my advice,
Crown him and say, "Long live our emperor!"

MARCUS With voices and applause of every sort,
Patricians and plebeians, we create
Lord Saturninus Rome's great emperor,
And say "Long live our Emperor Saturnine!"
[*A long flourish till they come down.*]

SATURNINUS Titus Andronicus, for thy favors done
To us in our election this day,
I give thee thanks in part of thy deserts,
And will with deeds requite thy gentleness:
And for an onset, Titus, to advance
Thy name and honorable family,
Lavinia will I make my empress,
Rome's royal mistress, mistress of my heart,
And in the sacred Pantheon her espouse.
Tell me, Andronicus, doth this motion please thee?

TITUS It doth, my worthy lord, and in this match

216 **meed** reward 221 **gratulate** rejoice at 222 **admits** approves 226 **Titan's** the sun god's 235 **election** (here, as often in Shakespeare, **-ion** is disyllabic) 236 **in** as 237 **gentleness** nobility 238 **onset** beginning 240 **empress** (here, and often elsewhere in *Titus*, trisyllabic: "em-per-es") 242 **Pantheon** temple dedicated to all the gods 243 **motion** proposal

I hold me highly honored of your grace,
And here in sight of Rome to Saturnine,
King and commander of our commonweal,
The wide world's emperor, do I consecrate
My sword, my chariot, and my prisoners,
Presents well worthy Rome's imperious lord.
Receive them then, the tribute that I owe,
Mine honor's ensigns humbled at thy feet.

SATURNINUS Thanks, noble Titus, father of my life!
How proud I am of thee and of thy gifts
Rome shall record, and when I do forget
The least of these unspeakable deserts,
Romans, forget your fealty to me.

TITUS [*To Tamora*] Now, madam, are you prisoner to an emperor,
To him that, for your honor and your state,
Will use you nobly and your followers.

SATURNINUS [*Aside*] A goodly lady, trust me, of the hue
That I would choose, were I to choose anew.
[*Aloud*] Clear up, fair Queen, that cloudy countenance.
Though chance of war hath wrought this change of cheer,
Thou com'st not to be made a scorn in Rome.
Princely shall be thy usage every way.
Rest on my word, and let not discontent
Daunt all your hopes. Madam, he comforts you
Can make you greater than the Queen of Goths.
Lavinia, you are not displeased with this?

LAVINIA Not I, my lord, sith true nobility
Warrants these words in princely courtesy.

SATURNINUS Thanks, sweet Lavinia. Romans, let us go.

250 **imperious** imperial 252 **ensigns** tokens 257 **fealty** loyalty 264 **cheer** countenance 268 **he** he who 271 **sith** since 272 **Warrants** justifies

Ransomless here we set our prisoners free.
Proclaim our honors, lords, with trump and drum.

BASSIANUS Lord Titus, by your leave, this maid is mine.

TITUS How, sir! Are you in earnest then, my lord?

BASSIANUS Ay, noble Titus, and resolved withal
To do myself this reason and this right.

MARCUS *Suum cuique* is our Roman justice.
This prince in justice seizeth but his own.

LUCIUS And that he will, and shall, if Lucius live.

TITUS Traitors, avaunt! Where is the Emperor's guard?
Treason, my lord! Lavinia is surprised!

SATURNINUS Surprised! By whom?

BASSIANUS By him that justly may
Bear his betrothed from all the world away.
[*Exeunt Marcus and Bassianus, with Lavinia.*]

MUTIUS Brothers, help to convey her hence away,
And with my sword I'll keep this door safe.
[*Exeunt Lucius, Quintus, and Martius.*]

TITUS Follow, my lord, and I'll soon bring her back.
[*During the fray, exeunt Saturninus, Tamora, Demetrius, Chiron, and Aaron.*]

MUTIUS My lord, you pass not here.

TITUS What, villain boy! Barr'st me my way in Rome?
[*He stabs Mutius.*]

MUTIUS [*Dying*] Help, Lucius, help!

[*Enter Lucius.*]

LUCIUS My lord, you are unjust; and more than so,

280 Suum cuique to each his own (Latin) **283 avaunt** be gone **284 surprised** suddenly taken **288 door** (disyllabic)

In wrongful quarrel you have slain your son.

TITUS Nor thou, nor he, are any sons of mine:
My sons would never so dishonor me.
Traitor, restore Lavinia to the Emperor.

LUCIUS Dead if you will, but not to be his wife
That is another's lawful promised love. [*Exit*.]

Enter aloft the Emperor with Tamora and her two sons and Aaron the Moor.

SATURNINUS No, Titus, no; the Emperor needs her not,
Nor her, nor thee, nor any of thy stock:
I'll trust by leisure him that mocks me once;
Thee never, nor thy traitorous haughty sons,
Confederates all thus to dishonor me.
Was none in Rome to make a stale
But Saturnine? Full well, Andronicus,
Agree these deeds with that proud brag of thine,
That saidst I begged the empire at thy hands.

TITUS O monstrous! What reproachful words are these?

SATURNINUS But go thy ways, go, give that changing piece
To him that flourished for her with his sword:
A valiant son-in-law thou shalt enjoy,
One fit to bandy with thy lawless sons,
To ruffle in the commonwealth of Rome.

TITUS These words are razors to my wounded heart.

SATURNINUS And therefore, lovely Tamora, Queen of Goths,
That like the stately Phoebe 'mongst her nymphs
Dost overshine the gallant'st dames of Rome,
If thou be pleased with this my sudden choice,
Behold, I choose thee, Tamora, for my bride,

302 **by leisure** slowly 305 **stale** laughingstock 310 **changing piece** fickle wench 313 **bandy** contend, bicker 314 **ruffle** brawl 317 **Phoebe** Diana, goddess of the moon

And will create thee Empress of Rome.
Speak, Queen of Goths, dost thou applaud my choice?
And here I swear by all the Roman gods,
Sith priest and holy water are so near,
And tapers burn so bright, and everything
In readiness for Hymenaeus stand,
I will not re-salute the streets of Rome,
Or climb my palace, till from forth this place
I lead espoused my bride along with me.

TAMORA And here in sight of heaven to Rome I swear,
If Saturnine advance the Queen of Goths,
She will a handmaid be to his desires,
A loving nurse, a mother to his youth.

SATURNINUS Ascend, fair Queen, Pantheon. Lords, accompany
Your noble emperor and his lovely bride,
Sent by the heavens for Prince Saturnine,
Whose wisdom hath her fortune conquerèd.
There shall we consummate our spousal rites.
Exeunt omnes [except Titus].

TITUS I am not bid to wait upon this bride.
Titus, when wert thou wont to walk alone,
Dishonored thus and challengèd of wrongs?

Enter Marcus and Titus' sons [Lucius, Quintus, and Martius].

MARCUS O Titus, see, O, see, what thou hast done!
In a bad quarrel slain a virtuous son.

TITUS No, foolish tribune, no; no son of mine,
Nor thou, not these, confederates in the deed
That hath dishonored all our family,
Unworthy brother, and unworthy sons!

326 **Hymenaeus** god of marriage 338 s.d. **omnes** all (Latin) 339 **bid** asked 341 **challengèd** accused

LUCIUS But let us give him burial as becomes;
Give Mutius burial with our brethren.

TITUS Traitors, away! He rests not in this tomb:
This monument five hundred years hath stood,
Which I have sumptuously re-edified:
Here none but soldiers and Rome's servitors
Repose in fame; none basely slain in brawls.
Bury him where you can, he comes not here.

MARCUS My lord, this is impiety in you.
My nephew Mutius' deeds do plead for him;
He must be buried with his brethren.

Titus' two sons speak:

[QUINTUS, MARTIUS] And shall, or him we will accompany.

TITUS And shall? What villain was it spake that word?

Titus' son speaks.

[QUINTUS.] He that would vouch it in any place but here.

TITUS What, would you bury him in my despite?

MARCUS No, noble Titus, but entreat of thee
To pardon Mutius and to bury him.

TITUS Marcus, even thou hast stroke upon my crest,
And with these boys mine honor thou hast wounded.
My foes I do repute you every one,
So trouble me no more, but get you gone.

MARTIUS He is not with himself; let us withdraw.

QUINTUS Not I, till Mutius' bones be buried.
The brother and the sons kneel.

MARCUS Brother, for in that name doth nature plead—

QUINTUS Father, and in that name doth nature speak—

348 becomes is fitting **352 re-edified** rebuilt **362 in my despite** in spite of me **367 repute** consider

TITUS Speak thou no more, if all the rest will speed.

MARCUS Renownèd Titus, more than half my soul——

LUCIUS Dear father, soul and substance of us all——

MARCUS Suffer thy brother Marcus to inter
His noble nephew here in virtue's nest,
That died in honor and Lavinia's cause.
Thou art a Roman, be not barbarous:
The Greeks upon advice did bury Ajax
That slew himself; and wise Laertes' son
Did graciously plead for his funerals:
Let not young Mutius then, that was thy joy,
Be barred his entrance here.

TITUS Rise, Marcus, rise.
The dismal'st day is this that e'er I saw,
To be dishonored by my sons in Rome!
Well, bury him, and bury me the next.
They put him in the tomb.

LUCIUS There lie thy bones, sweet Mutius, with thy friends,
Till we with trophies do adorn thy tomb.
They all kneel and say:

[ALL] No man shed tears for noble Mutius,
He lives in fame that died in virtue's cause.

MARCUS My lord, to step out of these dreary dumps,
How comes it that the subtle Queen of Goths
Is of a sudden thus advanced in Rome?

TITUS I know not, Marcus, but I know it is;
(Whether by device or no, the heavens can tell.)
Is she not then beholding to the man
That brought her for this high good turn so far?
Yes, and will nobly him remunerate.

373 **if all the rest will speed** if the rest is to go well (?) if the rest of you wish to live (?) 376 **Suffer** allow 380 **advice** deliberation 380 **Ajax** (when Achilles' arms were given to Odysseus, Ajax in a fury stabbed himself) 381 **Laertes' son** Odysseus 392 **dumps** blues, melancholy state 396 **Whether** (probably pronounced "where") 396 **device** plot 397 **beholding** beholden, indebted

Enter the Emperor, Tamora and her two sons, with the Moor at one door. Enter at the other door Bassianus and Lavinia, with others.

SATURNINUS So Bassianus, you have played your
prize: God give you joy, sir, of your gallant bride!

BASSIANUS And you of yours, my lord! I say no more,
Nor wish no less, and so I take my leave.

SATURNINUS Traitor, if Rome have law, or we have
power,
Thou and thy faction shall repent this rape.

BASSIANUS Rape, call you it, my lord, to seize my own,
My true-betrothèd love, and now my wife?
But let the laws of Rome determine all;
Meanwhile am I possessed of that is mine.

SATURNINUS 'Tis good, sir; you are very short with us,
But if we live we'll be as sharp with you.

BASSIANUS My lord, what I have done, as best I may
Answer I must, and shall do with my life.
Only thus much I give your grace to know—
By all the duties that I owe to Rome,
This noble gentleman, Lord Titus here,
Is in opinion and in honor wronged,
That, in the rescue of Lavinia,
With his own hand did slay his youngest son,
In zeal to you, and highly moved to wrath
To be controlled in that he frankly gave.
Receive him then to favor, Saturnine,
That hath expressed himself in all his deeds
A father and a friend to thee and Rome.

TITUS Prince Bassianus, leave to plead my deeds;
'Tis thou and those that have dishonored me.
Rome and the righteous heavens be my judge,
How I have loved and honored Saturnine!

400 **played your prize** won your contest 417 **opinion** reputation 421 **controlled** opposed 421 **frankly** generously 425 **leave to plead** cease pleading

TAMORA My worthy lord, if ever Tamora
Were gracious in those princely eyes of thine,
Then hear me speak indifferently for all;
And at my suit, sweet, pardon what is past.

SATURNINUS What, madam! Be dishonored openly,
And basely put it up without revenge?

TAMORA Not so, my lord, the gods of Rome forfend
I should be author to dishonor you!
But on mine honor dare I undertake
For good Lord Titus' innocence in all,
Whose fury not dissembled speaks his griefs:
Then at my suit look graciously on him;
Lose not so noble a friend on vain suppose,
Nor with sour looks afflict his gentle heart.
[*Aside*] My lord, be ruled by me, be won at last,
Dissemble all your griefs and discontents—
You are but newly planted in your throne—
Lest then the people, and patricians too,
Upon a just survey, take Titus' part,
And so supplant you for ingratitude,
Which Rome reputes to be a heinous sin.
Yield at entreats: and then let me alone.
I'll find a day to massacre them all,
And race their faction and their family,
The cruel father and his traitorous sons,
To whom I suèd for my dear son's life;
And make them know what 'tis to let a queen
Kneel in the streets and beg for grace in vain.
[*Aloud*] Come, come, sweet Emperor—come, Andronicus—
Take up this good old man, and cheer the heart
That dies in tempest of thy angry frown.

SATURNINUS Rise, Titus, rise, my empress hath prevailed.

431 **indifferently** impartially 434 **put it up** (the figure is of putting up, or sheathing, a sword) 435 **forfend** forbid 436 **author** agent 437 **undertake** assert 441 **vain suppose** empty supposition 450 **at entreats** to entreaties 450 **let me alone** i.e., leave it to me 452 **race** root out

TITUS I thank your Majesty, and her, my lord.
These words, these looks, infuse new life in me.

TAMORA Titus, I am incorporate in Rome,
A Roman now adopted happily,
And must advise the Emperor for his good.
This day all quarrels die, Andronicus.
And let it be mine honor, good my lord,
That I have reconciled your friends and you.
For you, Prince Bassianus, I have passed
My word and promise to the Emperor
That you will be more mild and tractable.
And fear not, lords, and you, Lavinia;
By my advice, all humbled on your knees,
You shall ask pardon of his Majesty.

[LUCIUS.] We do, and vow to heaven, and to his highness,
That what we did was mildly as we might,
Tend'ring our sister's honor and our own.

MARCUS That on mine honor here do I protest.

SATURNINUS Away, and talk not, trouble us no more.

TAMORA Nay, nay, sweet Emperor, we must all be friends.
The tribune and his nephews kneel for grace.
I will not be denied. Sweet heart, look back.

SATURNINUS Marcus, for thy sake, and thy brother's here,
And at my lovely Tamora's entreats,
I do remit these young men's heinous faults.
Stand up.
Lavinia, though you left me like a churl,
I found a friend, and sure as death I swore
I would not part a bachelor from the priest.
Come, if the Emperor's court can feast two brides,
You are my guest, Lavinia, and your friends.

476 **mildly as we might** as mild as we might do 477 **Tend'ring** having regard for 489 **part** depart

This day shall be a love-day, Tamora.

TITUS Tomorrow, and it please your Majesty
To hunt the panther and the hart with me,
With horn and hound we'll give your Grace bonjour.

SATURNINUS Be it so, Titus, and gramercy too.
Exeunt.

Sound trumpets. Manet [*Aaron the*] *Moor.*

492 **love-day** day appointed to settle disputes (with a pun on day for love) 493 **and if** 495 **bonjour** good morning (French) 496 **gramercy** thanks 496 s.d. **Manet** remains (Latin. Clearly this and the next scene are continuous; the Folio's incorrect division into acts is retained merely to facilitate reference)

[ACT II

Scene I. *Rome. Before the palace. Aaron alone.*]

AARON Now climbeth Tamora Olympus' top,
Safe out of fortune's shot, and sits aloft,
Secure of thunder's crack or lightning flash,
Advanced above pale envy's threat'ning reach.
As when the golden sun salutes the morn,
And having gilt the ocean with his beams,
Gallops the zodiac in his glistering coach,
And overlooks the highest-peering hills;
So Tamora:
Upon her wit doth earthly honor wait,
And virtue stoops and trembles at her frown.
Then, Aaron, arm thy heart, and fit thy thoughts
To mount aloft with thy imperial mistress,
And mount her pitch, whom thou in triumph long
Hast prisoner held, fettered in amorous chains,
And faster bound to Aaron's charming eyes
Than is Prometheus tied to Caucasus.
Away with slavish weeds and servile thoughts!
I will be bright and shine in pearl and gold
To wait upon this new-made empress.
To wait, said I? To wanton with this queen,

II.i.1 **Olympus** Mount Olympus (reputed home of the gods) 3 **of** from 4 **envy's** hate's 7 **Gallops** gallops through 8 **overlooks** looks down upon 14 **mount her pitch** rise to the highest point of her flight (a term from falconry) 16 **charming** spellbinding 17 **Prometheus** a Titan fettered to a rock in the Caucasus because he stole fire from heaven 18 **weeds** apparel

This goddess, this Semiramis, this nymph,
This siren, that will charm Rome's Saturnine
And see his shipwrack and his commonweal's.
Hollo! What storm is this?

Enter Chiron and Demetrius, braving.

DEMETRIUS Chiron, thy years wants wit, thy wits wants edge,
And manners, to intrude where I am graced,
And may for aught thou knowest affected be.

CHIRON Demetrius, thou dost overween in all,
And so in this, to bear me down with braves.
'Tis not the difference of a year or two
Makes me less gracious, or thee more fortunate;
I am as able and as fit as thou
To serve, and to deserve my mistress' grace;
And that my sword upon thee shall approve,
And plead my passions for Lavinia's love.

AARON Clubs, clubs! These lovers will not keep the peace.

DEMETRIUS Why, boy, although our mother, unadvised,
Gave you a dancing-rapier by your side,
Are you so desperate grown, to threat your friends?
Go to; have your lath glued within your sheath,
Till you know better how to handle it.

CHIRON Meanwhile, sir, with the little skill I have,
Full well shalt thou perceive how much I dare.
They draw.

DEMETRIUS Ay, boy, grow ye so brave?

AARON Why, how now, lords!

22 **Semiramis** legendary Assyrian queen, noted for her lust and beauty 25 s.d. **braving** challenging 26 **wants** (the ending -s is frequently found with a plural subject) 27 **graced** favored 28 **affected** loved 29 **overween** arrogantly presume 30 **braves** threats 32 **gracious** acceptable 35 **approve** prove 37 **Clubs, clubs** (the cry raised to call the watch to separate brawlers in London) 38 **unadvised** unwisely 39 **dancing-rapier** ornamental light sword 41 **lath** wooden (stage) sword

So near the Emperor's palace dare ye draw,
And maintain such a quarrel openly?
Full well I wot the ground of all this grudge.
I would not for a million of gold
The cause were known to them it most concerns,
Nor would your noble mother for much more
Be so dishonored in the court of Rome.
For shame, put up.

DEMETRIUS Not I, till I have sheathed
My rapier in his bosom, and withal
Thrust those reproachful speeches down his throat,
That he hath breathed in my dishonor here.

CHIRON For that I am prepared and full resolved,
Foul-spoken coward, that thund'rest with thy tongue
And with thy weapon nothing dar'st perform.

AARON Away, I say!
Now, by the gods that warlike Goths adore,
This petty brabble will undo us all.
Why, lords, and think you not how dangerous
It is to jet upon a prince's right?
What, is Lavinia then become so loose,
Or Bassianus so degenerate,
That for her love such quarrels may be broached
Without controlment, justice, or revenge?
Young lords, beware! And should the Empress know
This discord's ground, the music would not please.

CHIRON I care not, I, knew she and all the world:
I love Lavinia more than all the world.

DEMETRIUS Youngling, learn thou to make some meaner choice.
Lavinia is thine elder brother's hope.

AARON Why, are ye mad? Or know ye not, in Rome
How furious and impatient they be,

48 **wot** know 53 **put up** sheathe your weapons 62 **brabble** brawl 64 **jet** encroach 70 **ground** reason (with a pun on the musical meaning: bass to a descant) 73 **meaner** lower

And cannot brook competitors in love?
I tell you, lords, you do but plot your deaths
By this device.

CHIRON Aaron, a thousand deaths
Would I propose to achieve her whom I love.

AARON To achieve her how?

DEMETRIUS Why makes thou it so strange?
She is a woman, therefore may be wooed;
She is a woman, therefore may be won;
She is Lavinia, therefore must be loved.
What, man! More water glideth by the mill
Than wots the miller of, and easy it is
Of a cut loaf to steal a shive, we know:
Though Bassianus be the Emperor's brother,
Better than he have worn Vulcan's badge.

AARON [*Aside*] Ay, and as good as Saturninus may.

DEMETRIUS Then why should he despair that knows to court it
With words, fair looks, and liberality?
What, hast not thou full often stroke a doe,
And borne her cleanly by the keeper's nose?

AARON Why then, it seems, some certain snatch or so
Would serve your turns.

CHIRON Ay, so the turn were served.

DEMETRIUS Aaron, thou hast hit it.

AARON Would you had hit it too,
Then should not we be tired with this ado.
Why, hark ye, hark ye! And are you such fools
To square for this? Would it offend you then
That both should speed?

80 **propose** be willing to meet 81 **Why makes thou it so strange** why do you seem surprised 87 **shive** slice 89 **Vulcan's badge** i.e., the horns of cuckoldry (Vulcan's wife, Venus, deceived him with Mars) 95 **snatch** catch (the likelihood that there is also a sexual meaning here is increased by **turns** in the next line, a word often denoting sexual acts) 100 **square** quarrel 101 **speed** prosper

CHIRON Faith, not me.

DEMETRIUS Nor me, so I were one.

AARON For shame, be friends, and join for that you jar.
'Tis policy and stratagem must do
That you affect, and so must you resolve,
That what you cannot as you would achieve,
You must perforce accomplish as you may.
Take this of me, Lucrece was not more chaste
Than this Lavinia, Bassianus' love.
A speedier course than ling'ring languishment
Must we pursue, and I have found the path.
My lords, a solemn hunting is in hand.
There will the lovely Roman ladies troop:
The forest walks are wide and spacious,
And many unfrequented plots there are
Fitted by kind for rape and villainy.
Single you thither then this dainty doe,
And strike her home by force, if not by words:
This way, or not at all, stand you in hope.
Come, come, our empress, with her sacred wit
To villainy and vengeance consecrate,
Will we acquaint withal what we intend,
And she shall file our engines with advice,
That will not suffer you to square yourselves,
But to your wishes' height advance you both.
The Emperor's court is like the House of Fame,
The palace full of tongues, of eyes, and ears:
The woods are ruthless, dreadful, deaf, and dull;
There speak, and strike, brave boys, and take your turns,
There serve your lust shadowed from heaven's eye,
And revel in Lavinia's treasury.

103 **for that you jar** to get what you quarrel over 104 **policy** cunning 105 **affect** desire 107 **perforce** necessarily 108 **Lucrece** Roman lady noted for her chastity; she killed herself when Sextus Tarquinius raped her 112 **solemn** ceremonious 115 **unfrequented plots** unvisited areas 116 **kind** nature 117 **Single** single out (a hunting term) 123 **file our engines** sharpen our minds 126 **House of Fame** (Ovid and Chaucer have notable poems on it; Fame = Rumor, and the House of Fame is full of gossip) 128 **ruthless** pitiless

CHIRON Thy counsel, lad, smells of no cowardice.

DEMETRIUS *Sit fas aut nefas*, till I find the stream
To cool this heat, a charm to calm these fits,
Per Stygia, per manes vehor. *Exeunt.*

[Scene II. *A forest near Rome.*]

Enter Titus Andronicus and his three sons [*and Marcus*], *making a noise with hounds and horns.*

TITUS The hunt is up, the morn is bright and gray,
The fields are fragrant, and the woods are green:
Uncouple here, and let us make a bay,
And wake the Emperor and his lovely bride,
And rouse the Prince, and ring a hunter's peal,
That all the court may echo with the noise.
Sons, let it be your charge, as it is ours,
To atttend the Emperor's person carefully:
I have been troubled in my sleep this night,
But dawning day new comfort hath inspired.

Here a cry of hounds, and wind horns in a peal: then enter Saturninus, Tamora, Bassianus, Lavinia, Chiron, Demetrius, and their attendants.

Many good morrows to your Majesty!
Madam, to you as many and as good!
I promisèd your Grace a hunter's peal.

SATURNINUS And you have rung it lustily, my lords,
Somewhat too early for new-married ladies.

BASSIANUS Lavinia, how say you?

133 **Sit fas aut nefas** be it right or wrong (Latin) 135 **Per Stygia, per manes vehor** I am carried through Stygian (infernal) regions, through ghosts (Latin, derived from Seneca's *Hippolytus*, line 1177) II.ii.1 **gray** sky blue (?) 3 **Uncouple** unleash the hounds 3 **make a bay** keep up the cry of the hounds 10 s.d. **cry** deep barking

LAVINIA I say, no;
I have been broad awake two hours and more.

SATURNINUS Come on then, horse and chariots let us have,
And to our sport. [*To Tamora*] Madam, now shall ye see
Our Roman hunting.

MARCUS I have dogs, my lord,
Will rouse the proudest panther in the chase,
And climb the highest promontory top.

TITUS And I have horse will follow where the game
Makes way and runs like swallows o'er the plain.

DEMETRIUS Chiron, we hunt not, we, with horse nor hound,
But hope to pluck a dainty doe to ground. *Exeunt.*

[Scene III. *The forest.*]

Enter Aaron alone, [*with a bag of gold*].

AARON He that had wit would think that I had none,
To bury so much gold under a tree
And never after to inherit it.
Let him that thinks of me so abjectly
Know that this gold must coin a stratagem,
Which, cunningly effected, will beget
A very excellent piece of villainy.
And so repose, sweet gold, for their unrest,
That have their alms out of the Empress' chest.
[*Hides the gold.*]

Enter Tamora alone to the Moor.

TAMORA My lovely Aaron, wherefore look'st thou sad

II.iii.3 inherit possess 4 abjectly contemptuously

When every thing doth make a gleeful boast?
The birds chaunt melody on every bush,
The snakes lies rollèd in the cheerful sun,
The green leaves quiver with the cooling wind,
And make a checkered shadow on the ground:
Under their sweet shade, Aaron, let us sit,
And whilst the babbling echo mocks the hounds,
Replying shrilly to the well-tuned horns
As if a double hunt were heard at once,
Let us sit down and mark their yellowing noise:
And after conflict such as was supposed
The wandering prince and Dido once enjoyed,
When with a happy storm they were surprised
And curtained with a counsel-keeping cave,
We may, each wreathèd in the other's arms,
(Our pastimes done) possess a golden slumber,
Whiles hounds and horns and sweet melodious birds
Be unto us as is a nurse's song
Of lullaby to bring her babe asleep.

AARON Madam, though Venus govern your desires,
Saturn is dominator over mine:
What signifies my deadly-standing eye,
My silence and my cloudy melancholy,
My fleece of woolly hair that now uncurls
Even as an adder when she doth unroll
To do some fatal execution?
No, madam, these are no venereal signs:
Vengeance is in my heart, death in my hand,
Blood and revenge are hammering in my head.
Hark, Tamora, the empress of my soul,
Which never hopes more heaven than rests in thee,
This is the day of doom for Bassianus:
His Philomel must lose her tongue today,

11 **boast** display 20 **yellowing** loudly calling 22 **The wandering prince and Dido** Aeneas and the Queen of Carthage (see Virgil's *Aeneid* IV) 31 **Saturn is dominator** the planet Saturn (whose influence allegedly caused sluggishness) dominates 32 **deadly-standing** fixed in a deathlike stare (?) 37 **venereal** erotic 43 **Philomel** (Philomela was ravished by Tereus, who then cut out her tongue; later she communicated her plight by weaving the story into a tapestry. See II.iv.26–27, 38–39; IV.i.47–48; V.ii.195–6)

Thy sons make pillage of her chastity,
And wash their hands in Bassianus' blood.
Seest thou this letter? Take it up, I pray thee,
And give the King this fatal-plotted scroll.
Now question me no more; we are espied.
Here comes a parcel of our hopeful booty,
Which dreads not yet their lives' destruction.

Enter Bassianus and Lavinia.

TAMORA Ah, my sweet Moor, sweeter to me than life!

AARON No more, great Empress, Bassianus comes.
Be cross with him, and I'll go fetch thy sons
To back thy quarrels whatso'er they be. [*Exit.*]

BASSIANUS Who have we here? Rome's royal Empress,
Unfurnished of her well-beseeming troop?
Or is it Dian, habited like her,
Who hath abandonèd her holy groves
To see the general hunting in this forest?

TAMORA Saucy controller of my private steps!
Had I the power that some say Dian had,
Thy temples should be planted presently
With horns, as was Actaeon's, and the hounds
Should drive upon thy new-transformèd limbs,
Unmannerly intruder as thou art!

LAVINIA Under your patience, gentle Empress,
'Tis thought you have a goodly gift in horning,
And to be doubted that your Moor and you
Are singled forth to try experiments:
Jove shield your husband from his hounds today!
'Tis pity they should take him for a stag.

BASSIANUS Believe me, Queen, your swart Cimmerian

49 **parcel of our hopeful booty** part of the victims we hope for 56 **Unfurnished of** unaccompanied by 57 **habited** dressed 60 **controller** critic 62 **presently** immediately 63 **Actaeon** legendary hunter who spied on Diana bathing; she transformed him into a stag and his own hounds killed him 67 **horning** (an unfaithful wife was said to give her husband horns) 68 **doubted** suspected 72 **Cimmerian** dweller in darkness

Doth make your honor of his body's hue,
Spotted, detested, and abominable.
Why are you sequest'rèd from all your train,
Dismounted from your snow-white goodly steed,
And wand'red hither to an obscure plot,
Accompanied but with a barbarous Moor,
If foul desire had not conducted you?

LAVINIA And, being intercepted in your sport,
Great reason that my noble lord be rated
For sauciness. I pray you, let us hence,
And let her joy her raven-colored love;
This valley fits the purpose passing well.

BASSIANUS The King my brother shall have notice of
this.

LAVINIA Ay, for these slips have made him noted long.
Good king, to be so mightily abused!

TAMORA Why, I have patience to endure all this.

Enter Chiron and Demetrius.

DEMETRIUS How now, dear sovereign, and our
gracious mother,
Why doth your Highness look so pale and wan?

TAMORA Have I not reason, think you, to look pale?
These two have ticed me hither to this place,
A barren detested vale, you see it is;
The trees, though summer, yet forlorn and lean,
Overcome with moss and baleful mistletoe:
Here never shines the sun; here nothing breeds,
Unless the nightly owl or fatal raven:
And when they showed me this abhorrèd pit,
They told me, here, at dead time of the night
A thousand fiends, a thousand hissing snakes,
Ten thousand swelling toads, as many urchins,
Would make such fearful and confusèd cries,

74 **Spotted** infected 81 **rated** berated, rebuked 83 **joy** enjoy 85 **notice** (monosyllabic, pronounced "notes") 86 **noted** notorious 92 **ticed** enticed 101 **urchins** hedgehogs

As any mortal body hearing it
Should straight fall mad, or else die suddenly.
No sooner had they told this hellish tale,
But straight they told me they would bind me here
Unto the body of a dismal yew,
And leave me to this miserable death.
And then they called me foul adulteress,
Lascivious Goth, and all the bitterest terms
That ever ear did hear to such effect.
And, had you not by wondrous fortune come,
This vengeance on me had they executed:
Revenge it, as you love your mother's life,
Or be ye not henceforth called my children.

DEMETRIUS This is a witness that I am thy son.
Stab[s] him.

CHIRON And this for me, struck home to show my strength. [*Stabs Bassianus.*]

LAVINIA Ay come, Semiramis, nay, barbarous Tamora!
For no name fits thy nature but thy own!

TAMORA Give me the poniard! You shall know, my boys,
Your mother's hand shall right your mother's wrong.

DEMETRIUS Stay, madam; here is more belongs to her.
First thrash the corn, then after burn the straw.
This minion stood upon her chastity,
Upon her nuptial vow, her loyalty,
And with that painted hope she braves your mightiness:
And shall she carry this unto her grave?

CHIRON And if she do, I would I were an eunuch.
Drag hence her husband to some secret hole,
And make his dead trunk pillow to our lust.

110 **Goth** (possibly a pun on "goat," an animal believed to be lascivious)
124 **minion stood upon** hussy made a fuss about 126 **painted** specious, unreal

TAMORA But when ye have the honey we desire,
Let not this wasp outlive us both to sting.

CHIRON I warrant you, madam, we will make that sure.
Come, mistress, now perforce we will enjoy
That nice-preservèd honesty of yours.

LAVINIA O Tamora! Thou bearest a woman's face——

TAMORA I will not hear her speak; away with her.

LAVINIA Sweet lords, entreat her hear me but a word.

DEMETRIUS Listen, fair madam, let it be your glory
To see her tears, but be your heart to them
As unrelenting flint to drops of rain.

LAVINIA When did the tiger's young ones teach the dam?
O, do not learn her wrath; she taught it thee.
The milk thou suck'st from her did turn to marble;
Even at thy teat thou hadst thy tyranny.
Yet every mother breeds not sons alike,
[*To Chiron*] Do thou entreat her show a woman's pity.

CHIRON What! Wouldst thou have me prove myself a bastard?

LAVINIA 'Tis true; the raven doth not hatch a lark:
Yet have I heard—O could I find it now!—
The lion, moved with pity, did endure
To have his princely paws pared all away.
Some say that ravens foster forlorn children,
The whilst their own birds famish in their nests:
O, be to me, though thy hard heart say no,
Nothing so kind but something pitiful!

TAMORA I know not what it means; away with her!

135 **nice-preservèd honesty** fastidiously guarded chastity 142 **dam** mother 143 **learn** teach 156 **Nothing so kind but something pitiful** i.e., not so kind as the raven, but somewhat pitying

LAVINIA O, let me teach thee for my father's sake,
That gave thee life when well he might have slain thee.
Be not obdurate, open thy deaf ears.

TAMORA Hadst thou in person ne'er offended me,
Even for his sake am I pitiless.
Remember, boys, I poured forth tears in vain
To save your brother from the sacrifice,
But fierce Andronicus would not relent.
Therefore away with her, and use her as you will;
The worse to her, the better loved of me.

LAVINIA O Tamora, be called a gentle queen,
And with thine own hands kill me in this place!
For 'tis not life that I have begged so long;
Poor I was slain when Bassianus died.

TAMORA What begg'st thou then? Fond woman, let me go.

LAVINIA 'Tis present death I beg, and one thing more
That womanhood denies my tongue to tell.
O, keep me from their worse than killing lust,
And tumble me into some loathsome pit,
Where never man's eye may behold my body.
Do this, and be a charitable murderer.

TAMORA So should I rob my sweet sons of their fee.
No, let them satisfy their lust on thee.

DEMETRIUS Away! For thou hast stayed us here too long.

LAVINIA No grace? No womanhood? Ah beastly creature!
The blot and enemy to our general name!
Confusion fall——

CHIRON Nay, then I'll stop your mouth. Bring thou her husband.

172 **Fond** foolish 174 **denies** forbids 183 **our general name** i.e., womankind 184 **Confusion** destruction

This is the hole where Aaron bid us hide him.
[Demetrius throws the corpse into a pit and then covers it with branches. Exeunt Demetrius and Chiron, dragging Lavinia.]

TAMORA Farewell, my sons, see that you make her sure.
Ne'er let my heart know merry cheer indeed
Till all the Andronici be made away.
Now will I hence to seek my lovely Moor,
And let my spleenful sons this trull deflower. [*Exit.*]

Enter Aaron with two of Titus' sons [Quintus and Martius].

[AARON] Come on, my lords, the better foot before!
Straight will I bring you to the loathsome pit
Where I espied the panther fast asleep.

QUINTUS My sight is very dull, whate'er it bodes.

MARTIUS And mine, I promise you. Were it not for shame,
Well could I leave our sport to sleep awhile.
[*He falls into the pit.*]

QUINTUS What, art thou fallen? What subtle hole is this,
Whose mouth is covered with rude-growing briers,
Upon whose leaves are drops of new-shed blood
As fresh as morning dew distilled on flowers?
A very fatal place it seems to me.
Speak, brother, hast thou hurt thee with the fall?

MARTIUS O, brother, with the dismal'st object hurt
That ever eye with sight made heart lament.

AARON [*Aside*] Now will I fetch the King to find them here,
That he thereby may have a likely guess
How these were they that made away his brother.
Exit.

189 **made away** killed 191 **spleenful** lustful 191 **trull** strumpet

MARTIUS Why dost not comfort me and help me out
From this unhallowed and bloodstainèd hole?

QUINTUS I am surprisèd with an uncouth fear,
A chilling sweat o'erruns my trembling joints;
My heart suspects more than mine eye can see.

MARTIUS To prove thou hast a true-divining heart,
Aaron and thou look down into this den
And see a fearful sight of blood and death.

QUINTUS Aaron is gone, and my compassionate heart
Will not permit mine eyes once to behold
The thing whereat it trembles by surmise.
O, tell me who it is, for ne'er till now
Was I a child to fear I know not what.

MARTIUS Lord Bassianus lies berayed in blood,
All on a heap, like to a slaughtered lamb,
In this detested, dark, blood-drinking pit.

QUINTUS If it be dark, how dost thou know 'tis he?

MARTIUS Upon his bloody finger he doth wear
A precious ring that lightens all this hole,
Which, like a taper in some monument,
Doth shine upon the dead man's earthy cheeks,
And shows the ragged entrails of this pit:
So pale did shine the moon on Pyramus,
When he by night lay bathed in maiden blood.
O brother, help me with thy fainting hand—
If fear hath made thee faint, as me it hath—
Out of this fell devouring receptacle,
As hateful as Cocytus' misty mouth.

QUINTUS Reach me thy hand, that I may help thee out;
Or, wanting strength to do thee so much good,
I may be plucked into the swallowing womb
Of this deep pit, poor Bassianus' grave.
I have no strength to pluck thee to the brink.

211 **surprisèd** dumbfounded 211 **uncouth** strange 222 **berayed** defiled 230 **ragged entrails** rugged interior 235 **fell** savage 236 **Cocytus** river in Hades 238 **wanting** lacking

MARTIUS Nor I no strength to climb without thy help.

QUINTUS Thy hand once more; I will not loose again
Till thou art here aloft or I below:
Thou canst not come to me; I come to thee.
[*Falls in.*]

Enter the Emperor and Aaron the Moor.

SATURNINUS Along with me! I'll see what hole is here,
And what he is that now is leaped into it.
Say, who are thou, that lately didst descend
Into this gaping hollow of the earth?

MARTIUS The unhappy sons of old Andronicus,
Brought hither in a most unlucky hour,
To find thy brother Bassianus dead.

SATURNINUS My brother dead! I know thou dost but jest:
He and his lady both are at the lodge,
Upon the north side of this pleasant chase;
'Tis not an hour since I left them there.

MARTIUS We know not where you left them all alive,
But, out alas! Here have we found him dead.

Enter Tamora, Andronicus, and Lucius.

TAMORA Where is my lord the King?

SATURNINUS Here, Tamora, though grieved with killing grief.

TAMORA Where is thy brother, Bassianus?

SATURNINUS Now to the bottom dost thou search my wound;
Poor Bassianus here lies murderèd.

TAMORA Then all too late I bring this fatal writ,
The complot of this timeless tragedy;
And wonder greatly that man's face can fold

262 search probe **265 complot** plot **265 timeless** untimely **266 fold** hide (in the creases of a hypocritical smile)

In pleasing smiles such murderous tyranny.
She giveth Saturnine a letter.

SATURNINUS (*Reads the letter.*) "And if we miss to meet him handsomely—
Sweet huntsman, Bassianus 'tis we mean—
Do thou so much as dig the grave for him.
Thou know'st our meaning. Look for thy reward
Among the nettles at the elder tree
Which overshades the mouth of that same pit
Where we decreed to bury Bassianus.
Do this and purchase us thy lasting friends."
O, Tamora! Was ever heard the like?
This is the pit, and this the elder tree.
Look, sirs, if you can find the huntsman out
That should have murdered Bassianus here.

AARON My gracious lord, here is the bag of gold.

SATURNINUS [*To Titus*] Two of thy whelps, fell curs of bloody kind,
Have here bereft my brother of his life.
Sirs, drag them from the pit unto the prison,
There let them bide until we have devised
Some never-heard-of torturing pain for them.

TAMORA What, are they in this pit? O wondrous thing!
How easily murder is discoverèd!

TITUS High Emperor, upon my feeble knee
I beg this boon, with tears not lightly shed,
That this fell fault of my accursèd sons,
Accursèd, if the faults be proved in them——

SATURNINUS If it be proved! You see, it is apparent.
Who found this letter? Tamora, was it you?

TAMORA Andronicus himself did take it up.

TITUS I did, my lord, yet let me be their bail,
For by my father's reverend tomb I vow
They shall be ready at your Highness' will

268 And if if **268 handsomely** handily **279 should** was to **281 fell** savage **281 kind** nature **292 apparent** obvious

To answer their suspicion with their lives.

SATURNINUS Thou shalt not bail them; see thou follow me.
Some bring the murdered body, some the murderers.
Let them not speak a word; the guilt is plain,
For by my soul were there worse end than death,
That end upon them should be executed.

TAMORA Andronicus, I will entreat the King.
Fear not thy sons; they shall do well enough.

TITUS Come, Lucius, come, stay not to talk with them.
[*Exeunt.*]

[Scene IV. *The forest.*]

Enter the Empress' sons with Lavinia, her hands cut off, and her tongue cut out, and ravished.

DEMETRIUS So, now go tell, and if thy tongue can speak,
Who 'twas that cut thy tongue and ravished thee.

CHIRON Write down thy mind, bewray thy meaning so,
And if thy stumps will let thee play the scribe.

DEMETRIUS See how with signs and tokens she can scrowl.

CHIRON Go home, call for sweet water, wash thy hands.

DEMETRIUS She hath no tongue to call nor hands to wash,
And so let's leave her to her silent walks.

298 **their suspicion** i.e., the suspicion they are under 305 **Fear not** do not fear for II.iv.1 **and if** if (as in line 4) 3 **bewray** reveal 5 **scrowl** scrawl (with a pun on "scroll"?) 6 **sweet** perfumed

CHIRON And 'twere my cause, I should go hang myself.

DEMETRIUS If thou hadst hands to help thee knit the cord. *Exeunt* [*Chiron and Demetrius*].

Enter Marcus from hunting.

MARCUS Who is this? My niece, that flies away so fast!
Cousin, a word, where is your husband?
If I do dream, would all my wealth would wake me!
If I do wake, some planet strike me down,
That I may slumber an eternal sleep!
Speak, gentle niece, what stern ungentle hands
Hath lopped and hewed and made thy body bare
Of her two branches, those sweet ornaments,
Whose circling shadows kings have sought to sleep in,
And might not gain so great a happiness
As half thy love? Why dost not speak to me?
Alas, a crimson river of warm blood,
Like to a bubbling fountain stirred with wind,
Doth rise and fall between thy rosèd lips,
Coming and going with thy honey breath.
But, sure, some Tereus hath deflowered thee,
And, lest thou shouldst detect him, cut thy tongue.
Ah, now thou turn'st away thy face for shame!
And, notwithstanding all this loss of blood,
As from a conduit with three issuing spouts,
Yet do thy cheeks look red as Titan's face
Blushing to be encount'red with a cloud.
Shall I speak for thee? Shall I say 'tis so?
O, that I knew thy heart, and knew the beast,
That I might rail at him to ease my mind!
Sorrow concealèd, like an oven stopped,
Doth burn the heart to cinders where it is.
Fair Philomela, why she but lost her tongue,

9 **cause** case 12 **Cousin** (commonly used of any near relative other than a parent, child, or sibling) 26 **Tereus** ravisher of Philomela (see note to II.iii.43) 27 **detect** expose 31 **Titan's** the sun god's

And in a tedious sampler sewed her mind:
But lovely niece, that mean is cut from thee;
A craftier Tereus, cousin, hast thou met,
And he hath cut those pretty fingers off,
That could have better sewed than Philomel.
O, had the monster seen those lily hands
Tremble like aspen leaves upon a lute,
And make the silken strings delight to kiss them,
He would not then have touched them for his life!
Or, had he heard the heavenly harmony
Which that sweet tongue hath made,
He would have dropped his knife, and fell asleep
As Cerberus at the Thracian poet's feet.
Come, let us go and make thy father blind,
For such a sight will blind a father's eye.
One hour's storm will drown the fragrant meads;
What will whole months of tears thy father's eyes?
Do not draw back, for we will mourn with thee:
O, could our mourning ease thy misery! *Exeunt.*

39 **tedious sampler** laboriously executed tapestry 51 **Cerberus** three-headed dog who guarded the entrance to Hades; he was lulled by Orpheus, **the Thracian poet**

[ACT III

Scene I. *Rome. A street.*]

Enter the Judges and Senators with Titus' two sons bound, passing on the stage to the place of execution, and Titus going before, pleading.

TITUS Hear me, grave fathers! Noble tribunes, stay!
For pity of mine age, whose youth was spent
In dangerous wars, whilst you securely slept;
For all my blood in Rome's great quarrel shed,
For all the frosty nights that I have watched,
And for these bitter tears, which now you see
Filling the agèd wrinkles in my cheeks,
Be pitiful to my condemnèd sons,
Whose souls are not corrupted as 'tis thought.
For two and twenty sons I never wept,
Because they died in honor's lofty bed;

Andronicus lieth down and the Judges pass by him.

For these, tribunes, in the dust I write
My heart's deep languor and my soul's sad tears:
Let my tears staunch the earth's dry appetite;
My sons' sweet blood will make it shame and blush.
O earth, I will befriend thee more with rain,
That shall distill from these two ancient ruins,
Than youthful April shall with all his show'rs:
In summer's drought I'll drop upon thee still,

III.i.11 s.d. **lieth down** i.e., prostrates himself 13 **languor** grief 14 **staunch** satisfy, satiate 19 **still** continuously

In winter with warm tears I'll melt the snow,
And keep eternal springtime on thy face,
So thou refuse to drink my dear sons' blood.

Enter Lucius, with his weapon drawn.

O reverend tribunes! O gentle agèd men!
Unbind my sons, reverse the doom of death,
And let me say, that never wept before,
My tears are now prevailing orators.

LUCIUS O noble father, you lament in vain,
The tribunes hear you not, no man is by,
And you recount your sorrows to a stone.

TITUS Ah, Lucius, for thy brothers let me plead.
Grave tribunes, once more I entreat of you.

LUCIUS My gracious lord, no tribune hears you speak.

TITUS Why, 'tis no matter, man, if they did hear
They would not mark me, if they did mark
They would not pity me, yet plead I must,
And bootless unto them.
Therefore I tell my sorrows to the stones,
Who though they cannot answer my distress,
Yet in some sort they are better than the tribunes,
For that they will not intercept my tale:
When I do weep they humbly at my feet
Receive my tears and seem to weep with me;
And were they but attirèd in grave weeds,
Rome could afford no tribunes like to these.
A stone is soft as wax, tribunes more hard than stones:
A stone is silent and offendeth not,
And tribunes with their tongues doom men to death.
But wherefore stand'st thou with thy weapon drawn?

LUCIUS To rescue my two brothers from their death,
For which attempt the judges have pronounced
My everlasting doom of banishment.

22 **So** provided that 24 **doom** judgment 36 **bootless** in vain 40 **intercept** interrupt 43 **grave weeds** solemn apparel

TITUS O happy man! They have befriended thee.
Why, foolish Lucius, dost thou not perceive
That Rome is but a wilderness of tigers?
Tigers must prey, and Rome affords no prey
But mine and mine. How happy art thou then,
From these devourers to be banishèd!
But who comes with our brother Marcus here?

Enter Marcus with Lavinia.

MARCUS Titus, prepare thy agèd eyes to weep,
Or if not so, thy noble heart to break.
I bring consuming sorrow to thine age.

TITUS Will it consume me? Let me see it then.

MARCUS This was thy daughter.

TITUS Why, Marcus, so she is.

LUCIUS Ay me! This object kills me!

TITUS Faint-hearted boy, arise, and look upon her.
Speak, Lavinia, what accursèd hand
Hath made thee handless in thy father's sight?
What fool hath added water to the sea,
Or brought a faggot to bright-burning Troy?
My grief was at the height before thou cam'st,
And now like Nilus it disdaineth bounds.
Give me a sword, I'll chop off my hands too,
For they have fought for Rome, and all in vain;
And they have nursed this woe, in feeding life;
In bootless prayer have they been held up,
And they have served me to effectless use.
Now all the service I require of them
Is that the one will help to cut the other.
'Tis well, Lavinia, that thou hast no hands,
For hands to do Rome service is but vain.

LUCIUS Speak, gentle sister, who hath mart'red thee?

MARCUS O, that delightful engine of her thoughts,

64 **object** sight 71 **Nilus** the Nile 81 **mart'red** mutilated 82 **engine** instrument

That blabbed them with such pleasing eloquence,
Is torn from forth that pretty hollow cage,
Where like a sweet melodious bird it sung
Sweet varied notes, enchanting every ear!

LUCIUS O, say thou for her, who hath done this deed?

MARCUS O, thus I found her, straying in the park,
Seeking to hide herself, as doth the deer
That hath received some unrecuring wound.

TITUS It was my dear, and he that wounded her
Hath hurt me more than had he killed me dead:
For now I stand as one upon a rock,
Environed with a wilderness of sea,
Who marks the waxing tide grow wave by wave,
Expecting ever when some envious surge
Will in his brinish bowels swallow him.
This way to death my wretched sons are gone,
Here stands my other son, a banished man,
And here my brother weeping at my woes:
But that which gives my soul the greatest spurn
Is dear Lavinia, dearer than my soul.
Had I but seen thy picture in this plight,
It would have madded me: what shall I do
Now I behold thy lively body so?
Thou hast no hands to wipe away thy tears,
Nor tongue to tell me who hath mart'red thee.
Thy husband he is dead, and for his death
Thy brothers are condemned, and dead by this.
Look, Marcus! Ah, son Lucius, look on her!
When I did name her brothers, then fresh tears
Stood on her cheeks, as doth the honey-dew
Upon a gath'red lily almost withered.

MARCUS Perchance she weeps because they killed her husband,
Perchance because she knows them innocent.

83 **blabbed** freely spoke 90 **unrecuring** incurable 96 **envious** malicious 101 **spurn** thrust 105 **lively** living 109 **by this** by this time

TITUS If they did kill thy husband, then be joyful,
Because the law hath ta'en revenge on them.
No, no, they would not do so foul a deed;
Witness the sorrow that their sister makes.
Gentle Lavinia, let me kiss thy lips,
Or make some sign how I may do thee ease.
Shall thy good uncle, and thy brother Lucius,
And thou, and I, sit round about some fountain,
Looking all downwards, to behold our cheeks
How they are stained, like meadows yet not dry
With miry slime left on them by a flood?
And in the fountain shall we gaze so long
Till the fresh taste be taken from that clearness,
And made a brine-pit with our bitter tears?
Or shall we cut away our hands, like thine?
Or shall we bite our tongues, and in dumb shows
Pass the remainder of our hateful days?
What shall we do? Let us, that have our tongues,
Plot some device of further misery,
To make us wondered at in time to come.

LUCIUS Sweet father, cease your tears, for at your grief
See how my wretched sister sobs and weeps.

MARCUS Patience, dear niece. Good Titus, dry thine eyes.

TITUS Ah, Marcus, Marcus! Brother, well I wot
Thy napkin cannot drink a tear of mine,
For thou, poor man, hast drowned it with thine own.

LUCIUS Ah, my Lavinia, I will wipe thy cheeks.

TITUS Mark, Marcus, mark! I understand her signs:
Had she a tongue to speak, now would she say
That to her brother which I said to thee:
His napkin, with his true tears all bewet,
Can do no service on her sorrowful cheeks.
O, what a sympathy of woe is this!

121 do thee ease bring you relief **128 clearness** i.e., clear pool **131 dumb shows** silent signs **140 napkin** handkerchief **148 sympathy** agreement

As far from help as Limbo is from bliss!

Enter Aaron the Moor alone.

AARON Titus Andronicus, my lord the Emperor
Sends thee this word, that, if thou love thy sons,
Let Marcus, Lucius, or thyself, old Titus,
Or any one of you, chop off your hand
And send it to the King: he for the same
Will send thee hither both thy sons alive,
And that shall be the ransom for their fault.

TITUS O, gracious Emperor! O, gentle Aaron!
Did ever raven sing so like a lark,
That gives sweet tidings of the sun's uprise?
With all my heart, I'll send the Emperor my hand.
Good Aaron, wilt thou help to chop it off?

LUCIUS Stay, father! For that noble hand of thine
That hath thrown down so many enemies
Shall not be sent; my hand will serve the turn.
My youth can better spare my blood than you,
And therefore mine shall save my brothers' lives.

MARCUS Which of your hands hath not defended Rome
And reared aloft the bloody battle-ax,
Writing destruction on the enemy's castle?
O, none of both but are of high desert:
My hand hath been but idle; let it serve
To ransom my two nephews from their death,
Then have I kept it to a worthy end.

AARON Nay, come, agree whose hand shall go along,
For fear they die before their pardon come.

MARCUS My hand shall go.

LUCIUS By heaven, it shall not go.

TITUS Sirs, strive no more; such with'red herbs as these
Are meet for plucking up, and therefore mine.

LUCIUS Sweet father, if I shall be thought thy son,
Let me redeem my brothers both from death.

178 meet fit

MARCUS And, for our father's sake and mother's care,
Now let me show a brother's love to thee.

TITUS Agree between you; I will spare my hand.

LUCIUS Then I'll go fetch an ax.

MARCUS But I will use the ax.
Exeunt [Lucius and Marcus].

TITUS Come hither, Aaron. I'll deceive them both;
Lend me thy hand, and I will give thee mine.

AARON [*Aside*] If that be called deceit, I will be honest,
And never whilst I live deceive men so:
But I'll deceive you in another sort,
And that you'll say, ere half an hour pass.
He cuts off Titus' hand.

Enter Lucius and Marcus again.

TITUS Now stay your strife, what shall be is dispatched.
Good Aaron, give his Majesty my hand;
Tell him it was a hand that warded him
From thousand dangers; bid him bury it;
More hath it merited, that let it have.
As for my sons, say I account of them
As jewels purchased at an easy price,
And yet dear too because I bought mine own.

AARON I go, Andronicus, and for thy hand
Look by and by to have thy sons with thee.
[*Aside*] Their heads, I mean. O, how this villainy
Doth fat me with the very thoughts of it!
Let fools do good, and fair men call for grace,
Aaron will have his soul black like his face. *Exit.*

TITUS O, here I lift this one hand up to heaven,
And bow this feeble ruin to the earth.
If any power pities wretched tears,
To that I call! [*To Lavinia*] What, wouldst thou kneel with me?

194 warded guarded **203 fat** delight (literally: "nourish")

Do then, dear heart, for heaven shall hear our
prayers,
Or with our sighs we'll breathe the welkin dim,
And stain the sun with fog, as sometime clouds
When they do hug him in their melting bosoms.

MARCUS O brother, speak with possibility,
And do not break into these deep extremes.

TITUS Is not my sorrow deep, having no bottom?
Then be my passions bottomless with them.

MARCUS But yet let reason govern thy lament.

TITUS If there were reason for these miseries,
Then into limits could I bind my woes:
When heaven doth weep, doth not the earth
o'erflow?
If the winds rage, doth not the sea wax mad,
Threat'ning the welkin with his big-swoll'n face?
And wilt thou have a reason for this coil?
I am the sea; hark, how her sighs doth flow!
She is the weeping welkin, I the earth:
Then must my sea be movèd with her sighs,
Then must my earth with her continual tears
Become a deluge, overflowed and drowned,
For why my bowels cannot hide her woes,
But like a drunkard must I vomit them.
Then give me leave, for losers will have leave
To ease their stomachs with their bitter tongues.

Enter a Messenger, with two heads and a hand.

MESSENGER Worthy Andronicus, ill art thou repaid
For that good hand thou sent'st the Emperor.
Here are the heads of thy two noble sons,
And here's thy hand in scorn to thee sent back;
Thy griefs their sports, thy resolution mocked:

211 **breathe the welkin dim** becloud the heavens with our breath 217 **passions** outbursts 224 **coil** fuss 230 **For why** because 230 **bowels** (thought to be the seat of compassion; akin to the modern use of "heart") 233 **stomachs** feeling

That woe is me to think upon thy woes,
More than remembrance of my father's death.
[*Exit.*]

MARCUS Now let hot Etna cool in Sicily,
And be my heart an ever-burning hell!
These miseries are more than may be borne!
To weep with them that weep doth ease some deal,
But sorrow flouted at is double death.

LUCIUS Ah, that this sight should make so deep a wound,
And yet detested life not shrink thereat!
That ever death should let life bear his name,
Where life hath no more interest but to breathe!
[*Lavinia kisses Titus.*]

MARCUS Alas, poor heart, that kiss is comfortless
As frozen water to a starvèd snake.

TITUS When will this fearful slumber have an end?

MARCUS Now, farewell, flatt'ry, die Andronicus,
Thou dost not slumber: see thy two sons' heads,
Thy warlike hand, thy mangled daughter here,
Thy other banished son with this dear sight
Struck pale and bloodless, and thy brother, I,
Even like a stony image cold and numb.
Ah! Now no more will I control thy griefs:
Rend off thy silver hair, thy other hand
Gnawing with thy teeth, and be this dismal sight
The closing up of our most wretched eyes:
Now is a time to storm; why art thou still?

TITUS Ha, ha, ha!

MARCUS Why dost thou laugh? It fits not with this hour.

TITUS Why, I have not another tear to shed.
Besides, this sorrow is an enemy,

239 **That** so that 244 **some deal** somewhat 247 **shrink** slip away 248 **bear his name** i.e., be called "life" 251 **starvèd** numbed 252 **fearful slumber** i.e., nightmare existence 256 **dear** heartfelt

And would usurp upon my wat'ry eyes
And make them blind with tributary tears;
Then which way shall I find Revenge's Cave?
For these two heads do seem to speak to me,
And threat me I shall never come to bliss
Till all these mischiefs be returned again,
Even in their throats that hath committed them.
Come, let me see what task I have to do.
You heavy people, circle me about,
That I may turn me to each one of you,
And swear unto my soul to right your wrongs.
The vow is made. Come, brother, take a head;
And in this hand the other will I bear.
And Lavinia, thou shalt be employed in these arms,
Bear thou my hand, sweet wench, between thy teeth:
As for thee, boy, go, get thee from my sight.
Thou art an exile, and thou must not stay.
Hie to the Goths, and raise an army there,
And, if ye love me, as I think you do,
Let's kiss and part, for we have much to do.
Exeunt [all but Lucius].

LUCIUS Farewell, Andronicus, my noble father,
The woefull'st man that ever lived in Rome!
Farewell, proud Rome, till Lucius come again;
He loves his pledges dearer than his life.
Farewell, Lavinia, my noble sister;
O, would thou wert as thou tofore hast been!
But now nor Lucius nor Lavinia lives
But in oblivion and hateful griefs.
If Lucius live, he will require your wrongs,
And make proud Saturnine and his empress
Beg at the gates, like Tarquin and his queen.

269 **tributary** paid as tribute 276 **heavy** sad 282 **teeth** (possibly Shakespeare intended to delete "teeth" from the manuscript, and substituted the less grotesque "arms" above it; if so, the compositor mistakenly took "arms" to be part of the previous line, and to make sense of it he perhaps altered something like "employed in this" to "employed in these arms") 293 **tofore** formerly 294 **nor ... nor** neither ... nor 298 **Tarquin** Roman king whose rule was overthrown when his son (of the same name) raped Lucrece

Now will I to the Goths and raise a pow'r,
To be revenged on Rome and Saturnine.
Exit Lucius.

[Scene II. *Rome. Within Titus' house.*]

A banket. Enter Andronicus, Marcus, Lavinia, and the boy [*Lucius*].

TITUS So, so, now sit, and look you eat no more
Than will preserve just so much strength in us
As will revenge these bitter woes of ours.
Marcus, unknit that sorrow-wreathen knot:
Thy niece and I, poor creatures, want our hands,
And cannot passionate our tenfold grief
With folded arms. This poor right hand of mine
Is left to tyrannize upon my breast;
Who, when my heart all mad with misery
Beats in this hollow prison of my flesh,
Then thus I thump it down.
[*To Lavinia*] Thou map of woe, that thus dost talk in signs,
When thy poor heart beats with outrageous beating,
Thou canst not strike it thus to make it still.
Wound it with sighing, girl, kill it with groans;
Or get some little knife between thy teeth,
And just against thy heart make thou a hole,
That all the tears that thy poor eyes let fall
May run into that sink, and soaking in
Drown the lamenting fool in sea-salt tears.

MARCUS Fie, brother, fie! Teach her not thus to lay
Such violent hands upon her tender life.

III.ii.s.d. **banket** light meal 4 **knot** i.e., Marcus' folded arms, a sign of heavy thoughts 6 **passionate** passionately express 12 **map** picture 15 **wound it with sighing** (sighing was believed to shorten life) 19 **sink** sewer 20 **fool** (here, as often, implying affection and pity)

TITUS How now! Has sorrow made thee dote already?
Why, Marcus, no man should be mad but I.
What violent hands can she lay on her life!
Ah, wherefore dost thou urge the name of hands,
To bid Aeneas tell the tale twice o'er,
How Troy was burnt and he made miserable?
O, handle not the theme, to talk of hands,
Lest we remember still that we have none.
Fie, fie, how franticly I square my talk,
As if we should forget we had no hands,
If Marcus did not name the word of hands!
Come, let's fall to; and, gentle girl, eat this.
Here is no drink? Hark, Marcus, what she says—
I can interpret all her martyred signs—
She says she drinks no other drink but tears,
Brewed with her sorrow, meshed upon her cheeks.
Speechless complainer, I will learn thy thought;
In thy dumb action will I be as perfect
As begging hermits in their holy prayers:
Thou shalt not sigh, nor hold thy stumps to heaven,
Nor wink, nor nod, nor kneel, nor make a sign,
But I of these will wrest an alphabet,
And by still practice learn to know thy meaning.

BOY Good grandsire, leave these bitter deep laments.
Make my aunt merry with some pleasing tale.

MARCUS Alas, the tender boy, in passion moved,
Doth weep to see his grandsire's heaviness.

TITUS Peace, tender sapling, thou art made of tears,
And tears will quickly melt thy life away.
Marcus strikes the dish with a knife.
What dost thou strike at, Marcus, with thy knife?

MARCUS At that that I have killed, my lord—a fly.

TITUS Out on thee, murderer! Thou kill'st my heart;
Mine eyes are cloyed with view of tyranny:
A deed of death done on the innocent

27 **Aeneas** (see Virgil's *Aeneid* II.2) 31 **square** shape 38 **meshed** mashed, brewed 40 **perfect** fully knowing 43 **wink** shut the eyes 45 **still** constant

Becomes not Titus' brother. Get thee gone;
I see thou art not for my company.

MARCUS Alas, my lord, I have but killed a fly.

TITUS "But!" How, if that fly had a father and mother?
How would he hang his slender gilded wings,
And buzz lamenting doings in the air!
Poor harmless fly,
That, with his pretty buzzing melody,
Came here to make us merry! And thou has killed
him.

MARCUS Pardon me, sir; it was a black ill-favored fly,
Like to the Empress' Moor. Therefore I killed him.

TITUS O, O, O,
Then pardon me for reprehending thee,
For thou hast done a charitable deed.
Give me thy knife, I will insult on him,
Flattering myself, as if it were the Moor,
Come hither purposely to poison me.
[*He strikes at it.*]
There's for thyself, and that's for Tamora.
Ah, sirrah!
Yet I think we are not brought so low
But that between us we can kill a fly
That comes in likeness of a coal-black Moor.

MARCUS Alas, poor man! Grief has so wrought on him,
He takes false shadows for true substances.

TITUS Come, take away. Lavinia, go with me:
I'll to thy closet, and go read with thee
Sad stories chancèd in the times of old.
Come, boy, and go with me; thy sight is young,
And thou shalt read when mine begin to dazzle.
Exeunt.

66 **ill-favored** ugly 71 **insult on** exult over 75 **sirrah** (common term of address to an inferior) 81 **take away** clear the table 82 **closet** private room 83 **chancèd** that happened

[ACT IV

Scene I. *Rome. Before Titus' house.*]

Enter Lucius' son and Lavinia running after him; and the boy flies from her with his books under his arm. Enter Titus and Marcus.

BOY Help, grandsire, help! My aunt Lavinia
Follows me everywhere, I know not why.
Good uncle Marcus, see how swift she comes.
Alas, sweet aunt, I know not what you mean.

MARCUS Stand by me, Lucius, do not fear thine aunt.

TITUS She loves thee, boy, too well to do thee harm.

BOY Ay, when my father was in Rome she did.

MARCUS What means my niece Lavinia by these signs?

TITUS Fear her not, Lucius. Somewhat doth she mean.
See, Lucius, see, how much she makes of thee:
Somewhither would she have thee go with her.
Ah, boy, Cornelia never with more care
Read to her sons than she hath read to thee
Sweet poetry and Tully's *Orator*.
Canst thou not guess wherefore she plies thee thus?

BOY My lord, I know not, I, nor can I guess,
Unless some fit or frenzy do possess her:
For I have heard my grandsire say full oft,

IV.i.12 **Cornelia** mother of the Gracchi, two famous tribunes 14 **Tully's Orator** Cicero's *De oratore* (or his *Orator ad M. Brutum*)

Extremity of griefs would make men mad;
And I have read that Hecuba of Troy
Ran mad for sorrow. That made me to fear,
Although, my lord, I know my noble aunt
Loves me as dear as e'er my mother did,
And would not, but in fury, fright my youth,
Which made me down to throw my books and fly,
Causeless perhaps. But pardon me, sweet aunt:
And, madam, if my uncle Marcus go,
I will most willingly attend your ladyship.

MARCUS Lucius, I will.

TITUS How now, Lavinia? Marcus, what means this?
Some book there is that she desires to see.
Which is it, girl, of these? Open them, boy.
But thou art deeper read, and better skilled.
Come, and take choice of all my library,
And so beguile thy sorrow, till the heavens
Reveal the damned contriver of this deed.
Why lifts she up her arms in sequence thus?

MARCUS I think she means that there were more than one
Confederate in the fact. Ay, more there was,
Or else to heaven she heaves them for revenge.

TITUS Lucius, what book is that she tosseth so?

BOY Grandsire, 'tis Ovid's *Metamorphosis*;
My mother gave it me.

MARCUS For love of her that's gone,
Perhaps she culled it from among the rest.

TITUS Soft! So busily she turns the leaves!
Help her! What would she find? Lavinia, shall I read?
This is the tragic tale of Philomel,
And treats of Tereus' treason and his rape;

24 **but in fury** except in madness 28 **attend** wait on 39 **fact** crime 41 **tosseth** turns the pages of 42 **Metamorphosis** (so spelled in the title of an Elizabethan translation by Golding, with which Shakespeare was familiar; properly *Metamorphoses*)

And rape, I fear, was root of thy annoy.

MARCUS See, brother, see, note how she quotes the leaves.

TITUS Lavinia, wert thou thus surprised, sweet girl,
Ravished and wronged, as Philomela was,
Forced in the ruthless, vast, and gloomy woods?
See, see!
Ay, such a place there is, where we did hunt—
O, had we never, never hunted there—
Patterned by that the poet here describes,
By nature made for murders and for rapes.

MARCUS O, why should nature build so foul a den,
Unless the gods delight in tragedies?

TITUS Give signs, sweet girl, for here are none but friends,
What Roman lord it was durst do the deed:
Or slunk not Saturnine, as Tarquin erst,
That left the camp to sin in Lucrece' bed?

MARCUS Sit down, sweet niece: brother, sit down by me.
Apollo, Pallas, Jove, or Mercury,
Inspire me, that I may this treason find!
My lord, look here: look here, Lavinia.

He writes his name with his staff, and guides it with feet and mouth.

This sandy plot is plain; guide if thou canst,
This after me. I have writ my name
Without the help of any hand at all.
Cursed be that heart that forced us to this shift!
Write thou, good niece, and here display at last
What God will have discovered for revenge.
Heaven guide thy pen to print thy sorrows plain,
That we may know the traitors and the truth!

She takes the staff in her mouth and guides it with her stumps and writes.

50 quotes examines 53 vast desolate 57 Patterned by after the pattern 63 erst once 69 plain flat 70 after me as I do 72 shift device 74 discovered revealed

O, do ye read, my lord, what she hath writ?

[TITUS] "*Stuprum*. Chiron. Demetrius."

MARCUS What, what! The lustful sons of Tamora
Performers of this heinous, bloody deed?

TITUS *Magni Dominator poli,*
Tam lentus audis scelera? tam lentus vides?

MARCUS O, calm thee, gentle lord! Although I know
There is enough written upon this earth
To stir a mutiny in the mildest thoughts,
And arm the minds of infants to exclaims.
My lord, kneel down with me; Lavinia, kneel;
And kneel, sweet boy, the Roman Hector's hope;
And swear with me, as, with the woeful fere
And father of that chaste dishonored dame,
Lord Junius Brutus sware for Lucrece' rape,
That we will prosecute by good advice
Mortal revenge upon these traitorous Goths,
And see their blood, or die with this reproach.

TITUS 'Tis sure enough, and you knew how,
But if you hunt these bear-whelps, then beware:
The dam will wake; and if she wind ye once,
She's with the lion deeply still in league,
And lulls him whilst she playeth on her back,
And when he sleeps will she do what she list.
You are a young huntsman, Marcus, let alone;
And, come, I will go get a leaf of brass,
And with a gad of steel will write these words,
And lay it by. The angry northern wind
Will blow these sands like Sibyl's leaves abroad,
And where's our lesson then? Boy, what say you?

78 **Stuprum** rape (Latin) 81–82 **Magni Dominator . . . lentus vides?** ruler of the great heavens, are you so slow to hear and to see crimes? (Latin; derived from Seneca's *Hippolytus*, lines 668–69) 86 **exclaims** exclamations 88 **the Roman Hector's** i.e., Andronicus (Titus is compared to Hector, Troy's champion) 89 **fere** spouse 91 **Junius Brutus** chief of those who drove the Tarquins from Rome 92 **by good advice** after careful deliberation 97 **and if she wind ye** if she get wind of (smell) you 100 **list** please 103 **gad** spike, stylus 105 **Sibyl's leaves** leaves on which the Sibyl wrote prophecies

BOY I say, my lord, that if I were a man,
Their mother's bedchamber should not be safe
For these base bondmen to the yoke of Rome.

MARCUS Ay, that's my boy! Thy father hath full oft
For his ungrateful country done the like.

BOY And, uncle, so will I, and if I live.

TITUS Come, go with me into mine armory:
Lucius, I'll fit thee, and withal my boy
Shall carry from me to the Empress' sons
Presents that I intend to send them both.
Come, come; thou'lt do my message, wilt thou not?

BOY Ay, with my dagger in their bosoms, grandsire.

TITUS No, boy, not so; I'll teach thee another course.
Lavinia, come. Marcus, look to my house.
Lucius and I'll go brave it at the court;
Ay, marry, will we, sir; and we'll be waited on.
Exeunt.

MARCUS O heavens, can you hear a good man groan,
And not relent, or not compassion him?
Marcus, attend him in his ecstasy,
That hath more scars of sorrow in his heart
Than foemen's marks upon his batt'red shield,
But yet so just that he will not revenge.
Revenge the heavens for old Andronicus! *Exit.*

121 **brave it** behave defiantly 122 **marry** (an interjection, from "By the Virgin Mary") 122 **be waited on** i.e., not be ignored 125 **ecstasy** fit of madness 129 **Revenge the heavens** may the heavens take revenge

[Scene II. *Rome. Within the palace.*]

Enter Aaron, Chiron, and Demetrius, at one door, and at the other door young Lucius and another, with a bundle of weapons and verses writ upon them.

CHIRON Demetrius, here's the son of Lucius,
He hath some message to deliver us.

AARON Ay, some mad message from his mad grandfather.

BOY My lords, with all the humbleness I may,
I greet your honors from Andronicus.
[*Aside*] And pray the Roman gods confound you both.

DEMETRIUS Gramercy, lovely Lucius, what's the news?

BOY [*Aside*] That you are both deciphered, that's the news,
For villains marked with rape. [*Aloud*] May it please you,
My grandsire, well-advised, hath sent by me
The goodliest weapons of his armory
To gratify your honorable youth,
The hope of Rome; for so he bid me say;
And so I do, and with his gifts present
Your lordships; whenever you have need,
You may be armèd and appointed well.
And so I leave you both, [*aside*] like bloody villains.
Exit.

DEMETRIUS What's here? A scroll, and written round about?

IV.ii.6 **confound** destroy 7 **Gramercy** thanks 10 **well-advised** in sound mind 16 **appointed** equipped

Let's see:
Integer vitae, scelerisque purus,
Non eget Mauri jaculis, nec arcu.

CHIRON O, 'tis a verse in Horace; I know it well:
I read it in the grammar long ago.

AARON Ay, just; a verse in Horace; right, you have it.
[*Aside*] Now, what a thing it is to be an ass!
Here's no sound jest! The old man hath found their guilt,
And sends them weapons wrapped about with lines
That wound, beyond their feeling, to the quick.
But were our witty empress well afoot,
She would applaud Andronicus' conceit.
But let her rest in her unrest awhile.
[*Aloud*] And now, young lords, was't not a happy star
Led us to Rome, strangers, and more than so,
Captives, to be advancèd to this height?
It did me good, before the palace gate
To brave the tribune in his brother's hearing.

DEMETRIUS But me more good, to see so great a lord
Basely insinuate and send us gifts.

AARON Had he not reason, Lord Demetrius?
Did you not use his daughter very friendly?

DEMETRIUS I would we had a thousand Roman dames
At such a bay, by turn to serve our lust.

CHIRON A charitable wish and full of love.

AARON Here lacks but your mother for to say amen.

CHIRON And that would she for twenty thousand more.

DEMETRIUS Come, let us go, and pray to all the gods
For our belovèd mother in her pains.

20–21 **Integer vitae . . . nec arcu** the man of upright life and free from crime has no need of a Moor's javelins or bow (Latin; from Horace, *Odes*, I.xxii.1–2) 29 **witty** wise 30 **conceit** idea, design 38 **insinuate** curry favor 42 **At such a bay** thus cornered

AARON [*Aside*] Pray to the devils, the gods have given us over.

Trumpets sound.

DEMETRIUS Why do the Emperor's trumpets flourish thus?

CHIRON Belike, for joy the Emperor hath a son.

DEMETRIUS Soft! Who comes here?

Enter Nurse with a blackamoor child.

NURSE God morrow, lords.
O, tell me, did you see Aaron the Moor?

AARON Well, more or less, or ne'er a whit at all,
Here Aaron is; and what with Aaron now?

NURSE O gentle Aaron, we are all undone!
Now help, or woe betide thee evermore!

AARON Why, what a caterwauling dost thou keep!
What dost thou wrap and fumble in thy arms?

NURSE O, that which I would hide from heaven's eye,
Our empress' shame and stately Rome's disgrace!
She is delivered, lords, she is delivered.

AARON To whom?

NURSE I mean, she is brought abed.

AARON Well, God give her good rest! What hath he sent her?

NURSE A devil.

AARON Why, then she is the devil's dam;
A joyful issue.

NURSE A joyless, dismal, black, and sorrowful issue!
Here is the babe, as loathsome as a toad
Amongst the fair-faced breeders of our clime.
The Empress sends it thee, thy stamp, thy seal,

50 **Belike** probably 58 **fumble** clumsily bundle up 64 **dam** mother

And bids thee christen it with thy dagger's point.

AARON Zounds, ye whore! Is black so base a hue?
Sweet blowse, you are a beauteous blossom, sure.

DEMETRIUS Villain, what hast thou done?

AARON That which thou canst not undo.

CHIRON Thou has undone our mother.

AARON Villain, I have done thy mother.

DEMETRIUS And therein, hellish dog, thou hast undone her.
Woe to her chance, and damned her loathèd choice!
Accursed the offspring of so foul a fiend!

CHIRON It shall not live.

AARON It shall not die.

NURSE Aaron, it must; the mother wills it so.

AARON What, must it, nurse? Then let no man but I
Do execution on my flesh and blood.

DEMETRIUS I'll broach the tadpole on my rapier's point.
Nurse, give it me; my sword shall soon dispatch it.

AARON Sooner this sword shall plow thy bowels up.
Stay, murderous villains! Will you kill your brother?
Now, by the burning tapers of the sky,
That shone so brightly when this boy was got,
He dies upon my scimitar's sharp point
That touches this my first-born son and heir!
I tell you, younglings, not Enceladus,
With all his threat'ning band of Typhon's brood,
Nor great Alcides, nor the god of war,
Shall seize this prey out of his father's hands.

71 **Zounds** (an interjection, from "By God's wounds") 72 **blowse** ruddy wench (here, ironic) 76 **done** had sexual intercourse with 78 **chance** luck 85 **broach** impale 90 **got** begat 93 **Enceladus** one of the Titans (sons of Typhon) who fought the Olympians 95 **Alcides** Hercules

What, what, ye sanguine, shallow-hearted boys!
Ye white-limed walls! Ye alehouse painted signs!
Coal-black is better than another hue,
In that it scorns to bear another hue;
For all the water in the ocean
Can never turn the swan's black legs to white,
Although she lave them hourly in the flood.
Tell the Empress from me, I am of age
To keep mine own, excuse it how she can.

DEMETRIUS Wilt thou betray thy noble mistress thus?

AARON My mistress is my mistress, this my self,
The vigor and the picture of my youth:
This before all the world do I prefer;
This mauger all the world will I keep safe,
Or some of you shall smoke for it in Rome.

DEMETRIUS By this our mother is forever shamed.

CHIRON Rome will despise her for this foul escape.

NURSE The Emperor in his rage will doom her death.

CHIRON I blush to think upon this ignomy.

AARON Why, there's the privilege your beauty bears:
Fie, treacherous hue, that will betray with blushing
The close enacts and counsels of thy heart!
Here's a young lad framed of another leer:
Look, how the black slave smiles upon the father,
As who should say, "Old lad, I am thine own."
He is your brother, lords, sensibly fed
Of that self blood that first gave life to you,
And from your womb where you imprisoned were
He is enfranchisèd and come to light:
Nay, he is your brother by the surer side,
Although my seal be stampèd in his face.

97 **sanguine** pink-cheeked 98 **white-limed walls** (perhaps a reference to the "whited sepulchers" of Matthew 23:27) 103 **lave** wash 110 **mauger** in spite of 111 **smoke** suffer 113 **escape** escapade 115 **ignomy** ignominy 118 **close enacts** secret resolutions 119 **leer** complexion 122–23 **sensibly fed/Of that self blood** i.e., his body draws on the same blood 126 **the surer side** i.e., the mother's side

NURSE Aaron, what shall I say unto the Empress?

DEMETRIUS Advise thee, Aaron, what is to be done,
And we will all subscribe to thy advice:
Save thou the child, so we may all be safe.

AARON Then sit we down and let us all consult.
My son and I will have the wind of you:
Keep there; now talk at pleasure of your safety.

DEMETRIUS How many women saw this child of his?

AARON Why, so, brave lords! When we join in league,
I am a lamb: but if you brave the Moor,
The chafèd boar, the mountain lioness,
The ocean swells not so as Aaron storms.
But say again, how many saw the child?

NURSE Cornelia the midwife, and myself,
And no one else but the delivered Empress.

AARON The Empress, the midwife, and yourself:
Two may keep counsel when the third's away.
Go to the Empress, tell her this I said.
He kills her.
Wheak, wheak!
So cries a pig preparèd to the spit.

DEMETRIUS What mean'st thou, Aaron? Wherefore did'st thou this?

AARON O, lord, sir, 'tis a deed of policy!
Shall she live to betray this guilt of ours?
A long-tongued babbling gossip? No, lords, no.
And now be it known to you my full intent.
Not far one Muliteus my countryman
His wife but yesternight was brought to bed;
His child is like to her, fair as you are.
Go pack with him, and give the mother gold,
And tell them both the circumstance of all,

130 **subscribe** agree 131 so provided that 133 **have the wind of you** i.e., keep you safely in our view (as game is watched, down wind) 138 **chafèd** enraged 149 **policy** cunning 153–54 **countryman/His** countryman's 156 **pack** conspire 157 **circumstance of all** all the details

And how by this their child shall be advancèd,
And be receivèd for the Emperor's heir,
And substituted in the place of mine,
To calm this tempest whirling in the court;
And let the Emperor dandle him for his own.
Hark ye, lords; you see I have given her physic,
And you must needs bestow her funeral;
The fields are near, and you are gallant grooms.
This done, see that you take no longer days,
But send the midwife presently to me.
The midwife and the nurse well made away,
Then let the ladies tattle what they please.

CHIRON Aaron, I see, thou wilt not trust the air
With secrets.

DEMETRIUS For this care of Tamora,
Herself and hers are highly bound to thee. *Exeunt.*

AARON Now to the Goths, as swift as swallow flies,
There to dispose this treasure in mine arms,
And secretly to greet the Empress' friends.
Come on, you thick-lipped slave, I'll bear you hence;
For it is you that puts us to our shifts.
I'll make you feed on berries and on roots,
And feed on curds and whey, and suck the goat,
And cabin in a cave, and bring you up
To be a warrior and command a camp. *Exit.*

163 physic medicine **166 days** time **177 puts us to our shifts** causes us to use stratagems **180 cabin** dwell

[Scene III. *Rome. A street.*]

Enter Titus, old Marcus, [*his son Publius,*] *young Lucius, and other gentlemen, with bows; and Titus bears the arrows with letters on the ends of them.*

TITUS Come, Marcus, come; kinsmen, this is the way.
Sir boy, let me see your archery;
Look ye draw home enough, and 'tis there straight.
Terras Astraea reliquit.
Be you rememb'red, Marcus: she's gone, she's fled.
Sirs, take you to your tools. You, cousins, shall
Go sound the ocean, and cast your nets;
Happily you may catch her in the sea;
Yet there's as little justice as at land:
No, Publius and Sempronius, you must do it;
'Tis you must dig with mattock and with spade,
And pierce the inmost center of the earth:
Then, when you come to Pluto's region,
I pray you deliver him this petition:
Tell him, it is for justice and for aid,
And that it comes from old Andronicus,
Shaken with sorrows in ungrateful Rome.
Ah, Rome! Well, well; I made thee miserable
What time I threw the people's suffrages
On him that thus doth tyrannize o'er me.
Go, get you gone, and pray be careful all,
And leave you not a man of war unsearched:
This wicked emperor may have shipped her hence,
And, kinsmen, then we may go pipe for justice.

MARCUS O, Publius, is not this a heavy case,

IV.iii.3 **home** fully 4 **Terras Astraea reliquit** Astraea (goddess of justice) has left the earth (Latin; from Ovid, *Metamorphoses*, I.150) 5 **Be you remembʼred** remember 8 **Happily** perhaps 13 **Pluto's region** Hades 19 **What time** when 24 **pipe for** i.e., whistle vainly for

To see thy noble uncle thus distract?

PUBLIUS Therefore, my lords, it highly us concerns
By day and night t' attend him carefully,
And feed his humor kindly as we may,
Till time beget some careful remedy.

MARCUS Kinsmen, his sorrows are past remedy.
But . . .
Join with the Goths, and with revengeful war
Take wreak on Rome for this ingratitude,
And vengeance on the traitor Saturnine.

TITUS Publius, how now! How now, my masters!
What, have you met with her?

PUBLIUS No, my good lord, but Pluto sends you word,
If you will have revenge from hell, you shall:
Marry, for Justice, she is so employed,
He thinks, with Jove in heaven, or somewhere else,
So that perforce you must needs stay a time.

TITUS He doth me wrong to feed me with delays.
I'll dive into the burning lake below,
And pull her out of Acheron by the heels.
Marcus, we are but shrubs, no cedars we,
No big-boned men framed of the Cyclops' size;
But metal, Marcus, steel to the very back,
Yet wrung with wrongs more than our backs can
bear:
And sith there's no justice in earth nor hell,
We will solicit heaven, and move the gods
To send down Justice for to wreak our wrongs.
Come, to this gear. You are a good archer, Marcus.
He gives them the arrows.
Ad Jovem, that's for you: here, *Ad Apollinem*:
Ad Martem, that's for myself:

29 **humor** mood, caprice 32 **But** (a catchword indicates that the line begins "But," though the line itself was omitted) 34 **wreak** vengeance 45 **Acheron** river in Hades 47 **Cyclops** giants (in Homer's *Odyssey*) 50 **sith** since 52 **wreak** avenge 53 **gear** affair 54–55 **Ad Jovem . . . Ad Apollinem:/Ad Martem** to Jove . . . to Apollo; to Mars (Latin)

Here, boy, to Pallas: here, to Mercury:
To Saturn, Caius, not to Saturnine;
You were as good to shoot against the wind.
To it, boy! Marcus, loose when I bid.
Of my word, I have written to effect;
There's not a god left unsolicited.

MARCUS Kinsmen, shoot all your shafts into the court:
We will afflict the Emperor in his pride.

TITUS Now, masters, draw. O, well said, Lucius!
Good boy, in Virgo's lap; give it Pallas.

MARCUS My lord, I aim a mile beyond the moon;
Your letter is with Jupiter by this.

TITUS Ha, ha!
Publius, Publius, what hast thou done!
See, see, thou hast shot off one of Taurus' horns.

MARCUS This was the sport, my lord: when Publius shot,
The bull being galled, gave Aries such a knock
That down fell both the Ram's horns in the court,
And who should find them but the Empress' villain?
She laughed, and told the Moor he should not choose
But give them to his master for a present.

TITUS Why, there it goes! God give his lordship joy!

Enter the Clown, with a basket and two pigeons in it.

News, news from heaven! Marcus, the post is come.
Sirrah, what tidings? Have you any letters?
Shall I have justice? What says Jupiter?

CLOWN Ho, the gibbet maker! He says that he hath

58 **You were as good to shoot** you would do as much good by shooting 65 **Virgo's** the Virgin's (sign of the zodiac, as are **Taurus**—the bull—in line 70, and **Aries**—the ram—in line 72) 77 s.d. **Clown** rustic fellow 81 **gibbet maker** (apparently "Jupiter"—which in the original text is spelled "Jubiter"—was pronounced rather like "gibbeter," i.e., gibbet maker)

taken them down again, for the man must not be hanged till the next week.

TITUS But what says Jupiter, I ask thee?

CLOWN Alas, sir, I know not Jupiter; I never drank with him in all my life.

TITUS Why, villain, art not thou the carrier?

CLOWN Ay, of my pigeons, sir, nothing else.

TITUS Why, didst thou not come from heaven?

CLOWN From heaven? Alas, sir, I never came there! God forbid, I should be so bold to press to heaven in my young days. Why, I am going with my pigeons to the tribunal plebs, to take up a matter of brawl betwixt my uncle and one of the Emperal's men.

MARCUS Why, sir, that is as fit as can be to serve for your oration; and let him deliver the pigeons to the Emperor from you.

TITUS Tell me, can you deliver an oration to the Emperor with a grace?

CLOWN Nay, truly, sir, I could never say grace in all my life.

TITUS Sirrah, come hither: make no more ado,
But give your pigeons to the Emperor:
By me thou shalt have justice at his hands.
Hold, hold, meanwhile, here's money for thy
charges.
Give me pen and ink. Sirrah, can you with a grace deliver up a supplication?

CLOWN Ay, sir.

TITUS Then here is a supplication for you. And when you come to him, at the first approach you must

93 **tribunal plebs** (malaprop for *tribunus plebis*, "Tribune of the plebs"; **Emperal**, later in the sentence, is another malaprop) 106 **charges** i.e., pigeons

kneel, then kiss his foot, then deliver up your pigeons, and then look for your reward. I'll be at hand, sir! See you do it bravely.

CLOWN I warrant you, sir, let me alone.

TITUS Sirrah, has thou a knife? Come, let me see it.
Here, Marcus, fold it in the oration,
For thou hast made it like an humble suppliant.
And when thou hast given it to the Emperor,
Knock at my door, and tell me what he says.

CLOWN God be with you, sir; I will. *Exit.*

TITUS Come, Marcus, let us go. Publius, follow me.
Exeunt.

[Scene IV. *Rome. Before the palace.*]

Enter Emperor and Empress and her two sons. The Emperor brings the arrows in his hand that Titus shot at him.

SATURNINUS Why, lords, what wrongs are these! Was ever seen
An emperor in Rome thus overborne,
Troubled, confronted thus, and for the extent
Of egal justice used in such contempt?
My lords, you know, as know the mightful gods,
However these disturbers of our peace
Buzz in the people's ears, there naught hath passed
But even with law against the willful sons
Of old Andronicus. And what and if
His sorrows have so overwhelmed his wits,
Shall we be thus afflicted in his wreaks,
His fits, his frenzy, and his bitterness?

114 **bravely** well IV.iv.3 **extent** exercise 4 **egal** equal 8 **even** agreeing 11 **wreaks** vengeful acts

And now he writes to heaven for his redress!
See, here's to Jove, and this to Mercury,
This to Apollo, this to the god of war.
Sweet scrolls to fly about the streets of Rome!
What's this but libeling against the Senate,
And blazoning our unjustice everywhere?
A goodly humor, is it not, my lords?
As who would say, in Rome no justice were.
But if I live, his feignèd ecstasies
Shall be no shelter to these outrages,
But he and his shall know that justice lives
In Saturninus' health; whom, if he sleep,
He'll so awake, as he in fury shall
Cut off the proud'st conspirator that lives.

TAMORA My gracious lord, my lovely Saturnine,
Lord of my life, commander of my thoughts,
Calm thee, and bear the faults of Titus' age,
Th' effects of sorrow for his valiant sons,
Whose loss hath pierced him deep and scarred his heart,
And rather comfort his distressèd plight
Than prosecute the meanest or the best
For these contempts. [*Aside*] Why, thus it shall become
High-witted Tamora to gloze with all.
But, Titus, I have touched thee to the quick,
Thy lifeblood out: if Aaron now be wise,
Then is all safe, the anchor in the port.

Enter Clown.

How now, good fellow? Wouldst thou speak with us?

CLOWN Yea, forsooth, and your mistress-ship be emperial.

TAMORA Empress I am, but yonder sits the Emperor.

CLOWN 'Tis he. God and Saint Stephen give you

18 **blazoning** proclaiming 21 **ecstasies** fits of madness 35 **gloze** use specious words 37 **Thy lifeblood out** when your blood is out

godden. I have brought you a letter and a couple of pigeons here.

He [i.e., Saturninus] reads the letter.

SATURNINUS Go, take him away, and hang him presently.

CLOWN How much money must I have?

TAMORA Come, sirrah, you must be hanged.

CLOWN Hanged! By lady, then I have brought up a neck to a fair end. *Exit [with guards].*

SATURNINUS Despiteful and intolerable wrongs!
Shall I endure this monstrous villainy?
I know from whence this same device proceeds.
May this be borne as if his traitorous sons,
That died by law for murder of our brother,
Have by my means been butchered wrongfully.
Go, drag the villain hither by the hair,
Nor age nor honor shall shape privilege:
For this proud mock I'll be thy slaughter-man—
Sly frantic wretch, that holp'st to make me great,
In hope thyself should govern Rome and me.

Enter nuntius, Aemilius.

What news with thee, Aemilius?

AEMILIUS Arm, my lords. Rome never had more cause.
The Goths have gathered head, and with a power
Of high-resolvèd men, bent to the spoil,
They hither march amain, under conduct
Of Lucius, son to old Andronicus;
Who threats, in course of this revenge, to do
As much as ever Coriolanus did.

44 **godden** good evening 49 **By lady** (an interjection, from "By Our Lady") 50 **neck** (possibly with a pun on "knack," which means "deceitful trick") 58 **shape privilege** provide immunity 61 s.d. **nuntius** messenger (Latin) 64 **gathered head** raised an army 64 **power** army 66 **conduct** leadership 69 **Coriolanus** (this Roman hero who became Rome's enemy is the protagonist in Shakespeare's last tragedy)

SATURNINUS Is warlike Lucius general of the Goths?
These tidings nip me, and I hang the head
As flowers with frost or grass beat down with storms.
Ay, now begins our sorrows to approach:
'Tis he the common people love so much;
Myself hath often heard them say,
When I have walkèd like a private man,
That Lucius' banishment was wrongfully,
And they have wished that Lucius were their emperor.

TAMORA Why should you fear? Is not your city strong?

SATURNINUS Ay, but the citizens favor Lucius,
And will revolt from me to succor him.

TAMORA King, be thy thoughts imperious, like thy name.
Is the sun dimmed, that gnats do fly in it?
The eagle suffers little birds to sing
And is not careful what they mean thereby,
Knowing that with the shadow of his wings
He can at pleasure stint their melody:
Even so mayst thou the giddy men of Rome.
Then cheer thy spirit: for know, thou Emperor,
I will enchant the old Andronicus
With words more sweet, and yet more dangerous,
Than baits to fish, or honey-stalks to sheep;
Whenas the one is wounded with the bait,
The other rotted with delicious feed.

SATURNINUS But he will not entreat his son for us.

TAMORA If Tamora entreat him, then he will:
For I can smooth, and fill his agèd ears
With golden promises, that, were his heart
Almost impregnable, his old ears deaf,
Yet should both ear and heart obey my tongue.

85 **careful** worried 87 **stint** stop 92 **honey-stalks** clover

[*To Aemilius*] Go thou before to be our ambassador:
Say that the Emperor requests a parley
Of warlike Lucius, and appoint the meeting
Even at his father's house, the old Andronicus.

SATURNINUS Aemilius, do this message honorably,
And if he stand in hostage for his safety,
Bid him demand what pledge will please him best.

AEMILIUS Your bidding shall I do effectually. *Exit.*

TAMORA Now will I to that old Andronicus,
And temper him with all the art I have,
To pluck proud Lucius from the warlike Goths.
And now, sweet Emperor, be blithe again,
And bury all thy fear in my devices.

SATURNINUS Then go successantly, and plead to him.

Exeunt.

106 stand in insist upon **110 temper** work upon **114 successantly** one after the other (?)

[ACT V

Scene I. *A plain near Rome.*]

Enter Lucius, with an army of Goths, with drums and soldiers.

LUCIUS Approvèd warriors, and my faithful friends,
I have receivèd letters from great Rome,
Which signifies what hate they bear their emperor,
And how desirous of our sight they are.
Therefore, great lords, be, as your titles witness,
Imperious, and impatient of your wrongs;
And wherein Rome hath done you any scath,
Let him make treble satisfaction.

GOTH Brave slip, sprung from the great Andronicus,
Whose name was once our terror, now our comfort,
Whose high exploits and honorable deeds
Ingrateful Rome requites with foul contempt,
Be bold in us: we'll follow where thou lead'st,
Like stinging bees in hottest summer's day,
Led by their master to the flow'red fields,
And be avengèd on cursèd Tamora.

[OTHER GOTHS] And as he saith, so say we all with him.

LUCIUS I humbly thank him, and I thank you all.
But who comes here, led by a lusty Goth?

V.i.1 Approvèd tested   7 scath harm   9 slip offshoot   13 bold confident

Enter a Goth, leading of Aaron with his child in his arms.

GOTH Renownèd Lucius, from our troops I strayed
To gaze upon a ruinous monastery,
And, as I earnestly did fix mine eye
Upon the wasted building, suddenly
I heard a child cry underneath a wall.
I made unto the noise, when soon I heard
The crying babe controlled with this discourse:
"Peace, tawny slave, half me and half thy dame.
Did not thy hue bewray whose brat thou art,
Had nature lent thee but thy mother's look,
Villain, thou mightst have been an emperor:
But where the bull and cow are both milk-white,
They never do beget a coal-black calf.
Peace, villain, peace!" Even thus he rates the babe,
"For I must bear thee to a trusty Goth,
Who, when he knows thou art the Empress' babe,
Will hold thee dearly for thy mother's sake."
With this, my weapon drawn, I rushed upon him,
Surprised him suddenly, and brought him hither,
To use as you think needful of the man.

LUCIUS O worthy Goth, this is the incarnate devil
That robbed Andronicus of his good hand.
This is the pearl that pleased your empress' eye,
And here's the base fruit of her burning lust.
Say, wall-eyed slave, whither wouldst thou convey
This growing image of thy fiendlike face?
Why dost not speak? What, deaf? Not a word?
A halter, soldiers! Hang him on this tree,
And by his side his fruit of bastardy.

AARON Touch not the boy; he is of royal blood.

LUCIUS Too like the sire for ever being good.
First hang the child, that he may see it sprawl—
A sight to vex the father's soul withal.

23 **wasted** ruined 27 **tawny** black 27 **dame** mother 28 **bewray** reveal 28 **brat** young offspring 33 **rates** berates 44 **wall-eyed** glaring (literally: having a whitish iris)

AARON Get me a ladder. Lucius, save the child,
And bear it from me to the Empress.
If thou do this, I'll show thee wondrous things
That highly may advantage thee to hear.
If thou wilt not, befall what may befall,
I'll speak no more but "Vengeance rot you all!"

LUCIUS Say on, and if it please me which thou speak'st,
Thy child shall live, and I will see it nourished.

AARON And if it please thee! Why, assure thee, Lucius,
'Twill vex thy soul to hear what I shall speak;
For I must talk of murders, rapes, and massacres,
Acts of black night, abominable deeds,
Complots of mischief, treason, villainies
Ruthful to hear, yet piteously performed:
And this shall all be buried in my death,
Unless thou swear to me my child shall live.

LUCIUS Tell on thy mind, I say thy child shall live.

AARON Swear that he shall, and then I will begin.

LUCIUS Who should I swear by? Thou believest no god:
That granted, how canst thou believe an oath?

AARON What if I do not? As indeed I do not;
Yet, for I know thou art religious,
And hast a thing within thee callèd conscience,
With twenty popish tricks and ceremonies,
Which I have seen thee careful to observe,
Therefore I urge thy oath; for that I know
An idiot holds his bauble for a god,
And keeps the oath which by that god he swears,
To that I'll urge him: therefore thou shalt vow
By that same god, what god soe'er it be,
That thou adorest and hast in reverence,

53 **Get me a ladder** i.e., hang me rather than the child 66 **Ruthful** pitiful 66 **piteously performed** i.e., performed, which excites pity 79 **bauble** carved head at the end of a court fool's stick

To save my boy, to nourish and bring him up;
Or else I will discover naught to thee.

LUCIUS Even by my god I swear to thee I will.

AARON First know thou, I begot him on the Empress.

LUCIUS O most insatiate and luxurious woman!

AARON Tut, Lucius, this was but a deed of charity
To that which thou shalt hear of me anon.
'Twas her two sons that murdered Bassianus;
They cut thy sister's tongue and ravished her,
And cut her hands, and trimmed her as thou sawest.

LUCIUS O detestable villain! Call'st thou that
trimming?

AARON Why, she was washed, and cut, and trimmed,
and 'twas
Trim sport for them which had the doing of it.

LUCIUS O barbarous, beastly villains, like thyself!

AARON Indeed, I was their tutor to instruct them.
That codding spirit had they from their mother,
As sure a card as ever won the set.
That bloody mind, I think, they learned of me,
As true a dog as ever fought at head.
Well, let my deeds be witness of my worth.
I trained thy brethren to that guileful hole,
Where the dead corpse of Bassianus lay;
I wrote the letter that thy father found,
And hid the gold within that letter mentioned,
Confederate with the Queen and her two sons;
And what not done, that thou hast cause to rue,
Wherein I had no stroke of mischief in it?
I played the cheater for thy father's hand,
And when I had it drew myself apart,

88 **luxurious** lustful 90 To in comparison with 99 **codding** lustful 100 **set** game 102 **at head** (a courageous bulldog went for the bull's nose) 104 **trained** lured 111 **cheater** officer appointed to look after escheats or property forfeited to the Crown

And almost broke my heart with extreme laughter.
I pried me through the crevice of a wall,
When for his hand he had his two sons' heads;
Beheld his tears and laughed so heartily
That both mine eyes were rainy like to his:
And when I told the Empress of this sport,
She sounded almost at my pleasing tale,
And for my tidings gave me twenty kisses.

GOTH What, canst thou say all this and never blush?

AARON Ay, like a black dog, as the saying is.

LUCIUS Art thou not sorry for these heinous deeds?

AARON Ay, that I had not done a thousand more.
Even now I curse the day—and yet, I think,
Few come within the compass of my curse—
Wherein I did not some notorious ill:
As kill a man or else devise his death,
Ravish a maid or plot the way to do it,
Accuse some innocent and forswear myself,
Set deadly enmity between two friends,
Make poor men's cattle break their necks,
Set fire on barns and haystalks in the night,
And bid the owners quench them with their tears.
Oft have I digged up dead men from their graves
And set them upright at their dear friends' door,
Even when their sorrows almost was forgot,
And on their skins, as on the bark of trees,
Have with my knife carvèd in Roman letters,
"Let not your sorrow die, though I am dead."
But, I have done a thousand dreadful things
As willingly as one would kill a fly,
And nothing grieves me heartily indeed,
But that I cannot do ten thousand more.

LUCIUS Bring down the devil, for he must not die
So sweet a death as hanging presently.

AARON If there be devils, would I were a devil,
To live and burn in everlasting fire,

119 sounded swooned **130 forswear** perjure

So I might have your company in hell,
But to torment you with my bitter tongue!

LUCIUS Sirs, stop his mouth, and let him speak no
more.

Enter Aemilius.

GOTH My lord, there is a messenger from Rome
Desires to be admitted to your presence.

LUCIUS Let him come near.
Welcome, Aemilius, what's the news from Rome?

AEMILIUS Lord Lucius, and you princes of the Goths,
The Roman Emperor greets you all by me;
And, for he understands you are in arms,
He craves a parley at your father's house,
Willing you to demand your hostages,
And they shall be immediately delivered.

GOTH What says our general?

LUCIUS Aemilius, let the Emperor give his pledges
Unto my father and my uncle Marcus,
And we will come. March away. [*Exeunt.*]

[Scene II. *Rome. Before Titus' house.*]

Enter Tamora and her two sons, disguised
[*as Revenge attended by Rape and Murder*].

TAMORA Thus, in this strange and sad habiliment,
I will encounter with Andronicus,
And say I am Revenge, sent from below
To join with him and right his heinous wrongs.
Knock at his study, where, they say, he keeps
To ruminate strange plots of dire revenge;
Tell him Revenge is come to join with him,
And work confusion on his enemies.

V.ii.1 **sad habiliment** dismal apparel 5 **keeps** dwells 8 **confusion** destruction

They knock, and Titus [above] opens his study door.

TITUS Who doth molest my contemplation?
Is it your trick to make me ope the door,
That so my sad decrees may fly away,
And all my study be to no effect?
You are deceived: for what I mean to do
See here in bloody lines I have set down.
And what is written shall be executed.

TAMORA Titus, I am come to talk with thee.

TITUS No, not a word. How can I grace my talk,
Wanting a hand to give that accord?
Thou hast the odds of me, therefore no more.

TAMORA If thou didst know me, thou wouldst talk
with me.

TITUS I am not mad, I know thee well enough.
Witness this wretched stump, witness these crimson
lines,
Witness these trenches made by grief and care,
Witness the tiring day and heavy night,
Witness all sorrow, that I know thee well
For our proud empress, mighty Tamora:
Is not thy coming for my other hand?

TAMORA Know thou, sad man, I am not Tamora;
She is thy enemy, and I thy friend.
I am Revenge, sent from th' infernal kingdom
To ease the gnawing vulture of thy mind,
By working wreakful vengeance on thy foes.
Come down and welcome me to this world's light;
Confer with me of murder and of death:
There's not a hollow cave or lurking place,
No vast obscurity or misty vale,
Where bloody murder or detested rape
Can couch for fear, but I will find them out,

18 **give that accord** i.e., provide appropriate gestures 19 **odds of** advantage over 32 **wreakful** avenging 38 **couch** lie hidden

And in their ears tell them my dreadful name,
Revenge, which makes the foul offender quake.

TITUS Art thou Revenge? And art thou sent to me,
To be a torment to mine enemies?

TAMORA I am, therefore come down and welcome me.

TITUS Do me some service ere I come to thee.
Lo, by thy side where Rape and Murder stands;
Now give some surance that thou art Revenge;
Stab them, or tear them on thy chariot wheels;
And then I'll come and be thy wagoner,
And whirl along with thee about the globes.
Provide thee two proper palfreys, black as jet,
To hale thy vengeful wagon swift away,
And find out murder in their guilty caves:
And when thy car is loaden with their heads,
I will dismount, and by thy wagon wheel
Trot like a servile footman all day long,
Even from Hyperion's rising in the east,
Until his very downfall in the sea.
And day by day I'll do this heavy task,
So thou destroy Rapine and Murder there.

TAMORA These are my ministers and come with me.

TITUS Are them thy ministers? What are they called?

TAMORA Rape and Murder; therefore callèd so,
'Cause they take vengeance of such kind of men.

TITUS Good Lord, how like the Empress' sons they are!
And you the Empress! But we worldly men
Have miserable, mad, mistaking eyes.
O sweet Revenge, now do I come to thee:
And, if one arm's embracement will content thee,
I will embrace thee in it by and by. [*Exit above.*]

TAMORA This closing with him fits his lunacy.

46 **surance** assurance 50 **proper palfreys** excellent horses 53 **car** chariot 56 **Hyperion's** the sun god's 59 **So** provided that 59 **Rapine** rape 65 **worldly** mortal, of this world 70 **closing** agreement

Whate'er I forge to feed his brainsick humors,
Do you uphold and maintain in your speeches,
For now he firmly takes me for Revenge,
And, being credulous in this mad thought,
I'll make him send for Lucius his son;
And, whilst I at a banket hold him sure,
I'll find some cunning practice out of hand,
To scatter and disperse the giddy Goths,
Or at the least make them his enemies.
See, here he comes, and I must ply my theme.

[*Enter Titus.*]

TITUS Long have I been forlorn, and all for thee.
Welcome, dread Fury, to my woeful house:
Rapine and Murder, you are welcome too:
How like the Empress and her sons you are!
Well are you fitted, had you but a Moor:
Could not all hell afford you such a devil?
For well I wot the Empress never wags
But in her company there is a Moor;
And, would you represent our queen aright,
It were convenient you had such a devil:
But welcome, as you are. What shall we do?

TAMORA What wouldst thou have us do, Andronicus?

DEMETRIUS Show me a murderer, I'll deal with him.

CHIRON Show me a villain that hath done a rape,
And I am sent to be revenged on him.

TAMORA Show me a thousand that hath done thee wrong,
And I will be revengèd on them all.

TITUS Look round about the wicked streets of Rome,
And when thou find'st a man that's like thyself,
Good Murder, stab him; he's a murderer.
Go thou with him, and when it is thy hap
To find another that is like to thee,

71 **forge** invent 77 **practice** scheme 77 **out of hand** on the spur of the moment 87 **wags** moves 90 **convenient** fitting 101 **hap** chance

Good Rapine, stab him; he is a ravisher.
Go thou with them, and in the Emperor's court
There is a queen attended by a Moor;
Well shalt thou know her by thine own proportion,
For up and down she doth resemble thee;
I pray thee, do on them some violent death;
They have been violent to me and mine.

TAMORA Well hast thou lessoned us; this shall we do.
But would it please thee, good Andronicus,
To send for Lucius, thy thrice valiant son,
Who leads towards Rome a band of warlike Goths,
And bid him come and banquet at thy house:
When he is here, even at thy solemn feast,
I will bring in the Empress and her sons,
The Emperor himself, and all thy foes,
And at thy mercy shall they stoop and kneel,
And on them shalt thou ease thy angry heart.
What says Andronicus to this device?

TITUS Marcus, my brother! 'Tis sad Titus calls.

Enter Marcus.

Go, gentle Marcus, to thy nephew Lucius;
Thou shalt inquire him out among the Goths.
Bid him repair to me and bring with him
Some of the chiefest princes of the Goths:
Bid him encamp his soldiers where they are;
Tell him the Emperor and the Empress too
Feast at my house, and he shall feast with them.
This do thou for my love, and so let him,
As he regards his agèd father's life.

MARCUS This will I do, and soon return again. [*Exit.*]

TAMORA Now will I hence about thy business,
And take my ministers along with me.

TITUS Nay, nay, let Rape and Murder stay with me,
Or else I'll call my brother back again,
And cleave to no revenge but Lucius.

115 solemn ceremonious 124 repair come

TAMORA [*Aside to her sons*] What say you, boys? Will you abide with him,
Whiles I go tell my lord the Emperor
How I have governed our determined jest?
Yield to his humor, smooth and speak him fair,
And tarry with him till I turn again.

TITUS [*Aside*] I knew them all, though they supposed me mad;
And will o'erreach them in their own devices,
A pair of cursèd hellhounds and their dame.

DEMETRIUS Madam, depart at pleasure, leave us here.

TAMORA Farewell, Andronicus: Revenge now goes
To lay a complot to betray thy foes.

TITUS I know thou dost; and, sweet Revenge, farewell.
[*Exit Tamora.*]

CHIRON Tell us, old man, how shall we be employed?

TITUS Tut, I have work enough for you to do.
Publius, come hither, Caius, and Valentine!

[*Enter Publius and others.*]

PUBLIUS What is your will?

TITUS Know you these two?

PUBLIUS The Empress' sons, I take them: Chiron,
Demetrius.

TITUS Fie, Publius, fie! Thou art too much deceived;
The one is Murder, and Rape is the other's name:
And therefore bind them, gentle Publius:
Caius and Valentine, lay hands on them:
Oft have you heard me wish for such an hour,
And now I find it: therefore bind them sure;
And stop their mouths if they begin to cry. [*Exit.*]

139 governed our determined jest managed the jest we agreed ("determined") upon **140 smooth and speak him fair** flatter and speak courteously to him **147 complot** plot

CHIRON Villains, forbear! We are the Empress' sons.

PUBLIUS And therefore do we what we are commanded.
Stop close their mouths, let them not speak a word:
Is he sure bound? Look that you bind them fast.

Enter Titus Andronicus with a knife, and Lavinia with a basin.

TITUS Come, come, Lavinia; look, thy foes are bound.
Sirs, stop their mouths, let them not speak to me,
But let them hear what fearful words I utter.
O villains, Chiron and Demetrius!
Here stands the spring whom you have stained with mud,
This goodly summer with your winter mixed.
You killed her husband, and, for that vile fault
Two of her brothers were condemned to death,
My hand cut off and made a merry jest:
Both her sweet hands, her tongue, and that more dear
Than hands or tongue, her spotless chastity,
Inhuman traitors, you constrained and forced.
What would you say if I should let you speak?
Villains, for shame you could not beg for grace.
Hark, wretches, how I mean to martyr you.
This one hand yet is left to cut your throats,
Whiles that Lavinia 'tween her stumps doth hold
The basin that receives your guilty blood.
You know your mother means to feast with me,
And calls herself Revenge, and thinks me mad:
Hark, villains, I will grind your bones to dust,
And with your blood and it I'll make a paste,
And of the paste a coffin I will rear,
And make two pasties of your shameful heads,
And bid that strumpet, your unhallowed dam,
Like to the earth, swallow her own increase.
This is the feast that I have bid her to,
And this the banket she shall surfeit on;
For worse than Philomel you used my daughter,

189 coffin pie crust **192 increase** offspring

And worse than Progne I will be revenged.
And now prepare your throats. Lavinia, come,
Receive the blood; and when that they are dead,
Let me go grind their bones to powder small,
And with this hateful liquor temper it,
And in that paste let their vile heads be baked.
Come, come, be every one officious
To make this banket, which I wish may prove
More stern and bloody than the Centaurs' feast.
He cuts their throats.
So, now bring them in, for I'll play the cook,
And see them ready against their mother comes.
Exeunt.

[Scene III. *Rome. Within Titus' house.*]

Enter Lucius, Marcus, and the Goths [with Aaron a prisoner, and an Attendant bearing Aaron's child].

LUCIUS Uncle Marcus, since 'tis my father's mind
That I repair to Rome, I am content.

GOTH And ours with thine, befall what fortune will.

LUCIUS Good uncle, take you in this barbarous Moor,
This ravenous tiger, this accursèd devil;
Let him receive no sust'nance, fetter him,
Till he be brought unto the Empress' face
For testimony of her foul proceedings:
And see the ambush of our friends be strong;
I fear the Emperor means no good to us.

196 **Progne** wife of Tereus (Tereus raped and mutilated Progne's sister, Philomela, and in revenge Progne slaughtered Tereus'—and her own—son and served him to Tereus) 200 **temper** mix 202 **officious** busy 204 **Centaurs' feast** (a battle followed the marriage feast to which the Lapiths invited the Centaurs) 206 **against** in preparation for the time when V.iii.2 **repair** return

AARON Some devil whisper curses in my ear,
And prompt me, that my tongue may utter forth
The venomous malice of my swelling heart!

LUCIUS Away, inhuman dog! Unhallowed slave!
Sirs, help our uncle to convey him in.
[*Goths lead Aaron in. Trumpets sound.*]
The trumpets show the Emperor is at hand.

Sound trumpets. Enter Emperor and Empress, with Tribunes and others.

SATURNINUS What, hath the firmament mo suns than one?

LUCIUS What boots it thee to call thyself a sun?

MARCUS Rome's Emperor, and nephew, break the parle;
These quarrels must be quietly debated.
The feast is ready, which the careful Titus
Hath ordained to an honorable end,
For peace, for love, for league, and good to Rome.
Please you, therefore, draw nigh, and take your places.

SATURNINUS Marcus, we will.

Trumpets sounding, enter Titus, like a cook, placing the dishes, and Lavinia with a veil over her face, [*young Lucius, and others*].

TITUS Welcome, my lord; welcome, dread Queen;
Welcome, ye warlike Goths; welcome, Lucius;
And welcome, all: although the cheer be poor,
'Twill fill your stomachs; please you eat of it.

SATURNINUS Why art thou thus attired, Andronicus?

TITUS Because I would be sure to have all well,
To entertain your Highness and your empress.

TAMORA We are beholding to you, good Andronicus.

17 **mo** more 18 **boots** avails 19 **break the parle** interrupt the talk (i.e., cease quarreling) 21 **careful** full of sorrow 28 **cheer** hospitality

TITUS And if your Highness knew my heart, you were.
My lord the Emperor, resolve me this:
Was it well done of rash Virginius
To slay his daughter with his own right hand,
Because she was enforced, stained, and deflow'r'd?

SATURNINUS It was, Andronicus.

TITUS Your reason, mighty lord!

SATURNINUS Because the girl should not survive her shame,
And by her presence still renew his sorrows.

TITUS A reason mighty, strong, and effectual,
A pattern, precedent, and lively warrant,
For me, most wretched, to perform the like.
Die, die, Lavinia, and thy shame with thee,
And with thy shame thy father's sorrow die!
[*He kills her.*]

SATURNINUS What has thou done, unnatural and unkind?

TITUS Killed her for whom my tears have made me blind.
I am as woeful as Virginius was,
And have a thousand times more cause than he
To do this outrage, and it now is done.

SATURNINUS What, was she ravished? Tell who did the deed.

TITUS Will't please you eat? Will't please your Highness feed?

TAMORA Why hast thou slain thine only daughter thus?

TITUS Not I; 'twas Chiron and Demetrius:
They ravished her and cut away her tongue;
And they, 'twas they, that did her all this wrong.

SATURNINUS Go, fetch them hither to us presently.

35 **resolve** answer 38 **enforced** forced, raped 48 **unkind** (1) unnatural (2) cruel

TITUS Why, there they are, both bakèd in this pie,
Whereof their mother daintily hath fed,
Eating the flesh that she herself hath bred.
'Tis true, 'tis true; witness my knife's sharp point.
He stabs the Empress.

SATURNINUS Die, frantic wretch, for this accursèd deed.
[*Kills Titus.*]

LUCIUS Can the son's eye behold his father bleed?
There's meed for meed, death for a deadly deed.
[*Kills Saturninus.*]

MARCUS You sad-faced men, people and sons of Rome,
By uproars severed, as a flight of fowl
Scattered by winds and high tempestuous gusts,
O, let me teach you how to knit again
This scattered corn into one mutual sheaf,
These broken limbs again into one body.

ROMAN LORD Let Rome herself be bane unto herself,
And she whom mighty kingdoms curtsy to,
Like a forlorn and desperate castaway,
Do shameful execution on herself,
But if my frosty signs and chaps of age,
Grave witnesses of true experience,
Cannot induce you to attend my words.
[*To Lucius*] Speak, Rome's dear friend, as erst our ancestor,
When with his solemn tongue he did discourse
To lovesick Dido's sad attending ear
The story of that baleful burning night,
When subtle Greeks surprised King Priam's Troy;
Tell us what Sinon hath bewitched our ears,
Or who hath brought the fatal engine in
That gives our Troy, our Rome, the civil wound.
My heart is not compact of flint nor steel;

66 **meed for meed** measure for measure 73 **bane** destruction 77 **But if** unless 77 **frosty signs and chaps of age** i.e., white hair and cracked (wrinkled) skin 80 **erst** formerly 80 **our ancestor** i.e., Aeneas 82 **sad attending** seriously listening 83 **baleful** injurious 85 **Sinon** Greek who persuaded the Trojans to admit the wooden horse 88 **compact** composed

Nor can I utter all our bitter grief,
But floods of tears will drown my oratory
And break my utt'rance, even in the time
When it should move ye to attend me most,
And force you to commiseration.
Here's Rome's young captain, let him tell the tale,
While I stand by and weep to hear him speak.

LUCIUS Then, gracious auditory, be it known to you
That Chiron and the damned Demetrius
Were they that murd'red our emperor's brother;
And they it were that ravishèd our sister.
For their fell faults our brothers were beheaded,
Our father's tears despised, and basely cozened
Of that true hand that fought Rome's quarrel out
And sent her enemies unto the grave.
Lastly, myself unkindly banishèd,
The gates shut on me, and turned weeping out,
To beg relief among Rome's enemies,
Who drowned their enmity in my true tears
And oped their arms to embrace me as a friend:
I am the turned-forth, be it known to you,
That have preserved her welfare in my blood,
And from her bosom took the enemy's point,
Sheathing the steel in my advent'rous body.
Alas, you know I am no vaunter, I;
My scars can witness, dumb although they are,
That my report is just and full of truth.
But, soft! Methinks, I do digress too much,
Citing my worthless praise. O, pardon me,
For when no friends are by, men praise themselves.

MARCUS Now is my turn to speak. Behold the child:
Of this was Tamora deliverèd,
The issue of an irreligious Moor,
Chief architect and plotter of these woes:
The villain is alive in Titus' house,

100 **fell** savage 101 **cozened** cheated 113 **vaunter** braggart 116 **soft** hold (a common interjection)

And as he is to witness, this is true.
Now judge what cause had Titus to revenge
These wrongs, unspeakable, past patience,
Or more than any living man could bear.
Now have you heard the truth. What say you, Romans?
Have we done aught amiss, show us wherein,
And, from the place where you behold us pleading,
The poor remainder of Andronici
Will, hand in hand, all headlong hurl ourselves
And on the ragged stones beat forth our souls,
And make a mutual closure of our house.
Speak, Romans, speak, and if you say we shall,
Lo, hand in hand, Lucius and I will fall.

AEMILIUS Come, come, thou reverend man of Rome,
And bring our emperor gently in thy hand,
Lucius our emperor; for well I know
The common voice do cry it shall be so.

MARCUS Lucius, all hail, Rome's royal Emperor!
[*To soldiers*] Go, go into old Titus' sorrowful house,
And hither hale that misbelieving Moor,
To be adjudged some direful slaught'ring death,
As punishment for his most wicked life.
[*Exeunt Attendants.*]
Lucius, all hail, Rome's gracious governor!
[*Cries of approval.*]

LUCIUS Thanks, gentle Romans: may I govern so,
To heal Rome's harms and wipe away her woe!
But, gentle people, give me aim awhile,
For nature puts me to a heavy task.
Stand all aloof; but, uncle, draw you near
To shed obsequious tears upon this trunk.
O, take this warm kiss on thy pale cold lips,
These sorrowful drops upon thy bloodstained face,
The last true duties of thy noble son!

133 **ragged** rugged 134 **mutual closure** common end 149 **give me aim** assist me 152 **obsequious** mourning

MARCUS Tear for tear and loving kiss for kiss
Thy brother Marcus tenders on thy lips:
O, were the sum of these that I should pay
Countless and infinite, yet would I pay them!

LUCIUS Come hither, boy; come, come, and learn of us
To melt in showers. Thy grandsire loved thee well;
Many a time he danced thee on his knee,
Sung thee asleep, his loving breast thy pillow;
Many a story hath he told to thee,
And bid thee bear his pretty tales in mind,
And talk of them when he was dead and gone.

MARCUS How many thousand times hath these poor lips,
When they were living, warmed themselves on thine!
O, now, sweet boy, give them their latest kiss.
Bid him farewell; commit him to the grave;
Do them that kindness, and take leave of them.

BOY O, grandsire, grandsire! Ev'n with all my heart
Would I were dead, so you did live again!
O Lord, I cannot speak to him for weeping;
My tears will choke me if I ope my mouth.

[*Enter Attendants with Aaron.*]

ROMAN You sad Andronici, have done with woes;
Give sentence on this execrable wretch
That hath been breeder of these dire events.

LUCIUS Set him breast-deep in earth and famish him;
There let him stand and rave and cry for food:
If anyone relieves or pities him,
For the offense he dies. This is our doom.
Some stay, to see him fast'ned in the earth.

AARON Ah, why should wrath be mute, and fury dumb?
I am no baby, I, that with base prayers
I should repent the evils I have done:

169 **latest** last 171 **them** i.e., "these poor lips" of line 167 182 **doom** sentence

Ten thousand worse than ever yet I did
Would I perform, if I might have my will:
If one good deed in all my life I did,
I do repent it from my very soul.

LUCIUS Some loving friends convey the Emperor hence,
And give him burial in his father's grave:
My father and Lavinia shall forthwith
Be closèd in our household's monument.
As for that ravenous tiger, Tamora,
No funeral rite, nor man in mourning weed,
No mournful bell shall ring her burial;
But throw her forth to beasts and birds of prey.
Her life was beastly and devoid of pity,
And being dead, let birds on her take pity. *Exeunt.*

FINIS

Textual Note

THERE is an allusion to a Roman hero named Titus in *A Knack to Know a Knave*, acted in June 1592. Though the allusion may, of course, be to an earlier play on the subject rather than to Shakespeare's play, there is no need to multiply entities; Shakespeare's *Titus Andronicus* may have been on the stage before 1592. The next bit of evidence is a reference of 23 January 1594 in Henslowe's *Diary* to the effect that Sussex's men acted a new piece, "titus & ondronicus." If the allusion in *A Knave* is not to Shakespeare's play, quite possibly *Titus Andronicus* was indeed new in 1594, but it is equally possible that it was "new" only to Sussex's company, or that it had been newly revised. On 6 February 1594 the Stationers' Register entered "a book intituled a Noble Roman Historye of Titus Andronicus." Perhaps this entry alludes to the play, which indeed was published in 1594, though possibly the entry is to some other piece on the same subject. In 1614 Ben Jonson, in the Induction to *Bartholomew Fair*, mentions that Andronicus was seen on the stage as long ago as "fiue and twentie or thirtie yeeres"; strictly, Jonson's reference would date the play 1584–89, though probably he is speaking loosely and his evidence surely does not prohibit a date in the early nineties. The date widely favored is 1592–94, but there is no compelling reason to believe that *Titus* could not have been written in the late eighties.

Only one copy of the first quarto (1594) is known to be extant. Apparently Q1 (i.e., the first quarto) was printed from Shakespeare's manuscript or from a copy of it; a number of stage directions—such as "Enter . . . as many as can be"—suggest an author's hand. In 1600 a second quarto (Q2) was issued. It omits a few lines, adds some, and alters a good deal of punctuation. There is no reason to believe that the alterations represent Shakespeare's revisions; probably all the revisions are a compositor's tamperings. Q3, issued in 1611, was set up from Q2 and therefore has no authority. The version in the First Folio

(F) is based on Q3 but makes numerous small alterations (especially in stage directions) and adds the entire scene (III.ii). The new scene is of sufficient excellence to be Shakespeare's, and though the other changes in F do not suggest that great effort was made to give the play in a version much different from that of Q3, the new scene shows that the editors had access to some unpublished material. The present edition is based on Q1, except for III.ii, which is, of course, based on F. It regularizes speech prefixes (for example, Q1's "Saturnine," "Saturninus," "King," "Satur," are all given here as "Saturninus"); it slightly alters the position of a few stage directions, and it modernizes spelling and punctuation. The act divisions were first established by F; the scene divisions are the work of later editors and though of no authenticity they provide a convenient device for reference. Departures from Q1, other than those mentioned above and corrections of obvious typographical errors, are listed below, the adopted reading first, in bold type, followed by the original reading in roman. If the adopted reading is from Q2, Q3, or F, that fact is indicated in a bracket following the reading. If there is no such indication, the adopted reading is an editor's conjecture.

I.i.35 [for the three and a half lines that follow these words in Q1 see footnote to the line] 69 s.d. **her three sons** her two sonnes 98 **manes** manus 226 **Titan's** [Q2] Tytus 242 **Pantheon** Pathan 264 **chance** [Q2] change 280 **cuique** cuiqum 317 **Phoebe** Thebe 358 s.d. **speak** speakes 369 **Martius** 3. Sonne 370 **Quintus** 2. Sonne 372 **Quintus** 2. sonne 391 [Q1 follows with s.d.: "Exit all but Marcus and Titus," and the other early texts also indicate an exit] 399 **Yes . . . remunerate** [F; omitted in the quartos]

II.i.110 **than** this

II.ii.1 **morn** [F] Moone

II.iii.69 **try** [Q2] trie thy 72 **swart** swartie 160 **ears** [Q3] yeares 210 **unhallowed** [F] vnhollow 222 **berayed** bereaud 231 **Pyramus** [Q2] Priamus 236 **Cocytus** Ocitus

II.iv.27 **him** them 30 **three** their

TEXTUAL NOTE

III.i.146 **his true** her true

III.ii [this scene is found only in F] 39 **complainer** complayne 52 **thy knife** knife 53 **fly** Flys 55 **are cloyed** cloi'd 72 **myself** my selfes

IV.i.50 **quotes** [Q2] coates 88 **hope** [Q2] hop [or "I op"]

IV.ii.95 **Alcides** [Q2] Alciades

IV.iii.57 **Saturn** Saturnine 78 **News** [Q2] Clowne. Newes

IV.iv.5 **know, as know** know 49 **By** be 99 **ears** [F] yeares

V.ii.52 **caves** cares 56 **Hyperion's** Epeons 65 **worldly** [Q2] wordlie

V.iii.125 **cause** course 144 **adjudged** [F] adiudge 154 **bloodstained** blood slaine 163 **Sung** [Q2] Song

WILLIAM SHAKESPEARE

THE HISTORY OF TROILUS AND CRESSIDA

Edited by Daniel Seltzer

A NEVER WRITER, TO AN EVER READER. NEWS.

Eternal reader, you have here a new play, never staled with the stage, never clapperclawed with the palms of the vulgar, and yet passing full of the palm comical; for it is a birth of your brain[1] that never undertook anything comical vainly. And were but the vain names of comedies changed for the titles of commodities, or of plays for pleas, you should see all those grand censors, that now style them such vanities, flock to them for the main grace of their gravities—especially this author's comedies, that are so framed to the life that they serve for the most common commentaries of all the actions of our lives, showing such a dexterity and power of wit that the most displeased with plays are pleased with his comedies. And all such dull and heavy-witted worldlings as were never capable of the wit of a comedy, coming by report of them to his representations, have found that wit there that they never found in themselves and have parted better witted than they came, feeling an edge of wit set upon them more than ever they dreamed they had brain to grind it on. So much and such savored salt of wit is in his comedies that they seem, for their height of pleasure, to be born in that sea that brought forth Venus. Amongst all there is none more witty than this; and had I time I would comment upon it, though I know it needs not, for so much as will make you think your testern well bestowed, but for so much worth as even poor I know to be stuffed in it. It deserves such a labor as well as the best comedy

1. Footnotes are keyed to the text by line number. Text references are printed in bold type; the annotation follows in roman type. 4 **your brain** i.e., Shakespeare's brain 23 **Venus** (the Greek goddess Aphrodite, who, according to Hesiod, was born in ocean foam) 26 **testern** sixpence (slang)

in Terence or Plautus. And believe this, that when he is gone and his comedies out of sale, you will scramble for them and set up a new English Inquisition. Take this for a warning, and at the peril of your pleasure's loss, and judgment's, refuse not, nor like this the less for not being sullied with the smoky breath of the multitude; but thank fortune for the 'scape it hath made amongst you, since by the grand possessors' wills I believe you should have prayed for them rather than been prayed. And so I leave all such to be prayed for, for the state of their wits' healths, that will not praise it. *Vale.*

36 grand possessors (presumably, the actor-sharers of the King's Men, who may have tried to stop publication)

[*Dramatis Personae*

PRIAM, King of Troy

HECTOR, TROILUS, PARIS, DEIPHOBUS, HELENUS — his sons

MARGARELON, a bastard son of Priam

AENEAS, ANTENOR — Trojan commanders

CALCHAS, a Trojan priest, taking part with the Greeks

PANDARUS, uncle to Cressida

AGAMEMNON, the Greek general

MENELAUS, his brother

ACHILLES, AJAX, ULYSSES, NESTOR, DIOMEDES, PATROCLUS — Greek commanders

THERSITES, a deformed and scurrilous Greek

ALEXANDER, servant to Cressida

SERVANT TO TROILUS

SERVANT TO PARIS

SERVANT TO DIOMEDES

HELEN, wife to Menelaus

ANDROMACHE, wife to Hector

CASSANDRA, daughter to Priam; a prophetess

CRESSIDA, daughter to Calchas

TROJAN and GREEK SOLDIERS and ATTENDANTS

Scene: Troy, and the Greek camp before it]

THE HISTORY OF TROILUS AND CRESSIDA

THE PROLOGUE

[*Enter the Prologue, armed for battle.*]

In Troy there lies the scene. From isles of Greece
The princes orgulous, their high blood chafed,
Have to the port of Athens sent their ships,
Fraught with the ministers and instruments
Of cruel war. Sixty and nine, that wore
Their crownets regal, from th' Athenian bay
Put forth toward Phrygia; and their vow is made
To ransack Troy, within whose strong immures
The ravished Helen, Menelaus' queen,
With wanton Paris sleeps—and that's the quarrel.
To Tenedos they come,
And the deep-drawing barks do there disgorge
Their warlike fraughtage. Now on Dardan plains
The fresh and yet unbruisèd Greeks do pitch

Prologue 2 **orgulous** proud 7 **Phrygia** western Asia Minor 8 **immures** walls 11 **Tenedos** the port of Troy 13 **fraughtage** freight, i.e., soldiers 13 **Dardan** Trojan (after Dardanus, son of Zeus and the Pleiad Electra, and ancestor of Priam)

Their brave pavilions. Priam's six-gated city,
Dardan, and Timbria, Helias, Chetas, Troien,
And Antenonidus, with massy staples
And corresponsive and fulfilling bolts,
Sperr up the sons of Troy.
Now expectation, tickling skittish spirits,
On one and other side, Troyan and Greek,
Sets all on hazard. And hither am I come,
A prologue armed, but not in confidence
Of author's pen or actor's voice, but suited
In like conditions as our argument,
To tell you, fair beholders, that our play
Leaps o'er the vaunt and firstlings of those broils,
Beginning in the middle, starting thence away
To what may be digested in a play.
Like or find fault; do as your pleasures are;
Now good or bad, 'tis but the chance of war.

16–17 **Dardan . . . Antenonidus** (names of the gates of Troy) 18 **fulfilling** filling tightly 19 **Sperr up** shut up 20 **skittish** nervous 23 **armed** equipped for fight 24 **suited** dressed 25 **argument** subject 27 **vaunt** beginning

[ACT I

Scene I. *Within Troy.*]

Enter Pandarus and Troilus.

TROILUS Call here my varlet, I'll unarm again.
Why should I war without the walls of Troy
That find such cruel battle here within?
Each Troyan that is master of his heart,
Let him to field; Troilus, alas, hath none.

PANDARUS Will this gear ne'er be mended?

TROILUS The Greeks are strong, and skillful to their strength,
Fierce to their skill, and to their fierceness valiant;
But I am weaker than a woman's tear,
Tamer than sleep, fonder than ignorance,
Less valiant than the virgin in the night,
And skilless as unpracticed infancy.

PANDARUS Well, I have told you enough of this. For my part, I'll not meddle nor make no farther. He that will have a cake out of the wheat must tarry the grinding.

I.i.1 varlet servant **2 without** outside **6 gear** business **7 to** in addition to, in proportion to **10 fonder** more unsophisticated, simpler **12 skilless** inept, naïve

TROILUS Have I not tarried?

PANDARUS Ay, the grinding; but you must tarry the bolting.

TROILUS Have I not tarried?

PANDARUS Ay, the bolting; but you must tarry the leavening.

TROILUS Still have I tarried.

PANDARUS Ay, to the leavening; but here's yet in the word "hereafter" the kneading, the making of the cake, the heating the oven, and the baking. Nay, you must stay the cooling too, or ye may chance burn your lips.

TROILUS Patience herself, what goddess e'er she be,
Doth lesser blench at suff'rance than I do.
At Priam's royal table do I sit,
And when fair Cressid comes into my thoughts—
So, traitor, then she comes when she is thence.

PANDARUS Well, she looked yesternight fairer than ever I saw her look, or any woman else.

TROILUS I was about to tell thee, when my heart,
As wedgèd with a sigh, would rive in twain,
Lest Hector or my father should perceive me—
I have, as when the sun doth light a-scorn,
Buried this sigh in wrinkle of a smile;
But sorrow, that is couched in seeming gladness,
Is like that mirth fate turns to sudden sadness.

PANDARUS An her hair were not somewhat darker than Helen's—well, go to—there were no more comparison between the women; but, for my part, she is my kinswoman: I would not, as they term it, praise her, but I would somebody had heard her talk

19 bolting sifting **30 blench** flinch **33 traitor** (a self-rebuke, for suggesting that she is sometimes absent) **33 then she comes when she is thence** i.e., she returns immediately whenever she is absent **37 rive** split **39 a-scorn** mockingly (?), grudgingly (?) **43 An** if

yesterday, as I did. I will not dispraise your sister Cassandra's wit, but——

TROILUS O Pandarus! I tell thee, Pandarus,
When I do tell thee, there my hopes lie drowned,
Reply not in how many fathoms deep
They lie indrenched. I tell thee I am mad
In Cressid's love; thou answer'st she is fair,
Pour'st in the open ulcer of my heart
Her eyes, her hair, her cheek, her gait, her voice;
Handlest in thy discourse, O, that her hand
In whose comparison all whites are ink,
Writing their own reproach; to whose soft seizure
The cygnet's down is harsh, and spirit of sense
Hard as the palm of plowman. This thou tell'st me,
As true thou tell'st me, when I say I love her;
But, saying thus, instead of oil and balm,
Thou lay'st in every gash that love hath given me
The knife that made it.

PANDARUS I speak no more than truth.

TROILUS Thou dost not speak so much.

PANDARUS Faith, I'll not meddle in it; let her be as she is. If she be fair, 'tis the better for her; and she be not, she has the mends in her own hands.

TROILUS Good Pandarus, how now, Pandarus?

PANDARUS I have had my labor for my travail; ill thought on of her, and ill thought of you; gone between and between, but small thanks for my labor.

TROILUS What, art thou angry, Pandarus? What, with me?

PANDARUS Because she's kin to me, therefore she's not so fair as Helen. An she were not kin to me,

57 **that her hand** that hand of hers 59 **seizure** grasp 60 **cygnet's** young swan's 60 **spirit** (the thin bodily substance believed to transmit sense impressions through the nerves) 70 **mends** (1) remedies (2) cosmetics 72 **travail** (punning on "travel" ["gone between and between"])

she would be as fair a' Friday as Helen is on Sunday. But what care I? I care not an she were a blackamoor; 'tis all one to me.

TROILUS Say I she is not fair?

PANDARUS I do not care whether you do or no. She's a fool to stay behind her father. Let her to the Greeks, and so I'll tell her the next time I see her. For my part, I'll meddle nor make no more i' th' matter.

TROILUS Pandarus——

PANDARUS Not I.

TROILUS Sweet Pandarus——

PANDARUS Pray you, speak no more to me. I will leave all as I found it, and there an end.

Exit. Sound alarum.

TROILUS Peace, you ungracious clamors! Peace, rude sounds!
Fools on both sides! Helen must needs be fair,
When with your blood you daily paint her thus.
I cannot fight upon this argument;
It is too starved a subject for my sword.
But Pandarus—O gods, how do you plague me!
I cannot come to Cressid but by Pandar;
And he's as tetchy to be wooed to woo
As she is stubborn, chaste, against all suit.
Tell me, Apollo, for thy Daphne's love,
What Cressid is, what Pandar, and what we.
Her bed is India; there she lies, a pearl.
Between our Ilium and where she resides
Let it be called the wild and wand'ring flood,
Ourself the merchant, and this sailing Pandar

79 **a'** on 79–80 **on Sunday** i.e., in her Sunday best 84 **father** (Calchas, who had deserted to the Greeks) 95 **argument** theme 99 **tetchy** peevish 101 **Daphne** (the nymph who was changed into a bay tree as she ran to escape Apollo) 104 **Ilium** (here, Priam's palace; generally, Troy [for Ilus, founder of the city, Priam's grandfather])

Our doubtful hope, our convoy and our bark.

Alarum. Enter Aeneas.

AENEAS How now, Prince Troilus, wherefore not afield?

TROILUS Because not there. This woman's answer sorts,
For womanish it is to be from thence.
What news, Aeneas, from the field today?

AENEAS That Paris is returnèd home, and hurt.

TROILUS By whom, Aeneas?

AENEAS Troilus, by Menelaus.

TROILUS Let Paris bleed; 'tis but a scar to scorn:
Paris is gored with Menelaus' horn. *Alarum.*

AENEAS Hark what good sport is out of town today!

TROILUS Better at home, if "would I might" were "may."
But to the sport abroad; are you bound thither?

AENEAS In all swift haste.

TROILUS Come, go we then together.
Exeunt.

109 sorts is appropriate **114 but a scar to scorn** i.e., considering its source, the kind of scar to be scorned **115 horn** (of a cuckold)

[Scene II. *Within Troy.*]

Enter Cressida and [*Alexander,*] *her man.*

CRESSIDA Who were those went by?

MAN Queen Hecuba and Helen.

CRESSIDA And whither go they?

MAN Up to the eastern tower,
Whose height commands as subject all the vale,
To see the battle. Hector, whose patience
Is as a virtue fixed, today was moved.
He chid Andromache, and struck his armorer,
And, like as there were husbandry in war,
Before the sun rose he was harnessed light,
And to the field goes he, where every flower
Did, as a prophet, weep what it foresaw
In Hector's wrath.

CRESSIDA What was his cause of anger?

MAN The noise goes, this: there is among the Greeks
A lord of Troyan blood, nephew to Hector;
They call him Ajax.

CRESSIDA Good; and what of him?

MAN They say he is a very man per se
And stands alone.

CRESSIDA So do all men unless they are drunk, sick, or have no legs.

MAN This man, lady, hath robbed many beasts of their particular additions. He is as valiant as the

I.ii.7 husbandry good management, thrift **8 harnessed** armored **20 additions** distinctive qualities, characteristics

lion, churlish as the bear, slow as the elephant; a man into whom nature hath so crowded humors that his valor is crushed into folly, his folly sauced with discretion. There is no man hath a virtue that he hath not a glimpse of, nor any man an attaint but he carries some stain of it. He is melancholy without cause and merry against the hair. He hath the joints of everything, but everything so out of joint that he is a gouty Briareus, many hands and no use, or purblind Argus, all eyes and no sight.

CRESSIDA But how should this man that makes me smile make Hector angry?

MAN They say he yesterday coped Hector in the battle and struck him down, the disdain and shame whereof hath ever since kept Hector fasting and waking.

Enter Pandarus.

CRESSIDA Who comes here?

MAN Madam, your uncle Pandarus.

CRESSIDA Hector's a gallant man.

MAN As may be in the world, lady.

PANDARUS What's that? What's that?

CRESSIDA Good morrow, uncle Pandarus.

PANDARUS Good morrow, cousin Cressid. What do you talk of? Good morrow, Alexander. How do you, cousin? When were you at Ilium?

CRESSIDA This morning, uncle.

22 **humors** (bodily fluids which, in excess, were thought to cause emotional disorder) 25 **glimpse** momentary shining 25 **attaint** imputation of dishonor 27 **against the hair** contrary to natural tendency (cf. "against the grain") 29 **Briareus** (a hundred-handed giant) 30 **Argus** (a herdsman with eyes covering his body) 33 **coped** engaged, encountered 43 **cousin** (a term of familiarity; here, niece)

PANDARUS What were you talking of when I came? Was Hector armed and gone ere ye came to Ilium? Helen was not up, was she?

CRESSIDA Hector was gone, but Helen was not up.

PANDARUS E'en so, Hector was stirring early.

CRESSIDA That were we talking of, and of his anger.

PANDARUS Was he angry?

CRESSIDA So he says here.

PANDARUS True, he was so; I know the cause too. He'll lay about him today, I can tell them that; and there's Troilus will not come far behind him. Let them take heed of Troilus, I can tell them that too.

CRESSIDA What, is he angry too?

PANDARUS Who, Troilus? Troilus is the better man of the two.

CRESSIDA O Jupiter! There's no comparison.

PANDARUS What, not between Troilus and Hector? Do you know a man if you see him?

CRESSIDA Ay, if I ever saw him before and knew him.

PANDARUS Well, I say Troilus is Troilus.

CRESSIDA Then you say as I say, for I am sure he is not Hector.

PANDARUS No, nor Hector is not Troilus in some degrees.

CRESSIDA 'Tis just to each of them; he is himself.

PANDARUS Himself? Alas, poor Troilus, I would he were.

69–70 **in some degrees** by some distance; in some (specific) ways (?)
72–73 **I would he were** i.e., I wish he were himself, and not in love

CRESSIDA So he is.

PANDARUS Condition, I had gone barefoot to India.

CRESSIDA He is not Hector.

PANDARUS Himself? No, he's not himself. Would 'a were himself. Well, the gods are above; time must friend or end. Well, Troilus, well, I would my heart were in her body. No, Hector is not a better man than Troilus.

CRESSIDA Excuse me.

PANDARUS He is elder.

CRESSIDA Pardon me, pardon me.

PANDARUS Th' other's not come to't; you shall tell me another tale when th' other's come to't. Hector shall not have his will this year.

CRESSIDA He shall not need it if he have his own.

PANDARUS Nor his qualities.

CRESSIDA No matter.

PANDARUS Nor his beauty.

CRESSIDA 'Twould not become him. His own's better.

PANDARUS You have no judgment, niece. Helen herself swore th' other day that Troilus, for a brown favor—for so 'tis, I must confess—not brown neither——

CRESSIDA No, but brown.

PANDARUS Faith, to say truth, brown and not brown.

CRESSIDA To say the truth, true and not true.

PANDARUS She praised his complexion above Paris.

CRESSIDA Why, Paris hath color enough.

75 **Condition** i.e., even if to bring that about 77 **'a** he 86 **come to't** reached manhood 87 **will** (some editors emend to wit, i.e., intelligence) 94 **brown favor** dark complexion

PANDARUS So he has.

CRESSIDA Then Troilus should have too much. If she praised him above, his complexion is higher than his. He having color enough, and the other higher, is too flaming a praise for a good complexion. I had as lief Helen's golden tongue had commended Troilus for a copper nose.

PANDARUS I swear to you, I think Helen loves him better than Paris.

CRESSIDA Then she's a merry Greek indeed.

PANDARUS Nay, I am sure she does. She came to him th' other day into the compassed window—and, you know, he has not past three or four hairs on his chin——

CRESSIDA Indeed, a tapster's arithmetic may soon bring his particulars therein to a total.

PANDARUS Why, he is very young; and yet will he, within three pound, lift as much as his brother Hector.

CRESSIDA Is he so young a man, and so old a lifter?

PANDARUS But to prove to you that Helen loves him, she came and puts me her white hand to his cloven chin——

CRESSIDA Juno have mercy; how came it cloven?

PANDARUS Why, you know 'tis dimpled; I think his smiling becomes him better than any man in all Phrygia.

CRESSIDA O, he smiles valiantly.

PANDARUS Does he not?

CRESSIDA O, yes, an 'twere a cloud in autumn.

110 a merry Greek i.e., one of frivolous or loose behavior (slang) **112 compassed** bay **120 so old a lifter** so experienced a thief (cf. "shoplifter")

PANDARUS Why, go to then. But to prove to you that Helen loves Troilus——

CRESSIDA Troilus will stand to the proof if you'll prove it so.

PANDARUS Troilus? Why, he esteems her no more than I esteem an addle egg.

CRESSIDA If you love an addle egg as well as you love an idle head, you would eat chickens i' the shell.

PANDARUS I cannot choose but laugh to think how she tickled his chin. Indeed, she has a marvel's white hand, I must needs confess.

CRESSIDA Without the rack.

PANDARUS And she takes upon her to spy a white hair on his chin.

CRESSIDA Alas poor chin, many a wart is richer.

PANDARUS But there was such laughing. Queen Hecuba laughed that her eyes ran o'er.

CRESSIDA With millstones.

PANDARUS And Cassandra laughed.

CRESSIDA But there was a more temperate fire under the pot of her eyes. Did her eyes run o'er too?

PANDARUS And Hector laughed.

CRESSIDA At what was all this laughing?

PANDARUS Marry, at the white hair that Helen spied on Troilus' chin.

CRESSIDA An't had been a green hair, I should have laughed too.

PANDARUS They laughed not so much at the hair as at his pretty answer.

133 **stand** (a bawdy pun; cf. Sonnet 151) 136 **addle** rotten 140 **marvel's** marvelous 142 **rack** torture 154 **Marry** (an interjection, from the oath, "By the Virgin Mary")

CRESSIDA What was his answer?

PANDARUS Quoth she, "Here's but two-and-fifty hairs on your chin, and one of them is white."

CRESSIDA This is her question.

PANDARUS That's true, make no question of that. "Two-and-fifty hairs," quoth he, "and one white. That white hair is my father, and all the rest are his sons." "Jupiter!" quoth she, "which of these hairs is Paris, my husband?" "The forked one," quoth he; "pluck't out, and give it him." But there was such laughing, and Helen so blushed, and Paris so chafed, and all the rest so laughed, that it passed.

CRESSIDA So let it now, for it has been a great while going by.

PANDARUS Well, cousin, I told you a thing yesterday; think on't.

CRESSIDA So I do.

PANDARUS I'll be sworn 'tis true; he will weep you, an 'twere a man born in April. *Sound a retreat.*

CRESSIDA And I'll spring up in his tears, an 'twere a nettle against May.

PANDARUS Hark, they are coming from the field. Shall we stand up here and see them as they pass toward Ilium? Good niece, do; sweet niece, Cressida.

CRESSIDA At your pleasure.

PANDARUS Here, here, here's an excellent place; here we may see most bravely. I'll tell you them all by their names as they pass by, but mark Troilus above the rest.

Enter Aeneas [and passes across the stage].

168 **forked** (resembling a cuckold's horns [?]) 178 **an** as if 180 **against** in advance of 186 **bravely** excellently

CRESSIDA Speak not so loud.

PANDARUS That's Aeneas. Is not that a brave man? He's one of the flowers of Troy, I can tell you. But mark Troilus; you shall see anon.

Enter Antenor [*and passes across the stage*].

CRESSIDA Who's that?

PANDARUS That's Antenor. He has a shrewd wit, I can tell you; and he's man good enough—he's one o' the soundest judgments in Troy whosoever, and a proper man of person. When comes Troilus? I'll show you Troilus anon. If he see me, you shall see him nod at me.

CRESSIDA Will he give you the nod?

PANDARUS You shall see.

CRESSIDA If he do, the rich shall have more.

Enter Hector [*and passes across the stage*].

PANDARUS That's Hector, that, that, look you, that; there's a fellow! Go thy way, Hector! There's a brave man, niece. O brave Hector! Look how he looks; there's a countenance! Is't not a brave man?

CRESSIDA O, a brave man.

PANDARUS Is 'a not? It does a man's heart good. Look you what hacks are on his helmet. Look you yonder, do you see? Look you there. There's no jesting; there's laying on, take't off who will, as they say. There be hacks!

CRESSIDA Be those with swords?

190 **brave** fine 197 **proper** handsome 200 **nod** (play on "noddy," simpleton) 202 **the rich shall have more** i.e., the fool shall become more foolish 211 **take't off who will** i.e., whoever cares to say otherwise (to "lay on" and "take off" were common colloquial tags)

PANDARUS Swords, anything, he cares not; an the devil come to him, it's all one. By God's lid, it does one's heart good.

Enter Paris [*and passes across the stage*].

Yonder comes Paris, yonder comes Paris. Look ye yonder, niece. Is't not a gallant man too, is't not? Why, this is brave now. Who said he came hurt home today? He's not hurt. Why, this will do Helen's heart good now, ha? Would I could see Troilus now. You shall see Troilus anon.

CRESSIDA Who's that?

Enter Helenus [*and passes across the stage*].

PANDARUS That's Helenus. I marvel where Troilus is. That's Helenus. I think he went not forth today. That's Helenus.

CRESSIDA Can Helenus fight, uncle?

PANDARUS Helenus? No. Yes, he'll fight indifferent well. I marvel where Troilus is. Hark, do you not hear the people cry "Troilus"? Helenus is a priest.

CRESSIDA What sneaking fellow comes yonder?

Enter Troilus [*and passes across the stage*].

PANDARUS Where? Yonder? That's Deiphobus. 'Tis Troilus! There's a man, niece, hem? Brave Troilus, the prince of chivalry!

CRESSIDA Peace, for shame, peace!

PANDARUS Mark him, note him. O brave Troilus! Look well upon him, niece. Look you how his sword is bloodied, and his helm more hacked than Hector's—and how he looks, and how he goes. O

218 **gallant** (general term of praise, as "brave')

admirable youth! He never saw three-and-twenty. Go thy way, Troilus, go thy way! Had I a sister were a grace, or a daughter a goddess, he should take his choice. O admirable man! Paris? Paris is dirt to him; and I warrant Helen, to change, would give an eye to boot.

Enter Common Soldiers.

CRESSIDA Here comes more.

PANDARUS Asses, fools, dolts; chaff and bran, chaff and bran; porridge after meat. I could live and die in the eyes of Troilus. Ne'er look, ne'er look. The eagles are gone; crows and daws, crows and daws. I had rather be such a man as Troilus than Agamemnon and all Greece.

CRESSIDA There is amongst the Greeks Achilles, a better man than Troilus.

PANDARUS Achilles? A drayman, a porter, a very camel.

CRESSIDA Well, well.

PANDARUS "Well, well"? Why, have you any discretion, have you any eyes, do you know what a man is? Is not birth, beauty, good shape, discourse, manhood, learning, gentleness, virtue, youth, liberality, and such like, the spice and salt that season a man?

CRESSIDA Ay, a minced man; and then to be baked with no date in the pie, for then the man's date is out.

242 **grace** attendant goddess 255 **drayman** one who draws a cart 255 **camel** i.e., beast of burden 263 **minced** (1) mincing, affected (2) overspiced (3) divided into parts beyond recognition 263–65 **then to be baked ... out** (dates were a common ingredient in most pastries; Cressida's pun implies that Troilus, as Pandarus compounds hm, could contain no substance and be of no interest, out of date)

PANDARUS You are such a woman a man knows not at what ward you lie.

CRESSIDA Upon my back, to defend my belly; upon my wit, to defend my wiles; upon my secrecy, to defend mine honesty; my mask, to defend my beauty; and you, to defend all these. And at all these wards I lie, at a thousand watches.

PANDARUS Say one of your watches.

CRESSIDA Nay, I'll watch you for that; and that's one of the chiefest of them too. If I cannot ward what I would not have hit, I can watch you for telling how I took the blow; unless it swell past hiding, and then it's past watching.

PANDARUS You are such another!

Enter [Troilus'] Boy.

BOY Sir, my lord would instantly speak with you.

PANDARUS Where?

BOY At your own house. There he unarms him.

PANDARUS Good boy, tell him I come. [*Exit Boy.*]
I doubt he be hurt. Fare ye well, good niece.

CRESSIDA Adieu, uncle.

PANDARUS I will be with you, niece, by and by.

CRESSIDA To bring, uncle.

PANDARUS Ay, a token from Troilus.

267 **ward** position of defense in swordplay 270 **honesty** chastity 272 **watches** periods of the night 276 **watch you for telling** i.e., to make certain you do not tell 277 **swell past hiding** (Cressida thus completes her ribald play on words) 284 **doubt** suspect that, fear that 287 **To bring** (an idiomatic intensifier, now obsolete, meaning roughly, "indeed" or "with a vengeance"; Cressida says, with mild sarcasm, "yes, I am sure you will," although Pandarus picks up the word in its normal verbal sense)

CRESSIDA By the same token, you are a bawd.

Exit Pandarus.

Words, vows, gifts, tears, and love's full sacrifice
He offers in another's enterprise;
But more in Troilus thousandfold I see
Than in the glass of Pandar's praise may be.
Yet hold I off. Women are angels, wooing;
Things won are done, joy's soul lies in the doing.
That she beloved knows nought that knows not this:
Men prize the thing ungained more than it is;
That she was never yet, that ever knew
Love got so sweet as when desire did sue.
Therefore this maxim out of love I teach:
Achievement is command; ungained, beseech.
Then, though my heart's content firm love
doth bear,
Nothing of that shall from mine eyes appear. *Exit.*

[Scene III. *The Greek camp.*]

Sennet. Enter Agamemnon, Nestor, Ulysses, Diomedes, Menelaus, with others.

AGAMEMNON Princes,
What grief hath set these jaundies o'er your cheeks?
The ample proposition that hope makes
In all designs begun on earth below
Fails in the promised largeness. Checks and disasters

294 **wooing** while being wooed 296 **That she** that woman 297 **it is** its value 299 **got** i.e., by men 300 **out of love** from love's teaching 301 **Achievement . . . beseech** when men achieve love, they command; while still trying to gain it, they will beg I.iii.s.d. **Sennet** (a trumpet call announcing specific personages in a procession) 2 **jaundies** jaundice (an obsolete plural)

Grow in the veins of actions highest reared,
As knots, by the conflux of meeting sap,
Infects the sound pine and diverts his grain
Tortive and errant from his course of growth.
Nor, princes, is it matter new to us
That we come short of our suppose so far
That after seven years' siege yet Troy walls stand;
Sith every action that hath gone before,
Whereof we have record, trial did draw
Bias and thwart, not answering the aim
And that unbodied figure of the thought
That gave't surmisèd shape. Why then, you princes,
Do you with cheeks abashed behold our works
And call them shames, which are indeed nought
  else
But the protractive trials of great Jove
To find persistive constancy in men?
The fineness of which metal is not found
In Fortune's love; for then, the bold and coward,
The wise and fool, the artist and unread,
The hard and soft, seem all affined and kin.
But, in the wind and tempest of her frown,
Distinction, with a broad and powerful fan,
Puffing at all, winnows the light away,
And what hath mass or matter by itself
Lies rich in virtue and unmingled.

NESTOR With due observance of thy godlike seat,
Great Agamemnon, Nestor shall apply
Thy latest words. In the reproof of chance
Lies the true proof of men. The sea being smooth,
How many shallow bauble boats dare sail
Upon her patient breast, making their way
With those of nobler bulk?

7 **conflux** flowing together 9 **Tortive and errant** twisted and wandering 11 **suppose** anticipation 15 **Bias and thwart** to one side and crosswise 18 **cheeks abashed** i.e., faces turned aside in confusion and shame 20 **protractive** extended 24 **artist** scholar 25 **affined** in affinity, related 30 **unmingled** unmixed with other essences 32 **apply** show examples of (as in a rhetorical exercise) 33 **reproof** rebuff

But let the ruffian Boreas once enrage
The gentle Thetis, and anon behold
The strong-ribbed bark through liquid mountains cut,
Bounding between the two moist elements
Like Perseus' horse, where's then the saucy boat,
Whose weak untimbered sides but even now
Corrivaled greatness? Either to harbor fled,
Or made a toast for Neptune. Even so
Doth valor's show and valor's worth divide
In storms of fortune. For in her ray and brightness
The herd hath more annoyance by the breese
Than by the tiger; but when the splitting wind
Makes flexible the knees of knotted oaks,
And flies fled under shade, why then the thing of courage,
As roused with rage, with rage doth sympathize,
And with an accent tuned in selfsame key
Returns to chiding fortune.

ULYSSES Agamemnon,
Thou great commander, nerves and bone of Greece,
Heart of our numbers, soul and only sprite,
In whom the tempers and the minds of all
Should be shut up, hear what Ulysses speaks.
Besides th' applause and approbation
The which [*to Agamemnon*], most mighty for thy place and sway,
[*to Nestor*] And thou most reverend for thy stretched-out life,
I give to both your speeches—which were such
As Agamemnon and the hand of Greece
Should hold up high in brass; and such again

38 **Boreas** (the north wind) 39 **Thetis** (a sea maiden, Achilles' mother, but here personifying the sea) 42 **Perseus' horse** (Pegasus, the winged horse) 45 **toast** (a piece of toast was usually soaked in wine) 46 **show** outward appearance 48 **breese** gadfly 52 **sympathize** becomes similar to 54 **Returns** replies 55 **nerves** sinews 56 **sprite** spirit 58 **shut up** gathered in

As venerable Nestor, hatched in silver,
Should with a bond of air, strong as the axletree
On which heaven rides, knit all the Greekish ears
To his experienced tongue—yet let it please both,
Thou great, and wise, to hear Ulysses speak.

AGAMEMNON Speak, Prince of Ithaca; and be't of less
expect
That matter needless, of importless burden,
Divide thy lips than we are confident,
When rank Thersites opes his mastic jaws,
We shall hear music, wit, and oracle.

ULYSSES Troy, yet upon his basis, had been down,
And the great Hector's sword had lacked a master,
But for these instances.
The specialty of rule hath been neglected;
And look, how many Grecian tents do stand
Hollow upon this plain, so many hollow factions.
When that the general is not like the hive
To whom the foragers shall all repair,
What honey is expected? Degree being vizarded,
Th' unworthiest shows as fairly in the mask.
The heavens themselves, the planets, and this center
Observe degree, priority, and place,
Insisture, course, proportion, season, form,
Office, and custom, in all line of order.
And therefore is the glorious planet Sol
In noble eminence enthroned and sphered
Amidst the other; whose med'cinable eye
Corrects the influence of evil planets,

65 **hatched in silver** (referring to the silver lines in his hair) 73 **mastic** abusive, scourging (sometimes emended to "mastiff") 77 **instances** reasons 78 **The specialty of rule** the particular organization of ruling, the distinction of rights in a chain of authority 81–83 **When ... expected** i.e., when the endeavors of the general populace are not similar to those of the agent which rules them, and to which they are responsible, what profit can be expected? (?); when the ruling general is dissimilar in kind to the soldiers in his army, what profit, etc. (?) 83 **Degree being vizarded** the hierarchy of authority being hidden 87 **Insisture** regularity of position 89 **Sol** the sun 91 **other** others 92 **influence** astrological effect

And posts, like the commandment of a king,
Sans check, to good and bad. But when the planets
In evil mixture to disorder wander,
What plagues, and what portents, what mutiny,
What raging of the sea, shaking of earth,
Commotion in the winds, frights, changes, horrors,
Divert and crack, rend and deracinate
The unity and married calm of states
Quite from their fixure? O, when degree is shaked,
Which is the ladder of all high designs,
The enterprise is sick. How could communities,
Degrees in schools, and brotherhoods in cities,
Peaceful commerce from dividable shores,
The primogenity and due of birth,
Prerogative of age, crowns, scepters, laurels,
But by degree, stand in authentic place?
Take but degree away, untune that string,
And hark what discord follows. Each thing meets
In mere oppugnancy. The bounded waters
Should lift their bosoms higher than the shores
And make a sop of all this solid globe;
Strength should be lord of imbecility,
And the rude son should strike his father dead;
Force should be right, or rather right and wrong—
Between whose endless jar justice resides—
Should lose their names, and so should justice too.
Then everything include itself in power,
Power into will, will into appetite,
And appetite, an universal wolf,
So doubly seconded with will and power,
Must make perforce an universal prey
And last eat up himself. Great Agamemnon,
This chaos, when degree is suffocate,
Follows the choking.
And this neglection of degree it is

95 **evil mixture** unlucky or malignant relationship (astrological) 99 **deracinate** uproot 106 **primogenity** right of the eldest son to succeed to his father's estate 111 **mere oppugnancy** total strife 113 **sop** pulp 114 **imbecility** i.e., weakness 117 **jar** discord 119 **include itself in power** enclose itself within power, i.e., become power

That by a pace goes backward with a purpose
It hath to climb. The general's disdained
By him one step below, he by the next,
That next by him beneath; so every step,
Exampled by the first pace that is sick
Of his superior, grows to an envious fever
Of pale and bloodless emulation;
And 'tis this fever that keeps Troy on foot,
Not her own sinews. To end a tale of length,
Troy in our weakness stands, not in her strength.

NESTOR Most wisely hath Ulysses here discovered
The fever whereof all our power is sick.

AGAMEMNON The nature of the sickness found,
Ulysses,
What is the remedy?

ULYSSES The great Achilles, whom opinion crowns
The sinew and the forehand of our host,
Having his ear full of his airy fame,
Grows dainty of his worth, and in his tent
Lies mocking our designs. With him Patroclus
Upon a lazy bed the livelong day
Breaks scurril jests,
And with ridiculous and silly action
(Which, slanderer, he imitation calls)
He pageants us. Sometimes, great Agamemnon,
Thy topless deputation he puts on,
And, like a strutting player, whose conceit
Lies in his hamstring, and doth think it rich
To hear the wooden dialogue and sound
'Twixt his stretched footing and the scaffoldage,

127–29 **And this neglection . . . climb** this neglect of hierarchy causes a step toward disintegration each time an attempt is made to climb upward 134 **emulation** rivalry 145 **dainty of** finicky about 149–50 **silly action . . . imitation** (Ulysses contrasts such charades with true imitation to the life, presumably the goal of the excellent actor) 151 **pageants** mimics 152 **topless deputation** unlimited office 153–54 **conceit Lies in his hamstring** imagination lies in the tendon of his leg 155 **wooden dialogue** i.e., the thumps of heavy footfalls on the wooden stage floor 156 **stretched footing** absurdly long strides 156 **scaffoldage** scaffold, stage

Such to-be-pitied and o'erwrested seeming
He acts thy greatness in; and when he speaks,
'Tis like a chime a-mending, with terms unsquared,
Which, from the tongue of roaring Typhon dropped,
Would seem hyperboles. At this fusty stuff
The large Achilles, on his pressed bed lolling,
From his deep chest laughs out a loud applause,
Cries, "Excellent! 'tis Agamemnon right.
Now play me Nestor; hem, and stroke thy beard,
As he being drest to some oration."
That's done, as near as the extremest ends
Of parallels, as like as Vulcan and his wife,
Yet god Achilles still cries, "Excellent!
'Tis Nestor right. Now play him me, Patroclus,
Arming to answer in a night alarm."
And then, forsooth, the faint defects of age
Must be the scene of mirth; to cough and spit,
And with a palsy fumbling on his gorget,
Shake in and out the rivet. And at this sport
Sir Valor dies; cries, "O, enough, Patroclus,
Or give me ribs of steel; I shall split all
In pleasure of my spleen!" And in this fashion
All our abilities, gifts, natures, shapes,
Severals and generals of grace exact,
Achievements, plots, orders, preventions,
Excitements to the field or speech for truce,
Success or loss, what is or is not, serves
As stuff for these two to make paradoxes.

157 **o'erwrested seeming** overstrained impersonation 159 **chime a-mending** (1) chime being repaired (2) dissonant combination of sounds just following the ringing of many chimes (?) 159 **unsquared** inappropriate 160 **roaring Typhon** (a monster with serpents' heads and a tremendous voice) 161 **fusty** stale, second-rate 166 **drest** carefully prepared for, addressed 168 **Vulcan and his wife** (Vulcan, god of the smithy and forge, was depicted as sooty, and was lame besides; his "wife" was Venus, who cuckolded him with Mars) 170 **me** i.e., for me 174 **gorget** throat armor 178 **spleen** (supposed the seat of the emotions of anger and hilarity) 180 **Severals and generals** individual and general qualities 184 **paradoxes** absurdities

NESTOR And in the imitation of these twain,
Who, as Ulysses says, opinion crowns
With an imperial voice, many are infect.
Ajax is grown self-willed, and bears his head
In such a rein, in full as proud a place
As broad Achilles; keeps his tent like him;
Makes factious feasts; rails on our state of war,
Bold as an oracle, and sets Thersites,
A slave whose gall coins slanders like a mint,
To match us in comparisons with dirt,
To weaken and discredit our exposure,
How rank soever rounded in with danger.

ULYSSES They tax our policy and call it cowardice,
Count wisdom as no member of the war,
Forestall prescience, and esteem no act
But that of hand. The still and mental parts
That do contrive how many hands shall strike
When fitness calls them on, and know by measure
Of their observant toil the enemies' weight—
Why, this hath not a finger's dignity.
They call this bed-work, mapp'ry, closet war;
So that the ram that batters down the wall,
For the great swinge and rudeness of his poise,
They place before his hand that made the engine,
Or those that with the fineness of their souls
By reason guide his execution.

NESTOR Let this be granted, and Achilles' horse
Makes many Thetis' sons. *Tucket.*

AGAMEMNON What trumpet? Look, Menelaus.

MENELAUS From Troy.

189 **In such a rein** i.e., so high 193 **gall** (the source of bile, which was thought to produce rancor and abuse) 196 **rank** densely, abundantly 197 **tax** criticize 199 **Forestall prescience** discount foresight 202 **fitness** readiness 205 **mapp'ry** map work 207 **swinge** impetus, whirling force 211 **Achilles' horse** (either literally, or collectively, for his soldiers, the Myrmidons) 212 s.d. **Tucket** trumpet call

Enter Aeneas.

AGAMEMNON What would you 'fore our tent?

AENEAS Is this great Agamemnon's tent, I pray you?

AGAMEMNON Even this.

AENEAS May one that is a herald and a prince
Do a fair message to his kingly eyes?

AGAMEMNON With surety stronger than Achilles' arm
'Fore all the Greekish heads, which with one voice
Call Agamemnon head and general.

AENEAS Fair leave and large security. How may
A stranger to those most imperial looks
Know them from eyes of other mortals?

AGAMEMNON How?

AENEAS Ay.
I ask, that I might waken reverence,
And bid the cheek be ready with a blush
Modest as morning when she coldly eyes
The youthful Phoebus.
Which is that god in office, guiding men?
Which is the high and mighty Agamemnon?

AGAMEMNON This Troyan scorns us, or the men of Troy
Are ceremonious courtiers.

AENEAS Courtiers as free, as debonair, unarmed,
As bending angels; that's their fame in peace.
But when they would seem soldiers, they have galls,
Good arms, strong joints, true swords—and, great Jove's accord,
Nothing so full of heart. But peace, Aeneas;
Peace, Troyan; lay thy finger on thy lips.
The worthiness of praise distains his worth,

219 **to his kingly eyes** i.e., in his presence 230 **Phoebus** Phoebus Apollo (the sun god) 236 **bending** bowing 238 **Jove's accord** i.e., with Jove on their side 241 **distains** sullies

If that the praised himself bring the praise forth.
But what the repining enemy commends,
That breath fame blows; that praise, sole pure,
transcends.

AGAMEMNON Sir, you of Troy, call you yourself
Aeneas?

AENEAS Ay, Greek, that is my name.

AGAMEMNON What's your affair, I pray you?

AENEAS Sir, pardon; 'tis for Agamemnon's ears.

AGAMEMNON He hears nought privately that comes
from Troy.

AENEAS Nor I from Troy come not to whisper him.
I bring a trumpet to awake his ear,
To set his seat on the attentive bent,
And then to speak.

AGAMEMNON Speak frankly as the wind;
It is not Agamemnon's sleeping hour.
That thou shalt know, Troyan, he is awake,
He tells thee so himself.

AENEAS Trumpet, blow loud,
Send thy brass voice through all these lazy tents;
And every Greek of mettle, let him know,
What Troy means fairly shall be spoke aloud.
Sound trumpet.
We have, great Agamemnon, here in Troy
A prince called Hector—Priam is his father—
Who in this dull and long-continued truce
Is rusty grown. He bade me take a trumpet,
And to this purpose speak: kings, princes, lords,
If there be one among the fair'st of Greece
That holds his honor higher than his ease,
That seeks his praise more than he fears his peril,
That knows his valor and knows not his fear,
That loves his mistress more than in confession

252 To . . . bent i.e., to make him, and his place of government, pay attention **263 trumpet** i.e., a trumpeter in attendance

With truant vows to her own lips he loves,
And dare avow her beauty and her worth
In other arms than hers—to him this challenge;
Hector, in view of Troyans and of Greeks,
Shall make it good, or do his best to do it;
He hath a lady wiser, fairer, truer,
Than ever Greek did compass in his arms;
And will tomorrow with his trumpet call,
Midway between your tents and walls of Troy,
To rouse a Grecian that is true in love.
If any come, Hector shall honor him;
If none, he'll say in Troy when he retires,
The Grecian dames are sunburnt and not worth
The splinter of a lance. Even so much.

AGAMEMNON This shall be told our lovers, Lord Aeneas;
If none of them have soul in such a kind,
We left them all at home. But we are soldiers;
And may that soldier a mere recreant prove,
That means not, hath not, or is not in love!
If then one is, or hath, or means to be,
That one meets Hector; if none else, I am he.

NESTOR Tell him of Nestor, one that was a man
When Hector's grandsire sucked. He is old now,
But if there be not in our Grecian host
A nobleman that hath one spark of fire
To answer for his love, tell him from me,
I'll hide my silver beard in a gold beaver,
And in my vantbrace put my withered brawns,
And, meeting him, will tell him that my lady
Was fairer than his grandam, and as chaste
As may be in the world. His youth in flood,
I'll prove this truth with my three drops of blood.

269–70 **That loves ... lips he loves,** i.e., one that loves his mistress even more than the false oaths of lip service (?); more than enough to swear false vows that he loves her (?) 272 **In other arms than hers** i.e., with weapons 282 **sunburnt** dark (for the Elizabethans, ugly) 296 **beaver** movable face-guard of a helmet 297 **vantbrace** armor fitting the forearm 297 **brawns** arm (or leg) muscles (an obsolete plural)

AENEAS Now heavens forfend such scarcity of youth!

ULYSSES Amen.

[AGAMEMNON] Fair Lord Aeneas, let me touch your
hand;
To our pavilion shall I lead you first.
Achilles shall have word of this intent;
So shall each lord of Greece, from tent to tent.
Yourself shall feast with us before you go,
And find the welcome of a noble foe.

Exeunt. Manent Ulysses and Nestor.

ULYSSES Nestor.

NESTOR What says Ulysses?

ULYSSES I have a young conception in my brain;
Be you my time to bring it to some shape.

NESTOR What is't?

ULYSSES This 'tis:
Blunt wedges rive hard knots; the seeded pride
That hath to this maturity blown up
In rank Achilles, must or now be cropped
Or, shedding, breed a nursery of like evil
To overbulk us all.

NESTOR Well, and how?

ULYSSES This challenge that the gallant Hector sends,
However it is spread in general name,
Relates in purpose only to Achilles.

NESTOR True, the purpose is perspicuous as substance
Whose grossness little characters sum up;
And, in the publication, make no strain
But that Achilles, were his brain as barren
As banks of Libya—though, Apollo knows,
'Tis dry enough—will with great speed of judgment,

309 s.d. Manent (they) remain **312–13 I have . . . some shape** i.e., I have the beginning of an idea; let me develop it as you listen **319 shedding** i.e., scattering seed **325 Whose grossness . . . sum up** whose large size can be defined by small figures **326 make no strain** you may be sure

Ay with celerity, find Hector's purpose
Pointing on him.

ULYSSES And wake him to the answer, think you?

NESTOR Why, 'tis most meet. Who may you else
oppose
That can from Hector bring his honor off,
If not Achilles? Though't be a sportful combat,
Yet in the trial much opinion dwells;
For here the Troyans taste our dear'st repute
With their fin'st palate; and trust to me, Ulysses,
Our imputation shall be oddly poised
In this vild action. For the success,
Although particular, shall give a scantling
Of good or bad unto the general;
And in such indexes, although small pricks
To their subsequent volumes, there is seen
The baby figure of the giant mass
Of things to come at large. It is supposed
He that meets Hector issues from our choice;
And choice, being mutual act of all our souls,
Makes merit her election, and doth boil,
As 'twere from forth us all, a man distilled
Out of our virtues—who miscarrying,
What heart receives from hence a conquering part,
To steel a strong opinion to themselves;
Which entertained, limbs are his instruments,
In no less working than are swords and bows
Directive by the limbs.

ULYSSES Give pardon to my speech. Therefore 'tis
meet
Achilles meet not Hector. Let us, like merchants,
First show foul wares, and think perchance they'll
sell;

336 **opinion** reputation 337–38 **taste ... palate** put our most valued reputation to the test of their most careful, sensitive observation 339–40 **Our ... action** our reputation shall be unequally balanced in this trivial action 341 **scantling** sample 342 **general** (1) general view (2) entire army 343–44 **small ... volumes** small markings compared to the great significance to follow 349 **election** criteria for choice 354 **his** i.e., of the strong opinion

If not, the luster of the better shall exceed
By showing the worse first. Do not consent
That ever Hector and Achilles meet;
For both our honor and our shame in this
Are dogged with two strange followers.

NESTOR I see them not with my old eyes; what are
they?

ULYSSES What glory our Achilles shares from Hector,
Were he not proud, we all should share with him.
But he already is too insolent,
And it were better parch in Afric sun
Than in the pride and salt scorn of his eyes,
Should he 'scape Hector fair. If he were foiled,
Why then we do our main opinion crush
In taint of our best man. No, make a lott'ry;
And by device let blockish Ajax draw
The sort to fight with Hector; among ourselves
Give him allowance for the better man,
For that will physic the great Myrmidon
Who broils in loud applause, and make him fall
His crest that prouder than blue Iris bends.
If the dull brainless Ajax comes safe off,
We'll dress him up in voices; if he fail,
Yet go we under our opinion still
That we have better men. But, hit or miss,
Our project's life this shape of sense assumes:
Ajax employed plucks down Achilles' plumes.

NESTOR Now, Ulysses, I begin to relish thy advice,
And I will give a taste thereof forthwith
To Agamemnon. Go we to him straight.
Two curs shall tame each other; pride alone
Must tarre the mastiffs on, as 'twere a bone.

Exeunt.

364 **followers** consequences 370 **salt** bitter 372 **our main opinion** the mainstay of our reputation 373 **In taint of** to the loss of, with the shame of 375 **sort** lot 377 **the great Myrmidon** (Achilles, whose father, Peleus, had subjects called Myrmidons) 387 **broils** bakes; i.e., suns himself 379 **Iris** (the rainbow) 390 **tarre** incite, provoke

[ACT II

Scene I. *The Greek camp.*]

Enter Ajax and Thersites.

AJAX Thersites!

THERSITES Agamemnon, how if he had boils—full, all over, generally?

AJAX Thersites!

THERSITES And those boils did run?—say so—did not the general run then? Were not that a botchy core?

AJAX Dog!

THERSITES Then would come some matter from him. I see none now.

AJAX Thou bitch-wolf's son, canst thou not hear? Feel then. *Strikes him.*

THERSITES The plague of Greece upon thee, thou mongrel beef-witted lord!

AJAX Speak then, thou vinewed'st leaven, speak. I will beat thee into handsomeness.

II.i.6 botchy core erupted boil 14 vinewed'st leaven most mildewed dough

THERSITES I shall sooner rail thee into wit and holiness; but I think thy horse will sooner con an oration than thou learn a prayer without book. Thou canst strike, canst thou? A red murrain o' thy jade's tricks!

AJAX Toadstool, learn me the proclamation.

THERSITES Dost thou think I have no sense, thou strikest me thus?

AJAX The proclamation!

THERSITES Thou art proclaimed fool, I think.

AJAX Do not, porpentine, do not; my fingers itch.

THERSITES I would thou didst itch from head to foot; an I had the scratching of thee, I would make thee the loathsomest scab in Greece. When thou art forth in the incursions, thou strikest as slow as another.

AJAX I say, the proclamation!

THERSITES Thou grumblest and railest every hour on Achilles, and thou art as full of envy at his greatness as Cerberus is at Proserpina's beauty, ay, that thou bark'st at him.

AJAX Mistress Thersites!

THERSITES Thou shouldst strike him.

AJAX Cobloaf!

THERSITES He would pun thee into shivers with his fist, as a sailor breaks a biscuit.

AJAX You whoreson cur! [*Beating him.*]

17 **con** memorize 18 **without book** by heart 19 **red murrain** (form of plague manifested in red skin eruptions) 20 **jade's** nag's 21 **learn me** find out for me 26 **porpentine** porcupine 30 **incursions** battle raids, attacks 35 **Cerberus** (the monstrous watchdog of Hades) 35 **Proserpina** (a beautiful goddess carried off by Pluto to the underworld) 39 **Cobloaf** a badly baked, crusty loaf of bread 40 **pun** pound

THERSITES Do, do.

AJAX Thou stool for a witch!

THERSITES Ay, do, do, thou sodden-witted lord! thou hast no more brain than I have in mine elbows; an asinico may tutor thee. Thou scurvy-valiant ass, thou art here but to thrash Troyans, and thou art bought and sold among those of any wit like a barbarian slave. If thou use to beat me, I will begin at thy heel, and tell what thou art by inches, thou thing of no bowels, thou!

AJAX You dog!

THERSITES You scurvy lord!

AJAX You cur! [*Beating him.*]

THERSITES Mars his idiot! Do, rudeness; do, camel; do, do.

Enter Achilles and Patroclus.

ACHILLES Why, how now, Ajax, wherefore do you thus? How now, Thersites, what's the matter, man?

THERSITES You see him there? Do you?

ACHILLES Ay, what's the matter?

THERSITES Nay, look upon him.

ACHILLES So I do. What's the matter?

THERSITES Nay, but regard him well.

ACHILLES "Well"—why so I do.

THERSITES But yet you look not well upon him; for, whosomever you take him to be, he is Ajax.

ACHILLES I know that, fool.

47 **asinico** ass, simpleton 49 **bought and sold** i.e., made fun of 52 **bowels** mercy (the bowels were thought to be the source of compassion) 56 **Mars his** Mars's 67 **whosomever** whomsoever

THERSITES Ay, but that fool knows not himself.

AJAX Therefore I beat thee.

THERSITES Lo, lo, lo, lo, what modicums of wit he utters! His evasions have ears thus long. I have bobbed his brain more than he has beat my bones. I will buy nine sparrows for a penny, and his pia mater is not worth the ninth part of a sparrow. This lord, Achilles, Ajax, who wears his wit in his belly and his guts in his head, I'll tell you what I say of him.

ACHILLES What?

THERSITES I say, this Ajax——

[*Ajax threatens to strike him.*]

ACHILLES Nay, good Ajax.

THERSITES Has not so much wit——

[*Ajax threatens again to strike him.*]

ACHILLES Nay, I must hold you.

THERSITES As will stop the eye of Helen's needle, for whom he comes to fight.

ACHILLES Peace, fool!

THERSITES I would have peace and quietness, but the fool will not—he there, that he. Look you there.

AJAX O thou damned cur, I shall——

ACHILLES Will you set your wit to a fool's?

THERSITES No, I warrant you; the fool's will shame it.

PATROCLUS Good words, Thersites.

ACHILLES What's the quarrel?

69 **that fool** (as though Achilles had said "I know that fool") 72 **thus long** i.e., as long as those of an ass 74–75 **pia mater** i.e., brain (literally, the membrane covering the brain) 90 **set** match

AJAX I bade the vile owl go learn me the tenor of the proclamation, and he rails upon me.

THERSITES I serve thee not.

AJAX Well, go to, go to.

THERSITES I serve here voluntary.

ACHILLES Your last service was suff'rance, 'twas not voluntary; no man is beaten voluntary. Ajax was here the voluntary, and you as under an impress.

THERSITES E'en so. A great deal of your wit, too, lies in your sinews, or else there be liars. Hector shall have a great catch if he knock out either of your brains. 'A were as good crack a fusty nut with no kernel.

ACHILLES What, with me too, Thersites?

THERSITES There's Ulysses and old Nestor, whose wit was moldy ere your grandsires had nails on their toes, yoke you like draft oxen and make you plow up the wars.

ACHILLES What, what?

THERSITES Yes, good sooth. To, Achilles! To, Ajax! To——

AJAX I shall cut out your tongue.

THERSITES 'Tis no matter, I shall speak as much as thou afterwards.

PATROCLUS No more words, Thersites; peace!

THERSITES I will hold my peace when Achilles' brach bids me, shall I?

ACHILLES There's for you, Patroclus.

THERSITES I will see you hanged like clotpoles, ere

101 impress (pun on impressment, compulsory military service) **113–114 To, Achilles! To, Ajax! To** (imitation of the shouts of a driver, urging on his horses) **119 brach** bitch **122 clotpoles** blockheads

I come any more to your tents. I will keep where there is wit stirring and leave the faction of fools.
Exit.

PATROCLUS A good riddance.

ACHILLES Marry, this, sir, is proclaimed through all our host:
That Hector, by the fifth hour of the sun,
Will, with a trumpet, 'twixt our tents and Troy
Tomorrow morning call some knight to arms
That hath a stomach, and such a one that dare
Maintain—I know not what; 'tis trash. Farewell.

AJAX Farewell? Who shall answer him?

ACHILLES I know not. 'Tis put to lott'ry. Otherwise,
He knew his man.
[*Exeunt Achilles and Patroclus.*]

AJAX O, meaning you? I will go learn more of it.
Exit.

[Scene II. *Troy; Priam's palace.*]

Enter Priam, Hector, Troilus, Paris, and Helenus.

PRIAM After so many hours, lives, speeches spent,
Thus once again says Nestor from the Greeks:
"Deliver Helen, and all damage else,
As honor, loss of time, travail, expense,
Wounds, friends, and what else dear that is consumed
In hot digestion of this cormorant war,
Shall be struck off." Hector, what say you to't?

127 **fifth hour** i.e., eleven in the morning 130 **stomach** temperament or relish (here, for chivalric achievement) II.ii.6 **cormorant** ravenous, rapacious

HECTOR Though no man lesser fears the Greeks than I,
As far as toucheth my particular,
Yet, dread Priam,
There is no lady of more softer bowels,
More spongy to suck in the sense of fear,
More ready to cry out, "Who knows what follows?"
Than Hector is. The wound of peace is surety,
Surety secure; but modest doubt is called
The beacon of the wise, the tent that searches
To the bottom of the worst. Let Helen go.
Since the first sword was drawn about this question,
Every tithe soul, 'mongst many thousand dismes,
Hath been as dear as Helen. I mean, of ours.
If we have lost so many tenths of ours
To guard a thing not ours nor worth to us,
Had it our name, the value of one ten,
What merit's in that reason which denies
The yielding of her up?

TROILUS Fie, fie, my brother!
Weigh you the worth and honor of a king
So great as our dread father in a scale
Of common ounces? Will you with counters sum
The past proportion of his infinite,
And buckle in a waist most fathomless
With spans and inches so diminutive
As fears and reasons? Fie, for godly shame!

HELENUS No marvel, though you bite so sharp at reasons,
You are so empty of them. Should not our father

9 **my particular** me, personally 11 **of more softer bowels** more averse to violence 14 **The wound of peace is surety** peace is endangered by a sense of safety 16 **tent** (roll of absorbent material, for cleaning or probing wounds) 19 **Every . . . dismes** every tenth soul, among many thousand tens (?); every soul taken by war as its tenth among many thousand such tenths (?) 23 **one ten** i.e., one in ten 28 **counters** pieces of worthless metal used for computation 29 **The past . . . infinite** i.e., his infinite greatness which is past all measurement 30 **fathomless** i.e., immeasurable 31 **spans** (units of measure averaging nine inches)

Bear the great sway of his affairs with reason,
Because your speech hath none that tell him so?

TROILUS You are for dreams and slumbers, brother priest;
You fur your gloves with reason. Here are your reasons:
You know an enemy intends you harm;
You know a sword employed is perilous,
And reason flies the object of all harm.
Who marvels then, when Helenus beholds
A Grecian and his sword, if he do set
The very wings of reason to his heels
And fly like chidden Mercury from Jove,
Or like a star disorbed? Nay, if we talk of reason,
Let's shut our gates and sleep! Manhood and honor
Should have hare-hearts, would they but fat their thoughts
With this crammed reason. Reason and respect
Make livers pale and lustihood deject.

HECTOR Brother, she is not worth what she doth cost
The keeping.

TROILUS What's aught but as 'tis valued?

HECTOR But value dwells not in particular will.
It holds his estimate and dignity
As well wherein 'tis precious of itself
As in the prizer. 'Tis mad idolatry
To make the service greater than the god;
And the will dotes that is attributive
To what infectiously itself affects,
Without some image of th' affected merit.

38 **You fur your gloves with reason** i.e., you use reason as a comfortable word with which to decorate your speech, much as fur lines gloves 41 **object** (here, presentation, sight) 46 **disorbed** thrown from its sphere 49 **crammed** filled to excess, doughy 50 **livers** (thought to be the seats of passions) 53 **particular will** the individual's inclination 54 **his** its 54 **dignity** value 56 **prizer** appraiser 58 **attributive** dependent, subservient 59–60 **To what . . . merit** to what it, to its own infection, desires, with no objective perception of the worth of the thing desired

TROILUS I take today a wife, and my election
Is led on in the conduct of my will—
My will enkindled by mine eyes and ears,
Two traded pilots 'twixt the dangerous shores
Of will and judgment. How may I avoid,
Although my will distaste what it elected,
The wife I chose? There can be no evasion
To blench from this and to stand firm by honor.
We turn not back the silks upon the merchant
When we have soiled them, nor the remainder viands
We do not throw in unrespective sieve
Because we now are full. It was thought meet
Paris should do some vengeance on the Greeks.
Your breath with full consent bellied his sails;
The seas and winds, old wranglers, took a truce
And did him service; he touched the ports desired,
And for an old aunt whom the Greeks held captive
He brought a Grecian queen, whose youth and freshness
Wrinkles Apollo's and makes pale the morning.
Why keep we her? The Grecians keep our aunt.
Is she worth keeping? Why, she is a pearl
Whose price hath launched above a thousand ships
And turned crowned kings to merchants.
If you'll avouch 'twas wisdom Paris went—
As you must needs, for you all cried, "Go, go"—
If you'll confess he brought home worthy prize—
As you must needs, for you all clapped your hands
And cried, "Inestimable!"—why do you now
The issue of your proper wisdoms rate,
And do a deed that never Fortune did:
Beggar the estimation which you prized

61–62 **I take ... my will—** (Troilus is setting forth, rhetorically, an example to prove his point; whatever he may be thinking, he is not announcing, of course, his approaching liaison with Cressida) 64 **traded** experienced 68 **blench** shrink 71 **unrespective sieve** common receptacle 77 **aunt** (Hesione, Priam's sister and Ajax's mother, married to Telamon; another son was Teucer, greatest archer among the Greeks) 89 **The issue ... rate** condemn the result of your own judgments 91 **estimation** thing esteemed

Richer than sea and land? O theft most base,
That we have stol'n what we do fear to keep!
But thieves unworthy of a thing so stol'n,
That in their country did them that disgrace
We fear to warrant in our native place.

Enter Cassandra raving with her hair about her ears.

CASSANDRA Cry, Troyans, cry!

PRIAM What noise? What shriek is this?

TROILUS 'Tis our mad sister. I do know her voice.

CASSANDRA Cry, Troyans!

HECTOR It is Cassandra.

CASSANDRA Cry, Troyans, cry! Lend me ten thousand eyes,
And I will fill them with prophetic tears.

HECTOR Peace, sister, peace!

CASSANDRA Virgins and boys, mid-age and wrinkled eld,
Soft infancy, that nothing canst but cry,
Add to my clamors! Let us pay betimes
A moiety of that mass of moan to come.
Cry, Troyans, cry! Practice your eyes with tears!
Troy must not be, nor goodly Ilion stand;
Our firebrand brother, Paris, burns us all.
Cry, Troyans, cry! A Helen and a woe!
Cry, cry! Troy burns, or else let Helen go. *Exit.*

HECTOR Now, youthful Troilus, do not these high strains
Of divination in our sister work
Some touches of remorse? Or is your blood

95 **disgrace** i.e., the abduction of Helen 96 **warrant** justify by defense 98 **our mad sister** (when Cassandra refused Apollo's love, he destroyed his former gift of prophecy by causing her never to be believed) 107 **moiety** part 110 **firebrand** (Hecuba dreamed she was delivered of a firebrand when Paris was born)

So madly hot that no discourse of reason,
Nor fear of bad success in a bad cause,
Can qualify the same?

TROILUS Why, brother Hector,
We may not think the justness of each act
Such and no other than event doth form it,
Nor once deject the courage of our minds
Because Cassandra's mad. Her brainsick raptures
Cannot distaste the goodness of a quarrel
Which hath our several honors all engaged
To make it gracious. For my private part,
I am no more touched than all Priam's sons;
And Jove forbid there should be done amongst us
Such things as might offend the weakest spleen
To fight for and maintain.

PARIS Else might the world convince of levity
As well my undertakings as your counsels;
But I attest the gods, your full consent
Gave wings to my propension and cut off
All fears attending on so dire a project.
For what, alas, can these my single arms?
What propugnation is in one man's valor
To stand the push and enmity of those
This quarrel would excite? Yet, I protest,
Were I alone to pass the difficulties,
And had as ample power as I have will,
Paris should ne'er retract what he hath done
Nor faint in the pursuit.

PRIAM Paris, you speak
Like one besotted on your sweet delights.
You have the honey still, but these the gall;
So to be valiant is no praise at all.

PARIS Sir, I propose not merely to myself

118 **qualify** moderate 120 **event** outcome 122 **brainsick raptures** fits of prophecy 123 **distaste** make distasteful 128 **spleen** temper, temperament 130 **convince** convict 133 **propension** inclination 136 **propugnation** defense 139 **pass** suffer, undergo

The pleasure such a beauty brings with it;
But I would have the soil of her fair rape
Wiped off in honorable keeping her.
What treason were it to the ransacked queen,
Disgrace to your great worths, and shame to me,
Now to deliver her possession up
On terms of base compulsion! Can it be
That so degenerate a strain as this
Should once set footing in your generous bosoms?
There's not the meanest spirit on our party
Without a heart to dare or sword to draw
When Helen is defended, nor none so noble
Whose life were ill bestowed or death unfamed
Where Helen is the subject. Then, I say,
Well may we fight for her whom we know well
The world's large spaces cannot parallel.

HECTOR Paris and Troilus, you have both said well,
And on the cause and question now in hand
Have glozed—but superficially: not much
Unlike young men, whom Aristotle thought
Unfit to hear moral philosophy.
The reasons you allege do more conduce
To the hot passion of distempered blood
Than to make up a free determination
'Twixt right and wrong; for pleasure and revenge
Have ears more deaf than adders to the voice
Of any true decision. Nature craves
All dues be rendered to their owners. Now,
What nearer debt in all humanity
Than wife is to the husband? If this law
Of nature be corrupted through affection,
And that great minds, of partial indulgence

148 **rape** carrying off 150 **ransacked** carried off 155 **generous** nobly born (therefore magnanimous) 165 **glozed** commented, glossed 167 **moral** (Aristotle wrote "political" [*Nicomachean Ethics*, I.3], but the use of "moral" here is paralleled in Erasmus, Bacon, and many other contemporary translations and commentaries; the two words were roughly interchangeable in sixteenth-century terminology) 172 **more deaf than adders** (cf. Psalm 58:4–5) 177 **affection** appetite 178 **partial** biased, favoring

To their benumbèd wills, resist the same,
There is a law in each well-ordered nation
To curb those raging appetites that are
Most disobedient and refractory.
If Helen, then, be wife to Sparta's king,
As it is known she is, these moral laws
Of nature and of nations speak aloud
To have her back returned. Thus to persist
In doing wrong extenuates not wrong,
But makes it much more heavy. Hector's opinion
Is this in way of truth. Yet ne'ertheless,
My spritely brethren, I propend to you
In resolution to keep Helen still;
For 'tis a cause that hath no mean dependence
Upon our joint and several dignities.

TROILUS Why, there you touched the life of our design!
Were it not glory that we more affected
Than the performance of our heaving spleens,
I would not wish a drop of Troyan blood
Spent more in her defense. But, worthy Hector,
She is a theme of honor and renown,
A spur to valiant and magnanimous deeds,
Whose present courage may beat down our foes
And fame in time to come canonize us;
For I presume brave Hector would not lose
So rich advantage of a promised glory
As smiles upon the forehead of this action
For the wide world's revenue.

HECTOR I am yours,
You valiant offspring of great Priamus.
I have a roisting challenge sent amongst
The dull and factious nobles of the Greeks
Will strike amazement to their drowsy spirits.
I was advertised their great general slept

179 **benumbèd** paralyzed (by affection and appetite) 187 **extenuates** lessens 190 **spritely** spirited 190 **propend** incline 193 **joint and several** collective and individual 196 **heaving spleens** angry passions 208 **roisting** noisy, clamorous 211 **advertised** informed

Whilst emulation in the army crept;
This, I presume, will wake him. *Exeunt.*

[Scene III. *The Greek camp; near Achilles' tent.*]

Enter Thersites solus.

THERSITES How now, Thersites? What, lost in the labyrinth of thy fury? Shall the elephant Ajax carry it thus? He beats me, and I rail at him. O worthy satisfaction! Would it were otherwise—that I could beat him, whilst he railed at me. 'Sfoot, I'll learn to conjure and raise devils, but I'll see some issue of my spiteful execrations. Then there's Achilles, a rare enginer. If Troy be not taken till these two undermine it, the walls will stand till they fall of themselves. O thou great thunder-darter of Olympus, forget that thou art Jove, the king of gods; and, Mercury, lose all the serpentine craft of thy caduceus, if ye take not that little, little, less than little wit from them that they have; which short-armed ignorance itself knows is so abundant scarce it will not in circumvention deliver a fly from a spider, without drawing their massy irons and cutting the web. After this, the vengeance on the whole camp! Or, rather, the Neapolitan bone-ache, for that, methinks, is the curse depending on those that war for a placket. I have said my prayers, and devil Envy say "Amen." What ho, my Lord Achilles!

212 **emulation** envious rivalry (see I.iii.134) II.iii.2–3 **carry it** carry it off, come out on top 5 **'Sfoot** (an oath; "God's foot") 6 **but I'll see** rather than not see 8 **enginer** (a soldier in a company used for ditch digging, tunneling, and otherwise undermining the battlements of an enemy camp) 13 **caduceus** (Mercury's staff, twined with serpents) 19 **Neapolitan bone-ache** syphilis 21 **placket** opening in a petticoat (used obscenely, with anatomical suggestion)

Enter Patroclus.

PATROCLUS Who's there? Thersites? Good Thersites, come in and rail.

THERSITES If I could 'a' rememb'red a gilt counterfeit, thou wouldst not have slipped out of my contemplation. But it is no matter; thyself upon thyself! The common curse of mankind, folly and ignorance, be thine in great revenue. Heaven bless thee from a tutor, and discipline come not near thee. Let thy blood be thy direction till thy death. Then, if she that lays thee out says thou art a fair corse, I'll be sworn and sworn upon't she never shrouded any but lazars. Amen. Where's Achilles?

PATROCLUS What, art thou devout? Wast thou in prayer?

THERSITES Ay, the heavens hear me!

PATROCLUS Amen.

Enter Achilles.

ACHILLES Who's there?

PATROCLUS Thersites, my lord.

ACHILLES Where? Where? O, where? Art thou come? Why, my cheese, my digestion, why hast thou not served thyself in to my table so many meals? Come, what's Agamemnon?

THERSITES Thy commander, Achilles. Then tell me, Patroclus, what's Achilles?

PATROCLUS Thy lord, Thersites. Then tell me, I pray thee, what's thyself?

27 **slipped** (pun on "slip," a counterfeit coin of brass, covered with silver or gold) 30 **bless** i.e., save 32 **blood** passion 33 **corse** corpse 35 **lazars** lepers (with decayed bodies) 43 **my cheese, my digestion** (cheese served as the final course of a meal was thought to aid digestion)

THERSITES Thy knower, Patroclus. Then tell me, Patroclus, what art thou?

PATROCLUS Thou must tell that knowest.

ACHILLES O tell, tell.

THERSITES I'll decline the whole question. Agamemnon commands Achilles, Achilles is my lord, I am Patroclus' knower, and Patroclus is a fool.

PATROCLUS You rascal!

THERSITES Peace, fool! I have not done.

ACHILLES He is a privileged man. Proceed, Thersites.

THERSITES Agamemnon is a fool, Achilles is a fool, Thersites is a fool, and, as aforesaid, Patroclus is a fool.

ACHILLES Derive this; come.

THERSITES Agamemnon is a fool to offer to command Achilles, Achilles is a fool to be commanded of Agamemnon, Thersites is a fool to serve such a fool, and this Patroclus is a fool positive.

PATROCLUS Why am I a fool?

THERSITES Make that demand of the Creator; it suffices me thou art. Look you, who comes here?

Enter Agamemnon, Ulysses, Nestor, Diomedes, Ajax, and Calchas.

ACHILLES Patroclus, I'll speak with nobody. Come in with me, Thersites. *Exit.*

THERSITES Here is such patchery, such juggling, and such knavery. All the argument is a whore and a cuckold, a good quarrel to draw emulous factions

54 **decline** run through (in the grammatical sense, as to decline a noun) 59 **He is a privileged man** (in the sense that the railing of a professional jester or fool was "allowed") 64 **offer** attempt 73 **patchery** roguery 75 **emulous** jealous

and bleed to death upon. Now, the dry serpigo on the subject, and war and lechery confound all!

[*Exit.*]

AGAMEMNON Where is Achilles?

PATROCLUS Within his tent, but ill-disposed, my lord.

AGAMEMNON Let it be known to him that we are here.
He shent our messengers, and we lay by
Our appertainments, visiting of him.
Let him be told so, lest perchance he think
We dare not move the question of our place
Or know not what we are.

PATROCLUS I shall so say to him.

[*Exit.*]

ULYSSES We saw him at the opening of his tent. He is not sick.

AJAX Yes, lion-sick, sick of proud heart. You may call it melancholy if you will favor the man; but, by my head, 'tis pride. But why, why? Let him show us a cause. A word, my lord.

[*Takes Agamemnon aside.*]

NESTOR What moves Ajax thus to bay at him?

ULYSSES Achilles hath inveigled his fool from him.

NESTOR Who, Thersites?

ULYSSES He.

NESTOR Then will Ajax lack matter, if he have lost his argument.

ULYSSES No, you see, he is his argument that has his argument, Achilles.

NESTOR All the better. Their fraction is more our

76 **serpigo** a quickly spreading skin disease, with eruptions 81 **shent** rebuked 82 **appertainments** rights of rank 84 **move** raise 97 **argument** subject matter 100 **fraction** fracture, break

wish than their faction. But it was a strong composure a fool could disunite.

ULYSSES The amity that wisdom knits not, folly may easily untie.

Enter Patroclus.

Here comes Patroclus.

NESTOR No Achilles with him?

ULYSSES The elephant hath joints, but none for courtesy. His legs are legs for necessity, not for flexure.

PATROCLUS Achilles bids me say he is much sorry
If anything more than your sport and pleasure
Did move your greatness and this noble state
To call upon him. He hopes it is no other
But, for your health and your digestion sake,
An after-dinner's breath.

AGAMEMNON Hear you, Patroclus.
We are too well acquainted with these answers;
But his evasion, winged thus swift with scorn,
Cannot outfly our apprehensions.
Much attribute he hath, and much the reason
Why we ascribe it to him; yet all his virtues,
Not virtuously on his own part beheld,
Do in our eyes begin to lose their gloss—
Yea, like fair fruit in an unwholesome dish,
Are like to rot untasted. Go and tell him
We come to speak with him; and you shall not sin
If you do say we think him overproud
And underhonest, in self-assumption greater
Than in the note of judgment, and worthier than himself

101 **faction** union 101–02 **composure** union 108 **flexure** bending 111 **noble state** assemblage of noblemen 114 **breath** exercise 117 **apprehensions** perceptions 120 **Not ... beheld** not carried with modesty 126 **underhonest** calculating, not open 127 **the note of judgment** the opinion of men of judgment

Here tend the savage strangeness he puts on,
Disguise the holy strength of their command,
And underwrite in an observing kind
His humorous predominance; yea, watch
His pettish lunes, his ebbs and flows, as if
The passage and whole carriage of this action
Rode on his tide. Go tell him this; and add
That, if he overhold his price so much,
We'll none of him; but let him, like an engine
Not portable, lie under this report:
"Bring action hither, this cannot go to war."
A stirring dwarf we do allowance give
Before a sleeping giant. Tell him so.

PATROCLUS I shall, and bring his answer presently.
[*Exit*.]

AGAMEMNON In second voice we'll not be satisfied;
We come to speak with him. Ulysses, enter you.
Exit Ulysses.

AJAX What is he more than another?

AGAMEMNON No more than what he thinks he is.

AJAX Is he so much? Do you not think he thinks himself a better man than I am?

AGAMEMNON No question.

AJAX Will you subscribe his thought, and say he is?

AGAMEMNON No, noble Ajax; you are as strong, as valiant, as wise, no less noble, much more gentle, and altogether more tractable.

AJAX Why should a man be proud? How doth pride grow? I know not what pride is.

128 **tend the savage strangeness** wait upon the rude aloofness 129–31 **Disguise ... predominance** allow to be hidden the divine authority of their command, and, in a form of acquiescence, subscribe to his eccentric notion of superiority 132 **pettish lunes** capricious variations (like the changes of the moon) 135 **overhold** overvalue 136 **engine** mechanical contrivance (here, military) 139 **allowance** praise

AGAMEMNON Your mind is the clearer and your virtues the fairer. He that is proud eats up himself. Pride is his own glass, his own trumpet, his own chronicle; and whatever praises itself but in the deed, devours the deed in the praise.

Enter Ulysses.

AJAX I do hate a proud man as I hate the engend'ring of toads.

NESTOR [*Aside*] And yet he loves himself. Is't not strange?

ULYSSES Achilles will not to the field tomorrow.

AGAMEMNON What's his excuse?

ULYSSES He doth rely on none,
But carries on the stream of his dispose
Without observance or respect of any,
In will peculiar and in self-admission.

AGAMEMNON Why will he not upon our fair request
Untent his person and share th'air with us?

ULYSSES Things small as nothing, for request's sake only,
He makes important. Possessed he is with greatness,
And speaks not to himself but with a pride
That quarrels at self-breath. Imagined worth
Holds in his blood such swoln and hot discourse
That 'twixt his mental and his active parts
Kingdomed Achilles in commotion rages
And batters down himself. What should I say?

157 **glass** mirror 166 **dispose** inclination 168 **In . . . self-admission** i.e., with will exclusively his own and with self-approval 171 **for request's sake only** only because requested 174 **That quarrels at self-breath** that quarrels with speech itself 177 **Kingdomed** i.e., as though Achilles were himself a kingdom engaged in civil strife

He is so plaguy proud that the death-tokens of it
Cry "No recovery."

AGAMEMNON Let Ajax go to him.
Dear lord, go you and greet him in his tent;
'Tis said he holds you well, and will be led
At your request a little from himself.

ULYSSES O Agamemnon, let it not be so!
We'll consecrate the steps that Ajax makes
When they go from Achilles. Shall the proud lord
That bastes his arrogance with his own seam
And never suffers matter of the world
Enter his thoughts, save such as doth revolve
And ruminate himself—shall he be worshiped
Of that we hold an idol more than he?
No, this thrice-worthy and right valiant lord
Shall not so stale his palm, nobly acquired,
Nor, by my will, assubjugate his merit,
As amply titled as Achilles' is,
By going to Achilles.
That were to enlard his fat-already pride,
And add more coals to Cancer when he burns
With entertaining great Hyperion.
This lord go to him! Jupiter forbid,
And say in thunder, "Achilles, go to him."

NESTOR [*Aside*] O, this is well. He rubs the vein of him.

DIOMEDES [*Aside*] And how his silence drinks up his applause!

AJAX If I go to him, with my armèd fist
I'll pash him o'er the face.

AGAMEMNON O, no! You shall not go.

179 **death-tokens** external symptoms of the plague preceding death 187 **seam** grease, fat 193 **stale his palm** detract from his glory 194 **assubjugate** debase 198 **Cancer** i.e., summer, which begins under this sign of the zodiac 199 **Hyperion** the sun 202 **vein** mood 205 **pash** bash

AJAX An he be proud with me, I'll pheese his pride. Let me go to him.

ULYSSES Not for the worth that hangs upon our quarrel.

AJAX A paltry, insolent fellow!

NESTOR [*Aside*] How he describes himself!

AJAX Can he not be sociable?

ULYSSES [*Aside*] The raven chides blackness.

AJAX I'll let his humor's blood.

AGAMEMNON [*Aside*] He will be the physician that should be the patient.

AJAX An all men were of my mind——

ULYSSES [*Aside*] Wit would be out of fashion.

AJAX 'A should not bear it so, 'a should eat swords first! Shall pride carry it?

NESTOR [*Aside*] An 'twould, you'd carry half.

ULYSSES [*Aside*] 'A would have ten shares.

AJAX I will knead him; I'll make him supple.

NESTOR [*Aside*] He's not yet through warm. Force him with praises; pour in, pour, his ambition is dry.

ULYSSES [*To Agamemnon*] My lord, you feed too much on this dislike.

NESTOR Our noble general, do not do so.

DIOMEDES You must prepare to fight without Achilles.

ULYSSES Why, 'tis this naming of him does him harm.
Here is a man—but 'tis before his face;
I will be silent.

207 pheese settle the business of **214 let his humor's blood** i.e., cure him by letting blood, thus decreasing the strength of Achilles' humor, his mood of pride **219 'A** he **224 through** thoroughly **224 Force** stuff

NESTOR Wherefore should you so?
He is not emulous, as Achilles is.

ULYSSES Know the whole world, he is as valiant——

AJAX A whoreson dog, that shall palter with us thus!
Would he were a Troyan!

NESTOR What a vice were it in Ajax now——

ULYSSES If he were proud——

DIOMEDES Or covetous of praise——

ULYSSES Ay, or surly borne——

DIOMEDES Or strange, or self-affected!

ULYSSES Thank the heavens, lord, thou art of sweet
composure;
Praise him that gat thee, she that gave thee suck;
Famed be thy tutor, and thy parts of nature
Thrice-famed beyond, beyond all erudition;
But he that disciplined thine arms to fight,
Let Mars divide eternity in twain
And give him half; and, for thy vigor,
Bull-bearing Milo his addition yield
To sinewy Ajax. I will not praise thy wisdom,
Which, like a bourn, a pale, a shore, confines
Thy spacious and dilated parts. Here's Nestor,
Instructed by the antiquary times,
He must, he is, he cannot but be wise;
But pardon, father Nestor, were your days
As green as Ajax, and your brain so tempered,
You should not have the eminence of him,
But be as Ajax.

232 **emulous** jealously competitive 234 **palter** play shifty games, dodge 240 **strange, or self-affected** haughty, or self-centered 242 **gat** begat 243–44 **thy parts . . . erudition** your natural attributes three times more famous (i.e., than your tutor), even more famous than all learning itself 248 **Milo** (a famous Greek athlete, said to have carried a bull upon his shoulders for forty yards) 248 **addition** title, i.e., "Bull-bearing" 250 **a bourn, a pale** a boundary, a fence 252 **Instructed by the antiquary times** i.e., his wisdom learned from olden times, all the years of his old age

AJAX Shall I call you father?

NESTOR Ay, my good son.

DIOMEDES Be ruled by him, Lord Ajax.

ULYSSES There is no tarrying here; the hart Achilles
Keeps thicket. Please it our great general
To call together all his state of war;
Fresh kings are come to Troy. Tomorrow,
We must with all our main of power stand fast.
And here's a lord—come knights from east to west,
And cull their flower, Ajax shall cope the best.

AGAMEMNON Go we to council. Let Achilles sleep;
Light boats sail swift, though greater hulks draw
deep. *Exeunt.*

261 state noblemen in council **263 main** might

[ACT III

Scene I. *Troy; Priam's palace.*]

Music sounds within. Enter Pandarus and a Servant.

PANDARUS Friend you, pray you a word. Do you not follow the young Lord Paris?

SERVANT Ay, sir, when he goes before me.

PANDARUS You depend upon him, I mean.

SERVANT Sir, I do depend upon the Lord.

PANDARUS You depend upon a notable gentleman; I must needs praise him.

SERVANT The Lord be praised!

PANDARUS You know me, do you not?

SERVANT Faith, sir, superficially.

PANDARUS Friend, know me better. I am the Lord Pandarus.

SERVANT I hope I shall know your honor better.

PANDARUS I do desire it.

III.i.4 **depend** i.e., serve, in a position of dependence

SERVANT You are in the state of grace.

PANDARUS Grace? Not so, friend. Honor and lordship are my titles. What music is this?

SERVANT I do but partly know, sir. It is music in parts.

PANDARUS Know you the musicians?

SERVANT Wholly, sir.

PANDARUS Who play they to?

SERVANT To the hearers, sir.

PANDARUS At whose pleasure, friend?

SERVANT At mine, sir, and theirs that love music.

PANDARUS Command, I mean, friend.

SERVANT Who shall I command, sir?

PANDARUS Friend, we understand not one another. I am too courtly, and thou too cunning. At whose request do these men play?

SERVANT That's to't, indeed, sir. Marry, sir, at the request of Paris, my lord, who is there in person; with him the mortal Venus, the heartblood of beauty, love's invisible soul.

PANDARUS Who? My cousin Cressida?

SERVANT No, sir, Helen. Could not you find out that by her attributes?

PANDARUS It should seem, fellow, that thou hast not seen the Lady Cressid. I come to speak with Paris from the Prince Troilus. I will make a

15 **You . . . grace** (pretending that Pandarus meant that he desired his own honor to be better; also, perhaps, the servant is hinting for a gratuity) 16 **Grace** (the courtly title of a duke, etc.) 18–19 **music in parts** music containing several vocal or instrumental parts in counterpoint

complimental assault upon him, for my business seethes.

SERVANT Sodden business! There's a stewed phrase, indeed.

Enter Paris and Helen [*with courtiers*].

PANDARUS Fair be to you, my lord, and to all this fair company. Fair desires in all fair measure fairly guide them. Especially to you, fair queen, fair thoughts be your fair pillow.

HELEN Dear lord, you are full of fair words.

PANDARUS You speak your fair pleasure, sweet queen. Fair prince, here is good broken music.

PARIS You have broke it, cousin; and, by my life, you shall make it whole again; you shall piece it out with a piece of your performance. Nell, he is full of harmony.

PANDARUS Truly, lady, no.

HELEN O, sir!

PANDARUS Rude, in sooth; in good sooth, very rude.

PARIS Well said, my lord. Well, you say so in fits.

PANDARUS I have business to my lord, dear queen. My lord, will you vouchsafe me a word?

HELEN Nay, this shall not hedge us out. We'll hear you sing, certainly.

PANDARUS Well, sweet queen, you are pleasant with me. But, marry, thus, my lord: my dear lord and most esteemed friend, your brother Troilus——

42 **seethes** boils, i.e., demands immediate attention 43 **stewed** (1) boiled (2) pertaining to stews, or brothels (?) 51 **broken music** music the parts of which are written for different solo instruments, or groups of different instruments 58 **Rude** unpolished, rough 59 **fits** sections or divisions of a song (perhaps Paris means, "you say so only at times")

HELEN My Lord Pandarus, honey-sweet lord——

PANDARUS Go to, sweet queen, go to—commends himself most affectionately to you.

HELEN You shall not bob us out of our melody. If you do, our melancholy upon your head!

PANDARUS Sweet queen, sweet queen, that's a sweet queen, i' faith.

HELEN And to make a sweet lady sad is a sour offense.

PANDARUS Nay, that shall not serve your turn; that shall it not, in truth, la. Nay, I care not for such words; no, no. And, my lord, he desires you that, if the king call for him at supper, you will make his excuse.

HELEN My Lord Pandarus——

PANDARUS What says my sweet queen, my very, very sweet queen?

PARIS What exploit's in hand? Where sups he tonight?

HELEN Nay, but my Lord——

PANDARUS What says my sweet queen? My cousin will fall out with you.

HELEN You must not know where he sups.

PARIS I'll lay my life, with my disposer Cressida.

PANDARUS No, no; no such matter; you are wide. Come your disposer is sick.

PARIS Well, I'll make excuse.

PANDARUS Ay, good my lord. Why should you say Cressida? No, your poor disposer's sick.

PARIS I spy.

70 **bob** cheat 85–86 **My cousin . . . you** (Pandarus lightly pretends that Paris, his "cousin," will become jealous if Helen continues to flirt with him, Pandarus) 88 **disposer** i.e., she who rules him (Paris jokingly uses an excessively gallant term) 89 **wide** wide of the mark

PANDARUS You spy? What do you spy? Come, give me an instrument now, sweet queen.

HELEN Why, this is kindly done.

PANDARUS My niece is horribly in love with a thing you have, sweet queen.

HELEN She shall have it, my lord, if it be not my Lord Paris.

PANDARUS He? No, she'll none of him; they two are twain.

HELEN Falling in, after falling out, may make them three.

PANDARUS Come, come, I'll hear no more of this. I'll sing you a song now.

HELEN Ay, ay, prithee. Now by my troth, sweet lord, thou hast a fine forehead.

PANDARUS Ay, you may, you may.

HELEN Let thy song be love. This love will undo us all. O Cupid, Cupid, Cupid!

PANDARUS Love! Ay, that it shall, i' faith.

PARIS Ay, good now, "Love, love, nothing but love."

PANDARUS In good troth, it begins so: [*Sings.*]
Love, love, nothing but love, still love still more!
For, O, love's bow shoots buck and doe.
The shaft confounds not that it wounds,
But tickles still the sore.
These lovers cry, O ho! they die!
Yet that which seems the wound to kill

98–99 **My niece is . . . sweet queen** i.e., Cressida loves, or would love to have, a sexual partner such as Paris is to Helen 103 **twain** at odds, having nothing in common 104–05 **Falling in . . . them three** (Helen's bawdy joke picks up the train of thought begun by Pandarus) 110 **you may,** i.e., have your joke 118 **confounds not that** does not distress because 119 **sore** wound (perhaps a pun on the term for a buck in his fourth year)

Doth turn O ho! to Ha, ha, he!
So dying love lives still.
O ho! a while, but Ha, ha, ha!
O ho! groans out for Ha, ha, ha!—Heigh ho!

HELEN In love, i' faith, to the very tip of the nose.

PARIS He eats nothing but doves, love, and that breeds hot blood, and hot blood begets hot thoughts, and hot thoughts beget hot deeds, and hot deeds is love.

PANDARUS Is this the generation of love—hot blood, hot thoughts, and hot deeds? Why, they are vipers. Is love a generation of vipers? Sweet lord, who's a-field today?

PARIS Hector, Deiphobus, Helenus, Antenor, and all the gallantry of Troy. I would fain have armed today, but my Nell would not have it so. How chance my brother Troilus went not?

HELEN He hangs the lip at something. You know all, Lord Pandarus.

PANDARUS Not I, honey-sweet queen. I long to hear how they sped today. You'll remember your brother's excuse?

PARIS To a hair.

PANDARUS Farewell, sweet queen.

HELEN Commend me to your niece.

PANDARUS I will, sweet queen. [*Exit.*] *Sound a retreat.*

PARIS They're come from the field. Let us to Priam's hall
To greet the warriors. Sweet Helen, I must woo you
To help unarm our Hector. His stubborn buckles,
With these your white enchanting fingers touched,

132 a generation of vipers (cf. Matthew 3:7) **141 how they sped** i.e., the results of their action **143 To a hair** (does Paris jokingly recall Troilus' "pretty answer" about the hairs on his chin [see I.ii.167–69]?)

Shall more obey than to the edge of steel
Or force of Greekish sinews. You shall do more
Than all the island kings—disarm great Hector.

HELEN 'Twill make us proud to be his servant, Paris;
Yea, what he shall receive of us in duty
Gives us more palm in beauty than we have,
Yea, overshines ourself.

PARIS Sweet, above thought I love thee. *Exeunt.*

[Scene II. *Within Troy.*]

Enter Pandarus and Troilus' Man.

PANDARUS How now, where's thy master? At my cousin Cressida's?

MAN No, sir; he stays for you to conduct him thither.

Enter Troilus.

PANDARUS O, here he comes. How now, how now?

TROILUS Sirrah, walk off. [*Exit Man.*]

PANDARUS Have you seen my cousin?

TROILUS No, Pandarus. I stalk about her door
Like a strange soul upon the Stygian banks
Staying for waftage. O, be thou my Charon,
And give me swift transportance to those fields
Where I may wallow in the lily beds
Proposed for the deserver. O gentle Pandar,
From Cupid's shoulder pluck his painted wings,
And fly with me to Cressid.

153 **island kings** i.e., kings of the Grecian islands III.ii.8 **Stygian** (from Styx, the principal river of the underworld) 9 **waftage** passage across water 9 **Charon** (ferryman of the dead, across the Styx to Hades) 12 **Proposed** promised

PANDARUS Walk here i' th' orchard. I'll bring her straight. *Exit Pandarus.*

TROILUS I am giddy; expectation whirls me round.
Th' imaginary relish is so sweet
That it enchants my sense. What will it be
When that the wat'ry palates taste indeed
Love's thrice-repurèd nectar? Death, I fear me,
Sounding destruction, or some joy too fine,
Too subtle, potent, tuned too sharp in sweetness
For the capacity of my ruder powers.
I fear it much; and I do fear besides
That I shall lose distinction in my joys,
As doth a battle, when they charge on heaps
The enemy flying.

Enter Pandarus.

PANDARUS She's making her ready; she'll come straight; you must be witty now. She does so blush, and fetches her wind so short as if she were frayed with a spirit. I'll fetch her. It is the prettiest villain; she fetches her breath as short as a new-ta'en sparrow. *Exit Pandarus.*

TROILUS Even such a passion doth embrace my bosom.
My heart beats thicker than a feverous pulse,
And all my powers do their bestowing lose,
Like vassalage at unawares encount'ring
The eye of majesty.

Enter Pandarus and Cressida.

PANDARUS Come, come, what need you blush? Shame's a baby. Here she is now; swear the oaths now to

20 **wat'ry** watering (cf. mouth "watering" with appetite) 21 **thrice-repurèd** distilled again and again (i.e., to extract the purest essence) 22 **Sounding** swooning 24 **ruder** physical 26 **distinction** ability to distinguish 30 **be witty** be alert, have your wits about you 31–32 **frayed with a spirit** frightened by a ghost 33 **villain** (here a term of endearment) 37 **bestowing** proper use 38 **vassalage** vassals

her that you have sworn to me. What! Are you gone again? You must be watched ere you be made tame, must you? Come your ways, come your ways; an you draw backward, we'll put you i' the fills. Why do you not speak to her? Come, draw this curtain, and let's see your picture. Alas the day, how loath you are to offend daylight! An 'twere dark, you'd close sooner. So, so; rub on, and kiss the mistress. How now, a kiss in fee-farm! Build there, carpenter; the air is sweet. Nay, you shall fight your hearts out ere I part you. The falcon as the tercel, for all the ducks i' the river. Go to, go to.

TROILUS You have bereft me of all words, lady.

PANDARUS Words pay no debts, give her deeds; but she'll bereave you o' the deeds too if she call your activity in question. What, billing again? Here's "In witness whereof the parties interchangeably"— Come in, come in. I'll go get a fire. [*Exit*.]

CRESSIDA Will you walk in, my lord?

TROILUS O Cressid, how often have I wished me thus!

CRESSIDA Wished, my lord? The gods grant—O my lord!

TROILUS What should they grant? What makes this pretty abruption? What too curious dreg espies my sweet lady in the fountain of our love?

43–44 **watched ere you be made tame** i.e., prodded on until made submissive (a hawk was tamed by "watching" it, i.e., keeping it constantly awake) 46 **fills** shafts (of a cart) 47 **curtain** i.e., her veil 49 **close** move together 49–50 **rub ... mistress** (terms from bowling, where "to rub" was to meet obstacles in the way of the small object-ball, called the "mistress"; bowls are still said "to kiss" when they touch gently) 50–51 **a kiss in fee-farm** i.e., a long kiss (a fee-farm was a grant of lands in perpetuity) 52–53 **The falcon ... river** i.e., I will bet on the falcon (the term applied only to the female of the species) against the tercel (the male) to bring down any game 59 **"In witness ... interchangeably"** (a legal formula, usually ending with the words "have set their hands and seals") 66 **abruption** breaking off 66 **too curious** overly cautious, anxious, or inquisitive

CRESSIDA More dregs than water, if my fears have eyes.

TROILUS Fears make devils of cherubins; they never see truly.

CRESSIDA Blind fear, that seeing reason leads, finds safer footing than blind reason stumbling without fear. To fear the worst oft cures the worse.

TROILUS O, let my lady apprehend no fear; in all Cupid's pageant there is presented no monster.

CRESSIDA Nor nothing monstrous neither?

TROILUS Nothing but our undertakings when we vow to weep seas, live in fire, eat rocks, tame tigers, thinking it harder for our mistress to devise imposition enough than for us to undergo any difficulty imposed. This is the monstruosity in love, lady, that the will is infinite and the execution confined; that the desire is boundless and the act a slave to limit.

CRESSIDA They say all lovers swear more performance than they are able, and yet reserve an ability that they never perform, vowing more than the perfection of ten and discharging less than the tenth part of one. They that have the voice of lions and the act of hares—are they not monsters?

TROILUS Are there such? Such are not we. Praise us as we are tasted, allow us as we prove; our head shall go bare till merit crown it. No perfection in reversion shall have a praise in present; we will not name desert before his birth, and, being born, his addition shall be humble. Few words to fair faith. Troilus shall be such to Cressid, as what envy

75–76 **apprehend . . . no monster** (Troilus refers to some type of dramatic allegory such as Cupid might be depicted as "presenting," or the emblematic characters, such as Fear, in pageants or court masques) 93 **tasted** tested 95 **reversion** right or anticipation of future possession 97 **his addition shall be humble** it shall be given no high or pompous titles

can say worst shall be a mock for his truth, and what truth can speak truest not truer than Troilus.

CRESSIDA Will you walk in, my lord?

Enter Pandarus.

PANDARUS What, blushing still? Have you not done talking yet?

CRESSIDA Well, uncle, what folly I commit, I dedicate to you.

PANDARUS I thank you for that. If my lord get a boy of you, you'll give him me. Be true to my lord; if he flinch, chide me for it.

TROILUS You know now your hostages: your uncle's word and my firm faith.

PANDARUS Nay, I'll give my word for her too. Our kindred, though they be long ere they be wooed, they are constant being won. They are burrs, I can tell you; they'll stick where they are thrown.

CRESSIDA Boldness comes to me now and brings me
heart.
Prince Troilus, I have loved you night and day
For many weary months.

TROILUS Why was my Cressid then so hard to win?

CRESSIDA Hard to seem won; but I was won, my lord,
With the first glance that ever—pardon me;
If I confess much you will play the tyrant.
I love you now, but, till now, not so much
But I might master it. In faith, I lie;
My thoughts were like unbridled children grown
Too headstrong for their mother. See, we fools!
Why have I blabbed? Who shall be true to us
When we are so unsecret to ourselves?

98–100 as what envy . . . Troilus so that the worst malice can do is sneer at his constancy, and even the best truth that truth can speak will not be truer than Troilus

But, though I loved you well, I wooed you not;
And yet, good faith, I wished myself a man,
Or that we women had men's privilege
Of speaking first. Sweet, bid me hold my tongue,
For in this rapture I shall surely speak
The thing I shall repent. See, see! Your silence,
Cunning in dumbness, from my weakness draws
My very soul of counsel. Stop my mouth.

TROILUS And shall, albeit sweet music issues thence.

PANDARUS Pretty, i'faith.

CRESSIDA My lord, I do beseech you, pardon me;
'Twas not my purpose thus to beg a kiss.
I am ashamed. O heavens, what have I done?
For this time will I take my leave, my lord.

TROILUS Your leave, sweet Cressid?

PANDARUS Leave! An you take leave till tomorrow morning——

CRESSIDA Pray you, content you.

TROILUS What offends you, lady?

CRESSIDA Sir, mine own company.

TROILUS You cannot shun yourself.

CRESSIDA Let me go and try.
I have a kind of self resides with you;
But an unkind self, that itself will leave
To be another's fool. I would be gone.
Where is my wit? I know not what I speak.

TROILUS Well know they what they speak that speak so wisely.

CRESSIDA Perchance, my lord, I show more craft than love,
And fell so roundly to a large confession

135 very soul of counsel inmost thoughts and secrets **151 fool** dupe **155 roundly** frankly, openly **155 large** unrestrained

To angle for your thoughts. But you are wise,
Or else you love not, for to be wise and love
Exceeds man's might; that dwells with gods above.

TROILUS O that I thought it could be in a woman—
As, if it can, I will presume in you—
To feed for aye her lamp and flames of love;
To keep her constancy in plight and youth,
Outliving beauty's outward, with a mind
That doth renew swifter than blood decays;
Or that persuasion could but thus convince me
That my integrity and truth to you
Might be affronted with the match and weight
Of such a winnowed purity in love;
How were I then uplifted! But, alas,
I am as true as truth's simplicity,
And simpler than the infancy of truth.

CRESSIDA In that I'll war with you.

TROILUS O virtuous fight,
When right with right wars who shall be most right!
True swains in love shall in the world to come
Approve their truth by Troilus. When their rhymes,
Full of protest, of oath and big compare,
Wants similes, truth tired with iteration,
"As true as steel, as plantage to the moon,
As sun to day, as turtle to her mate,
As iron to adamant, as earth to the center,"
Yet, after all comparisons of truth,
As truth's authentic author to be cited,
"As true as Troilus" shall crown up the verse
And sanctify the numbers.

156–58 **But you are wise . . . man's might** i.e., you are reasonable, which means you are not in love, for no man can follow reason and love at the same time 162 **in plight and youth** as it was when it was plighted, and as fresh 163 **beauty's outward** external, transitory beauty 167 **affronted** confronted, i.e., equaled 168 **winnowed** i.e., distilled 175 **Approve** attest 178 **plantage to the moon** (the moon was thought to influence plantage, or vegetation) 179 **turtle** turtledove (an emblem of eternally faithful love) 180 **adamant** the loadstone (magnetic) 184 **numbers** metrical verses

CRESSIDA Prophet may you be!
If I be false or swerve a hair from truth,
When time is old and hath forgot itself,
When waterdrops have worn the stones of Troy,
And blind oblivion swallowed cities up,
And mighty states characterless are grated
To dusty nothing, yet let memory,
From false to false among false maids in love,
Upbraid my falsehood! When they've said, "As false
As air, as water, wind or sandy earth,
As fox to lamb, as wolf to heifer's calf,
Pard to the hind, or stepdame to her son,"
Yea, let them say, to stick the heart of falsehood,
"As false as Cressid."

PANDARUS Go to, a bargain made. Seal it, seal it; I'll be the witness. Here I hold your hand, here my cousin's. If ever you prove false one to another, since I have taken such pains to bring you together, let all pitiful goers-between be called to the world's end after my name; call them all Pandars. Let all constant men be Troiluses, all false women Cressids, and all brokers-between Pandars! Say, "Amen."

TROILUS Amen.

CRESSIDA Amen.

PANDARUS Amen. Whereupon I will show you a chamber which bed, because it shall not speak of your pretty encounters, press it to death. Away!

Exeunt [Troilus and Cressida].

And Cupid grant all tongue-tied maidens here
Bed, chamber, Pandar to provide this gear! *Exit.*

189 **characterless** without an identifying mark 195 **Pard to the hind** leopard to the doe 210 **which bed** the bed in which 210 **because** (1) for the reason that (normal usage) (2) in order that (?)

[Scene III. *The Greek camp.*]

Enter Ulysses, Diomedes, Nestor, Agamemnon,
[*Menelaus, Ajax, and*] *Calchas. Flourish* [*of trumpets.*]

CALCHAS Now, princes, for the service I have done,
Th' advantage of the time prompts me aloud
To call for recompense. Appear it to mind
That through the sight I bear in things to come,
I have abandoned Troy, left my possession,
Incurred a traitor's name, exposed myself,
From certain and possessed conveniences,
To doubtful fortunes, sequest'ring from me all
That time, acquaintance, custom, and condition
Made tame and most familiar to my nature;
And here, to do you service, am become
As new into the world, strange, unacquainted.
I do beseech you, as in way of taste,
To give me now a little benefit
Out of those many registered in promise,
Which, you say, live to come in my behalf.

AGAMEMNON What wouldst thou of us, Troyan? Make demand.

CALCHAS You have a Troyan prisoner, called Antenor,
Yesterday took; Troy holds him very dear.
Oft have you—often have you thanks therefor—
Desired my Cressid in right great exchange,
Whom Troy hath still denied; but this Antenor

III.iii.4 **sight** i.e., foresight 8 **sequest'ring** putting aside 10 **tame** familiar, comfortable 13 **taste** foretaste 21 **right great exchange** exchange for someone sufficiently great 22 **still** always

I know is such a wrest in their affairs
That their negotiations all must slack,
Wanting his manage; and they will almost
Give us a prince of blood, a son of Priam,
In change of him. Let him be sent, great princes,
And he shall buy my daughter; and her presence
Shall quite strike off all service I have done
In most accepted pain.

AGAMEMNON Let Diomedes bear him,
And bring us Cressid hither; Calchas shall have
What he requests of us. Good Diomed,
Furnish you fairly, for this interchange.
Withal bring word if Hector will tomorrow
Be answered in his challenge. Ajax is ready.

DIOMEDES This shall I undertake, and 'tis a burden
Which I am proud to bear. *Exit* [*with Calchas*].

Achilles and Patroclus stand in their tent.

ULYSSES Achilles stands i' th' entrance of his tent.
Please it our general pass strangely by him,
As if he were forgot; and, princes all,
Lay negligent and loose regard upon him.
I will come last. 'Tis like he'll question me
Why such unplausive eyes are bent, why turned, on him.
If so, I have derision medicinable
To use between your strangeness and his pride,
Which his own will shall have desire to drink.
It may do good; pride hath no other glass
To show itself but pride, for supple knees
Feed arrogance and are the proud man's fees.

AGAMEMNON We'll execute your purpose, and put on
A form of strangeness as we pass along.
So do each lord, and either greet him not

23 **wrest** a key used for tuning stringed instruments (i.e., the influence of harmony in Trojan discussions) 30 **accepted** cheerfully endured 37 s.d. **stand in their tent** i.e., appear and stand in the entrance of their tent 39 **strangely** aloofly 43 **unplausive** disapproving 48 **show** mirror

Or else disdainfully, which shall shake him more
Than if not looked on. I will lead the way.

ACHILLES What comes the general to speak with me?
You know my mind; I'll fight no more 'gainst Troy.

AGAMEMNON What says Achilles? Would he aught with
us?

NESTOR Would you, my lord, aught with the general?

ACHILLES No.

NESTOR Nothing, my lord.

AGAMEMNON The better.

ACHILLES Good day, good day.

MENELAUS How do you? How do you?

ACHILLES What, does the cuckold scorn me?

AJAX How now, Patroclus?

ACHILLES Good morrow, Ajax.

AJAX Ha?

ACHILLES Good morrow.

AJAX Ay, and good next day too.

Exeunt.

ACHILLES What mean these fellows? Know they not
Achilles?

PATROCLUS They pass by strangely. They were used to
bend,
To send their smiles before them to Achilles,
To come as humbly as they used to creep
To holy altars.

ACHILLES What, am I poor of late?
'Tis certain, greatness, once fall'n out with fortune,
Must fall out with men too. What the declined is
He shall as soon read in the eyes of others
As feel in his own fall; for men, like butterflies,

Show not their mealy wings but to the summer,
And not a man, for being simply man,
Hath any honor, but honor for those honors
That are without him, as place, riches, and favor,
Prizes of accident as oft as merit;
Which when they fall, as being slippery standers,
The love that leaned on them as slippery too,
Doth one pluck down another, and together
Die in the fall. But 'tis not so with me;
Fortune and I are friends. I do enjoy
At ample point all that I did possess,
Save these men's looks—who do, methinks, find out
Something not worth in me such rich beholding
As they have often given. Here is Ulysses;
I'll interrupt his reading.
How now, Ulysses.

ULYSSES Now, great Thetis' son.

ACHILLES What are you reading?

ULYSSES A strange fellow here
Writes me that man, how dearly ever parted,
How much in having, or without or in,
Cannot make boast to have that which he hath,
Nor feels not what he owes but by reflection;
As when his virtues aiming upon others
Heat them, and they retort that heat again
To the first giver.

ACHILLES This is not strange, Ulysses.
The beauty that is borne here in the face
The bearer knows not, but commends itself
To others' eyes; nor doth the eye itself,
That most pure spirit of sense, behold itself,
Not going from itself; but eye to eye opposed

79 **mealy** powdery 82 **without** external to 89 **At ample point** in full measure, in every way 96 **how dearly ever parted** however excellently endowed by nature 97 **How much ... or in** however much in possession, whether externally or internally 99 **Nor feels ... by reflection** and understands what he himself possesses (**owes** = "owns") only as it is reflected

Salutes each other with each other's form;
For speculation turns not to itself
Till it hath traveled and is married there
Where it may see itself. This is not strange at all.

ULYSSES I do not strain at the position—
It is familiar—but at the author's drift;
Who in his circumstance expressly proves
That no man is the lord of anything—
Though in and of him there be much consisting—
Till he communicate his parts to others.
Nor doth he of himself know them for aught
Till he behold them formèd in th' applause
Where they're extended; who, like an arch, reverb'rate
The voice again, or, like a gate of steel
Fronting the sun, receives and renders back
His figure and his heat. I was much rapt in this,
And apprehended here immediately
Th' unknown Ajax.
Heavens, what a man is there! A very horse,
That has he knows not what. Nature, what things there are
Most abject in regard and dear in use!
What things again most dear in the esteem
And poor in worth! Now shall we see tomorrow,
An act that very chance doth throw upon him:
Ajax renowned. O heavens, what some men do,
While some men leave to do!
How some men creep in skittish Fortune's hall,
While others play the idiots in her eyes!
How one man eats into another's pride,
While pride is fasting in his wantonness!
To see these Grecian lords—why, even already

109 **speculation** power of sight 112 **position** i.e., that of the writer whom Ulysses paraphrases above 114 **circumstance** detailed discussion 116 **Though . . . consisting** although much exists in him and also because of him 120 **Where they're extended** in which his natural attributes are noised abroad 120 **who** which 128 **Most . . . use** most despised and yet invaluable 134 **in** into 134 **skittish** i.e., unreliable 137 **his wantonness** its own self-satisfaction

They clap the lubber Ajax on the shoulder,
As if his foot were on brave Hector's breast,
And great Troy shrinking.

ACHILLES I do believe it; for they passed by me
As misers do by beggars, neither gave to me
Good word nor look. What, are my deeds forgot?

ULYSSES Time hath, my lord, a wallet at his back,
Wherein he puts alms for oblivion,
A great-sized monster of ingratitudes.
Those scraps are good deeds past, which are devoured
As fast as they are made, forgot as soon
As done. Perseverance, dear my lord,
Keeps honor bright. To have done, is to hang
Quite out of fashion, like a rusty mail
In monumental mock'ry. Take the instant way;
For honor travels in a strait so narrow
Where one but goes abreast. Keep, then, the path;
For emulation hath a thousand sons
That one by one pursue. If you give way,
Or hedge aside from the direct forthright,
Like to an ent'red tide they all rush by
And leave you hindmost;
Or, like a gallant horse fall'n in first rank,
Lie there for pavement to the abject rear,
O'errun and trampled on. Then what they do in present,
Though less than yours in past, must o'ertop yours.
For time is like a fashionable host,
That slightly shakes his parting guest by the hand,
And with his arms outstretched, as he would fly,
Grasps in the comer. The welcome ever smiles,
And farewell goes out sighing. Let not virtue seek
Remuneration for the thing it was. For beauty, wit,
High birth, vigor of bone, desert in service,

152 **mail** piece of armor 153 **instant** most immediate 158 **direct forthright** course of action clearly at hand, the path straight ahead 162 **the abject rear** the miserable, degraded members of the rear (as in a military charge or parade)

Love, friendship, charity, are subjects all
To envious and calumniating time.
One touch of nature makes the whole world kin,
That all with one consent praise newborn gauds,
Though they are made and molded of things past,
And give to dust that is a little gilt
More laud than gilt o'erdusted.
The present eye praises the present object.
Then marvel not, thou great and complete man,
That all the Greeks begin to worship Ajax;
Since things in motion sooner catch the eye
Than what stirs not. The cry went once on thee,
And still it might, and yet it may again,
If thou wouldst not entomb thyself alive
And case thy reputation in thy tent;
Whose glorious deeds, but in these fields of late,
Made emulous missions 'mongst the gods themselves
And drave great Mars to faction.

ACHILLES Of this my privacy
I have strong reasons.

ULYSSES But 'gainst your privacy
The reasons are more potent and heroical.
'Tis known, Achilles, that you are in love
With one of Priam's daughters.

ACHILLES Ha! Known!

ULYSSES Is that a wonder?
The providence that's in a watchful state
Knows almost every grain of Pluto's gold
Finds bottom in th' uncomprehensive deeps,

174 **One touch of nature** a natural inclination, common to all men (to praise according to superficial values) 175 **gauds** toys, trifles 178 **More laud than gilt o'erdusted** more praise than gold covered with dust 183 **cry** public opinion 186 **case** encase 188 **emulous missions** competitive and jealous warfare (the gods took sides in the Trojan war, fighting among themselves) 189 **to faction** to become a partisan 193 **one of Priam's daughters** (Polyxena) 196 **providence** careful and timely understanding 197 **Pluto's** (Shakespeare's error for Plutus, god of wealth; Pluto was god of the underworld) 198 **uncomprehensive** unfathomable

Keeps place with thought, and almost, like the gods,
Do thoughts unveil in their dumb cradles.
There is a mystery—with whom relation
Durst never meddle—in the soul of state,
Which hath an operation more divine
Than breath or pen can give expressure to.
All the commerce that you have had with Troy
As perfectly is ours as yours, my lord;
And better would it fit Achilles much
To throw down Hector than Polyxena.
But it must grieve young Pyrrhus now at home,
When fame shall in our islands sound her trump,
And all the Greekish girls shall tripping sing,
"Great Hector's sister did Achilles win,
But our great Ajax bravely beat down him."
Farewell, my lord; I as your lover speak;
The fool slides o'er the ice that you should break.
[*Exit*.]

PATROCLUS To this effect, Achilles, have I moved you.
A woman impudent and mannish grown
Is not more loathed than an effeminate man
In time of action. I stand condemned for this;
They think my little stomach to the war
And your great love to me restrains you thus.
Sweet, rouse yourself; and the weak wanton Cupid
Shall from your neck unloose his amorous fold
And, like a dewdrop from the lion's mane,
Be shook to air.

ACHILLES Shall Ajax fight with Hector?

PATROCLUS Ay, and perhaps receive much honor by him.

ACHILLES I see my reputation is at stake.
My fame is shrewdly gored.

199 **Keeps place** keeps up, runs parallel 201 **relation** open statement 209 **Pyrrhus** (Achilles' son, also called Neoptolemus) 228 **shrewdly gored** sorely wounded

PATROCLUS O, then, beware!
Those wounds heal ill that men do give themselves.
Omission to do what is necessary
Seals a commision to a blank of danger;
And danger, like an ague, subtly taints
Even then when they sit idly in the sun.

ACHILLES Go call Thersites hither, sweet Patroclus.
I'll send the fool to Ajax and desire him
T' invite the Troyan lords after the combat
To see us here unarmed. I have a woman's longing,
An appetite that I am sick withal,
To see great Hector in his weeds of peace,
To talk with him and to behold his visage,
Even to my full of view.

Enter Thersites.

A labor saved!

THERSITES A wonder!

ACHILLES What?

THERSITES Ajax goes up and down the field, asking for himself.

ACHILLES How so?

THERSITES He must fight singly tomorrow with Hector, and is so prophetically proud of an heroical cudgeling that he raves in saying nothing.

ACHILLES How can that be?

THERSITES Why, he stalks up and down like a peacock—a stride and a stand; ruminates like an

231 **Seals . . . danger** i.e., binds one to confront unnamed danger (royal officers sometimes carried blank warrants for arrest, already bearing the commissioning seal of authority, which could be filled in as necessary) 232 **taints** infects 237 **woman's** i.e., pregnant woman's (?) 239 **weeds** apparel 240–41 **to behold . . . view** (since in full armor Hector's face would have been hidden behind the closed beaver of his helmet) 244–45 **asking for himself** (here "Ajax" is probably a pun on a jakes, i.e., a privy)

hostess that hath no arithmetic but her brain to set down her reckoning; bites his lip with a politic regard, as who should say, "There were wit in his head an 'twould out"; and so there is, but it lies as coldly in him as fire in a flint, which will not show without knocking. The man's undone forever, for if Hector break not his neck i' the combat, he'll break't himself in vainglory. He knows not me. I said, "Good morrow, Ajax"; and he replies, "Thanks, Agamemnon." What think you of this man that takes me for the general? He's grown a very land-fish, languageless, a monster. A plague of opinion! A man may wear it on both sides like a leather jerkin.

ACHILLES Thou must be my ambassador to him, Thersites.

THERSITES Who, I? Why, he'll answer nobody. He professes not answering. Speaking is for beggars; he wears his tongue in's arms. I will put on his presence; let Patroclus make demands to me, you shall see the pageant of Ajax.

ACHILLES To him, Patroclus. Tell him I humbly desire the valiant Ajax to invite the most valorous Hector to come unarmed to my tent, and to procure safe-conduct for his person of the magnanimous and most illustrious, six-or-seven-times-honored captain-general of the Grecian army, Agamemnon, et cetera. Do this.

PATROCLUS Jove bless great Ajax!

THERSITES Hum.

PATROCLUS I come from the worthy Achilles——

THERSITES Ha!

PATROCLUS Who most humbly desires you to invite Hector to his tent——

254–55 **politic regard** expression of shrewd judgment 266 **jerkin** close-fitting jacket 271 **put on** imitate

THERSITES Hum!

PATROCLUS And to procure safe-conduct from Agamemnon.

THERSITES Agamemnon?

PATROCLUS Ay, my lord.

THERSITES Ha!

PATROCLUS What say you to't?

THERSITES God b'wi'you, with all my heart.

PATROCLUS Your answer, sir.

THERSITES If tomorrow be a fair day, by eleven of the clock it will go one way or other; howsoever, he shall pay for me ere he has me.

PATROCLUS Your answer, sir.

THERSITES Fare ye well, with all my heart.

ACHILLES Why, but he is not in this tune, is he?

THERSITES No, but out of tune thus. What music will be in him when Hector has knocked out his brains, I know not; but I am sure none, unless the fiddler Apollo get his sinews to make catlings on.

ACHILLES Come, thou shalt bear a letter to him straight.

THERSITES Let me bear another to his horse, for that's the more capable creature.

ACHILLES My mind is troubled, like a fountain stirred,
And I myself see not the bottom of it.
[*Exeunt Achilles and Patroclus.*]

THERSITES Would the fountain of your mind were clear again, that I might water an ass at it! I had rather be a tick in a sheep than such a valiant ignorance.
[*Exit.*]

305 **catlings** strings of catgut 309 **capable** intelligent

[ACT IV

Scene I. *Within Troy.*]

Enter, at one door, Aeneas [with a torch;] at another, Paris, Deiphobus, Antenor, Diomed the Grecian, [and others,] with torches.

PARIS See, ho! Who is that there?

DEIPHOBUS It is the Lord Aeneas.

AENEAS Is the prince there in person?
Had I so good occasion to lie long
As you, Prince Paris, nothing but heavenly business
Should rob my bedmate of my company.

DIOMEDES That's my mind too. Good morrow, Lord Aeneas.

PARIS A valiant Greek, Aeneas; take his hand.
Witness the process of your speech, wherein
You told how Diomed, a whole week by days,
Did haunt you in the field.

AENEAS Health to you, valiant sir,
During all question of the gentle truce;

IV.i.8 **process** gist, drift 9 **by days** day by day 11 **question of the gentle truce** i.e., intercourse made possible by the truce

But when I meet you armed, as black defiance
As heart can think or courage execute.

DIOMEDES The one and other Diomed embraces.
Our bloods are now in calm, and, so long, health!
But when contention and occasion meet,
By Jove, I'll play the hunter for thy life
With all my force, pursuit, and policy.

AENEAS And thou shalt hunt a lion that will fly
With his face backward. In humane gentleness,
Welcome to Troy. Now, by Anchises' life,
Welcome indeed! By Venus' hand I swear,
No man alive can love in such a sort
The thing he means to kill more excellently.

DIOMEDES We sympathize. Jove, let Aeneas live,
If to my sword his fate be not the glory,
A thousand complete courses of the sun!
But, in mine emulous honor, let him die
With every joint a wound, and that tomorrow!

AENEAS We know each other well.

DIOMEDES We do, and long to know each other worse.

PARIS This is the most despiteful gentle greeting,
The noblest hateful love, that e'er I heard of.
What business, lord, so early?

AENEAS I was sent for to the king; but why, I know not.

PARIS His purpose meets you; it was to bring this
Greek
To Calchas' house, and there to render him,
For the enfreed Antenor, the fair Cressid.
Let's have your company; or, if you please,
Haste there before us. I constantly do think—
Or rather call my thought a certain knowledge—
My brother Troilus lodges there tonight.

16 **occasion** opportunity 18 **policy** cunning 21 **Anchises** (Aeneas' father) 22 **Venus' hand** (Diomedes was supposed to have wounded Venus, Aeneas' mother, in the hand) 25 **sympathize** have the same feeling 40 **constantly** firmly

Rouse him and give him note of our approach,
With the whole quality wherefore. I fear
We shall be much unwelcome.

AENEAS That I assure you.
Troilus had rather Troy were borne to Greece
Than Cressid borne from Troy.

PARIS There is no help.
The bitter disposition of the time
Will have it so. On, lord; we'll follow you.

AENEAS Good morrow, all. *Exit Aeneas.*

PARIS And tell me, noble Diomed; faith, tell me true,
Even in the soul of sound good-fellowship,
Who, in your thoughts, deserves fair Helen best,
Myself or Menelaus?

DIOMEDES Both alike.
He merits well to have her that doth seek her,
Not making any scruple of her soilure,
With such a hell of pain and world of charge;
And you as well to keep her that defend her,
Not palating the taste of her dishonor,
With such a costly loss of wealth and friends.
He, like a puling cuckold, would drink up
The lees and dregs of a flat tamèd piece;
You, like a lecher, out of whorish loins
Are pleased to breed out your inheritors.
Both merits poised, each weighs nor less nor more;
But he as he, the heavier for a whore.

PARIS You are too bitter to your countrywoman.

DIOMEDES She's bitter to her country! Hear me,
Paris—

44 **quality** occasion, explanation 57 **charge** cost 59 **Not palating** insensible to 62 **flat tamèd piece** (1) cask of wine opened so long that the wine has gone flat (2) woman so promiscuous that she can no longer excite or be excited sexually 65 **poised** weighed 66 **But he . . . a whore** (1) but he, i.e., Menelaus, as heavy as his small merit may be, plus the weight of the whore who is, after all, his legal possession (?); (2) but he, whoever wins her, heavier only by the weight of a whore (to be "light" was to be morally loose) (?)

For every false drop in her bawdy veins
A Grecian's life hath sunk; for every scruple
Of her contaminated carrion weight
A Troyan hath been slain. Since she could speak,
She hath not given so many good words breath
As for her Greeks and Troyans suffered death.

PARIS Fair Diomed, you do as chapmen do,
Dispraise the thing that you desire to buy;
But we in silence hold this virtue well,
We'll not commend what we intend to sell.
Here lies our way. *Exeunt.*

[Scene II. *Within Troy; Calchas' house.*]

Enter Troilus and Cressida.

TROILUS Dear, trouble not yourself; the morn is cold.

CRESSIDA Then, sweet my lord, I'll call mine uncle down;
He shall unbolt the gates.

TROILUS Trouble him not;
To bed, to bed. Sleep kill those pretty eyes,
And give as soft attachment to thy senses
As infants' empty of all thought!

CRESSIDA Good morrow then.

TROILUS I prithee now, to bed.

CRESSIDA Are you aweary of me?

TROILUS O Cressida! But that the busy day,

70 **scruple** (the smallest possible unit of weight) 75 **chapmen** hawkers of cheap wares 78 **We'll not . . . to sell** i.e., we'll not practice the seller's tricks although you practice the buyer's (Paris does not imply that Helen is for sale) IV.ii.4 **kill** overpower 5 **attachment** seizure

Waked by the lark, hath roused the ribald crows,
And dreaming night will hide our joys no longer,
I would not from thee.

CRESSIDA Night hath been too brief.

TROILUS Beshrew the witch! With venomous wights she stays
As tediously as hell, but flies the grasps of love
With wings more momentary-swift than thought.
You will catch cold and curse me.

CRESSIDA Prithee, tarry;
You men will never tarry.
O foolish Cressid! I might have still held off,
And then you would have tarried. Hark, there's one up.

PANDARUS (*Within*) What's all the doors open here?

TROILUS It is your uncle.

CRESSIDA A pestilence on him! Now will he be mocking.
I shall have such a life.

Enter Pandarus.

PANDARUS How now, how now! How go maidenheads?
Here, you maid, where's my cousin Cressid?

CRESSIDA Go hang yourself, you naughty mocking uncle.
You bring me to do—and then you flout me too.

PANDARUS To do what? To do what? Let her say what.
What have I brought you to do?

CRESSIDA Come come; beshrew your heart! You'll ne'er be good,
Nor suffer others.

PANDARUS Ha, ha! Alas, poor wretch! A poor capocchia!

12 **venomous weights** malignant witches (or, simply, evil creatures) 26 **do** (used sometimes in obscene sense) 31 **capocchia** simpleton

Hast not slept tonight? Would he not, a naughty man, let it sleep? A bugbear take him!

CRESSIDA Did not I tell you? Would he were knocked i' the head! *One knocks.*
Who's that at door? Good uncle, go and see.
My lord, come you again into my chamber.
You smile and mock me, as if I meant naughtily.

TROILUS Ha, ha!

CRESSIDA Come, you are deceived, I think of no such thing. *Knock.*
How earnestly they knock! Pray you, come in.
I would not for half Troy have you seen here.
Exeunt [*Troilus and Cressida*].

PANDARUS Who's there? What's the matter? Will you beat down the door? How now, what's the matter?

[*Enter Aeneas.*]

AENEAS Good morrow, lord, good morrow.

PANDARUS Who's there? My Lord Aeneas! By my troth,
I knew you not. What news with you so early?

AENEAS Is not Prince Troilus here?

PANDARUS Here? What should he do here?

AENEAS Come, he is here, my lord. Do not deny him.
It doth import him much to speak with me.

PANDARUS Is he here, say you? 'Tis more than I know, I'll be sworn. For my own part, I came in late. What should he do here?

AENEAS Who! Nay, then. Come, come, you'll do him wrong ere you are ware. You'll be so true to him, to

33 **bugbear** hobgoblin 50 **doth import** is important to 54 **Who!** (an exclamation of impatience; sometimes as to call "stop!" to a horse)

be false to him. Do not you know of him, but yet go fetch him hither; go.

Enter Troilus.

TROILUS How now, what's the matter?

AENEAS My lord, I scarce have leisure to salute you,
My matter is so rash. There is at hand
Paris your brother, and Deiphobus,
The Grecian Diomed, and our Antenor
Delivered to us; and for him forthwith,
Ere the first sacrifice, within this hour,
We must give up to Diomedes' hand
The Lady Cressida.

TROILUS Is it so concluded?

AENEAS By Priam, and the general state of Troy.
They are at hand and ready to effect it.

TROILUS How my achievements mock me!
I will go meet them. And, my Lord Aeneas,
We met by chance; you did not find me here.

AENEAS Good, good, my lord; the secrets of nature
Have not more gift in taciturnity.
Exeunt [*Troilus and Aeneas*].

PANDARUS Is't possible? No sooner got but lost? The devil take Antenor! The young prince will go mad. A plague upon Antenor! I would they had broke 's neck!

Enter Cressida.

CRESSIDA How now? What's the matter? Who was here?

PANDARUS Ah, ah!

CRESSIDA Why sigh you so profoundly? Where's my

60 **rash** urgent 67 **general state** noblemen in council 72 **secrets** most unknown parts

lord? Gone? Tell me, sweet uncle, what's the matter?

PANDARUS Would I were as deep under the earth as I am above!

CRESSIDA O the gods! What's the matter?

PANDARUS Pray thee, get thee in. Would thou hadst ne'er been born! I knew thou wouldst be his death. O poor gentleman! A plague upon Antenor!

CRESSIDA Good uncle, I beseech you on my knees, what's the matter?

PANDARUS Thou must be gone, wench, thou must be gone; thou art changed for Antenor. Thou must to thy father and be gone from Troilus. 'Twill be his death; 'twill be his bane; he cannot bear it.

CRESSIDA O you immortal gods! I will not go.

PANDARUS Thou must.

CRESSIDA I will not, uncle. I have forgot my father;
I know no touch of consanguinity—
No kin, no love, no blood, no soul so near me
As the sweet Troilus. O you gods divine,
Make Cressid's name the very crown of falsehood
If ever she leave Troilus! Time, force, and death,
Do to this body what extremes you can;
But the strong base and building of my love
Is as the very center of the earth,
Drawing all things to it. I will go in and weep——

PANDARUS Do, do.

CRESSIDA —Tear my bright hair, and scratch my praisèd cheeks,
Crack my clear voice with sobs, and break my heart
With sounding Troilus. I will not go from Troy.
Exeunt.

93 changed exchanged **95 bane** poison, destruction **99 no touch of consanguinity** no sense of relationship

[Scene III. *Within Troy; near Calchas' house.*]

Enter Paris, Troilus, Aeneas, Deiphobus, Antenor, Diomedes.

PARIS It is great morning, and the hour prefixed
For her delivery to this valiant Greek
Comes fast upon. Good my brother Troilus,
Tell you the lady what she is to do,
And haste her to the purpose.

TROILUS Walk into her house.
I'll bring her to the Grecian presently;
And to his hand when I deliver her,
Think it an altar, and thy brother Troilus
A priest there off'ring to it his own heart.

PARIS I know what 'tis to love;
And would, as I shall pity, I could help.
Please you walk in, my lords. *Exeunt.*

[Scene IV. *Within Troy; Calchas' house.*]

Enter Pandarus and Cressida.

PANDARUS Be moderate, be moderate.

CRESSIDA Why tell you me of moderation?
The grief is fine, full, perfect, that I taste,
And violenteth in a sense as strong
As that which causeth it. How can I moderate it?
If I could temporize with my affections,

IV.iii.1 **great morning** broad daylight 6 **presently** immediately IV.iv.4 **violenteth** rages

Or brew it to a weak and colder palate,
The like allayment could I give my grief.
My love admits no qualifying dross;
No more my grief, in such a precious loss.

Enter Troilus.

PANDARUS Here, here, here he comes. Ah, sweet ducks!

CRESSIDA O Troilus! Troilus!

PANDARUS What a pair of spectacles is here! Let me embrace too. "O heart," as the goodly saying is—
O heart, heavy heart,
Why sigh'st thou without breaking?
where he answers again,
Because thou canst not ease thy smart
By friendship nor by speaking.
There was never a truer rhyme. Let us cast away nothing, for we may live to have need of such a verse. We see it, we see it. How now, lambs!

TROILUS Cressid, I love thee in so strained a purity,
That the blest gods, as angry with my fancy,
More bright in zeal than the devotion which
Cold lips blow to their deities, take thee from me.

CRESSIDA Have the gods envy?

PANDARUS Ay, ay, ay, ay, 'tis too plain a case.

CRESSIDA And is it true that I must go from Troy?

TROILUS A hateful truth.

CRESSIDA What, and from Troilus too?

TROILUS From Troy and Troilus.

CRESSIDA Is't possible?

7 **palate** taste 9 **qualifying dross** moderating impurity 14 **spectacles** (a pun) 24 **strained** distilled, filtered 25 **fancy** love

TROILUS And suddenly, where injury of chance
Puts back leave-taking, justles roughly by
All time of pause, rudely beguiles our lips
Of all rejoindure, forcibly prevents
Our locked embrasures, strangles our dear vows
Even in the birth of our own laboring breath.
We two, that with so many thousand sighs
Did buy each other, must poorly sell ourselves
With the rude brevity and discharge of one.
Injurious time now with a robber's haste
Crams his rich thievery up, he knows not how;
As many farewells as be stars in heaven,
With distinct breath and consigned kisses to them,
He fumbles up into a loose adieu,
And scants us with a single famished kiss,
Distasted with the salt of broken tears.

AENEAS (*Within*) My lord, is the lady ready?

TROILUS Hark! You are called. Some say the Genius
Cries so to him that instantly must die.
Bid them have patience; she shall come anon.

PANDARUS Where are my tears? Rain, to lay this wind,
or my heart will be blown up by the root! [*Exit.*]

CRESSIDA I must, then, to the Grecians?

TROILUS No remedy.

CRESSIDA A woeful Cressid 'mongst the merry Greeks!
When shall we see again?

TROILUS Hear me, love. Be thou but true of heart——

CRESSIDA I true! How now! What wicked deem is this?

TROILUS Nay, we must use expostulation kindly,

33 **injury of chance** injurious accident 36 **rejoindure** reunion 45 **With distinct . . . to them** with the words of each farewell and the kisses which ratify each of them 46 **fumbles** wraps clumsily 48 **Distasted** the taste (of the kiss) ruined 50 **Genius** guardian spirit 59 **deem** thought

For it is parting from us.
I speak not "be thou true" as fearing thee,
For I will throw my glove to Death himself
That there's no maculation in thy heart;
But "be thou true," say I, to fashion in
My sequent protestation: be thou true,
And I will see thee.

CRESSIDA O, you shall be exposed, my lord, to dangers
As infinite as imminent; but I'll be true.

TROILUS And I'll grow friend with danger. Wear this
sleeve.

CRESSIDA And you this glove. When shall I see you?

TROILUS I will corrupt the Grecian sentinels,
To give thee nightly visitation.
But yet, be true.

CRESSIDA O heavens! "Be true" again!

TROILUS Hear why I speak it, love.
The Grecian youths are full of quality;
They're loving, well composed with gift of nature,
And swelling o'er with arts and exercise.
How novelty may move, and parts with person,
Alas! A kind of godly jealousy—
Which, I beseech you, call a virtuous sin—
Makes me afeared.

CRESSIDA O heavens, you love me not!

TROILUS Die I a villain then!
In this I do not call your faith in question
So mainly as my merit. I cannot sing,

60–61 **Nay, we . . . from us** we must be gentle in all remonstrance, for we are now saying good-bye 63 **throw my glove** give challenge 64 **maculation** taint, blemish (i.e., disloyalty) 65–66 **to fashion in . . . sequent protestation** as introduction for my own promise to follow 76 **quality** qualities 77 **loving** adept in the arts of love 78 **arts and exercise** talents both in theory and practice 79 **parts with person** specific qualities and talents, combined with personal charm

Nor heel the high lavolt, nor sweeten talk,
Nor play at subtle games—fair virtues all,
To which the Grecians are most prompt and pregnant;
But I can tell that in each grace of these
There lurks a still and dumb-discoursive devil
That tempts most cunningly. But be not tempted.

CRESSIDA Do you think I will?

TROILUS No!
But something may be done that we will not;
And sometimes we are devils to ourselves
When we will tempt the frailty of our powers,
Presuming on their changeful potency.

AENEAS (*Within*) Nay, good my lord!

TROILUS Come, kiss; and let us part.

PARIS (*Within*) Brother Troilus!

TROILUS Good brother, come you hither;
And bring Aeneas and the Grecian with you.

CRESSIDA My lord, will you be true?

TROILUS Who? I? Alas, it is my vice, my fault.
Whiles others fish with craft for great opinion,
I with great truth catch mere simplicity;
Whilst some with cunning gild their copper crowns,
With truth and plainness I do wear mine bare.
Fear not my truth; the moral of my wit
Is "plain and true"—there's all the reach of it.

[*Enter Aeneas, Paris, Antenor, Deiphobus and Diomedes.*]

Welcome, Sir Diomed. Here is the lady

86 **the high lavolt** (the lavolt was a dance for two persons, requiring many high steps and bounds) 88 **pregnant** ready, fully able 90 **dumb-discoursive** articulate even in silence 97 **changeful potency** power which may alter to failure 103 **opinion** reputation 104 **catch** achieve; i.e., achieve a reputation for 107 **moral** maxim

Which for Antenor we deliver you.
At the port, lord, I'll give her to thy hand,
And by the way possess thee what she is.
Entreat her fair; and, by my soul, fair Greek,
If e'er thou stand at mercy of my sword,
Name Cressid, and thy life shall be as safe
As Priam is in Ilion.

DIOMEDES Fair Lady Cressid,
So please you, save the thanks this prince expects.
The luster in your eye, heaven in your cheek,
Pleads your fair usage; and to Diomed
You shall be mistress, and command him wholly.

TROILUS Grecian, thou dost not use me courteously,
To shame the seal of my petition to thee
In praising her. I tell thee, lord of Greece,
She is as far high-soaring o'er thy praises
As thou unworthy to be called her servant.
I charge thee use her well, even for my charge;
For, by the dreadful Pluto, if thou dost not,
Though the great bulk Achilles be thy guard,
I'll cut thy throat.

DIOMEDES O, be not moved, Prince Troilus.
Let me be privileged by my place and message
To be a speaker free. When I am hence,
I'll answer to my lust; and know you, lord,
I'll nothing do on charge. To her own worth
She shall be prized; but that you say "be't so,"
I speak it in my spirit and honor, "no."

TROILUS Come, to the port. I'll tell thee, Diomed,
This brave shall oft make thee to hide thy head.
Lady, give me your hand, and, as we walk,
To our own selves bend we our needful talk.
[*Exeunt Troilus, Cressida, and Diomedes.*]
Sound trumpet.

111 **port** gate (of the city) 112 **possess** inform 113 **Entreat** treat 122 **To shame the seal of my petition** to disdain the worth of my charge and promise 126 **even for my charge** simply because I say so 132 **answer to my lust** do as I please 137 **brave** boast

PARIS Hark! Hector's trumpet.

AENEAS How have we spent this
morning!
The prince must think me tardy and remiss,
That swore to ride before him to the field.

PARIS 'Tis Troilus' fault. Come, come, to field with
him.

DEIPHOBUS Let us make ready straight.

AENEAS Yea, with a bridegroom's fresh alacrity,
Let us address to tend on Hector's heels.
The glory of our Troy doth this day lie
On his fair worth and single chivalry. *Exeunt.*

[Scene V. *The Greek camp.*]

Enter Ajax, armed; Achilles, Patroclus, Agamemnon, Menelaus, Ulysses, Nestor, Calchas, &c.

AGAMEMNON Here art thou in appointment fresh and
fair,
Anticipating time. With starting courage,
Give with thy trumpet a loud note to Troy,
Thou dreadful Ajax, that the appallèd air
May pierce the head of the great combatant
And hale him hither.

AJAX Thou, trumpet, there's my
purse.
Now crack thy lungs, and split thy brazen pipe.
Blow, villain, till thy spherèd bias cheek
Outswell the colic of puffed Aquilon!

146 **address** prepare IV.v.1 **appointment** equipment and apparel 2 **starting** active, prompt 6 **trumpet** trumpeter 8 **bias** puffed-out 9 **the colic of puffed Aquilon** the north wind, distended as if by colic

Come, stretch thy chest, and let thy eyes spout blood;
Thou blow'st for Hector. [*Trumpet sounds.*]

ULYSSES No trumpet answers.

ACHILLES 'Tis but early days.

AGAMEMNON Is not yond Diomed with Calchas' daughter?

ULYSSES 'Tis he, I ken the manner of his gait;
He rises on the toe. That spirit of his
In aspiration lifts him from the earth.

[*Enter Diomedes, with Cressida.*]

AGAMEMNON Is this the Lady Cressid?

DIOMEDES Even she.

AGAMEMNON Most dearly welcome to the Greeks, sweet lady.

NESTOR Our general doth salute you with a kiss.

ULYSSES Yet is the kindness but particular.
'Twere better she were kissed in general.

NESTOR And very courtly counsel. I'll begin.
So much for Nestor.

ACHILLES I'll take that winter from your lips, fair lady.
Achilles bids you welcome.

MENELAUS I had good argument for kissing once.

PATROCLUS But that's no argument for kissing now;
For thus popped Paris in his hardiment,
And parted thus you and your argument.

ULYSSES O, deadly gall, and theme of all our scorns,

12 days in the day **20 particular** single **21 in general** (1) by the general (2) universally **24 that winter** i.e., Nestor's kiss (cold from old age) **28 hardiment** boldness **29 argument** i.e., Helen

For which we lose our heads to gild his horns.

PATROCLUS The first was Menelaus' kiss; this, mine.
Patroclus kisses you.

MENELAUS O, this is trim.

PATROCLUS Paris and I kiss evermore for him.

MENELAUS I'll have my kiss, sir. Lady, by your leave.

CRESSIDA In kissing, do you render or receive?

PATROCLUS Both take and give.

CRESSIDA I'll make my match to live,
The kiss you take is better than you give;
Therefore no kiss.

MENELAUS I'll give you boot; I'll give you three for one.

CRESSIDA You are an odd man; give even, or give none.

MENELAUS An odd man, lady? Every man is odd.

CRESSIDA No, Paris is not, for you know 'tis true
That you are odd and he is even with you.

MENELAUS You fillip me o' the head.

CRESSIDA No, I'll be sworn.

ULYSSES It were no match, your nail against his horn.
May I, sweet lady, beg a kiss of you?

CRESSIDA You may.

ULYSSES I do desire it.

CRESSIDA Why, beg then.

37 I'll . . . match to live I'll bet my life **40 boot** odds **41 odd** i.e., single and singular **45 fillip** tap **46 It . . . horn** your nail, in tapping, would be no match for his hard cuckold's horn

ULYSSES Why, then, for Venus' sake, give me a kiss,
When Helen is a maid again, and his.

CRESSIDA I am your debtor; claim it when 'tis due.

ULYSSES Never's my day, and then a kiss of you.

DIOMEDES Lady, a word. I'll bring you to your father.
[*Exeunt Diomedes and Cressida.*]

NESTOR A woman of quick sense.
ULYSSES Fie, fie upon her!
There's language in her eye, her cheek, her lip;
Nay, her foot speaks. Her wanton spirits look out
At every joint and motive of her body.
O, these encounterers, so glib of tongue,
That give a coasting welcome ere it comes,
And wide unclasp the tables of their thoughts
To every ticklish reader, set them down
For sluttish spoils of opportunity
And daughters of the game.

Flourish. Enter all of Troy [*Hector, Paris, Aeneas, Helenus, Troilus, and Attendants*].

ALL The Troyans' trumpet.

AGAMEMNON Yonder comes the troop.

AENEAS Hail, all the state of Greece. What shall be done
To him that victory commands? Or do you purpose
A victor shall be known? Will you the knights
Shall to the edge of all extremity
Pursue each other, or shall they be divided

54 **Fie, fie upon her!** (Ulysses' exclamation does not imply disagreement with Nestor's observation; the following nine lines elaborate "quick sense") 57 **motive** moving part 59 **a coasting welcome ere it comes** a sidelong, flirtatious greeting before being greeted 60 **tables** tablets 62 **sluttish spoils of opportunity** harlots who yield at every opportunity 63 **daughters of the game** whores 63 **The Troyans' trumpet** (in the theater, this line becomes a pun on "strumpet") 69 **divided** i.e., separated during the fight

By any voice or order of the field?
Hector bade ask.

AGAMEMNON Which way would Hector have it?

AENEAS He cares not; he'll obey conditions.

ACHILLES 'Tis done like Hector; but securely done,
A little proudly, and great deal misprising
The knight opposed.

AENEAS If not Achilles, sir.
What is your name?

ACHILLES If not Achilles, nothing.

AENEAS Therefore Achilles; but, whate'er, know this:
In the extremity of great and little,
Valor and pride excel themselves in Hector;
The one almost as infinite as all,
The other blank as nothing. Weigh him well;
And that which looks like pride is courtesy.
This Ajax is half made of Hector's blood,
In love whereof half Hector stays at home;
Half heart, half hand, half Hector comes to seek
This blended knight, half Troyan, and half Greek.

ACHILLES A maiden battle, then? O, I perceive you.

[*Enter Diomedes.*]

AGAMEMNON Here is Sir Diomed. Go, gentle knight,
Stand by our Ajax. As you and Lord Aeneas
Consent upon the order of their fight,
So be it; either to the uttermost,
Or else a breath. The combatants being kin
Half stints their strife before their strokes begin.

[*Ajax and Hector enter the lists.*]

ULYSSES They are opposed already.

73 **securely** overconfidently 83 **Hector's blood** (see note to II.ii.77) 87 **maiden** bloodless (as of novices or men in training, who do not intend to kill) 92 **breath** exercise

AGAMEMNON What Troyan is that same that looks so
heavy?

ULYSSES The youngest son of Priam, a true knight,
Not yet mature, yet matchless; firm of word,
Speaking in deeds and deedless in his tongue,
Not soon provoked, nor being provoked soon
calmed;
His heart and hand both open and both free,
For what he has he gives, what thinks he shows;
Yet gives he not till judgment guide his bounty,
Nor dignifies an impare thought with breath;
Manly as Hector, but more dangerous;
For Hector, in his blaze of wrath, subscribes
To tender objects, but he in heat of action
Is more vindicative than jealous love.
They call him Troilus, and on him erect
A second hope as fairly built as Hector.
Thus says Aeneas, one that knows the youth
Even to his inches, and with private soul
Did in great Ilion thus translate him to me.
Alarum. [*Hector and Ajax fight.*]

AGAMEMNON They are in action.

NESTOR Now, Ajax, hold thine own!

TROILUS Hector, thou
sleep'st; awake thee!

AGAMEMNON His blows are well disposed. There, Ajax!

DIOMEDES You must no more. *Trumpets cease.*

AENEAS Princes, enough, so please
you.

95 **heavy** heavyhearted 98 **deedless in his tongue** free of boasts 100 **free** generous 103 **impare thought** (1) ill-considered thought (2) thought unequal to the dignity of his character 105–06 **subscribes/To tender objects** grants merciful terms to the defenseless 111 **Even to his inches** i.e., from head to toe 111 **with private soul** in confidence 115 **well disposed** well aimed, well placed

AJAX I am not warm yet; let us fight again.

DIOMEDES As Hector pleases.

HECTOR Why, then will I no more.
Thou art, great lord, my father's sister's son,
A cousin-german to great Priam's seed;
The obligation of our blood forbids
A gory emulation 'twixt us twain.
Were thy commixtion Greek and Troyan so
That thou couldst say, "This hand is Grecian all,
And this is Troyan; the sinews of this leg
All Greek, and this all Troy; my mother's blood
Runs on the dexter cheek, and this sinister
Bounds in my father's," by Jove multipotent,
Thou shouldst not bear from me a Greekish member
Wherein my sword had not impressure made
Of our rank feud. But the just gods gainsay
That any drop thou borrow'dst from thy mother,
My sacred aunt, should by my mortal sword
Be drained! Let me embrace thee, Ajax—
By him that thunders, thou hast lusty arms;
Hector would have them fall upon him thus.
Cousin, all honor to thee!

AJAX I thank thee, Hector;
Thou art too gentle and too free a man.
I came to kill thee, cousin, and bear hence
A great addition earnèd in thy death.

HECTOR Not Neoptolemus so mirable,
On whose bright crest Fame with her loud'st
"Oyes"
Cries, "This is he!" could promise to himself
A thought of added honor torn from Hector.

123 **commixtion** composition 127 **dexter** right 127 **sinister** left 128 **multipotent** of many powers 135 **him that thunders** i.e., Jove (Zeus) 136 **thus** i.e., embracing him 141 **Neoptolemus** (this name probably applies here to Achilles himself, and not to his son, Pyrrhus) 141 **mirable** wonderful 142 **Oyes** cries beginning the proclamations of heralds or sessions of a court

AENEAS There is expectance here from both the sides,
What further you will do.

HECTOR We'll answer it.
The issue is embracement. Ajax, farewell.

AJAX If I might in entreaties find success—
As seld I have the chance—I would desire
My famous cousin to our Grecian tents.

DIOMEDES 'Tis Agamemnon's wish; and great Achilles
Doth long to see unarmed the valiant Hector.

HECTOR Aeneas, call my brother Troilus to me,
And signify this loving interview
To the expecters of our Troyan part.
Desire them home. Give me thy hand, my cousin;
I will go eat with thee and see your knights.

[*Agamemnon and the rest approach them.*]

AJAX Great Agamemnon comes to meet us here.

HECTOR The worthiest of them tell me name by name;
But for Achilles, my own searching eyes
Shall find him by his large and portly size.

AGAMEMNON Worthy all arms [*embraces him*], as welcome as to one
That would be rid of such an enemy—
But that's no welcome. Understand more clear,
What's past and what's to come is strewed with husks
And formless ruin of oblivion;
But in this extant moment, faith and troth,
Strained purely from all hollow bias-drawing,
Bids thee, with most divine integrity,
From heart of very heart, great Hector, welcome.

147 **issue** result, outcome 149 **seld** seldom 154 **signify** expound, explain 155 **the expecters of our Troyan part** those on our side, the Trojans, awaiting news 156 **Desire them home** ask them to go home 167 **extant** present 168 **all hollow bias-drawing** all fruitless and tortuous dealings (in the course of the war, as in the course given by the bias of a bowl in bowling)

HECTOR I thank thee, most imperious Agamemnon.

AGAMEMNON [*To Troilus*] My well-famed lord of Troy, no less to you.

MENELAUS Let me confirm my princely brother's greeting.
You brace of warlike brothers, welcome hither.

HECTOR Who must we answer?

AENEAS The noble Menelaus.

HECTOR O, you, my lord? By Mars his gauntlet, thanks!
Mock not that I affect th' untraded oath;
Your quondam wife swears still by Venus' glove.
She's well, but bade me not commend her to you.

MENELAUS Name her not now, sir; she's a deadly theme.

HECTOR O, pardon! I offend.

NESTOR I have, thou gallant Troyan, seen thee oft,
Laboring for destiny, make cruel way
Through ranks of Greekish youth; and I have seen thee,
As hot as Perseus, spur thy Phrygian steed,
Despising many forfeits and subduements,
When thou hast hung thy advancèd sword i' th' air,
Not letting it decline on the declinèd,
That I have said to some my standers-by,
"Lo, Jupiter is yonder, dealing life!"
And I have seen thee pause and take thy breath,

177 **untraded** unusual, unfamiliar (Hector, apologizing for what might appear to be an affected oath, gives his reason for using it in the following line, in which he completes a satirical reference to Menelaus and Helen by alluding to the liaison between Mars and Venus) 178 **quondam** former 183 **Laboring for destiny** working in behalf of destiny, i.e., causing destined deaths 186 **Despising many forfeits and subduements** ignoring or disdaining those already vanquished, whose lives were forfeit 187 **hung** held suspended 190 **dealing life** dispensing life (as a god might do by not causing death)

When that a ring of Greeks have shraped thee in,
Like an Olympian wrestling. This have I seen;
But this thy countenance, still locked in steel,
I never saw till now. I knew thy grandsire,
And once fought with him. He was a soldier good;
But, by great Mars, the captain of us all,
Never like thee. O, let an old man embrace thee;
And, worthy warrior, welcome to our tents.

AENEAS 'Tis the old Nestor.

HECTOR Let me embrace thee, good old chronicle,
That has so long walked hand in hand with time.
Most reverend Nestor, I am glad to clasp thee.

NESTOR I would my arms could match thee in contention,
As they contend with thee in courtesy.

HECTOR I would they could.

NESTOR Ha,
By this white beard, I'd fight with thee tomorrow.
Well, welcome, welcome. I have seen the time——

ULYSSES I wonder now how yonder city stands,
When we have here her base and pillar by us.

HECTOR I know your favor, Lord Ulysses, well.
Ah, sir, there's many a Greek and Troyan dead,
Since first I saw yourself and Diomed
In Ilion, on your Greekish embassy.

ULYSSES Sir, I foretold you then what would ensue.
My prophecy is but half his journey yet;
For yonder walls, that pertly front your town,
Yon towers, whose wanton tops do buss the clouds,
Must kiss their own feet.

HECTOR I must not believe you.
There they stand yet, and modestly I think,

192 shraped trapped **194 still** always **195 grandsire** (Laomedon, the builder of Troy) **212 favor** face, features **219 buss** kiss

The fall of every Phrygian stone will cost
A drop of Grecian blood. The end crowns all,
And that old common arbitrator, Time,
Will one day end it.

ULYSSES So to him we leave it.
Most gentle and most valiant Hector, welcome.
After the general, I beseech you next
To feast with me and see me at my tent.

ACHILLES I shall forestall thee, Lord Ulysses, thou!
Now, Hector, I have fed mine eyes on thee;
I have with exact view perused thee, Hector,
And quoted joint by joint.

HECTOR Is this Achilles?

ACHILLES I am Achilles.

HECTOR Stand fair, I pray thee; let me look on thee.

ACHILLES Behold thy fill.

HECTOR Nay, I have done already.

ACHILLES Thou art too brief. I will the second time,
As I would buy thee, view thee limb by limb.

HECTOR O, like a book of sport thou'lt read me o'er;
But there's more in me than thou understand'st.
Why dost thou so oppress me with thine eye?

ACHILLES Tell me, you heavens, in which part of his body
Shall I destroy him, whether there, or there, or there?
That I may give the local wound a name,
And make distinct the very breach whereout
Hector's great spirit flew. Answer me, heavens!

HECTOR It would discredit the blessed gods, proud man,
To answer such a question. Stand again.

232 quoted made exact mental note, scrutinized **234 Stand fair** stand openly, face me

Think'st thou to catch my life so pleasantly
As to prenominate in nice conjecture
Where thou wilt hit me dead?

ACHILLES I tell thee, yea.

HECTOR Wert thou an oracle to tell me so,
I'd not believe thee. Henceforth guard thee well,
For I'll not kill thee there, nor there, nor there;
But, by the forge that stithied Mars his helm,
I'll kill thee everywhere, yea, o'er and o'er.
You wisest Grecians, pardon me this brag.
His insolence draws folly from my lips;
But I'll endeavor deeds to match these words,
Or may I never——

AJAX Do not chafe thee, cousin;
And you, Achilles, let these threats alone,
Till accident or purpose bring you to't.
You may have every day enough of Hector,
If you have stomach. The general state, I fear,
Can scarce entreat you to be odd with him.

HECTOR I pray you, let us see you in the field.
We have had pelting wars since you refused
The Grecians' cause.

ACHILLES Dost thou entreat me, Hector?
Tomorrow do I meet thee, fell as death;
Tonight all friends.

HECTOR Thy hand upon that match.

AGAMEMNON First, all you peers of Greece, go to my
tent;
There in the full convive we. Afterwards,
As Hector's leisure and your bounties shall
Concur together, severally entreat him

248 **pleasantly** casually, merrily 249 **prenominate in nice conjecture** name beforehand in detailed conjecture 254 **stithied** forged 263 **stomach** inclination, relish 263 **general state** commanders in council 264 **odd** at odds, engaged in combat 266 **pelting** paltry, petty 267 **entreat** invite 268 **fell** fierce 271 **convive** feast 273 **severally** individually

To taste your bounties. Let the trumpets blow,
That this great soldier may his welcome know.
Exeunt [*all except Troilus and Ulysses*].

TROILUS My Lord Ulysses, tell me, I beseech you,
In what place of the field doth Calchas keep?

ULYSSES At Menelaus' tent, most princely Troilus.
There Diomed doth feast with him tonight—
Who neither looks upon the heaven nor earth,
But gives all gaze and bent of amorous view
On the fair Cressid.

TROILUS Shall I, sweet lord, be bound to you so much,
After we part from Agamemnon's tent,
To bring me thither?

ULYSSES You shall command me, sir.
But gentle tell me, of what honor was
This Cressida in Troy? Had she no lover there
That wails her absence?

TROILUS O, sir, to such as boasting show their scars
A mock is due. Will you walk on, my lord?
She was beloved, she loved; she is, and doth;
But still sweet love is food for fortune's tooth.
Exeunt.

277 **keep** dwell

[ACT V

Scene I. *The Greek camp.*]

Enter Achilles and Patroclus.

ACHILLES I'll heat his blood with Greekish wine tonight,
Which with my scimitar I'll cool tomorrow.
Patroclus, let us feast him to the height.

Enter Thersites.

PATROCLUS Here comes Thersites.

ACHILLES How now, thou cur of envy!
Thou crusty batch of nature, what's the news?

THERSITES Why, thou picture of what thou seemest, and idol of idiot-worshipers, here's a letter for thee.

ACHILLES From whence, fragment?

THERSITES Why, thou full dish of fool, from Troy.

V.i.5 **batch** (a mass of anything baked together, or baked without reheating the oven) 6 **thou picture of what thou seemest** (i.e., who is nothing more than one glance sufficiently reveals)

PATROCLUS Who keeps the tent now?

THERSITES The surgeon's box or the patient's wound.

PATROCLUS Well said, adversity, and what needs these tricks?

THERSITES Prithee, be silent, boy; I profit not by thy talk. Thou art said to be Achilles' male varlet.

PATROCLUS Male varlet, you rogue! What's that?

THERSITES Why, his masculine whore. Now, the rotten diseases of the south, the guts-griping ruptures, catarrhs, loads o' gravel in the back, lethargies, cold palsies, raw eyes, dirt-rotten livers, wheezing lungs, bladders full of imposthume, sciaticas, lime-kilns i'the palm, incurable bone-ache, and the riveled fee-simple of the tetter, and the like, take and take again such preposterous discoveries!

PATROCLUS Why, thou damnable box of envy, thou, what means thou to curse thus?

THERSITES Do I curse thee?

PATROCLUS Why, no, you ruinous butt, you whoreson indistinguishable cur, no.

THERSITES No? Why art thou then exasperate, thou idle immaterial skein of sleave silk, thou green sarcenet flap for a sore eye, thou tassel of a prodigal's purse, thou? Ah, how the poor world is

10 **Who keeps the tent now?** (Thersites can no longer taunt Achilles for refusing to leave his tent) 11 **The surgeon's . . . wound** (from the play on "tent," a surgeon's probe for wounds) 18 **diseases of the south** i.e., venereal diseases 19–20 **gravel . . . palsies** kidney stones, apoplectic strokes, paralysis of the limbs 21 **imposthume** internal abscess 22 **lime-kilns** psoriasis (burning red patches covered with scales) 23 **riveled** wrinkled 23 **fee-simple of the tetter** chronic ringworm (?) ("fee-simple" implies unlimited possession) 24 **discoveries** (referring generally to—in Thersites' opinion—such absurd monstrosities as Patroclus) 28 **ruinous butt** dilapidated cask 29 **indistinguishable** shapeless (here suggesting mongrel) 31 **sleave silk** soft silk floss 32 **sarcenet** (a fine silk taffeta)

pestered with such water-flies, diminutives of nature.

PATROCLUS Out, gall!

THERSITES Finch egg!

ACHILLES My sweet Patroclus, I am thwarted quite
From my great purpose in tomorrow's battle.
Here is a letter from Queen Hecuba,
A token from her daughter, my fair love,
Both taxing me and gaging me to keep
An oath that I have sworn. I will not break it.
Fall Greeks, fail fame, honor or go or stay,
My major vow lies here; this I'll obey.
Come, come, Thersites, help to trim my tent;
This night in banqueting must all be spent.
Away, Patroclus! *Exit [with Patroclus].*

THERSITES With too much blood and too little brain, these two may run mad; but if with too much brain and too little blood they do, I'll be a curer of madmen. Here's Agamemnon, an honest fellow enough, and one that loves quails, but he has not so much brain as ear-wax; and the goodly transformation of Jupiter there, his brother, the bull, the primitive statue and oblique memorial of cuckolds—a thrifty shoeing-horn in a chain, hanging at his brother's leg—to what form but that he is should wit larded with malice and malice forced with wit turn him to? To an ass, were nothing; he is both ass and ox. To an ox, were nothing; he is both ox and ass. To be a dog, a mule, a cat, a fitchew,

42 **taxing** censuring 42 **gaging** engaging to a promise 44 **or go or** either go or 53 **quails** prostitutes 54–55 **transformation of Jupiter** (i.e., into a bull, in which shape he seduced Europa) 55–56 **the primitive statue . . . of cuckolds** (in having horns, the emblem or symbol of cuckoldry, although since Europa was not married, the parallel to Paris' rape of Helen is "oblique") 57 **thrifty** stingy 57–58 **hanging at his brother's leg** (1) as Agamemnon's tool, appropriately enough a "horn," his pretext for war (2) as being entirely dependent on Agamemnon 59 **forced** stuffed, intermixed 62 **fitchew** polecat

a toad, a lizard, an owl, a puttock, or a herring without a roe, I would not care; but to be Menelaus! I would conspire against destiny. Ask me not what I would be, if I were not Thersites, for I care not to be the louse of a lazar, so I were not Menelaus. Hey-day, sprites and fires!

Enter Agamemnon, Ulysses, Nestor, [Hector, Ajax, Troilus, Menelaus,] and Diomedes, with lights.

AGAMEMNON We go wrong, we go wrong.

AJAX No, yonder 'tis;
There, where we see the lights.

HECTOR I trouble you.

AJAX No, not a whit.

ULYSSES Here comes himself to guide you.

Enter Achilles.

ACHILLES Welcome, brave Hector; welcome, princes all.

AGAMEMNON So now, fair prince of Troy, I bid good night.
Ajax commands the guard to tend on you.

HECTOR Thanks and good night to the Greeks' general.

MENELAUS Good night, my lord.

HECTOR Good night, sweet Lord Menelaus.

THERSITES Sweet draught! "Sweet," quoth 'a! Sweet sink, sweet sewer.

ACHILLES Good night and welcome both at once, to those
That go or tarry.

63 **puttock** kite, a small hawk feeding on carrion 66–67 **I care not to be** I wouldn't mind being 67 **lazar** leper 78 **draught** privy, cesspool

AGAMEMNON Good night.

Exeunt Agamemnon, Menelaus.

ACHILLES Old Nestor tarries, and you too, Diomed,
Keep Hector company an hour or two.

DIOMEDES I cannot, lord; I have important business,
The tide whereof is now. Good night, great Hector.

HECTOR Give me your hand.

ULYSSES [*Aside to Troilus*] Follow his torch; he goes to
Calchas' tent.
I'll keep you company.

TROILUS Sweet sir, you honor me.

HECTOR And so, good night.

[*Exeunt Diomedes, then Ulysses and Troilus.*]

ACHILLES Come, come, enter my tent.

Exeunt [*Achilles, Hector, Ajax, and Nestor*].

THERSITES That same Diomed's a false-hearted rogue, a most unjust knave; I will no more trust him when he leers than I will a serpent when he hisses. He will spend his mouth and promise like Brabbler the hound; but when he performs, astronomers foretell it. It is prodigious, there will come some changes. The sun borrows of the moon when Diomed keeps his word. I will rather leave to see Hector than not to dog him. They say he keeps a Troyan drab, and uses the traitor Calchas' tent. I'll after—nothing but lechery! All incontinent varlets! [*Exit.*]

86 tide time **95–96 Brabbler the hound** (a hunting hound who would "spend his mouth" in barking while not on the scent would be called "babbler" or "brabbler" by his master) **99 leave to see** miss seeing

[Scene II. *The Greek camp.*]

Enter Diomed.

DIOMEDES What, are you up here, ho? Speak.

CALCHAS [*Within*] Who calls?

DIOMEDES Diomed. Calchas, I think. Where's your daughter?

CALCHAS [*Within*] She comes to you.

Enter Troilus and Ulysses; [*after them Thersites.*]

ULYSSES Stand where the torch may not discover us.

Enter Cressid.

TROILUS Cressid comes forth to him.

DIOMEDES How now, my charge!

CRESSIDA Now, my sweet guardian! Hark, a word with you. [*Whispers.*]

TROILUS Yea, so familiar!

ULYSSES She will sing any man at first sight.

THERSITES And any man may sing her, if he can take her cliff; she's noted.

DIOMEDES Will you remember?

CRESSIDA Remember? Yes.

DIOMEDES Nay, but do, then;
And let your mind be coupled with your words.

V.ii.11 **cliff** clef (signifying the musical key; with an obscene pun on "cleft")
11 **noted** reputed a loose woman (with a pun on musical notes)

TROILUS What shall she remember?

ULYSSES List!

CRESSIDA Sweet honey Greek, tempt me no more to folly.

THERSITES Roguery!

DIOMEDES Nay, then——

CRESSIDA I'll tell you what——

DIOMEDES Foh, foh! Come, tell a pin. You are forsworn.

CRESSIDA In faith, I cannot. What would you have me do?

THERSITES A juggling trick—to be secretly open.

DIOMEDES What did you swear you would bestow on me?

CRESSIDA I prithee, do not hold me to mine oath;
Bid me do anything but that, sweet Greek.

DIOMEDES Good night.

TROILUS Hold, patience!

ULYSSES How now, Troyan?

CRESSIDA Diomed——

DIOMEDES No, no, good night; I'll be your fool no more

TROILUS Thy better must.

CRESSIDA Hark, a word in your ear.

TROILUS O plague and madness!

ULYSSES You are moved, prince; let us depart, I pray,
Lest your displeasure should enlarge itself

23 **secretly** privately, sexually

To wrathful terms. This place is dangerous;
The time right deadly. I beseech you, go.

TROILUS Behold, I pray you!

ULYSSES Nay, good my lord, go off;
You flow to great distraction. Come, my lord.

TROILUS I prithee, stay.

ULYSSES You have not patience; come.

TROILUS I pray you, stay! By hell, and all hell's torments,
I will not speak a word!

DIOMEDES And so, good night.

CRESSIDA Nay, but you part in anger.

TROILUS Doth that grieve thee?
O withered truth!

ULYSSES How now, my lord!

TROILUS By Jove,
I will be patient.

CRESSIDA Guardian! Why, Greek!

DIOMEDES Foh, foh! Adieu; you palter.

CRESSIDA In faith, I do not. Come hither once again.

ULYSSES You shake, my lord, at something. Will you go?
You will break out.

TROILUS She strokes his cheek!

ULYSSES Come, come.

TROILUS Nay, stay; by Jove, I will not speak a word.
There is between my will and all offenses
A guard of patience. Stay a little while.

THERSITES How the devil Luxury, with his fat rump

53 **Luxury** lechery

and potato finger, tickles these together. Fry, lechery, fry!

DIOMEDES But will you, then?

CRESSIDA In faith, I will, la; never trust me else.

DIOMEDES Give me some token for the surety of it.

CRESSIDA I'll fetch you one. *Exit.*

ULYSSES You have sworn patience.

TROILUS Fear me not, my lord;
I will not be myself, nor have cognition
Of what I feel. I am all patience.

Enter Cressida.

THERSITES Now the pledge! Now, now now!

CRESSIDA Here, Diomed, keep this sleeve.

TROILUS O beauty, where is thy faith?

ULYSSES My lord——

TROILUS I will be patient; outwardly I will.

CRESSIDA You look upon that sleeve; behold it well.
He loved me—O false wench! Give't me again.

DIOMEDES Whose was't?

CRESSIDA It is no matter, now I have't again.
I will not meet with you tomorrow night.
I prithee, Diomed, visit me no more.

THERSITES Now she sharpens. Well said, whetstone!

DIOMEDES I shall have it.

CRESSIDA What, this?

DIOMEDES Ay, that.

CRESSIDA O, all you gods! O pretty, pretty pledge!

54 **potato** (potatoes were thought to be aphrodisiac) 72 **sharpens** i.e., whets Diomedes' desire

Thy master now lies thinking on his bed
Of thee and me, and sighs, and takes my glove,
And gives memorial dainty kisses to it,
As I kiss thee. Nay, do not snatch it from me;
He that takes that doth take my heart withal.

DIOMEDES I had your heart before; this follows it.

TROILUS I did swear patience.

CRESSIDA You shall not have it, Diomed; faith, you shall not;
I'll give you something else.

DIOMEDES I will have this. Whose was it?

CRESSIDA It is no matter.

DIOMEDES Come, tell me whose it was.

CRESSIDA 'Twas one's that loved me better than you will.
But, now you have it, take it.

DIOMEDES Whose was it?

CRESSIDA By all Diana's waiting-women yond,
And by herself, I will not tell you whose.

DIOMEDES Tomorrow will I wear it on my helm,
And grieve his spirit that dares not challenge it.

TROILUS Wert thou the devil, and wor'st it on thy horn,
It should be challenged.

CRESSIDA Well, well, 'tis done, 'tis past. And yet it is not;
I will not keep my word.

DIOMEDES Why then, farewell;
Thou never shalt mock Diomed again.

CRESSIDA You shall not go. One cannot speak a word
But it straight starts you.

77 **memorial** in remembrance 88 **Diana's waiting-women** i.e., the stars clustered about the moon 98 **straight starts you** immediately makes you start angrily away

DIOMEDES I do not like this fooling.

THERSITES Nor I, by Pluto; but that that likes not
you
Pleases me best.

DIOMEDES What, shall I come? The hour?

CRESSIDA Ay, come—O Jove!—
Do come—I shall be plagued.

DIOMEDES Farewell till then.

CRESSIDA Good night. I prithee, come.
Exit [*Diomedes*].
Troilus, farewell. One eye yet looks on thee,
But with my heart the other eye doth see.
Ah, poor our sex! This fault in us I find,
The error of our eye directs our mind.
What error leads must err. O, then conclude,
Minds swayed by eyes are full of turpitude. *Exit*.

THERSITES A proof of strength she could not publish
more,
Unless she said, "My mind is now turned whore."

ULYSSES All's done, my lord.

TROILUS It is.

ULYSSES Why stay we, then?

TROILUS To make a recordation to my soul
Of every syllable that here was spoke.
But if I tell how these two did coact,
Shall I not lie in publishing a truth?
Sith yet there is a credence in my heart,
An esperance so obstinately strong,
That doth invert th' attest of eyes and ears,
As if those organs had deceptious functions,
Created only to calumniate.

99 **likes** pleases 102 **plagued** punished 106 **poor our sex** our poor sex 107 **error** wandering (here, physically and morally) 110 **proof of strength** strong proof 110 **publish more** confess more clearly 118 **esperance** hope 119 **attest** testimony 120 **deceptious** deceiving

Was Cressid here?

ULYSSES I cannot conjure, Troyan.

TROILUS She was not, sure.

ULYSSES Most sure she was.

TROILUS Why, my negation hath no taste of madness.

ULYSSES Nor mine, my lord. Cressid was here but now.

TROILUS Let it not be believed for womanhood!
Think we had mothers; do not give advantage
To stubborn critics, apt, without a theme,
For depravation, to square the general sex
By Cressid's rule. Rather think this not Cressid.

ULYSSES What hath she done, prince, that can soil our mothers?

TROILUS Nothing at all, unless that this were she.

THERSITES Will 'a swagger himself out on's own eyes?

TROILUS This she? No, this is Diomed's Cressida.
If beauty have a soul, this is not she;
If souls guide vows, if vows be sanctimonies,
If sanctimony be the gods' delight,
If there be rule in unity itself,
This was not she. O madness of discourse,
That cause sets up with and against itself:
Bifold authority, where reason can revolt

122 **conjure** raise spirits 124 **negation** denial 126 **for** for the sake of 128–29 **apt ... For depravation** ready and eager to claim the depravity of women, but lacking examples 129–30 **square the ... Cressid's rule** take the measure of womankind by Cressida's standard 133 **Will 'a ... on's own eyes?** i.e., will he bluff himself out of trusting his own sight? 138 **If there ... unity itself** i.e., if it is a true principle that one cannot be two (that Cressida may not be divided into two persons) 139 **discourse** reasonable sequence of thought 140–41 **That cause ... Bifold authority** that case of principle wherein divided authority both supports and confutes the question

Without perdition, and loss assume all reason
Without revolt. This is, and is not, Cressid.
Within my soul there doth conduce a fight
Of this strange nature that a thing inseparate
Divides more wider than the sky and earth;
And yet the spacious breadth of this division
Admits no orifex for a point as subtle
As Ariachne's broken woof to enter.
Instance, O instance, strong as Pluto's gates;
Cressid is mine, tied with the bonds of heaven.
Instance, O instance, strong as heaven itself;
The bonds of heaven are slipped, dissolved, and
  loosed,
And with another knot, five-finger-tied,
The fractions of her faith, orts of her love,
The fragments, scraps, the bits, and greasy relics
Of her o'ereaten faith, are given to Diomed.

ULYSSES May worthy Troilus be half attached
With that which here his passion doth express?

TROILUS Ay, Greek! And that shall be divulgèd well
In characters as red as Mars his heart
Inflamed with Venus. Never did young man fancy
With so eternal and so fixed a soul.
Hark, Greek. Much as I do Cressid love,
So much by weight hate I her Diomed;
That sleeve is mine that he'll bear on his helm;
Were it a casque composed by Vulcan's skill,
My sword should bite it. Not the dreadful spout

141–43 **where reason . . . Without revolt** where reason can rebel without subsequent chaos, and loss of understanding assume the appearance of reason without reason itself objecting 144 **conduce** go on 145 **thing inseparate** that which is indivisible; i.e., Cressida 148 **orifex** opening 148 **subtle** finely sharp 149 **Ariachne's broken woof** (Arachne was a Lydian woman who challenged Athene to a weaving contest, but the goddess, angered, tore her work to shreds and changed her to a spider) 150 **Instance** example, proof (here, in the sense of "for instance") 154 **five-finger-tied** (1) so tied because Cressida's hand is now Diomedes' (?) (2) i.e., impossible to untie (?) 155 **orts** scraps, pieces (as of food) 157 **o'ereaten** eaten through, picked over (as a dog will eat the best pieces first, the last scraps left over) 158 **half attached** i.e., half so much affected (as it appears) 167 **casque** helmet

Which shipmen do the hurricano call,
Constringed in mass by the almighty sun,
Shall dizzy with more clamor Neptune's ear
In his descent than shall my prompted sword
Falling on Diomed.

THERSITES He'll tickle it for his concupy.

TROILUS O Cressid! O false Cressid! False, false, false!
Let all untruths stand by thy stainèd name,
And they'll seem glorious.

ULYSSES O, contain yourself;
Your passion draws ears hither.

Enter Aeneas.

AENEAS I have been seeking you this hour, my lord.
Hector, by this, is arming him in Troy;
Ajax, your guard, stays to conduct you home.

TROILUS Have with you, prince. My courteous lord, adieu.
Farewell, revolted fair; and Diomed,
Stand fast, and wear a castle on thy head!

ULYSSES I'll bring you to the gates.

TROILUS Accept distracted thanks.

Exeunt Troilus, Aeneas, and Ulysses.

THERSITES Would I could meet that rogue Diomed. I would croak like a raven; I would bode, I would bode. Patroclus will give me anything for the intelligence of this whore. The parrot will not do more for an almond than he for a commodious drab. Lechery, lechery; still wars and lechery; nothing else holds fashion. A burning devil take them! *Exit.*

170 **Constringed** drawn together 172 **prompted** i.e., urged on, as having its own motive 174 **He'll tickle it for his concupy** he'll be well tickled for his concupiscence ("it" refers contemptuously to Diomedes) 180 **him** himself 182 **Have with you** let's go along 188 **bode** portend disaster 191–92 **commodious drab** serviceable whore 193 **burning devil** venereal disease

[Scene III. *Troy; Priam's palace.*]

Enter Hector and Andromache.

ANDROMACHE When was my lord so much ungently tempered,
To stop his ears against admonishment?
Unarm, unarm, and do not fight today.

HECTOR You train me to offend you; get you in.
By all the everlasting gods, I'll go.

ANDROMACHE My dreams will, sure, prove ominous to the day.

HECTOR No more, I say.

Enter Cassandra.

CASSANDRA Where is my brother Hector?

ANDROMACHE Here, sister; armed and bloody in intent.
Consort with me in loud and dear petition;
Pursue we him on knees, for I have dreamed
Of bloody turbulence, and this whole night
Hath nothing been but shapes and forms of slaughter.

CASSANDRA O, 'tis true.

HECTOR Ho, bid my trumpet sound.

CASSANDRA No notes of sally, for the heavens, sweet brother.

HECTOR Be gone, I say; the gods have heard me swear.

V.iii.4 train tempt **4 offend** injure, insult **6 ominous to the day** omens applicable to this day

CASSANDRA The gods are deaf to hot and peevish vows.
They are polluted offerings, more abhorred
Than spotted livers in the sacrifice.

ANDROMACHE O, be persuaded! Do not count it holy
To hurt by being just. It is as lawful,
For we would give much, to use violent thefts,
And rob in the behalf of charity.

CASSANDRA It is the purpose that makes strong the vow;
But vows to every purpose must not hold.
Unarm, sweet Hector.

HECTOR Hold you still, I say.
Mine honor keeps the weather of my fate.
Life every man holds dear; but the dear man
Holds honor far more precious-dear than life.

Enter Troilus.

How now, young man; mean'st thou to fight today?

ANDROMACHE Cassandra, call my father to persuade.
Exit Cassandra.

HECTOR No, faith, young Troilus; doff thy harness, youth.
I am today i' the vein of chivalry.
Let grow thy sinews till their knots be strong,
And tempt not yet the brushes of the war.
Unarm thee; go, and doubt thou not, brave boy,
I'll stand today for thee and me and Troy.

TROILUS Brother, you have a vice of mercy in you,
Which better fits a lion than a man.

16 **peevish** brash, perverse 18 **spotted** i.e., spoiled 21 **For** because 24 **But vows . . . not hold** i.e., vows sworn indiscriminately or to unlawful purpose should not bind the swearer 26 **keeps the weather** i.e., maintains the position of advantage 27 **dear** valuable, worthy 34 **brushes** encounters

HECTOR What vice is that? Good Troilus, chide me for it.

TROILUS When many times the captive Grecian falls,
Even in the fan and wind of your fair sword,
You bid them rise and live.

HECTOR O, 'tis fair play.

TROILUS Fool's play, by heaven, Hector.

HECTOR How now? How now?

TROILUS For the love of all the gods,
Let's leave the hermit pity with our mother,
And when we have our armors buckled on,
The venomed vengeance ride upon our swords,
Spur them to ruthful work, rein them from ruth.

HECTOR Fie, savage, fie!

TROILUS Hector, then 'tis wars.

HECTOR Troilus, I would not have you fight today.

TROILUS Who should withhold me?
Not fate, obedience, nor the hand of Mars
Beck'ning with fiery truncheon my retire;
Not Priamus and Hecuba on knees,
Their eyes o'ergallèd with recourse of tears;
Nor you, my brother, with your true sword drawn,
Opposed to hinder me, should stop my way,
But by my ruin.

Enter Priam and Cassandra.

CASSANDRA Lay hold upon him, Priam, hold him fast;
He is thy crutch. Now if thou lose thy stay,
Thou on him leaning, and all Troy on thee,
Fall all together.

48 ruthful i.e., to be pitied, woeful **48 ruth** pity **49 then 'tis wars** that's what war is **53 truncheon** (a kind of baton used by the referee of a combat to signal the end of the fight) **55 o'er-gallèd** inflamed **55 recourse** repeated coursing down, constant flowing **60 stay** support

PRIAM Come, Hector, come; go back.
Thy wife hath dreamt, thy mother hath had visions,
Cassandra doth foresee, and I myself
Am like a prophet suddenly enrapt
To tell thee that this day is ominous.
Therefore, come back.

HECTOR Aeneas is afield;
And I do stand engaged to many Greeks,
Even in the faith of valor, to appear
This morning to them.

PRIAM Ay, but thou shalt not go.

HECTOR I must not break my faith.
You know me dutiful; therefore, dear sir,
Let me not shame respect, but give me leave
To take that course by your consent and voice,
Which you do here forbid me, royal Priam.

CASSANDRA O Priam, yield not to him!

ANDROMACHE Do not, dear father.

HECTOR Andromache, I am offended with you.
Upon the love you bear me, get you in.
Exit Andromache.

TROILUS This foolish, dreaming, superstitious girl
Makes all these bodements.

CASSANDRA O farewell, dear Hector!
Look, how thou diest; look, how thy eye turns pale;
Look, how thy wounds do bleed at many vents!
Hark, how Troy roars, how Hecuba cries out,
How poor Andromache shrills her dolors forth!
Behold, distraction, frenzy, and amazement,
Like witless antics, one another meet,
And all cry Hector! Hector's dead! O Hector!

TROILUS Away! Away!

69 the faith of valor a brave man's promise **73 shame respect** i.e., disgrace the respect due to a parent **80 bodements** evil omens **86 antics** madmen

CASSANDRA Farewell. Yet, soft; Hector, I take my leave.
Thou dost thyself and all our Troy deceive. *Exit.*

HECTOR You are amazed, my liege, at her exclaim.
Go in and cheer the town. We'll forth and fight;
Do deeds worth praise and tell you them at night.

PRIAM Farewell. The gods with safety stand about thee. [*Exeunt Priam and Hector.*] *Alarum.*

TROILUS They are at it, hark. Proud Diomed, believe,
I come to lose my arm, or win my sleeve.

Enter Pandar.

PANDARUS Do you hear, my lord? Do you hear?

TROILUS What now?

PANDARUS Here's a letter come from yond poor girl.

TROILUS Let me read.

PANDARUS A whoreson tisick, a whoreson rascally tisick so troubles me, and the foolish fortune of this girl; and what one thing, what another, that I shall leave you one o'th'se days; and I have a rheum in mine eyes too, and such an ache in my bones that, unless a man were cursed, I cannot tell what to think on't. What says she there?

TROILUS Words, words, mere words, no matter from the heart;
Th' effect doth operate another way.
[*Tearing the letter.*]
Go, wind to wind, there turn and change together.
My love with words and errors still she feeds,
But edifies another with her deeds. *Exeunt.*

101 tisick cough **111 errors** meanderings, i.e., underhanded tricks (?)

[Scene IV. *The battlefield.*]

[Alarum.] Enter Thersites. Excursions.

THERSITES Now they are clapperclawing one another; I'll go look on. That dissembling abominable varlet, Diomed, has got that same scurvy doting foolish young knave's sleeve of Troy there in his helm. I would fain see them meet, that that same young Troyan ass, that loves the whore there, might send that Greekish whoremasterly villain with the sleeve back to the dissembling luxurious drab, of a sleeveless errand. O' th' t'other side, the policy of those crafty swearing rascals—that stale old mouse-eaten dry cheese, Nestor, and that same dog-fox, Ulysses—is not proved worth a blackberry. They set me up, in policy, that mongrel cur, Ajax, against that dog of as bad a kind, Achilles; and now is the cur Ajax prouder than the cur Achilles, and will not arm today. Whereupon the Grecians begin to proclaim barbarism, and policy grows into an ill opinion.

Enter Diomedes and Troilus.

Soft, here comes sleeve, and t'other.

TROILUS Fly not; for shouldst thou take the river Styx,
I would swim after.

DIOMEDES Thou dost miscall retire.

V.iv.8–9 **sleeveless** futile, fruitless 10 **crafty swearing** craftily swearing, i.e., crafty to the extent of perjury 17 **proclaim barbarism** i.e., recognize the authority of chaos (to replace policy)

I do not fly, but advantageous care
Withdrew me from the odds of multitude.
Have at thee!

THERSITES Hold thy whore, Grecian! Now for thy whore,
Troyan! Now the sleeve, now the sleeve!

[*Exeunt Troilus and Diomedes, fighting.*]

Enter Hector.

HECTOR What art thou, Greek? Art thou for Hector's match?
Art thou of blood and honor?

THERSITES No, no, I am a rascal, a scurvy railing knave, a very filthy rogue.

HECTOR I do believe thee; live. [*Exit.*]

THERSITES God-a-mercy, that thou wilt believe me; but a plague break thy neck—for frighting me. What's become of the wenching rogues? I think they have swallowed one another. I would laugh at that miracle—yet, in a sort, lechery eats itself. I'll seek them. *Exit.*

[Scene V. *The battlefield.*]

Enter Diomed and Servant.

DIOMEDES Go, go, my servant, take thou Troilus' horse;
Present the fair steed to my Lady Cressid.
Fellow, commend my service to her beauty;

22–23 but advantageous . . . of multitude care for my own advantage led me to avoid facing absurdly heavy odds

Tell her I have chastised the amorous Troyan,
And am her knight by proof.

SERVANT I go, my lord. [*Exit.*]

Enter Agamemnon.

AGAMEMNON Renew, renew! The fierce Polydamas
Hath beat down Menon; bastard Margarelon
Hath Doreus prisoner,
And stands colossus-wise, waving his beam,
Upon the pashèd corses of the kings
Epistrophus and Cedius; Polyxenes is slain,
Amphimachus and Thoas deadly hurt,
Patroclus ta'en or slain, and Palamedes
Sore hurt and bruised. The dreadful Sagittary
Appals our numbers. Haste we, Diomed,
To reinforcement, or we perish all.

Enter Nestor.

NESTOR Go, bear Patroclus' body to Achilles,
And bid the snail-paced Ajax arm for shame.
There is a thousand Hectors in the field;
Now here he fights on Galathe his horse,
And there lacks work; anon he's there afoot,
And there they fly or die, like scalèd sculls
Before the belching whale; then is he yonder,
And there the strawy Greeks, ripe for his edge,
Fall down before him, like a mower's swath.
Here, there, and everywhere, he leaves and takes,
Dexterity so obeying appetite
That what he will he does, and does so much
That proof is called impossibility.

V.v.9 **beam** spear 10 **pashèd corses** battered corpses 14 **Sagittary** (a centaur [half man, half horse], who was a splendid archer and aided the Trojans) 22 **scalèd sculls** scaly schools of fish 24 **strawy . . . edge** i.e., Greeks who are like straw, ripe for the edge of the scythe 29 **proof** visible fact

Enter Ulysses.

ULYSSES O, courage, courage, princes! Great Achilles
Is arming, weeping, cursing, vowing vengeance!
Patroclus' wounds have roused his drowsy blood,
Together with his mangled Myrmidons,
That noseless, handless, hacked and chipped, come to him,
Crying on Hector. Ajax hath lost a friend,
And foams at mouth, and he is armed and at it,
Roaring for Troilus, who hath done today
Mad and fantastic execution,
Engaging and redeeming of himself
With such a careless force and forceless care
As if that luck, in very spite of cunning,
Bade him win all.

Enter Ajax.

AJAX Troilus, thou coward Troilus! *Exit.*

DIOMEDES Ay, there, there.

NESTOR So, so, we draw together. *Exit.*

Enter Achilles.

ACHILLES Where is this Hector?
Come, come, thou boy-queller, show thy face;
Know what it is to meet Achilles angry.
Hector, where's Hector? I will none but Hector.
Exit.

40 forceless casual, reckless **45 boy-queller** boy-killer

[Scene VI. *The battlefield.*]

Enter Ajax.

AJAX Troilus, thou coward Troilus, show thy head!

Enter Diomedes.

DIOMEDES Troilus, I say, where's Troilus?

AJAX What wouldst thou?

DIOMEDES I would correct him.

AJAX Were I the general, thou shouldst have my office
Ere that correction. Troilus, I say! What, Troilus!

Enter Troilus.

TROILUS O traitor Diomed! Turn thy false face, thou traitor,
And pay thy life thou owest me for my horse.

DIOMEDES Ha, art thou there?

AJAX I'll fight with him alone. Stand, Diomed.

DIOMEDES He is my prize; I will not look upon.

TROILUS Come, both you cogging Greeks; have at you both! [*Exeunt, fighting.*]

[*Enter Hector.*]

HECTOR Yea, Troilus? O, well fought, my youngest brother!

V.vi.5 **correction** i.e., privilege to correct 7 **horse** (with a pun on whore?) 10 **look upon** stand by 11 **cogging** deceitful

Enter Achilles.

ACHILLES Now do I see thee, ha! Have at thee,
Hector! [*They fight; Achilles tires.*]

HECTOR Pause, if thou wilt.

ACHILLES I do disdain thy courtesy, proud Troyan;
Be happy that my arms are out of use.
My rest and negligence befriends thee now,
But thou anon shalt hear of me again;
Till when, go seek thy fortune. *Exit.*

HECTOR Fare thee well;
I would have been much more a fresher man,
Had I expected thee.

Enter Troilus

How now, my brother!

TROILUS Ajax hath ta'en Aeneas! Shall it be?
No, by the flame of yonder glorious heaven,
He shall not carry him; I'll be ta'en too,
Or bring him off. Fate, hear me what I say!
I reck not though thou end my life today. *Exit.*

Enter one in armor.

HECTOR Stand, stand, thou Greek; thou art a goodly
mark.
No? Wilt thou not? I like thy armor well;
I'll frush it and unlock the rivets all,
But I'll be master of it. Wilt thou not, beast, abide?
Why then, fly on, I'll hunt thee for thy hide.
Exit [in pursuit].

22 ta'en taken captive **24 carry him** prevail over him **29 frush** smash

[Scene VII. *The battlefield.*]

Enter Achilles with Myrmidons.

ACHILLES Come here about me, you my Myrmidons;
Mark what I say. Attend me where I wheel.
Strike not a stroke, but keep yourselves in breath.
And when I have the bloody Hector found,
Empale him with your weapons round about;
In fellest manner execute your arms.
Follow me, sirs, and my proceedings eye;
It is decreed Hector the great must die.
Exit [with Myrmidons].

Enter Thersites, Menelaus, Paris [the last two fighting].

THERSITES The cuckold and the cuckold-maker are at it. Now, bull! Now, dog! 'Loo, Paris, 'loo! Now, my double-horned Spartan! 'Loo, Paris, 'loo! The bull has the game; 'ware horns, ho!
Exeunt Paris and Menelaus.

Enter Bastard [Margarelon].

BASTARD Turn, slave, and fight.

THERSITES What art thou?

BASTARD A bastard son of Priam's.

THERSITES I am a bastard too; I love bastards. I am bastard begot, bastard instructed, bastard in mind, bastard in valor, in everything illegitimate. One bear will not bite another, and wherefore should one bas-

V.vii.5 **Empale him** hem him in 6 **fellest** cruelest 6 **execute** use 10 **Now, bull! Now, dog! 'Loo** (Thersites compares the combat of Menelaus and Paris to the baiting of a bull by a dog, as it was done in such arenas as the Paris Garden) 12 **has the game** wins

tard? Take heed, the quarrel's most ominous to us. If the son of a whore fight for a whore, he tempts judgment. Farewell, bastard.

BASTARD The devil take thee, coward! *Exeunt.*

[Scene VIII. *The battlefield.*]

Enter Hector.

HECTOR Most putrefièd core, so fair without,
Thy goodly armor thus hath cost thy life.
Now is my day's work done; I'll take my breath.
Rest, sword; thou hast thy fill of blood and death.
[*Puts off his helmet, and hangs his shield behind him.*]

Enter Achilles and Myrmidons.

ACHILLES Look, Hector, how the sun begins to set,
How ugly night comes breathing at his heels.
Even with the vail and dark'ning of the sun,
To close the day up, Hector's life is done.

HECTOR I am unarmed; forgo this vantage, Greek.

ACHILLES Strike, fellows, strike. This is the man I seek.
[*Hector falls.*]
So, Ilion, fall thou next! Come, Troy, sink down!
Here lies thy heart, thy sinews, and thy bone.
On, Myrmidons, and cry you all amain,
"Achilles hath the mighty Hector slain!" *Retreat.*
Hark, a retire upon our Grecian part.

V.viii.7 vail sinking, going down

ONE GREEK The Troyans' trumpets sound the like, my lord.

ACHILLES The dragon wing of night o'erspreads the earth.
And, sticklerlike, the armies separates.
My half-supped sword, that frankly would have fed,
Pleased with this dainty bait, thus goes to bed.
[*Sheathes his sword.*]
Come, tie his body to my horse's tail;
Along the field I will the Troyan trail. *Exeunt.*

[Scene IX. *The battlefield.*]

Enter Agamemnon, Ajax, Menelaus, Nestor, Diomed, and the rest, marching. [*Sound retreat. Shout.*]

AGAMEMNON Hark, hark, what shout is that?

NESTOR Peace, drums!

SOLDIERS (*Within*) Achilles!
Achilles! Hector's slain! Achilles!

DIOMEDES The bruit is, Hector's slain, and by Achilles.

AJAX If it be so, yet bragless let it be;
Great Hector was as good a man as he.

AGAMEMNON March patiently along. Let one be sent
To pray Achilles see us at our tent.
If in his death the gods have us befriended,
Great Troy is ours, and our sharp wars are ended.
Exeunt.

18 **sticklerlike** like an umpire separating combatants, and ordering the field 19 **frankly** freely, abundantly V.ix.3 **bruit** rumor

[Scene X. *The battlefield.*]

Enter Aeneas, Paris, Antenor, Deiphobus.

AENEAS Stand, ho! Yet are we masters of the field.
Never go home; here starve we out the night.

Enter Troilus.

TROILUS Hector is slain.

ALL Hector! The dogs forbid!

TROILUS He's dead and at the murderer's horse's tail,
In beastly sort, dragged through the shameful field.
Frown on, you heavens, effect your rage with speed;
Sit, gods, upon your thrones, and smile at Troy.
I say, at once let your brief plagues be mercy,
And linger not our sure destructions on.

AENEAS My lord, you do discomfort all the host.

TROILUS You understand me not that tell me so.
I do not speak of flight, of fear, of death,
But dare all imminence that gods and men
Address their dangers in. Hector is gone.
Who shall tell Priam so, or Hecuba?
Let him that will a screech-owl aye be called
Go in to Troy, and say there Hector's dead.
There is a word will Priam turn to stone,
Make wells and Niobes of the maids and wives,

V.x.7 **smile** i.e., in derision 8 **let . . . mercy** be merciful in letting the plagues you send destroy us quickly 13–14 **But dare . . . dangers in** but instead dare whatever imminent dangers gods and men may be preparing 16 **screech-owl** (a bearer of ill omen) 19 **Niobes** (Niobe wept for her slain children until she was turned into a column of stone, from which tears continued to flow)

Cold statues of the youth, and in a word
Scare Troy out of itself. But march away.
Hector is dead; there is no more to say.
Stay yet. You vile abominable tents,
Thus proudly pitched upon our Phrygian plains,
Let Titan rise as early as he dare,
I'll through and through you! And, thou great-sized coward,
No space of earth shall sunder our two hates.
I'll haunt thee like a wicked conscience still,
That moldeth goblins swift as frenzy's thoughts.
Strike a free march to Troy. With comfort go;
Hope of revenge shall hide our inward woe.

Enter Pandarus.

PANDARUS But hear you, hear you!

TROILUS Hence, broker, lackey! Ignominy and shame
Pursue thy life, and live aye with thy name.
Exeunt all but Pandarus.

PANDARUS A goodly medicine for my aching bones! O world, world! Thus is the poor agent despised. O traders and bawds, how earnestly are you set awork, and how ill requited! Why should our endeavor be so loved, and the performance so loathed? What verse for it? What instance for it? Let me see.

Full merrily the humble-bee doth sing,
Till he hath lost his honey and his sting;
And being once subdued in armèd tail,
Sweet honey and sweet notes together fail.

Good traders in the flesh, set this in your painted cloths:

"As many as be here of Pandar's hall,
Your eyes, half out, weep out at Pandar's fall;
Or if you cannot weep, yet give some groans,

25 **Titan** (Helios, the sun, one of the Titans) 26 **coward** i.e., Achilles 46 **painted cloths** painted cloth hangings, used in brothels, sometimes bearing mottoes

Though not for me, yet for your aching bones."
Brethren and sisters of the hold-door trade,
Some two months hence my will shall here be made.
It should be now, but that my fear is this,
Some gallèd goose of Winchester would hiss.
Till then I'll sweat and seek about for eases,
And at that time bequeath you my diseases.
[*Exit.*]

FINIS

51 **hold-door trade** prostitution 54 **gallèd goose of Winchester** angry prostitute (the Bishop of Winchester had once held jurisdiction over the area of London called Southwark, where many brothels stood; a prostitute—and sometimes a venereal disease—was called a "Winchester goose") 55 **sweat** (a treatment for gout or rheumatism, as well as for venereal disease)

Textual Note

IT IS NOW generally believed that the 1609 quarto of *Troilus and Cressida* was printed from a transcript made from Shakespeare's original draft of the play. It omits about forty-five lines, the Prologue, and many stage directions that appear in the Folio, but on the whole contains a text that stands closer to Shakespeare's original than does that of the Folio. Since the compositors of the Folio apparently worked not only from the Quarto but from Shakespeare's autograph manuscript, it is surprising that they did not produce the better text; their readings are mainly inferior to those of the Quarto.

The relative values of the two texts (both of them, in different ways, stemming from Shakespeare's manuscript, and both of them, therefore, authoritative) depend on the nature of the copy used by the compositors, and the care and intelligence with which they worked. It is possible that the Quarto represents the play as it was shortened for performance, but more likely that the transcriber of the original manuscript was confused by Shakespeare's own second thoughts and deletions and failed to record some revisions and added speeches. On the other hand, although the compositors of the Folio probably had for reference and collation not only the Quarto but the original manuscript itself, their goal was speed and not always accuracy. While they added many lines omitted in the Quarto, they also introduced many mistaken readings; one compositor in particular evidently suited himself in interpreting difficult words and phrases, and made hash of most of them. Other portions of the Folio text were printed with greater care, however, and since the manuscript at hand may have been used in the playhouse, these portions include more complete stage directions and speech heads than appear in the Quarto. The Folio, therefore, supplies the fuller text; it should be used occasionally to emend the Quarto, but the earlier edition remains the better text. Its readings are frequently superior to those of the Folio, although, naturally, where the Folio prints speeches entirely omitted in the Quarto, these must be considered authoritative. Similarly, those readings in the Folio which introduce corrections on the basis of copy which was either Shakespeare's or very close to his should be followed.

The present edition is based on the Quarto but adds passages from the Folio. (These additions are recorded in the list of departures printed below.) Act and scene divisions (none is given for this play in Quarto or Folio) have been added in square brackets, along with simple indications of locale. Abbreviations have been amplified, spelling and punctuation have been modernized, and "and" is printed "an" when it means "if." The position of a few stage directions has been slightly altered when necessary. Other departures from the Quarto are listed below, the adopted reading first in bold, and then the original reading in roman. The adopted reading is most often from the Folio; when it is not, it is followed by (ed) to indicate that it is an editor's conjecture rather than an authoritative reading.

Dedicatory address 39 **state** (ed) states

Prologue (Q omits) 12 **barks** (ed; F has "Barke") 19 **Sperr** (ed; F has "Stirre")

I.i.77 **she were not** she were 80 **what care I** what I

I.ii.17 **they** the 36 s.d. **Enter Pandarus** (Q omits) 183 **Ilium** Ilion 208 **man's heart** man heart 245 s.d. **Enter Common Soldiers** (Q omits) 289 s.d. **Exit Pandarus** (Q omits)

I.iii.i. s.d. **Sennet** (Q omits) 13 **every** euer 31 **thy** the 36 **patient** ancient 54 **Returns** (ed) Retires 61 **thy** the 70–74 **Agamemnon. Speak ... oracle** (Q omits) 75 **basis** bases 110 **meets** melts 159 **unsquared** vnsquare 195 **and discredit** our discredit 212 s.d. **Tucket** (Q omits) 214 s.d. **Enter Aeneas** (Q omits) 247 **affair** affaires 250 **whisper him** whisper with him 252 **the attentive** that attentiue 256 **loud** alowd 263 **rusty** restie 267 **That seeks** And feeds 276 **compass** couple 294 **one** no 298 **will tell** tell 302 **youth** men 305 **first** sir 309 s.d. **Exeunt. Manent Ulysses and Nestor** (Q omits) 315 **This** 'tis (Q omits) 334 **his honor** those honours 354–56 **which ... the limbs** (F emended from "in his" to "his"; Q omits) 390 **tarre** arre

II.i.11 s.d. **Strikes him** (Q omits) 14 **vinewed'st** (F: whinid'st) vnsalted 18 **oration** oration without booke 18 **a prayer** praier 42–43 **Ajax . . . Do, do** (Q assigns to Thersites as one speech) 47 **Thou scurvy-valiant** you scuruy valiant 57 s.d. **Enter Achilles and Patroclus** (Q omits) 58 **do you** do yee 74 **I** It 77 **I'll** I 104 **if he knock out** and knocke at 109 **your grandsires had nails on their toes** (F emended from "their" to "your") their grandsiers had nailes 119 **brach** (ed) brooch 127 **fifth** first 135 s.d. **Exit** (Q omits)

II.ii.14–15 **surety, Surety** surely Surely 27 **father** fathers 33 **at reasons** of reasons 47 **Let's** Sets 64 **shores** shore 75 **truce** ttuce 86 **he** be 96 s.d. **with her hair about her ears** (Q omits) 104 **eld** (ed; F has "old") elders 210 **strike** shrike

II.iii.23 s.d. **Enter Patroclus** (Q omits) 27 **wouldst** couldst 33 **art** art not 49 **thyself** Thersites 57–62 **Patroclus. You . . . a fool** (Q omits) 65 **commanded of Agamemnon** commanded 69 **Creator** Prouer 71 **Patroclus** Come Patroclus 72 s.d. **Exit** (Q omits) 76–77 **Now . . . all** (Q omits) 81 **shent** (ed; F has "sent") sate 82 **appertainments** appertainings 91 **A word, my lord** (Q omits) 104 s.d. **Enter Patroclus** (Q omits) 132 **pettish lunes** (F emended from "lines" to "lunes") course, and time 132 **as** if and if 133 **carriage of this action** streame of his commencement 143 **enter you** entertaine 143 s.d. **Exit Ulysses** (Q omits) 160 **I do hate** I hate 193 **stale** (ed) staule 195 **titled** liked 205 **pash** push 214 **let his humor's** tell his humorous 222 **'A would . . . shares** (Q gives to Ajax) 224 **He's . . . warm** (ed; Q and F give to Ajax) 225 **praises** praiers 244 **beyond, beyond all erudition** beyond all thy erudition 250 **bourn** boord 251 **Thy** This 265 **cull** call

III.i. s.d. **Music . . . Servant** Enter Pandarus 24 **friend** (Q omits) 38 **that thou** thou 93 **your poor disposer's** your disposers 108 **lord** lad 115 **In . . . so** (Q omits) 118 **shaft confounds** shafts confound 150 **these** this 158 **thee** her

III.ii.1 s.d. **and Troilus'** Troylus 3 **he stays** stayes 3 s.d. **Enter Troilus** (Q omits) 8 **Like** like to 10 **those** these 16 s.d. **Exit Pandarus** (Q omits) 28 s.d. **Enter Pandarus** (Q omits) 34 s.d. **Exit Pandarus** (Q omits) 38 **unawares** vnwares 68 **fears** (ed) teares 82 **This is** This 94 **merit crown it. No perfection** merit louer part no affection 101 s.d. **Enter Pandarus** (Q omits) 134 **Cunning** (ed) Comming 161 **aye** age 181 **Yet, after** After 186 **and** or 194 **as wolf** or Wolfe 201 **pains** paine

III.iii. s.d. **Flourish** (Q omits) 4 **come** (ed) loue 102 **giver** giuers 128 **abject** obiect 140 **on** one 141 **shrinking** shriking 155 **one** on 158 **hedge** turne 160 **hindmost** him, most 161–63 **Or . . . on** (F emended from "neere" to "rear"; Q omits) 164 **past** passe 177 **give** (ed) goe 183 **Than** That 197 **every grain of Pluto's gold** euery thing 198 **th' uncomprehensive deeps** the vncomprehensiue depth 224 **a dewdrop** dew drop 251 **he** a 267 **ambassador to him** Ambassador 275 **most valorous** valorous 279 **Grecian army** armie 279–80 **Agamemnon, et cetera** Agamemnon 294 **God b'wi' you** (ed) God buy you

IV.i.4 **you** your 16 **But** Lul'd 36 **it was** twas 40 **do think** beleeue 50 s.d. **Exit Aeneas** (Q omits) 52 **the soul** soule 56 **soilure** soyle 76 **you** they

IV.ii.19 s.d. **Within** (Q omits) 22 s.d. **Enter Pandarus** (F places after line 20; Q omits) 51 **'Tis** Its 57 s.d. **Enter Troilus** (Q omits) 63 **to us; and for him forthwith** to him, and forth-with 72 **nature** neighbor Pandar 107 **I will** Ile 112 s.d. **Exeunt** (Q omits)

IV.iv.54 **the root** my throate 64 **there's** there is 77 **They're ... nature** (Q omits) 79 **person** portion 139 s.d. **Sound trumpet** (Q omits) 144–48 **Deiphobus. Let us ... chivalry** (F, with 144 assigned to Diomedes; Q omits)

IV.v.94 **Ulysses. They ... already** (Q omits) 95 **Agamemnon** Vlises 98 **in deeds** deeds 131 **Of our rank feud** (Q omits) 132 **drop** day 164–69 **But that's ... integrity** (Q omits) 177 **that I affect th' untraded oath** thy affect, the vntraded earth 187 **thy** th' 192 **shraped** (ed) shruped 205 **As they ... courtesy** (Q omits) 254 **stithied** stichied 291 **she loved** my Lord

V.i.12 **these** this 14 **boy** box 19 **catarrhs** (Q omits) 23 **and the like** (Q omits) 48 s.d. **Exit** (Q omits) 55 **brother** be 57–58 **hanging at his brother's leg** at his bare legge 59 **forced** faced 61 **he is** her's 62 **dog, a mule** day, a Moyle 62 **fitchew** Fichooke 65 **Ask me not** aske me 71 s.d. **Enter Achilles** (Q omits) 73 **good** God 79 **sewer** (ed) sure 80 **both at once** both

V.ii.4 s.d. **Enter ... Ulysses** (Q omits) 13 **Cressida** Cal 38 **Nay** Now 39 **distraction** distruction 46 **Adieu** (Q omits) 54 **these together** together 56 **But will** Will 57 **la** (ed) lo 66 **Troilus. I ... will** (Q omits) 67 **Cressida** Troy 78 **Nay ... me** (Q, F assigned to Diomedes 82 **Cressida** (Q omits) 88 **By** And by 103 s.d. **Exit** (Q omits) 115 **coact** Court 120 **had deceptious** were deceptions 131 **soil** spoile 154 **five** finde 164 **Much as** as much

V.iii.14 **Cassandra** Cres 20–22 **To hurt ... charity** (F emended from "would count" to "would," and from "as" to "use"; Q omits) 23–25 **It is ... sweet Hector** (Q assigns to Andromache) 29 **mean'st** meanest 58 **But by my ruin** (Q omits) 85 **distraction** destruction 90 **Exit** (Q omits)

V.iv.4 **young knave's** knaues 9 **errand** (F has "errant") arrant 9 **O' th'** Ath 17 **begin** (ed) began 18 s.d. **Enter Diomedes and Troilus** (Q omits) 27 **art thou** art

V.v. 22 **scalèd** scaling 41 **luck** lust

V.vii.11 **double-horned** (ed) double-hen'd 12 s.d. **Exeunt** (ed) Exit 23 **Exeunt** Exit

V.viii.16 **One Greek** (F has "Gree.") One

V.ix.1 **what shout is that** what is this

V.x.2 **Never ... night** (Q assigns to Troilus, and places his entrance before the line) 21–22 **But march away. Hector is dead** (Q omits) 23 **Vile** proud 32–34 **Pandarus. But hear you! ... aye with thy name** (in F these lines appear as well after V.iii.112, concluding that scene) 33 **Ignominy and** ignominy 37 **traders** (ed) traitors 50 **your aching** my aking 51 **hold-door** hold-ore

WILLIAM SHAKESPEARE

THE TRAGEDY OF JULIUS CAESAR

Edited by William and Barbara Rosen

[*Dramatis Personae*

JULIUS CAESAR

OCTAVIUS CAESAR
MARCUS ANTONIUS
M. AEMILIUS LEPIDUS
} triumvirs after the death of Julius Caesar

CICERO
PUBLIUS
POPILIUS LENA
} senators

MARCUS BRUTUS
CASSIUS
CASCA
TREBONIUS
LIGARIUS
DECIUS BRUTUS
METELLUS CIMBER
CINNA
} conspirators against Julius Caesar

FLAVIUS
MARULLUS
} tribunes

ARTEMIDORUS OF CNIDOS, a teacher of rhetoric
A SOOTHSAYER
CINNA, a poet
ANOTHER POET

LUCILIUS
TITINIUS
MESSALA
YOUNG CATO
VOLUMNIUS
} friends to Brutus and Cassius

VARRO
CLITUS
CLAUDIUS
STRATO
LUCIUS
DARDANIUS
} servants to Brutus

PINDARUS, servant to Cassius
CALPHURNIA, wife to Caesar
PORTIA, wife to Brutus
SENATORS, CITIZENS, GUARDS, ATTENDANTS, &c.

Scene: During most of the play, at Rome; afterward near Sardis, and near Philippi]

THE TRAGEDY OF JULIUS CAESAR

ACT I

Scene I. [*Rome. A street.*]

Enter Flavius, Marullus, and certain Commoners over the stage.

FLAVIUS Hence! Home, you idle creatures, get you home!
Is this a holiday? What, know you not,
Being mechanical,[1] you ought not walk
Upon a laboring day without the sign
Of your profession? Speak, what trade art thou?

CARPENTER Why, sir, a carpenter.

MARULLUS Where is thy leather apron and thy rule?
What dost thou with thy best apparel on?
You, sir, what trade are you?

COBBLER Truly, sir, in respect of a fine workman, I am but, as you would say, a cobbler.

MARULLUS But what trade art thou? Answer me directly.

COBBLER A trade, sir, that, I hope, I may use with a

1. Text references are printed in **bold** type; the annotation follows in roman type.
I.i.3 **mechanical** of the working class 4–5 **sign/Of your profession** mark of your trade, i.e., working clothes 10 **in respect of a fine** in comparison with a skilled 11 **cobbler** (1) shoemaker (2) bungler 12 **directly** straightforwardly

safe conscience, which is indeed, sir, a mender of bad soles.

FLAVIUS What trade, thou knave? Thou naughty knave, what trade?

COBBLER Nay, I beseech you, sir, be not out with me: yet, if you be out, sir, I can mend you.

MARULLUS What mean'st thou by that? Mend me, thou saucy fellow?

COBBLER Why, sir, cobble you.

FLAVIUS Thou art a cobbler, art thou?

COBBLER Truly, sir, all that I live by is with the awl: I meddle with no tradesman's matters, nor women's matters; but withal, I am indeed, sir, a surgeon to old shoes: when they are in great danger, I recover them. As proper men as ever trod upon neat's leather have gone upon my handiwork.

FLAVIUS But wherefore art not in thy shop today?
Why dost thou lead these men about the streets?

COBBLER Truly, sir, to wear out their shoes, to get myself into more work. But indeed, sir, we make holiday to see Caesar and to rejoice in his triumph.

MARULLUS Wherefore rejoice? What conquest brings he home?
What tributaries follow him to Rome,
To grace in captive bonds his chariot wheels?
You block, you stones, you worse than senseless things!
O you hard hearts, you cruel men of Rome,
Knew you not Pompey? Many a time and oft
Have you climbed up to walls and battlements,

15 **soles** (pun on "souls") 16 **naughty** worthless 18 **out** angry 19 **be out** i.e., have worn-out shoes 19 **mend you** (1) mend your shoes (2) improve your character 26 **withal** (1) nevertheless (2) with awl (3) with all 27 **recover** (1) resole (2) cure 28–29 **neat's leather** cattle's hide 34 **triumph** triumphal celebration 36 **tributaries** captives 40 **Pompey** (defeated by Caesar in 48 B.C., later murdered)

To tow'rs and windows, yea, to chimney tops,
Your infants in your arms, and there have sat
The livelong day, with patient expectation,
To see great Pompey pass the streets of Rome.
And when you saw his chariot but appear,
Have you not made an universal shout,
That Tiber trembled underneath her banks
To hear the replication of your sounds
Made in her concave shores?
And do you now put on your best attire?
And do you now cull out a holiday?
And do you now strew flowers in his way
That comes in triumph over Pompey's blood?
Be gone!
Run to your houses, fall upon your knees,
Pray to the gods to intermit the plague
That needs must light on this ingratitude.

FLAVIUS Go, go, good countrymen, and, for this fault,
Assemble all the poor men of your sort;
Draw them to Tiber banks and weep your tears
Into the channel, till the lowest stream
Do kiss the most exalted shores of all.
Exeunt all the Commoners.
See, whe'r their basest mettle be not moved;
They vanish tongue-tied in their guiltiness.
Go you down that way towards the Capitol;
This way will I. Disrobe the images,
If you do find them decked with ceremonies.

MARULLUS May we do so?
You know it is the feast of Lupercal.

FLAVIUS It is no matter; let no images
Be hung with Caesar's trophies. I'll about

49 **replication** echo 50 **concave shores** hollowed-out banks 54 **in triumph over Pompey's blood** as the conqueror of Pompey's sons 57 **intermit** hold back 63 **most exalted shores of all** highest water mark 64 **whe'r** whether 64 **mettle** (1) substance (2) disposition 68 **ceremonies** robes (or ornaments) 70 **Lupercal** (fertility festival held on February 15; Caesar's triumph really took place in the preceding October, but Shakespeare combines events and shortens time spans for dramatic effect)

And drive away the vulgar from the streets;
So do you too, where you perceive them thick.
These growing feathers plucked from Caesar's wing
Will make him fly an ordinary pitch,
Who else would soar above the view of men
And keep us all in servile fearfulness. *Exeunt.*

[Scene II. *A public place.*]

Enter Caesar, Antony (for the course), Calphurnia, Portia, Decius, Cicero, Brutus, Cassius, Casca, a Soothsayer; after them, Marullus and Flavius.

CAESAR Calphurnia!

CASCA Peace, ho! Caesar speaks.

CAESAR Calphurnia!

CALPHURNIA Here, my lord.

CAESAR Stand you directly in Antonius' way
When he doth run his course. Antonius!

ANTONY Caesar, my lord?

CAESAR Forget not in your speed, Antonius,
To touch Calphurnia; for our elders say
The barren, touchèd in this holy chase,
Shake off their sterile curse.

ANTONY I shall remember:
When Caesar says "Do this," it is performed.

CAESAR Set on, and leave no ceremony out.

SOOTHSAYER Caesar!

CAESAR Ha! Who calls?

73 vulgar common people 76 pitch height

CASCA Bid every noise be still; peace yet again!

CAESAR Who is it in the press that calls on me?
I hear a tongue, shriller than all the music,
Cry "Caesar." Speak; Caesar is turned to hear.

SOOTHSAYER Beware the ides of March.

CAESAR What man is that?

BRUTUS A soothsayer bids you beware the ides of March.

CAESAR Set him before me; let me see his face.

CASSIUS Fellow, come from the throng; look upon Caesar.

CAESAR What say'st thou to me now? Speak once again.

SOOTHSAYER Beware the ides of March.

CAESAR He is a dreamer, let us leave him. Pass.
Sennet. Exeunt. Mane[n]t Brutus and Cassius.

CASSIUS Will you go see the order of the course?

BRUTUS Not I.

CASSIUS I pray you do.

BRUTUS I am not gamesome: I do lack some part
Of that quick spirit that is in Antony.
Let me not hinder, Cassius, your desires;
I'll leave you.

CASSIUS Brutus, I do observe you now of late;
I have not from your eyes that gentleness
And show of love as I was wont to have;
You bear too stubborn and too strange a hand
Over your friend that loves you.

I.ii.15 **press** crowd 18 **ides of March** March 15 24 s.d. **Sennet** flourish of trumpets marking ceremonial entrance or exit 24 s.d. **Mane[n]t** (they) remain 25 **order of the course** progress of the race 28 **gamesome** (1) fond of sport (2) merry 29 **quick spirit** (1) lively nature (2) prompt obedience 34 **wont** accustomed 35 **bear . . . hand** treat too haughtily and distantly, keep at arm's length (the metaphor is from horsemanship)

BRUTUS Cassius,
Be not deceived: if I have veiled my look,
I turn the trouble of my countenance
Merely upon myself. Vexèd I am
Of late with passions of some difference,
Conceptions only proper to myself,
Which give some soil, perhaps, to my behaviors;
But let not therefore my good friends be grieved
(Among which number, Cassius, be you one)
Nor construe any further my neglect
Than that poor Brutus, with himself at war,
Forgets the shows of love to other men.

CASSIUS Then, Brutus, I have much mistook your passion;
By means whereof this breast of mine hath buried
Thoughts of great value, worthy cogitations.
Tell me, good Brutus, can you see your face?

BRUTUS No, Cassius; for the eye sees not itself
But by reflection, by some other things.

CASSIUS 'Tis just:
And it is very much lamented, Brutus,
That you have no such mirrors as will turn
Your hidden worthiness into your eye,
That you might see your shadow. I have heard
Where many of the best respect in Rome
(Except immortal Caesar), speaking of Brutus,
And groaning underneath this age's yoke,
Have wished that noble Brutus had his eyes.

BRUTUS Into what dangers would you lead me, Cassius,
That you would have me seek into myself
For that which is not in me?

37–39 **if I have ... upon myself** i.e., if I have seemed withdrawn, it is because I am displeased with myself and no one else (**Merely** = wholly) 40 **passions of some difference** conflicting emotions 41 **Conceptions ... myself** ideas concerning me only 42 **soil** blemish 45 **construe** interpret 47 **shows** manifestations 48 **passion** feelings 49 **By means whereof** as a consequence of which 54 **just** true 58 **shadow** reflection, i.e., yourself as others see you 59 **best respect** highest reputation

CASSIUS Therefore, good Brutus, be prepared to hear;
And since you know you cannot see yourself
So well as by reflection, I, your glass
Will modestly discover to yourself
That of yourself which you yet know not of.
And be not jealous on me, gentle Brutus:
Were I a common laughter, or did use
To stale with ordinary oaths my love
To every new protester; if you know
That I do fawn on men and hug them hard,
And after scandal them; or if you know
That I profess myself in banqueting
To all the rout, then hold me dangerous.
Flourish and shout.

BRUTUS What means this shouting? I do fear the people
Choose Caesar for their king.

CASSIUS Aye, do you fear it?
Then must I think you would not have it so.

BRUTUS I would not, Cassius, yet I love him well.
But wherefore do you hold me here so long?
What is it that you would impart to me?
If it be aught toward the general good,
Set honor in one eye and death i' th' other,
And I will look on both indifferently;
For let the gods so speed me, as I love
The name of honor more than I fear death.

CASSIUS I know that virtue to be in you, Brutus,
As well as I do know your outward favor.
Well, honor is the subject of my story.
I cannot tell what you and other men
Think of this life, but for my single self,

68 **glass** mirror 71 **jealous on** suspicious of 72 **laughter** object of mockery 72–74 **did use . . . protester** were accustomed to make cheap with glib and frequent avowals to every new promiser of friendship (**ordinary** = [1] tavern [2] everyday) 76 **scandal** slander 77 **profess myself** declare my friendship 78 **rout** vulgar crowd 78 s.d. **Flourish** ceremonial sounding of trumpets 85 **general good** public welfare 87 **indifferently** impartially 88 **speed me** make me prosper 91 **favor** appearance

I had as lief not be, as live to be
In awe of such a thing as I myself.
I was born free as Caesar; so were you:
We both have fed as well, and we can both
Endure the winter's cold as well as he:
For once, upon a raw and gusty day,
The troubled Tiber chafing with her shores,
Caesar said to me "Dar'st thou, Cassius, now
Leap in with me into this angry flood,
And swim to yonder point?" Upon the word,
Accout'red as I was, I plungèd in
And bade him follow: so indeed he did.
The torrent roared, and we did buffet it
With lusty sinews, throwing it aside
And stemming it with hearts of controversy.
But ere we could arrive the point proposed,
Caesar cried "Help me, Cassius, or I sink!"
I, as Aeneas, our great ancestor,
Did from the flames of Troy upon his shoulder
The old Anchises bear, so from the waves of Tiber
Did I the tired Caesar. And this man
Is now become a god, and Cassius is
A wretched creature, and must bend his body
If Caesar carelessly but nod on him.
He had a fever when he was in Spain,
And when the fit was on him, I did mark
How he did shake. 'Tis true, this god did shake.
His coward lips did from their color fly,
And that same eye whose bend doth awe the world
Did lose his luster. I did hear him groan;
Ay, and that tongue of his, that bade the Romans
Mark him and write his speeches in their books,
Alas, it cried, "Give me some drink, Titinius,"

95 **as lief not be** just as soon not exist 96 **such a thing as I myself** i.e., another human being (Caesar) 101 **chafing with** raging against 105 **Accout'red** fully armed 109 **stemming . . . controversy** moving forward against it (1) aggressively (2) in rivalry 112 **Aeneas** (legendary founder of the Roman state and hero of Virgil's *Aeneid.* Anchises was his feeble father) 122 **His coward . . . fly** the color fled from his lips like a deserter fleeing from his banner in battle (**color** = [1] hue [2] banner) 123 **bend** glance 124 **his** its

As a sick girl. Ye gods! It doth amaze me,
A man of such a feeble temper should
So get the start of the majestic world,
And bear the palm alone. *Shout. Flourish.*

BRUTUS Another general shout?
I do believe that these applauses are
For some new honors that are heaped on Caesar.

CASSIUS Why, man, he doth bestride the narrow world
Like a Colossus, and we petty men
Walk under his huge legs and peep about
To find ourselves dishonorable graves.
Men at some time are masters of their fates:
The fault, dear Brutus, is not in our stars,
But in ourselves, that we are underlings.
Brutus and Caesar: what should be in that "Caesar"?
Why should that name be sounded more than yours?
Write them together, yours is as fair a name;
Sound them, it doth become the mouth as well;
Weigh them, it is as heavy; conjure with 'em,
"Brutus" will start a spirit as soon as "Caesar."
Now, in the names of all the gods at once,
Upon what meat doth this our Caesar feed,
That he is grown so great? Age, thou art shamed!
Rome, thou hast lost the breed of noble bloods!
When went there by an age, since the great flood,
But it was famed with more than with one man?
When could they say (till now) that talked of Rome,
That her wide walks encompassed but one man?
Now is it Rome indeed, and room enough,

129 **feeble temper** weak constitution 130 **get the start of** outdistance 131 **bear the palm** carry off the victor's prize 136 **Colossus** (an immense statue of Apollo, said to straddle the entrance to the harbor of Rhodes so that ships sailed under its legs) 138 **dishonorable** (because we are dominated by Caesar) 140 **stars** destinies (in Shakespeare's day one's temperament and therefore one's actions and course of life, were thought to be largely determined by the position of the planets at one's birth) 143 **sounded** (1) spoken (2) proclaimed by trumpet 147 **start** raise 152 **great flood** (classical story told of the drowning of all mankind except Deucalion and his wife Pyrrha, spared by Zeus because of their virtue) 153 **But it was famed with** without the age being made famous by 156 **Rome . . . room** (homonyms, hence a pun)

When there is in it but one only man.
O, you and I have heard our fathers say,
There was a Brutus once that would have brooked
Th' eternal devil to keep his state in Rome
As easily as a king.

BRUTUS That you do love me, I am nothing jealous;
What you would work me to, I have some aim;
How I have thought of this, and of these times,
I shall recount hereafter. For this present,
I would not so (with love I might entreat you)
Be any further moved. What you have said
I will consider; what you have to say
I will with patience hear, and find a time
Both meet to hear and answer such high things.
Till then, my noble friend, chew upon this:
Brutus had rather be a villager
Than to repute himself a son of Rome
Under these hard conditions as this time
Is like to lay upon us.

CASSIUS I am glad
That my weak words have struck but thus much show
Of fire from Brutus.

Enter Caesar and his Train.

BRUTUS The games are done, and Caesar is returning.

CASSIUS As they pass by, pluck Casca by the sleeve,
And he will (after his sour fashion) tell you
What hath proceeded worthy note today.

BRUTUS I will do so. But look you, Cassius,
The angry spot doth glow on Caesar's brow,
And all the rest look like a chidden train:
Calphurnia's cheek is pale, and Cicero

159 **a Brutus** (Lucius Junius Brutus helped expel the Tarquins and found the Republic in 509 B.C.) 159 **brooked** tolerated 162 **nothing jealous** not at all doubtful 163 **work me to** persuade me of 163 **aim** idea 170 **meet** suitable 171 **chew** reflect 177 s.d. **Train** retinue

Looks with such ferret and such fiery eyes
As we have seen him in the Capitol,
Being crossed in conference by some senators.

CASSIUS Casca will tell us what the matter is.

CAESAR Antonius.

ANTONY Caesar?

CAESAR Let me have men about me that are fat,
Sleek-headed men, and such as sleep a-nights.
Yond Cassius has a lean and hungry look;
He thinks too much: such men are dangerous.

ANTONY Fear him not, Caesar, he's not dangerous;
He is a noble Roman, and well given.

CAESAR Would he were fatter! But I fear him not.
Yet if my name were liable to fear,
I do not know the man I should avoid
So soon as that spare Cassius. He reads much,
He is a great observer, and he looks
Quite through the deeds of men. He loves no plays,
As thou dost, Antony; he hears no music;
Seldom he smiles, and smiles in such a sort
As if he mocked himself, and scorned his spirit
That could be moved to smile at anything.
Such men as he be never at heart's ease
Whiles they behold a greater than themselves,
And therefore are they very dangerous.
I rather tell thee what is to be feared
Than what I fear; for always I am Caesar.
Come on my right hand, for this ear is deaf,
And tell me truly what thou think'st of him.

Sennet. Exeunt Caesar and his Train.

186 **ferret** ferretlike (a ferret is a vicious, weasel-like animal with red eyes) 188 **conference** debate 197 **given** disposed 199 **if my name . . . to fear** i.e., if the idea of fear could ever be associated with me 203 **through the deeds** i.e., to the hidden motives of actions 204 **hears no music** (cf. *Merchant of Venice*, V.i.83ff: "The man that hath no music in himself,/Nor is not moved with concord of sweet sounds,/Is fit for treasons. . . . Let no such man be trusted") 205 **sort** manner

CASCA You pulled me by the cloak; would you speak with me?

BRUTUS Ay, Casca; tell us what hath chanced today, That Caesar looks so sad.

CASCA Why, you were with him, were you not?

BRUTUS I should not then ask Casca what had chanced.

CASCA Why, there was a crown offered him; and being offered him, he put it by with the back of his hand, thus; and then the people fell a-shouting.

BRUTUS What was the second noise for?

CASCA Why, for that too.

CASSIUS They shouted thrice; what was the last cry for?

CASCA Why, for that too.

BRUTUS Was the crown offered him thrice?

CASCA Ay, marry, was't, and he put it by thrice, every time gentler than other; and every putting-by mine honest neighbors shouted.

CASSIUS Who offered him the crown?

CASCA Why, Antony.

BRUTUS Tell us the manner of it, gentle Casca.

CASCA I can as well be hanged as tell the manner of it: it was mere foolery; I did not mark it. I saw Mark Antony offer him a crown—yet 'twas not a crown neither, 'twas one of these coronets—and, as I told you, he put it by once; but for all that, to my thinking, he would fain have had it. Then he offered it to him again; then he put it by again; but to my thinking, he was very loath to lay his fingers off it. And

217 sad serious **221 put it by** pushed it aside **228 marry** truly (originally an oath, "By the Virgin Mary") **237 coronets** small crowns **239 fain** gladly

then he offered it the third time. He put it the third time by; and still as he refused it, the rabblement hooted, and clapped their chopt hands, and threw up their sweaty nightcaps, and uttered such a deal of stinking breath because Caesar refused the crown, that it had, almost, choked Caesar; for he swounded and fell down at it. And for mine own part, I durst not laugh, for fear of opening my lips and receiving the bad air.

CASSIUS But, soft, I pray you; what, did Caesar swound?

CASCA He fell down in the market place, and foamed at mouth, and was speechless.

BRUTUS 'Tis very like he hath the falling-sickness.

CASSIUS No, Caesar hath it not; but you, and I,
And honest Casca, we have the falling-sickness.

CASCA I know not what you mean by that, but I am sure Caesar fell down. If the tag-rag people did not clap him and hiss him, according as he pleased and displeased them, as they use to do the players in the theater, I am no true man.

BRUTUS What said he when he came unto himself?

CASCA Marry, before he fell down, when he perceived the common herd was glad he refused the crown, he plucked me ope his doublet and offered them his throat to cut. An I had been a man of any occupation, if I would not have taken him at a word, I would I might go to hell among the rogues. And so he fell. When he came to himself again, he said, if he had

243 **still** every time 244 **chopt** rough, chapped 245 **nightcaps** (contemptuous term for workingmen's caps) 247 **swounded** fainted 251 **soft** slowly, "wait a minute" 254 **falling-sickness** epilepsy 256 **we have the falling-sickness** i.e., we are becoming powerless and are declining under Caesar's rule 258 **tag-rag people** ragged mob 260 **use** are accustomed 265 **ope his doublet** open his jacket 266 **man of any occupation** (1) workingman, i.e., one of those to whom Caesar's speech was addressed (2) "man of action"

done or said anything amiss, he desired their worships to think it was his infirmity. Three or four wenches, where I stood, cried "Alas, good soul!" and forgave him with all their hearts; but there's no heed to be taken of them; if Caesar had stabbed their mothers, they would have done no less.

BRUTUS And after that, he came thus sad away?

CASCA Ay.

CASSIUS Did Cicero say anything?

CASCA Ay, he spoke Greek.

CASSIUS To what effect?

CASCA Nay, an I tell you that, I'll ne'er look you i' th' face again. But those that understood him smiled at one another and shook their heads; but for mine own part, it was Greek to me. I could tell you more news too: Marullus and Flavius, for pulling scarfs off Caesar's images, are put to silence. Fare you well. There was more foolery yet, if I could remember it.

CASSIUS Will you sup with me tonight, Casca?

CASCA No, I am promised forth.

CASSIUS Will you dine with me tomorrow?

CASCA Ay, if I be alive, and your mind hold, and your dinner worth the eating.

CASSIUS Good; I will expect you.

CASCA Do so. Farewell, both. *Exit.*

BRUTUS What a blunt fellow is this grown to be!
He was quick mettle when he went to school.

CASSIUS So is he now in execution
Of any bold or noble enterprise,

286 **put to silence** silenced (by being stripped of their tribuneships, and perhaps exiled or executed) 289 **am promised forth** have a previous engagement 291 **hold** does not change 296 **quick mettle** of a lively disposition

However he puts on this tardy form.
This rudeness is a sauce to his good wit,
Which gives men stomach to disgest his words
With better appetite.

BRUTUS And so it is. For this time I will leave you.
Tomorrow, if you please to speak with me,
I will come home to you; or if you will,
Come home to me, and I will wait for you.

CASSIUS I will do so. Till then, think of the world.
Exit Brutus.
Well, Brutus, thou art noble; yet I see
Thy honorable mettle may be wrought
From that it is disposed; therefore it is meet
That noble minds keep ever with their likes;
For who so firm that cannot be seduced?
Caesar doth bear me hard, but he loves Brutus.
If I were Brutus now, and he were Cassius,
He should not humor me. I will this night,
In several hands, in at his windows throw,
As if they came from several citizens,
Writings, all tending to the great opinion
That Rome holds of his name; wherein obscurely
Caesar's ambition shall be glancèd at.
And after this, let Caesar seat him sure;
For we will shake him, or worse days endure. *Exit.*

299 **tardy form** sluggish appearance 300 **wit** intelligence 301 **stomach** appetite 301 **disgest** digest 307 **the world** i.e., the current state of affairs 309 **mettle** (1) disposition (2) metal 309–10 **wrought ... disposed** shaped (like iron) contrary to its natural form 310 **meet** fitting 313 **bear me hard** hold a grudge against me 315 **humor** cajole, influence by flattery 316 **several hands** different handwritings 318 **tending to** bearing on 320 **glancèd at** indirectly touched upon 321 **seat him sure** make his position secure

[Scene III. *A street.*]

Thunder and lightning. Enter [*from opposite sides,*] *Casca and Cicero.*

CICERO Good even, Casca; brought you Caesar home?
Why are you breathless? And why stare you so?

CASCA Are not you moved, when all the sway of earth
Shakes like a thing unfirm? O Cicero,
I have seen tempests, when the scolding winds
Have rived the knotty oaks, and I have seen
Th' ambitious ocean swell and rage and foam,
To be exalted with the threat'ning clouds;
But never till tonight, never till now,
Did I go through a tempest dropping fire.
Either there is a civil strife in heaven,
Or else the world, too saucy with the gods,
Incenses them to send destruction.

CICERO Why, saw you anything more wonderful?

CASCA A common slave—you know him well by sight—
Held up his left hand, which did flame and burn
Like twenty torches joined, and yet his hand,
Not sensible of fire, remained unscorched.
Besides—I ha' not since put up my sword—
Against the Capitol I met a lion,
Who glazed upon me and went surly by
Without annoying me. And there were drawn
Upon a heap a hundred ghastly women,

I.iii.3 **all the sway of earth** i.e., the whole scheme of things (sway: ruling principle) 6 **rived** split 8 **exalted with** elevated to 12 **saucy** presumptuous 18 **sensible of** sensitive to 20 **Against** directly opposite (?) near (?) 21 **glazed** stared 22–23 **drawn/Upon a heap** huddled together 23 **ghastly** white as ghosts

Transformèd with their fear, who swore they saw
Men, all in fire, walk up and down the streets.
And yesterday the bird of night did sit
Even at noonday upon the market place,
Hooting and shrieking. When these prodigies
Do so conjointly meet, let not men say,
"These are their reasons, they are natural,"
For I believe they are portentous things
Unto the climate that they point upon.

CICERO Indeed, it is a strange-disposèd time:
But men may construe things after their fashion,
Clean from the purpose of the things themselves.
Comes Caesar to the Capitol tomorrow?

CASCA He doth; for he did bid Antonius
Send word to you he would be there tomorrow.

CICERO Good night then, Casca; this disturbèd sky
Is not to walk in.

CASCA Farewell, Cicero. *Exit Cicero.*

Enter Cassius.

CASSIUS Who's there?

CASCA A Roman.

CASSIUS Casca, by your voice.

CASCA Your ear is good. Cassius, what night is this?

CASSIUS A very pleasing night to honest men.

CASCA Who ever knew the heavens menace so?

CASSIUS Those that have known the earth so full of
faults.
For my part, I have walked about the streets,
Submitting me unto the perilous night,

26 **bird of night** owl (a bird of ill omen) 28 **prodigies** unnatural events 29 **conjointly meet** coincide 32 **climate** region 33 **strange-disposèd** abnormal 34 **after their fashion** in their own way 35 **Clean from the purpose** quite contrary to the real meaning

And thus unbracèd, Casca, as you see,
Have bared my bosom to the thunder-stone;
And when the cross blue lightning seemed to open
The breast of heaven, I did present myself
Even in the aim and very flash of it.

CASCA But wherefore did you so much tempt the heavens?
It is the part of men to fear and tremble
When the most mighty gods by tokens send
Such dreadful heralds to astonish us.

CASSIUS You are dull, Casca, and those sparks of life
That should be in a Roman you do want,
Or else you use not. You look pale, and gaze,
And put on fear, and cast yourself in wonder,
To see the strange impatience of the heavens;
But if you would consider the true cause
Why all these fires, why all these gliding ghosts,
Why birds and beasts from quality and kind,
Why old men, fools, and children calculate,
Why all these things change from their ordinance,
Their natures and preformèd faculties,
To monstrous quality, why, you shall find
That heaven hath infused them with these spirits
To make them instruments of fear and warning
Unto some monstrous state.
Now could I, Casca, name to thee a man
Most like this dreadful night,
That thunders, lightens, opens graves, and roars
As doth the lion in the Capitol;
A man no mightier than thyself, or me,

48 **unbracèd** with doublet unfastened 49 **thunder-stone** lightning bolt 50 **cross** jagged 54 **part** role 55 **tokens** prophetic signs 56 **astonish** stun 58 **want** lack 60 **put on** display 60 **cast yourself in wonder** are amazed 64 **from quality and kind** (act) against their natures 65 **old men** i.e., the senile, in second childhood 65 **calculate** make predictions (cf. proverb, "Fools and children often do prophesy") 66 **ordinance** natural order of behavior 67 **preformèd faculties** innate qualities 68 **monstrous quality** unnatural condition 69 **spirits** supernatural powers 71 **monstrous state** abnormal state of affairs

In personal action, yet prodigious grown
And fearful, as these strange eruptions are.

CASCA 'Tis Caesar that you mean, is it not, Cassius?

CASSIUS Let it be who it is; for Romans now
Have thews and limbs like to their ancestors;
But, woe the while! Our fathers' minds are dead,
And we are governed with our mothers' spirits;
Our yoke and sufferance show us womanish.

CASCA Indeed, they say the senators tomorrow
Mean to establish Caesar as a king;
And he shall wear his crown by sea and land,
In every place save here in Italy.

CASSIUS I know where I will wear this dagger then;
Cassius from bondage will deliver Cassius.
Therein, ye gods, you make the weak most strong;
Therein, ye gods, you tyrants do defeat.
Nor stony tower, nor walls of beaten brass,
Nor airless dungeon, nor strong links of iron,
Can be retentive to the strength of spirit;
But life, being weary of these worldly bars,
Never lacks power to dismiss itself.
If I know this, know all the world besides,
That part of tyranny that I do bear
I can shake off at pleasure. *Thunder still.*

CASCA So can I;
So every bondman in his own hand bears
The power to cancel his captivity.

CASSIUS And why should Caesar be a tyrant then?
Poor man, I know he would not be a wolf
But that he sees the Romans are but sheep;
He were no lion, were not Romans hinds.

77 **prodigious** ominous 78 **fearful** causing fear 78 **eruptions** disturbances of nature 81 **thews** sinews 82 **woe the while** alas for the times 84 **yoke and sufferance** servitude and the meek endurance of it 91 **Therein** i.e., in suicide 95 **be retentive to** hold in 106 **hinds** (1) female deer (2) peasants (3) servants

Those that with haste will make a mighty fire
Begin it with weak straws. What trash is Rome,
What rubbish and what offal, when it serves
For the base matter to illuminate
So vile a thing as Caesar! But, O grief,
Where hast thou led me? I, perhaps, speak this
Before a willing bondman; then I know
My answer must be made. But I am armed,
And dangers are to me indifferent.

CASCA You speak to Casca, and to such a man
That is no fleering tell-tale. Hold, my hand.
Be factious for redress of all these griefs,
And I will set this foot of mine as far
As who goes farthest. [*They clasp hands.*]

CASSIUS There's a bargain made.
Now know you, Casca, I have moved already
Some certain of the noblest-minded Romans
To undergo with me an enterprise
Of honorable dangerous consequence;
And I do know, by this they stay for me
In Pompey's porch; for now, this fearful night,
There is no stir or walking in the streets,
And the complexion of the element
In favor's like the work we have in hand,
Most bloody, fiery, and most terrible.

Enter Cinna.

CASCA Stand close awhile, for here comes one in haste.

CASSIUS 'Tis Cinna; I do know him by his gait;
He is a friend. Cinna, where haste you so?

114 **My answer must be made** I shall have to answer for my words 115 **indifferent** unimportant 117 **fleering** flattering 118 **factious** active in forming a political party 123 **undergo** undertake 125 **by this** by this time 126 **Pompey's porch** portico of Pompey's Theater 128 **complexion of the element** condition of the sky 129 **In favor's like** in appearance is like 131 **close** hidden

CINNA To find out you. Who's that? Metellus Cimber?

CASSIUS No, it is Casca, one incorporate
To our attempts. Am I not stayed for, Cinna?

CINNA I am glad on't. What a fearful night is this!
There's two or three of us have seen strange sights.

CASSIUS Am I not stayed for? Tell me.

CINNA Yes, you are.
O Cassius, if you could
But win the noble Brutus to our party——

CASSIUS Be you content. Good Cinna, take this paper,
And look you lay it in the praetor's chair,
Where Brutus may but find it; and throw this
In at his window; set this up with wax
Upon old Brutus' statue. All this done,
Repair to Pompey's porch, where you shall find us.
Is Decius Brutus and Trebonius there?

CINNA All but Metellus Cimber, and he's gone
To seek you at your house. Well, I will hie,
And so bestow these papers as you bade me.

CASSIUS That done, repair to Pompey's Theater.
Exit Cinna.
Come, Casca, you and I will yet ere day
See Brutus at his house; three parts of him
Is ours already, and the man entire
Upon the next encounter yields him ours.

135–36 **incorporate/To** intimately bound up with 136 **stayed** waited 137 **on't** of it (i.e., that Casca has joined the conspiracy) 143 **praetor's chair** official chair in which Brutus would sit as chief magistrate, an office next in rank to consul 144 **Where Brutus may but find it** where only Brutus may find it 146 **old Brutus** (Lucius Junius Brutus, founder of the Roman Republic) 147 **Repair** go 148 **Decius** (actually Decimus, a kinsman of Marcus Brutus; the error is found in North's Plutarch) 150 **hie** hurry

CASCA O, he sits high in all the people's hearts;
And that which would appear offense in us,
His countenance, like richest alchemy,
Will change to virtue and to worthiness.

CASSIUS Him, and his worth, and our great need of him,
You have right well conceited. Let us go,
For it is after midnight, and ere day
We will awake him and be sure of him. *Exeunt.*

159 countenance support **159 alchemy** (the "science" by which many experimenters tried to turn base metals into gold) **162 conceited** (1) understood (2) described in an elaborate simile

ACT II

[Scene I. *Rome.*]

Enter Brutus in his orchard.

BRUTUS What, Lucius, ho!
I cannot, by the progress of the stars,
Give guess how near to day. Lucius, I say!
I would it were my fault to sleep so soundly.
When, Lucius, when? Awake, I say! What, Lucius!

Enter Lucius.

LUCIUS Called you, my lord?

BRUTUS Get me a taper in my study, Lucius.
When it is lighted, come and call me here.

LUCIUS I will, my lord. *Exit.*

BRUTUS It must be by his death; and for my part,
I know no personal cause to spurn at him,
But for the general. He would be crowned.
How that might change his nature, there's the question.
It is the bright day that brings forth the adder,
And that craves wary walking. Crown him that,
And then I grant we put a sting in him

II.i.s.d. orchard garden **7 taper** candle **11 spurn at** rebel (literally "kick") against **12 general** public welfare **15 craves** demands

That at his will he may do danger with.
Th' abuse of greatness is when it disjoins
Remorse from power; and, to speak truth of Caesar,
I have not known when his affections swayed
More than his reason. But 'tis a common proof
That lowliness is young ambition's ladder,
Whereto the climber upward turns his face;
But when he once attains the upmost round,
He then unto the ladder turns his back,
Looks in the clouds, scorning the base degrees
By which he did ascend. So Caesar may;
Then lest he may, prevent. And, since the quarrel
Will bear no color for the thing he is,
Fashion it thus: that what he is, augmented,
Would run to these and these extremities;
And therefore think him as a serpent's egg
Which hatched, would as his kind grow mischievous,
And kill him in the shell.

Enter Lucius.

LUCIUS The taper burneth in your closet, sir.
Searching the window for a flint, I found
This paper thus sealed up, and I am sure
It did not lie there when I went to bed.
Gives him the letter.

BRUTUS Get you to bed again; it is not day.
Is not tomorrow, boy, the ides of March?

LUCIUS I know not, sir.

BRUTUS Look in the calendar and bring me word.

LUCIUS I will, sir. *Exit.*

17 **danger** harm 18–19 **disjoins/Remorse** separates mercy 20 **affections swayed** emotions ruled 21 **common proof** matter of common experience 22 **lowliness** humility 24 **round** rung 26 **base degrees** (1) low steps of the ladder (2) less important grades of office (3) common people 28 **prevent** take action to forestall 28 **quarrel** cause of complaint 29 **bear no color** have no excuse 30 **Fashion it** construct the case 31 **these and these extremities** such and such extremes (of tyranny) 33 **as his kind** according to its nature 35 **closet** study

BRUTUS The exhalations whizzing in the air
Give so much light that I may read by them.
Opens the letter and reads.

"Brutus, thou sleep'st; awake, and see thyself.
Shall Rome, &c. Speak, strike, redress.
Brutus, thou sleep'st; awake."

Such instigations have been often dropped
Where I have took them up.
"Shall Rome, &c." Thus must I piece it out:
Shall Rome stand under one man's awe? What, Rome?
My ancestors did from the streets of Rome
The Tarquin drive, when he was called a king.
"Speak, strike, redress." Am I entreated
To speak and strike? O Rome, I make thee promise,
If the redress will follow, thou receivest
Thy full petition at the hand of Brutus!

Enter Lucius.

LUCIUS Sir, March is wasted fifteen days. *Knock within.*

BRUTUS 'Tis good. Go to the gate; somebody knocks.
[*Exit Lucius.*]
Since Cassius first did whet me against Caesar,
I have not slept.
Between the acting of a dreadful thing
And the first motion, all the interim is
Like a phantasma, or a hideous dream.
The genius and the mortal instruments
Are then in council, and the state of a man,
Like to a little kingdom, suffers then
The nature of an insurrection.

44 **exhalations** meteors 47, 51 **&c.** (read "et cetera") 51 **piece it out** develop the meaning 52 **under one man's awe** in awe of one man 58 **Thy full ... hand of** all you ask from 61 **whet** incite 64 **motion** prompting 65 **phantasma** hallucination 66 **genius** guardian spirit (?) reasoning spirit (?) 66 **mortal instruments** the emotions and physical powers (which should be ruled and guided by reason) 69 **nature of an insurrection** a kind of insurrection

Enter Lucius.

LUCIUS Sir, 'tis your brother Cassius at the door,
Who doth desire to see you.

BRUTUS Is he alone?

LUCIUS No, sir, there are moe with him.

BRUTUS Do you know them?

LUCIUS No, sir; their hats are plucked about their ears,
And half their faces buried in their cloaks,
That by no means I may discover them
By any mark of favor.

BRUTUS Let 'em enter. [*Exit Lucius.*]
They are the faction. O conspiracy,
Sham'st thou to show thy dang'rous brow by night,
When evils are most free? O, then by day
Where wilt thou find a cavern dark enough
To mask thy monstrous visage? Seek none, conspiracy;
Hide it in smiles and affability:
For if thou path, thy native semblance on,
Not Erebus itself were dim enough
To hide thee from prevention.

Enter the conspirators, Cassius, Casca, Decius, Cinna, Metellus [*Cimber*], *and Trebonius.*

CASSIUS I think we are too bold upon your rest.
Good morrow, Brutus; do we trouble you?

BRUTUS I have been up this hour, awake all night.
Know I these men that come along with you?

CASSIUS Yes, every man of them; and no man here
But honors you; and every one doth wish

70 **brother** i.e., brother-in-law (Cassius was married to Brutus' sister) 72 **moe** more 75 **discover** recognize 76 **favor** appearance 79 **evils are most free** evil things roam most freely 83 **path** walk (verb) 83 **native semblance** true appearance 84 **Erebus** dark region between earth and Hades 85 **from prevention** from being forestalled and hindered 86 **upon** in intruding on

You had but that opinion of yourself
Which every noble Roman bears of you.
This is Trebonius.

BRUTUS He is welcome hither.

CASSIUS This, Decius Brutus.

BRUTUS He is welcome too.

CASSIUS This, Casca; this, Cinna; and this, Metellus Cimber.

BRUTUS They are all welcome.
What watchful cares do interpose themselves
Betwixt your eyes and night?

CASSIUS Shall I entreat a word? *They whisper.*

DECIUS Here lies the east; doth not the day break here?

CASCA No.

CINNA O, pardon, sir, it doth; and yon gray lines
That fret the clouds are messengers of day.

CASCA You shall confess that you are both deceived
Here, as I point my sword, the sun arises,
Which is a great way growing on the south,
Weighing the youthful season of the year.
Some two months hence, up higher toward the north
He first presents his fire; and the high east
Stands as the Capitol, directly here.

BRUTUS Give me your hands all over, one by one.

CASSIUS And let us swear our resolution.

BRUTUS No, not an oath. If not the face of men,
The sufferance of our souls, the time's abuse—

98 **watchful cares** cares that keep you awake 104 **fret** pattern, interlace 107 **growing on** tending toward 108 **Weighing** considering 110 **high** due 114 **the face of men** i.e., the sincere and resolute appearance of the conspirators, which should not be distrusted 115 **sufferance** patient endurance 115 **time's abuse** corruption of the age (i.e., Caesar's assumption of unconstitutional powers)

If these be motives weak, break off betimes,
And every man hence to his idle bed.
So let high-sighted tyranny range on
Till each man drop by lottery. But if these
(As I am sure they do) bear fire enough
To kindle cowards and to steel with valor
The melting spirits of women, then, countrymen,
What need we any spur but our own cause
To prick us to redress? What other bond
Than secret Romans that have spoke the word,
And will not palter? And what other oath
Than honesty to honesty engaged
That this shall be, or we will fall for it?
Swear priests and cowards and men cautelous,
Old feeble carrions and such suffering souls
That welcome wrongs; unto bad causes swear
Such creatures as men doubt; but do not stain
The even virtue of our enterprise,
Nor th' insuppressive mettle of our spirits,
To think that or our cause or our performance
Did need an oath; when every drop of blood
That every Roman bears, and nobly bears,
Is guilty of a several bastardy
If he do break the smallest particle
Of any promise that hath passed from him.

CASSIUS But what of Cicero? Shall we sound him?
I think he will stand very strong with us.

CASCA Let us not leave him out.

CINNA No, by no means.

METELLUS O, let us have him, for his silver hairs

116 **betimes** immediately 118 **high-sighted** arrogant (viewing widely from on high, like a falcon ready to swoop on prey) 118 **range** rove or fly in search of prey 119 **by lottery** by chance, i.e., at the tyrant's whim 124 **prick** urge 125 **secret Romans** the fact that we are Romans capable of maintaining secrecy 126 **palter** equivocate 127 **honesty** personal honor 127 **engaged** pledged 129 **Swear** bind by oath 129 **cautelous** deceitful 130 **carrions** wretches almost dead and rotting 133 **even** unblemished, perfect 134 **insuppressive mettle** indomitable temper 135 **or . . . or** either . . . or 138 **guilty . . . bastardy** i.e., guilty of an act not truly Roman

Will purchase us a good opinion,
And buy men's voices to commend our deeds.
It shall be said his judgment ruled our hands;
Our youths and wildness shall no whit appear,
But all be buried in his gravity.

BRUTUS O, name him not! Let us not break with him;
For he will never follow anything
That other men begin.

CASSIUS Then leave him out.

CASCA Indeed, he is not fit.

DECIUS Shall no man else be touched but only Caesar?

CASSIUS Decius, well urged. I think it is not meet
Mark Antony, so well beloved of Caesar,
Should outlive Caesar; we shall find of him
A shrewd contriver; and you know, his means;
If he improve them, may well stretch so far
As to annoy us all; which to prevent,
Let Antony and Caesar fall together.

BRUTUS Our course will seem too bloody, Caius Cassius,
To cut the head off and then hack the limbs,
Like wrath in death and envy afterwards;
For Antony is but a limb of Caesar.
Let's be sacrificers, but not butchers, Caius.
We all stand up against the spirit of Caesar,
And in the spirit of men there is no blood.
O, that we then could come by Caesar's spirit,
And not dismember Caesar! But, alas,
Caesar must bleed for it. And, gentle friends,
Let's kill him boldly, but not wrathfully;

145 **opinion** reputation 148 **no whit** not in the slightest 149 **gravity** sobriety and stability (Latin *gravitas*) 150 **break with him** divulge our plan to him 155 **urged** suggested 157 **of** in 158 **shrewd contriver** cunning and malicious plotter 159 **improve** make good use of 160 **annoy** harm 160 **prevent** forestall 164 **envy** malice, i.e., as though we were killing Caesar for personal spite and hatred 167 **the spirit of Caesar** the principles (of tyranny) for which Caesar stands 169 **come by** get possession of 171 **gentle** noble

Let's carve him as a dish fit for the gods,
Not hew him as a carcass fit for hounds.
And let our hearts, as subtle masters do,
Stir up their servants to an act of rage,
And after seem to chide 'em. This shall make
Our purpose necessary, and not envious;
Which so appearing to the common eyes,
We shall be called purgers, not murderers.
And for Mark Antony, think not of him;
For he can do no more than Caesar's arm
When Caesar's head is off.

CASSIUS Yet I fear him;
For in the ingrafted love he bears to Caesar——

BRUTUS Alas, good Cassius, do not think of him.
If he love Caesar, all that he can do
Is to himself—take thought and die for Caesar.
And that were much he should, for he is given
To sports, to wildness, and much company.

TREBONIUS There is no fear in him; let him not die,
For he will live and laugh at this hereafter.
Clock strikes.

BRUTUS Peace! Count the clock.

CASSIUS The clock hath stricken three.

TREBONIUS 'Tis time to part.

CASSIUS But it is doubtful yet
Whether Caesar will come forth today or no;
For he is superstitious grown of late,
Quite from the main opinion he held once
Of fantasy, of dreams, and ceremonies.
It may be these apparent prodigies,
The unaccustomed terror of this night,

176 **servants** (1) the hands (2) the passions 178 **envious** malicious 180 **purgers** healers 184 **ingrafted** firmly rooted 187 **take thought** grow melancholy with brooding 188 **that were much he should** that would be too much to expect of him 190 **no fear** nothing to fear 196 **Quite from the main** at variance with the strong 197 **ceremonies** omens 198 **apparent prodigies** obvious signs of disaster

And the persuasion of his augurers
May hold him from the Capitol today.

DECIUS Never fear that. If he be so resolved,
I can o'ersway him; for he loves to hear
That unicorns may be betrayed with trees,
And bears with glasses, elephants with holes,
Lions with toils, and men with flatterers;
But when I tell him he hates flatterers,
He says he does, being then most flatterèd.
Let me work;
For I can give his humor the true bent,
And I will bring him to the Capitol.

CASSIUS Nay, we will all of us be there to fetch him.

BRUTUS By the eighth hour; is that the uttermost?

CINNA Be that the uttermost, and fail not then.

METELLUS Caius Ligarius doth bear Caesar hard,
Who rated him for speaking well of Pompey.
I wonder none of you have thought of him.

BRUTUS Now, good Metellus, go along by him.
He loves me well, and I have given him reasons;
Send him but hither, and I'll fashion him.

CASSIUS The morning comes upon 's; we'll leave you,
Brutus.
And, friends, disperse yourselves; but all remember
What you have said, and show yourselves true
Romans.

BRUTUS Good gentlemen, look fresh and merrily.
Let not our looks put on our purposes,

200 **augurers** augurs (priests who foretold, from omens, the future) 203 **o'ersway him** persuade him to change his mind 204 **betrayed with trees** i.e., tricked into running at a tree (at the last moment its prey steps aside so that the horn is deeply embedded and the unicorn is helpless) 205 **glasses** mirrors 205 **holes** pitfalls 206 **toils** nets, snares 210 **humor** temperament 210 **bent** direction 213 **uttermost** latest 215 **bear Caesar hard** has a grudge against Caesar 216 **rated** berated 218 **him** his house 220 **fashion** shape (to our designs) 225 **put on** display

But bear it as our Roman actors do,
With untired spirits and formal constancy.
And so good morrow to you every one.
Exeunt. Manet Brutus.
Boy! Lucius! Fast asleep? It is no matter;
Enjoy the honey-heavy dew of slumber.
Thou hast no figures nor no fantasies
Which busy care draws in the brains of men;
Therefore thou sleep'st so sound.

Enter Portia.

PORTIA Brutus, my lord.

BRUTUS Portia, what mean you? Wherefore rise you now?
It is not for your health thus to commit
Your weak condition to the raw cold morning.

PORTIA Nor for yours neither. Y'have ungently, Brutus,
Stole from my bed; and yesternight at supper
You suddenly arose and walked about,
Musing and sighing, with your arms across;
And when I asked you what the matter was,
You stared upon me with ungentle looks.
I urged you further; then you scratched your head,
And too impatiently stamped with your foot.
Yet I insisted, yet you answered not,
But with an angry wafter of your hand
Gave sign for me to leave you. So I did,
Fearing to strengthen that impatience
Which seemed too much enkindled, and withal
Hoping it was but an effect of humor,
Which sometime hath his hour with every man.
It will not let you eat, nor talk, nor sleep,
And could it work so much upon your shape

226 **bear it** play our parts 227 **formal constancy** consistent decorum 228 s.d. **Manet** remains 230 **dew** i.e., refreshment 231 **figures . . . fantasies** (both words specify figments of the imagination) 237 **ungently** discourteously 240 **across** folded (a sign of melancholy) 246 **wafter** waving 249 **withal** also 250 **effect of humor** i.e., sign of a temporary mood 251 **his** its

As it hath much prevailed on your condition,
I should not know you Brutus. Dear my lord,
Make me acquainted with your cause of grief.

BRUTUS I am not well in health, and that is all.

PORTIA Brutus is wise and, were he not in health,
He would embrace the means to come by it.

BRUTUS Why, so I do. Good Portia, go to bed.

PORTIA Is Brutus sick, and is it physical
To walk unbracèd and suck up the humors
Of the dank morning? What, is Brutus sick,
And will he steal out of his wholesome bed,
To dare the vile contagion of the night,
And tempt the rheumy and unpurgèd air
To add unto his sickness? No, my Brutus;
You have some sick offense within your mind,
Which by the right and virtue of my place
I ought to know of; and upon my knees
I charm you, by my once commended beauty,
By all your vows of love, and that great vow
Which did incorporate and make us one,
That you unfold to me, your self, your half,
Why you are heavy, and what men tonight
Have had resort to you; for here have been
Some six or seven, who did hide their faces
Even from darkness.

BRUTUS Kneel not, gentle Portia.

PORTIA I should not need, if you were gentle Brutus.
Within the bond of marriage, tell me, Brutus,
Is it excepted I should know no secrets
That appertain to you? Am I your self

254 **condition** disposition 255 **know you** recognize you as 261 **physical** healthy 262 **unbracèd** with doublet unfastened 262 **humors** dampness, mist 265 **night** (night air was thought to be harmful, even poisonous) 266 **tempt . . . air** risk the damp and unpurified (by the sun) air 268 **sick offense** sickness that harms 269 **place** situation (as wife) 271 **charm** entreat 273 **incorporate** make us one flesh (cf. Matthew 19:5, "they twain shall be one flesh") 275 **heavy** dejected 281 **excepted** made an exception that

But, as it were, in sort or limitation,
To keep with you at meals, comfort your bed,
And talk to you sometimes? Dwell I but in the
    suburbs
Of your good pleasure? If it be no more,
Portia is Brutus' harlot, not his wife.

BRUTUS You are my true and honorable wife,
As dear to me as are the ruddy drops
That visit my sad heart.

PORTIA If this were true, then should I know this secret.
I grant I am a woman; but withal
A woman that Lord Brutus took to wife.
I grant I am a woman; but withal
A woman well reputed, Cato's daughter.
Think you I am no stronger than my sex,
Being so fathered and so husbanded?
Tell me your counsels, I will not disclose 'em.
I have made strong proof of my constancy,
Giving myself a voluntary wound
Here in the thigh; can I bear that with patience,
And not my husband's secrets?

BRUTUS O ye gods,
Render me worthy of this noble wife! *Knock.*
Hark, hark! One knocks. Portia, go in a while,
And by and by thy bosom shall partake
The secrets of my heart.
All my engagements I will construe to thee,
All the charactery of my sad brows.
Leave me with haste. *Exit Portia.*

283 **in sort or limitation** after a fashion or within a certain restriction (legal terms) 285 **suburbs** outlying districts (where the brothels and least respectable taverns were found) 292 **withal** at the same time 295 **Cato's daughter** (Marcus Porcius Cato was famous for his integrity; he joined Pompey against Caesar and killed himself at Utica in 46 B.C. to avoid capture; he was Brutus' uncle as well as father-in-law) 298 **counsels** secrets 299 **proof of my constancy** trial of my resolution 307 **engagements** commitments 307 **construe** explain 308 **charactery** of writing upon, i.e., wrinkles of grief and worry

Enter Lucius and [*Caius*] *Ligarius.*

Lucius, who's that knocks?

LUCIUS Here is a sick man that would speak with you.

BRUTUS Caius Ligarius, that Metellus spake of.
Boy, stand aside. Caius Ligarius! How?

CAIUS Vouchsafe good morrow from a feeble tongue.

BRUTUS O, what a time have you chose out, brave Caius.
To wear a kerchief! Would you were not sick!

CAIUS I am not sick, if Brutus have in hand
Any exploit worthy the name of honor.

BRUTUS Such an exploit have I in hand, Ligarius,
Had you a healthful ear to hear of it.

CAIUS By all the gods that Romans bow before,
I here discard my sickness! Soul of Rome,
Brave son, derived from honorable loins,
Thou, like an exorcist, hast conjured up
My mortifièd spirit. Now bid me run,
And I will strive with things impossible,
Yea, get the better of them. What's to do?

BRUTUS A piece of work that will make sick men whole.

CAIUS But are not some whole that we must make sick?

BRUTUS That must we also. What it is, my Caius,
I shall unfold to thee, as we are going
To whom it must be done.

CAIUS Set on your foot,
And with a heart new-fired I follow you,

312 **How** how are you 313 **Vouchsafe** please accept 314 **brave** noble 315 **To wear a kerchief** (as a protection against drafts), i.e., to be sick 322 **from honorable loins** i.e., descent from Lucius Junius Brutus, founder of the Roman Republic 323 **exorcist** conjurer 324 **mortifièd** deadened 327 **whole** healthy 331 **To whom** to the house of him to whom 331 **Set on** advance

To do I know not what; but it sufficeth
That Brutus leads me on. *Thunder.*

BRUTUS Follow me, then. *Exeunt.*

[Scene II. *Caesar's house.*]

Thunder and lightning. Enter Julius Caesar in his nightgown.

CAESAR Nor heaven nor earth have been at peace tonight:
Thrice hath Calphurnia in her sleep cried out,
"Help, ho! They murder Caesar!" Who's within?

Enter a Servant.

SERVANT My lord?

CAESAR Go bid the priests do present sacrifice,
And bring me their opinions of success.

SERVANT I will, my lord. *Exit.*

Enter Calphurnia.

CALPHURNIA What mean you, Caesar? Think you to walk forth?
You shall not stir out of your house today.

CAESAR Caesar shall forth. The things that threatened me
Ne'er looked but on my back; when they shall see
The face of Caesar, they are vanishèd.

CALPHURNIA Caesar, I never stood on ceremonies,
Yet now they fright me. There is one within,
Besides the things that we have heard and seen,
Recounts most horrid sights seen by the watch.

II.ii. s.d. **nightgown** dressing gown 5 **present** immediate 6 **opinions of success** judgment as to the future course of events 13 **stood on ceremonies** paid attention to omens 16 **watch** nightwatchmen

A lioness hath whelpèd in the streets,
And graves have yawned, and yielded up their dead;
Fierce fiery warriors fought upon the clouds
In ranks and squadrons and right form of war,
Which drizzled blood upon the Capitol;
The noise of battle hurtled in the air,
Horses did neigh and dying men did groan,
And ghosts did shriek and squeal about the streets.
O Caesar, these things are beyond all use,
And I do fear them.

CAESAR What can be avoided
Whose end is purposed by the mighty gods?
Yet Caesar shall go forth; for these predictions
Are to the world in general as to Caesar.

CALPHURNIA When beggars die, there are no comets seen;
The heavens themselves blaze forth the death of princes.

CAESAR Cowards die many times before their deaths;
The valiant never taste of death but once.
Of all the wonders that I yet have heard,
It seems to me most strange that men should fear,
Seeing that death, a necessary end,
Will come when it will come.

Enter a Servant.

What say the augurers?

SERVANT They would not have you to stir forth today.
Plucking the entrails of an offering forth,
They could not find a heart within the beast.

CAESAR The gods do this in shame of cowardice:
Caesar should be a beast without a heart
If he should stay at home today for fear.
No, Caesar shall not; Danger knows full well
That Caesar is more dangerous than he.

20 **right form** proper military formation 22 **hurtled** clashed 25 **use** normal experience 29 **Are to** apply to 31 **blaze forth** i.e., proclaim (by comets and meteors) 42 **should** would 42 **heart** (the organ of courage)

We are two lions littered in one day,
And I the elder and more terrible,
And Caesar shall go forth.

CALPHURNIA Alas, my lord,
Your wisdom is consumed in confidence.
Do not go forth today. Call it my fear
That keeps you in the house and not your own.
We'll send Mark Antony to the Senate House,
And he shall say you are not well today.
Let me, upon my knee, prevail in this.

CAESAR Mark Antony shall say I am not well,
And for thy humor, I will stay at home.

Enter Decius.

Here's Decius Brutus, he shall tell them so.

DECIUS Caesar, all hail! Good morrow, worthy Caesar;
I come to fetch you to the Senate House.

CAESAR And you are come in very happy time
To bear my greeting to the senators,
And tell them that I will not come today.
Cannot, is false; and that I dare not, falser:
I will not come today. Tell them so, Decius.

CALPHURNIA Say he is sick.

CAESAR Shall Caesar send a lie?
Have I in conquest stretched mine arm so far
To be afeard to tell graybeards the truth?
Decius, go tell them Caesar will not come.

DECIUS Most mighty Caesar, let me know some cause,
Lest I be laughed at when I tell them so.

CAESAR The cause is in my will: I will not come.
That is enough to satisfy the Senate.
But for your private satisfaction,
Because I love you, I will let you know.

49 **consumed in confidence** destroyed by too much confidence 56 **humor** whim 59 **fetch** escort 60 **happy time** favorable time (i.e., just at the right moment)

Calphurnia here, my wife, stays me at home.
She dreamt tonight she saw my statue,
Which, like a fountain with an hundred spouts,
Did run pure blood, and many lusty Romans
Came smiling and did bathe their hands in it.
And these does she apply for warning and portents
And evils imminent, and on her knee
Hath begged that I will stay at home today.

DECIUS This dream is all amiss interpreted;
It was a vision fair and fortunate:
Your statue spouting blood in many pipes,
In which so many smiling Romans bathed,
Signifies that from you great Rome shall suck
Reviving blood, and that great men shall press
For tinctures, stains, relics, and cognizance.
This by Calphurnia's dream is signified.

CAESAR And this way have you well expounded it.

DECIUS I have, when you have heard what I can say;
And know it now, the Senate have concluded
To give this day a crown to mighty Caesar.
If you shall send them word you will not come,
Their minds may change. Besides, it were a mock
Apt to be rendered, for someone to say
"Break up the Senate till another time,
When Caesar's wife shall meet with better dreams."
If Caesar hide himself, shall they not whisper
"Lo, Caesar is afraid"?
Pardon me, Caesar, for my dear dear love
To your proceeding bids me tell you this,
And reason to my love is liable.

75 **stays** keeps 76 **tonight** i.e., last night 76 **statue** (trisyllabic; pronounced "stat-u-a") 80 **apply for** explain as 80 **portents** (accent on last syllable) 89 **tinctures ... cognizance** (Samuel Johnson paraphrases the line: "The Romans, says Decius, all come to you, as to a saint, for relics; as to a prince, for honors") **tinctures** (1) alchemical elixirs (2) colors, metals, etc. used in heraldry **stains** colors in a coat of arms **relics** venerated property of a martyr **cognizance** mark of identification worn by a nobleman's followers 96–97 **mock ... rendered** jeering remark likely to be made 103 **proceeding** advancement 104 **reason ... liable** i.e., my affection proves stronger than my judgment (of impropriety) in telling you this (**liable** = subordinate)

CAESAR How foolish do your fears seem now,
Calphurnia!
I am ashamèd I did yield to them.
Give me my robe, for I will go.

Enter Brutus, Ligarius, Metellus [*Cimber*], *Casca, Trebonius, Cinna, and Publius.*

And look where Publius is come to fetch me.

PUBLIUS Good morrow, Caesar.

CAESAR Welcome, Publius.
What, Brutus, are you stirred so early too?
Good morrow, Casca. Caius Ligarius,
Caesar was ne'er so much your enemy
As that same ague which hath made you lean.
What is't o'clock?

BRUTUS Caesar, 'tis strucken eight.

CAESAR I thank you for your pains and courtesy.

Enter Antony.

See! Antony, that revels long a-nights,
Is notwithstanding up. Good morrow, Antony.

ANTONY So to most noble Caesar.

CAESAR Bid them prepare within.
I am to blame to be thus waited for.
Now, Cinna; now, Metellus; what, Trebonius,
I have an hour's talk in store for you;
Remember that you call on me today;
Be near me, that I may remember you.

TREBONIUS Caesar, I will [*aside*] and so near will I be,
That your best friends shall wish I had been further.

107 **robe** toga 112 **enemy** (Ligarius had supported Pompey against Caesar in the Civil War and had recently been pardoned by Caesar) 118 **prepare** i.e., set out the wine mentioned in line 126

CAESAR Good friends, go in and taste some wine with me,
And we (like friends) will straightway go together.

BRUTUS [*Aside*] That every like is not the same, O Caesar,
The heart of Brutus earns to think upon. *Exeunt.*

[Scene III. *A street near the Capitol, close to Brutus' house.*]

Enter Artemidorus [*reading a paper*].

[ARTEMIDORUS] "Caesar, beware of Brutus; take heed of Cassius; come not near Casca; have an eye to Cinna; trust not Trebonius; mark well Metellus Cimber; Decius Brutus loves thee not; thou hast wronged Caius Ligarius. There is but one mind in all these men, and it is bent against Caesar. If thou beest not immortal, look about you: security gives way to conspiracy. The mighty gods defend thee!
Thy lover, ARTEMIDORUS."
Here will I stand till Caesar pass along,
And as a suitor will I give him this.
My heart laments that virtue cannot live
Out of the teeth of emulation.
If thou read this, O Caesar, thou mayest live;
If not, the Fates with traitors do contrive. *Exit.*

128 **That every like is not the same** i.e., what a pity that those who appear like friends may actually be enemies 129 **earns** grieves II.iii.6 **bent** directed 7–8 **security gives way to conspiracy** overconfidence gives conspiracy its opportunity 9 **lover** devoted friend 11 **as a suitor** like a petitioner 13 **Out of the teeth of emulation** beyond the reach of envious rivalry 15 **contrive** conspire

[Scene IV. *Another part of the street.*]

Enter Portia and Lucius.

PORTIA I prithee, boy, run to the Senate House;
Stay not to answer me, but get thee gone.
Why dost thou stay?

LUCIUS To know my errand, madam.

PORTIA I would have had thee there and here again
Ere I can tell thee what thou shouldst do there.
O constancy, be strong upon my side;
Set a huge mountain 'tween my heart and tongue!
I have a man's mind, but a woman's might.
How hard it is for women to keep counsel!
Art thou here yet?

LUCIUS Madam, what should I do?
Run to the Capitol, and nothing else?
And so return to you, and nothing else?

PORTIA Yes, bring me word, boy, if thy lord look well,
For he went sickly forth; and take good note
What Caesar doth, what suitors press to him.
Hark, boy, what noise is that?

LUCIUS I hear none, madam.

PORTIA Prithee, listen well.
I heard a bustling rumor like a fray,
And the wind brings it from the Capitol.

LUCIUS Sooth, madam, I hear nothing.

II.iv.6 **constancy** resolution 8 **might** physical strength 9 **counsel** secret (Brutus has obviously told her of the conspiracy, though "stage time" has allowed no opportunity for this; the inconsistency is not noticeable during a performance) 18 **bustling rumor like a fray** confused noise as of battle 20 **Sooth** truly

Enter the Soothsayer.

PORTIA Come hither, fellow. Which way hast thou been?

SOOTHSAYER At mine own house, good lady.

PORTIA What is't o'clock?

SOOTHSAYER About the ninth hour, lady.

PORTIA Is Caesar yet gone to the Capitol?

SOOTHSAYER Madam, not yet; I go to take my stand,
To see him pass on to the Capitol.

PORTIA Thou hast some suit to Caesar, hast thou not?

SOOTHSAYER That I have, lady; if it will please Caesar
To be so good to Caesar as to hear me,
I shall beseech him to befriend himself.

PORTIA Why, know'st thou any harm's intended towards him?

SOOTHSAYER None that I know will be, much that I fear may chance.
Good morrow to you. Here the street is narrow;
The throng that follows Caesar at the heels,
Of senators, of praetors, common suitors,
Will crowd a feeble man almost to death.
I'll get me to a place more void, and there
Speak to great Caesar as he comes along. *Exit.*

PORTIA I must go in. Ay me, how weak a thing
The heart of woman is! O Brutus,
The heavens speed thee in thine enterprise!
Sure, the boy heard me—Brutus hath a suit
That Caesar will not grant—O, I grow faint.
Run, Lucius, and commend me to my lord;
Say I am merry; come to me again,
And bring me word what he doth say to thee.
Exeunt [*severally*].

32 **chance** happen 37 **more void** more empty (less crowded) 41 **speed** prosper 44 **commend me** give my love 45 **merry** cheerful

ACT III

[Scene I. *Rome. Before the Capitol.*]

Flourish. Enter Caesar, Brutus, Cassius, Casca, Decius, Metellus [*Cimber*], *Trebonius, Cinna, Antony, Lepidus, Artemidorus, Publius,* [*Popilius,*] *and the Soothsayer.*

CAESAR The ides of March are come.

SOOTHSAYER Ay, Caesar, but not gone.

ARTEMIDORUS Hail, Caesar! Read this schedule.

DECIUS Trebonius doth desire you to o'er-read,
At your best leisure, this his humble suit.

ARTEMIDORUS O Caesar, read mine first; for mine's a suit
That touches Caesar nearer. Read it, great Caesar.

CAESAR What touches us ourself shall be last served.

ARTEMIDORUS Delay not, Caesar; read it instantly.

CAESAR What, is the fellow mad?

PUBLIUS Sirrah, give place.

CASSIUS What, urge you your petitions in the street?
Come to the Capitol.

[*Caesar goes to the Capitol, the rest following.*]

III.i.3 schedule scroll **7 touches** concerns **10 Sirrah, give place** fellow, get out of the way

POPILIUS I wish your enterprise today may thrive.

CASSIUS What enterprise, Popilius?

POPILIUS Fare you well.
[*Advances to Caesar.*]

BRUTUS What said Popilius Lena?

CASSIUS He wished today our enterprise might thrive.
I fear our purpose is discoverèd.

BRUTUS Look how he makes to Caesar; mark him.

CASSIUS Casca, be sudden, for we fear prevention.
Brutus, what shall be done? If this be known,
Cassius or Caesar never shall turn back,
For I will slay myself.

BRUTUS Cassius, be constant.
Popilius Lena speaks not of our purposes;
For look, he smiles, and Caesar doth not change.

CASSIUS Trebonius knows his time; for look you, Brutus,
He draws Mark Antony out of the way.
[*Exeunt Antony and Trebonius.*]

DECIUS Where is Metellus Cimber? Let him go
And presently prefer his suit to Caesar.

BRUTUS He is addressed. Press near and second him.

CINNA Casca, you are the first that rears your hand.

CAESAR Are we all ready? What is now amiss
That Caesar and his Senate must redress?

METELLUS Most high, most mighty, and most puissant Caesar,
Metellus Cimber throws before thy seat
An humble heart. [*Kneeling.*]

18 **makes to** heads for 19 **sudden** swift 19 **prevention** being forestalled 21 **turn back** i.e., return alive 22 **constant** calm 24 **change** change his expression 28 **presently prefer** immediately present 29 **addressed** ready 33 **puissant** powerful

CAESAR I must prevent thee, Cimber.
These couchings and these lowly courtesies
Might fire the blood of ordinary men,
And turn preordinance and first decree
Into the law of children. Be not fond
To think that Caesar bears such rebel blood
That will be thawed from the true quality
With that which melteth fools—I mean sweet words,
Low-crookèd curtsies, and base spaniel fawning.
Thy brother by decree is banishèd.
If thou dost bend and pray and fawn for him,
I spurn thee like a cur out of my way.
Know, Caesar doth not wrong, nor without cause
Will he be satisfied.

METELLUS Is there no voice more worthy than my own,
To sound more sweetly in great Caesar's ear
For the repealing of my banished brother?

BRUTUS I kiss thy hand, but not in flattery, Caesar,
Desiring thee that Publius Cimber may
Have an immediate freedom of repeal.

CAESAR What, Brutus?

CASSIUS Pardon, Caesar; Caesar, pardon!
As low as to thy foot doth Cassius fall
To beg enfranchisement for Publius Cimber.

CAESAR I could be well moved, if I were as you;
If I could pray to move, prayers would move me;
But I am constant as the Northern Star,
Of whose true-fixed and resting quality

36 **couchings** low bowings 36 **lowly courtesies** humble obeisances 38 **preordinance and first decree** customs and laws established from antiquity 39 **fond** so foolish as 40 **bears such rebel blood** has such uncontrolled emotions 41 **true quality** proper quality (i.e., firmness) 42 **With that** by those things 43 **spaniel** doglike, cringing 51 **repealing** recalling 54 **freedom of repeal** permission to be recalled from exile 57 **enfranchisement** recall, freedom 59 **pray to move** i.e., beg others to change their minds 60 **constant as the Northern Star** unchanging as the pole-star 61 **resting** changeless

There is no fellow in the firmament.
The skies are painted with unnumb'red sparks,
They are all fire and every one doth shine;
But there's but one in all doth hold his place.
So in the world; 'tis furnished well with men,
And men are flesh and blood, and apprehensive;
Yet in the number I do know but one
That unassailable holds on his rank,
Unshaked of motion; and that I am he,
Let me a little show it, even in this—
That I was constant Cimber should be banished,
And constant do remain to keep him so.

CINNA O Caesar——

CAESAR Hence! Wilt thou lift up Olympus?

DECIUS Great Caesar——

CAESAR Doth not Brutus bootless kneel?

CASCA Speak hands for me! *They stab Caesar.*

CAESAR *Et tu, Brutè?* Then fall Caesar. *Dies.*

CINNA Liberty! Freedom! Tyranny is dead!
Run hence, proclaim, cry it about the streets.

CASSIUS Some to the common pulpits, and cry out
"Liberty, freedom, and enfranchisement!"

BRUTUS People, and senators, be not affrighted.
Fly not; stand still; ambition's debt is paid.

CASCA Go to the pulpit, Brutus.

DECIUS And Cassius too.

62 **fellow** equal 63 **unnumb'red** innumerable 65 **hold** keep 67 **apprehensive** capable of reason 69 **holds on his rank** maintains his position 70 **Unshaked of motion** i.e., unmoved by internal or external forces 72 **constant** firmly determined 74 **Olympus** a mountain in Greece where the gods lived and held court 75 **bootless** in vain 77 **Et tu, Brutè** and you (too), Brutus 80 **pulpits** platforms for public speakers 83 **ambition's debt is paid** ambition has received what was due to it

BRUTUS Where's Publius?

CINNA Here, quite confounded with this mutiny.

METELLUS Stand fast together, lest some friend of Caesar's
Should chance——

BRUTUS Talk not of standing. Publius, good cheer;
There is no harm intended to your person,
Nor to no Roman else. So tell them, Publius.

CASSIUS And leave us, Publius, lest that the people
Rushing on us should do your age some mischief.

BRUTUS Do so; and let no man abide this deed
But we the doers.

Enter Trebonius.

CASSIUS Where is Antony?

TREBONIUS Fled to his house amazed.
Men, wives, and children stare, cry out and run,
As it were doomsday.

BRUTUS Fates, we will know your pleasures.
That we shall die, we know; 'tis but the time,
And drawing days out, that men stand upon.

CASCA Why, he that cuts off twenty years of life
Cuts off so many years of fearing death.

BRUTUS Grant that, and then is death a benefit.
So are we Caesar's friends, that have abridged
His time of fearing death. Stoop, Romans, stoop,
And let us bathe our hands in Caesar's blood
Up to the elbows, and besmear our swords.
Then walk we forth, even to the market place,

85 **Publius** an old senator, too infirm to flee 86 **confounded with this mutiny** overwhelmed by this uproar 89 **Talk not of standing** i.e., don't worry about making a stand, organizing resistance 94 **abide** bear the consequences of 96 **amazed** utterly confused 98 **As** as if 100 **drawing . . . upon** (hope of) prolonging life, that men are concerned about 108 **the market place** the Roman Forum, center of business and public affairs

And waving our red weapons o'er our heads,
Let's all cry "Peace, freedom, and liberty!"

CASSIUS Stoop then, and wash. How many ages hence
Shall this our lofty scene be acted over
In states unborn and accents yet unknown!

BRUTUS How many times shall Caesar bleed in sport,
That now on Pompey's basis lies along
No worthier than the dust!

CASSIUS So oft as that shall be,
So often shall the knot of us be called
The men that gave their country liberty.

DECIUS What, shall we forth?

CASSIUS Ay, every man away.
Brutus shall lead, and we will grace his heels
With the most boldest and best hearts of Rome.

Enter a Servant.

BRUTUS Soft, who comes here? A friend of Antony's.

SERVANT Thus, Brutus, did my master bid me kneel;
Thus did Mark Antony bid me fall down;
And, being prostrate, thus he bade me say:
Brutus is noble, wise, valiant, and honest;
Caesar was mighty, bold, royal, and loving.
Say I love Brutus and I honor him;
Say I feared Caesar, honored him, and loved him.
If Brutus will vouchsafe that Antony
May safely come to him and be resolved
How Caesar hath deserved to lie in death,
Mark Antony shall not love Caesar dead
So well as Brutus living; but will follow
The fortunes and affairs of noble Brutus
Thorough the hazards of this untrod state

114 **in sport** for entertainment, i.e., as part of a play 115 **basis** pedestal of statue 115 **along** stretched out 117 **knot** closely bound group 120 **grace** do honor to 122 **Soft** wait a moment 126 **honest** honorable 127 **royal** of princely generosity 131 **be resolved** have it explained to his satisfaction 136 **Thorough** through 136 **untrod state** new and uncertain state of affairs

With all true faith. So says my master Antony.

BRUTUS Thy master is a wise and valiant Roman;
I never thought him worse.
Tell him, so please him come unto this place,
He shall be satisfied and, by my honor,
Depart untouched.

SERVANT I'll fetch him presently.

Exit Servant.

BRUTUS I know that we shall have him well to friend.

CASSIUS I wish we may. But yet have I a mind
That fears him much; and my misgiving still
Falls shrewdly to the purpose.

Enter Antony.

BRUTUS But here comes Antony. Welcome, Mark
Antony.

ANTONY O mighty Caesar! Dost thou lie so low?
Are all thy conquests, glories, triumphs, spoils,
Shrunk to this little measure? Fare thee well.
I know not, gentlemen, what you intend,
Who else must be let blood, who else is rank.
If I myself, there is no hour so fit
As Caesar's death's hour, nor no instrument
Of half that worth as those your swords, made rich
With the most noble blood of all this world.
I do beseech ye, if you bear me hard,
Now, whilst your purpled hands do reek and smoke,
Fulfill your pleasure. Live a thousand years,
I shall not find myself so apt to die;

140 so if it should 142 **presently** immediately 143 **well to friend** as a good friend 145–46 **misgiving . . . purpose** my forebodings always turn out to be justified 152 **let blood** (1) bled, purged (common Elizabethan practice of drawing blood to cure those swollen with disease) (2) put to death 152 **rank** (1) swollen with disease (2) overgrown, i.e., too powerful 157 **bear me hard** have a grudge against me 158 **purpled** (1) made scarlet (with blood) (2) made royal (?) 158 **reek and smoke** i.e., steam (with freshly shed warm blood) 159 **Live** though I live 160 **apt** prepared

No place will please me so, no mean of death,
As here by Caesar, and by you cut off,
The choice and master spirits of this age.

BRUTUS O Antony, beg not your death of us!
Though now we must appear bloody and cruel,
As by our hands and this our present act
You see we do, yet see you but our hands
And this the bleeding business they have done.
Our hearts you see not; they are pitiful;
A pity to the general wrong of Rome—
As fire drives out fire, so pity pity—
Hath done this deed on Caesar. For your part,
To you our swords have leaden points, Mark
Antony:
Our arms in strength of malice, and our hearts
Of brothers' temper, do receive you in
With all kind love, good thoughts, and reverence.

CASSIUS Your voice shall be as strong as any man's
In the disposing of new dignities.

BRUTUS Only be patient till we have appeased
The multitude, beside themselves with fear,
And then we will deliver you the cause
Why I, that did love Caesar when I struck him,
Have thus proceeded.

ANTONY I doubt not of your wisdom.
Let each man render me his bloody hand.
First, Marcus Brutus, will I shake with you;
Next, Caius Cassius, do I take your hand;
Now, Decius Brutus, yours; now yours, Metellus;
Yours, Cinna; and, my valiant Casca, yours;
Though last, not least in love, yours, good Trebonius.
Gentlemen all—alas, what shall I say?
My credit now stands on such slippery ground

161 **mean** manner 169 **pitiful** full of pity 171 **pity pity** pity for Rome's subjection drove out pity for Caesar 173 **leaden** blunt 174–75 **Our arms ... temper** our arms, strong with the might inspired by enmity, and our hearts, full of brotherly feeling 177 **voice** vote 178 **dignities** offices 181 **deliver** communicate to 191 **credit** reputation

That one of two bad ways you must conceit me,
Either a coward or a flatterer.
That I did love thee, Caesar, O, 'tis true!
If then thy spirit look upon us now,
Shall it not grieve thee dearer than thy death
To see thy Antony making his peace,
Shaking the bloody fingers of thy foes,
Most noble, in the presence of thy corse?
Had I as many eyes as thou hast wounds,
Weeping as fast as they stream forth thy blood,
It would become me better than to close
In terms of friendship with thine enemies.
Pardon me, Julius! Here wast thou bayed, brave
hart;
Here didst thou fall, and here thy hunters stand,
Signed in thy spoil and crimsoned in thy lethe.
O world, thou wast the forest to this hart;
And this indeed, O world, the heart of thee.
How like a deer, stroken by many princes,
Dost thou here lie!

CASSIUS Mark Antony——

ANTONY Pardon me, Caius Cassius.
The enemies of Caesar shall say this;
Then, in a friend, it is cold modesty.

CASSIUS I blame you not for praising Caesar so;
But what compact mean you to have with us?
Will you be pricked in number of our friends,
Or shall we on, and not depend on you?

ANTONY Therefore I took your hands, but was indeed
Swayed from the point by looking down on Caesar.

192 **conceit** judge 196 **dearer** more deeply 199 **corse** corpse 202 **close** make an agreement 204 **bayed** brought to bay 204 **hart** (1) deer (2) heart 206 **Signed in thy spoil** marked with the signs of your slaughter 206 **lethe** (dissyllabic; the river of oblivion from which the dead drank in Hades; here, by extension, "stream of death," or "lifeblood") 209 **stroken** struck down 213 **modesty** moderation 216 **pricked in number** marked down (the modern "ticks off names"; the Roman made small holes in his wax-covered tablets) 217 **on** proceed

Friends am I with you all, and love you all,
Upon this hope, that you shall give me reasons
Why, and wherein, Caesar was dangerous.

BRUTUS Or else were this a savage spectacle.
Our reasons are so full of good regard
That were you, Antony, the son of Caesar,
You should be satisfied.

ANTONY That's all I seek;
And am moreover suitor that I may
Produce his body to the market place,
And in the pulpit, as becomes a friend,
Speak in the order of his funeral.

BRUTUS You shall, Mark Antony.

CASSIUS Brutus, a word with you.
[*Aside to Brutus*] You know not what you do; do not consent
That Antony speak in his funeral.
Know you how much the people may be moved
By that which he will utter?

BRUTUS By your pardon:
I will myself into the pulpit first,
And show the reason of our Caesar's death.
What Antony shall speak, I will protest
He speaks by leave and by permission,
And that we are contented Caesar shall
Have all true rites and lawful ceremonies.
It shall advantage more than do us wrong.

CASSIUS I know not what may fall; I like it not.

BRUTUS Mark Antony, here, take you Caesar's body.
You shall not in your funeral speech blame us,
But speak all good you can devise of Caesar,
And say you do't by our permission;

224 **good regard** sound considerations 228 **Produce** bring forth 230 **order** course of ceremonies 238 **protest** declare 241 **true** proper 242 **advantage** benefit 242 **wrong** harm 243 **fall** happen

Else shall you not have any hand at all
About his funeral. And you shall speak
In the same pulpit whereto I am going,
After my speech is ended.

ANTONY Be it so;
I do desire no more.

BRUTUS Prepare the body then, and follow us.
Exeunt. Manet Antony.

ANTONY O pardon me, thou bleeding piece of earth,
That I am meek and gentle with these butchers!
Thou art the ruins of the noblest man
That ever livèd in the tide of times.
Woe to the hand that shed this costly blood!
Over thy wounds now do I prophesy
(Which like dumb mouths do ope their ruby lips
To beg the voice and utterance of my tongue),
A curse shall light upon the limbs of men;
Domestic fury and fierce civil strife
Shall cumber all the parts of Italy;
Blood and destruction shall be so in use,
And dreadful objects so familiar,
That mothers shall but smile when they behold
Their infants quartered with the hands of war,
All pity choked with custom of fell deeds;
And Caesar's spirit, ranging for revenge,
With Atè by his side come hot from hell,
Shall in these confines with a monarch's voice
Cry "Havoc," and let slip the dogs of war,
That this foul deed shall smell above the earth
With carrion men, groaning for burial.

Enter Octavius' Servant.

You serve Octavius Caesar, do you not?

257 **tide of times** course (ebb and flow) of history 264 **cumber** burden, oppress 265 **in use** customary 269 **custom of fell deeds** habituation to cruel acts 270 **ranging** roving widely in search of prey 271 **Atè** Greek goddess of discord and vengeance 272 **confines** boundaries, regions 273 **Cry "Havoc"** give the signal for unrestricted slaughter and looting 273 **let slip** unleash 275 **carrion** dead and rotting

SERVANT I do, Mark Antony.

ANTONY Caesar did write for him to come to Rome.

SERVANT He did receive his letters and is coming,
And bid me say to you by word of mouth—
O Caesar! [*Seeing the body*.]

ANTONY Thy heart is big; get thee apart and weep.
Passion, I see, is catching, for mine eyes,
Seeing those beads of sorrow stand in thine,
Began to water. Is thy master coming?

SERVANT He lies tonight within seven leagues of Rome.

ANTONY Post back with speed, and tell him what hath chanced.
Here is a mourning Rome, a dangerous Rome,
No Rome of safety for Octavius yet.
Hie hence and tell him so. Yet stay awhile;
Thou shalt not back till I have borne this corse
Into the market place; there shall I try
In my oration how the people take
The cruel issue of these bloody men;
According to the which, thou shalt discourse
To young Octavius of the state of things.
Lend me your hand. *Exeunt*.

282 **big** swollen (with grief) 283 **Passion** intense emotion, grief 287 **Post** ride (with relays of horses), hasten 287 **chanced** happened 289 **Rome** (another play on the pronunciation "room"; cf. I.ii.156) 290 **Hie** hurry 292 **try** test 294 **cruel issue** outcome of the cruelty

[Scene II. *The Forum.*]

Enter Brutus and goes into the pulpit, and Cassius, with the Plebeians.

PLEBEIANS We will be satisfied! Let us be satisfied!

BRUTUS Then follow me, and give me audience, friends.
Cassius, go you into the other street
And part the numbers.
Those that will hear me speak, let 'em stay here;
Those that will follow Cassius, go with him;
And public reasons shall be renderèd
Of Caesar's death.

FIRST PLEBEIAN I will hear Brutus speak.

SECOND PLEBEIAN I will hear Cassius, and compare their reasons,
When severally we hear them renderèd.

[*Exit Cassius, with some of the Plebeians.*]

THIRD PLEBEIAN The noble Brutus is ascended. Silence!

BRUTUS Be patient till the last.
Romans, countrymen, and lovers, hear me for my cause, and be silent, that you may hear. Believe me for mine honor, and have respect to mine honor, that you may believe. Censure me in your wisdom, and awake your senses, that you may the better judge. If there be any in this assembly, any dear friend of Caesar's, to him I say that Brutus' love to Caesar was no less than his. If then that friend demand why

III.ii.1 **will be satisfied** want a full explanation 4 **part the numbers** divide the crowd 10 **severally** separately 12 **last** conclusion (of my speech) 13 **lovers** dear friends 15 **respect** regard 16 **Censure** judge 17 **senses** powers of understanding, reason

Brutus rose against Caesar, this is my answer: Not that I love Caesar less, but that I loved Rome more. Have you rather Caesar were living, and die all slaves, than that Caesar were dead, to live all free men? As Caesar loved me, I weep for him; as he was fortunate, I rejoice at it; as he was valiant, I honor him; but as he was ambitious, I slew him. There is tears, for his love; joy, for his fortune; honor, for his valor; and death, for his ambition. Who is here so base, that would be a bondman? If any, speak; for him have I offended. Who is here so rude, that would not be a Roman? If any, speak; for him have I offended. Who is here so vile, that will not love his country? If any, speak; for him have I offended. I pause for a reply.

ALL None, Brutus, none!

BRUTUS Then none have I offended. I have done no more to Caesar than you shall do to Brutus. The question of his death is enrolled in the Capitol; his glory not extenuated, wherein he was worthy, nor his offenses enforced, for which he suffered death.

Enter Mark Antony, with Caesar's body.

Here comes his body, mourned by Mark Antony, who, though he had no hand in his death, shall receive the benefit of his dying, a place in the commonwealth, as which of you shall not? With this I depart, that, as I slew my best lover for the good of Rome, I have the same dagger for myself, when it shall please my country to need my death.

ALL Live, Brutus! Live, live!

FIRST PLEBEIAN Bring him with triumph home unto his house

30 **bondman** slave 31 **rude** barbarous 38 **shall do** i.e., if I should become equally tyrannical 38–39 **The question . . . enrolled** the considerations that made necessary his death are recorded 40 **extenuated** depreciated 41 **enforced** exaggerated 44 **place** i.e., as a free citizen 46 **lover** friend

SECOND PLEBEIAN Give him a statue with his ancestors.

THIRD PLEBEIAN Let him be Caesar.

FOURTH PLEBEIAN Caesar's better parts
Shall be crowned in Brutus.

FIRST PLEBEIAN We'll bring him to his house with shouts and clamors.

BRUTUS My countrymen——

SECOND PLEBEIAN Peace! Silence! Brutus speaks.

FIRST PLEBEIAN Peace, ho!

BRUTUS Good countrymen, let me depart alone,
And, for my sake, stay here with Antony.
Do grace to Caesar's corpse, and grace his speech
Tending to Caesar's glories, which Mark Antony
By our permission, is allowed to make.
I do entreat you, not a man depart,
Save I alone, till Antony have spoke. *Exit.*

FIRST PLEBEIAN Stay, ho! And let us hear Mark Antony.

THIRD PLEBEIAN Let him go up into the public chair;
We'll hear him. Noble Antony, go up.

ANTONY For Brutus' sake, I am beholding to you.

FOURTH PLEBEIAN What does he say of Brutus?

THIRD PLEBEIAN He says, for Brutus' sake,
He finds himself beholding to us all.

FOURTH PLEBEIAN 'Twere best he speak no harm of Brutus here!

FIRST PLEBEIAN This Caesar was a tyrant.

THIRD PLEBEIAN Nay, that's certain.
We are blest that Rome is rid of him.

52 **parts** qualities 59 **Do . . . speech** show respect to dead Caesar and listen respectfully to Antony's speech 60 **Tending** relating 65 **public chair** pulpit, rostrum 67 **beholding** beholden, indebted

SECOND PLEBEIAN Peace! Let us hear what Antony can say.

ANTONY You gentle Romans——

ALL Peace, ho! Let us hear him.

ANTONY Friends, Romans, countrymen, lend me your ears;
I come to bury Caesar, not to praise him.
The evil that men do lives after them,
The good is oft interrèd with their bones;
So let it be with Caesar. The noble Brutus
Hath told you Caesar was ambitious.
If it were so, it was a grievous fault,
And grievously hath Caesar answered it.
Here, under leave of Brutus and the rest
(For Brutus is an honorable man,
So are they all, all honorable men),
Come I to speak in Caesar's funeral.
He was my friend, faithful and just to me;
But Brutus says he was ambitious,
And Brutus is an honorable man.
He hath brought many captives home to Rome,
Whose ransoms did the general coffers fill;
Did this in Caesar seem ambitious?
When that the poor have cried, Caesar hath wept;
Ambition should be made of sterner stuff.
Yet Brutus says he was ambitious;
And Brutus is an honorable man.
You all did see that on the Lupercal
I thrice presented him a kingly crown,
Which he did thrice refuse. Was this ambition?
Yet Brutus says he was ambitious;
And sure he is an honorable man.
I speak not to disprove what Brutus spoke,
But here I am to speak what I do know.
You all did love him once, not without cause;
What cause withholds you then to mourn for him?
O judgment, thou art fled to brutish beasts,

82 **answered** paid the penalty for 91 **general coffers** public treasury

And men have lost their reason! Bear with me;
My heart is in the coffin there with Caesar,
And I must pause till it come back to me.

FIRST PLEBEIAN Methinks there is much reason in his sayings.

SECOND PLEBEIAN If thou consider rightly of the matter,
Caesar has had great wrong.

THIRD PLEBEIAN Has he, masters?
I fear there will a worse come in his place.

FOURTH PLEBEIAN Marked ye his words? He would not take the crown,
Therefore 'tis certain he was not ambitious.

FIRST PLEBEIAN If it be found so, some will dear abide it.

SECOND PLEBEIAN Poor soul, his eyes are red as fire with weeping.

THIRD PLEBEIAN There's not a nobler man in Rome than Antony.

FOURTH PLEBEIAN Now mark him, he begins again to speak.

ANTONY But yesterday the word of Caesar might
Have stood against the world; now lies he there,
And none so poor to do him reverence.
O masters! If I were disposed to stir
Your hearts and minds to mutiny and rage,
I should do Brutus wrong and Cassius wrong,
Who, you all know, are honorable men.
I will not do them wrong; I rather choose
To wrong the dead, to wrong myself and you,
Than I will wrong such honorable men.
But here's a parchment with the seal of Caesar;
I found it in his closet; 'tis his will.
Let but the commons hear this testament,
Which, pardon me, I do not mean to read,

116 **dear abide it** pay dearly for it 122 **so poor to** so low in rank as to 131 **closet** study (?) desk (?) 132 **commons** plebeians

And they would go and kiss dead Caesar's wounds,
And dip their napkins in his sacred blood;
Yea, beg a hair of him for memory,
And dying, mention it within their wills,
Bequeathing it as a rich legacy
Unto their issue.

FOURTH PLEBEIAN We'll hear the will; read it, Mark Antony.

ALL The will, the will! We will hear Caesar's will!

ANTONY Have patience, gentle friends, I must not read it.
It is not meet you know how Caesar loved you.
You are not wood, you are not stones, but men;
And being men, hearing the will of Caesar,
It will inflame you, it will make you mad.
'Tis good you know not that you are his heirs;
For if you should, O, what would come of it?

FOURTH PLEBEIAN Read the will! We'll hear it, Antony!
You shall read us the will, Caesar's will!

ANTONY Will you be patient? Will you stay awhile?
I have o'ershot myself to tell you of it.
I fear I wrong the honorable men
Whose daggers have stabbed Caesar; I do fear it.

FOURTH PLEBEIAN They were traitors. Honorable men!

ALL The will! The testament!

SECOND PLEBEIAN They were villains, murderers! The will! Read the will!

ANTONY You will compel me then to read the will?
Then make a ring about the corpse of Caesar,
And let me show you him that made the will.
Shall I descend? And will you give me leave?

ALL Come down.

SECOND PLEBEIAN Descend. [*Antony comes down.*]

135 **napkins** handkerchiefs 139 **issue** heirs 143 **meet** fitting 151 **stay** wait 152 **o'ershot myself** gone further than I intended

THIRD PLEBEIAN You shall have leave.

FOURTH PLEBEIAN A ring! Stand round.

FIRST PLEBEIAN Stand from the hearse, stand from the body!

SECOND PLEBEIAN Room for Antony, most noble Antony!

ANTONY Nay, press not so upon me; stand far off.

ALL Stand back! Room! Bear back.

ANTONY If you have tears, prepare to shed them now.
You all do know this mantle; I remember
The first time ever Caesar put it on:
'Twas on a summer's evening, in his tent,
That day he overcame the Nervii.
Look, in this place ran Cassius' dagger through;
See what a rent the envious Casca made;
Through this the well-belovèd Brutus stabbed,
And as he plucked his cursèd steel away,
Mark how the blood of Caesar followed it,
As rushing out of doors, to be resolved
If Brutus so unkindly knocked, or no;
For Brutus, as you know, was Caesar's angel.
Judge, O you gods, how dearly Caesar loved him!
This was the most unkindest cut of all;
For when the noble Caesar saw him stab,
Ingratitude, more strong than traitors' arms,
Quite vanquished him. Then burst his mighty heart;
And, in his mantle muffling up his face,
Even at the base of Pompey's statue
(Which all the while ran blood) great Caesar fell.
O, what a fall was there, my countrymen!
Then I, and you, and all of us fell down,
Whilst bloody treason flourished over us.

169 **far** farther 172 **mantle** cloak (here, the toga) 175 **Nervii** (a fierce tribe decisively conquered by Caesar in 57 B.C.) 177 **envious** spiteful 181 **As** as though 181 **to be resolved** to learn for certain 182 **unkindly** (1) cruelly (2) unnaturally 183 **angel** favorite (i.e., considered incapable of evil) 185 **most unkindest** most cruel and unnatural 190 **base** pedestal 190 **statue** (pronounced "stat-u-a") 194 **flourished** (1) swaggered (2) brandished a sword in triumph

O, now you weep, and I perceive you feel
The dint of pity; these are gracious drops.
Kind souls, what weep you when you but behold
Our Caesar's vesture wounded? Look you here,
Here is himself, marred as you see with traitors.

FIRST PLEBEIAN O piteous spectacle!

SECOND PLEBEIAN O noble Caesar!

THIRD PLEBEIAN O woeful day!

FOURTH PLEBEIAN O traitors, villains!

FIRST PLEBEIAN O most bloody sight!

SECOND PLEBEIAN We will be revenged.

[ALL] Revenge! About! Seek! Burn! Fire! Kill! Slay!
Let not a traitor live!

ANTONY Stay, countrymen.

FIRST PLEBEIAN Peace there! Hear the noble Antony.

SECOND PLEBEIAN We'll hear him, we'll follow him, we'll die with him!

ANTONY Good friends, sweet friends, let me not stir you up
To such a sudden flood of mutiny.
They that have done this deed are honorable.
What private griefs they have, alas, I know not,
That made them do it. They are wise and honorable,
And will, no doubt, with reasons answer you.
I come not, friends, to steal away your hearts;
I am no orator, as Brutus is;
But (as you know me all) a plain blunt man
That love my friend, and that they know full well
That gave me public leave to speak of him.
For I have neither writ, nor words, nor worth,

196 **dint** stroke 197 **what** why 198 **vesture** clothing 199 **marred** mangled 199 **with** by 206 **About** let's go 215 **private griefs** personal grievances 222 **public leave to speak** permission to speak in public

Action, nor utterance, nor the power of speech
To stir men's blood; I only speak right on.
I tell you that which you yourselves do know,
Show you sweet Caesar's wounds, poor poor dumb mouths,
And bid them speak for me. But were I Brutus,
And Brutus Antony, there were an Antony
Would ruffle up your spirits, and put a tongue
In every wound of Caesar that should move
The stones of Rome to rise and mutiny.

ALL We'll mutiny.

FIRST PLEBEIAN We'll burn the house of Brutus.

THIRD PLEBEIAN Away, then! Come, seek the conspirators.

ANTONY Yet hear me, countrymen. Yet hear me speak.

ALL Peace, ho! Hear Antony, most noble Antony!

ANTONY Why, friends, you go to you know not what:
Wherein hath Caesar thus deserved your loves?
Alas, you know not; I must tell you then:
You have forgot the will I told you of.

ALL Most true, the will! Let's stay and hear the will.

ANTONY Here is the will, and under Caesar's seal.
To every Roman citizen he gives,
To every several man, seventy-five drachmas.

SECOND PLEBEIAN Most noble Caesar! We'll revenge his death!

THIRD PLEBEIAN O royal Caesar!

ANTONY Hear me with patience.

ALL Peace, ho!

223–24 **neither ... utterance** neither a written speech, nor fluency, nor reputation, nor (an orator's) gestures, nor good delivery (perhaps **writ** should be emended to **wit**, "intellectual cleverness") 225 **right on** directly, without premeditation 230 **ruffle up** incite to rage 244 **several** individual 246 **royal** nobly generous

ANTONY Moreover, he hath left you all his walks,
His private arbors, and new-planted orchards,
On this side Tiber; he hath left them you,
And to your heirs forever: common pleasures,
To walk abroad and recreate yourselves.
Here was a Caesar! When comes such another?

FIRST PLEBEIAN Never, never! Come, away, away!
We'll burn his body in the holy place,
And with the brands fire the traitors' houses.
Take up the body.

SECOND PLEBEIAN Go fetch fire.

THIRD PLEBEIAN Pluck down benches.

FOURTH PLEBEIAN Pluck down forms, windows, anything! *Exeunt Plebeians [with the body].*

ANTONY Now let it work: Mischief, thou art afoot,
Take thou what course thou wilt.

Enter Servant.

How now, fellow?

SERVANT Sir, Octavius is already come to Rome.

ANTONY Where is he?

SERVANT He and Lepidus are at Caesar's house.

ANTONY And thither will I straight to visit him;
He comes upon a wish. Fortune is merry,
And in this mood will give us anything.

SERVANT I heard him say, Brutus and Cassius
Are rid like madmen through the gates of Rome.

ANTONY Belike they had some notice of the people,
How I had moved them. Bring me to Octavius.

Exeunt.

249 **walks** parks 250 **orchards** gardens 252 **common pleasures** public places of recreation 261 **forms, windows** long benches (and) shutters 263 **work** (1) ferment (as yeast) (2) work itself out 268 **will I straight** will I (go) at once 269 **upon a wish** just as I wished 272 **Are rid** have ridden 273 **Belike** probably 273 **notice of** news about

[Scene III. *A street.*]

Enter Cinna the Poet, and after him the Plebeians.

CINNA I dreamt tonight that I did feast with Caesar,
And things unluckily charge my fantasy.
I have no will to wander forth of doors,
Yet something leads me forth.

FIRST PLEBEIAN What is your name?

SECOND PLEBEIAN Whither are you going?

THIRD PLEBEIAN Where do you dwell?

FOURTH PLEBEIAN Are you a married man or a bachelor?

SECOND PLEBEIAN Answer every man directly.

FIRST PLEBEIAN Ay, and briefly.

FOURTH PLEBEIAN Ay, and wisely.

THIRD PLEBEIAN Ay, and truly, you were best.

CINNA What is my name? Whither am I going? Where do I dwell? Am I a married man or a bachelor? Then, to answer every man directly and briefly, wisely and truly: wisely I say, I am a bachelor.

SECOND PLEBEIAN That's as much as to say, they are fools that marry: you'll bear me a bang for that, I fear. Proceed directly.

CINNA Directly, I am going to Caesar's funeral.

FIRST PLEBEIAN As a friend or an enemy?

III.iii.1 **tonight** last night 2 **things . . . fantasy** events give ominous weight to my imaginings 3 **forth** out 9 **directly** straightforwardly 18 **bear me a bang** get a blow from me

CINNA As a friend.

SECOND PLEBEIAN That matter is answered directly.

FOURTH PLEBEIAN For your dwelling, briefly.

CINNA Briefly, I dwell by the Capitol.

THIRD PLEBEIAN Your name, sir, truly.

CINNA Truly, my name is Cinna.

FIRST PLEBEIAN Tear him to pieces! He's a conspirator.

CINNA I am Cinna the poet! I am Cinna the poet!

FOURTH PLEBEIAN Tear him for his bad verses! Tear him for his bad verses!

CINNA I am not Cinna the conspirator.

FOURTH PLEBEIAN It is no matter, his name's Cinna; pluck but his name out of his heart, and turn him going.

THIRD PLEBEIAN Tear him, tear him! [*They attack him.*] Come, brands, ho! Firebrands! To Brutus', to Cassius'! Burn all! Some to Decius' house, and some to Casca's; some to Ligarius'! Away, go!

Exeunt all the Plebeians [*with Cinna*].

34–35 turn him going dispatch him

ACT IV

[Scene I. *A house in Rome.*]

Enter Antony, Octavius, and Lepidus.

ANTONY These many then shall die; their names are pricked.

OCTAVIUS Your brother too must die; consent you, Lepidus?

LEPIDUS I do consent——

OCTAVIUS Prick him down, Antony.

LEPIDUS Upon condition Publius shall not live,
Who is your sister's son, Mark Antony.

ANTONY He shall not live; look, with a spot I damn him.
But, Lepidus, go you to Caesar's house;
Fetch the will hither, and we shall determine
How to cut off some charge in legacies.

LEPIDUS What, shall I find you here?

OCTAVIUS Or here or at the Capitol. *Exit Lepidus.*

IV.i.1 **pricked** ticked off, marked on the list 6 **with a spot I damn him** with a dot (on the wax tablet) I condemn him 9 **cut off some charge** reduce expenses (by altering the amount left in bequests) 11 **Or** either

ANTONY This is a slight unmeritable man,
Meet to be sent on errands; is it fit,
The threefold world divided, he should stand
One of the three to share it?

OCTAVIUS So you thought him,
And took his voice who should be pricked to die
In our black sentence and proscription.

ANTONY Octavius, I have seen more days than you;
And though we lay these honors on this man,
To ease ourselves of divers sland'rous loads,
He shall but bear them as the ass bears gold,
To groan and sweat under the business,
Either led or driven, as we point the way;
And having brought our treasure where we will,
Then take we down his load, and turn him off,
(Like to the empty ass) to shake his ears
And graze in commons.

OCTAVIUS You may do your will;
But he's a tried and valiant soldier.

ANTONY So is my horse, Octavius, and for that
I do appoint him store of provender.
It is a creature that I teach to fight,
To wind, to stop, to run directly on,
His corporal motion governed by my spirit.
And, in some taste, is Lepidus but so.
He must be taught, and trained, and bid go forth.
A barren-spirited fellow; one that feeds

12 **slight unmeritable** insignificant and undeserving 13 **Meet** fit 14 **threefold world** three areas of the Roman empire, Europe, Asia, and Africa 16 **voice** vote 17 **black sentence** sentence of death 17 **proscription** condemnation to death or exile 18 **have seen more days** am older (and more experienced) 20 **divers sland'rous loads** blame which will be laid upon us for our various actions 22 **business** hard labor 25 **turn him off** drive him away 26 **empty** unburdened 27 **in commons** on public pasture 28 **soldier** (trisyllabic) 30 **appoint him store** allot him a supply 32 **wind** turn 33 **corporal** physical 33 **spirit** mind 34 **taste** measure 34 **so** the same 36 **barren-spirited** lacking initiative or ideas of his own

On objects, arts, and imitations,
Which, out of use and staled by other men,
Begin his fashion. Do not talk of him
But as a property. And now, Octavius,
Listen great things. Brutus and Cassius
Are levying powers; we must straight make head.
Therefore let your alliance be combined,
Our best friends made, our means stretched;
And let us presently go sit in council
How covert matters may be best disclosed,
And open perils surest answerèd.

OCTAVIUS Let us do so; for we are at the stake,
And bayed about with many enemies;
And some that smile have in their hearts, I fear,
Millions of mischiefs. *Exeunt.*

[Scene II. *Camp near Sardis.*]

Drum. Enter Brutus, Lucilius, [*Lucius,*] *and the Army. Titinius and Pindarus meet them.*

BRUTUS Stand ho!

LUCILIUS Give the word, ho! and stand.

BRUTUS What now, Lucilius, is Cassius near?

37 **objects, arts, and imitations** curiosities, artifices, and fashions (or styles) 38 **staled** made common 39 **Begin his fashion** i.e., he is always far behind the times 40 **property** mere tool (a thing rather than a person) 42 **powers** armed forces 42 **straight make head** immediately gather troops 44 **Our best friends made** let our closest allies be selected 44 **stretched** be used to the fullest advantage 45 **presently** immediately 46–47 **How . . . answerèd** to decide how hidden dangers may best be discovered and open dangers most safely encountered 48 **at the stake** (metaphor derived from Elizabethan sport of bearbaiting) i.e., like a bear tied to a stake and set upon by many dogs 51 **mischiefs** plans to injure us

LUCILIUS He is at hand, and Pindarus is come
To do you salutation from his master.

BRUTUS He greets me well. Your master, Pindarus,
In his own change, or by ill officers,
Hath given me some worthy cause to wish
Things done undone; but if he be at hand,
I shall be satisfied.

PINDARUS I do not doubt
But that my noble master will appear
Such as he is, full of regard and honor.

BRUTUS He is not doubted. A word, Lucilius,
How he received you; let me be resolved.

LUCILIUS With courtesy and with respect enough,
But not with such familiar instances,
Nor with such free and friendly conference
As he hath used of old.

BRUTUS Thou has described
A hot friend cooling. Ever note, Lucilius,
When love begins to sicken and decay
It useth an enforcèd ceremony.
There are no tricks in plain and simple faith;
But hollow men, like horses hot at hand,
Make gallant show and promise of their mettle;
Low march within.
But when they should endure the bloody spur,
They fall their crests, and like deceitful jades
Sink in the trial. Comes his army on?

LUCILIUS They mean this night in Sardis to be
quartered;

IV.ii.6 **He greets me well** he sends greetings by a very good man 7 **In his . . . officers** either from a change in his feelings toward me or through the actions of bad subordinates 8 **worthy** substantial 10 **be satisfied** receive a satisfactory explanation 12 **full of regard** worthy of respect 14 **resolved** fully informed 16 **familiar instances** marks of friendship 17 **conference** conversation 21 **enforcèd ceremony** strained formality 23 **hollow** insincere 23 **hot at hand** overspirited at the start 24 **mettle** quality, courage 26 **fall their crests** let fall the ridges of their necks 26 **jades** nags 27 **Sink in the trial** fail when put to the test

The greater part, the horse in general,
Are come with Cassius.

Enter Cassius and his Powers.

BRUTUS Hark! He is arrived.
March gently on to meet him.

CASSIUS Stand, ho!

BRUTUS Stand, ho! Speak the word along.

[FIRST SOLDIER] Stand!

[SECOND SOLDIER] Stand!

[THIRD SOLDIER] Stand!

CASSIUS Most noble brother, you have done me wrong.

BRUTUS Judge me, you gods! Wrong I mine enemies?
And if not so, how should I wrong a brother.

CASSIUS Brutus, this sober form of yours hides wrongs;
And when you do them——

BRUTUS Cassius, be content.
Speak your griefs softly; I do know you well.
Before the eyes of both our armies here
(Which should perceive nothing but love from us)
Let us not wrangle. Bid them move away;
Then in my tent, Cassius, enlarge your griefs,
And I will give you audience.

CASSIUS Pindarus,
Bid our commanders lead their charges off
A little from this ground.

BRUTUS Lucilius, do you the like, and let no man
Come to our tent till we have done our conference.
Let Lucius and Titinius guard our door.

Exeunt. Mane[n]t Brutus and Cassius.

29 **the horse in general** all the cavalry 31 **gently** slowly 40 **sober form** staid manner 41 **be content** keep calm 42 **griefs** grievances 46 **enlarge** freely express 48 **charges** troops

[Scene III. *Brutus' tent.*]

CASSIUS That you have wronged me doth appear in this:
You have condemned and noted Lucius Pella
For taking bribes here of the Sardians;
Wherein my letters, praying on his side,
Because I knew the man, was slighted off.

BRUTUS You wronged yourself to write in such a case.

CASSIUS In such a time as this it is not meet
That every nice offense should bear his comment.

BRUTUS Let me tell you, Cassius, you yourself
Are much condemned to have an itching palm,
To sell and mart your offices for gold
To undeservers.

CASSIUS I an itching palm?
You know that you are Brutus that speaks this,
Or, by the gods, this speech were else your last.

BRUTUS The name of Cassius honors this corruption,
And chastisement doth therefore hide his head.

CASSIUS Chastisement!

BRUTUS Remember March, the ides of March
remember.
Did not great Julius bleed for justice' sake?
What villain touched his body, that did stab,
And not for justice? What, shall one of us,
That struck the foremost man of all this world

IV.iii.2. **noted** publicly disgraced 4 **praying on his side** appealing on his behalf 5 **was slighted off** was contemptuously disregarded ("letters" takes a singular verb because of its singular meaning) 8 **nice ... comment** trivial fault should receive criticism (his = its) 10 **condemned ... palm** accused of being mercenary 11 **mart** traffic in 15 **honors** lends an air of respectability 21 **And not** except

But for supporting robbers, shall we now
Contaminate our fingers with base bribes,
And sell the mighty space of our large honors
For so much trash as may be graspèd thus?
I had rather be a dog, and bay the moon,
Than such a Roman.

CASSIUS Brutus, bait not me;
I'll not endure it. You forget yourself
To hedge me in. I am a soldier, I,
Older in practice, abler than yourself
To make conditions.

BRUTUS Go to! You are not, Cassius.

CASSIUS I am.

BRUTUS I say you are not.

CASSIUS Urge me no more, I shall forget myself;
Have mind upon your health; tempt me no farther.

BRUTUS Away, slight man!

CASSIUS Is't possible?

BRUTUS Hear me, for I will speak.
Must I give way and room to your rash choler?
Shall I be frighted when a madman stares?

CASSIUS O ye gods, ye gods! Must I endure all this?

23 **supporting robbers** i.e., protecting dishonest officials (a point made by Plutarch but mentioned only now by Shakespeare) 25 **mighty ... honors** vast capacity to be honorable and magnanimous (with suggestion of potentiality for making other men free, and honorable in office) 26 **trash** rubbish, i.e., money 26 **graspèd thus** (the small confined area of the closed fist contrasts with the "mighty space" gained by their honorable deeds in abolishing injustice and corruption) 27 **bay** howl at 28 **bait** harass and worry (as a bear tied to a stake is baited by dogs) 30 **hedge me in** limit my freedom of action 32 **make conditions** manage practical matters 35 **Urge** drive, bully 36 **health** safety 36 **tempt** provoke 37 **slight** insignificant 39 **give ... choler** let your hasty temper have free vent and run its course unchecked 40 **stares** glares

BRUTUS All this? Ay, more: fret till your proud heart
break.
Go show your slaves how choleric you are,
And make your bondmen tremble. Must I budge?
Must I observe you? Must I stand and crouch
Under your testy humor? By the gods,
You shall digest the venom of your spleen,
Though it do split you; for, from this day forth,
I'll use you for my mirth, yea, for my laughter,
When you are waspish.

CASSIUS Is it come to this?

BRUTUS You say you are a better soldier:
Let it appear so; make your vaunting true,
And it shall please me well. For mine own part,
I shall be glad to learn of noble men.

CASSIUS You wrong me every way; you wrong me, Brutus;
I said, an elder soldier, not a better.
Did I say, better?

BRUTUS If you did, I care not.

CASSIUS When Caesar lived, he durst not thus have
moved me.

BRUTUS Peace, peace, you durst not so have tempted
him.

CASSIUS I durst not?

BRUTUS No.

CASSIUS What? Durst not tempt him?

BRUTUS For your life you durst not.

44 **budge** defer to it 45 **observe** wait on 45 **crouch** bow 46 **testy humor** irritability 47 **digest the venom** swallow the poison 47 **spleen** (considered the source of sudden passions) i.e., fiery temper 52 **vaunting** boasting 54 **learn of** (1) hear about the exploits of (2) take lessons from 58 **moved** exasperated 59 **tempted** provoked

CASSIUS Do not presume too much upon my love;
I may do that I shall be sorry for.

BRUTUS You have done that you should be sorry for.
There is no terror, Cassius, in your threats;
For I am armed so strong in honesty
That they pass by me as the idle wind,
Which I respect not. I did send to you
For certain sums of gold, which you denied me;
For I can raise no money by vile means.
By heaven, I had rather coin my heart
And drop my blood for drachmas than to wring
From the hard hands of peasants their vile trash
By any indirection. I did send
To you for gold to pay my legions,
Which you denied me. Was that done like Cassius?
Should I have answered Caius Cassius so?
When Marcus Brutus grows so covetous
To lock such rascal counters from his friends,
Be ready, gods, with all your thunderbolts,
Dash him to pieces!

CASSIUS I denied you not.

BRUTUS You did.

CASSIUS I did not. He was but a fool
That brought my answer back. Brutus hath rived my heart.
A friend should bear his friend's infirmities;
But Brutus makes mine greater than they are.

BRUTUS I do not, till you practice them on me.

CASSIUS You love me not.

BRUTUS I do not like your faults.

CASSIUS A friendly eye could never see such faults.

67 **honesty** integrity 69 **respect** heed 75 **indirection** irregular methods 80 **rascal counters** base (and worthless) coins 84 **rived** broken

BRUTUS A flatterer's would not, though they do appear
As huge as high Olympus.

CASSIUS Come, Antony, and young Octavius, come,
Revenge yourselves alone on Cassius,
For Cassius is aweary of the world:
Hated by one he loves; braved by his brother;
Checked like a bondman; all his faults observed,
Set in a notebook, learned and conned by rote
To cast into my teeth. O, I could weep
My spirit from mine eyes! There is my dagger,
And here my naked breast; within, a heart
Dearer than Pluto's mine, richer than gold;
If that thou be'st a Roman, take it forth.
I, that denied thee gold, will give my heart.
Strike as thou didst at Caesar; for I know,
When thou didst hate him worst, thou lovedst him
better
Than ever thou lovedst Cassius.

BRUTUS Sheathe your dagger.
Be angry when you will, it shall have scope.
Do what you will, dishonor shall be humor.
O Cassius, you are yokèd with a lamb
That carries anger as the flint bears fire,
Who, much enforcèd, shows a hasty spark,
And straight is cold again.

CASSIUS Hath Cassius lived
To be but mirth and laughter to his Brutus
When grief and blood ill-tempered vexeth him?

BRUTUS When I spoke that, I was ill-tempered too.

93 **alone** only 95 **braved** defied 96 **Checked** rebuked 97 **conned by rote** learned by heart 98 **cast into my teeth** i.e., throw in my face 101 **Dearer than Pluto's mine** more precious than all the riches in the earth (Pluto, god of the underworld, and Plutus, god of riches, were frequently confused) 107 **shall have scope** (your anger) shall have free play 108 **dishonor shall be humor** insults shall be regarded as quirks of temperament 111 **much enforcèd** greatly provoked 112 **straight** immediately 114 **blood ill-tempered** i.e., a "black mood"

CASSIUS Do you confess so much? Give me your hand.

BRUTUS And my heart too.

CASSIUS O Brutus!

BRUTUS What's the matter?

CASSIUS Have not you love enough to bear with me
When that rash humor which my mother gave me
Makes me forgetful?

BRUTUS Yes, Cassius, and from henceforth,
When you are over-earnest with your Brutus,
He'll think your mother chides, and leave you so.

Enter a Poet, [followed by Lucilius, Titinius, and Lucius].

POET Let me go in to see the generals;
There is some grudge between 'em; 'tis not meet
They be alone.

LUCILIUS You shall not come to them.

POET Nothing but death shall stay me.

CASSIUS How now. What's the matter?

POET For shame, you generals! What do you mean?
Love, and be friends, as two such men should be;
For I have seen more years, I'm sure, than ye.

CASSIUS Ha, ha! How vilely doth this cynic rhyme!

BRUTUS Get you hence, sirrah! Saucy fellow, hence!

CASSIUS Bear with him, Brutus, 'tis his fashion.

BRUTUS I'll know his humor when he knows his time.
What should the wars do with these jigging fools?
Companion, hence!

119 **rash humor** hasty temperament 122 **your mother** i.e., your inherited temperament 122 **leave you so** leave it at that 124 **grudge** bad feeling 132 **cynic** rude fellow 133 **Saucy** impertinent 135 **I'll . . . time** I'll accept his eccentricity when he can judge the suitable time for it 136 **jigging** doggerel-writing, rhyming 137 **Companion** base fellow

CASSIUS Away, away, be gone!
Exit Poet.

BRUTUS Lucilius and Titinius, bid the commanders
Prepare to lodge their companies tonight.

CASSIUS And come yourselves, and bring Messala with you
Immediately to us. [*Exeunt Liucilius and Titinius.*]

BRUTUS Lucius, a bowl of wine.
[*Exit Lucius.*]

CASSIUS I did not think you could have been so angry.

BRUTUS O Cassius, I am sick of many griefs.

CASSIUS Of your philosophy you make no use,
If you give place to accidental evils.

BRUTUS No man bears sorrow better. Portia is dead.

CASSIUS Ha? Portia?

BRUTUS She is dead.

CASSIUS How scaped I killing when I crossed you so?
O insupportable and touching loss!
Upon what sickness?

BRUTUS Impatient of my absence,
And grief that young Octavius with Mark Antony
Have made themselves so strong—for with her death
That tidings came—with this she fell distract,
And (her attendants absent) swallowed fire.

CASSIUS And died so?

BRUTUS Even so.

145 **place** way 145 **accidental evils** misfortunes brought on by chance (Brutus seems not to be behaving as a Stoic philosopher should) 149 **crossed** contradicted 150 **touching** wounding, grievous 151 **Upon** as a result of 151 **Impatient of** unable to endure 153–54 **for . . . came** i.e., news of her death came at the same time as news of their strength 154 **fell distract** became distraught 155 **swallowed fire** (according to Plutarch she choked herself by putting hot coals into her mouth)

CASSIUS O ye immortal gods!

Enter Boy [Lucius], with wine and tapers.

BRUTUS Speak no more of her. Give me a bowl of wine.
In this I bury all unkindness, Cassius. *Drinks.*

CASSIUS My heart is thirsty for that noble pledge.
Fill, Lucius, till the wine o'erswell the cup;
I cannot drink too much of Brutus' love.
[*Drinks. Exit Lucius.*]

Enter Titinius and Messala.

BRUTUS Come in, Titinius! Welcome, good Messala.
Now sit we close about this taper here,
And call in question our necessities.

CASSIUS Portia, art thou gone?

BRUTUS No more, I pray you.
Messala, I have here receivèd letters
That young Octavius and Mark Antony
Come down upon us with a mighty power,
Bending their expedition toward Philippi.

MESSALA Myself have letters of the selfsame tenure.

BRUTUS With what addition?

MESSALA That by proscription and bills of outlawry
Octavius, Antony, and Lepidus
Have put to death an hundred senators.

BRUTUS Therein our letters do not well agree.
Mine speak of seventy senators that died
By their proscriptions, Cicero being one.

CASSIUS Cicero one?

MESSALA Cicero is dead,
And by that order of proscription.
Had you your letters from your wife, my lord?

164 **call in question** consider 168 **power** army 169 **Bending their expedition** directing their rapid march 170 **tenure** tenor, general meaning 172 **proscription** proclamation of the death sentence 172 **bills of outlawry** lists of those proscribed

BRUTUS No, Messala.

MESSALA Nor nothing in your letters writ of her?

BRUTUS Nothing, Messala.

MESSALA That methinks is strange.

BRUTUS Why ask you? Hear you aught of her in yours?

MESSALA No, my lord.

BRUTUS Now as you are a Roman, tell me true.

MESSALA Then like a Roman bear the truth I tell,
For certain she is dead, and by strange manner.

BRUTUS Why, farewell, Portia. We must die, Messala.
With meditating that she must die once,
I have the patience to endure it now.

MESSALA Even so great men great losses should endure.

CASSIUS I have as much of this in art as you,
But yet my nature could not bear it so.

BRUTUS Well, to our work alive. What do you think
Of marching to Philippi presently?

CASSIUS I do not think it good.

BRUTUS Your reason?

CASSIUS This it is:
'Tis better that the enemy seek us;
So shall he waste his means, weary his soldiers,
Doing himself offense, whilst we, lying still,
Are full of rest, defense, and nimbleness.

BRUTUS Good reasons must of force give place to better.
The people 'twixt Philippi and this ground

190 **once** at some time 193 **this in art** i.e., this Stoicism in theory 180–94 **Had ... so** (some editors suggest that this was the original version of Shakespeare's account of Portia's death and that he later deleted this and wrote in lines 142–57, preferring to demonstrate Brutus' humanity rather than his Stoicism; the Folio printer then set up both versions by mistake. Line 158 would follow 141—as 195 would follow 179—neatly enough to make this an attractive theory) 195 **alive** as men still living 196 **presently** immediately 200 **offense** harm 202 **force** necessity

Do stand but in a forced affection;
For they have grudged us contribution.
The enemy, marching along by them,
By them shall make a fuller number up,
Come on refreshed, new-added and encouraged;
From which advantage shall we cut him off
If at Philippi we do face him there,
These people at our back.

CASSIUS Hear me, good brother.

BRUTUS Under your pardon. You must note beside
That we have tried the utmost of our friends,
Our legions are brimful, our cause is ripe.
The enemy increaseth every day;
We, at the height, are ready to decline.
There is a tide in the affairs of men
Which, taken at the flood, leads on to fortune;
Omitted, all the voyage of their life
Is bound in shallows and in miseries.
On such a full sea are we now afloat,
And we must take the current when it serves,
Or lose our ventures.

CASSIUS Then, with your will, go on;
We'll along ourselves and meet them at Philippi.

BRUTUS The deep of night is crept upon our talk,
And nature must obey necessity,
Which we will niggard with a little rest.
There is no more to say?

CASSIUS No more. Good night.
Early tomorrow will we rise and hence.

Enter Lucius.

204 **Do . . . affection** i.e., support us only under compulsion 208 **new-added** reinforced 212 **Under your pardon** excuse me 219 **Omitted** neglected 220 **bound in** limited to 223 **ventures** shipping trade, i.e., risks 223 **with your will** as you wish 227 **niggard with a little rest** i.e., put off with the shortest possible sleep 229 **hence** leave this place

BRUTUS Lucius, my gown. *Exit Lucius.*
Farewell, good Messala.
Good night, Titinius. Noble, noble Cassius,
Good night, and good repose.

CASSIUS O my dear brother,
This was an ill beginning of the night.
Never come such division 'tween our souls!
Let it not, Brutus.

Enter Lucius, with the gown.

BRUTUS Everything is well.

CASSIUS Good night, my lord.

BRUTUS Good night, good brother.

TITINIUS, MESSALA Good night, Lord Brutus.

BRUTUS Farewell, every one.
Exeunt.
Give me the gown. Where is thy instrument?

LUCIUS Here in the tent.

BRUTUS What, thou speak'st drowsily?
Poor knave, I blame thee not; thou art o'erwatched.
Call Claudius and some other of my men;
I'll have them sleep on cushions in my tent.

LUCIUS Varro and Claudius!

Enter Varro and Claudius.

VARRO Calls my lord?

BRUTUS I pray you, sirs, lie in my tent and sleep.
It may be I shall raise you by and by
On business to my brother Cassius.

VARRO So please you, we will stand and watch your pleasure.

230 **gown** dressing gown 234 **Never come** may there never again come 238 **instrument** (probably a lute) 240 **knave** boy 240 **o'erwatched** tired out from lack of sleep 246 **raise** rouse 248 **watch your pleasure** be on the watch for your command

BRUTUS I will not have it so; lie down, good sirs;
It may be I shall otherwise bethink me.
[*Varro and Claudius lie down.*]
Look, Lucius, here's the book I sought for so;
I put it in the pocket of my gown.

LUCIUS I was sure your lordship did not give it me.

BRUTUS Bear with me, good boy, I am much forgetful.
Canst thou hold up thy heavy eyes awhile,
And touch thy instrument a strain or two?

LUCIUS Ay, my lord, an't please you.

BRUTUS It does, my boy.
I trouble thee too much, but thou art willing.

LUCIUS It is my duty, sir.

BRUTUS I should not urge thy duty past thy might;
I know young bloods look for a time of rest.

LUCIUS I have slept, my lord, already.

BRUTUS It was well done, and thou shalt sleep again;
I will not hold thee long. If I do live,
I will be good to thee.
Music, and a song.
This is a sleepy tune. O murd'rous slumber!
Layest thou thy leaden mace upon my boy,
That plays thee music? Gentle knave, good night;
I will not do thee so much wrong to wake thee.
If thou dost nod, thou break'st thy instrument;
I'll take it from thee; and, good boy, good night.
Let me see, let me see; is not the leaf turned down
Where I left reading? Here it is, I think.

Enter the Ghost of Caesar.

250 **otherwise bethink me** change my mind 256 **touch** play on 256 **strain** tune 257 **an't** if it 261 **young bloods** youthful constitutions 266 **murd'rous** deathlike 267 **leaden** heavy (association also with death, for lead was used in coffin-making) 267 **mace** staff of office (with which a man was touched on the shoulder when arrested)

How ill this taper burns. Ha! Who comes here?
I think it is the weakness of mine eyes
That shapes this monstrous apparition.
It comes upon me. Art thou anything?
Art thou some god, some angel, or some devil,
That mak'st my blood cold, and my hair to stare?
Speak to me what thou art.

GHOST Thy evil spirit, Brutus.

BRUTUS Why com'st thou?

GHOST To tell thee thou shalt see me at Philippi.

BRUTUS Well; then I shall see thee again?

GHOST Ay, at Philippi.

BRUTUS Why, I will see thee at Philippi then.
[*Exit Ghost*.]
Now I have taken heart thou vanishest.
Ill spirit, I would hold more talk with thee.
Boy! Lucius! Varro! Claudius! Sirs, awake!
Claudius!

LUCIUS The strings, my lord, are false.

BRUTUS He thinks he still is at his instrument.
Lucius, awake!

LUCIUS My lord?

BRUTUS Didst thou dream, Lucius, that thou so criedst out?

LUCIUS My lord, I do not know that I did cry.

BRUTUS Yes, that thou didst. Didst thou see anything?

LUCIUS Nothing, my lord.

BRUTUS Sleep again, Lucius. Sirrah Claudius!
[*To Varro*] Fellow thou, awake!

274 **How . . . burns** (lights allegedly burned dimly or blue in the presence of a supernatural being) 277 **upon** toward 279 **stare** stand on end 290 **false** out of tune

VARRO My lord?

CLAUDIUS My lord?

BRUTUS Why did you so cry out, sirs, in your sleep?

BOTH Did we, my lord?

BRUTUS Ay. Saw you anything?

VARRO No, my lord, I saw nothing.

CLAUDIUS Nor I, my lord.

BRUTUS Go and commend me to my brother Cassius;
Bid him set on his pow'rs betimes before,
And we will follow.

BOTH It shall be done, my lord.

Exeunt.

305 **commend me** give my greetings 306 **set ... before** advance his forces early in the morning before me

ACT V

[Scene I. *The plains of Philippi.*]

Enter Octavius, Antony, and their Army.

OCTAVIUS Now, Antony, our hopes are answerèd;
You said the enemy would not come down,
But keep the hills and upper regions.
It proves not so; their battles are at hand;
They mean to warn us at Philippi here,
Answering before we do demand of them.

ANTONY Tut, I am in their bosoms, and I know
Wherefore they do it. They could be content
To visit other places, and come down
With fearful bravery, thinking by this face
To fasten in our thoughts that they have courage;
But 'tis not so.

Enter a Messenger.

MESSENGER Prepare you, generals,
The enemy comes on in gallant show;
Their bloody sign of battle is hung out,

V.i.4 **battles** armies 5 **warn** challenge 6 **Answering . . . demand** appearing in opposition before we force a meeting 7 **I am in their bosoms** I understand their inmost thoughts 8–9 **They could . . . places** they would prefer to be somewhere else 10 **fearful** (1) frightened (2) awe-inspiring 10 **bravery** bravado (and show of splendor) 10 **face** appearance 11 **fasten in our thoughts** persuade us 14 **bloody sign** red flag

And something to be done immediately.

ANTONY Octavius, lead your battle softly on
Upon the left hand of the even field.

OCTAVIUS Upon the right hand I; keep thou the left.

ANTONY Why do you cross me in this exigent?

OCTAVIUS I do not cross you; but I will do so. *March.*

Drum. Enter Brutus, Cassius, and their Army;
[*Lucilius, Titinius, Messala, and others*].

BRUTUS They stand, and would have parley.

CASSIUS Stand fast, Titinius, we must out and talk.

OCTAVIUS Mark Antony, shall we give sign of battle?

ANTONY No, Caesar, we will answer on their charge.
Make forth; the generals would have some words.

OCTAVIUS Stir not until the signal.

BRUTUS Words before blows; is it so, countrymen?

OCTAVIUS Not that we love words better, as you do.

BRUTUS Good words are better than bad strokes,
Octavius.

ANTONY In your bad strokes, Brutus, you give good
words;
Witness the hole you made in Caesar's heart,
Crying "Long live! Hail, Caesar!"

CASSIUS Antony,
The posture of your blows are yet unknown;
But for your words, they rob the Hybla bees,
And leave them honeyless.

ANTONY Not stingless too.

16 **battle softly** army slowly 17 **even** level 19 **cross** oppose, contradict 19 **exigent** crisis 24 **answer on their charge** meet them when they attack 25 **Make forth** go forward 33 **posture** nature, quality 34 **Hybla** a Sicilian town famous for its sweet honey

BRUTUS O, yes, and soundless too;
For you have stol'n their buzzing, Antony,
And very wisely threat before you sting.

ANTONY Villains! You did not so, when your vile daggers
Hacked one another in the sides of Caesar.
You showed your teeth like apes, and fawned like hounds,
And bowed like bondmen, kissing Caesar's feet;
Whilst damnèd Casca, like a cur, behind
Struck Caesar on the neck. O you flatterers!

CASSIUS Flatterers! Now, Brutus, thank yourself;
This tongue had not offended so today,
If Cassius might have ruled.

OCTAVIUS Come, come, the cause. If arguing make us sweat,
The proof of it will turn to redder drops.
Look,
I draw a sword against conspirators.
When think you that the sword goes up again?
Never, till Caesar's three and thirty wounds
Be well avenged; or till another Caesar
Have added slaughter to the sword of traitors.

BRUTUS Caesar, thou canst not die by traitors' hands,
Unless thou bring'st them with thee.

OCTAVIUS So I hope.
I was not born to die on Brutus' sword.

BRUTUS O, if thou wert the noblest of thy strain,
Young man, thou couldst not die more honorable.

41 **showed your teeth** grinned 47 **ruled** had his way (i.e., in urging that Antony be slain) 48 **cause** business at hand 49 **proof** test 52 **up** into the sheath 54 **another Caesar** i.e., Octavius himself 55 **Have added slaughter to** has also been killed by 59 **strain** family, line of descent

CASSIUS A peevish schoolboy, worthless of such honor,
Joined with a masker and a reveler.

ANTONY Old Cassius still!

OCTAVIUS Come, Antony; away!
Defiance, traitors, hurl we in your teeth.
If you dare fight today, come to the field;
If not, when you have stomachs.

Exit Octavius, Antony, and Army.

CASSIUS Why, now blow wind, swell billow, and swim bark!
The storm is up, and all is on the hazard.

BRUTUS Ho, Lucilius, hark, a word with you.

Lucilius and Messala stand forth.

LUCILIUS My lord?

[*Brutus and Lucilius converse apart.*]

CASSIUS Messala.

MESSALA What says my general?

CASSIUS Messala,
This is my birthday; as this very day
Was Cassius born. Give me thy hand, Messala:
Be thou my witness that against my will
(As Pompey was) am I compelled to set
Upon one battle all our liberties.
You know that I held Epicurus strong,
And his opinion; now I change my mind,
And partly credit things that do presage.
Coming from Sardis, on our former ensign

61 **peevish** childish (Octavius was 21) 61 **worthless** unworthy 62 **masker and a reveler** i.e., the dissipated Antony, who loved participating in masques and wild parties (cf. I.ii.203–04, II.i.189, II.ii.116) 66 **stomachs** inclination, appetite 68 **on the hazard** at stake 74 **As Pompey was** (at Pharsalus where, having been persuaded to give battle against his will, he was decisively defeated and later murdered) 74 **set** stake 76 **held Epicurus strong** believed strongly in the philosophy of Epicurus (a materialist who believed that because the gods were not interested in human affairs omens were to be discounted) 78 **presage** foretell the future 79 **former** foremost

Two mighty eagles fell, and there they perched,
Gorging and feeding from our soldiers' hands,
Who to Philippi here consorted us.
This morning are they fled away and gone,
And in their stead do ravens, crows, and kites
Fly o'er our heads and downward look on us
As we were sickly prey; their shadows seem
A canopy most fatal, under which
Our army lies, ready to give up the ghost.

MESSALA Believe not so.

CASSIUS I but believe it partly,
For I am fresh of spirit and resolved
To meet all perils very constantly.

BRUTUS Even so, Lucilius.

CASSIUS Now, most noble Brutus,
The gods today stand friendly, that we may,
Lovers in peace, lead on our days to age!
But since the affairs of men rests still incertain,
Let's reason with the worst that may befall.
If we do lose this battle, then is this
The very last time we shall speak together.
What are you then determinèd to do?

BRUTUS Even by the rule of that philosophy
By which I did blame Cato for the death
Which he did give himself; I know not how,
But I do find it cowardly and vile,
For fear of what might fall, so to prevent
The time of life, arming myself with patience
To stay the providence of some high powers
That govern us below.

80 **fell** swooped down 82 **consorted** accompanied 84 **ravens, crows, and kites** (scavengers; traditionally, they know when a battle is pending and accompany the armies) 86 **sickly** ready for death 87 **fatal** presaging death 91 **constantly** resolutely 94 **Lovers** devoted friends 95 **rests still incertain** always stand in doubt 96 **reason . . . befall** consider what must be done if the worst happens 100 **that philosophy** i.e., Stoicism 104 **fall** befall 104 **prevent** anticipate 105 **time** term, natural end 106 **stay the providence** await the ordained fate

CASSIUS Then, if we lose this battle,
You are contented to be led in triumph
Thorough the streets of Rome?

BRUTUS No, Cassius, no; think not, thou noble Roman,
That ever Brutus will go bound to Rome;
He bears too great a mind. But this same day
Must end that work the ides of March begun;
And whether we shall meet again I know not.
Therefore our everlasting farewell take.
Forever, and forever, farewell, Cassius!
If we do meet again, why, we shall smile;
If not, why then this parting was well made.

CASSIUS Forever, and forever, farewell, Brutus!
If we do meet again, we'll smile indeed;
If not, 'tis true this parting was well made.

BRUTUS Why then, lead on. O, that a man might know
The end of this day's business ere it come!
But it sufficeth that the day will end,
And then the end is known. Come, ho! Away!
Exeunt.

[Scene II. *The field of battle.*]

Alarum. Enter Brutus and Messala.

BRUTUS Ride, ride, Messala, ride, and give these bills
Unto the legions on the other side. *Loud alarum.*
Let them set on at once; for I perceive
But cold demeanor in Octavius' wing,
And sudden push gives them the overthrow.
Ride, ride, Messala! Let them all come down. *Exeunt.*

108 **in triumph** (as a captive) in the victor's procession V.ii.1 s.d. **Alarum** call to arms (drums or trumpets) 1 **bills** written orders 2 **side** wing (commanded by Cassius) 4 **But cold demeanor** marked lack of spirit in fighting 5 **push** attack

[Scene III. *The field of battle.*]

Alarums. Enter Cassius and Titinius.

CASSIUS O, look, Titinius, look, the villains fly!
Myself have to mine own turned enemy.
This ensign here of mine was turning back;
I slew the coward, and did take it from him.

TITINIUS O Cassius, Brutus gave the word too early,
Who, having some advantage on Octavius,
Took it too eagerly; his soldiers fell to spoil,
Whilst we by Antony are all enclosed.

Enter Pindarus.

PINDARUS Fly further off, my lord, fly further off!
Mark Antony is in your tents, my lord.
Fly, therefore, noble Cassius, fly far off!

CASSIUS This hill is far enough. Look, look, Titinius!
Are those my tents where I perceive the fire?

TITINIUS They are, my lord.

CASSIUS Titinius, if thou lovest me,
Mount thou my horse and hide thy spurs in him
Till he have brought thee up to yonder troops
And here again, that I may rest assured
Whether yond troops are friend or enemy.

TITINIUS I will be here again even with a thought.
Exit.

CASSIUS Go, Pindarus, get higher on that hill;

V.iii.1 **villains** i.e., cowardly soldiers of his own side 2 **mine own** my own men 3 **ensign** standard-bearer 4 **it** i.e., the standard 7 **spoil** looting 11 **far** farther 19 **even with a thought** as quickly as thought

My sight was ever thick. Regard Titinius,
And tell me what thou not'st about the field.
[*Exit Pindarus.*]
This day I breathèd first. Time is come round,
And where I did begin, there shall I end.
My life is run his compass. Sirrah, what news?

PINDARUS (*Above*) O my lord!

CASSIUS What news?

PINDARUS [*Above*] Titinius is enclosèd round about
With horsemen that make to him on the spur;
Yet he spurs on. Now they are almost on him.
Now, Titinius! Now some light. O, he lights too!
He's ta'en! (*Shout.*) And, hark! They shout for joy.

CASSIUS Come down; behold no more.
O, coward that I am, to live so long,
To see my best friend ta'en before my face!

Enter Pindarus.

Come hither, sirrah.
In Parthia did I take thee prisoner;
And then I swore thee, saving of thy life,
That whatsoever I did bid thee do,
Thou shouldst attempt it. Come now, keep thine oath.
Now be a freeman, and with this good sword,
That ran through Caesar's bowels, search this bosom.
Stand not to answer. Here, take thou the hilts,
And when my face is covered, as 'tis now,
Guide thou the sword—Caesar, thou art revenged,
Even with the sword that killed thee. [*Dies.*]

PINDARUS So, I am free; yet would not so have been,
Durst I have done my will. O Cassius!
Far from this country Pindarus shall run,
Where never Roman shall take note of him. [*Exit.*]

21 **My . . . thick** I have always been nearsighted 25 **is run his compass** has completed its circuit 26 s.d. **Above** on the upper stage 29 **make . . . spur** ride toward him at top speed 31 **light** dismount 32 **ta'en** taken, captured 38 **swore . . . of** made you swear, when I spared 42 **search** penetrate 43 **Stand** delay

Enter Titinius and Messala.

MESSALA It is but change, Titinius; for Octavius
Is overthrown by noble Brutus' power,
As Cassius' legions are by Antony.

TITINIUS These tidings will well comfort Cassius.

MESSALA Where did you leave him?

TITINIUS All disconsolate,
With Pindarus his bondman, on this hill.

MESSALA Is not that he that lies upon the ground?

TITINIUS He lies not like the living. O my heart!

MESSALA Is not that he?

TITINIUS No, this was he, Messala,
But Cassius is no more. O setting sun,
As in thy red rays thou dost sink to night,
So in his red blood Cassius' day is set.
The sun of Rome is set. Our day is gone;
Clouds, dews, and dangers come; our deeds are done!
Mistrust of my success hath done this deed.

MESSALA Mistrust of good success hath done this deed.
O hateful Error, Melancholy's child,
Why dost thou show to the apt thoughts of men
The things that are not? O Error, soon conceived,
Thou never com'st unto a happy birth,
But kill'st the mother that engend'red thee!

TITINIUS What, Pindarus! Where art thou, Pindarus?

MESSALA Seek him, Titinius, whilst I go to meet
The noble Brutus, thrusting this report
Into his ears. I may say "thrusting" it;

51 **change** exchange (of fortune) 64 **dews** (considered unwholesome) 65 **Mistrust of** lack of confidence in 67 **Melancholy's child** (i.e., those of despondent temperament are liable to be introspective and full of imaginary fears) 68 **apt** easily impressed 71 **mother** i.e., the melancholy person, Cassius, who conceived the error

For piercing steel and darts envenomèd
Shall be as welcome to the ears of Brutus
As tidings of this sight.

TITINIUS Hie you, Messala,
And I will seek for Pindarus the while.
[*Exit Messala.*]
Why didst thou send me forth, brave Cassius?
Did I not meet thy friends, and did not they
Put on my brows this wreath of victory,
And bid me give it thee? Didst thou not hear their shouts?
Alas, thou hast misconstrued everything!
But hold thee, take this garland on thy brow;
Thy Brutus bid me give it thee, and I
Will do his bidding. Brutus, come apace,
And see how I regarded Caius Cassius.
By your leave, gods. This is a Roman's part:
Come, Cassius' sword, and find Titinius' heart. *Dies.*

Alarum. Enter Brutus, Messala, young Cato, Strato, Volumnius, and Lucilius.

BRUTUS Where, where, Messala, doth his body lie?

MESSALA Lo, yonder, and Titinius mourning it.

BRUTUS Titinius' face is upward.

CATO He is slain.

BRUTUS O Julius Caesar, thou art mighty yet!
Thy spirit walks abroad, and turns our swords
In our own proper entrails. *Low alarums.*

CATO Brave Titinius!
Look, whe'r he have not crowned dead Cassius.

BRUTUS Are yet two Romans living such as these?
The last of all the Romans, fare thee well!

78 **Hie** hasten 80 **brave** noble 85 **hold thee** wait a moment 87 **apace** quickly 88 **regarded** honored 89 **By your leave** with your permission (because he is ending his life before the time appointed by the gods) 89 **part** role, duty 96 **own proper** (emphatic) very own 96 **Brave** noble 97 **whe'r** whether

It is impossible that ever Rome
Should breed thy fellow. Friends, I owe moe tears
To this dead man than you shall see me pay.
I shall find time, Cassius; I shall find time.
Come, therefore, and to Thasos send his body;
His funerals shall not be in our camp,
Lest it discomfort us. Lucilius, come,
And come, young Cato; let us to the field.
Labeo and Flavius set our battles on.
'Tis three o'clock; and, Romans, yet ere night
We shall try fortune in a second fight. *Exeunt.*

[Scene IV. *The field of battle.*]

Alarum. Enter Brutus, Messala, [*young*] *Cato, Lucilius, and Flavius.*

BRUTUS Yet, countrymen, O, yet hold up your heads!
[*Exit, with followers.*]
CATO What bastard doth not? Who will go with me?
I will proclaim my name about the field.
I am the son of Marcus Cato, ho!
A foe to tyrants, and my country's friend.
I am the son of Marcus Cato, ho!

Enter Soldiers and fight.

LUCILIUS And I am Brutus, Marcus Brutus, I;
Brutus, my country's friend; know me for Brutus!
[*Young Cato falls.*]

101 **fellow** equal 101 **moe** more 104 **Thasos** an island near Philippi 106 **discomfort us** dishearten our troops 108 **battles** armies V.iv.2 **What bastard** who is such a low fellow that he 4 **son of Marcus Cato** son of Cato of Utica, hence, brother of Brutus' wife 7 **Lucilius** (the Folio fails to provide a speech prefix for lines 7–8, but because it is clear from Plutarch and from line 14 that Lucilius impersonates Brutus it is plausible to attribute 7–8 to Lucilius)

O young and noble Cato, art thou down?
Why, now thou diest as bravely as Titinius,
And mayst be honored, being Cato's son.

[FIRST] SOLDIER Yield, or thou diest.

LUCILIUS Only I yield to die.
There is so much that thou wilt kill me straight;
Kill Brutus, and be honored in his death.

[FIRST] SOLDIER We must not. A noble prisoner!

Enter Antony.

SECOND SOLDIER Room, ho! Tell Antony, Brutus is ta'en.

FIRST SOLDIER I'll tell thee news. Here comes the general.
Brutus is ta'en, Brutus is ta'en, my lord.

ANTONY Where is he?

LUCILIUS Safe, Antony; Brutus is safe enough.
I dare assure thee that no enemy
Shall ever take alive the noble Brutus.
The gods defend him from so great a shame!
When you do find him, or alive or dead,
He will be found like Brutus, like himself.

ANTONY This is not Brutus, friend, but, I assure you,
A prize no less in worth. Keep this man safe;
Give him all kindness. I had rather have
Such men my friends than enemies. Go on,
And see whe'r Brutus be alive or dead,
And bring us word unto Octavius' tent
How everything is chanced. *Exeunt.*

12 **Only I yield to die** I yield only to die 13 **so much** so great an inducement, i.e., gaining great honor by killing Brutus (?), so much to be blamed for (?), a sum of money (offered to the soldier) (?) 13 **straight** immediately 25 **like himself** i.e., behaving in accordance with his noble nature 32 **is chanced** has turned out

[Scene V. *The field of battle.*]

Enter Brutus, Dardanius, Clitus, Strato, and Volumnius.

BRUTUS Come, poor remains of friends, rest on this rock.

CLITUS Statilius showed the torchlight, but, my lord,
He came not back; he is or ta'en or slain.

BRUTUS Sit thee down, Clitus. Slaying is the word;
It is a deed in fashion. Hark thee, Clitus.
[*Whispers.*]

CLITUS What, I, my lord? No, not for all the world!

BRUTUS Peace then, no words.

CLITUS I'll rather kill myself.

BRUTUS Hark thee, Dardanius. [*Whispers.*]

DARDANIUS Shall I do such a deed?

CLITUS O Dardanius!

DARDANIUS O Clitus!

CLITUS What ill request did Brutus make to thee?

DARDANIUS To kill him, Clitus. Look, he meditates.

CLITUS Now is that noble vessel full of grief,
That it runs over even at his eyes.

V.v. 1 **poor remains** wretched survivors 2 **showed the torchlight** (Statilius had volunteered to see if Cassius' camp was occupied by the enemy; he signaled on arrival there but was obviously captured thereafter) 13 **vessel** (figurative for "human being." Also an allusion to the small jars of tears offered to the dead)

BRUTUS Come hither, good Volumnius; list a word.

VOLUMNIUS What says my lord?

BRUTUS Why, this, Volumnius:
The ghost of Caesar hath appeared to me
Two several times by night; at Sardis once,
And this last night here in Philippi fields.
I know my hour is come.

VOLUMNIUS Not so, my lord.

BRUTUS Nay, I am sure it is, Volumnius.
Thou seest the world, Volumnius, how it goes;
Our enemies have beat us to the pit. *Low alarums.*
It is more worthy to leap in ourselves
Than tarry till they push us. Good Volumnius,
Thou know'st that we two went to school together;
Even for that our love of old, I prithee
Hold thou my sword-hilts whilst I run on it.

VOLUMNIUS That's not an office for a friend, my lord.
Alarum still.

CLITUS Fly, fly, my lord, there is no tarrying here.

BRUTUS Farewell to you; and you; and you, Volumnius.
Strato, thou hast been all this while asleep;
Farewell to thee too, Strato. Countrymen,
My heart doth joy that yet in all my life
I found no man but he was true to me.
I shall have glory by this losing day
More than Octavius and Mark Antony
By this vile conquest shall attain unto.
So fare you well at once, for Brutus' tongue
Hath almost ended his life's history.
Night hangs upon mine eyes; my bones would rest,

15 **list** hear 18 **several** separate 23 **pit** (1) trap for capturing wild animals (2) grave 29 s.d. **still** continuing 38 **vile conquest** i.e., overthrow of the revolution against tyranny 39 **at once** without further delay

That have but labored to attain this hour.
Alarum. Cry within, "Fly, fly, fly!"

CLITUS Fly, my lord, fly!

BRUTUS Hence! I will follow.
[*Exeunt Clitus, Dardanius, and Volumnius.*]
I prithee, Strato, stay thou by thy lord,
Thou art a fellow of a good respect.
Thy life hath had some smatch of honor in it;
Hold then my sword, and turn away thy face,
While I do run upon it. Wilt thou, Strato?

STRATO Give me your hand first. Fare you well, my lord.

BRUTUS Farewell, good Strato—Caesar, now be still;
I killed not thee with half so good a will. *Dies.*

Alarum. Retreat. Enter Antony, Octavius, Messala, Lucilius, and the Army.

OCTAVIUS What man is that?

MESSALA My master's man. Strato, where is thy master?

STRATO Free from the bondage you are in, Messala;
The conquerors can but make a fire of him.
For Brutus only overcame himself,
And no man else hath honor by his death.

LUCILIUS So Brutus should be found. I thank thee,
Brutus,
That thou hast proved Lucilius' saying true.

OCTAVIUS All that served Brutus, I will entertain them.
Fellow, wilt thou bestow thy time with me?

STRATO Ay, if Messala will prefer me to you.

OCTAVIUS Do so, good Messala.

42 **but . . . hour** i.e., worked hard only to reach this goal of death (which brings, for a Stoic, rest from life's trials) 45 **respect** reputation 46 **smatch** smack, taste 53 **man** servant 56 **Brutus only overcame himself** only Brutus overcame Brutus 59 **saying** (see V.iv.21–25) 60 **entertain** take into service 61 **bestow** spend 62 **prefer** recommend

MESSALA How died my master, Strato?

STRATO I held the sword, and he did run on it.

MESSALA Octavius, then take him to follow thee,
That did the latest service to my master.

ANTONY This was the noblest Roman of them all.
All the conspirators save only he
Did that they did in envy of great Caesar;
He, only in a general honest thought
And common good to all, made one of them.
His life was gentle, and the elements
So mixed in him that Nature might stand up
And say to all the world, "This was a man!"

OCTAVIUS According to his virtue, let us use him
With all respect and rites of burial.
Within my tent his bones tonight shall lie,
Most like a soldier ordered honorably.
So call the field to rest, and let's away
To part the glories of this happy day. *Exeunt omnes.*

FINIS

67 **latest** last 71–72 **He only ... them** he, moved only by impersonal motives directed to the good of the community, joined the conspirators 73 **gentle** noble 73 **elements** (the four opposed elements, of which all nature was thought to be composed, were represented in the human body by the four liquids, bile, phlegm, blood, and choler; the dominance of one of these determined a man's temperament—melancholic, phlegmatic, sanguine, or choleric) 74 **So mixed** i.e., so well-balanced 76 **virtue** excellence 76 **use** treat 79 **ordered honorably** arrayed (and treated) with all honor 80 **field** army 81 **part** divide

Textual Note

THE FIRST FOLIO of 1623 provides us with the text for *Julius Caesar*; there are no early quarto editions. In setting this play for the press, the printer's compositors probably worked from the playhouse promptbook, for the Folio text contains remarkably few misprints, serious errors in punctuation, or misattribution of speeches. The stage directions, unusually numerous and detailed, also suggest a stage manager's prompt copy; stage directions like "Alarum still" and "Enter Boy with wine and tapers" are obviously closely connected with actual performance.

In the present edition, the names of characters have been normalized so that *Marullus* appears for the Folio Murellus (and Murrellus), *Casca* for Caska, *Lucilius* for Lucillius. Occasionally the Folio uses the forms "Antonio" (I.ii.3, 4, 6, 190; I.iii.37), "Claudio" (IV.iii.241, 243 s.d., 288), "Flavio," "Labio" (V.iii.108), "Octavio" (III.i.275 s.d., V.ii.4), "Varrus" (IV.iii.243, 243 s.d., 288); these are standardized, appearing as *Antonius*, *Claudius*, *Flavius*, *Labeo*, *Octavius*, and *Varro*. The present edition modernizes spelling and punctuation, corrects a few obvious misprints, translates the act divisions from Latin into English, expands the speech prefixes, and alters the lineation of a few passages. The only other substantial departures from the Folio are listed below, the present reading in bold and then the Folio's reading in roman.

I.iii.129 **In favor's** Is Fauors

II.i.40 **ides** first 213 **eighth** eight

II.ii. 19 **fought** fight 23 **did neigh** do neigh 46 **are** heare

III.i.39 **law** lane 113 **states** State 115 **lies** lye 283 **for** from

III.ii.106 **art** are

IV.iii.253 **not** it not

V.i.41 **teeth** teethes

V.iii.104 **Thasos** Tharsus

V.iv.7 **Lucilius** [F omits, and prints "Lucilius" as the prefix to line 9]

WILLIAM SHAKESPEARE

THE TRAGEDY OF ANTONY AND CLEOPATRA

Edited by Barbara Everett

[*Dramatis Personae*

MARK ANTONY, OCTAVIUS CAESAR, M. AEMILIUS LEPIDUS — triumvirs
SEXTUS POMPEIUS
DOMITIUS ENOBARBUS, VENTIDIUS, EROS, SCARUS, DECRETAS, DEMETRIUS, PHILO — friends to Antony
CANIDIUS, lieutenant general to Antony
SILIUS, an officer in Ventidius' army
MAECENAS, AGRIPPA, DOLABELLA, PROCULEIUS, THIDIAS, GALLUS — friends to Caesar
TAURUS, lieutenant general to Caesar
MENAS, MENECRATES, VARRIUS — friends to Pompey
ROMAN OFFICER under Ventidius
AN AMBASSADOR from Antony to Caesar
ALEXAS, MARDIAN, SELEUCUS, DIOMEDES — attendants on Cleopatra
A SOOTHSAYER
A CLOWN
CLEOPATRA, Queen of Egypt
OCTAVIA, sister to Caesar and wife to Antony
CHARMIAN, IRAS — attendants on Cleopatra
OFFICERS, SOLDIERS, MESSENGERS, ATTENDANTS

Scene: several parts of the Roman Empire]

THE TRAGEDY OF ANTONY AND CLEOPATRA

ACT I

Scene I. [*Alexandria. Cleopatra's palace.*]

Enter Demetrius and Philo.

PHILO Nay, but this dotage of our general's
O'erflows the measure. Those his goodly eyes
That o'er the files and musters of the war
Have glowed like plated Mars, now bend, now turn
The office and devotion of their view
Upon a tawny front. His captain's heart,
Which in the scuffles of great fights hath burst
The buckles on his breast, reneges all temper
And is become the bellows and the fan
To cool a gypsy's lust.

Flourish. Enter Antony, Cleopatra, her Ladies, the Train, with Eunuchs fanning her.

Look where they come:

A footnote is keyed to the text by line number. Text references are printed in **bold** type; the annotation follows in roman type.

I.i.4 **plated** armored 5 **office** service 6 **tawny front** dark face (with a pun on the military sense of **front**, "first line of battle") 8 **reneges all temper** gives up all self-control 10 **gypsy's** (gypsies were believed to have come from Egypt, hence "'gyptians"; they had a reputation for trickery, sorcery, and lechery) 10 s.d. **Flourish** fanfare of trumpets

Take but good note, and you shall see in him
The triple pillar of the world transformed
Into a strumpet's fool. Behold and see.

CLEOPATRA If it be love indeed, tell me how much.

ANTONY There's beggary in the love that can be reckoned.

CLEOPATRA I'll set a bourn how far to be beloved.

ANTONY Then must thou needs find out new heaven, new earth.

Enter a Messenger.

MESSENGER News, my good lord, from Rome.

ANTONY Grates me! The sum.

CLEOPATRA Nay, hear them, Antony.
Fulvia perchance is angry; or who knows
If the scarce-bearded Caesar have not sent
His pow'rful mandate to you, "Do this, or this;
Take in that kingdom, and enfranchise that.
Perform't, or else we damn thee."

ANTONY How, my love?

CLEOPATRA Perchance? Nay, and most like:
You must not stay here longer, your dismission
Is come from Caesar; therefore hear it, Antony.
Where's Fulvia's process? Caesar's I would say? Both?
Call in the messengers. As I am Egypt's Queen,
Thou blushest, Antony, and that blood of thine
Is Caesar's homager: else so thy cheek pays shame
When shrill-tongued Fulvia scolds. The messengers!

12 **The triple pillar** i.e., one of the triumvirs who ruled the world 16 **bourn** limit 18 **Grates me! The sum** It's irritating! Be brief 20 **Fulvia** Antony's wife 21 **scarce-bearded Caesar** (Octavius, then twenty-three, was some twenty years younger than Antony) 23 **Take in** occupy 23 **enfranchise** set free from slavery 24 **How** (a common exclamation, like "What!") 26 **dismission** dismissal 28 **process** summons (i.e., to appear in court) 31 **homager** vassal 31 **else so** or else

ANTONY Let Rome in Tiber melt, and the wide arch
Of the ranged empire fall! Here is my space,
Kingdoms are clay: our dungy earth alike
Feeds beast as man. The nobleness of life
Is to do thus; when such a mutual pair
And such a twain can do't, in which I bind,
On pain of punishment, the world to weet
We stand up peerless.

CLEOPATRA Excellent falsehood!
Why did he marry Fulvia, and not love her?
I'll seem the fool I am not. Antony
Will be—himself.

ANTONY But stirred by Cleopatra.
Now for the love of Love and her soft hours,
Let's not confound the time with conference harsh.
There's not a minute of our lives should stretch
Without some pleasure now. What sport tonight?

CLEOPATRA Hear the ambassadors.

ANTONY Fie, wrangling queen!
Whom everything becomes—to chide, to laugh,
To weep; whose every passion fully strives
To make itself, in thee, fair and admired.
No messenger but thine; and all alone
Tonight we'll wander through the streets and note
The qualities of people. Come, my queen;
Last night you did desire it. [*To Attendants*] Speak not to us.

Exeunt [*Antony and Cleopatra*] *with the Train.*

DEMETRIUS Is Caesar with Antonius prized so slight?

PHILO Sir, sometimes, when he is not Antony,
He comes too short of that great property
Which still should go with Antony.

37 **thus** (perhaps they embrace, but perhaps **thus** alludes to their way of life) 39 **weet** know 43 **himself** (1) the peerless Antony (2) the fool he is 43 **stirred** (1) angered (2) inspired, inflamed 45 **confound** waste 50 **fully** absolutely and successfully 56 **with** by 58 **property** quality 59 **still** always

DEMETRIUS I am full sorry
That he approves the common liar, who
Thus speaks of him at Rome; but I will hope
Of better deeds tomorrow. Rest you happy! *Exeunt.*

[Scene II. *Alexandria. Cleopatra's palace.*]

Enter Enobarbus, Lamprius, a Soothsayer, Rannius, Lucillius, Charmian, Iras, Mardian the Eunuch, and Alexas.

CHARMIAN Lord Alexas, sweet Alexas, most anything Alexas, almost most absolute Alexas, where's the soothsayer that you praised so to th' Queen? O, that I knew this husband, which, you say, must charge his horns with garlands!

ALEXAS Soothsayer!

SOOTHSAYER Your will?

CHARMIAN Is this the man? Is't you, sir, that know things?

SOOTHSAYER In Nature's infinite book of secrecy
A little I can read.

ALEXAS Show him your hand.

ENOBARBUS Bring in the banquet quickly: wine enough
Cleopatra's health to drink.

CHARMIAN Good sir, give me good fortune.

60 **approves** corroborates I.ii.4–5 **charge his horns with garlands** be a blindly happy cuckold of a husband (**charge** = load; **horns** = symbol of a cuckold; **garlands** = bridegroom's chaplet, and sign of happy prosperity) 11 **banquet** light refreshment of fruit and wine

SOOTHSAYER I make not, but foresee.

CHARMIAN Pray then, foresee me one.

SOOTHSAYER You shall be yet far fairer than you are.

CHARMIAN He means in flesh.

IRAS No, you shall paint when you are old.

CHARMIAN Wrinkles forbid!

ALEXAS Vex not his prescience; be attentive.

CHARMIAN Hush!

SOOTHSAYER You shall be more beloving than beloved.

CHARMIAN I had rather heat my liver with drinking.

ALEXAS Nay, hear him.

CHARMIAN Good now, some excellent fortune! Let me be married to three kings in a forenoon and widow them all; let me have a child at fifty, to whom Herod of Jewry may do homage; find me to marry me with Octavius Caesar, and companion me with my mistress.

SOOTHSAYER You shall outlive the lady whom you serve.

CHARMIAN O excellent! I love long life better than figs.

SOOTHSAYER You have seen and proved a fairer former fortune
Than that which is to approach.

CHARMIAN Then belike my children shall have no names. Prithee, how many boys and wenches must I have?

16 **fairer** more beautiful (though in the next line Charmian pretends to take it another way, "plumper") 23 **liver** (believed to be the seat of sexual desire) 27–28 **Herod of Jewry** i.e., even that blustering tyrant who slaughtered the innocents of Judea 33 **figs** (phallic allusion) 36–37 **have no names** be bastards

SOOTHSAYER If every of your wishes had a womb,
And fertile every wish, a million.

CHARMIAN Out, fool! I forgive thee for a witch.

ALEXAS You think none but your sheets are privy to your wishes.

CHARMIAN Nay, come, tell Iras hers.

ALEXAS We'll know all our fortunes.

ENOBARBUS Mine, and most of our fortunes, tonight, shall be—drunk to bed.

IRAS There's a palm presages chastity, if nothing else.

CHARMIAN E'en as the o'erflowing Nilus presageth famine.

IRAS Go, you wild bedfellow, you cannot soothsay.

CHARMIAN Nay, if an oily palm be not a fruitful prognostication, I cannot scratch mine ear. Prithee, tell her but a workyday fortune.

SOOTHSAYER Your fortunes are alike.

IRAS But how, but how? Give me particulars.

SOOTHSAYER I have said.

IRAS Am I not an inch of fortune better than she?

CHARMIAN Well, if you were but an inch of fortune better than I, where would you choose it?

IRAS Not in my husband's nose.

CHARMIAN Our worser thoughts Heavens mend! Alexas—come, his fortune, his fortune! O, let him marry a woman that cannot go, sweet Isis, I

41 **I forgive thee for a witch** (1) you have no power of prophecy, so I absolve you from the charge of being a witch (2) a sorcerer like you is allowed to be outspoken 52 **oily palm** (sign of a lascivious nature) 52–53 **fruitful prognostication** omen of fertility 54 **workyday** commonplace 61 **husband's nose** (bawdy, hence **worser thoughts** in next line) 64 **go** satisfactorily copulate (?) bear children (?) 64 **Isis** goddess of fertility and the moon

beseech thee, and let her die too, and give him a worse, and let worse follow worse till the worst of all follow him laughing to his grave, fiftyfold a cuckold! Good Isis, hear me this prayer, though thou deny me a matter of more weight: good Isis, I beseech thee!

IRAS Amen. Dear goddess, hear that prayer of the people! For, as it is a heartbreaking to see a handsome man loose-wived, so it is a deadly sorrow to behold a foul knave uncuckolded. Therefore, dear Isis, keep decorum, and fortune him accordingly!

CHARMIAN Amen.

ALEXAS Lo, now, if it lay in their hands to make me a cuckold, they would make themselves whores but they'd do't.

ENOBARBUS Hush, here comes Antony.

CHARMIAN Not he, the Queen.

Enter Cleopatra.

CLEOPATRA Saw you my lord?

ENOBARBUS No, lady.

CLEOPATRA Was he not here?

CHARMIAN No, madam.

CLEOPATRA He was disposed to mirth; but on the sudden
A Roman thought hath struck him. Enobarbus!

ENOBARBUS Madam?

CLEOPATRA Seek him, and bring him hither. Where's Alexas?

ALEXAS Here at your service. My lord approaches.

Enter Antony with a Messenger [and Attendants].

73 **loose-wived** with a faithless, lecherous wife 74 **foul** ugly 75 **keep decorum** i.e., act like a just goddess 84 **Roman thought** (1) thought of Rome (2) serious reflection

CLEOPATRA We will not look upon him. Go with us.
Exeunt [*all but Antony, Messenger, and Attendants*].

MESSENGER Fulvia thy wife first came into the field.

ANTONY Against my brother Lucius?

MESSENGER Ay.
But soon that war had end, and the time's state
Made friends of them, jointing their force 'gainst Caesar,
Whose better issue in the war, from Italy
Upon the first encounter drave them.

ANTONY Well, what worst?

MESSENGER The nature of bad news infects the teller.

ANTONY When it concerns the fool or coward. On.
Things that are past are done, with me. 'Tis thus:
Who tells me true, though in his tale lie death,
I hear him as he flattered.

MESSENGER Labienus—
This is stiff news—hath with his Parthian force
Extended Asia: from Euphrates
His conquering banner shook, from Syria
To Lydia and to Ionia,
Whilst——

ANTONY Antony, thou wouldst say——

MESSENGER O, my lord.

ANTONY Speak to me home, mince not the general tongue:
Name Cleopatra as she is called in Rome;
Rail thou in Fulvia's phrase, and taunt my faults
With such full license as both truth and malice
Have power to utter. O, then we bring forth weeds

94 **better issue** greater success 100 **as** as if 102 **Extended** seized upon 102 **Euphrates** (accented on first syllable) 106 **Speak . . . tongue** be blunt, don't diminish what everyone is saying

When our quick winds lie still, and our ills told us
Is as our earing. Fare thee well awhile.

MESSENGER At your noble pleasure. *Exit Messenger.*

ANTONY From Sicyon, ho, the news! Speak there!

FIRST ATTENDANT The man from Sicyon—is there such
an one?

SECOND ATTENDANT He stays upon your will.

ANTONY Let him appear.
These strong Egyptian fetters I must break
Or lose myself in dotage.

Enter another Messenger, with a letter.

What are you?

MESSENGER Fulvia thy wife is dead.

ANTONY Where died she?

MESSENGER In Sicyon.
Her length of sickness, with what else more serious
Importeth thee to know, this bears. [*Gives a letter.*]

ANTONY Forbear me. [*Exit Messenger.*]
There's a great spirit gone! Thus did I desire it:
What our contempts doth often hurl from us,
We wish it ours again. The present pleasure,
By revolution low'ring, does become
The opposite of itself: she's good, being gone;
The hand could pluck her back that shoved her on.
I must from this enchanting queen break off:
Ten thousand harms, more than the ills I know,
My idleness doth hatch. Ho now, Enobarbus!

111 **quick winds** lively winds (that ventilate the soil) 111–12 **our ills . . . earing** i.e., when our faults are told to us, it is like plowing (that makes the ground fertile) 116 **stays upon your will** awaits your pleasure 122 **Forbear me** leave me 126 **By revolution low'ring** sinking in our estimation (as the wheel of time turns and spins the present moment downward) 128 **could** would like to 129 **enchanting** spellbinding

Enter Enobarbus.

ENOBARBUS What's your pleasure, sir?

ANTONY I must with haste from hence.

ENOBARBUS Why, then we kill all our women. We see how mortal an unkindness is to them. If they suffer our departure, death's the word.

ANTONY I must be gone.

ENOBARBUS Under a compelling occasion let women die. It were pity to cast them away for nothing, though between them and a great cause they should be esteemed nothing. Cleopatra, catching but the least noise of this, dies instantly; I have seen her die twenty times upon far poorer moment. I do think there is mettle in death, which commits some loving act upon her, she hath such a celerity in dying.

ANTONY She is cunning past man's thought.

ENOBARBUS Alack, sir, no; her passions are made of nothing but the finest part of pure love. We cannot call her winds and waters sighs and tears; they are greater storms and tempests than almanacs can report. This cannot be cunning in her; if it be, she makes a show'r of rain as well as Jove.

ANTONY Would I had never seen her!

ENOBARBUS O, sir, you had then left unseen a wonderful piece of work, which not to have been blest withal would have discredited your travel.

ANTONY Fulvia is dead.

ENOBARBUS Sir?

ANTONY Fulvia is dead.

ENOBARBUS Fulvia?

139 **die** (throughout this speech Enobarbus puns on a second meaning of die, "to experience sexual orgasm") 143 **moment** cause 144 **mettle** strength

ANTONY Dead.

ENOBARBUS Why, sir, give the gods a thankful sacrifice. When it pleaseth their deities to take the wife of a man from him, it shows to man the tailors of the earth; comforting therein, that when old robes are worn out, there are members to make new. If there were no more women but Fulvia, then had you indeed a cut, and the case to be lamented. This grief is crowned with consolation: your old smock brings forth a new petticoat, and indeed the tears live in an onion that should water this sorrow.

ANTONY The business she hath broachèd in the state
Cannot endure my absence.

ENOBARBUS And the business you have broached here cannot be without you; especially that of Cleopatra's, which wholly depends on your abode.

ANTONY No more light answers. Let our officers
Have notice what we purpose. I shall break
The cause of our expedience to the Queen
And get her leave to part. For not alone
The death of Fulvia, with more urgent touches,
Do strongly speak to us, but the letters too
Of many our contriving friends in Rome
Petition us at home. Sextus Pompeius
Hath given the dare to Caesar and commands
The empire of the sea. Our slippery people,
Whose love is never linked to the deserver
Till his deserts are past, begin to throw
Pompey the Great and all his dignities
Upon his son; who, high in name and power,

169 **cut** (1) severe blow (2) pudendum (the entire speech infuses bawdy meanings [e.g., of **tailors** and **members**] into the conceit of the world as a tailor's shop, with the gods as tailors cutting new clothes out of old, replacing old people with new; the tailor's shop is where men make love and breed) 175–77 **And the business ... abode** (bawdy again) 178 **light** indecent 178 **our** (royal plural) 179 **break** tell 180 **expedience** (1) haste (2) expedition 182 **more urgent touches** more pressing reasons 184 **many our contriving friends** many who plot on my behalf 189–91 **throw ... /Upon** transfer ... to

Higher than both in blood and life, stands up
For the main soldier; whose quality, going on,
The sides o' th' world may danger. Much is breeding,
Which, like the courser's hair, hath yet but life
And not a serpent's poison. Say our pleasure,
To such whose places under us require,
Our quick remove from hence.

ENOBARBUS I shall do't. [*Exeunt*.]

[Scene III. *Alexandria. Cleopatra's palace*.]

Enter Cleopatra, Charmian, Alexas, and Iras.

CLEOPATRA Where is he?

CHARMIAN I did not see him since.

CLEOPATRA See where he is, who's with him, what he does:
I did not send you. If you find him sad,
Say I am dancing; if in mirth, report
That I am sudden sick. Quick, and return.
[*Exit Alexas*.]

CHARMIAN Madam, methinks, if you did love him dearly,
You do not hold the method to enforce
The like from him.

CLEOPATRA What should I do, I do not?

192 **blood and life** courage and energy 192–93 **stands ... soldier** sets himself up as the greatest soldier in the world 193–94 **whose quality ... danger** whose character may, if his fortunes prosper, threaten the structure of the world 195 **courser's hair** (a horse's hair placed in water was thought to turn into a serpent) I.iii.1 **since** recently 3 **sad** serious

CHARMIAN In each thing give him way, cross him in nothing.

CLEOPATRA Thou teachest like a fool: the way to lose him!

CHARMIAN Tempt him not so too far. I wish, forbear.
In time we hate that which we often fear.

Enter Antony.

But here comes Antony.

CLEOPATRA I am sick and sullen.

ANTONY I am sorry to give breathing to my purpose—

CLEOPATRA Help me away, dear Charmian! I shall fall.
It cannot be thus long; the sides of nature
Will not sustain it.

ANTONY Now, my dearest queen——

CLEOPATRA Pray you, stand farther from me.

ANTONY What's the matter?

CLEOPATRA I know by that same eye there's some good news.
What, says the married woman you may go?
Would she had never given you leave to come!
Let her not say 'tis I that keep you here.
I have no power upon you; hers you are.

ANTONY The gods best know—

CLEOPATRA O, never was there queen
So mightily betrayed! Yet at the first
I saw the treasons planted.

ANTONY Cleopatra——

CLEOPATRA Why should I think you can be mine, and true

11 **Tempt** try 14 **breathing** utterance 16–17 **the sides ... it** the human frame will not stand it 26 **planted** (like seeds, and like mines)

(Though you in swearing shake the thronèd gods)
Who have been false to Fulvia? Riotous madness,
To be entangled with those mouth-made vows
Which break themselves in swearing.

ANTONY Most sweet queen——

CLEOPATRA Nay, pray you seek no color for your going,
But bid farewell, and go. When you sued staying,
Then was the time for words: no going then;
Eternity was in our lips and eyes,
Bliss in our brows' bent, none our parts so poor
But was a race of heaven; they are so still,
Or thou, the greatest soldier of the world,
Art turned the greatest liar.

ANTONY How now, lady?

CLEOPATRA I would I had thy inches; thou shouldst know
There were a heart in Egypt.

ANTONY Hear me, Queen:
The strong necessity of time commands
Our services awhile; but my full heart
Remains in use with you. Our Italy
Shines o'er with civil swords; Sextus Pompeius
Makes his approaches to the port of Rome;
Equality of two domestic powers
Breed scrupulous faction; the hated, grown to strength,
Are newly grown to love; the condemned Pompey,
Rich in his father's honor, creeps apace

31 **Which ... swearing** which are broken the second they are uttered 32 **color** pretext 33 **sued staying** pleaded to stay 36 **brows' bent** eyebrows' arch 37 **a race of heaven** (1) of heavenly flavor (2) of heavenly origin, rooted in heaven 41 **Egypt** (here, as elsewhere, Cleopatra as well as the country) 44 **in use with you** for you to possess 45 **civil swords** swords drawn in civil war 47–48 **Equality ... faction** where the rule at home is equally divided between two, parties grow up, quarreling over tiny points 48–49 **the hated ... to love** the hated begin to be loved as they gain power

Into the hearts of such as have not thrived
Upon the present state, whose numbers threaten;
And quietness, grown sick of rest, would purge
By any desperate change. My more particular,
And that which most with you should safe my going,
Is Fulvia's death.

CLEOPATRA Though age from folly could not give me freedom,
It does from childishness. Can Fulvia die?

ANTONY She's dead, my queen.
Look here, and at thy sovereign leisure read
The garboils she awaked. At the last, best,
See when and where she died.

CLEOPATRA O most false love!
Where be the sacred vials thou shouldst fill
With sorrowful water? Now I see, I see,
In Fulvia's death, how mine received shall be.

ANTONY Quarrel no more, but be prepared to know
The purposes I bear; which are, or cease,
As you shall give th' advice. By the fire
That quickens Nilus' slime, I go from hence
Thy soldier-servant, making peace or war
As thou affects.

CLEOPATRA Cut my lace, Charmian, come—
But let it be: I am quickly ill, and well,
So Antony loves.

ANTONY My precious queen, forbear,

53–54 **quietness ... change** i.e., a long peace has developed disease in the body politic, which demands to be made well by the blood-letting of war and revolution 54 **My more particular** my own more personal reason 61 **garboils** commotion 61 **best** i.e., best news of all 63 **sacred vials** (the bottles of tears supposedly placed by Romans in friends' tombs) 68–69 **By the fire ... slime** by the sun that generates life in the Nile's mud 71 **affects** choosest 71 **Cut my lace** (of her tight bodice, i.e., "Give me air") 73 **So Antony loves** (1) if Antony loves me (2) in just such a changeable way does Antony love me

And give true evidence to his love, which stands
An honorable trial.

CLEOPATRA So Fulvia told me.
I prithee turn aside and weep for her;
Then bid adieu to me, and say the tears
Belong to Egypt. Good now, play one scene
Of excellent dissembling, and let it look
Like perfect honor.

ANTONY You'll heat my blood: no more.

CLEOPATRA You can do better yet; but this is meetly.

ANTONY Now by my sword——

CLEOPATRA And target. Still he mends.
But this is not the best. Look, prithee, Charmian,
How this Herculean Roman does become
The carriage of his chafe.

ANTONY I'll leave you, lady.

CLEOPATRA Courteous lord, one word.
Sir, you and I must part, but that's not it:
Sir, you and I have loved, but there's not it:
That you know well. Something it is I would—
O, my oblivion is a very Antony,
And I am all forgotten.

ANTONY But that your royalty
Holds idleness your subject, I should take you
For idleness itself.

CLEOPATRA 'Tis sweating labor
To bear such idleness so near the heart
As Cleopatra this. But, sir, forgive me,
Since my becomings kill me when they do not

74 **stands** sustains 81 **meetly** suitable 82 **target** small shield 84–85 **How this ... his chafe** how gracefully this descendant of Hercules acts out his rage 90–91 **my oblivion ... forgotten** (1) my forgetful memory is like Antony and has deserted me (2) my forgetfulness even, like my memory, is consumed by the image of Antony, and my mind is empty of all else 91–92 **But that ... subject** if you were not queen over trifling 93–94 **labor/To bear** (pun on childbirth) 96 **becomings** graces

Eye well to you. Your honor calls you hence;
Therefore be deaf to my unpitied folly,
And all the gods go with you. Upon your sword
Sit laurel victory, and smooth success
Be strewed before your feet!

ANTONY Let us go. Come:
Our separation so abides and flies
That thou residing here goes yet with me,
And I hence fleeting here remain with thee.
Away! *Exeunt.*

[Scene IV. *Rome. Caesar's house.*]

Enter Octavius [*Caesar*], *reading a letter, Lepidus, and their Train.*

CAESAR You may see, Lepidus, and henceforth know
It is not Caesar's natural vice to hate
Our great competitor. From Alexandria
This is the news: he fishes, drinks, and wastes
The lamps of night in revel; is not more manlike
Than Cleopatra, nor the queen of Ptolemy
More womanly than he; hardly gave audience, or
Vouchsafed to think he had partners. You shall
find there
A man who is th' abstract of all faults
That all men follow.

LEPIDUS I must not think there are
Evils enow to darken all his goodness;
His faults, in him, seem as the spots of heaven,
More fiery by night's blackness, hereditary

I.iv.3 **competitor** partner 6 **queen of Ptolemy** (Cleopatra had nominally married her brother Ptolemy, who was only a child, at the command of Julius Caesar) 9–10 **abstract . . . follow** symbol of universal weakness 11 **enow** enough

Rather than purchased, what he cannot change
Than what he chooses.

CAESAR You are too indulgent. Let's grant it is not
Amiss to tumble on the bed of Ptolemy,
To give a kingdom for a mirth, to sit
And keep the turn of tippling with a slave,
To reel the streets at noon, and stand the buffet
With knaves that smells of sweat. Say this becomes him
(As his composure must be rare indeed
Whom these things cannot blemish); yet must Antony
No way excuse his foils when we do bear
So great weight in his lightness. If he filled
His vacancy with his voluptuousness,
Full surfeits and the dryness of his bones
Call on him for't. But to confound such time
That drums him from his sport and speaks as loud
As his own state and ours, 'tis to be chid
As we rate boys who, being mature in knowledge,
Pawn their experience to their present pleasure
And so rebel to judgment.

Enter a Messenger.

LEPIDUS Here's more news.

MESSENGER Thy biddings have been done, and every hour,
Most noble Caesar, shalt thou have report
How 'tis abroad. Pompey is strong at sea,
And it appears he is beloved of those
That only have feared Caesar: to the ports

14 **purchased** acquired 19 **keep the turn of tippling** exchange toasts 22 **composure** character 24 **foils** stains 24–25 **when we ... lightness** when his triviality throws such a burden on us 26 **vacancy** leisure 27–28 **Full ... for't** let him pay the price in sickness and syphilis 28 **confound** waste 30–33 **'tis to be ... judgment** deserves the considered rebuke we give to boys who, though old enough to know better, give up all the wisdom they have learned in exchange for a moment's pleasure

The discontents repair, and men's reports
Give him much wronged.

CAESAR I should have known no less.
It hath been taught us from the primal state
That he which is was wished until he were;
And the ebbed man, ne'er loved till ne'er worth
love,
Comes deared by being lacked. This common
body,
Like to a vagabond flag upon the stream,
Goes to and back, lackeying the varying tide,
To rot itself with motion.

MESSENGER Caesar, I bring thee word
Menecrates and Menas, famous pirates,
Makes the sea serve them, which they ear and
wound
With keels of every kind. Many hot inroads
They make in Italy; the borders maritime
Lack blood to think on't, and flush youth revolt.
No vessel can peep forth but 'tis as soon
Taken as seen; for Pompey's name strikes more
Than could his war resisted.

CAESAR Antony,
Leave thy lascivious wassails. When thou once
Was beaten from Modena, where thou slew'st
Hirtius and Pansa, consuls, at thy heel
Did famine follow, whom thou fought'st against
(Though daintily brought up) with patience more
Than savages could suffer. Thou didst drink
The stale of horses and the gilded puddle
Which beasts would cough at. Thy palate then did
deign

39 **discontents** malcontents 40 **Give him** say he is 41 **from the primal state** since government began 42 **That he . . . were** that a man in power had supporters until he gained power 44 **common body** populace 45 **vagabond flag** aimlessly drifting iris 49 **ear** plow 52 **flush** vigorous, lusty 56 **wassails** revelry 57 **Modena** (accented on second syllable) 61 **suffer** summon up 62 **stale** urine 62 **gilded** i.e., yellow with scum 63 **deign** not disdain

The roughest berry on the rudest hedge.
Yea, like the stag when snow the pasture sheets,
The barks of trees thou browsed. On the Alps
It is reported thou didst eat strange flesh,
Which some did die to look on. And all this
(It wounds thine honor that I speak it now)
Was borne so like a soldier that thy cheek
So much as lanked not.

LEPIDUS 'Tis pity of him.

CAESAR Let his shames quickly
Drive him to Rome. 'Tis time we twain
Did show ourselves i' th' field; and to that end
Assemble we immediate council. Pompey
Thrives in our idleness.

LEPIDUS Tomorrow, Caesar,
I shall be furnished to inform you rightly
Both what by sea and land I can be able
To front this present time.

CAESAR Till which encounter,
It is my business too. Farewell.

LEPIDUS Farewell, my lord. What you shall know meantime
Of stirs abroad, I shall beseech you, sir,
To let me be partaker.

CAESAR Doubt not, sir;
I knew it for my bond *Exeunt*.

71 **lanked** thinned 78 **I can be able** my powers can be 79 **front** confront 84 **bond** duty

[Scene V. *Alexandria. Cleopatra's palace.*]

Enter Cleopatra, Charmian, Iras, and Mardian.

CLEOPATRA Charmian!

CHARMIAN Madam?

CLEOPATRA [*Yawning*] Ha, ha.
Give me to drink mandragora.

CHARMIAN Why, madam?

CLEOPATRA That I might sleep out this great gap of time
My Antony is away.

CHARMIAN You think of him too much.

CLEOPATRA O, 'tis treason!

CHARMIAN Madam, I trust, not so.

CLEOPATRA Thou, eunuch Mardian!

MARDIAN What's your Highness' pleasure?

CLEOPATRA Not now to hear thee sing. I take no pleasure
In aught an eunuch has: 'tis well for thee
That, being unseminared, thy freer thoughts
May not fly forth of Egypt. Hast thou affections?

MARDIAN Yes, gracious madam.

CLEOPATRA Indeed?

MARDIAN Not in deed, madam; for I can do nothing
But what indeed is honest to be done:

I.v.4 **mandragora** mandrake (a strong narcotic) 11 **unseminared** unsexed 12 **affections** passions 16 **honest** chaste

Yet have I fierce affections, and think
What Venus did with Mars.

CLEOPATRA O, Charmian,
Where think'st thou he is now? Stands he, or sits he?
Or does he walk? Or is he on his horse?
O happy horse, to bear the weight of Antony!
Do bravely, horse, for wot'st thou whom thou mov'st?
The demi-Atlas of this earth, the arm
And burgonet of men. He's speaking now,
Or murmuring, "Where's my serpent of old Nile?"
(For so he calls me.) Now I feed myself
With most delicious poison. Think on me,
That am with Phoebus' amorous pinches black
And wrinkled deep in time. Broad-fronted Caesar,
When thou wast here above the ground, I was
A morsel for a monarch; and great Pompey
Would stand and make his eyes grow in my brow;
There would he anchor his aspect, and die
With looking on his life.

Enter Alexas from Antony.

ALEXAS Sovereign of Egypt, hail!

CLEOPATRA How much unlike art thou Mark Antony!
Yet, coming from him, that great med'cine hath
With his tinct gilded thee.
How goes it with my brave Mark Antony?

ALEXAS Last thing he did, dear Queen,
He kissed—the last of many doubled kisses—
This orient pearl. His speech sticks in my heart.

18 **Venus ... Mars** (Venus, goddess of love, and Mars, god of war, were lovers) 22 **wot'st** knowest 23 **demi-Atlas** (the Titan Atlas supported the heavens on his shoulders) 24 **burgonet** visored helmet 28 **Phoebus'** the sun's 29 **Broad-fronted Caesar** wide-browed Caesar (i.e., Julius Caesar, whose mistress she had been in youth) 31 **great Pompey** Cneius Pompeius (son of Pompey the Great) 33 **aspect** gaze (accented on second syllable) 36–37 **that great med'cine ... thee** (alchemists long tried to make or discover the "philosopher's stone" or *elixir vitae*—known as the "great medicine" and the "tincture"—which had the property of turning base metals to gold, and of restoring youth) 41 **orient** eastern, bright

CLEOPATRA Mine ear must pluck it thence.

ALEXAS "Good friend," quoth he,
"Say the firm Roman to great Egypt sends
This treasure of an oyster; at whose foot,
To mend the petty present, I will piece
Her opulent throne with kingdoms. All the East
(Say thou) shall call her mistress." So he nodded,
And soberly did mount an arm-gaunt steed,
Who neighed so high that what I would have spoke
Was beastly dumbed by him.

CLEOPATRA What was he, sad or merry?

ALEXAS Like to the time o' th' year between the extremes
Of hot and cold, he was nor sad nor merry.

CLEOPATRA O well-divided disposition! Note him,
Note him, good Charmian, 'tis the man; but note him.
He was not sad, for he would shine on those
That make their looks by his; he was not merry,
Which seemed to tell them his remembrance lay
In Egypt with his joy; but between both.
O heavenly mingle! Be'st thou sad or merry,
The violence of either thee becomes,
So does it no man else.—Met'st thou my posts?

ALEXAS Ay, madam, twenty several messengers.
Why do you send so thick?

CLEOPATRA Who's born that day
When I forget to send to Antony
Shall die a beggar. Ink and paper, Charmian.
Welcome, my good Alexas. Did I, Charmian,
Ever love Caesar so?

CHARMIAN O, that brave Caesar!

43 **firm** constant 45 **piece** add to 48 **arm-gaunt** battle-worn (?) battle-hungry (?) 50 **beastly dumbed** silenced by a beast 53 **disposition** temperament 54 **'tis the man** that's exactly what he is like 61 **posts** messengers 62 **several** separate 67 **brave** splendid, fine

CLEOPATRA Be choked with such another emphasis!
Say "the brave Antony."

CHARMIAN The valiant Caesar!

CLEOPATRA By Isis, I will give thee bloody teeth
If thou with Caesar paragon again
My man of men.

CHARMIAN By your most gracious pardon,
I sing but after you.

CLEOPATRA My salad days,
When I was green in judgment, cold in blood,
To say as I said then. But come, away,
Get me ink and paper.
He shall have every day a several greeting,
Or I'll unpeople Egypt *Exeunt*.

68 **emphasis** forceful statement 71 **paragon** compare 74 **green** young, silly

[ACT II

Scene I. *Messina. Pompey's house.*]

Enter Pompey, Menecrates, and Menas, in war-like manner.

POMPEY If the great gods be just, they shall assist
The deeds of justest men.

MENECRATES Know, worthy Pompey,
That what they do delay, they not deny.

POMPEY Whiles we are suitors to their throne, decays
The thing we sue for.

MENECRATES We, ignorant of ourselves
Beg often our own harms, which the wise pow'rs
Deny us for our good; so find we profit
By losing of our prayers.

POMPEY I shall do well:
The people love me, and the sea is mine;
My powers are crescent, and my auguring hope

II.i.1 **shall** surely must 3 **what they . . . deny** i.e., delay in performing does not necessarily imply a refusal 5 **sue** beg 10 **crescent** growing (i.e., waxing like the moon—hence the following image) 10 **auguring** prophesying

Says it will come to th' full. Mark Antony
In Egypt sits at dinner, and will make
No wars without doors. Caesar gets money where
He loses hearts. Lepidus flatters both,
Of both is flattered, but he neither loves,
Nor either cares for him.

MENAS Caesar and Lepidus
Are in the field; a mighty strength they carry.

POMPEY Where have you this? 'Tis false.

MENAS From Silvius, sir.

POMPEY He dreams: I know they are in Rome together,
Looking for Antony. But all the charms of love,
Salt Cleopatra, soften thy waned lip!
Let witchcraft join with beauty, lust with both!
Tie up the libertine in a field of feasts,
Keep his brain fuming. Epicurean cooks
Sharpen with cloyless sauce his appetite,
That sleep and feeding may prorogue his honor
Even till a Lethe'd dullness——

Enter Varrius.

How now, Varrius?

VARRIUS This is most certain, that I shall deliver:
Mark Antony is every hour in Rome
Expected. Since he went from Egypt 'tis
A space for farther travel.

POMPEY I could have given less matter
A better ear. Menas, I did not think
This amorous surfeiter would have donned his helm
For such a petty war. His soldiership

13 **without doors** out-of-doors (contrasted with the indoor "wars" of love) 17 **in the field** ready for battle 20 **charms** spells 21 **Salt** lustful 21 **waned** pale and thin (like the old moon) 26 **prorogue** suspend 27 **Lethe'd** oblivious (from Lethe, a river in Hades; those who drank of the water forgot all) 30–31 **'tis . . . travel** there has been time for an even longer journey

Is twice the other twain; but let us rear
The higher our opinion, that our stirring
Can from the lap of Egypt's widow pluck
The ne'er-lust-wearied Antony.

MENAS I cannot hope
Caesar and Antony shall well greet together;
His wife that's dead did trespasses to Caesar;
His brother warred upon him—although I think
Not moved by Antony.

POMPEY I know not, Menas,
How lesser enmities may give way to greater.
Were't not that we stand up against them all,
'Twere pregnant they should square between themselves,
For they have entertainèd cause enough
To draw their swords; but how the fear of us
May cement their divisions and bind up
The petty difference, we yet not know.
Be't as our gods will have't! It only stands
Our lives upon, to use our strongest hands.
Come, Menas. *Exeunt.*

[Scene II. *Rome. Lepidus' house.*]

Enter Enobarbus and Lepidus.

LEPIDUS Good Enobarbus, 'tis a worthy deed,
And shall become you well, to entreat your captain
To soft and gentle speech.

ENOBARBUS I shall entreat him

35–36 **let us . . . opinion** let us think all the better of ourselves 38 **hope** believe 39 **well greet** meet amiably 42 **moved** encouraged 44–45 **Were't not . . . themselves** had we not challenged them (and thus united them) they would probably have quarreled among themselves 48 **cement** (accented on first syllable) 50–51 **It only . . . upon** only, it is a matter of life and death to us all

To answer like himself: if Caesar move him,
Let Antony look over Caesar's head
And speak as loud as Mars. By Jupiter,
Were I the wearer of Antonio's beard,
I would not shave't today!

LEPIDUS 'Tis not a time
For private stomaching.

ENOBARBUS Every time
Serves for the matter that is then born in't.

LEPIDUS But small to greater matters must give way.

ENOBARBUS Not if the small come first.

LEPIDUS Your speech is passion;
But pray you stir no embers up. Here comes
The noble Antony.

Enter Antony and Ventidius [*in conversation*].

ENOBARBUS And yonder, Caesar.

Enter [*from the other side*] *Caesar, Maecenas, and Agrippa* [*in conversation*].

ANTONY If we compose well here, to Parthia.
Hark, Ventidius.

CAESAR I do not know,
Maecenas; ask Agrippa.

LEPIDUS Noble friends,
That which combined us was most great, and let not
A leaner action rend us. What's amiss,
May it be gently heard. When we debate
Our trivial difference loud, we do commit
Murder in healing wounds. Then, noble partners,
The rather for I earnestly beseech,

II.ii.4 **move** irritate 8 **I would not shave't today** (1) I would not do him the courtesy of clean-shaving (2) I would not remove the temptation of plucking it (an incitement to fight) 9 **private stomaching** personal resentment 15 **compose** come to an agreement

Touch you the sourest points with sweetest terms,
Nor curstness grow to th' matter.

ANTONY 'Tis spoken well.
Were we before our armies, and to fight,
I should do thus. *Flourish.*

CAESAR Welcome to Rome.

ANTONY Thank you.

CAESAR Sit.

ANTONY Sit, sir.

CAESAR Nay then. [*They sit.*]

ANTONY I learn you take things ill which are not so,
Or being, concern you not.

CAESAR I must be laughed at
If, or for nothing or a little, I
Should say myself offended, and with you
Chiefly i' th' world; more laughed at that I should
Once name you derogately, when to sound your name
It not concerned me.

ANTONY My being in Egypt, Caesar,
What was't to you?

CAESAR No more than my residing here at Rome
Might be to you in Egypt: yet if you there
Did practice on my state, your being in Egypt
Might be my question.

ANTONY How intend you? Practiced?

CAESAR You may be pleased to catch at mine intent
By what did here befall me. Your wife and brother

25 **Nor ... matter** and do not let ill temper be added to the problem at hand 27 **thus** (perhaps Antony embraces Caesar, but perhaps he means his words would be temperate in any circumstance) 35 **or ... or** either ... or 38 **derogately** disparagingly 43 **practice on my state** plot against my rule

Made wars upon me, and their contestation
Was theme for you; you were the word of war.

ANTONY You do mistake your business: my brother never
Did urge me in his act. I did inquire it
And have my learning from some true reports
That drew their swords with you. Did he not rather
Discredit my authority with yours,
And make the wars alike against my stomach,
Having alike your cause? Of this, my letters
Before did satisfy you. If you'll patch a quarrel,
As matter whole you have to make it with,
It must not be with this.

CAESAR You praise yourself
By laying defects of judgment to me, but
You patched up your excuses.

ANTONY Not so, not so:
I know you could not lack, I am certain on't,
Very necessity of this thought, that I,
Your partner in the cause 'gainst which he fought,
Could not with graceful eyes attend those wars
Which fronted mine own peace. As for my wife,
I would you had her spirit in such another;
The third o' th' world is yours, which with a snaffle
You may pace easy, but not such a wife.

ENOBARBUS Would we had all such wives, that the men might go to wars with the women.

ANTONY So much uncurbable, her garboils, Caesar,
Made out of her impatience—which not wanted
Shrewdness of policy too—I grieving grant

48 **Was theme for you** had you as root cause (?) provided you with a pretext (?) 48 **you were the word of war** the war was about you 50 **Did urge me** made use of my name 51 **reports** reporters 54 **stomach** desire 56–57 **If you'll . . . with** if you want to fabricate a quarrel out of odds and ends, though in fact you have more substantial materials for one 64 **with graceful eyes attend** look favorably on 65 **fronted** attacked 66 **I would . . . another** I wish you were married to just such a wife 68 **pace** train (used of horses)

Did you too much disquiet: for that you must
But say, I could not help it.

CAESAR I wrote to you;
When rioting in Alexandria you
Did pocket up my letters, and with taunts
Did gibe my missive out of audience.

ANTONY Sir,
He fell upon me, ere admitted, then:
Three kings I had newly feasted, and did want
Of what I was i' th' morning; but next day
I told him of myself, which was as much
As to have asked him pardon. Let this fellow
Be nothing of our strife: if we contend,
Out of our question wipe him.

CAESAR You have broken
The article of your oath, which you shall never
Have tongue to charge me with.

LEPIDUS Soft, Caesar!

ANTONY No,
Lepidus; let him speak.
The honor is sacred which he talks on now,
Supposing that I lacked it. But on, Caesar,
The article of my oath——

CAESAR To lend me arms and aid when I required
them,
The which you both denied.

ANTONY Neglected rather:
And then when poisonèd hours had bound me up
From mine own knowledge. As nearly as I may,
I'll play the penitent to you: but mine honesty
Shall not make poor my greatness, nor my power
Work without it. Truth is, that Fulvia,
To have me out of Egypt, made wars here,
For which myself, the ignorant motive, do

75 But only **78 missive** messenger **82 myself** my condition **84 Be nothing of** have no place in **86 article** precise terms **87 Soft** be careful **98 it** honesty (?)

So far ask pardon as befits mine honor
To stoop in such a case.

LEPIDUS 'Tis noble spoken.

MAECENAS If it might please you, to enforce no further
The griefs between ye: to forget them quite
Were to remember that the present need
Speaks to atone you.

LEPIDUS Worthily spoken, Maecenas.

ENOBARBUS Or, if you borrow one another's love for the instant, you may, when you hear no more words of Pompey, return it again: you shall have time to wrangle in when you have nothing else to do.

ANTONY Thou art a soldier only; speak no more.

ENOBARBUS That truth should be silent I had almost forgot.

ANTONY You wrong this presence; therefore speak no more.

ENOBARBUS Go to, then; your considerate stone.

CAESAR I do not much dislike the matter, but
The manner of his speech; for't cannot be
We shall remain in friendship, our conditions
So diff'ring in their acts. Yet if I knew
What hoop should hold us stanch, from edge to edge
O' th' world I would pursue it.

AGRIPPA Give me leave, Caesar.

CAESAR Speak, Agrippa.

AGRIPPA Thou hast a sister by the mother's side,
Admired Octavia: great Mark Antony
Is now a widower.

104 **griefs** grievances 106 **Speaks to atone you** demands your reconciliation 114 **presence** dignified company 115 **your considerate stone** I will be silent as stone about what I am thinking 118 **conditions** temperaments 123 **by the mother's side** i.e., half sister (though actually Octavia was a full sister of Octavius)

CAESAR Say not so, Agrippa:
If Cleopatra heard you, your reproof
Were well deserved of rashness.

ANTONY I am not married, Caesar: let me hear
Agrippa further speak.

AGRIPPA To hold you in perpetual amity,
To make you brothers, and to knit your hearts
With an unslipping knot, take Antony
Octavia to his wife; whose beauty claims
No worse a husband than the best of men;
Whose virtue and whose general graces speak
That which none else can utter. By this marriage
All little jealousies, which now seem great,
And all great fears, which now import their
dangers,
Would then be nothing: truths would be tales,
Where now half-tales be truths: her love to both
Would each to other, and all loves to both,
Draw after her. Pardon what I have spoke;
For 'tis a studied, not a present thought,
By duty ruminated.

ANTONY Will Caesar speak?

CAESAR Not till he hears how Antony is touched
With what is spoke already.

ANTONY What power is in Agrippa,
If I would say, "Agrippa, be it so,"
To make this good?

CAESAR The power of Caesar, and
His power unto Octavia.

ANTONY May I never
To this good purpose, that so fairly shows,
Dream of impediment! Let me have thy hand.

126–27 **your reproof . . . rashness** you would get a deserved reproof for being foolhardy 137 **jealousies** suspicions 138 **import** bring 139–40 **truths would . . . truths** things true would be disbelieved, whereas now half-truths are believed 143 **present** momentary 145 **touched** affected

Further this act of grace, and from this hour
The heart of brothers govern in our loves
And sway our great designs.

CAESAR There's my hand.
A sister I bequeath you, whom no brother
Did ever love so dearly. Let her live
To join our kingdoms and our hearts; and never
Fly off our loves again.

LEPIDUS Happily, amen.

ANTONY I did not think to draw my sword 'gainst
Pompey,
For he hath laid strange courtesies and great
Of late upon me. I must thank him only,
Lest my remembrance suffer ill report:
At heel of that, defy him.

LEPIDUS Time calls upon's.
Of us must Pompey presently be sought,
Or else he seeks out us.

ANTONY Where lies he?

CAESAR About the Mount Mesena.

ANTONY What is his strength by land?

CAESAR Great and increasing; but by sea
He is an absolute master.

ANTONY So is the fame.
Would we had spoke together! Haste we for it,
Yet, ere we put ourselves in arms, dispatch we
The business we have talked of.

CAESAR With most gladness;
And do invite you to my sister's view,
Whither straight I'll lead you.

152 **grace** reconciliation 158 **Fly off our loves** may our love for each other desert us 162 **remembrance** memory (of kindnesses done) 163 **At heel of that** immediately after 164 **presently** at once 166 **Mesena** Misenum, an Italian port 169 **fame** report

ANTONY Let us, Lepidus,
Not lack your company.

LEPIDUS Noble Antony,
Not sickness should detain me.

Flourish. Exit [*all but*] *Enobarbus, Agrippa, Maecenas.*

MAECENAS Welcome from Egypt, sir.

ENOBARBUS Half the heart of Caesar, worthy Maecenas. My honorable friend, Agrippa.

AGRIPPA Good Enobarbus.

MAECENAS We have cause to be glad that matters are so well disgested. You stayed well by't in Egypt.

ENOBARBUS Ay, sir, we did sleep day out of countenance and made the night light with drinking.

MAECENAS Eight wild boars roasted whole at a breakfast, and but twelve persons there; is this true?

ENOBARBUS This was but as a fly by an eagle: we had much more monstrous matter of feast, which worthily deserved noting.

MAECENAS She's a most triumphant lady, if report be square to her.

ENOBARBUS When she first met Mark Antony, she pursed up his heart, upon the river of Cydnus.

AGRIPPA There she appeared indeed; or my reporter devised well for her.

ENOBARBUS I will tell you.
The barge she sat in, like a burnished throne,
Burned on the water: the poop was beaten gold;
Purple the sails, and so perfumèd that

178 **Half the heart** dear friend (though possibly the idea is that Caesar is equally devoted to Agrippa and to Maecenas) 182 **disgested** digested 182 **stayed well by't** "lived it up" 183–84 **we did . . . countenance** we disconcerted the day by sleeping through it 187 **by** compared with 191 **square** just, true 193 **pursed up** put in her purse, took possession of 195 **devised** invented

The winds were lovesick with them; the oars were
silver,
Which to the tune of flutes kept stroke and made
The water which they beat to follow faster,
As amorous of their strokes. For her own person,
It beggared all description: she did lie
In her pavilion, cloth-of-gold of tissue,
O'erpicturing that Venus where we see
The fancy outwork nature: on each side her
Stood pretty dimpled boys, like smiling Cupids,
With divers-colored fans, whose wind did seem
To glow the delicate cheeks which they did cool,
And what they undid did.

AGRIPPA O, rare for Antony.

ENOBARBUS Her gentlewomen, like the Nereides,
So many mermaids, tended her i' th' eyes,
And made their bends adornings. At the helm
A seeming mermaid steers: the silken tackle
Swell with the touches of those flower-soft hands,
That yarely frame the office. From the barge
A strange invisible perfume hits the sense
Of the adjacent wharfs. The city cast
Her people out upon her; and Antony,
Enthroned i' th' marketplace, did sit alone,
Whistling to th' air; which, but for vacancy,
Had gone to gaze on Cleopatra too,
And made a gap in nature.

AGRIPPA Rare Egyptian!

ENOBARBUS Upon her landing, Antony sent to her,
Invited her to supper. She replied,

205 **cloth-of-gold of tissue** a rich fabric interwoven with gold threads 206–07 **O'erpicturing . . . nature** surpassing that painting of Venus where we can see the imagination excelling nature itself in creative ability 211 **And . . . did** i.e., and seemed to produce the warm color they were cooling 212 **Nereides** sea nymphs 213–14 **tended . . . adornings** stood before her and waited on her, their bowing movements being works of art in themselves 217 **yarely frame the office** deftly perform the task 219 **wharfs** banks 222 **but for vacancy** i.e., but for the law that nature abhors a vacuum

It should be better he became her guest;
Which she entreated. Our courteous Antony,
Whom ne'er the word of "No" woman heard speak,
Being barbered ten times o'er, goes to the feast,
And, for his ordinary, pays his heart
For what his eyes eat only.

AGRIPPA Royal wench!
She made great Caesar lay his sword to bed;
He plowed her, and she cropped.

ENOBARBUS I saw her once
Hop forty paces through the public street;
And having lost her breath, she spoke, and panted,
That she did make defect perfection,
And, breathless, pow'r breathe forth.

MAECENAS Now Antony must leave her utterly.

ENOBARBUS Never; he will not:
Age cannot wither her, nor custom stale
Her infinite variety: other women cloy
The appetites they feed, but she makes hungry
Where most she satisfies; for vilest things
Become themselves in her, that the holy priests
Bless her when she is riggish.

MAECENAS If beauty, wisdom, modesty, can settle
The heart of Antony, Octavia is
A blessèd lottery to him.

AGRIPPA Let us go.
Good Enobarbus, make yourself my guest
Whilst you abide here.

ENOBARBUS Humbly, sir, I thank you. *Exeunt.*

231 **ordinary** public dinner in a tavern 234 **she cropped** i.e., had a child (Caesarion) 237 **That** so that 245 **Become themselves** are becoming 246 **riggish** wanton 249 **lottery** allotment

[Scene III. *Rome. Caesar's house.*]

Enter Antony, Caesar, Octavia between them.

ANTONY The world and my great office will sometimes
Divide me from your bosom.

OCTAVIA All which time
Before the gods my knee shall bow my prayers
To them for you.

ANTONY Good night, sir. My Octavia,
Read not my blemishes in the world's report:
I have not kept my square, but that to come
Shall all be done by th' rule. Good night, dear lady.
Good night, sir.

CAESAR Good night. *Exit* [*with Octavia*].

Enter Soothsayer.

ANTONY Now, sirrah: you do wish yourself in Egypt?

SOOTHSAYER Would I had never come from thence, nor you thither.

ANTONY If you can, your reason?

SOOTHSAYER I see it in my motion, have it not in my tongue, but yet hie you to Egypt again.

ANTONY Say to me, whose fortunes shall rise higher,
Caesar's, or mine?

SOOTHSAYER Caesar's.
Therefore, O Antony, stay not by his side.

II.iii.6 kept my square kept straight **14 motion** mind

Thy daemon, that thy spirit which keeps thee, is
Noble, courageous, high, unmatchable,
Where Caesar's is not. But near him thy angel
Becomes afeard, as being o'erpow'red: therefore
Make space enough between you.

ANTONY Speak this no more.

SOOTHSAYER To none but thee; no more but when to
thee.
If thou dost play with him at any game,
Thou art sure to lose; and of that natural luck
He beats thee 'gainst the odds. Thy luster thickens
When he shines by: I say again, thy spirit
Is all afraid to govern thee near him;
But he away, 'tis noble.

ANTONY Get thee gone.
Say to Ventidius I would speak with him.

Exit [Soothsayer].

He shall to Parthia. Be it art or hap,
He hath spoken true. The very dice obey him,
And in our sports my better cunning faints
Under his chance: if we draw lots, he speeds;
His cocks do win the battle still of mine
When it is all to naught, and his quails ever
Beat mine, inhooped, at odds. I will to Egypt:
And though I make this marriage for my peace,
I' th' East my pleasure lies.

Enter Ventidius.

O, come, Ventidius,
You must to Parthia. Your commission's ready:
Follow me, and receive't. *Exeunt.*

20 **daemon** guardian angel 27 **of** by 28 **thickens** dims 33 **art or hap** skill or chance 36 **chance** luck 36 **speeds** is successful 37 **still** always 38 **it is all to naught** the odds are all to nothing (against him) 39 **inhooped** confined within a ring

[Scene IV. *Rome. A street.*]

Enter Lepidus, Maecenas, and Agrippa.

LEPIDUS Trouble yourselves no further: pray you, hasten
Your generals after.

AGRIPPA Sir, Mark Antony
Will e'en but kiss Octavia, and we'll follow.

LEPIDUS Till I shall see you in your soldier's dress,
Which will become you both, farewell.

MAECENAS We shall,
As I conceive the journey, be at Mount
Before you, Lepidus.

LEPIDUS Your way is shorter;
My purposes do draw me much about:
You'll win two days upon me.

BOTH Sir, good success.

LEPIDUS Farewell. *Exeunt.*

II.iv.6 **conceive** understand 6 **Mount** i.e., Misenum 8 **My purposes . . . about** my plans take me the long way around

[Scene V. *Alexandria. Cleopatra's palace.*]

Enter Cleopatra, Charmian, Iras, and Alexas.

CLEOPATRA Give me some music: music, moody food
Of us that trade in love.

OMNES The music, ho!

Enter Mardian the Eunuch.

CLEOPATRA Let it alone, let's to billiards: come, Charmian.

CHARMIAN My arm is sore; best play with Mardian.

CLEOPATRA As well a woman with an eunuch played
As with a woman. Come, you'll play with me, sir?

MARDIAN As well as I can, madam.

CLEOPATRA And when good will is showed, though't come too short,
The actor may plead pardon. I'll none now.
Give me mine angle, we'll to th' river: there,
My music playing far off, I will betray
Tawny-finned fishes. My bended hook shall pierce
Their slimy jaws; and as I draw them up,
I'll think them every one an Antony,
And say, "Ah, ha! y' are caught!"

CHARMIAN 'Twas merry when
You wagered on your angling, when your diver
Did hang a salt fish on his hook, which he
With fervency drew up.

II.v.1 **moody** melancholy (with pun on musical "mood" or key) 2 **Omnes** all (Latin) 10 **angle** fishing tackle 17 **salt** dried

CLEOPATRA That time—O times!—
I laughed him out of patience; and that night
I laughed him into patience; and next morn,
Ere the ninth hour, I drunk him to his bed;
Then put my tires and mantles on him, whilst
I wore his sword Philippan.

Enter a Messenger.

O, from Italy!
Ram thou thy fruitful tidings in mine ears,
That long time have been barren.

MESSENGER Madam, madam——

CLEOPATRA Antonio's dead! If thou say so, villain,
Thou kill'st thy mistress: but well and free,
If thou so yield him. There is gold and here
My bluest veins to kiss, a hand that kings
Have lipped, and trembled kissing.

MESSENGER First, madam, he is well.

CLEOPATRA Why, there's more gold.
But, sirrah, mark, we use
To say the dead are well: bring it to that,
The gold I give thee will I melt and pour
Down thy ill-uttering throat.

MESSENGER Good madam, hear me.

CLEOPATRA Well, go to, I will:
But there's no goodness in thy face if Antony
Be free and healthful; so tart a favor
To trumpet such good tidings? If not well,
Thou shouldst come like a Fury crowned with
snakes,
Not like a formal man.

MESSENGER Will't please you hear me?

22 **tires** headdresses 23 **Philippan** (Antony's sword is named after Philippi, where he conquered Brutus and Cassius) 33 **well** i.e., in having gone to heaven 38 **tart a favor** sour an expression 41 **formal** (1) sane (2) normally shaped

CLEOPATRA I have a mind to strike thee ere thou speak'st:
Yet, if thou say Antony lives, is well,
Or friends with Caesar, or not captive to him,
I'll set thee in a shower of gold, and hail
Rich pearls upon thee.

MESSENGER Madam, he's well.

CLEOPATRA Well said.

MESSENGER And friends with Caesar.

CLEOPATRA Th'art an honest man.

MESSENGER Caesar and he are greater friends than ever.

CLEOPATRA Make thee a fortune from me.

MESSENGER But yet, madam——

CLEOPATRA I do not like "But yet"; it does allay
The good precedence: fie upon "But yet";
"But yet" is as a jailer to bring forth
Some monstrous malefactor. Prithee, friend,
Pour out the pack of matter to mine ear,
The good and bad together: he's friends with Caesar,
In state of health, thou say'st, and thou say'st, free.

MESSENGER Free, madam, no: I made no such report;
He's bound unto Octavia.

CLEOPATRA For what good turn?

MESSENGER For the best turn i' th' bed.

CLEOPATRA I am pale, Charmian.

MESSENGER Madam, he's married to Octavia.

CLEOPATRA The most infectious pestilence upon thee!
Strikes him down.

50–51 **allay/The good precedence** qualify the good news before it 58 **For what good turn** (she takes his *bound* in the sense "indebted to"; he then takes up her *turn*, or "act," in a sexual sense)

MESSENGER Good madam, patience.

CLEOPATRA What say you?

Strikes him.

Hence,
Horrible villain! Or I'll spurn thine eyes
Like balls before me: I'll unhair thy head,

She hales him up and down.

Thou shalt be whipped with wire and stewed in brine,
Smarting in ling'ring pickle.

MESSENGER Gracious madam,
I that do bring the news made not the match.

CLEOPATRA Say 'tis not so, a province I will give thee,
And make thy fortunes proud: the blow thou hadst
Shall make thy peace for moving me to rage,
And I will boot thee with what gift beside
Thy modesty can beg.

MESSENGER He's married, madam.

CLEOPATRA Rogue, thou hast lived too long.

Draws a knife.

MESSENGER Nay, then I'll run.
What mean you, madam? I have made no fault.

Exit.

CHARMIAN Good madam, keep yourself within yourself,
The man is innocent.

CLEOPATRA Some innocents 'scape not the thunderbolt.
Melt Egypt into Nile, and kindly creatures
Turn all to serpents! Call the slave again:
Though I am mad, I will not bite him. Call!

CHARMIAN He is afeard to come.

CLEOPATRA I will not hurt him.

[*Exit Charmian.*]

63 **spurn** kick 66 **pickle** pickling solution (of painful salt or acid) 71 **boot thee** compensate you 72 **modesty** humble rank

These hands do lack nobility, that they strike
A meaner than myself; since I myself
Have given myself the cause.

Enter [Charmian and] the Messenger again.

Come hither, sir.
Though it be honest, it is never good
To bring bad news: give to a gracious message
An host of tongues, but let ill tidings tell
Themselves, when they be felt.

MESSENGER I have done my duty.

CLEOPATRA Is he married?
I cannot hate thee worser than I do
If thou again say "Yes."

MESSENGER He's married, madam.

CLEOPATRA The gods confound thee! Dost thou hold there still?

MESSENGER Should I lie, madam?

CLEOPATRA O, I would thou didst,
So half my Egypt were submerged and made
A cistern for scaled snakes! Go get thee hence;
Hadst thou Narcissus in thy face, to me
Thou wouldst appear most ugly. He is married?

MESSENGER I crave your Highness' pardon.

CLEOPATRA He is married?

MESSENGER Take no offense that I would not offend you:
To punish me for what you make me do
Seems much unequal: he's married to Octavia.

CLEOPATRA O, that his fault should make a knave of thee,

84 **the cause** i.e., by loving Antony 92 **confound** destroy 94 **So** even if 96 **Hadst . . . face** even if you were as handsome as Narcissus (Greek youth of great beauty) 99 **Take . . . offend you** do not be angry at me for hesitating to tell you what I know will anger you 101 **unequal** unjust

That art not what th' art sure of! Get thee hence,
The merchandise which thou hast brought from
Rome
Are all too dear for me. Lie they upon thy hand,
And be undone by 'em! [*Exit Messenger.*]

CHARMIAN Good your Highness, patience.

CLEOPATRA In praising Antony I have dispraised
Caesar.

CHARMIAN Many times, madam.

CLEOPATRA I am paid for't now.
Lead me from hence;
I faint. O, Iras, Charmian! 'Tis no matter.
Go to the fellow, good Alexas; bid him
Report the feature of Octavia: her years,
Her inclination, let him not leave out
The color of her hair. Bring me word quickly.
[*Exit Alexas.*]
Let him forever go!—let him not!—Charmian,
Though he be painted one way like a Gorgon,
The other way's a Mars. [*To Mardian*] Bid you
Alexas
Bring me word how tall she is.—Pity me,
Charmian,
But do not speak to me. Lead me to my chamber.
Exeunt.

103 **That art ... sure of** who are not really as wicked as the news you insist on 106 **undone** bankrupted 112 **feature** appearance (not limited to facial characteristics) 113 **inclination** character 116–17 **Though he ... Mars** (alluding to "perspective" pictures, trick paintings that showed contrasted figures – here a monstrous woman and the god of war—when looked at from opposite sides)

[Scene VI. *Near Misenum.*]

Flourish. Enter Pompey [*and Menas*] *at one door, with Drum and Trumpet: at another, Caesar, Lepidus, Antony, Enobarbus, Maecenas, Agrippa, with Soldiers marching.*

POMPEY Your hostages I have, so have you mine;
And we shall talk before we fight.

CAESAR Most meet
That first we come to words, and therefore have we
Our written purposes before us sent;
Which, if thou hast considered, let us know
If 'twill tie up thy discontented sword
And carry back to Sicily much tall youth
That else must perish here.

POMPEY To you all three,
The senators alone of this great world,
Chief factors for the gods: I do not know
Wherefore my father should revengers want,
Having a son and friends, since Julius Caesar,
Who at Philippi the good Brutus ghosted,
There saw you laboring for him. What was't
That moved pale Cassius to conspire? And what
Made all-honored, honest, Roman Brutus,
With the armed rest, courtiers of beauteous freedom,
To drench the Capitol—but that they would
Have one man but a man? And that is it
Hath made me rig my navy, at whose burden

II.vi.2 **meet** fit 7 **tall** brave 10 **factors** agents 11 **want** lack 13 **ghosted** haunted 19 **but a man** merely a man (and not a king or demigod)

The angered ocean foams; with which I meant
To scourge th' ingratitude that despiteful Rome
Cast on my noble father.

CAESAR Take your time.

ANTONY Thou canst not fear us, Pompey, with thy sails.
We'll speak with thee at sea. At land thou know'st
How much we do o'ercount thee.

POMPEY At land indeed
Thou dost o'ercount me of my father's house:
But since the cuckoo builds not for himself,
Remain in't as thou mayst.

LEPIDUS Be pleased to tell us
(For this is from the present) how you take
The offers we have sent you.

CAESAR There's the point.

ANTONY Which do not be entreated to, but weigh
What it is worth embraced.

CAESAR And what may follow,
To try a larger fortune.

POMPEY You have made me offer
Of Sicily, Sardinia; and I must
Rid all the sea of pirates; then, to send
Measures of wheat to Rome; this 'greed upon,
To part with unhacked edges and bear back
Our targes undinted.

24 **fear** frighten 25 **speak with thee** meet you 27 **o'ercount** cheat (Antony had used it in the sense of "outnumber," but Pompey punningly alludes to a house Antony bought from the elder Pompey but did not pay for) 28–29 **But since . . . mayst** but since cuckoos can't build (and therefore have to steal other birds' nests), keep it if you can hold on to it. (Pompey includes in this sentence a jeering suggestion that Antony is a cuckold, a lover of a faithless woman) 30 **from the present** beside the point 33 **embraced** if accepted 33–34 **And what . . . fortune** (1) and what the result may be, if you try to do better for yourself (i.e., risk war) (2) and the even greater things you may gain, if you join us and our affairs prosper 38 **edges** swords 39 **targes** shields

OMNES That's our offer.

POMPEY Know then
I came before you here a man prepared
To take this offer. But Mark Antony
Put me to some impatience. Though I lose
The praise of it by telling, you must know,
When Caesar and your brother were at blows,
Your mother came to Sicily and did find
Her welcome friendly.

ANTONY I have heard it, Pompey,
And am well studied for a liberal thanks,
Which I do owe you.

POMPEY Let me have your hand:
I did not think, sir, to have met you here.

ANTONY The beds i' th' East are soft; and thanks to you,
That called me timelier than my purpose hither;
For I have gained by't.

CAESAR Since I saw you last
There's a change upon you.

POMPEY Well, I know not
What counts harsh fortune casts upon my face,
But in my bosom shall she never come
To make my heart her vassal.

LEPIDUS Well met here.

POMPEY I hope so, Lepidus. Thus we are agreed.
I crave our composition may be written,
And sealed between us.

CAESAR That's the next to do.

39 **Omnes** i.e., Caesar, Antony, Lepidus 47–48 **am well . . . you** I am ready indeed to give you the free and full thanks that I owe you 51 **timelier** earlier 54 **counts** reckonings 54 **casts** (1) throws (2) sums up (the lines and wrinkles resulting from a hard life are compared to a bill of costs written out by a cruelly precise Fortune) 58 **composition** agreement

POMPEY We'll feast each other ere we part, and let's
Draw lots who shall begin.

ANTONY That will I, Pompey.

POMPEY No, Antony, take the lot:
But, first or last, your fine Egyptian cookery
Shall have the fame. I have heard that Julius Caesar
Grew fat with feasting there.

ANTONY You have heard much.

POMPEY I have fair meanings, sir.

ANTONY And fair words to them.

POMPEY Then so much have I heard:
And I have heard Apollodorus carried——

ENOBARBUS No more of that: he did so.

POMPEY What, I pray you?

ENOBARBUS A certain queen to Caesar in a mattress.

POMPEY I know thee now; how far'st thou, soldier?

ENOBARBUS Well;
And well am like to do, for I perceive
Four feasts are toward.

POMPEY Let me shake thy hand;
I never hated thee: I have seen thee fight
When I have envied thy behavior.

ENOBARBUS Sir,
I never loved you much; but I ha' praised ye
When you have well deserved ten times as much
As I have said you did.

POMPEY Enjoy thy plainness,
It nothing ill becomes thee.
Aboard my galley I invite you all:
Will you lead, lords?

ALL Show's the way, sir.

73 toward in the offing (accented "tòward") **79 It . . . thee** it suits you very well

POMPEY Come.

Exeunt. Manet Enobarbus and Menas.

MENAS [*Aside*] Thy father, Pompey, would ne'er have made this treaty.—You and I have known, sir.

ENOBARBUS At sea, I think.

MENAS We have, sir.

ENOBARBUS You have done well by water.

MENAS And you by land.

ENOBARBUS I will praise any man that will praise me; though it cannot be denied what I have done by land.

MENAS Nor what I have done by water.

ENOBARBUS Yes, something you can deny for your own safety: you have been a great thief by sea.

MENAS And you by land.

ENOBARBUS There I deny my land service. But give me your hand, Menas: if our eyes had authority, here they might take two thieves kissing.

MENAS All men's faces are true, whatsome'er their hands are.

ENOBARBUS But there is never a fair woman has a true face.

MENAS No slander; they steal hearts.

ENOBARBUS We came hither to fight with you.

MENAS For my part, I am sorry it is turned to a drinking. Pompey doth this day laugh away his fortune.

ENOBARBUS If he do, sure he cannot weep't back again.

81 s.d. **Manet** (Latin for "remains"; the plural is properly *manent*, but the singular is often used for the plural, just as "exit" is often used for "exeunt") 83 **known** met 95 **deny my land service** (a quibble: "I claim exemption from military service" and "I deny that I have been a thief") 96 **authority** authority to arrest 97 **two thieves kissing** (1) two crooks fraternizing (2) two thieving hands clasping 98 **true** (1) honest (2) natural, without make-up

MENAS Y' have said, sir. We looked not for Mark Antony here. Pray you, is he married to Cleopatra?

ENOBARBUS Caesar's sister is called Octavia.

MENAS True, sir, she was the wife of Caius Marcellus.

ENOBARBUS But she is now the wife of Marcus Antonius.

MENAS Pray ye, sir?

ENOBARBUS 'Tis true.

MENAS Then is Caesar and he forever knit together.

ENOBARBUS If I were bound to divine of this unity, I would not prophesy so.

MENAS I think the policy of that purpose made more in the marriage than the love of the parties.

ENOBARBUS I think so too. But you shall find the band that seems to tie their friendship together will be the very strangler of their amity: Octavia is of a holy, cold, and still conversation.

MENAS Who would not have his wife so?

ENOBARBUS Not he that himself is not so; which is Mark Antony. He will to his Egyptian dish again: then shall the sighs of Octavia blow the fire up in Caesar, and, as I said before, that which is the strength of their amity shall prove the immediate author of their variance. Antony will use his affection where it is. He married but his occasion here.

MENAS And thus it may be. Come, sir, will you aboard? I have a health for you.

ENOBARBUS I shall take it, sir: we have used our throats in Egypt.

MENAS Come, let's away. *Exeunt*

113 **Pray ye** pardon me (incredulous) 118 **policy** political expediency 123 **still conversation** quiet manner 131 **occasion** convenience

[Scene VII. *On board Pompey's galley, off Misenum.*]

Music plays. Enter two or three Servants, with a banquet.

FIRST SERVANT Here they'll be, man. Some o' their plants are ill-rooted already; the least wind i' th' world will blow them down.

SECOND SERVANT Lepidus is high-colored.

FIRST SERVANT They have made him drink alms drink.

SECOND SERVANT As they pinch one another by the disposition, he cries out "No more"; reconciles them to his entreaty, and himself to th' drink.

FIRST SERVANT But it raises the greater war between him and his discretion.

SECOND SERVANT Why, this it is to have a name in great men's fellowship. I had as lief have a reed that will do me no service, as a partisan I could not heave.

FIRST SERVANT To be called into a huge sphere, and not to be seen to move in't, are the holes where eyes should be, which pitifully disaster the cheeks.

A sennet sounded. Enter Caesar, Antony, Pompey, Lepidus, Agrippa, Maecenas, Enobarbus, Menas, with other Captains.

II.vii.2 **plants** (pun on foot or sole of foot) 5 **alms drink** (1) remains of liquor usually saved for alms people (2) drinking done kindly, i.e., toasts given to smooth over quarrels 7 **No more** (1) no more quarreling (2) no more to drink 13 **partisan** great long-handled spear 14 **sphere** (1) area of influence (2) revolving circle holding a star or planet, in the old astronomy 15 **move** (1) be active, influential (2) circle, like a planet 16 **disaster** ruin (with a suggestion of a star's malignant influence) 16 s.d. **sennet** trumpet call signaling the entrance of a great man

ANTONY Thus do they, sir: they take the flow o' th' Nile
By certain scales i' th' pyramid. They know
By th' height, the lowness, or the mean, if dearth
Or foison follow. The higher Nilus swells,
The more it promises; as it ebbs, the seedsman
Upon the slime and ooze scatters his grain,
And shortly comes to harvest.

LEPIDUS Y' have strange serpents there.

ANTONY Ay, Lepidus.

LEPIDUS Your serpent of Egypt is bred now of your mud by the operation of your sun: so is your crocodile.

ANTONY They are so.

POMPEY Sit—and some wine! A health to Lepidus!

LEPIDUS I am not so well as I should be, but I'll ne'er out.

ENOBARBUS Not till you have slept; I fear me you'll be in till then.

LEPIDUS Nay, certainly, I have heard the Ptolemies' pyramises are very goodly things; without contradiction I have heard that.

MENAS [*Aside to Pompey*] Pompey, a word.

POMPEY [*Aside to Menas*] Say in mine ear: what is't?

MENAS [*Aside to Pompey*] Forsake thy seat, I do beseech thee, captain,
And hear me speak a word.

17 **take** measure 18 **scales i'** degree marks on 19–20 **dearth/Or foison** famine or plenty 26 **Your** (a colloquialism suggesting casual knowledgeableness) 31–32 **I'll ne'er out** I won't give in 34 **in** (1) in the game (2) in liquor 36 **pyramises** (a false plural made up from the Latin singular; Lepidus is pretentious and drunk)

POMPEY [*Aside to Menas*] Forbear me till anon.
[*Menas*] *whispers in's ear.*
This wine for Lepidus!

LEPIDUS What manner o' thing is your crocodile?

ANTONY It is shaped, sir, like itself, and it is as broad as it hath breadth; it is just so high as it is, and moves with it own organs. It lives by that which nourisheth it, and the elements once out of it, it transmigrates.

LEPIDUS What color is it of?

ANTONY Of it own color too.

LEPIDUS 'Tis a strange serpent.

ANTONY 'Tis so; and the tears of it are wet.

CAESAR Will this description satisfy him?

ANTONY With the health that Pompey gives him; else he is a very epicure.

POMPEY [*Aside to Menas*] Go hang, sir, hang! Tell me of that? Away!
Do as I bid you.—Where's this cup I called for?

MENAS [*Aside to Pompey*] If for the sake of merit thou wilt hear me,
Rise from thy stool.

POMPEY [*Aside to Menas*] I think th' art mad. The matter? [*Rises and walks aside.*]

MENAS I have ever held my cap off to thy fortunes.

POMPEY Thou hast served me with much faith. What's else to say?
Be jolly, lords.

ANTONY These quicksands, Lepidus,
Keep off them, for you sink.

40 **Forbear me till anon** leave me alone for a minute 45 **it** its 59 **held my cap off to** treated respectfully

MENAS Wilt thou be lord of all the world?

POMPEY What say'st thou?

MENAS Wilt thou be lord of the whole world? That's twice.

POMPEY How should that be?

MENAS But entertain it,
And though thou think me poor, I am the man
Will give thee all the world.

POMPEY Hast thou drunk well?

MENAS No, Pompey, I have kept me from the cup.
Thou art, if thou dar'st be, the earthly Jove:
Whate'er the ocean pales, or sky inclips,
Is thine, if thou wilt ha't.

POMPEY Show me which way.

MENAS These three world-sharers, these competitors,
Are in thy vessel. Let me cut the cable;
And when we are put off, fall to their throats.
All there is thine.

POMPEY Ah, this thou shouldst have done,
And not have spoke on't. In me 'tis villainy,
In thee't had been good service. Thou must know,
'Tis not my profit that does lead mine honor;
Mine honor, it. Repent that e'er thy tongue
Hath so betrayed thine act. Being done unknown,
I should have found it afterwards well done,
But must condemn it now. Desist, and drink.

MENAS [*Aside*] For this,
I'll never follow thy palled fortunes more.
Who seeks, and will not take when once 'tis offered,
Shall never find it more.

POMPEY This health to Lepidus!

65 **But entertain it** only accept it 70 **pales** fences in 70 **inclips** embraces 72 **competitors** partners 84 **palled** decayed

ANTONY Bear him ashore. I'll pledge it for him, Pompey.

ENOBARBUS Here's to thee, Menas!

MENAS Enobarbus, welcome.

POMPEY Fill till the cup be hid.

ENOBARBUS There's a strong fellow, Menas.
[*Points to the Servant who carries off Lepidus.*]

MENAS Why?

ENOBARBUS 'A bears the third part of the world, man; seest not?

MENAS The third part then is drunk. Would it were all,
That it might go on wheels!

ENOBARBUS Drink thou: increase the reels.

MENAS Come.

POMPEY This is not yet an Alexandrian feast.

ANTONY It ripens towards it. Strike the vessels, ho!
Here's to Caesar!

CAESAR I could well forbear't.
It's monstrous labor when I wash my brain
And it grows fouler.

ANTONY Be a child o' th' time.

CAESAR Possess it, I'll make answer;
But I had rather fast from all, four days,
Than drink so much in one.

ENOBARBUS Ha, my brave emperor!
Shall we dance now the Egyptian bacchanals
And celebrate our drink?

92 'A he 95 **go on wheels** (1) go easily (2) spin wildly 96 **reels** (1) revels (2) staggering movements 99 **Strike the vessels** broach the casks 103 **Possess ... answer** master the time (rather than be mastered by it) is my answer 106 **bacchanals** riotous salute to Bacchus, god of wine

POMPEY Let's ha't, good soldier.

ANTONY Come, let's all take hands
Till that the conquering wine hath steeped our sense
In soft and delicate Lethe.

ENOBARBUS All take hands:
Make battery to our ears with the loud music;
The while I'll place you; then the boy shall sing.
The holding every man shall bear as loud
As his strong sides can volley.

Music plays. Enobarbus places them hand in hand.

The Song

Come, thou monarch of the vine,
Plumpy Bacchus with pink eyne!
In thy fats our cares be drowned,
With thy grapes our hairs be crowned.
Cup us till the world go round,
Cup us till the world go round!

CAESAR What would you more? Pompey, good night.
Good brother,
Let me request you off: our graver business
Frowns at this levity. Gentle lords, let's part;
You see we have burnt our cheeks: strong Enobarb
Is weaker than the wine, and mine own tongue
Splits what it speaks: the wild disguise hath almost
Anticked us all. What needs more words? Good
night.
Good Antony, your hand.

POMPEY I'll try you on the shore.

ANTONY And shall, sir. Give's your hand.

110 **Lethe** forgetfulness 113 **holding** refrain 116 **pink eyne** half-closed eyes 117 **fats** vats 122 **request you off** beg you leave the ship with me 126 **disguise** drunken revelry 127 **Anticked** made fools of 128 **try you** test your power (to hold liquor)

POMPEY O, Antony,
You have my father's house. But what, we are friends!
Come down into the boat.
[*Exeunt all but Enobarbus and Menas.*]

ENOBARBUS [*To Menas*] Take heed you fall not.

MENAS I'll not on shore; no, to my cabin!
These drums! These trumpets, flutes! What!
Let Neptune hear we bid a loud farewell
To these great fellows. Sound and be hanged, sound out! *Sound a flourish, with drums.*

ENOBARBUS Hoo, says 'a. There's my cap.
[*Throws his cap in the air.*]

MENAS Hoa! Noble captain, come. *Exeunt.*

[ACT III

Scene I. *A plain in Syria.*]

Enter Ventidius as it were in triumph, the dead body of Pacorus borne before him; [*with Silius and other Romans*].

VENTIDIUS Now, darting Parthia, art thou struck; and now
Pleased fortune does of Marcus Crassus' death
Make me revenger. Bear the King's son's body
Before our army. Thy Pacorus, Orodes,
Pays this for Marcus Crassus.

SILIUS Noble Ventidius,
Whilst yet with Parthian blood thy sword is warm,
The fugitive Parthians follow. Spur through Media,
Mesopotamia, and the shelters whither
The routed fly. So thy grand captain, Antony,
Shall set thee on triumphant chariots, and
Put garlands on thy head.

III.i.1 **darting** (the Parthians' method of attack was to fling darts and then retreat swiftly, shooting arrows) 2 **Marcus Crassus** (treacherously killed by Orodes, King of Parthia and father of Pacorus)

VENTIDIUS O Silius, Silius,
I have done enough: a lower place, note well,
May make too great an act. For learn this, Silius,
Better to leave undone, than by our deed
Acquire too high a fame when him we serve's away.
Caesar and Antony have ever won
More in their officer than person. Sossius,
One of my place in Syria, his lieutenant,
For quick accumulation of renown,
Which he achieved by th' minute, lost his favor.
Who does i' th' wars more than his captain can
Becomes his captain's captain; and ambition
(The soldier's virtue) rather makes choice of loss
Than gain which darkens him.
I could do more to do Antonius good,
But 'twould offend him, and in his offense
Should my performance perish.

SILIUS Thou hast, Ventidius, that
Without the which a soldier and his sword
Grants scarce distinction. Thou wilt write to Antony?

VENTIDIUS I'll humbly signify what in his name,
That magical word of war, we have effected;
How, with his banners and his well-paid ranks,
The ne'er-yet-beaten horse of Parthia
We have jaded out o' th' field.

SILIUS Where is he now?

VENTIDIUS He purposeth to Athens; whither, with what haste
The weight we must convey with's will permit,
We shall appear before him.—On, there; pass along.
Exeunt.

12 **lower place** subordinate 18 **place** rank 18 **his** i.e., Antony's 20 **by th' minute** every minute, incessantly 27 **perish** i.e., lose its value to me 27–29 **that . . . distinction** that quality (i.e., discretion) without which it is hard to see any difference between a soldier and his sword 34 **jaded** driven like nags

[Scene II. *Rome. Caesar's house.*]

Enter Agrippa at one door, Enobarbus at another.

AGRIPPA What, are the brothers parted?

ENOBARBUS They have dispatched with Pompey; he is gone;
The other three are sealing. Octavia weeps
To part from Rome; Caesar is sad, and Lepidus
Since Pompey's feast, as Menas says, is troubled
With the green-sickness.

AGRIPPA 'Tis a noble Lepidus.

ENOBARBUS A very fine one. O, how he loves Caesar!

AGRIPPA Nay, but how dearly he adores Mark Antony!

ENOBARBUS Caesar? Why, he's the Jupiter of men.

AGRIPPA What's Antony? The god of Jupiter.

ENOBARBUS Spake you of Caesar? How! The non-pareil!

AGRIPPA O Antony! O thou Arabian bird!

ENOBARBUS Would you praise Caesar, say "Caesar": go no further.

AGRIPPA Indeed, he plied them both with excellent praises.

ENOBARBUS But he loves Caesar best, yet he loves Antony:

III.ii.1 **parted** departed 3 **sealing** making the last arrangements 6 **green-sickness** anemia supposed to affect lovesick girls (Lepidus' hangover is attributed to his love of Antony and Octavius) 11 **non-pareil** unequaled thing 12 **Arabian bird** phoenix (unique and immortal)

Hoo! Hearts, tongues, figures, scribes, bards, poets, cannot
Think, speak, cast, write, sing, number—hoo!—
His love to Antony. But as for Caesar,
Kneel down, kneel down, and wonder.

AGRIPPA Both he loves.

ENOBARBUS They are his shards, and he their beetle.
[*Trumpet within.*] So—
This is to horse. Adieu, noble Agrippa.

AGRIPPA Good fortune, worthy soldier, and farewell!

Enter Caesar, Antony, Lepidus, and Octavia.

ANTONY No further, sir.

CAESAR You take from me a great part of myself;
Use me well in't. Sister, prove such a wife
As my thoughts make thee, and as my farthest band
Shall pass on thy approof. Most noble Antony,
Let not the piece of virtue which is set
Betwixt us as the cement of our love
To keep it builded, be the ram to batter
The fortress of it: for better might we
Have loved without this mean, if on both parts
This be not cherished.

ANTONY Make me not offended
In your distrust.

CAESAR I have said.

ANTONY You shall not find,
Though you be therein curious, the least cause
For what you seem to fear. So the gods keep you
And make the hearts of Romans serve your ends!
We will here part.

CAESAR Farewell, my dearest sister, fare thee well.

17 **cast** count 20 **shards** wings 26–27 **As my thoughts ... approof** as I believe you to be, and such as I would give my utmost bond that you will triumphantly prove to be 28 **piece** masterpiece 29 **cement** (accented on first syllable) 32 **mean** intermediary 34 **In** by 35 **curious** overscrupulous

The elements be kind to thee, and make
Thy spirits all of comfort. Fare thee well.

OCTAVIA My noble brother!

ANTONY The April's in her eyes: it is love's spring,
And these the showers to bring it on. Be cheerful.

OCTAVIA Sir, look well to my husband's house; and—

CAESAR What,
Octavia?

OCTAVIA I'll tell you in your ear.

ANTONY Her tongue will not obey her heart, nor can
Her heart inform her tongue; the swan's-down feather
That stands upon the swell at the full of tide,
And neither way inclines.

ENOBARBUS [*Aside to Agrippa*] Will Caesar weep?

AGRIPPA [*Aside to Enobarbus*] He has a cloud in's face.

ENOBARBUS [*Aside to Agrippa*] He were the worse for that, were he a horse;
So is he, being a man.

AGRIPPA [*Aside to Enobarbus*] Why, Enobarbus,
When Antony found Julius Caesar dead,
He cried almost to roaring; and he wept
When at Philippi he found Brutus slain.

ENOBARBUS [*Aside to Agrippa*] That year indeed he was troubled with a rheum.
What willingly he did confound he wailed,
Believe't, till I wept too.

CAESAR No, sweet Octavia,

48–50 **the swan's ... inclines** (pressure of feeling urges Octavia to speak but prevents her from finding the words; she hesitates—like a feather held immobile by cross-currents at the turn of the tide—between husband and brother, love and sorrow, speech and silence) 52 **horse** (a horse with a dark face, or without a white star on its face, was less prized) 57 **rheum** watering at the eyes 58 **confound** destroy

You shall hear from me still: the time shall not
Outgo my thinking on you.

ANTONY Come, sir, come,
I'll wrestle with you in my strength of love:
Look, here I have you; thus I let you go,
And give you to the gods.

CAESAR Adieu; be happy!

LEPIDUS Let all the number of the stars give light
To thy fair way!

CAESAR Farewell, farewell! *Kisses Octavia.*

ANTONY Farewell!
Trumpets sound. Exeunt.

[Scene III. *Alexandria. Cleopatra's palace.*]

Enter Cleopatra, Charmian, Iras, and Alexas.

CLEOPATRA Where is the fellow?

ALEXAS Half afeard to come.

CLEOPATRA Go to, go to.
Enter the Messenger as before.
Come hither, sir.

ALEXAS Good Majesty,
Herod of Jewry dare not look upon you
But when you are well pleased.

CLEOPATRA That Herod's head
I'll have: but how, when Antony is gone
Through whom I might command it? Come thou near.

III.iii.2 s.d. **as before** i.e., nervously, as he left her 3 **Herod of Jewry** i.e., even the fiercest of tyrants

MESSENGER Most gracious Majesty!

CLEOPATRA Didst thou behold Octavia?

MESSENGER Ay, dread queen.

CLEOPATRA Where?

MESSENGER Madam, in Rome.
I looked her in the face, and saw her led
Between her brother and Mark Antony.

CLEOPATRA Is she as tall as me?

MESSENGER She is not, madam.

CLEOPATRA Didst hear her speak? Is she shrill-tongued or low?

MESSENGER Madam, I heard her speak; she is low-voiced.

CLEOPATRA That's not so good. He cannot like her long.

CHARMIAN Like her? O Isis! 'Tis impossible.

CLEOPATRA I think so, Charmian. Dull of tongue, and dwarfish.
What majesty is in her gait? Remember,
If e'er thou look'st on majesty.

MESSENGER She creeps:
Her motion and her station are as one.
She shows a body rather than a life,
A statue than a breather.

CLEOPATRA Is this certain?

MESSENGER Or I have no observance.

CHARMIAN Three in Egypt
Cannot make better note.

CLEOPATRA He's very knowing,

17 **That's not so good** (1) that's a nuisance. Nevertheless ... (2) that's a bad thing to be 22 **Her motion** ... one moving and standing still are the same thing with her

I do perceive't. There's nothing in her yet.
The fellow has good judgment.

CHARMIAN Excellent.

CLEOPATRA Guess at her years, I prithee.

MESSENGER Madam,
She was a widow——

CLEOPATRA Widow? Charmian, hark.

MESSENGER And I do think she's thirty.

CLEOPATRA Bear'st thou her face in mind? Is't long or round?

MESSENGER Round, even to faultiness.

CLEOPATRA For the most part, too, they are foolish that are so.
Her hair, what color?

MESSENGER Brown, madam; and her forehead
As low as she would wish it.

CLEOPATRA There's gold for thee.
Thou must not take my former sharpness ill;
I will employ thee back again: I find thee
Most fit for business. Go, make thee ready;
Our letters are prepared. [*Exit Messenger*.]

CHARMIAN A proper man.

CLEOPATRA Indeed he is so: I repent me much
That so I harried him. Why, methinks, by him,
This creature's no such thing.

CHARMIAN Nothing, madam.

CLEOPATRA The man hath seen some majesty, and should know.

CHARMIAN Hath he seen majesty? Isis else defend,
And serving you so long!

31 **thirty** (Cleopatra, being thirty-eight, lets this pass) 37 **As low . . . it** (colloquial phrase: low enough, and I hope she's pleased with it) 41 **proper** excellent 44 **no such thing** nothing very much 46 **Isis else defend** Isis forbid

CLEOPATRA I have one thing more to ask him yet, good Charmian;
But 'tis no matter, thou shalt bring him to me
Where I will write. All may be well enough.

CHARMIAN I warrant you, madam. *Exeunt.*

[Scene IV. *Athens. Antony's house.*]

Enter Antony and Octavia.

ANTONY Nay, nay, Octavia, not only that,
That were excusable, that and thousands more
Of semblable import—but he hath waged
New wars 'gainst Pompey; made his will, and read it
To public ear;
Spoke scantly of me: when perforce he could not
But pay me terms of honor, cold and sickly
He vented them, most narrow measure lent me;
When the best hint was given him, he not took't,
Or did it from his teeth.

OCTAVIA O, my good lord,
Believe not all; or, if you must believe,
Stomach not all. A more unhappy lady,
If this division chance, ne'er stood between,
Praying for both parts.
The good gods will mock me presently
When I shall pray "O, bless my lord and husband!"—
Undo that prayer by crying out as loud
"O, bless my brother!" Husband win, win brother,
Prays, and destroys the prayer; no midway
'Twixt these extremes at all.

III.iv.3 **semblable import** similar significance 4–5 **made ... ear** i.e., like Julius Caesar, made a will benefiting the people and so worked up popular support 8 **narrow measure** little credit 10 **from his teeth** grudgingly 12 **Stomach** resent 15 **presently** immediately

ANTONY Gentle Octavia,
Let your best love draw to that point which seeks
Best to preserve it. If I lose mine honor,
I lose myself: better I were not yours
Than yours so branchless. But, as you requested,
Yourself shall go between's: the meantime, lady,
I'll raise the preparation of a war
Shall stain your brother. Make your soonest haste;
So your desires are yours.

OCTAVIA Thanks to my lord.
The Jove of power make me, most weak, most weak,
Your reconciler! Wars 'twixt you twain would be
As if the world should cleave, and that slain men
Should solder up the rift.

ANTONY When it appears to you where this begins,
Turn your displeasure that way, for our faults
Can never be so equal that your love
Can equally move with them. Provide your going;
Choose your own company, and command what cost
Your heart has mind to. *Exeunt.*

[Scene V. *Athens. Antony's house.*]

Enter Enobarbus and Eros.

ENOBARBUS How now, friend Eros?

EROS There's strange news come, sir.

ENOBARBUS What, man?

EROS Caesar and Lepidus have made wars upon Pompey.

ENOBARBUS This is old. What is the success?

24 **branchless** mutilated 27 **stain** eclipse (the reputation of) III.v.6 **success** sequel

EROS Caesar, having made use of him in the wars 'gainst Pompey, presently denied him rivality, would not let him partake in the glory of the action; and not resting here, accuses him of letters he had formerly wrote to Pompey; upon his own appeal, seizes him; so the poor third is up, till death enlarge his confine.

ENOBARBUS Then, world, thou hast a pair of chaps, no more;
And throw between them all the food thou hast,
They'll grind the one the other. Where's Antony?

EROS He's walking in the garden—thus, and spurns
The rush that lies before him; cries "Fool Lepidus!"
And threats the throat of that his officer
That murd'red Pompey.

ENOBARBUS Our great navy's rigged.

EROS For Italy and Caesar. More, Domitius:
My lord desires you presently. My news
I might have told hereafter.

ENOBARBUS 'Twill be naught;
But let it be. Bring me to Antony.

EROS Come, sir. *Exeunt.*

8 **rivality** partnership 11 **upon his own appeal** on his (Caesar's) own accusation 12 **up** shut up, imprisoned 14 **chaps** jaws 15–16 **And throw ... other** and feed them with all the victims in the world, they (Caesar and Antony) will nevertheless meet, and one consume the other 20 **Pompey** (Pompey has by now been murdered, according to Plutarch by Antony's command; Pompey would have proved useful to Antony in the coming war)

[Scene VI. *Rome. Caesar's house.*]

Enter Agrippa, Maecenas, and Caesar.

CAESAR Contemning Rome, he has done all this and more
In Alexandria. Here's the manner of't:
I' th' marketplace on a tribunal silvered,
Cleopatra and himself in chairs of gold
Were publicly enthroned; at the feet sat
Caesarion, whom they call my father's son,
And all the unlawful issue that their lust
Since then hath made between them. Unto her
He gave the stablishment of Egypt; made her
Of lower Syria, Cyprus, Lydia,
Absolute queen.

MAECENAS This in the public eye?

CAESAR I' th' common showplace, where they exercise.
His sons he there proclaimed the kings of kings:
Great Media, Parthia, and Armenia
He gave to Alexander; to Ptolemy he assigned
Syria, Cilicia, and Phoenicia. She
In th' habiliments of the goddess Isis
That day appeared, and oft before gave audience,
As 'tis reported, so.

MAECENAS Let Rome be thus informed.

AGRIPPA Who, queasy with his insolence already,
Will their good thoughts call from him.

III.vi.1 **Contemning** despising 6 **my father** (Octavius had been adopted by Julius Caesar) 9 **stablishment** possession 20 **queasy** disgusted

CAESAR The people knows it, and have now received
His accusations.

AGRIPPA Who does he accuse?

CAESAR Caesar: and that, having in Sicily
Sextus Pompeius spoiled, we had not rated him
His part o' th' isle. Then does he say he lent me
Some shipping, unrestored. Lastly, he frets
That Lepidus of the triumvirate
Should be deposed; and, being, that we detain
All his revenue.

AGRIPPA Sir, this should be answered.

CAESAR 'Tis done already, and the messenger gone.
I have told him Lepidus was grown too cruel,
That he his high authority abused
And did deserve his change; for what I have
conquered,
I grant him part; but then in his Armenia,
And other of his conquered kingdoms, I
Demand the like.

MAECENAS He'll never yield to that.

CAESAR Nor must not then be yielded to in this.

Enter Octavia with her Train.

OCTAVIA Hail, Caesar, and my lord, hail, most dear
Caesar!

CAESAR That ever I should call thee castaway!

OCTAVIA You have not called me so, nor have you
cause.

CAESAR Why have you stol'n upon us thus? You come
not
Like Caesar's sister. The wife of Antony
Should have an army for an usher, and
The neighs of horse to tell of her approach

25 **spoiled** despoiled 25 **rated** allotted 30 **revenue** (accented on second syllable)

Long ere she did appear. The trees by th' way
Should have borne men, and expectation fainted,
Longing for what it had not. Nay, the dust
Should have ascended to the roof of heaven,
Raised by your populous troops. But you are come
A market maid to Rome, and have prevented
The ostentation of our love; which, left unshown,
Is often left unloved. We should have met you
By sea and land, supplying every stage
With an augmented greeting.

OCTAVIA Good my lord,
To come thus was I not constrained, but did it
On my free will. My lord, Mark Antony,
Hearing that you prepared for war, acquainted
My grievèd ear withal; whereon I begged
His pardon for return.

CAESAR Which soon he granted,
Being an abstract 'tween his lust and him.

OCTAVIA Do not say so, my lord.

CAESAR I have eyes upon him,
And his affairs come to me on the wind.
Where is he now?

OCTAVIA My lord, in Athens.

CAESAR No, my most wrongèd sister, Cleopatra
Hath nodded him to her. He hath given his empire
Up to a whore, who now are levying
The kings o' th' earth for war. He hath assembled
Bocchus, the King of Libya; Archelaus,
Of Cappadocia; Philadelphos, King
Of Paphlagonia; the Thracian king, Adallas;
King Mauchus of Arabia; King of Pont;
Herod of Jewry; Mithridates, King
Of Comagene; Polemon and Amyntas,

52 **ostentation** public display 53 **left unloved** (1) unrequited (2) thought not to exist 61 **abstract** (1) immaterial, merely notional thing (2) short cut (3) symbol (of what prevented him from indulging his lust) 67 **who now** and they now

The Kings of Mede and Lycaonia;
With a more larger list of scepters.

OCTAVIA Ay me most wretched,
That have my heart parted betwixt two friends
That does afflict each other!

CAESAR Welcome hither.
Your letters did withhold our breaking forth,
Till we perceived both how you were wrong led
And we in negligent danger. Cheer your heart:
Be you not troubled with the time, which drives
O'er your content these strong necessities;
But let determined things to destiny
Hold unbewailed their way. Welcome to Rome,
Nothing more dear to me. You are abused
Beyond the mark of thought: and the high gods,
To do you justice, makes his ministers
Of us and those that love you. Best of comfort,
And ever welcome to us.

AGRIPPA Welcome, lady.

MAECENAS Welcome, dear madam.
Each heart in Rome does love and pity you.
Only th' adulterous Antony, most large
In his abominations, turns you off
And gives his potent regiment to a trull
That noises it against us.

OCTAVIA Is it so, sir?

CAESAR Most certain. Sister, welcome. Pray you
Be ever known to patience. My dear'st sister!
Exeunt.

81 **in negligent danger** endangered by doing nothing 86 **abused** deceived 87 **mark** reach 88–89 **makes . . . us** make us their agents of justice 93 **large** loose, licentious 95 **potent regiment to a trull** powerful authority to a prostitute 96 **noises it** is clamorous

[Scene VII. *Near Actium. Antony's camp.*]

Enter Cleopatra and Enobarbus.

CLEOPATRA I will be even with thee, doubt it not.

ENOBARBUS But why, why, why?

CLEOPATRA Thou hast forspoke my being in these wars,
And say'st it is not fit.

ENOBARBUS Well, is it, is it?

CLEOPATRA Is't not denounced against us? Why should not we
Be there in person?

ENOBARBUS [*Aside*] Well, I could reply:
If we should serve with horse and mares together,
The horse were merely lost; the mares would bear
A soldier and his horse.

CLEOPATRA What is't you say?

ENOBARBUS Your presence needs must puzzle Antony;
Take from his heart, take from his brain, from's time,
What should not then be spared. He is already
Traduced for levity; and 'tis said in Rome
That Photinus an eunuch and your maids
Manage this war.

CLEOPATRA Sink Rome, and their tongues rot
That speak against us! A charge we bear i' th' war,

III.vii.3 **forspoke** spoken against 5 **denounced against us** (Caesar had declared, or denounced—the technical term—war on Cleopatra personally) 8 **merely** utterly 10 **puzzle** bewilder, bring to a standstill

And as the president of my kingdom will
Appear there for a man. Speak not against it,
I will not stay behind.

Enter Antony and Canidius.

ENOBARBUS Nay, I have done.
Here comes the Emperor.

ANTONY Is it not strange, Canidius,
That from Tarentum and Brundusium
He could so quickly cut the Ionian sea
And take in Toryne?—You have heard on't, sweet?

CLEOPATRA Celerity is never more admired
Than by the negligent.

ANTONY A good rebuke,
Which might have well becomed the best of men
To taunt at slackness. Canidius, we
Will fight with him by sea.

CLEOPATRA By sea; what else?

CANIDIUS Why will my lord do so?

ANTONY For that he dares us to't.

ENOBARBUS So hath my lord dared him to single fight.

CANIDIUS Ay, and to wage this battle at Pharsalia,
Where Caesar fought with Pompey: but these offers,
Which serve not for his vantage, he shakes off;
And so should you.

ENOBARBUS Your ships are not well manned;
Your mariners are muleters, reapers, people
Ingrossed by swift impress. In Caesar's fleet
Are those that often have 'gainst Pompey fought;
Their ships are yare, yours, heavy: no disgrace
Shall fall you for refusing him at sea,
Being prepared for land.

23 **take in** conquer 29 **For that** because 35 **muleters** mule drivers 36 **Ingrossed by swift impress** collected by hasty conscription 38 **yare** swift, nimble

ANTONY By sea, by sea.

ENOBARBUS Most worthy sir, you therein throw away
The absolute soldiership you have by land,
Distract your army, which doth most consist
Of war-marked footmen, leave unexecuted
Your own renownèd knowledge, quite forgo
The way which promises assurance, and
Give up yourself merely to chance and hazard
From firm security.

ANTONY I'll fight at sea.

CLEOPATRA I have sixty sails, Caesar none better.

ANTONY Our overplus of shipping will we burn,
And with the rest full-manned, from th' head of Actium
Beat th' approaching Caesar. But if we fail,
We then can do't at land.

Enter a Messenger.

Thy business?

MESSENGER The news is true, my lord, he is descried;
Caesar has taken Toryne.

ANTONY Can he be there in person? 'Tis impossible;
Strange that his power should be. Canidius,
Our nineteen legions thou shalt hold by land
And our twelve thousand horse. We'll to our ship.
Away, my Thetis!

Enter a Soldier.

How now, worthy soldier?

SOLDIER O noble Emperor, do not fight by sea,
Trust not to rotten planks. Do you misdoubt
This sword and these my wounds? Let th' Egyptians
And the Phoenicians go a-ducking: we

43 **Distract** (1) divide (2) confuse 57 **power** army 60 **Thetis** sea goddess, mother of Achilles 64 **a-ducking** (1) swimming like ducks (2) tipped underwater

Have used to conquer standing on the earth
And fighting foot to foot.

ANTONY Well, well: away!

Exit Antony, Cleopatra, and Enobarbus.

SOLDIER By Hercules, I think I am i' th' right.

CANIDIUS Soldier, thou art; but his whole action grows
Not in the power on't: so our leader's led,
And we are women's men.

SOLDIER You keep by land
The legions and the horse whole, do you not?

CANIDIUS Marcus Octavius, Marcus Justeius,
Publicola, and Caelius are for sea;
But we keep whole by land. This speed of Caesar's
Carries beyond belief.

SOLDIER While he was yet in Rome,
His power went out in such distractions as
Beguiled all spies.

CANIDIUS Who's his lieutenant, hear you?

SOLDIER They say, one Taurus.

CANIDIUS Well I know the man.

Enter a Messenger.

MESSENGER The Emperor calls Canidius.

CANIDIUS With news the time's with labor, and throws forth
Each minute some. *Exeunt.*

68–69 **his whole . . . power on't** his entire plan of action has developed away from its sources of power 75 **Carries** shoots him forward 76 **distractions** divisions 80–81 **With news . . . some** i.e., more news is born every minute

[Scene VIII. *A plain near Actium.*]

Enter Caesar, with his Army, marching.

CAESAR Taurus!

TAURUS My lord?

CAESAR Strike not by land; keep whole, provoke not battle
Till we have done at sea. Do not exceed
The prescript of this scroll. Our fortune lies
Upon this jump. *Exit* [*with Taurus and the Army*].

[Scene IX. *Another part of the plain.*]

Enter Antony and Enobarbus.

ANTONY Set we our squadrons on yond side o' th' hill
In eye of Caesar's battle; from which place
We may the number of the ships behold,
And so proceed accordingly. *Exit* [*with Enobarbus*].

III.viii.6 **jump** risk III.ix.2 **battle** battle line

[Scene X. *Another part of the plain.*]

Canidius marcheth with his land army one way over the stage, and Taurus, the lieutenant of Caesar, [*with his army,*] *the other way. After their going in is heard the noise of a sea fight. Alarum. Enter Enobarbus.*

ENOBARBUS Naught, naught, all naught! I can behold
no longer.
Th' *Antoniad*, the Egyptian admiral,
With all their sixty, fly and turn the rudder:
To see't mine eyes are blasted.

Enter Scarus.

SCARUS Gods and goddesses,
All the whole synod of them!

ENOBARBUS What's thy passion?

SCARUS The greater cantle of the world is lost
With very ignorance; we have kissed away
Kingdoms and provinces.

ENOBARBUS How appears the fight?

SCARUS On our side like the tokened pestilence,
Where death is sure. Yon ribaudred nag of
Egypt—
Whom leprosy o'ertake!—i' th' midst o' th' fight,
When vantage like a pair of twins appeared,

III.x.1 **Naught** i.e., all's come to nothing 2 **admiral** flagship 5 **synod** assembly 6 **cantle** segment of a sphere 7 **With very ignorance** by utter stupidity 9 **tokened pestilence** first fatal symptoms of the plague 10 **ribaudred** (apparently from "ribald," but of uncertain meaning; probably just a cursing word; "filthy")

Both as the same, or rather ours the elder,
The breese upon her, like a cow in June,
Hoists sails, and flies.

ENOBARBUS That I beheld:
Mine eyes did sicken at the sight, and could not
Endure a further view.

SCARUS She once being loofed,
The noble ruin of her magic, Antony,
Claps on his sea wing, and (like a doting mallard)
Leaving the fight in height, flies after her.
I never saw an action of such shame;
Experience, manhood, honor, ne'er before
Did violate so itself.

ENOBARBUS Alack, alack!

Enter Canidius.

CANIDIUS Our fortune on the sea is out of breath,
And sinks most lamentably. Had our general
Been what he knew himself, it had gone well.
O, he has given example for our flight
Most grossly by his own.

ENOBARBUS Ay, are you thereabouts?
Why then, good night indeed.

CANIDIUS Toward Peloponnesus are they fled.

SCARUS 'Tis easy to 't; and there I will attend
What further comes.

CANIDIUS To Caesar will I render
My legions and my horse; six kings already
Show me the way of yielding.

13 **elder** greater 14 **breese** gadfly (with pun on "breeze," "wind") 17 **loofed** (1) luffed, i.e., with the head of a ship turned into the wind (2) aloofed, rapidly departing 19 **mallard** wild duck 26 **Been . . . himself** been his true self—and he knew what that was 28 **are you thereabouts** is that where your thoughts are

ENOBARBUS I'll yet follow
The wounded chance of Antony, though my reason
Sits in the wind against me. [*Exeunt.*]

[Scene XI. *Alexandria. Cleopatra's palace.*]

Enter Antony with Attendants.

ANTONY Hark! The land bids me tread no more upon't,
It is ashamed to bear me. Friends, come hither.
I am so lated in the world that I
Have lost my way forever. I have a ship
Laden with gold: take that, divide it; fly,
And make your peace with Caesar.

OMNES Fly? Not we.

ANTONY I have fled myself, and have instructed cowards
To run and show their shoulders. Friends, be gone.
I have myself resolved upon a course
Which has no need of you. Be gone.
My treasure's in the harbor. Take it. O,
I followed that I blush to look upon.
My very hairs do mutiny, for the white
Reprove the brown for rashness, and they them
For fear and doting. Friends, be gone; you shall
Have letters from me to some friends that will
Sweep your way for you. Pray you, look not sad,
Nor make replies of loathness; take the hint
Which my despair proclaims. Let that be left

35 **wounded chance** broken fortunes 36 **Sits ... me** is opposed to me
III.xi.3 **lated** belated (as of a traveler, caught by the encroaching night)
12 **that** what 14 **rashness** foolishness 18 **hint** opportunity

Which leaves itself. To the seaside straightway!
I will possess you of that ship and treasure.
Leave me, I pray, a little: pray you now,
Nay, do so; for indeed I have lost command,
Therefore I pray you. I'll see you by and by.
Sits down.

Enter Cleopatra led by Charmian, [*Iras,*] *and Eros.*

EROS Nay, gentle madam, to him, comfort him.

IRAS Do, most dear queen.

CHARMIAN Do: why, what else?

CLEOPATRA Let me sit down. O, Juno!

ANTONY No, no, no, no, no.

EROS See you here, sir?

ANTONY O, fie, fie, fie!

CHARMIAN Madam!

IRAS Madam, O, good empress!

EROS Sir, sir!

ANTONY Yes, my lord, yes. He at Philippi kept
His sword e'en like a dancer, while I struck
The lean and wrinkled Cassius; and 'twas I
That the mad Brutus ended: he alone
Dealt on lieutenantry, and no practice had
In the brave squares of war: yet now—No matter.

CLEOPATRA Ah, stand by.

EROS The Queen, my lord, the Queen.

19–20 **Let that . . . itself** leave the man who has taken leave of his senses (?); leave the man who has given himself up for lost (?) 23 **I have lost command** (1) my feelings are becoming uncontrollable (2) I have lost the right to order you 35 **He** i.e., Octavius 36 **like a dancer** i.e., for ornament only 39 **Dealt on lieutenantry** told his subordinates how to fight 40 **squares** squadrons

IRAS Go to him, madam, speak to him;
He is unqualitied with very shame.

CLEOPATRA Well then, sustain me. O!

EROS Most noble sir, arise. The Queen approaches.
Her head's declined, and death will seize her, but
Your comfort makes the rescue.

ANTONY I have offended reputation,
A most unnoble swerving.

EROS Sir, the Queen.

ANTONY O, whither hast thou led me, Egypt? See
How I convey my shame out of thine eyes
By looking back what I have left behind
'Stroyed in dishonor.

CLEOPATRA O my lord, my lord,
Forgive my fearful sails! I little thought
You would have followed.

ANTONY Egypt, thou knew'st too well
My heart was to thy rudder tied by th' strings,
And thou shouldst tow me after. O'er my spirit
Thy full supremacy thou knew'st, and that
Thy beck might from the bidding of the gods
Command me.

CLEOPATRA O, my pardon!

ANTONY Now I must
To the young man send humble treaties, dodge
And palter in the shifts of lowness, who
With half the bulk o' th' world played as I pleased,
Making and marring fortunes. You did know
How much you were my conqueror, and that
My sword, made weak by my affection, would
Obey it on all cause.

44 **unqualitied** beside himself 47 **but** unless 49 **reputation** honor 53 **By looking back** i.e., by averting my eyes and by lonely meditation on 63 **palter . . . lowness** employ the tricks of a man brought low 67 **affection** love

CLEOPATRA Pardon, pardon!

ANTONY Fall not a tear, I say; one of them rates
All that is won and lost. Give me a kiss;
Even this repays me. We sent our schoolmaster:
Is 'a come back? Love, I am full of lead.
Some wine, within there, and our viands! Fortune knows
We scorn her most when most she offers blows.

Exeunt.

[Scene XII. *Egypt. Caesar's camp.*]

Enter Caesar, Agrippa, Dolabella, [*Thidias,*] *with others.*

CAESAR Let him appear that's come from Antony.
Know you him?

DOLABELLA Caesar, 'tis his schoolmaster:
An argument that he is plucked, when hither
He sends so poor a pinion of his wing,
Which had superfluous kings for messengers
Not many moons gone by.

Enter Ambassador from Antony.

CAESAR Approach and speak.

AMBASSADOR Such as I am, I come from Antony.
I was of late as petty to his ends
As is the morn-dew on the myrtle leaf
To his grand sea.

69 **Fall** let fall 69 **rates** (1) is worth (2) berates, rebukes as unimportant 71 **our schoolmaster** i.e., the tutor of his and Cleopatra's children III.xii.10 **To his grand sea** (1) to the great sea that is its source and end (2) to the great sea that is Antony

CAESAR Be't so. Declare thine office.

AMBASSADOR Lord of his fortunes he salutes thee, and
Requires to live in Egypt; which not granted,
He lessons his requests, and to thee sues
To let him breathe between the heavens and earth,
A private man in Athens: this for him.
Next, Cleopatra does confess thy greatness,
Submits her to thy might, and of thee craves
The circle of the Ptolemies for her heirs,
Now hazarded to thy grace.

CAESAR For Antony,
I have no ears to his request. The Queen
Of audience nor desire shall fail, so she
From Egypt drive her all-disgracèd friend
Or take his life there. This if she perform,
She shall not sue unheard. So to them both.

AMBASSADOR Fortune pursue thee!

CAESAR Bring him through the bands.
[*Exit Ambassador.*]
[*To Thidias*] To try thy eloquence now 'tis time.
Dispatch.
From Antony win Cleopatra: promise,
And in our name, what she requires; add more,
From thine invention, offers. Women are not
In their best fortunes strong, but want will perjure
The ne'er-touched vestal. Try thy cunning,
Thidias;
Make thine own edict for thy pains, which we
Will answer as a law.

THIDIAS Caesar, I go.

12 **Requires** requests 13 **lessons** disciplines (though perhaps the word should be emended to "lessens") 18 **circle** crown 19 **Now hazarded to thy grace** now dependent for its fate on your favor 21 so provided that 27–29 **promise . . . offers** (possibly corrupt; rearranges to the much more lucid: "promise/What she requires; and in our name add more/Offers from thine invention") 30 **perjure** make a perjuror of 31 **ne'er-touched vestal** immaculate virgin 32 **Make thine own edict** decree what you think the right reward

CAESAR Observe how Antony becomes his flaw,
And what thou think'st his very action speaks
In every power that moves.

THIDIAS Caesar, I shall. *Exeunt.*

[Scene XIII. *Alexandria. Cleopatra's palace.*]

Enter Cleopatra, Enobarbus, Charmian, and Iras.

CLEOPATRA What shall we do, Enobarbus?

ENOBARBUS Think, and die.

CLEOPATRA Is Antony, or we, in fault for this?

ENOBARBUS Antony only, that would make his will
Lord of his reason. What though you fled
From that great face of war, whose several ranges
Frighted each other? Why should he follow?
The itch of his affection should not then
Have nicked his captainship, at such a point,
When half to half the world opposed, he being
The merèd question. 'Twas a shame no less
Than was his loss, to course your flying flags
And leave his navy gazing.

CLEOPATRA Prithee, peace.

Enter the Ambassador, with Antony.

ANTONY Is that his answer?

AMBASSADOR Ay, my lord.

ANTONY The Queen shall then have courtesy, so she

34 **becomes his flaw** takes his fall III.xiii.3 **will** desire, lust 7 **affection** passion 8 **nicked** (1) maimed (2) got the better of 10 **merèd question** sole ground of dispute 11 **course** pursue 15 **so** if

Will yield us up.

AMBASSADOR He says so.

ANTONY Let her know't.
To the boy Caesar send this grizzled head,
And he will fill thy wishes to the brim
With principalities.

CLEOPATRA That head, my lord?

ANTONY To him again! Tell him he wears the rose
Of youth upon him; from which the world should note
Something particular. His coin, ships, legions
May be a coward's, whose ministers would prevail
Under the service of a child as soon
As i' th' command of Caesar. I dare him therefore
To lay his gay comparisons apart
And answer me declined, sword against sword,
Ourselves alone. I'll write it: follow me.
[*Exeunt Antony and Ambassador*.]

ENOBARBUS [*Aside*] Yes, like enough: high-battled Caesar will
Unstate his happiness and be staged to th' show
Against a sworder! I see men's judgments are
A parcel of their fortunes, and things outward
Do draw the inward quality after them
To suffer all alike. That he should dream,
Knowing all measures, the full Caesar will
Answer his emptiness! Caesar, thou hast subdued
His judgment too.

Enter a Servant.

SERVANT A messenger from Caesar.

22 **Something particular** i.e., a fact concerning Caesar 26 **comparisons** i.e., the ships, etc., which make him Antony's superior by comparison 27 **declined** i.e., in years and fortunes 29 **high-battled** elev^ted high by great armies 30–31 **Unstate . . . sworder** strip his good fortune of all its power, and make a public exhibition of himself against a gladiator 32 **parcel** part 34 **suffer all alike** deteriorate together 35 **knowing all measures** having experienced every measure of fortune

CLEOPATRA What, no more ceremony? See, my women,
Against the blown rose may they stop their nose
That kneeled unto the buds. Admit him, sir.
[*Exit Servant.*]

ENOBARBUS [*Aside*] Mine honesty and I begin to square.
The loyalty well held to fools does make
Our faith mere folly: yet he that can endure
To follow with allegiance a fall'n lord
Does conquer him that did his master conquer
And earns a place i' th' story.

Enter Thidias.

CLEOPATRA Caesar's will?

THIDIAS Hear it apart.

CLEOPATRA None but friends: say boldly.

THIDIAS So, haply, are they friends to Antony.

ENOBARBUS He needs as many, sir, as Caesar has,
Or needs not us. If Caesar please, our master
Will leap to be his friend; for us, you know,
Whose he is we are, and that is Caesar's.

THIDIAS So.
Thus then, thou most renowned: Caesar entreats
Not to consider in what case thou stand'st
Further than he is Caesar.

CLEOPATRA Go on: right royal.

THIDIAS He knows that you embraced not Antony
As you did love, but as you feared him.

CLEOPATRA O!

THIDIAS The scars upon your honor therefore he
Does pity, as constrainèd blemishes,
Not as deserved.

CLEOPATRA He is a god, and knows

41 **square** quarrel 43 **faith** faithfulness 48 **haply** perhaps 55 **Caesar** i.e., famous for generosity

What is most right. Mine honor was not yielded,
But conquered merely.

ENOBARBUS [*Aside*] To be sure of that,
I will ask Antony. Sir, sir, thou art so leaky
That we must leave thee to thy sinking, for
Thy dearest quit thee. *Exit Enobarbus.*

THIDIAS Shall I say to Caesar
What you require of him? For he partly begs
To be desired to give. It much would please him
That of his fortunes you should make a staff
To lean upon. But it would warm his spirits
To hear from me you had left Antony,
And put yourself under his shroud,
The universal landlord.

CLEOPATRA What's your name?

THIDIAS My name is Thidias.

CLEOPATRA Most kind messenger,
Say to great Caesar this: in deputation
I kiss his conqu'ring hand; tell him I am prompt
To lay my crown at's feet, and there to kneel.
Tell him, from his all-obeying breath I hear
The doom of Egypt.

THIDIAS 'Tis your noblest course:
Wisdom and fortune combating together,
If that the former dare but what it can,
No chance may shake it. Give me grace to lay
My duty on your hand.

CLEOPATRA [*Giving her hand*] Your Caesar's father oft,
When he hath mused of taking kingdoms in,

62 **merely** utterly 66 **require** request 71 **shroud** protection 74 **in deputation** by proxy 77 **all-obeying** which all obey 78 **doom of Egypt** judgment of the Queen of Egypt 80 **If that . . . it can** if a wise man has the courage merely to go on being wise 82 **duty** i.e., a kiss

Bestowed his lips on that unworthy place,
As it rained kisses.

Enter Antony and Enobarbus.

ANTONY Favors, by Jove that thunders!
What art thou, fellow?

THIDIAS One that but performs
The bidding of the fullest man, and worthiest
To have command obeyed.

ENOBARBUS [*Aside*] You will be whipped.

ANTONY [*Cclling for Servants*] Approach there!—Ah, you kite! Now, gods and devils!
Authority melts from me. Of late, when I cried "Ho!"
Like boys unto a muss kings would start forth,
And cry "Your will?" Have you no ears? I am
Antony yet.

Enter a Servant [followed by others].

Take hence this Jack and whip him.

ENOBARBUS [*Aside*] 'Tis better playing with a lion's whelp
Than with an old one dying.

ANTONY Moon and stars!
Whip him! Were't twenty of the greatest tributaries
That do acknowledge Caesar, should I find them
So saucy with the hand of she here—what's her name
Since she was Cleopatra? Whip him, fellows,
Till like a boy you see him cringe his face
And whine aloud for mercy. Take him hence.

THIDIAS Mark Antony——

ANTONY Tug him away. Being whipped,

85 **As** as if 87 **fullest** greatest (in character and fortunes) 89 **kite** ignoble bird of prey 91 **muss** scramble; fighting heap of bodies 93 **Jack** fellow, knave

Bring him again. The Jack of Caesar's shall
Bear us an errand to him.

Exeunt [Servants] with Thidias.

You were half blasted ere I knew you. Ha!
Have I my pillow left unpressed in Rome,
Forborne the getting of a lawful race,
And by a gem of women, to be abused
By one that looks on feeders?

CLEOPATRA Good my lord——

ANTONY You have been a boggler ever:
But when we in our viciousness grow hard
(O misery on't!) the wise gods seel our eyes,
In our own filth drop our clear judgments, make us
Adore our errors, laugh at's while we strut
To our confusion.

CLEOPATRA O, is't come to this?

ANTONY I found you as a morsel cold upon
Dead Caesar's trencher: nay, you were a fragment
Of Gneius Pompey's, besides what hotter hours,
Unregist'red in vulgar fame, you have
Luxuriously picked out. For I am sure,
Though you can guess what temperance should be,
You know not what it is.

CLEOPATRA Wherefore is this?

ANTONY To let a fellow that will take rewards
And say "God quit you!" be familiar with
My playfellow, your hand, this kingly seal
And plighter of high hearts. O, that I were
Upon the hill of Basan to outroar

105 **blasted** worn out 107 **getting** begetting 109 **feeders** servants, parasites 110 **boggler** waverer 112 **seel** blind (in falconry, a hawk's eyelids are seeled, or sewn up, before it grows used to being hooded) 115 **confusion** destruction 117 **trencher** wooden dish 117 **fragment** leftover 119 **vulgar fame** common knowledge, popular rumor 120 **Luxuriously picked out** lecherously selected 124 **quit** reward

The hornèd herd! For I have savage cause,
And to proclaim it civilly were like
A haltered neck which does the hangman thank
For being yare about him.

Enter a Servant with Thidias.

Is he whipped?

SERVANT Soundly, my lord.

ANTONY Cried he? And begged 'a pardon?

SERVANT He did ask favor.

ANTONY If that thy father live, let him repent
Thou wast not made his daughter; and be thou sorry
To follow Caesar in his triumph, since
Thou hast been whipped for following him. Henceforth
The white hand of a lady fever thee,
Shake thou to look on't. Get thee back to Caesar,
Tell him thy entertainment: look thou say
He makes me angry with him; for he seems
Proud and disdainful, harping on what I am,
Not what he knew I was. He makes me angry,
And at this time most easy 'tis to do't,
When my good stars that were my former guides
Have empty left their orbs and shot their fires
Into th' abysm of hell. If he mislike
My speech and what is done, tell him he has
Hipparchus, my enfranchèd bondman, whom
He may at pleasure whip, or hang, or torture,
As he shall like, to quit me. Urge it thou.
Hence with thy stripes, be gone! *Exit Thidias.*

CLEOPATRA Have you done yet?

ANTONY Alack, our terrene moon

126–28 **O that ... hornèd herd** i.e., Antony is so well provided with the cuckold's horns that he should be among the "fat bulls of Basan" of Psalm 22 131 **yare** deft 140 **entertainment** reception 146 **orbs** spheres 149 **enfranchèd** freed 153 **terrene moon** earthly Isis (goddess of the moon)

Is now eclipsed, and it portends alone
The fall of Antony.

CLEOPATRA I must stay his time.

ANTONY To flatter Caesar, would you mingle eyes
With one that ties his points?

CLEOPATRA Not know me yet?

ANTONY Cold-hearted toward me?

CLEOPATRA Ah, dear, if I be so,
From my cold heart let heaven engender hail,
And poison it in the source, and the first stone
Drop in my neck: as it determines, so
Dissolve my life! The next Caesarion smite,
Till by degrees the memory of my womb,
Together with my brave Egyptians all,
By the discandying of this pelleted storm,
Lie graveless, till the flies and gnats of Nile
Have buried them for prey!

ANTONY I am satisfied.
Caesar sits down in Alexandria, where
I will oppose his fate. Our force by land
Hath nobly held; our severed navy too
Have knit again, and fleet, threat'ning most sea-like.
Where hast thou been, my heart? Dost thou hear,
lady?
If from the field I shall return once more
To kiss these lips, I will appear in blood;
I and my sword will earn our chronicle.
There's hope in't yet.

CLEOPATRA That's my brave lord!

155 **stay his time** i.e., wait till his rage ends 157 **one that ties his points** one who laces up his clothes, i.e., a valet 161 **determines** comes to an end, melts 163 **memory** memorials, heirs 165 **discandying** melting 169 **oppose his fate** challenge his destiny 171 **fleet** float 172 **heart** courage 174 **in blood** (1) covered with blood (2) in full vigor 175 **chronicle** place in history

ANTONY I will be treble-sinewed, hearted, breathed,
And fight maliciously; for when mine hours
Were nice and lucky, men did ransom lives
Of me for jests; but now I'll set my teeth
And send to darkness all that stop me. Come,
Let's have one other gaudy night: call to me
All my sad captains; fill our bowls once more;
Let's mock the midnight bell.

CLEOPATRA It is my birthday.
I had thought t' have held it poor. But since my lord
Is Antony again, I will be Cleopatra.

ANTONY We will yet do well.

CLEOPATRA Call all his noble captains to my lord.

ANTONY Do so, we'll speak to them; and tonight I'll force
The wine peep through their scars. Come on, my queen,
There's sap in't yet! The next time I do fight,
I'll make death love me, for I will contend
Even with his pestilent scythe.
Exeunt [all but Enobarbus].

ENOBARBUS Now he'll outstare the lightning. To be furious
Is to be frighted out of fear, and in that mood
The dove will peck the estridge; and I see still
A diminution in our captain's brain
Restores his heart. When valor preys on reason,
It eats the sword it fights with. I will seek
Some way to leave him. *Exit.*

178 **I will . . . breathed** I will have the strength, courage, and expertise of three men 180 **nice** delicate, wanton 183 **gaudy** joyful 197 **estridge** goshawk (?) ostrich (?)

ACT IV

Scene I. *Before Alexandria. Caesar's camp.*]

Enter Caesar, Agrippa, and Maecenas, with his Army, Caesar reading a letter.

CAESAR He calls me boy, and chides as he had power
To beat me out of Egypt. My messenger
He hath whipped with rods; dares me to personal
combat.
Caesar to Antony: let the old ruffian know
I have many other ways to die; meantime
Laugh at his challenge.

MAECENAS Caesar must think,
When one so great begins to rage, he's hunted
Even to falling. Give him no breath, but now
Make boot of his distraction: never anger
Made good guard for itself.

CAESAR Let our best heads
Know that tomorrow the last of many battles
We mean to fight. Within our files there are,
Of those that served Mark Antony but late,
Enough to fetch him in. See it done,

IV.i.7 **rage** grow mad 9 **Make boot of his distraction** profit from his rage
12 **files** ranks 14 **fetch him in** capture him

And feast the army; we have store to do't,
And they have earned the waste. Poor Antony!
Exeunt.

[Scene II. *Alexandria. Cleopatra's palace.*]

Enter Antony, Cleopatra, Enobarbus, Charmian, Iras, Alexas, with others.

ANTONY He will not fight with me, Domitius?

ENOBARBUS No.

ANTONY Why should he not?

ENOBARBUS He thinks, being twenty times of better fortune,
He is twenty men to one.

ANTONY Tomorrow, soldier,
By sea and land I'll fight: or I will live,
Or bathe my dying honor in the blood
Shall make it live again. Woo't thou fight well?

ENOBARBUS I'll strike, and cry "Take all!"

ANTONY Well said, come on;
Call forth my household servants; let's tonight
Be bounteous at our meal.

Enter three or four Servitors.

Give me thy hand,
Thou hast been rightly honest—so hast thou—
Thou—and thou—and thou: you have served me well,
And kings have been your fellows.

CLEOPATRA [*Aside to Enobarbus*] What means this?

IV.ii.5 or either 7 **Woo't** wilt 8 **Take all** all or nothing 13 **kings have been your fellows** kings have served me too, but no better

ENOBARBUS [*Aside to Cleopatra*] 'Tis one of those odd tricks which sorrow shoots
Out of the mind.

ANTONY And thou art honest too.
I wish I could be made so many men,
And all of you clapped up together in
An Antony, that I might do you service
So good as you have done.

OMNES The gods forbid!

ANTONY Well, my good fellows, wait on me tonight:
Scant not my cups, and make as much of me
As when mine empire was your fellow too
And suffered my command.

CLEOPATRA [*Aside to Enobarbus*] What does he mean?

ENOBARBUS [*Aside to Cleopatra*] To make his followers weep.

ANTONY Tend me tonight;
May be it is the period of your duty.
Haply you shall not see me more; or if,
A mangled shadow. Perchance tomorrow
You'll serve another master. I look on you
As one that takes his leave. Mine honest friends,
I turn you not away, but like a master
Married to your good service; stay till death.
Tend me tonight two hours, I ask no more,
And the gods yield you for't!

ENOBARBUS What mean you, sir,
To give them this discomfort? Look, they weep,
And I, an ass, am onion-eyed; for shame,
Transform us not to women.

ANTONY Ho, ho, ho!
Now the witch take me if I meant it thus!

23 **suffered my command** served under my authority 25 **period** end 26 **Haply** perhaps 33 **yield** reward 37 **the witch take me** may I be bewitched

Grace grow where those drops fall! My hearty friends,
You take me in too dolorous a sense,
For I spake to you for your comfort, did desire you
To burn this night with torches. Know, my hearts,
I hope well of tomorrow, and will lead you
Where rather I'll expect victorious life
Than death and honor. Let's to supper, come,
And drown consideration. *Exeunt.*

[Scene III. *Alexandria. Before Cleopatra's palace.*]

Enter a Company of Soldiers.

FIRST SOLDIER Brother, good night: tomorrow is the day.

SECOND SOLDIER It will determine one way: fare you well.
Heard you of nothing strange about the streets?

FIRST SOLDIER Nothing. What news?

SECOND SOLDIER Belike 'tis but a rumor. Good night to you.

FIRST SOLDIER Well, sir, good night.

They meet other Soldiers.

SECOND SOLDIER Soldiers, have careful watch.

THIRD SOLDIER And you. Good night, good night.

They place themselves in every corner of the stage.

SECOND SOLDIER Here we; and if tomorrow

38 **Grace** (1) God's grace, favor (2) herb of grace, rue 44 **death and honor** honorable death IV.iii.5 **Belike** probably 8 **Here we** here is our post

Our navy thrive, I have an absolute hope
Our landmen will stand up.

FIRST SOLDIER 'Tis a brave army,
And full of purpose.

Music of the hautboys is under the stage.

SECOND SOLDIER Peace! What noise?

FIRST SOLDIER List, list!

SECOND SOLDIER Hark!

FIRST SOLDIER Music i' th' air.

THIRD SOLDIER Under the earth.

FOURTH SOLDIER It signs well, does it not?

THIRD SOLDIER No.

FIRST SOLDIER Peace, I say!
What should this mean?

SECOND SOLDIER 'Tis the god Hercules, whom Antony loved,
Now leaves him.

FIRST SOLDIER Walk; let's see if other watchmen
Do hear what we do.

SECOND SOLDIER How now, masters?

OMNES (*Speak together*) How now? How now? Do you hear this?

FIRST SOLDIER Ay. Is't not strange?

THIRD SOLDIER Do you hear, masters? Do you hear?

FIRST SOLDIER Follow the noise so far as we have quarter.
Let's see how it will give off.

OMNES Content. 'Tis strange. *Exeunt.*

13 signs signifies **25 give off** cease

[Scene IV. *Alexandria. Cleopatra's palace.*]

Enter Antony and Cleopatra, with [*Charmian and*] *others* [*attending*].

ANTONY Eros! Mine armor, Eros!

CLEOPATRA Sleep a little.

ANTONY No, my chuck. Eros! Come, mine armor, Eros!

Enter Eros [*with armor*].

Come, good fellow, put thine iron on.
If fortune be not ours today, it is
Because we brave her. Come.

CLEOPATRA Nay, I'll help too.
What's this for?

ANTONY Ah, let be, let be! Thou art
The armorer of my heart. False, false; this, this.

CLEOPATRA Sooth, la, I'll help: thus it must be.

ANTONY Well, well,
We shall thrive now. Seest thou, my good fellow?
Go put on thy defenses.

EROS Briefly, sir.

CLEOPATRA Is not this buckled well?

ANTONY Rarely, rarely:
He that unbuckles this, till we do please
To daff't for our repose, shall hear a storm.

IV.iv.2 **chuck** chick 3 **thine iron** that armor (of mine) you hold 4–5 **If fortune . . . brave her** (1) if fortune is not friendly to us today, it will be because we defy her (2) we shall be fortunate today, or we shall defy fortune 7 **False** i.e., wrong piece 10 **Briefly** soon 13 **daff't** put it off

Thou fumblest, Eros, and my queen's a squire
More tight at this than thou. Dispatch. O, love,
That thou couldst see my wars today, and knew'st
The royal occupation: thou shouldst see
A workman in't.

Enter an armed Soldier.

Good morrow to thee; welcome:
Thou look'st like him that knows a warlike charge.
To business that we love we rise betime
And go to't with delight.

SOLDIER A thousand, sir,
Early though't be, have on their riveted trim,
And at the port expect you.

Shout. Trumpets flourish. Enter Captains and Soldiers.

CAPTAIN The morn is fair. Good morrow, General.

ALL Good morrow, General.

ANTONY 'Tis well blown, lads.
This morning, like the spirit of a youth
That means to be of note, begins betimes.
So, so. Come, give me that: this way; well said.
Fare thee well, dame; whate'er becomes of me,
This is a soldier's kiss. Rebukable
And worthy shameful check it were to stand
On more mechanic compliment. I'll leave thee
Now like a man of steel. You that will fight,
Follow me close; I'll bring you to't. Adieu.
Exeunt [all but Cleopatra and Charmian].

CHARMIAN Please you retire to your chamber?

CLEOPATRA Lead me.
He goes forth gallantly. That he and Caesar might

15 **tight** skilled 17 **royal occupation** kingly trade 18 **workman** professional 19 **charge** duty 22 **riveted trim** armor 23 **port** gate 25 **well blown** (1) i.e., on the trumpets (2) in full flower (of the morning) 28 **well said** well done 31 **shameful check** shaming rebuke 31–32 **to stand … compliment** to make a business of vulgar civilities

Determine this great war in single fight!
Then Antony—but now—Well, on *Exeunt.*

[Scene V. *Alexandria. Antony's camp.*]

Trumpets sound. Enter Antony and Eros,
[*a soldier meeting them*].

SOLDIER The gods make this a happy day to Antony!

ANTONY Would thou and those thy scars had once prevailed
To make me fight at land!

SOLDIER Hadst thou done so,
The kings that have revolted, and the soldier
That has this morning left thee, would have still
Followèd thy heels.

ANTONY Who's gone this morning?

SOLDIER Who?
One ever near thee: call for Enobarbus,
He shall not hear thee, or from Caesar's camp
Say "I am none of thine."

ANTONY What sayest thou?

SOLDIER Sir,
He is with Caesar.

EROS Sir, his chests and treasure
He has not with him.

ANTONY Is he gone?

SOLDIER Most certain.

ANTONY Go, Eros, send his treasure after; do it;
Detain no jot, I charge thee. Write to him

IV.v.1 **happy** fortunate

(I will subscribe) gentle adieus and greetings;
Say that I wish he never find more cause
To change a master. O, my fortunes have
Corrupted honest men! Dispatch. Enobarbus!
Exit [*with Eros and Soldier*].

[Scene VI. *Alexandria. Caesar's camp.*]

Flourish. Enter Agrippa, Caesar, with Enobarbus, and Dolabella.

CAESAR Go forth, Agrippa, and begin the fight.
Our will is Antony be took alive:
Make it so known.

AGRIPPA Caesar, I shall. [*Exit.*]

CAESAR The time of universal peace is near.
Prove this a prosp'rous day, the three-nooked world
Shall bear the olive freely.

Enter a Messenger.

MESSENGER Antony
Is come into the field.

CAESAR Go charge Agrippa
Plant those that have revolted in the vant,
That Antony may seem to spend his fury
Upon himself. *Exeunt* [*all but Enobarbus*].

ENOBARBUS Alexas did revolt and went to Jewry on
Affairs of Antony; there did dissuade
Great Herod to incline himself to Caesar
And leave his master Antony. For this pains

14 **subscribe** sign IV.vi.6 **three-nooked** three-cornered (Europe, Asia, Africa) 9 **vant** first lines 13 **dissuade** i.e., persuade to leave Antony

Caesar hath hanged him. Canidius and the rest
That fell away have entertainment, but
No honorable trust. I have done ill,
Of which I do accuse myself so sorely
That I will joy no more.

Enter a Soldier of Caesar's.

SOLDIER Enobarbus, Antony
Hath after thee sent all thy treasure, with
His bounty overplus. The messenger
Came on my guard, and at thy tent is now
Unloading of his mules.

ENOBARBUS I give it you.

SOLDIER Mock not, Enobarbus:
I tell you true: best you safed the bringer
Out of the host; I must attend mine office
Or would have done't myself. Your emperor
Continues still a Jove. *Exit.*

ENOBARBUS I am alone the villain of the earth,
And feel I am so most. O, Antony,
Thou mine of bounty, how wouldst thou have paid
My better service, when my turpitude
Thou dost so crown with gold! This blows my heart.
If swift thought break it not, a swifter mean
Shall outstrike thought; but thought will do't, I feel.
I fight against thee! No, I will go seek
Some ditch wherein to die: the foul'st best fits
My latter part of life. *Exit.*

26–27 best . . . host you had better see that the man who brought them has safe-conduct through enemy lines **30 alone the** the only **31 And feel I am so most** and no one could be more bitterly aware of it **34 blows** swells **35 thought** sorrow

[Scene VII. *Field of battle between the camps.*]

Alarum. Drums and Trumpets. Enter Agrippa [and Soldiers].

AGRIPPA Retire; we have engaged ourselves too far:
Caesar himself has work, and our oppression
Exceeds what we expected. *Exit [with Soldiers].*

Alarums. Enter Antony, and Scarus wounded.

SCARUS O my brave emperor, this is fought indeed!
Had we done so at first, we had droven them home
With clouts about their heads.

ANTONY Thou bleed'st apace.

SCARUS I had a wound here that was like a *T*,
But now 'tis made an *H*. [*Retreat sounded*] *far off.*

ANTONY They do retire.

SCARUS We'll beat 'em into bench holes. I have yet
Room for six scotches more.

Enter Eros.

EROS They are beaten, sir, and our advantage serves
For a fair victory.

SCARUS Let us score their backs
And snatch 'em up, as we take hares, behind:
'Tis sport to maul a runner.

ANTONY I will reward thee

IV.vii.2 **has work** is hard-pressed 2 **our oppression** the pressure on us 6 **clouts** (1) blows (2) bandages 8 ***H*** (pun on "ache," pronounced "aitch") 9 **bench holes** holes in a privy 10 **scotches** gashes 12 **score** slash

Once for thy sprightly comfort, and tenfold
For thy good valor. Come thee on.

SCARUS I'll halt after. *Exeunt.*

[Scene VIII. *Before Alexandria.*]

Alarum. Enter Antony again in a march; Scarus, with others.

ANTONY We have beat him to his camp. Run one before
And let the Queen know of our gests. Tomorrow,
Before the sun shall see's, we'll spill the blood
That has today escaped. I thank you all,
For doughty-handed are you, and have fought
Not as you served the cause, but as't had been
Each man's like mine: you have shown all Hectors.
Enter the city, clip your wives, your friends,
Tell them your feats, whilst they with joyful tears
Wash the congealment from your wounds, and kiss
The honored gashes whole.

Enter Cleopatra.

[*To Scarus*] Give me thy hand;
To this great fairy I'll commend thy acts,
Make her thanks bless thee.—O thou day o' th' world,
Chain mine armed neck; leap thou, attire and all,
Through proof of harness to my heart, and there
Ride on the pants triumphing.

15 **sprightly** high-hearted 16 **halt** limp IV.viii.2 **gests** deeds 8 **clip** embrace 12 **fairy** enchantress 15 **proof of harness** impenetrable armor

CLEOPATRA Lord of lords!
O infinite virtue, com'st thou smiling from
The world's great snare uncaught?

ANTONY Mine nightingale,
We have beat them to their beds. What, girl! Though gray
Do something mingle with our younger brown, yet ha' we
A brain that nourishes our nerves, and can
Get goal for goal of youth. Behold this man:
Commend unto his lips thy favoring hand.—
Kiss it, my warrior.—He hath fought today
As if a god in hate of mankind had
Destroyed in such a shape.

CLEOPATRA I'll give thee, friend,
An armor all of gold; it was a king's.

ANTONY He has deserved it, were it carbuncled
Like holy Phoebus' car. Give me thy hand.
Through Alexandria make a jolly march;
Bear our hacked targets like the men that owe them.
Had our great palace the capacity
To camp this host, we all would sup together
And drink carouses to the next day's fate,
Which promises royal peril. Trumpeters,
With brazen din blast you the city's ear,
Make mingle with our rattling tabourines,
That heaven and earth may strike their sounds together,
Applauding our approach. *Exeunt.*

17 **virtue** valor 22 **Get goal for goal of youth** keep pace with every point won by youth 28 **carbuncled** jeweled 29 **Phoebus' car** the sun god's chariot 31 **targets** shields 31 **owe** own 37 **tabourines** small drums

[Scene IX. *Caesar's camp.*]

Enter a Sentry and his Company. Enobarbus follows.

SENTRY If we be not relieved within this hour,
We must return to th' court of guard. The night
Is shiny, and they say we shall embattle
By th' second hour i' th' morn.

FIRST WATCH This last day was
A shrewd one to's.

ENOBARBUS O, bear me witness, night—

SECOND WATCH What man is this?

FIRST WATCH Stand close, and list him.

ENOBARBUS Be witness to me, O, thou blessèd moon,
When men revolted shall upon record
Bear hateful memory, poor Enobarbus did
Before thy face repent!

SENTRY Enobarbus?

SECOND WATCH Peace:
Hark further.

ENOBARBUS O sovereign mistress of true melancholy,
The poisonous damp of night disponge upon me,
That life, a very rebel to my will,
May hang no longer on me. Throw my heart
Against the flint and hardness of my fault,
Which, being dried with grief, will break to powder,
And finish all foul thoughts. O, Antony,
Nobler than my revolt is infamous,

IV.ix.5 **shrewd** curst, bad 12 **mistress** i.e., the moon 13 **disponge** drip

Forgive me in thine own particular,
But let the world rank me in register
A master-leaver and a fugitive.
O, Antony! O, Antony! [*Dies.*]

FIRST WATCH Let's speak to him.

SENTRY Let's hear him, for the things he speaks
May concern Caesar.

SECOND WATCH Let's do so. But he sleeps.

SENTRY Swoons rather, for so bad a prayer as his
Was never yet for sleep.

FIRST WATCH Go we to him.

SECOND WATCH Awake, sir, awake; speak to us.

FIRST WATCH Hear you, sir?

SENTRY The hand of death hath raught him.

Drums afar off.

Hark! The drums
Demurely wake the sleepers. Let us bear him
To th' court of guard: he is of note. Our hour
Is fully out.

SECOND WATCH Come on then; he may recover yet.

Exeunt [*with the body*].

[Scene X. *Between the two camps.*]

Enter Antony and Scarus, with their Army.

ANTONY Their preparation is today by sea;
We please them not by land.

20 in thine own particular yourself **21 in register** in its records **22 master-leaver** (1) supreme traitor (2) runaway servant **27 for** a prelude to **29 raught** reached **30 Demurely** soberly, with a low sound

SCARUS For both, my lord.

ANTONY I would they'd fight i' th' fire or i' th' air;
We'd fight there too. But this it is: our foot
Upon the hills adjoining to the city
Shall stay with us—order for sea is given;
They have put forth the haven—
Where their appointment we may best discover
And look on their endeavor. *Exeunt.*

[Scene XI. *Between the two camps.*]

Enter Caesar and his Army.

CAESAR But being charged, we will be still by land—
Which, as I take't, we shall, for his best force
Is forth to man his galleys. To the vales,
And hold our best advantage. *Exeunt.*

[Scene XII. *Before Alexandria.*]

Enter Antony and Scarus.

ANTONY Yet they are not joined. Where yond pine does stand
I shall discover all. I'll bring thee word
Straight how 'tis like to go. *Exit.*

IV.x.3 **i' th' fire or i' th' air** i.e., as well as the other two elements, earth and water (land and sea) IV.xi.1 **But being charged** unless we are attacked 4 **hold our best advantage** take up the best position we can IV.xii.1 **joined** i.e., in battle

Alarum afar off, as at a sea fight.

SCARUS Swallows have built
In Cleopatra's sails their nests. The augurers
Say they know not, they cannot tell, look grimly,
And dare not speak their knowledge. Antony
Is valiant, and dejected, and by starts
His fretted fortunes give him hope and fear
Of what he has, and has not.

Enter Antony.

ANTONY All is lost!
This foul Egyptian hath betrayèd me:
My fleet hath yielded to the foe, and yonder
They cast their caps up and carouse together
Like friends long lost. Triple-turned whore! 'Tis thou
Hast sold me to this novice, and my heart
Makes only wars on thee. Bid them all fly;
For when I am revenged upon my charm,
I have done all. Bid them all fly, be gone.
[*Exit Scarus.*]
O sun, thy uprise shall I see no more.
Fortune and Antony part here, even here
Do we shake hands. All come to this? The hearts
That spanieled me at heels, to whom I gave
Their wishes, do discandy, melt their sweets
On blossoming Caesar; and this pine is barked,
That overtopped them all. Betrayed I am.
O this false soul of Egypt! This grave charm,
Whose eye becked forth my wars, and called them home,
Whose bosom was my crownet, my chief end,

3 s.d. **Alarum . . . sea fight** (the Folio prints this direction just before the entrance of Antony and Scarus; if F's placement is correct, the noise fills the otherwise empty stage for a moment and makes ironic Antony's first line, but probably the direction should be placed either in its present position or in the middle of line 9) 8 **fretted** (1) checkered (2) worn, decayed 13 **Triple-turned** i.e., from Pompey, from Julius Caesar, from Antony 16 **charm** witch 22 **discandy** dissolve 23 **barked** stripped bare 25 **grave charm** deadly witch 27 **crownet, my chief end** crown and end of all I did

Like a right gypsy hath at fast and loose
Beguiled me, to the very heart of loss.
What, Eros, Eros!

Enter Cleopatra.

Ah, thou spell! Avaunt!

CLEOPATRA Why is my lord enraged against his love?

ANTONY Vanish, or I shall give thee thy deserving
And blemish Caesar's triumph. Let him take thee
And hoist thee up to the shouting plebeians;
Follow his chariot, like the greatest spot
Of all thy sex: most monsterlike be shown
For poor'st diminutives, for dolts, and let
Patient Octavia plow thy visage up
With her preparèd nails. *Exit Cleopatra.*
'Tis well th' art gone,
If it be well to live; but better 'twere
Thou fell'st into my fury, for one death
Might have prevented many. Eros, ho!
The shirt of Nessus is upon me; teach me,
Alcides, thou mine ancestor, thy rage.
Let me lodge Lichas on the horns o' th' moon,
And with those hands that grasped the heaviest club
Subdue my worthiest self. The witch shall die:
To the young Roman boy she hath sold me, and I fall
Under this plot: she dies for't. Eros, ho! *Exit.*

28 **right** true 28 **fast and loose** (a cheating game played by gypsies, in which the dupe inevitably fails to make fast a coiled rope) 30 **Avaunt** begone 34 **plebeians** (accented on first syllable) 35 **spot** blemish 37 **diminutives** little people, i.e., the populace 43–45 **Nessus . . . moon** (the death of Antony's ancestor Hercules—called Alcides in line 44—is here recalled. Hercules killed the centaur Nessus with a poisoned arrow, for trying to rape his wife Deianira; the dying Nessus in revenge gave his robe, soaked in poisoned blood, to Deianira, pretending it would act as a love charm. She sent it to her husband for this purpose; in his dying agonies Hercules hurled the bringer of it, Lichas, high in the air)

[Scene XIII. *Alexandria. Cleopatra's palace.*]

Enter Cleopatra, Charmian, Iras, Mardian.

CLEOPATRA Help me, my women! O, he's more mad
Than Telamon for his shield; the boar of Thessaly
Was never so embossed.

CHARMIAN To th' monument:
There lock yourself, and send him word you are dead.
The soul and body rive not more in parting
Than greatness going off.

CLEOPATRA To th' monument!
Mardian, go tell him I have slain myself:
Say that the last I spoke was "Antony"
And word it, prithee, piteously. Hence, Mardian,
And bring me how he takes my death. To th' monument! *Exeunt.*

IV.xiii.2 **Telamon** i.e., Ajax, who went mad and killed himself when he lost the contest between himself and Odysseus for the arms and shield of Achilles 2 **the boar of Thessaly** (sent by Artemis to ravage the country of King Oeneus, and killed by his son Meleager) 3 **embossed** (of a hunted animal) foaming at the mouth from fury and exhaustion 5 **rive** rend

[Scene XIV. *Alexandria. Cleopatra's palace.*]

Enter Antony and Eros.

ANTONY Eros, thou yet behold'st me?

EROS Ay, noble lord.

ANTONY Sometime we see a cloud that's dragonish,
A vapor sometime like a bear or lion,
A towered citadel, a pendant rock,
A forkèd mountain, or blue promontory
With trees upon't that nod unto the world
And mock our eyes with air. Thou hast seen these signs:
They are black vesper's pageants.

EROS Ay, my lord.

ANTONY That which is now a horse, even with a thought
The rack dislimns, and makes it indistinct
As water is in water.

EROS It does, my lord.

ANTONY My good knave Eros, now thy captain is
Even such a body: here I am Antony,
Yet cannot hold this visible shape, my knave.
I made these wars for Egypt; and the Queen—
Whose heart I thought I had, for she had mine,
Which, whilst it was mine, had annexed unto't
A million moe, now lost—she, Eros, has

IV.xiv.8 **black vesper's pageants** evening's brightly colored but unreal scenery (**pageants** = floats of the mystery plays, hence plays, masques, etc.) 9–10 **even ... dislimns** as swift as thought the cloud formation (**rack**) obliterates 12 **knave** boy 18 **moe** more

Packed cards with Caesar, and false-played my glory
Unto an enemy's triumph.
Nay, weep not, gentle Eros, there is left us
Ourselves to end ourselves.

Enter Mardian.

O, thy vile lady!
She has robbed me of my sword.

MARDIAN No, Antony;
My mistress loved thee, and her fortunes mingled
With thine entirely.

ANTONY Hence, saucy eunuch, peace!
She hath betrayed me and shall die the death.

MARDIAN Death of one person can be paid but once,
And that she has discharged. What thou wouldst do
Is done unto thy hand. The last she spake
Was "Antony! most noble Antony!"
Then in the midst a tearing groan did break
The name of Antony; it was divided
Between her heart and lips: she rend'red life,
Thy name so buried in her.

ANTONY Dead, then?

MARDIAN Dead.

ANTONY Unarm, Eros. The long day's task is done,
And we must sleep. [*To Mardian*] That thou depart'st hence safe
Does pay thy labor richly: go. *Exit Mardian.*
Off, pluck off:
The sevenfold shield of Ajax cannot keep
The battery from my heart. O, cleave, my sides!
Heart, once be stronger than thy continent,

19–20 **Packed cards ... triumph** stacked the cards to favor herself and Caesar, and so treacherously played her hand as to allow Caesar to trump my glory 23 **sword** i.e., soldiership, masculinity 29 **unto thy hand** already for you 33 **rend'red** surrendered 38 **sevenfold shield of Ajax** (made of brass and lined with seven layers of oxhide) 39 **battery** bombardment 40 **thy continent** what holds you in

Crack thy frail case! Apace, Eros, apace.
No more a soldier. Bruisèd pieces, go;
You have been nobly borne.—From me awhile.
Exit Eros.
I will o'ertake thee, Cleopatra, and
Weep for my pardon. So it must be, for now
All length is torture: since the torch is out,
Lie down, and stray no farther. Now all labor
Mars what it does; yea, very force entangles
Itself with strength. Seal then, and all is done.
Eros!—I come, my queen.—Eros!—Stay for me.
Where souls do couch on flowers, we'll hand in hand,
And with our sprightly port make the ghosts gaze:
Dido and her Aeneas shall want troops,
And all the haunt be ours.—Come, Eros, Eros!

Enter Eros.

EROS What would my lord?

ANTONY Since Cleopatra died,
I have lived in such dishonor that the gods
Detest my baseness. I, that with my sword
Quartered the world and o'er green Neptune's back
With ships made cities, condemn myself to lack
The courage of a woman; less noble mind
Than she which by her death our Caesar tells
"I am conqueror of myself." Thou art sworn, Eros,
That, when the exigent should come, which now
Is come indeed, when I should see behind me
Th' inevitable prosecution of
Disgrace and horror, that on my command
Thou then wouldst kill me. Do't, the time is come.

42 **pieces** armor 46 **length** length of life 48–49 **very force ... strength** (the image probably is of a creature caught more tightly in a net by the very violence of its struggles) 49 **Seal then** finish then (i.e., the final act of sealing a document, especially a will) 52 **sprightly** (1) high-hearted, gay (2) ghostly 52 **port** bearing 53 **Dido ... Aeneas** (the legendary lovers are brought together, though in Vergil, Dido repulses forever the faithless Aeneas) 53 **want troops** lack retinue 58 **Quartered** (1) covered with troops (2) carved up 59 **to lack** for lacking 63 **exigent** need 65 **inevitable prosecution** unescapable pursuit

Thou strik'st not me, 'tis Caesar thou defeat'st.
Put color in thy cheek.

EROS The gods withhold me!
Shall I do that which all the Parthian darts,
Though enemy, lost aim and could not?

ANTONY Eros,
Wouldst thou be windowed in great Rome and see
Thy master thus: with pleached arms, bending down
His corrigible neck, his face subdued
To penetrative shame, whilst the wheeled seat
Of fortunate Caesar, drawn before him, branded
His baseness that ensued?

EROS I would not see't.

ANTONY Come then; for with a wound I must be cured.
Draw that thy honest sword, which thou hast worn
Most useful for thy country.

EROS O, sir, pardon me.

ANTONY When I did make thee free, swor'st thou not then
To do this when I bade thee? Do it at once,
Or thy precedent services are all
But accidents unpurposed. Draw, and come.

EROS Turn from me then that noble countenance
Wherein the worship of the whole world lies.

ANTONY Lo thee! [*Turns from him.*]

EROS My sword is drawn.

ANTONY Then let it do at once
The thing why thou hast drawn it.

EROS My dear master,

73 **pleached** folded (twisted behind?) 74 **corrigible** submissive 74–75 **subdued/To penetrative shame** filled with the humiliation of deepest shame 76–77 **branded ... ensued** made as hideously clear as the mark branded on a criminal or animal the abject nature of the man who followed 83 **precedent** former 87 **Lo thee** there you are, then

My captain, and my emperor, let me say,
Before I strike this bloody stroke, farewell.

ANTONY 'Tis said, man, and farewell.

EROS Farewell, great chief. Shall I strike now?

ANTONY Now, Eros.

EROS Why, there then! Thus I do escape the sorrow
Of Antony's death. *Kills himself.*

ANTONY Thrice-nobler than myself,
Thou teachest me, O valiant Eros, what
I should, and thou couldst not. My queen and Eros
Have by their brave instruction got upon me
A nobleness in record. But I will be
A bridegroom in my death, and run into't
As to a lover's bed. Come then; and, Eros,
Thy master dies thy scholar. To do thus
[*Falls on his sword.*]
I learned of thee. How? Not dead? Not dead?
The guard, ho! O, dispatch me!

Enter [*Decretas and*] *a* [*Company of the*] *Guard.*

FIRST GUARD What's the noise?

ANTONY I have done my work ill, friends. O, make an end
Of what I have begun.

SECOND GUARD The star is fall'n.

FIRST GUARD And time is at his period.

ALL Alas, and woe!

ANTONY Let him that loves me strike me dead.

FIRST GUARD Not I.

SECOND GUARD Nor I.

THIRD GUARD Nor anyone. *Exeunt* [*Guard*].

DECRETAS Thy death and fortunes bid thy followers fly.

98–99 got . . . record beaten me in achieving a noble place in the story
107 period end

This sword but shown to Caesar, with this tidings,
Shall enter me with him.

Enter Diomedes.

DIOMEDES Where's Antony?

DECRETAS There, Diomed, there.

DIOMEDES Lives he?
Wilt thou not answer, man? [*Exit Decretas.*]

ANTONY Art thou there, Diomed? Draw thy sword, and give me
Sufficing strokes for death.

DIOMEDES Most absolute lord,
My mistress Cleopatra sent me to thee.

ANTONY When did she send thee?

DIOMEDES Now, my lord.

ANTONY Where is she?

DIOMEDES Locked in her monument. She had a prophesying fear
Of what hath come to pass; for when she saw
(Which never shall be found) you did suspect
She had disposed with Caesar, and that your rage
Would not be purged, she sent you word she was dead;
But, fearing since how it might work, hath sent
Me to proclaim the truth, and I am come,
I dread, too late.

ANTONY Too late, good Diomed. Call my guard, I prithee.

DIOMEDES What ho! The Emperor's guard! The guard, what ho!
Come, your lord calls!

Enter four or five of the Guard of Antony.

ANTONY Bear me, good friends, where Cleopatra bides;

113 enter recommend 123 disposed settled things 124 purged cured

'Tis the last service that I shall command you.

FIRST GUARD Woe, woe are we, sir, you may not live to wear
All your true followers out.

ALL Most heavy day!

ANTONY Nay, good my fellows, do not please sharp fate
To grace it with your sorrows. Bid that welcome
Which comes to punish us, and we punish it,
Seeming to bear it lightly. Take me up:
I have led you oft; carry me now, good friends,
And have my thanks for all.

Exit [the Guard,] bearing Antony.

[Scene XV. *Alexandria. The monument.*]

Enter Cleopatra and her Maids aloft, with Charmian and Iras.

CLEOPATRA O, Charmian, I will never go from hence.

CHARMIAN Be comforted, dear madam.

CLEOPATRA No, I will not.
All strange and terrible events are welcome,
But comforts we despise. Our size of sorrow,
Proportioned to our cause, must be as great
As that which makes it.

Enter Diomed [below].

How now? Is he dead?

DIOMEDES His death's upon him, but not dead.

133–34 **live . . . out** outlive all your faithful men IV.xv.s.d. **aloft** (presumably on the upper stage at the back of the main stage)

Look out o' th' other side your monument;
His guard have brought him thither.

Enter, [*below*,] *Antony, and the Guard* [*bearing him*].

CLEOPATRA O sun,
Burn the great sphere thou mov'st in: darkling stand
The varying shore o' th' world! O Antony,
Antony, Antony! Help, Charmian, help, Iras, help:
Help, friends below, let's draw him hither.

ANTONY Peace!
Not Caesar's valor hath o'erthrown Antony,
But Antony's hath triumphed on itself.

CLEOPATRA So it should be, that none but Antony
Should conquer Antony, but woe 'tis so!

ANTONY I am dying, Egypt, dying; only
I here importune death awhile, until
Of many thousand kisses the poor last
I lay upon thy lips.

CLEOPATRA I dare not, dear;
Dear my lord, pardon: I dare not,
Lest I be taken. Not th' imperious show
Of the full-fortuned Caesar ever shall
Be brooched with me, if knife, drugs, serpents have
Edge, sting, or operation. I am safe:
Your wife Octavia, with her modest eyes
And still conclusion, shall acquire no honor
Demuring upon me. But come, come, Antony—
Help me, my women—we must draw thee up:
Assist, good friends.

ANTONY O, quick, or I am gone.

10 **darkling** in darkness 12–13 **Help ... hither** (Shakespeare appears to have made a false start, afterwards left uncanceled, in lines 12–13, or even to line 29; Cleopatra's plan for getting Antony in is passed over, then repeated, in a curious way; and Antony's "I am dying" is also repeated) 19 **importune** beg 21 **dare not** i.e., dare not descend, or open the gates 25 **Be brooched with me** have me as its ornament 28 **still conclusion** (1) silent judgment (2) impassive finality 29 **Demuring** looking soberly

CLEOPATRA Here's sport indeed! How heavy weighs my lord!
Our strength is all gone into heaviness,
That makes the weight. Had I great Juno's power,
The strong-winged Mercury should fetch thee up
And set thee by Jove's side. Yet come a little,
Wishers were ever fools. O, come, come, come.
They heave Antony aloft to Cleopatra.
And welcome, welcome! Die when thou hast lived,
Quicken with kissing. Had my lips that power,
Thus would I wear them out.

ALL A heavy sight!

ANTONY I am dying, Egypt, dying.
Give me some wine, and let me speak a little.

CLEOPATRA No, let me speak, and let me rail so high
That the false housewife Fortune break her wheel,
Provoked by my offense.

ANTONY One word, sweet queen.
Of Caesar seek your honor, with your safety. O!

CLEOPATRA They do not go together.

ANTONY Gentle, hear me:
None about Caesar trust but Proculeius.

CLEOPATRA My resolution and my hands I'll trust,
None about Caesar.

ANTONY The miserable change now at my end
Lament nor sorrow at, but please your thoughts
In feeding them with those my former fortunes,
Wherein I lived; the greatest prince o' th' world,
The noblest; and do now not basely die,
Not cowardly put off my helmet to
My countryman; a Roman, by a Roman

33 **heaviness** (1) weight (2) sorrow 39 **Quicken** come to life 44 **false housewife** treacherous hussy, strumpet 44 **wheel** (1) spinning wheel (the especial property of a "housewife") (2) wheel of Fortune, whose turns govern the affairs of men 45 **offense** insults

Valiantly vanquished. Now my spirit is going,
I can no more.

CLEOPATRA Noblest of men, woo't die?
Hast thou no care of me? Shall I abide
In this dull world, which in thy absence is
No better than a sty? O, see, my women,
[*Antony dies.*]
The crown o' th' earth doth melt. My lord!
O, withered is the garland of the war,
The soldier's pole is fall'n: young boys and girls
Are level now with men. The odds is gone,
And there is nothing left remarkable
Beneath the visiting moon. [*Faints.*]

CHARMIAN O, quietness, lady!

IRAS She's dead too, our sovereign.

CHARMIAN Lady!

IRAS Madam!

CHARMIAN O madam, madam, madam!

IRAS Royal Egypt! Empress!

CHARMIAN Peace, peace, Iras!

CLEOPATRA No more but e'en a woman, and commanded
By such poor passion as the maid that milks
And does the meanest chares. It were for me
To throw my scepter at the injurious gods,
To tell them that this world did equal theirs
Till they had stol'n our jewel. All's but naught.
Patience is sottish, and impatience does
Become a dog that's mad: then is it sin
To rush into the secret house of death
Ere death dare come to us? How do you, women?
What, what, good cheer! Why, how now, Charmian?
My noble girls! Ah, women, women, look,

64 **garland** flower, crown 65 **pole** (1) standard (2) polestar (3) Maypole (suggested by "garland") 66 **odds** measure, distinctive value 67 **remarkable** wonderful 74 **chares** chores 78 **sottish** dully stupid

Our lamp is spent, it's out. Good sirs, take heart:
We'll bury him; and then, what's brave, what's noble,
Let's do't after the high Roman fashion,
And make death proud to take us. Come, away.
This case of that huge spirit now is cold.
Ah, women, women! Come; we have no friend
But resolution, and the briefest end.
Exeunt, bearing off Antony's body.

84 **sirs** (used of women, as of men) 90 **briefest** swiftest

[ACT V

Scene I. *Alexandria. Caesar's camp.*]

Enter Caesar, Agrippa, Dolabella, Maecenas, [Gallus, Proculeius,] with his Council of War.

CAESAR Go to him, Dolabella, bid him yield:
Being so frustrate, tell him, he mocks
The pauses that he makes.

DOLABELLA Caesar, I shall. [*Exit.*]

Enter Decretas, with the sword of Antony.

CAESAR Wherefore is that? And what art thou that dar'st
Appear thus to us?

DECRETAS I am called Decretas.
Mark Antony I served, who best was worthy
Best to be served. Whilst he stood up and spoke,
He was my master, and I wore my life
To spend upon his haters. If thou please
To take me to thee, as I was to him
I'll be to Caesar; if thou pleasest not,
I yield thee up my life.

CAESAR What is't thou say'st?

V.i.2–3 **Being so ... he makes** tell him that, since he is truly defeated, these delays are a mere mockery 5 **thus** i.e., holding a naked sword

DECRETAS I say, O Caesar, Antony is dead.

CAESAR The breaking of so great a thing should make
A greater crack. The round world
Should have shook lions into civil streets
And citizens to their dens. The death of Antony
Is not a single doom; in the name lay
A moiety of the world.

DECRETAS He is dead, Caesar,
Not by a public minister of justice
Nor by a hirèd knife; but that self hand
Which writ his honor in the acts it did
Hath, with the courage which the heart did lend it,
Splitted the heart. This is his sword,
I robbed his wound of it: behold it stained
With his most noble blood.

CAESAR [*Weeping*] Look you, sad friends.
The gods rebuke me, but it is tidings
To wash the eyes of kings.

AGRIPPA And strange it is
That nature must compel us to lament
Our most persisted deeds.

MAECENAS His taints and honors
Waged equal with him.

AGRIPPA A rarer spirit never
Did steer humanity; but you gods will give us
Some faults to make us men. Caesar is touched.

MAECENAS When such a spacious mirror's set before him,
He needs must see himself.

14 **breaking** (1) destruction (2) disclosure, report 15 **crack** (1) breach (2) explosive sound 16 **civil** city 19 **moiety** half 21 **self** selfsame 30 **persisted** persisted in 31 **Waged equal with** were equally matched in

CAESAR O Antony,
I have followed thee to this. But we do launch
Diseases in our bodies. I must perforce
Have shown to thee such a declining day
Or look on thine: we could not stall together
In the whole world. But yet let me lament
With tears as sovereign as the blood of hearts
That thou, my brother, my competitor
In top of all design, my mate in empire,
Friend and companion in the front of war,
The arm of mine own body, and the heart
Where mine his thoughts did kindle—that our stars,
Unreconciliable, should divide
Our equalness to this. Hear me, good friends—

Enter an Egyptian.

But I will tell you at some meeter season.
The business of this man looks out of him;
We'll hear him what he says. Whence are you?

EGYPTIAN A poor Egyptian yet. The Queen my mistress,
Confined in all she has, her monument,
Of thy intents desires instruction,
That she preparèdly may frame herself
To th' way she's forced to.

CAESAR Bid her have good heart:
She soon shall know of us, by some of ours,
How honorable and how kindly we
Determine for her. For Caesar cannot live
To be ungentle.

EGYPTIAN So the gods preserve thee! *Exit.*

CAESAR Come hither, Proculeius. Go and say
We purpose her no shame: give her what comforts
The quality of her passion shall require,

36 **followed** pursued 36 **launch** lance 39 **stall** dwell 41 **sovereign** potent 42–43 **my competitor ... design** my partner in noblest enterprise 46 **his** its 52 **yet** still (though Egypt will soon be Roman) 63 **passion** strong emotion (here, grief)

Lest, in her greatness, by some mortal stroke
She do defeat us. For her life in Rome
Would be eternal in our triumph. Go,
And with your speediest bring us what she says
And how you find of her.

PROCULEIUS Caesar, I shall.

Exit Proculeius.

CAESAR Gallus, go you along. [*Exit Gallus.*] Where's Dolabella,
To second Proculeius?

ALL Dolabella!

CAESAR Let him alone, for I remember now
How he's employed. He shall in time be ready.
Go with me to my tent, where you shall see
How hardly I was drawn into this war,
How calm and gentle I proceeded still
In all my writings. Go with me, and see
What I can show in this. *Exeunt.*

[Scene II. *Alexandria. The monument.*]

Enter Cleopatra, Charmian, Iras, and Mardian.

CLEOPATRA My desolation does begin to make
A better life. 'Tis paltry to be Caesar:
Not being Fortune, he's but Fortune's knave,
A minister of her will. And it is great
To do that thing that ends all other deeds,
Which shackles accidents and bolts up change;

65–66 **For her ... our triumph** alive, in Rome, walking in my triumphal procession, she would manifest my power to the end of time 74 **hardly** reluctantly V.ii.3 **knave** servant

Which sleeps, and never palates more the dung,
The beggar's nurse and Caesar's.

Enter, [*to the gates of the monument*,] *Proculeius*, [*Gallus, and Soldiers*].

PROCULEIUS Caesar sends greeting to the Queen of
Egypt,
And bids thee study on what fair demands
Thou mean'st to have him grant thee.

CLEOPATRA What's thy name?

PROCULEIUS My name is Proculeius.

CLEOPATRA Antony
Did tell me of you, bade me trust you, but
I do not greatly care to be deceived,
That have no use for trusting. If your master
Would have a queen his beggar, you must tell him
That majesty, to keep decorum, must
No less beg than a kingdom: if he please
To give me conquered Egypt for my son,
He gives me so much of mine own as I
Will kneel to him with thanks.

PROCULEIUS Be of good cheer:
Y' are fall'n into a princely hand, fear nothing.
Make your full reference freely to my lord,
Who is so full of grace that it flows over
On all that need. Let me report to him
Your sweet dependency, and you shall find
A conqueror that will pray in aid for kindness,
Where he for grace is kneeled to.

CLEOPATRA Pray you, tell him
I am his fortune's vassal, and I send him
The greatness he has got. I hourly learn
A doctrine of obedience, and would gladly
Look him i' th' face.

7 palates tastes **7–8 the dung ... Caesar's** the dungy earth, whose fruits are the source of life to beggar and to emperor **14 to be deceived** whether or not I am deceived **23 Make ... freely** hand your affairs fully **27 pray in aid for kindness** beg you to assist him to be kind to you

PROCULEIUS This I'll report, dear lady.
Have comfort, for I know your plight is pitied
Of him that caused it.

[*Enter Gallus and Soldiers behind.*]

You see how easily she may be surprised.
[*They seize Cleopatra.*]
Guard her till Caesar come.

IRAS Royal Queen!

CHARMIAN O, Cleopatra! Thou art taken, Queen.

CLEOPATRA Quick, quick, good hands!
[*Draws a dagger.*]

PROCULEIUS Hold, worthy lady, hold!
[*Disarms her.*]
Do not yourself such wrong, who are in this
Relieved, but not betrayed.

CLEOPATRA What, of death too,
That rids our dogs of languish?

PROCULEIUS Cleopatra,
Do not abuse my master's bounty by
Th' undoing of yourself: let the world see
His nobleness well acted, which your death
Will never let come forth.

CLEOPATRA Where art thou, death?
Come hither, come! Come, come, and take a queen
Worth many babes and beggars!

PROCULEIUS O, temperance, lady!

CLEOPATRA Sir, I will eat no meat, I'll not drink, sir—
If idle talk will once be necessary—
I'll not sleep neither. This mortal house I'll ruin,
Do Caesar what he can. Know, sir, that I
Will not wait pinioned at your master's court

34 s.d. (the Folio gives no stage direction here; it was presumably left to the stage performance to decide on the procedure by which the Romans capture the tomb) 41 **Relieved** rescued 42 **languish** lingering illness 46 **let come forth** allow to be revealed 53 **pinioned** with clipped wings

Nor once be chastised with the sober eye
Of dull Octavia. Shall they hoist me up
And show me to the shouting varletry
Of censuring Rome? Rather a ditch in Egypt
Be gentle grave unto me! Rather on Nilus' mud
Lay me stark nak'd and let the waterflies
Blow me into abhorring! Rather make
My country's high pyramides my gibbet
And hang me up in chains!

PROCULEIUS You do extend
These thoughts of horror further than you shall
Find cause in Caesar.

Enter Dolabella.

DOLABELLA Proculeius,
What thou hast done, thy master Caesar knows,
And he hath sent for thee. For the Queen,
I'll take her to my guard.

PROCULEIUS So, Dolabella,
It shall content me best: be gentle to her.
[*To Cleopatra*] To Caesar I will speak what you shall please,
If you'll employ me to him.

CLEOPATRA Say, I would die.

Exit Proculeius [*with Soldiers*].

DOLABELLA Most noble Empress, you have heard of me.

CLEOPATRA I cannot tell.

DOLABELLA Assuredly you know me.

CLEOPATRA No matter, sir, what I have heard or known.
You laugh when boys or women tell their dreams;
Is't not your trick?

DOLABELLA I understand not, madam.

CLEOPATRA I dreamt there was an Emperor Antony.

56 **varletry** mob 60 **Blow** swell 61 **pyramides** (four syllables, accented on second) 75 **trick** way

O, such another sleep, that I might see
But such another man.

DOLABELLA If it might please ye——

CLEOPATRA His face was as the heav'ns, and therein stuck
A sun and moon, which kept their course and lighted
The little *O*, th' earth.

DOLABELLA Most sovereign creature——

CLEOPATRA His legs bestrid the ocean: his reared arm
Crested the world: his voice was propertied
As all the tunèd spheres, and that to friends;
But when he meant to quail and shake the orb,
He was as rattling thunder. For his bounty,
There was no winter in't: an autumn 'twas
That grew the more by reaping. His delights
Were dolphinlike, they showed his back above
The element they lived in. In his livery
Walked crowns and crownets: realms and islands were
As plates dropped from his pocket.

DOLABELLA Cleopatra——

CLEOPATRA Think you there was or might be such a man
As this I dreamt of?

DOLABELLA Gentle madam, no.

CLEOPATRA You lie, up to the hearing of the gods.
But if there be nor ever were one such,
It's past the size of dreaming; nature wants stuff
To vie strange forms with fancy, yet t' imagine

83–84 **propertied ... spheres** musical as the spheres (referring to the belief in the music of the spheres, made by the harmonious blend of each planet's "note" and normally too fine for human ears to catch) 85 **quail** make quail 90 **livery** (1) service (2) possession, guardianship (legal term) 91 **crowns and crownets** i.e., kings and princes 92 **plates** silver coins 96–97 **But if ... dreaming** but suppose you were right, and no such man exists, and never did exist, how can I have imagined such a man, for no mere dreaming fantasy could make something so great

An Antony were nature's piece 'gainst fancy,
Condemning shadows quite.

DOLABELLA Hear me, good madam.
Your loss is as yourself, great; and you bear it
As answering to the weight. Would I might never
O'ertake pursued success, but I do feel,
By the rebound of yours, a grief that smites
My very heart at root.

CLEOPATRA I thank you, sir.
Know you what Caesar means to do with me?

DOLABELLA I am loath to tell you what I would you knew.

CLEOPATRA Nay, pray you, sir.

DOLABELLA Though he be honorable——

CLEOPATRA He'll lead me, then, in triumph?

DOLABELLA Madam, he will. I know't.

Flourish. Enter Proculeius, Caesar, Gallus, Maecenas, and others of his Train.

ALL Make way there! Caesar!

CAESAR Which is the Queen of Egypt?

DOLABELLA It is the Emperor, madam.

Cleopatra kneels.

CAESAR Arise! You shall not kneel:
I pray you rise; rise, Egypt.

CLEOPATRA Sir, the gods
Will have it thus. My master and my lord
I must obey.

CAESAR Take to you no hard thoughts.
The record of what injuries you did us,

97–100 **nature . . . quite** reality lacks the material to compete with imagination in the creation of strange forms, yet the creation of an Antony would be a masterpiece of conception on the part of reality, surpassing and discrediting all the illusions of imagination 103 **but I do** if I do not

Though written in our flesh, we shall remember
As things but done by chance.

CLEOPATRA Sole sir o' th' world,
I cannot project mine own cause so well
To make it clear, but do confess I have
Been laden with like frailties which before
Have often shamed our sex.

CAESAR Cleopatra, know,
We will extenuate rather than enforce.
If you apply yourself to our intents,
Which towards you are most gentle, you shall find
A benefit in this change; but if you seek
To lay on me a cruelty by taking
Antony's course, you shall bereave yourself
Of my good purposes, and put your children
To that destruction which I'll guard them from
If thereon you rely. I'll take my leave.

CLEOPATRA And may, through all the world: 'tis yours, and we,
Your scutcheons and your signs of conquest, shall
Hang in what place you please. Here, my good lord.
[*Hands him a paper*.]

CAESAR You shall advise me in all for Cleopatra.

CLEOPATRA This is the brief of money, plate, and jewels
I am possessed of. 'Tis exactly valued,
Not petty things admitted. [*Calling*] Where's Seleucus?

[*Enter Seleucus*.]

SELEUCUS Here, madam.

CLEOPATRA This is my treasurer; let him speak, my lord,
Upon his peril, that I have reserved
To myself nothing. Speak the truth, Seleucus.

121 **project** set forth (accented on first syllable) 122 **clear** innocent 125 **enforce** emphasize 126 **apply** conform 135 **scutcheons** armorial bearings (alluding to the captured shields displayed by a conqueror) 138 **brief** summary

SELEUCUS Madam,
I had rather seel my lips than to my peril
Speak that which is not.

CLEOPATRA What have I kept back?

SELEUCUS Enough to purchase what you have made known.

CAESAR Nay, blush not, Cleopatra, I approve
Your wisdom in the deed.

CLEOPATRA See, Caesar: O, behold,
How pomp is followed! Mine will now be yours,
And should we shift estates, yours would be mine.
The ingratitude of this Seleucus does
Even make me wild. O slave, of no more trust
Than love that's hired! What, goest thou back? Thou shalt
Go back, I warrant thee; but I'll catch thine eyes,
Though they had wings. Slave, soulless villain, dog!
O rarely base!

CAESAR Good Queen, let us entreat you.

CLEOPATRA O Caesar, what a wounding shame is this,
That thou vouchsafing here to visit me,
Doing the honor of thy lordliness
To one so meek, that mine own servant should
Parcel the sum of my disgraces by
Addition of his envy. Say, good Caesar,
That I some lady trifles have reserved,
Immoment toys, things of such dignity
As we greet modern friends withal; and say
Some nobler token I have kept apart
For Livia and Octavia, to induce
Their mediation—must I be unfolded
With one that I have bred? The gods! it smites me

146 **seel** sew up 151 **Mine** i.e., my followers 158 **rarely** exceptionally 163 **Parcel** piece out 164 **envy** malice 165 **lady** lady's 166 **Immoment** unimportant 167 **modern** ordinary 169 **Livia** Caesar's wife 170–71 **unfolded/With** exposed by

Beneath the fall I have. [*To Seleucus*] Prithee go hence,
Or I shall show the cinders of my spirits
Through th' ashes of my chance. Wert thou a man,
Thou wouldst have mercy on me.

CAESAR Forbear, Seleucus.
[*Exit Seleucus.*]

CLEOPATRA Be it known that we, the greatest, are misthought
For things that others do, and when we fall,
We answer others' merits in our name,
Are therefore to be pitied.

CAESAR Cleopatra,
Not what you have reserved, nor what acknowledged,
Put we i' th' roll of conquest: still be't yours,
Bestow it at your pleasure, and believe
Caesar's no merchant, to make prize with you
Of things that merchants sold. Therefore be cheered,
Make not your thoughts your prisons: no, dear Queen,
For we intend so to dispose you as
Yourself shall give us counsel. Feed and sleep:
Our care and pity is so much upon you
That we remain your friend; and so adieu.

CLEOPATRA My master, and my lord!

CAESAR Not so. Adieu.
Flourish. Exeunt Caesar and his Train.

CLEOPATRA He words me, girls, he words me, that I should not
Be noble to myself! But hark thee, Charmian.
[*Whispers to Charmian.*]

IRAS Finish, good lady, the bright day is done,
And we are for the dark.

173 **cinders** burning coals 174 **chance** fortune 176 **misthought** misjudged 178 **We ... name** (1) we have to be responsible for faults committed in our name (**merits** = deserts, acts deserving punishment) (2) our name is used to validate the actions of others 183 **make prize** haggle

CLEOPATRA Hie thee again:
I have spoke already, and it is provided;
Go put it to the haste.

CHARMIAN Madam, I will.

Enter Dolabella.

DOLABELLA Where is the Queen?

CHARMIAN Behold, sir. [*Exit.*]

CLEOPATRA Dolabella!

DOLABELLA Madam, as thereto sworn, by your command
(Which my love makes religion to obey)
I tell you this: Caesar through Syria
Intends his journey, and within three days
You with your children will he send before.
Make your best use of this. I have performed
Your pleasure, and my promise.

CLEOPATRA Dolabella,
I shall remain your debtor.

DOLABELLA I, your servant.
Adieu, good Queen; I must attend on Caesar.

CLEOPATRA Farewell, and thanks. *Exit* [*Dolabella*].
Now, Iras, what think'st thou?
Thou, an Egyptian puppet, shall be shown
In Rome as well as I: mechanic slaves
With greasy aprons, rules, and hammers shall
Uplift us to the view. In their thick breaths,
Rank of gross diet, shall we be enclouded,
And forced to drink their vapor.

IRAS The gods forbid!

CLEOPATRA Nay, 'tis most certain, Iras. Saucy lictors
Will catch at us like strumpets, and scald rhymers
Ballad us out o' tune. The quick comedians

208 **puppet** (she envisages Iras as a doll manipulated by the puppeteer, Octavius—i.e., a figure posed on a float following Caesar in the triumphal procession) 209 **mechanic slaves** vulgar workmen 212 **Rank of gross diet** stinking of bad food 214 **Saucy lictors** insolent officers 215 **scald** scurvy

Extemporally will stage us, and present
Our Alexandrian revels: Antony
Shall be brought drunken forth, and I shall see
Some squeaking Cleopatra boy my greatness
I' th' posture of a whore.

IRAS O, the good gods!

CLEOPATRA Nay, that's certain.

IRAS I'll never see't! For I am sure mine nails
Are stronger than mine eyes.

CLEOPATRA Why, that's the way
To fool their preparation, and to conquer
Their most absurd intents.

Enter Charmian.

Now, Charmian!
Show me, my women, like a queen: go fetch
My best attires. I am again for Cydnus,
To meet Mark Antony. Sirrah Iras, go.
Now, noble Charmian, we'll dispatch indeed,
And when thou hast done this chare, I'll give thee leave
To play till doomsday.—Bring our crown and all.
[*Exit Iras.*] *A noise within.*
Wherefore's this noise?

Enter a Guardsman.

GUARDSMAN Here is a rural fellow
That will not be denied your Highness' presence:
He brings you figs.

CLEOPATRA Let him come in. *Exit Guardsman.*
What poor an instrument
May do a noble deed! He brings me liberty.
My resolution's placed, and I have nothing

220 **boy my greatness** reduce my greatness to the crude imitation that a boy can manage (in England women's parts were acted by boys or young men) 229 **Sirrah** (an address to inferiors, used equally of men or women) 231 **chare** chore 236 **What poor an** what a poor 238 **placed** fixed

Of woman in me: now from head to foot
I am marble-constant: now the fleeting moon
No planet is of mine.

Enter Guardsman and Clown [*with basket*].

GUARDSMAN This is the man.

CLEOPATRA Avoid, and leave him. *Exit Guardsman.*
Hast thou the pretty worm of Nilus there,
That kills and pains not?

CLOWN Truly I have him; but I would not be the party that should desire you to touch him, for his biting is immortal: those that do die of it do seldom or never recover.

CLEOPATRA Remember'st thou any that have died on't?

CLOWN Very many, men and women too. I heard of one of them no longer than yesterday; a very honest woman, but something given to lie, as a woman should not do but in the way of honesty; how she died of the biting of it, what pain she felt; truly, she makes a very good report o' th' worm; but he that will believe all that they say shall never be saved by half that they do; but this is most falliable, the worm's an odd worm.

CLEOPATRA Get thee hence, farewell.

CLOWN I wish you all joy of the worm.
[*Sets down his basket.*]

CLEOPATRA Farewell.

CLOWN You must think this, look you, that the worm will do his kind.

CLEOPATRA Ay, ay, farewell.

240 **fleeting moon** (a symbol of fickleness, especially in women; and Cleopatra's special symbol, as being Isis or moon goddess) 241 s.d. **Clown** rustic 242 **Avoid** depart 243 **worm of Nilus** serpent of Nile, i.e., asp or small viper 247 **immortal** (his blunder for "mortal") 250 **heard of** heard from 251 **honest** (1) chaste (2) truthful (similar innuendoes fill the speech, with puns on "lie" and "die") 263 **do his kind** act according to his nature

CLOWN Look you, the worm is not to be trusted but in the keeping of wise people: for indeed there is no goodness in the worm.

CLEOPATRA Take thou no care; it shall be heeded.

CLOWN Very good. Give it nothing, I pray you, for it is not worth the feeding.

CLEOPATRA Will it eat me?

CLOWN You must not think I am so simple but I know the devil himself will not eat a woman. I know that a woman is a dish for the gods, if the devil dress her not. But truly, these same whoreson devils do the gods great harm in their women; for in every ten that they make, the devils mar five.

CLEOPATRA Well, get thee gone, farewell.

CLOWN Yes, forsooth. I wish you joy o' th' worm. *Exit.*

[*Enter Iras with a robe, crown, etc.*]

CLEOPATRA Give me my robe, put on my crown, I have
Immortal longings in me. Now no more
The juice of Egypt's grape shall moist this lip.
Yare, yare, good Iras; quick: methinks I hear
Antony call: I see him rouse himself
To praise my noble act. I hear him mock
The luck of Caesar, which the gods give men
To excuse their after wrath. Husband, I come:
Now to that name my courage prove my title!
I am fire, and air; my other elements
I give to baser life. So, have you done?
Come then, and take the last warmth of my lips.
Farewell, kind Charmian, Iras, long farewell.
[*Kisses them. Iras falls and dies.*]

274 **dress** (1) prepare (i.e., of food) (2) clothe, equip 281 **Immortal longings** (1) the desires of a goddess (2) longings for immortality 283 **Yare** quickly 287 **their after wrath** the retributive punishments heaped by the gods on those who have been too proud of their good fortune 289–90 **I am fire . . . life** (man was believed to be made up of four elements, two higher—fire and air—and two lower or baser—earth and water)

Have I the aspic in my lips? Dost fall?
If thou and nature can so gently part,
The stroke of death is as a lover's pinch,
Which hurts, and is desired. Dost thou lie still?
If thus thou vanishest, thou tell'st the world
It is not worth leave-taking.

CHARMIAN Dissolve, thick cloud, and rain, that I may say
The gods themselves do weep.

CLEOPATRA This proves me base:
If she first meet the curlèd Antony,
He'll make demand of her, and spend that kiss
Which is my heaven to have. Come, thou mortal wretch,
[*To an asp, which she applies to her breast.*]
With thy sharp teeth this knot intrinsicate
Of life at once untie. Poor venomous fool,
Be angry, and dispatch. O, couldst thou speak,
That I might hear thee call great Caesar ass
Unpolicied!

CHARMIAN O eastern star!

CLEOPATRA Peace, peace!
Dost thou not see my baby at my breast,
That sucks the nurse asleep?

CHARMIAN O, break! O, break!

CLEOPATRA As sweet as balm, as soft as air, as gentle—
O, Antony! Nay, I will take thee too:
[*Applies another asp to her arm.*]
What should I stay—— *Dies.*

293 **aspic** asp 301 **curlèd** freshly barbered 303 **thou mortal wretch** you deadly little object (**wretch**, like **fool** in line 305, is often an affectionate term, used especially of children) 304 **intrinsicate** intricate 306 **dispatch** quickly end it 308 **Unpolicied** lacking statecraft 308 **eastern star** morning star, Venus 313 **What** why 313 s.d. **Dies** (modern actresses prefer to die upright, seated regally, but Caesar's penultimate and final speeches suggest that Cleopatra dies—as in Plutarch—"upon a bed")

CHARMIAN In this wild world? So, fare thee well.
Now boast thee, death, in thy possession lies
A lass unparalleled. Downy windows, close;
And golden Phoebus never be beheld
Of eyes again so royal! Your crown's awry;
I'll mend it, and then play——

Enter the Guard, rustling in.

FIRST GUARD Where's the Queen?

CHARMIAN Speak softly, wake her not.

FIRST GUARD Caesar hath sent——

CHARMIAN Too slow a messenger.
[*Applies an asp.*]
O, come apace, dispatch; I partly feel thee.

FIRST GUARD Approach, ho! All's not well: Caesar's beguiled.

SECOND GUARD There's Dolabella sent from Caesar; call him.

FIRST GUARD What work is here! Charmian, is this well done?

CHARMIAN It is well done, and fitting for a princess
Descended of so many royal kings.
Ah, soldier! *Charmian dies.*

Enter Dolabella.

DOLABELLA How goes it here?

SECOND GUARD All dead.

DOLABELLA Caesar, thy thoughts
Touch their effects in this: thyself art coming
To see performed the dreaded act which thou
So sought'st to hinder.

Enter Caesar and all his Train, marching.

ALL A way there, a way for Caesar!

317 **Phoebus** sun god 330 **Touch their effects** meet with realization

DOLABELLA O, sir, you are too sure an augurer:
That you did fear is done.

CAESAR Bravest at the last,
She leveled at our purposes, and being royal,
Took her own way. The manner of their deaths?
I do not see them bleed.

DOLABELLA Who was last with them?

FIRST GUARD A simple countryman, that brought her figs.
This was his basket.

CAESAR Poisoned, then.

FIRST GUARD O, Caesar,
This Charmian lived but now, she stood and spake;
I found her trimming up the diadem
On her dead mistress; tremblingly she stood,
And on the sudden dropped.

CAESAR O, noble weakness!
If they had swallowed poison, 'twould appear
By external swelling; but she looks like sleep,
As she would catch another Antony
In her strong toil of grace.

DOLABELLA Here, on her breast,
There is a vent of blood, and something blown;
The like is on her arm.

FIRST GUARD This is an aspic's trail; and these fig leaves
Have slime upon them, such as th' aspic leaves
Upon the caves of Nile.

CAESAR Most probable
That so she died: for her physician tells me
She hath pursued conclusions infinite
Of easy ways to die. Take up her bed,
And bear her women from the monument.
She shall be buried by her Antony.

335 **leveled at** (1) guessed (2) fought against 347 **toil** snare 348 **vent** discharge 348 **blown** swollen 354 **conclusions** experiments

No grave upon the earth shall clip in it
A pair so famous. High events as these
Strike those that make them; and their story is
No less in pity, than his glory which
Brought them to be lamented. Our army shall
In solemn show attend this funeral,
And then to Rome. Come, Dolabella, see
High order in this great solemnity. *Exeunt omnes.*

FINIS

358 clip clasp **360 Strike** touch

Textual Note

Antony and Cleopatra was entered in the Stationers' Register in May, 1608. Though this procedure normally suggested that publication would follow shortly, the play remained, in fact, unprinted until 1623, when it appeared in the "Tragedies" section of the First Folio. This First Folio text of the play is therefore the single authoritative one, and all succeeding editions—including of course the present one—derive from it.

It is widely agreed that the Folio text of *Antony and Cleopatra* was almost certainly printed direct from Shakespeare's own manuscript, and not from a transcript or prompter's copy. The features of the Folio text that suggest a source in Shakespearean manuscript may be briefly summarized as follows. First, it contains unusual spellings and word usages, some of which seem to be peculiar to Shakespeare, and some of which were, at any rate, archaic by the time the Folio was printed. Secondly, many of the Folio misprints are of the kind (occurring also in other texts of the plays) that would seem to arise from the individual character of Shakespeare's own handwriting. Thirdly, it lacks all act and scene divisions, except for the opening "Actus Primus, Scoena Prima"; a lack which indicates copy prepared primarily for the theater. Fourthly, its stage directions are unusually full and detailed, and are often of the nature of an author's "notes on the text"; for example, "Alarum afar off, as at a sea fight." And lastly, the Folio text contains a passage in the first Monument scene (IV.xv.12–29) that suggests the direct carrying over of the author's deletions and rewritings. (See relevant footnote to text.) None of this is absolutely conclusive, but taken together the evidence leaves little doubt that the Folio text was printed direct from Shakespeare's manuscript.

As a text, it is relatively good: it contains many slips but few real difficulties. Its major flaw is the occurrence of very frequent mislineation. This has been silently adjusted in the present edition, as the "correct" lineation is either clear, or, where doubtful, immaterial. The present edition also adds a list of dramatis personae, which is lacking in the Folio; and it adds act and scene divisions, and indications of locality, except for the Folio's opening "Actus Primus, Scoena Prima" which is here translated. It also supplements the existing stage directions. All such additions and supplementations are indicated by square brackets. The positions of a few stage directions have been slightly altered; speech prefixes and other abbreviations are expanded, punctuation and spelling are modernized. The spelling of proper names is regularized: for example, "Cleopatra" is given, though in F "Cleopater" also appears; again, "Decretas" is given though in F "Decretus" also appears; "Canidius" is given for F's "Camidius," "Camidias," and "Camindius"; and so forth. (In a few instances, where the change is more marked, the reading is listed below.) All other departures from the Folio text are listed below, and utilize earlier editorial emendations; the adopted reading is given in bold, and then the original reading in roman. As in the footnotes to the text, a line number followed by "s.d." indicates the stage direction which follows the given line, or which interrupts it.

I.i.39 **On** One 50 **whose** who

I.ii.4 **Charge** change 40 **fertile** foretell 63 **Alexas** [F treats "Alexas" as a speech prefix and gives him the rest of the speech here given to Charmian] 81 **Saw** Saue 113 [F adds s.d.: Enter another Messenger] 114 **ho, the news!** how the newes? 115 **First Attendant** 1 Mes 116 **Second Attendant** 2 Mes 119 **Messenger** 3 Mes 131 **Ho now, Enobarbus!** How now Enobarbus. 138 **occasion** an occasion 181 **leave** loue 186 **Hath** Haue 195 **hair** heire

I.iii.25 **first** fitst 43 **services** Seruicles 82 **by my sword** by Sword

I.iv.3 **Our** One 8 **Vouchsafed** vouchsafe 9 **abstract** abstracts 44 **deared** fear'd 46 **lackeying** lacking 56 **wassails** Vassailes 58 **Pansa** Pausa 75 **we** me

I.v.34 s.d. **Antony** Caesar 50 **dumbed** dumbe 61 **man** mans

TEXTUAL NOTE

II.i.16,18,38 [F's speech prefix here, as for all speeches in the scene other than those of Pompey and Varrius, is "Mene." But the context clearly indicates that Menas as well as Menecrates speaks in the scene] 21 **waned** wand 41 **warred** wan'd

II.ii.125 **not so** not, say 126 **reproof** proofe 176 s.d. **Exit** Exit omnes. Manet 210 **glow** gloue 212 **gentlewomen** Gentlewoman 229 **heard** hard 238 **pow'r breathe** powr breath

II.iii.23 **afeard** a feare 31 **away** alway

II.v.12 **Tawny-finned** Tawny fine 43 **is** 'tis

II.vi.s.d. **Agrippa, with** Agrippa, Menas with 19 **is** his 52 **jailer** laylor 58 **composition** composion 66 **meanings** meaning 69 **more of** more

II.vii.1 **their** th' their 4 **high-colored** high Conlord 12 **lief** liue 36 **pyramises** Pyramisis 94 **then** then he 102 **grows** grow 113 **bear** beate 126 **Splits** Spleet's 130 **father's** Father 131–35 **Take heed ... sound out** [F gives all to Enobarbus, mistaking (?) speech prefix "Menas" for vocative]

III.i.5 **Silius** Romaine [so throughout scene] 8 **whither** whether

III.ii.10 **Agrippa** Ant 16 **figures** Figure 59 **wept** weepe

III.iv.9 **took't** look't 24 **yours** your 30 **Your** You 38 **has** he's

III.v.14 **world, thou hast** would thou hadst 16 **the one the other** the other

III.vi.13 **he there** hither 13 **kings of kings** King of Kings 74 **Comagene** Comageat

III.vii.4 **it is** it it 5 **Is't** If 23 **Toryne** Troine 35 **muleters** Militers 51 **Actium** Action 69 **led** leade 72 **Canidius** Ven

III.x.s.d. **Enobarbus** Enobarbus and Scarus 14 **June** Inne 27 **he** his

III.xi.19 **that** them 44 **He is** Hee's 47 **seize** cease 51 **whither** whether 58 **tow** stowe 59 **Thy** The

III.xiii.10 **merèd** meered 55 **Caesar** Caesars 56 **embraced** embrace 74 **deputation** disputation 104 **errand** arrant 162 **smite** smile 165 **discandying** discandering 168 **sits** sets 199 **preys on** prayes in 201 s.d. **Exit** Exeunt

IV.ii.1 **Domitius** Domitian

IV.iii.7 **Third Soldier** 1

IV.iv.5–8 **Nay, I'll help ... must be** [F gives all to Cleopatra, mistaking (?) speech prefix "Antony" for vocative, and misplacing (?) it after "help too"] 8 **Sooth, la** Sooth-law 13 **daff't** daft 24 **Captain** Alex

IV.v.1,3,6 **Soldier** Eros

IV.viii.2 **gests** guests 23 **favoring** sauoring

IV.xii.4 **augurers** Auguries 21 **spanieled** pannelled

TEXTUAL NOTE

IV.xiv.4 **towered** toward 10 **dislimns** dislimes 19 **Caesar** Caesars 104 **ho!** how?

IV.xv.72 **e'en** in 90 s.d. **off** of

V.i.s.d. **Maecenas** Menas 28,31 **Agrippa** Dol 59 **live** leaue

V.ii.56 **varletry** Varlotarie 81 **little O, th' earth** little o' th' earth 87 **autumn 'twas** Antony it was 104 **smites** suites 216 **Ballad** Ballads 216 **o' tune** a Tune 228 **Cydnus** Cidrus 318 **awry** away 319 s.d. **rustling in** rustling in and Dolabella

WILLIAM SHAKESPEARE

THE LIFE OF TIMON OF ATHENS

Edited by Maurice Charney

The Actors' Names

TIMON OF ATHENS
LUCIUS, and LUCULLUS } two flattering lords
SEMPRONIUS, another flattering lord
VENTIDIUS, one of Timon's false friends
APEMANTUS, a churlish philosopher
ALCIBIADES, an Athenian captain
POET
PAINTER
JEWELER
MERCHANT
[FLAVIUS, steward to Timon]
FLAMINIUS, one of Timon's servants
SERVILIUS, another
[LUCILIUS, another]
CAPHIS, PHILOTUS, TITUS, HORTENSIUS, [SERVANT TO] VARRO, [SERVANT TO] LUCIUS, [SERVANT TO ISIDORE] } several servants to usurers
[AN OLD ATHENIAN]
[THREE STRANGERS]
[A PAGE]
[A FOOL]
[PHRYNIA, [TIMANDRA } mistresses to Alcibiades]
CERTAIN MASKERS [AS] CUPID [AND AMAZONS]
CERTAIN SENATORS, CERTAIN THIEVES, WITH DIVERS OTHER SERVANTS AND ATTENDANTS, [LORDS, OFFICERS, SOLDIERS]

[*Scene*: Athens and the neighboring woods]

THE TRAGEDY OF TIMON OF ATHENS

ACT I

Scene I. [*Athens. Timon's house.*]

Enter Poet, Painter, Jeweler, Merchant at several doors.

POET Good day, sir.

PAINTER I am glad y'are well.

POET I have not seen you long; how goes the world?

PAINTER It wears, sir, as it grows.

POET Ay that's well known.
But what particular rarity? What strange,
Which manifold record not matches? See,
Magic of bounty, all these spirits thy power
Hath conjured to attend. I know the merchant.

PAINTER I know them both; th' other's a jeweler.

A footnote is keyed to the text by line number. Text references are printed in **bold** type; the annotation follows in roman type.
I.i.s.d. **several** separate (the Poet and Painter enter at one door, the Jeweler and Merchant at another) 3 **wears** wears out 5 **manifold record** many and varied records, history ("record" accented on second syllable) 6 **bounty** generosity

MERCHANT O 'tis a worthy lord.

JEWELER Nay that's most fixed.

MERCHANT A most incomparable man, breathed, as it were,
To an untirable and continuate goodness.
He passes.

JEWELER I have a jewel here——

MERCHANT O pray let's see't. For the Lord Timon, sir?

JEWELER If he will touch the estimate. But for that——

POET [*Aside to Painter*] When we for recompense have praised the vild,
It stains the glory in that happy verse
Which aptly sings the good.

MERCHANT [*Looking at the jewel*] 'Tis a good form.

JEWELER And rich. Here is a water, look ye.

PAINTER You are rapt, sir, in some work, some dedication
To the great lord.

POET A thing slipped idly from me.
Our poesy is as a gum, which oozes
From whence 'tis nourished. The fire i' th' flint
Shows not till it be struck; our gentle flame
Provokes itself, and like the current flies
Each bound it chases. What have you there?

PAINTER A picture, sir. When comes your book forth?

POET Upon the heels of my presentment, sir.
Let's see your piece.

9 **fixed** certain 10 **breathed** exercised, trained 11 **continuate** uninterrupted 12 **passes** surpasses 14 **touch the estimate** offer the expected price 15 **vild** vile 16 **happy** fortunate 18 **water** luster (of a jewel) 23–24 **our gentle flame/Provokes itself** i.e., the inspiration of poets is spontaneous, not externally provoked like the "fire i' th' flint" 25 **Each bound it chases** i.e., the stream flows towards the shore but rebounds upon contact 27 **presentment** presentation (to Timon)

PAINTER 'Tis a good piece.

POET So 'tis; this comes off well and excellent.

PAINTER Indifferent.

POET Admirable. How this grace
Speaks his own standing! What a mental power
This eye shoots forth! How big imagination
Moves in this lip! To th' dumbness of the gesture
One might interpret.

PAINTER It is a pretty mocking of the life.
Here is a touch—is't good?

POET I will say of it,
It tutors nature; artificial strife
Lives in these touches, livelier than life.

Enter certain Senators, [who pass over the stage and exeunt].

PAINTER How this lord is followed!

POET The senators of Athens, happy men!

PAINTER Look, moe!

POET You see this confluence, this great flood of visitors:
I have in this rough work shaped out a man
Whom this beneath world doth embrace and hug
With amplest entertainment. My free drift
Halts not particularly, but moves itself
In a wide sea of wax; no leveled malice

30 **Indifferent** neither good nor bad 31 **standing** dignity, social status 32 **big** (adverb) 33 **dumbness** silence (as in a dumb show) 34 **interpret** supply words 35 **mocking** imitation 37 **artificial strife** the striving of art to outdo nature 41 **moe** more 44 **beneath world** sublunary world (Timon as the moon) 46 **particularly** at individuals 47 **sea of wax** (either a sea of inspiration as easily molded as wax—not limited to a mere writing tablet of wax—or perhaps a waxing sea swelling with inspiration) 47 **leveled** aimed (at one person)

Infects one comma in the course I hold,
But flies an eagle flight, bold and forth on,
Leaving no tract behind.

PAINTER How shall I understand you?

POET I will unbolt to you.
You see how all conditions, how all minds,
As well of glib and slipp'ry creatures as
Of grave and austere quality, tender down
Their services to Lord Timon. His large fortune,
Upon his good and gracious nature hanging,
Subdues and properties to his love and tendance
All sorts of hearts; yea, from the glass-faced
flatterer
To Apemantus, that few things loves better
Than to abhor himself—even he drops down
The knee before him, and returns in peace
Most rich in Timon's nod.

PAINTER I saw them speak together.

POET Sir, I have upon a high and pleasant hill
Feigned Fortune to be throned. The base o' th'
mount
Is ranked with all deserts, all kind of natures
That labor on the bosom of this sphere
To propagate their states. Amongst them all,
Whose eyes are on this sovereign lady fixed,
One do I personate of Lord Timon's frame,
Whom Fortune with her ivory hand wafts to her,

50 **tract** (either "trace" or "track") 52 **conditions** (1) social classes (2) temperaments 54 **tender down** offer (as one offers money) 57 **properties** appropriates 57 **tendance** attendance 58 **glass-faced** mirror-faced 64 **Feigned** imagined 65 **deserts** degrees of worth 67 **propagate their states** increase their possessions 69 **frame** (1) disposition (2) physical stature 70 **ivory hand** hand white and smooth as ivory (this is the right hand of Fortune, with which she distributes her favors; with the left or dark hand she takes them away)

Whose present grace to present slaves and servants
Translates his rivals.

PAINTER 'Tis conceived to scope.
This throne, this Fortune, and this hill, methinks,
With one man beckoned from the rest below,
Bowing his head against the steepy mount
To climb his happiness, would be well expressed
In our condition.

POET Nay, sir, but hear me on.
All those which were his fellows but of late,
Some better than his value, on the moment
Follow his strides, his lobbies fill with tendance,
Rain sacrificial whisperings in his ear,
Make sacred even his stirrup, and through him
Drink the free air.

PAINTER Ay marry, what of these?

POET When Fortune in her shift and change of mood
Spurns down her late beloved, all his dependants
Which labored after him to the mountain's top,
Even on their knees and hands, let him slip down,
Not one accompanying his declining foot.

PAINTER 'Tis common.
A thousand moral paintings I can show
That shall demonstrate these quick blows of
Fortune's
More pregnantly than words. Yet you do well
To show Lord Timon that mean eyes have seen
The foot above the head.

71 **present** (1) existing now (2) immediate 71 **grace** graciousness, generosity 72 **Translates** transforms 72 **to scope** to the purpose, just right 81 **sacrificial whisperings** (lines 81–83 suggest the hieratic atmosphere surrounding Timon, now high in Fortune's favor) 83 **Drink** breathe 83 **marry** indeed (originally "By Mary") 90 **moral paintings** allegorical pictures (especially wall hangings) 91 **demonstrate** (accented on second syllable) 91 **quick** (1) swift (2) full of life 93 **mean** lowly 94 **The foot above the head** i.e., in the quick changes that Fortune brings, the foot of the lowliest may suddenly appear above the head of the highest

Trumpets sound. Enter Lord Timon, addressing himself courteously to every suitor; [a Messenger from Ventidius talking with him; Lucilius and other servants following].

TIMON Imprisoned is he, say you?

MESSENGER Ay, my good lord; five talents is his debt,
His means most short, his creditors most strait.
Your honorable letter he desires
To those have shut him up, which failing,
Periods his comfort.

TIMON Noble Ventidius—well.
I am not of that feather to shake off
My friend when he must need me. I do know him
A gentleman that well deserves a help,
Which he shall have. I'll pay the debt and free him.

MESSENGER Your lordship ever binds him.

TIMON Commend me to him; I will send his ransom,
And being enfranchised bid him come to me.
'Tis not enough to help the feeble up,
But to support him after. Fare you well.

MESSENGER All happiness to your honor. *Exit.*

Enter an Old Athenian.

OLD ATHENIAN Lord Timon, hear me speak.

TIMON Freely, good father.

OLD ATHENIAN Thou hast a servant named Lucilius.

TIMON I have so. What of him?

OLD ATHENIAN Most noble Timon, call the man before thee.

TIMON Attends he here or no? Lucilius!

LUCILIUS Here at your lordship's service.

96 **strait** strict 99 **Periods** puts an end to 100 **feather** character 104 **binds** attaches by ties of gratitude (with play on "free" in line 103)

OLD ATHENIAN This fellow here, Lord Timon, this thy creature,
By night frequents my house. I am a man
That from my first have been inclined to thrift,
And my estate deserves an heir more raised
Than one which holds a trencher.

TIMON Well; what further?

OLD ATHENIAN One only daughter have I, no kin else,
On whom I may confer what I have got.
The maid is fair, a th' youngest for a bride,
And I have bred her at my dearest cost
In qualities of the best. This man of thine
Attempts her love. I prithee, noble lord,
Join with me to forbid him her resort;
Myself have spoke in vain.

TIMON The man is honest.

OLD ATHENIAN Therefore he will be, Timon.
His honesty rewards him in itself;
It must not bear my daughter.

TIMON Does she love him?

OLD ATHENIAN She is young and apt.
Our own precedent passions do instruct us
What levity's in youth.

TIMON Love you the maid?

LUCILIUS Ay, my good lord, and she accepts of it.

OLD ATHENIAN If in her marriage my consent be missing,
I call the gods to witness, I will choose

116 **fellow, creature** (terms of contempt) 120 **trencher** wooden plate or shallow dish on which meat is served (a servant who waits on tables would hold a trencher) 123 **a** (a worn down form for "of") 127 **her resort** resort or access to her 129 **Therefore he will be** i.e., since Lucilius *is* honest (or honorable), he will therefore show his honesty by not pursuing the Old Athenian's daughter 131 **bear** carry away 133 **precedent** former (accented on second syllable)

Mine heir from forth the beggars of the world,
And dispossess her all.

TIMON How shall she be endowed,
If she be mated with an equal husband?

OLD ATHENIAN Three talents on the present; in future, all.

TIMON This gentleman of mine hath served me long.
To build his fortune I will strain a little,
For 'tis a bond in men. Give him thy daughter;
What you bestow, in him I'll counterpoise,
And make him weigh with her.

OLD ATHENIAN Most noble lord,
Pawn me to this your honor, she is his.

TIMON My hand to thee, mine honor on my promise.

LUCILIUS Humbly I thank your lordship; never may
That state or fortune fall into my keeping,
Which is not owed to you.

Exit [*Lucilius, with Old Athenian*].

POET Vouchsafe my labor, and long live your lordship.

TIMON I thank you; you shall hear from me anon.
Go not away. What have you there, my friend?

PAINTER A piece of painting, which I do beseech
Your lordship to accept.

TIMON Painting is welcome.
The painting is almost the natural man;
For since dishonor traffics with man's nature,
He is but outside. These penciled figures are

139 **all** completely 140 **equal** (either socially or financially) 141 **on the present** at once 144 **bond** obligation 145 **counterpoise** counterbalance 151 **owed** (1) acknowledged to you as the cause of it (2) due to you as a debt 152 **Vouchsafe** deign to accept 158 **traffics** deals (pejorative sense) 159 **but outside** merely external, a false semblance 159 **penciled** painted

Even such as they give out. I like your work,
And you shall find I like it. Wait attendance
Till you hear further from me.

PAINTER The gods preserve ye.

TIMON Well fare you, gentleman. Give me your hand;
We must needs dine together. Sir, your jewel
Hath suffered under praise.

JEWELER What, my lord, dispraise?

TIMON A mere satiety of commendations.
If I should pay you for't as 'tis extolled,
It would unclew me quite.

JEWELER My lord, 'tis rated
As those which sell would give. But you well know,
Things of like value, differing in the owners,
Are prizèd by their masters. Believe't, dear lord,
You mend the jewel by the wearing it.

TIMON Well mocked.

MERCHANT No, my good lord; he speaks the common tongue
Which all men speak with him.

Enter Apemantus.

TIMON Look who comes here; will you be chid?

JEWELER We'll bear with your lordship.

MERCHANT He'll spare none.

160 **Even such as they give out** i.e., painting, in contrast with human nature, is honest; it makes no pretense to be something other than what it appears to be 165 **under praise** in being praised, since the jewel is beyond praise (but the Jeweler takes it in the sense of "dispraise") 166 **mere** absolute 168 **unclew** undo 169 **As those which sell would give** i.e., at the wholesale price 171 **Are prizèd by their masters** are valued according to the social status of their owners 172 **mend** improve 173 **mocked** simulated (i.e., I know your flattery is only part of your sales talk) 174 **speaks the common tongue** says what everyone is saying

TIMON Good morrow to thee, gentle Apemantus.

APEMANTUS Till I be gentle, stay thou for thy good morrow——
When thou art Timon's dog, and these knaves honest.

TIMON Why dost thou call them knaves, thou know'st them not?

APEMANTUS Are they not Athenians?

TIMON Yes.

APEMANTUS Then I repent not.

JEWELER You know me, Apemantus?

APEMANTUS Thou know'st I do, I called thee by thy name.

TIMON Thou art proud, Apemantus.

APEMANTUS Of nothing so much as that I am not like Timon.

TIMON Whither art going?

APEMANTUS To knock out an honest Athenian's brains.

TIMON That's a deed thou't die for.

APEMANTUS Right, if doing nothing be death by th' law.

TIMON How lik'st thou this picture, Apemantus?

APEMANTUS The best, for the innocence.

TIMON Wrought he not well that painted it?

APEMANTUS He wrought better that made the painter, and yet he's but a filthy piece of work.

178 **gentle** (1) well-born (a conventional complimentary epithet) (2) mild
198 **innocence** (1) harmlessness (2) foolishness 201 **filthy** contemptible

PAINTER Y'are a dog.

APEMANTUS Thy mother's of my generation. What's she, if I be a dog?

TIMON Wilt dine with me, Apemantus?

APEMANTUS No. I eat not lords.

TIMON And thou shouldst, thou'dst anger ladies.

APEMANTUS O they eat lords; so they come by great bellies.

TIMON That's a lascivious apprehension.

APEMANTUS So, thou apprehend'st it, take it for thy labor.

TIMON How dost thou like this jewel, Apemantus?

APEMANTUS Not so well as plain-dealing, which will not cost a man a doit.

TIMON What dost thou think 'tis worth?

APEMANTUS Not worth my thinking. How now, poet?

POET How now, philosopher?

APEMANTUS Thou liest.

POET Art not one?

APEMANTUS Yes.

POET Then I lie not.

APEMANTUS Art not a poet?

POET Yes.

202 **dog** (Apemantus is a Cynic philosopher; "cynic" is derived from the Greek word for dog) 203 **generation** (1) breed (2) persons born at about the same time 207 **And** if 208–09 **come by great bellies** become pregnant 215 **doit** a small Dutch coin worth less than a farthing (used as a type expression for any very small sum)

APEMANTUS Then thou liest. Look in thy last work, where thou hast feigned him a worthy fellow.

POET That's not feigned, he is so.

APEMANTUS Yes, he is worthy of thee, and to pay thee for thy labor. He that loves to be flattered is worthy o' th' flatterer. Heavens, that I were a lord!

TIMON What wouldst do then, Apemantus?

APEMANTUS E'en as Apemantus does now: hate a lord with my heart.

TIMON What, thyself?

APEMANTUS Ay.

TIMON Wherefore?

APEMANTUS That I had no angry wit to be a lord. Art not thou a merchant?

MERCHANT Ay, Apemantus.

APEMANTUS Traffic confound thee, if the gods will not.

MERCHANT If traffic do it, the gods do it.

APEMANTUS Traffic's thy god, and thy god confound thee.

Trumpet sounds. Enter a Messenger.

TIMON What trumpet's that?

MESSENGER 'Tis Alcibiades and some twenty horse,
All of companionship.

TIMON Pray entertain them, give them guide to us.
[*Exeunt some Attendants.*]
You must needs dine with me. Go not you hence

225 **liest** (a play on the old idea that poetry is a *mimesis*, imitation, mocking, or feigning of reality and therefore a lie) 226 **him** i.e., Timon 237 **no angry wit to be a lord** no more wit in my anger than to wish to be a lord (?) 240 **Traffic** trade, business 245 **horse** horsemen 246 **All of companionship** all of the same party

Till I have thankèd you. When dinner's done
Show me this piece. I am joyful of your sights.

Enter Alcibiades with the rest.

Most welcome, sir.

APEMANTUS So, so.
Their aches contract and starve your supple joints!
That there should be small love amongst these sweet knaves,
And all this courtesy! The strain of man's bred out
Into baboon and monkey.

ALCIBIADES Sir, you have saved my longing, and I feed
Most hungerly on your sight.

TIMON Right welcome, sir.
Ere we depart, we'll share a bounteous time
In different pleasures. Pray you let us in.
Exeunt [all but Apemantus].

Enter two Lords.

FIRST LORD What time a day is't, Apemantus?

APEMANTUS Time to be honest.

FIRST LORD That time serves still.

APEMANTUS The most accursèd thou that still omit'st it.

SECOND LORD Thou art going to Lord Timon's feast?

APEMANTUS Ay, to see meat fill knaves and wine heat fools.

SECOND LORD Fare thee well, fare thee well.

250 **of your sights** at the sight of you 253 **Their** i.e., of Alcibiades and his soldiers 253 **aches** (the reference is probably to venereal disease—"aches" is dissyllabic, pronounced "aitches") 253 **starve** destroy 257 **saved** anticipated and so prevented 263 **still** always 264 **omit'st** neglects

APEMANTUS Thou art a fool to bid me farewell twice.

SECOND LORD Why, Apemantus?

APEMANTUS Shouldst have kept one to thyself, for I mean to give thee none.

FIRST LORD Hang thyself!

APEMANTUS No, I will do nothing at thy bidding.
Make thy requests to thy friend.

SECOND LORD Away, unpeaceable dog, or I'll spurn thee hence.

APEMANTUS I will fly like a dog the heels a th' ass.
[*Exit*.]

FIRST LORD He's opposite to humanity. Come, shall we in
And taste Lord Timon's bounty? He outgoes
The very heart of kindness.

SECOND LORD He pours it out. Plutus, the god of gold,
Is but his steward; no meed but he repays
Sevenfold above itself. No gift to him
But breeds the giver a return exceeding
All use of quittance.

FIRST LORD The noblest mind he carries
That ever governed man.

SECOND LORD Long may he live
In fortunes. Shall we in?

FIRST LORD I'll keep you company. *Exeunt*.

277 **unpeaceable** quarrelsome 280 **opposite to** (1) hostile to (2) the reverse of 284 **meed** (1) merit, desert (2) gift (?) 287 **All use of quittance** all the customary returns made in repayment of debts (one meaning of "use" is "interest") 287 **carries** bears

[Scene II. *Timon's house.*]

Hautboys playing loud music. A great banquet served in; and then enter Lord Timon, the States, the Athenian Lords, Ventidius (which Timon redeemed from prison), [*and Alcibiades. Steward and others attending.*] *Then comes dropping after all, Apemantus, discontentedly, like himself.*

VENTIDIUS Most honored Timon,
It hath pleased the gods to remember my father's age,
And call him to long peace.
He is gone happy, and has left me rich.
Then, as in grateful virtue I am bound
To your free heart, I do return those talents
Doubled with thanks and service, from whose help
I derived liberty.

TIMON O by no means,
Honest Ventidius. You mistake my love;
I gave it freely ever, and there's none
Can truly say he gives, if he receives.
If our betters play at that game, we must not dare
To imitate them; faults that are rich are fair.

VENTIDIUS A noble spirit.

TIMON Nay, my lords, ceremony was but devised at first
To set a gloss on faint deeds, hollow welcomes,
Recanting goodness, sorry ere 'tis shown.

I.ii.s.d. **Hautboys** oboes s.d. **the States** persons of state, the Senators 6 **free** generous 12 **our betters** those of higher rank 13 **faults that are rich are fair** i.e., the faults of rich persons are made to seem attractive because of their wealth 15 **ceremony** ceremonious attitudes

But where there is true friendship, there needs none.
Pray sit; more welcome are ye to my fortunes
Than my fortunes to me.

FIRST LORD My lord, we always have confessed it.

APEMANTUS Ho, ho, confessed it? Hanged it, have you not?

TIMON O Apemantus, you are welcome.

APEMANTUS No, you shall not make me welcome.
I come to have thee thrust me out of doors.

TIMON Fie, th'art a churl, y'have got a humor there
Does not become a man; 'tis much to blame.
They say, my lords, *Ira furor brevis est*, but yond man is ever angry. Go, let him have a table by himself, for he does neither affect company, nor is he fit for't indeed.

APEMANTUS Let me stay at thine apperil, Timon.
I come to observe, I give thee warning on't.

TIMON I take no heed of thee. Th'art an Athenian, therefore welcome. I myself would have no power; prithee let my meat make thee silent.

APEMANTUS I scorn thy meat; 'twould choke me, for I should ne'er flatter thee. O you gods! What a number of men eats Timon, and he sees 'em not! It grieves me to see so many dip their meat in one man's blood, and all the madness is, he cheers them up too.
I wonder men dare trust themselves with men.
Methinks they should invite them without knives:

22 confessed it? Hanged it (an allusion to the proverb "Confess and be hanged") **26 humor** temperamental quirk (in the old physiological sense of the four humors) **28 Ira furor brevis est** anger is a brief fury or madness (Horace, *Epistles*, I.ii.62) **30 affect** (1) like (2) seek out **32 apperil** peril **35 no power** i.e., to force you to be silent **37–38 'twould ... thee** i.e., Apemantus would prefer to choke on Timon's meat than to flatter him **44 knives** (dinner guests normally brought their own knives)

Good for their meat, and safer for their lives.
There's much example for't; the fellow that sits next him, now parts bread with him, pledges the breath of him in a divided draught, is the readiest man to kill him. 'T'as been proved. If I were a huge man, I should fear to drink at meals,
Lest they should spy my windpipe's dangerous notes;
Great men should drink with harness on their throats.

TIMON My lord, in heart; and let the health go round.

SECOND LORD Let it flow this way, my good lord.

APEMANTUS Flow this way? A brave fellow. He keeps his tides well. Those healths will make thee and thy state look ill, Timon.
Here's that which is too weak to be a sinner,
Honest water, which ne'er left man i' th' mire.
This and my food are equals, there's no odds;
Feasts are too proud to give thanks to the gods.

Apemantus' Grace.

Immortal gods, I crave no pelf;
I pray for no man but myself.
Grant I may never prove so fond
To trust man on his oath or bond,
Or a harlot for her weeping,
Or a dog that seems a-sleeping,
Or a keeper with my freedom,
Or my friends if I should need 'em.
Amen. So fall to't:

48 **a divided draught** a drink from a cup that is passed around the table 50 **huge** important 51 **Lest . . . notes** i.e., lest men should cut my throat when my head is tilted backward (with additional allusion to the windpipe as a musical instrument, like a bagpipe) 52 **harness** armor 53 **My lord, in heart** (a toast) 55 **brave** excellent 56 **tides** times (with play on the usual sense, linked to "flow") 57 **state** estate, fortune 61 **Feasts** i.e., those who give feasts 62 **pelf** possessions 64 **fond** foolish 68 **keeper** jailer

Rich men sin, and I eat root. [*Eats and drinks.*]
Much good dich thy good heart, Apemantus.

TIMON Captain Alcibiades, your heart's in the field now.

ALCIBIADES My heart is ever at your service, my lord,

TIMON You had rather be at a breakfast of enemies than a dinner of friends.

ALCIBIADES So they were bleeding new, my lord, there's no meat like 'em; I could wish my best friend at such a feast.

APEMANTUS Would all those flatterers were thine enemies then, that then thou mightst kill 'em—and bid me to 'em.

FIRST LORD Might we but have that happiness, my lord, that you would once use our hearts, whereby we might express some part of our zeals, we should think ourselves for ever perfect.

TIMON O no doubt, my good friends, but the gods themselves have provided that I shall have much help from you: how had you been my friends else? Why have you that charitable title from thousands, did not you chiefly belong to my heart? I have told more of you to myself than you can with modesty speak in your own behalf; and thus far I confirm you. O you gods, think I, what need we have any friends, if we should ne'er have need of 'em? They were the most needless creatures living should we ne'er have use for 'em, and would most resemble sweet instruments hung up in cases, that keeps their sounds to themselves. Why I have often wished myself poorer that I

72 **dich** may it do (?) 76 **of** consisting of (but later in the sentence it means "with") 78 **So** provided that 83 **bid** invite 85 **use our hearts** i.e., make trial of the feelings in our hearts 87 **perfect** i.e., in our happiness in demonstrating our love for Timon 91 **charitable** loving, kindly 91 **from** from among 95 **confirm** sanction, corroborate (your claims as friends)

might come nearer to you. We are born to do benefits; and what better or properer can we call our own than the riches of our friends? O what a precious comfort 'tis to have so many like brothers commanding one another's fortunes. O joy's e'en made away ere't can be born. Mine eyes cannot hold out water, methinks. To forget their faults, I drink to you.

APEMANTUS Thou weep'st to make them drink, Timon.

SECOND LORD Joy had the like conception in our eyes,
And at that instant like a babe sprung up.

APEMANTUS Ho, ho! I laugh to think that babe a bastard.

THIRD LORD I promise you, my lord, you moved me much.

APEMANTUS Much. *Sound tucket.*

TIMON What means that trump?

Enter Servant.

How now?

SERVANT Please you, my lord, there are certain ladies most desirous of admittance.

TIMON Ladies? What are their wills?

SERVANT There comes with them a forerunner, my lord, which bears that office to signify their pleasures.

102 **nearer** (1) closer to your hearts (2) closer to your financial status 106–07 **e'en . . . born** i.e., our weeping for joy seems to destroy joy before it properly exists 108 **hold out water** keep out tears 108 **faults** defects 110 **to make them drink** (1) to provide drink for them (they drink up your tears, and you and your estate, too) (2) to furnish a pretext for their carousing 111 **the like conception** a similar birth (i.e., accompanied with tears) 112 **like a babe sprung up** i.e., the sight of Timon's joy immediately caused the birth of a like joy in the eyes of his friends 115 s.d. **tucket** a flourish on a trumpet 121–22 **pleasures** wishes

TIMON I pray let them be admitted.

[*Enter Cupid.*]

CUPID Hail to thee, worthy Timon, and to all
That of his bounties taste. The five best senses
Acknowledge thee their patron, and come freely
To gratulate thy plenteous bosom. Th' ear,
Taste, touch, all, pleased from thy table rise;
They only now come but to feast thine eyes.

TIMON They're welcome all; let 'em have kind admittance.
Music make their welcome. [*Exit Cupid.*]

FIRST LORD You see, my lord, how ample y'are beloved.

[*Music.*] *Enter Cupid with the Masque of Ladies* [*as*] *Amazons, with lutes in their hands, dancing and playing.*

APEMANTUS Hoy-day!
What a sweep of vanity comes this way.
They dance? They are madwomen.
Like madness is the glory of this life,
As this pomp shows to a little oil and root.
We make ourselves fools to disport ourselves,
And spend our flatteries to drink those men
Upon whose age we void it up again
With poisonous spite and envy.
Who lives that's not depravèd or depraves?
Who dies that bears not one spurn to their graves

127 **gratulate** (1) greet (2) gratify, please 129 **but to feast thine eyes** i.e., only to appeal to the sense of sight, whereas at Timon's banquet all the senses were gratified 131 **Music** i.e., let music 132 s.d. **Masque** an elaborate allegorical show or entertainment with emphasis on spectacle, music, and dance 132 s.d. **Amazons** legendary female warriors 133 **Hoy-day** (exclamation of surprise) 134 **sweep** (in reference to the sweeping motion of the dancers) 136 **Like** similar 136 **glory** vainglory 137 **to** compared to 138 **disport** amuse 139 **drink** drink the health of 140 **void** vomit 141 **envy** malice 142 **depravèd or depraves** slandered or a slanderer 143 **spurn** insult

Of their friends' gift?
I should fear those that dance before me now
Would one day stamp upon me. 'T'as been done.
Men shut their doors against a setting sun.

The Lords rise from table, with much adoring of Timon, and to show their loves, each single out an Amazon, and all dance, men with women, a lofty strain or two to the hautboys, and cease.

TIMON You have done our pleasures much grace, fair ladies,
Set a fair fashion on our entertainment,
Which was not half so beautiful and kind.
You have added worth unto't and luster,
And entertained me with mine own device.
I am to thank you for't.

FIRST LADY My lord, you take us even at the best.

APEMANTUS Faith, for the worst is filthy, and would not hold taking, I doubt me.

TIMON Ladies, there is an idle banquet attends you,
Please you to dispose yourselves.

ALL LADIES Most thankfully, my lord.
Exeunt [*Cupid and Ladies*].

TIMON Flavius.

FLAVIUS My lord.

TIMON The little casket bring me hither.

FLAVIUS Yes, my lord. [*Aside*] More jewels yet?

144 **gift** giving 147 s.d. **adoring of** paying homage to 149 **Set a fair fashion on** given a pleasant semblance to 150 **kind** gracious 152 **mine own device** (suggests that Timon designed the masque or at least had the idea for it) 154 **take us even at the best** judge us in the most favorable and complimentary way 155–56 **would not hold taking** i.e., sexual "taking" is not possible because of rottenness caused by venereal disease 156 **doubt me** fear, suspect (reflexive) 157 **idle banquet** trifling dessert or light collation 158 **Please you to dispose yourselves** if you please to take your places

There is no crossing him in's humor,
Else I should tell him well, i' faith I should,
When all's spent, he'd be crossed then, and he could.
'Tis pity bounty had not eyes behind,
That man might ne'er be wretched for his mind.
Exit.

FIRST LORD Where be our men?

SERVANT Here, my lord, in readiness.

SECOND LORD Our horses.

Enter Flavius [*with the casket*].

TIMON O my friends,
I have one word to say to you. Look you, my good lord,
I must entreat you honor me so much
As to advance this jewel; accept it and wear it,
Kind my lord.

FIRST LORD I am so far already in your gifts—

ALL So are we all.

Enter a Servant.

SERVANT My lord, there are certain nobles of the senate newly alighted, and come to visit you.

TIMON They are fairly welcome.

FLAVIUS I beseech your honor, vouchsafe me a word; it does concern you near.

TIMON Near? Why then another time I'll hear thee. I prithee let's be provided to show them entertainment.

FLAVIUS [*Aside*] I scarce know how.

163 **no crossing him in's humor** no thwarting him in his capricious disposition 165 **crossed** (1) thwarted (2) have his debts canceled ("crossed" off a list) (3) be given money (have his palm "crossed") 165 **and** if 167 **for his mind** for his generous inclinations 174 **advance** enhance in value (by your wearing it) 180 **fairly** courteously

Enter another Servant.

SECOND SERVANT May it please your honor, Lord Lucius,
Out of his free love, hath presented to you
Four milk-white horses, trapped in silver.

TIMON I shall accept them fairly. Let the presents
Be worthily entertained.

Enter a third Servant.

How now? What news?

THIRD SERVANT Please you, my lord, that honorable gentleman Lord Lucullus entreats your company tomorrow to hunt with him, and has sent your honor two brace of greyhounds.

TIMON I'll hunt with him, and let them be received
Not without fair reward.

FLAVIUS [*Aside*] What will this come to?
He commands us to provide, and give great gifts,
And all out of an empty coffer;
Nor will he know his purse, or yield me this,
To show him what a beggar his heart is,
Being of no power to make his wishes good.
His promises fly so beyond his state
That what he speaks is all in debt; he owes for ev'ry word.
He is so kind that he now pays interest for't;
His land's put to their books. Well, would I were
Gently put out of office before I were forced out.
Happier is he that has no friend to feed
Than such that do e'en enemies exceed.
I bleed inwardly for my lord. *Exit.*

189 **trapped in silver** with harness coverings adorned in silver 191 **worthily entertained** appropriately received 195 **two brace** two pairs 200 **yield** grant 203 **state** estate, possessions 206 **put to their books** mortgaged (entered on creditors' account books) 209 **Than such that do e'en enemies exceed** (1) than such a number that surpasses the number of one's enemies (2) than such sort of friends whose demands go beyond those of one's enemies

TIMON You do yourselves much wrong,
You bate too much of your own merits.
Here, my lord, a trifle of our love.

SECOND LORD With more than common thanks I will receive it.

THIRD LORD O he's the very soul of bounty.

TIMON And now I remember, my lord, you gave good words the other day of a bay courser I rode on. 'Tis yours because you liked it.

FIRST LORD O I beseech you pardon me, my lord, in that.

TIMON You may take my word, my lord, I know no man can justly praise but what he does affect. I weigh my friend's affection with mine own. I'll tell you true, I'll call to you.

ALL LORDS O none so welcome.

TIMON I take all and your several visitations
So kind to heart, 'tis not enough to give.
Methinks I could deal kingdoms to my friends,
And ne'er be weary. Alcibiades,
Thou art a soldier, therefore seldom rich;
It comes in charity to thee, for all thy living
Is 'mongst the dead, and all the lands thou hast
Lie in a pitched field.

ALCIBIADES Ay, defiled land, my lord.

FIRST LORD We are so virtuously bound——

TIMON And so am I to you.

212 **bate** abate, undervalue 217 **bay courser** reddish-brown stallion 219–20 **in that** in accepting your gift (because I seemed to solicit it) 222 **affect** like, desire to possess 223 **weigh** consider 223 **with** equal with 223–24 **I'll tell you true, I'll call to you** I assure you I will call on you 226 **all and your several** the sum total (an intensive form) 227 **'tis not enough to give** i.e., mere gifts, no matter how great, cannot truly express the feeling in my heart 228 **deal** distribute 231 **It** what you receive, a gift 231 **living** (1) existence (2) property (3) livelihood 233 **pitched field** field prepared for a battle 234 **defiled land** (a quibble on the proverb, "He that toucheth pitch shall be defiled," *Ecclesiasticus* 13:1)

SECOND LORD So infinitely endeared——

TIMON All to you. Lights, more lights!

FIRST LORD The best of happiness, honor, and fortunes
Keep with you, Lord Timon.

TIMON Ready for his friends. *Exeunt Lords.*

APEMANTUS What a coil's here,
Serving of becks and jutting out of bums!
I doubt whether their legs be worth the sums
That are given for 'em. Friendship's full of dregs;
Methinks false hearts should never have sound legs.
Thus honest fools lay out their wealth on curtsies.

TIMON Now Apemantus, if thou wert not sullen,
I would be good to thee.

APEMANTUS No, I'll nothing; for if I should be bribed too, there would be none left to rail upon thee, and then thou wouldst sin the faster. Thou giv'st so long, Timon, I fear me thou wilt give away thyself in paper shortly. What needs these feasts, pomps, and vainglories?

TIMON Nay, and you begin to rail on society once, I am sworn not to give regard to you. Farewell, and come with better music. *Exit.*

APEMANTUS So. Thou wilt not hear me now, thou shalt not then.
I'll lock thy heaven from thee.
O that men's ears should be
To counsel deaf, but not to flattery. *Exit.*

237 **endeared** indebted 238 **All to you** i.e., I am all of these things to you rather than vice versa 241 **coil** fuss, bustle, confusion 242 **Serving of becks** offering of nods or curtsies 242 **bums** posteriors 243 **legs** (1) bows (cf. "to make a leg") (2) the limbs themselves 245 **sound legs** i.e., legs healthy enough to make obeisances 246 **curtsies** (1) bows (2) courtesies (a different spelling of the same word) 250 **rail upon** revile 253 **in paper** i.e., in promissory notes and other paper records of debts 258 **thou shalt not then** you will not be able to listen to me later, when you are bankrupt 259 **thy heaven** i.e., the advice by which I might have saved you from ruin

[ACT II

Scene I. *A Senator's house.*]

Enter a Senator.

SENATOR And late five thousand. To Varro and to Isidore
He owes nine thousand, besides my former sum,
Which makes it five and twenty. Still in motion
Of raging waste? It cannot hold, it will not.
If I want gold, steal but a beggar's dog
And give it Timon—why the dog coins gold.
If I would sell my horse and buy twenty moe
Better than he—why give my horse to Timon;
Ask nothing, give it him, it foals me straight,
And able horses. No porter at his gate,
But rather one that smiles, and still invites
All that pass by. It cannot hold; no reason
Can sound his state in safety. Caphis, ho!
Caphis, I say!

II.i.1 **late** lately 3 **Still** always 4 **hold** last 9 **straight** immediately 10 **No porter** (because a porter's function is to keep out undesirable persons) 12–13 **no reason/Can sound his state in safety** i.e., because Timon is insolvent, no reasonable person can safely fathom or test his estate ("sound" in its nautical sense)

Enter Caphis.

CAPHIS Here, sir, what is your pleasure?

SENATOR Get on your cloak, and haste you to Lord
Timon;
Importune him for my moneys; be not ceased
With slight denial; nor then silenced when
"Commend me to your master" and the cap
Plays in the right hand, thus—but tell him,
My uses cry to me; I must serve my turn
Out of mine own; his days and times are past,
And my reliances on his fracted dates
Have smit my credit. I love and honor him,
But must not break my back to heal his finger.
Immediate are my needs, and my relief
Must not be tossed and turned to me in words,
But find supply immediate. Get you gone;
Put on a most importunate aspect,
A visage of demand; for I do fear,
When every feather sticks in his own wing,
Lord Timon will be left a naked gull,
Which flashes now a phoenix. Get you gone.

CAPHIS I go, sir.

SENATOR Ay, go sir! Take the bonds along with you,
And have the dates in. Come!

CAPHIS I will, sir.

SENATOR Go!

Exeunt.

18–19 **"Commend me ..." ... thus** (examples of anticipated ceremonious delays by Timon) 20 **uses** financial needs 21 **mine own** i.e., my own money 21 **days and times** due dates of his debts 22 **fracted** broken 28 **aspect** (accented on second syllable) 30 **sticks in his own wing** is returned to the bird to which it belongs (i.e., when Timon's debts, and the security he has given for them, are settled) 31 **gull** (1) unfledged bird (2) credulous dupe 32 **phoenix** a rare legendary bird which immolated itself and was reborn from its own ashes; a unique or matchless person 35 **have the dates in** put in the exact dates when the bonds fall due

[Scene II. *Timon's house.*]

Enter [*Flavius, the*] *Steward, with many bills in his hand.*

FLAVIUS No care, no stop, so senseless of expense
That he will neither know how to maintain it,
Nor cease his flow of riot. Takes no accompt
How things go from him, nor resumes no care
Of what is to continue. Never mind
Was to be so unwise to be so kind.
What shall be done he will not hear, till feel.
I must be round with him, now he comes from hunting.
Fie, fie, fie, fie!

Enter Caphis, [*with the Servants of*] *Isidore and Varro.*

CAPHIS Good even, Varro. What, you come for money?

VARRO'S SERVANT Is't not your business too?

CAPHIS It is; and yours too, Isidore?

ISIDORE'S SERVANT It is so.

CAPHIS Would we were all discharged.

VARRO'S SERVANT I fear it.

CAPHIS Here comes the lord.

Enter Timon and his Train, [*and Alcibiades*].

TIMON So soon as dinner's done, we'll forth again,

II.ii.3 **riot** extravagance, irresponsible reveling 4 **resumes no care** has no concern 6 **to be so kind** (1) as to be so generous (2) in order to be so generous 8 **round** blunt 14 **discharged** paid (of a debt) 15 **I fear it** I doubt it

My Alcibiades. [*To Caphis*] With me, what is your will?

CAPHIS My lord, here is a note of certain dues.

TIMON Dues? Whence are you?

CAPHIS Of Athens here, my lord.

TIMON Go to my steward.

CAPHIS Please it your lordship, he hath put me off
To the succession of new days this month.
My master is awaked by great occasion
To call upon his own, and humbly prays you
That with your other noble parts you'll suit
In giving him his right.

TIMON Mine honest friend,
I prithee but repair to me next morning.

CAPHIS Nay, good my lord——

TIMON Contain thyself, good friend.

VARRO'S SERVANT One Varro's servant, my good lord—

ISIDORE'S SERVANT From Isidore; he humbly prays your speedy payment.

CAPHIS If you did know, my lord, my master's wants——

VARRO'S SERVANT 'Twas due on forfeiture, my lord, six weeks and past.

ISIDORE'S SERVANT Your steward puts me off, my lord, and I am sent expressly to your lordship.

TIMON Give me breath.
I do beseech you, good my lords, keep on;
I'll wait upon you instantly.
[*Exeunt Alcibiades and Lords.*]

23 **To the succession of new days** from one day to the next 26 **That . . . suit** i.e., that you will act in accordance with your other noble qualities 28 **repair** return 35 **on** on penalty of 40 **keep on** go ahead

[*To Flavius*] Come hither. Pray you,
How goes the world, that I am thus encount'red
With clamorous demands of broken bonds,
And the detention of long since due debts
Against my honor?

FLAVIUS Please you, gentlemen,
The time is unagreeable to this business.
Your importunacy cease till after dinner,
That I may make his lordship understand
Wherefore you are not paid.

TIMON Do so, my friends. See them well entertained.
Exit.

FLAVIUS Pray draw near. [*Exit.*]

Enter Apemantus and Fool.

CAPHIS Stay, stay, here comes the fool with Apemantus.
Let's ha' some sport with 'em.

VARRO'S SERVANT Hang him, he'll abuse us.

ISIDORE'S SERVANT A plague upon him, dog!

VARRO'S SERVANT How dost, fool?

APEMANTUS Dost dialogue with thy shadow?

VARRO'S SERVANT I speak not to thee.

APEMANTUS No, 'tis to thyself. [*To the Fool*] Come away.

ISIDORE'S SERVANT [*To Varro's Servant*] There's the fool hangs on your back already.

APEMANTUS No, thou stand'st single, th'art not on him yet.

CAPHIS Where's the fool now?

APEMANTUS He last asked the question. Poor rogues and usurers' men, bawds between gold and want.

42 **How goes the world** what is going on 44 **detention** withholding payment 47 **importunacy** urgent solicitation 64 **single** alone

ALL SERVANTS What are we, Apemantus?

APEMANTUS Asses.

ALL SERVANTS Why?

APEMANTUS That you ask me what you are, and do not know yourselves. Speak to 'em, fool.

FOOL How do you, gentlemen?

ALL SERVANTS Gramercies, good fool. How does your mistress?

FOOL She's e'en setting on water to scald such chickens as you are. Would we could see you at Corinth.

APEMANTUS Good, gramercy.

Enter Page.

FOOL Look you, here comes my mistress' page.

PAGE [*To the Fool*] Why, how now, captain? What do you in this wise company? How dost thou, Apemantus?

APEMANTUS Would I had a rod in my mouth, that I might answer thee profitably.

PAGE Prithee, Apemantus, read me the superscription of these letters. I know not which is which.

APEMANTUS Canst not read?

PAGE No.

APEMANTUS There will little learning die then that day thou art hanged. This is to Lord Timon, this to Alcibiades. Go, thou wast born a bastard, and thou'lt die a bawd.

75 **Gramercies** thanks 77 **scald** a method of removing feathers from chickens (with suggestions of loss of hair in venereal disease, and of sweating in a heated tub, which was one of the treatments of venereal disease) 78 **Corinth** ancient city noted for licentiousness (hence a cant term for brothel or red-light district) 84 **rod** stick to beat you 85 **profitably** for your profit or improvement 86–87 **superscription** address

PAGE Thou wast whelped a dog, and thou shalt famish a dog's death. Answer not, I am gone. *Exit.*

APEMANTUS E'en so thou outrun'st grace. Fool, I will go with you to Lord Timon's.

FOOL Will you leave me there?

APEMANTUS If Timon stay at home. You three serve three usurers?

ALL SERVANTS Ay; would they served us.

APEMANTUS So would I—as good a trick as ever hangman served thief.

FOOL Are you three usurers' men?

ALL SERVANTS Ay, fool.

FOOL I think no usurer but has a fool to his servant. My mistress is one, and I am her fool. When men come to borrow of your masters, they approach sadly, and go away merry; but they enter my mistress' house merrily, and go away sadly. The reason of this?

VARRO'S SERVANT I could render one.

APEMANTUS Do it then, that we may account thee a whoremaster and a knave, which notwithstanding, thou shalt be no less esteemed.

VARRO'S SERVANT What is a whoremaster, fool?

FOOL A fool in good clothes, and something like thee. 'Tis a spirit; sometime't appears like a lord, sometime like a lawyer, sometime like a philosopher, with two stones moe than's artificial one. He is very often like a knight; and generally, in all shapes

94–95 **famish a dog's death** die by famishing, a mean death appropriate for a dog 96 **E'en so thou outrun'st grace** i.e., by leaving now and not listening to my profitable answer, you will never receive grace 109 **sadly** gravely 120 **stones** testicles 120 **artificial one** philosopher's stone (a highly refined substance which could turn base metals into gold)

that man goes up and down in, from fourscore to thirteen, this spirit walks in.

VARRO'S SERVANT Thou are not altogether a fool.

FOOL Nor thou altogether a wise man. As much foolery as I have, so much wit thou lack'st.

APEMANTUS That answer might have become Apemantus.

Enter Timon and [*Flavius, the*] *Steward.*

ALL SERVANTS Aside, aside, here comes Lord Timon.

APEMANTUS Come with me, fool, come.

FOOL I do not always follow lover, elder brother, and woman; sometime the philosopher.

FLAVIUS Pray you, walk near: I'll speak with you anon.
Exeunt [*Apemantus, Fool, and Servants*].

TIMON You make me marvel wherefore ere this time
Had you not fully laid my state before me,
That I might so have rated my expense
As I had leave of means.

FLAVIUS You would not hear me.
At many leisures I proposed——

TIMON Go to.
Perchance some single vantages you took
When my indisposition put you back,
And that unaptness made your minister
Thus to excuse yourself.

FLAVIUS O my good lord,
At many times I brought in my accompts,

131–32 **lover, elder brother, and woman** (persons who might be expected to be generous) 133 **anon** soon 135 **state** financial situation 136 **rated** regulated 137 **As I had leave of means** as my means would allow 138 **At many leisures** i.e., when you were at leisure 138 **Go to** nonsense (an exclamation of impatience) 139 **vantages** opportunities 140 **indisposition** disinclination 141 **unaptness** unreadiness to listen 141 **minister** ministration, prompting

Laid them before you; you would throw them off,
And say you found them in mine honesty.
When for some trifling present you have bid me
Return so much, I have shook my head and wept;
Yea 'gainst th' authority of manners, prayed you
To hold your hand more close. I did endure
Not seldom, nor no slight checks, when I have
Prompted you in the ebb of your estate
And your great flow of debts. My loved lord,
Though you hear now, too late, yet now's a time:
The greatest of your having lacks a half
To pay your present debts.

TIMON Let all my land be sold.

FLAVIUS 'Tis all engaged, some forfeited and gone,
And what remains will hardly stop the mouth
Of present dues. The future comes apace.
What shall defend the interim? And at length
How goes our reck'ning?

TIMON To Lacedaemon did my land extend.

FLAVIUS O my good lord, the world is but a word;
Were it all yours to give it in a breath,
How quickly were it gone!

TIMON You tell me true.

FLAVIUS If you suspect my husbandry or falsehood,
Call me before th' exactest auditors,
And set me on the proof. So the gods bless me,
When all our offices have been oppressed
With riotous feeders, when our vaults have wept
With drunken spilth of wine, when every room
Hath blazed with lights and brayed with minstrelsy,

148 **th' authority of manners** the dictates of good manners 150 **checks** rebukes 151 **Prompted** (in its theatrical sense) 154 **The greatest of your having** your worth estimated at the highest possible figure 156 **engaged** mortgaged 158 **apace** swiftly 165 **suspect my husbandry or falsehood** suspect me of false husbandry or dishonest management 167 **on** to 168 **offices** service rooms of a household 168 **oppressed** crowded 169 **feeders** servants 169 **vaults** wine cellars 170 **spilth** spilling

I have retired me to a wasteful cock,
And set mine eyes at flow.

TIMON Prithee no more.

FLAVIUS Heavens, have I said, the bounty of this lord!
How many prodigal bits have slaves and peasants
This night englutted! Who is not Timon's?
What heart, head, sword, force, means, but is
Lord Timon's?
Great Timon, noble, worthy, royal Timon!
Ah, when the means are gone that buy this praise,
The breath is gone whereof this praise is made.
Feast-won, fast-lost; one cloud of winter show'rs,
These flies are couched.

TIMON Come, sermon me no further.
No villainous bounty yet hath passed my heart;
Unwisely, not ignobly, have I given.
Why dost thou weep? Canst thou the conscience
lack
To think I shall lack friends? Secure thy heart.
If I would broach the vessels of my love,
And try the argument of hearts by borrowing,
Men and men's fortunes could I frankly use
As I can bid thee speak.

FLAVIUS Assurance bless your thoughts.

TIMON And in some sort these wants of mine are
crowned,
That I account them blessings; for by these

172 **wasteful cock** spigot (of a wine cask) that has not been shut off 173 **And set mine eyes at flow** i.e., following the example of the "wasteful cock," I have added my tears to the general riot and superfluity 175 **prodigal bits** wasteful morsels 176 **englutted** gulped down 181 **Feast-won, fast-lost** the friendship that is won by giving feasts is quickly lost (with pun on "fast" as noun and adverb) 182 **couched** lying hidden 183 **villainous bounty** generosity for evil purposes 185 **conscience** reasonableness 186 **Secure** make free from care or apprehension 187 **broach the vessels** tap the casks 188 **try the argument** test the theme or contents 189 **frankly** freely 190 **Assurance** i.e., may assurance 191 **crowned** given a royal dignity

Shall I try friends. You shall perceive how you
Mistake my fortunes; I am wealthy in my friends.
Within there! Flaminius! Servilius!

Enter [*Flaminius, Servilius, and Third Servant*].

SERVANTS My lord, my lord.

TIMON I will dispatch you severally. [*To Servilius*]
You to Lord Lucius, [*to Flaminius*] to Lord Lucullus you; I hunted with his honor today. [*To Third Servant*] You to Sempronius. Commend me to their loves; and I am proud, say, that my occasions have found time to use 'em toward a supply of money. Let the request be fifty talents.

FLAMINIUS As you have said, my lord.
[*Exeunt Servants.*]

FLAVIUS [*Aside*] Lord Lucius and Lucullus? Humh!

TIMON Go you, sir, to the senators,
Of whom, even to the state's best health, I have
Deserved this hearing. Bid 'em send o' th' instant
A thousand talents to me.

FLAVIUS I have been bold,
For that I knew it the most general way,
To them to use your signet and your name;
But they do shake their heads, and I am here
No richer in return.

TIMON Is't true? Can't be?

FLAVIUS They answer in a joint and corporate voice,
That now they are at fall, want treasure, cannot
Do what they would, are sorry; you are honorable,
But yet they could have wished—they know not;
Something hath been amiss—a noble nature

197 **severally** separately 201 **occasions** needs 207 **even to the state's best health** i.e., Timon, because of his own generosity to the state in the past, now deserves a loan from them to the very outermost limit they can pay (?) 210 **general** usual 211 **signet** signet ring (as sign of authority to act) 215 **at fall** at ebb tide

May catch a wrench—would all were well—'tis
  pity—
And so, intending other serious matters,
After distasteful looks, and these hard fractions,
With certain half-caps and cold-moving nods,
They froze me into silence.

TIMON You gods reward them!
Prithee man look cheerly. These old fellows
Have their ingratitude in them hereditary.
Their blood is caked, 'tis cold, it seldom flows;
'Tis lack of kindly warmth they are not kind;
And nature, as it grows again toward earth,
Is fashioned for the journey, dull and heavy.
Go to Ventidius. Prithee be not sad;
Thou art true and honest; ingeniously I speak,
No blame belongs to thee. Ventidius lately
Buried his father, by whose death he's stepped
Into a great estate. When he was poor,
Imprisoned, and in scarcity of friends,
I cleared him with five talents. Greet him from me,
Bid him suppose some good necessity
Touches his friend, which craves to be remember'red
With those five talents. That had, give't these
  fellows
To whom 'tis instant due. Nev'r speak or think
That Timon's fortunes 'mong his friends can sink.

FLAVIUS I would I could not think it; that thought is
  bounty's foe.
Being free itself, it thinks all others so. *Exeunt.*

219 **catch a wrench** accidentally be twisted from its natural bent 220 **intending** pretending 221 **hard fractions** harsh fragments of speech (conveyed in the broken syntax) 222 **half-caps** half-courteous salutations 222 **cold-moving** producing cold, frigid 227 **kindly** (1) natural (2) generous 228 **grows again toward earth** approaches death and the grave 231 **ingeniously** ingenuously, candidly 237 **good necessity** valid need 240 **instant** instantly, immediately 241 **'mong** in the midst of 243 **free** bounteous

[ACT III

Scene I. *Lucullus' house.*]

Flaminius waiting to speak with Lord [Lucullus] from his Master, enters a Servant to him.

SERVANT I have told my lord of you; he is coming down to you.

FLAMINIUS I thank you, sir.

Enter Lucullus.

SERVANT Here's my lord.

LUCULLUS [*Aside*] One of Lord Timon's men? A gift I warrant. Why this hits right; I dreamt of a silver basin and ewer tonight.—Flaminius, honest Flaminius, you are very respectively welcome, sir. Fill me some wine. [*Exit Servant.*] And how does that honorable, complete, free-hearted gentleman of Athens, thy very bountiful good lord and master?

FLAMINIUS His health is well, sir.

III.i.7 **tonight** last night 8 **respectively** respectfully 10 **complete** fully equipped or endowed, perfect

LUCULLUS I am right glad that his health is well, sir. And what hast thou there under thy cloak, pretty Flaminius?

FLAMINIUS Faith, nothing but an empty box, sir, which in my lord's behalf I come to entreat your honor to supply; who, having great and instant occasion to use fifty talents, hath sent to your lordship to furnish him, nothing doubting your present assistance therein.

LUCULLUS La, la, la, la! "Nothing doubting," says he? Alas, good lord, a noble gentleman 'tis, if he would not keep so good a house. Many a time and often I ha' dined with him, and told him on't, and come again to supper to him of purpose to have him spend less, and yet he would embrace no counsel, take no warning by my coming. Every man has his fault, and honesty is his. I ha' told him on't, but I could ne'er get him from't.

Enter Servant, with wine.

SERVANT Please your lordship, here is the wine.

LUCULLUS Flaminius, I have noted thee always wise. Here's to thee.

FLAMINIUS Your lordship speaks your pleasure.

LUCULLUS I have observed thee always for a towardly prompt spirit, give thee thy due, and one that knows what belongs to reason; and canst use the time well, if the time use thee well. Good parts in thee. [*To Servant*] Get you gone, sirrah. [*Exit Servant.*] Draw nearer, honest Flaminius. Thy lord's a bountiful gentleman, but thou art wise, and thou know'st well enough, although thou

15 **pretty** (vague epithet of praise) 19 **supply** fill 21 **present** immediate 25 **so good a house** such lavish hospitality 30 **honesty** generosity 35 **speaks your pleasure** is pleased to say so 36–37 **towardly prompt spirit** well-disposed and well-inclined person 39 **if the time use thee well** if you strike good fortune 39 **parts** qualities

com'st to me, that this is no time to lend money, especially upon bare friendship without security. Here's three solidares for thee. Good boy, wink at me, and say thou saw'st me not. Fare thee well.

FLAMINIUS Is't possible the world should so much
differ,
And we alive that lived? Fly, damnèd baseness,
To him that worships thee.

[*Throws back the money.*]

LUCULLUS Ha? Now I see thou art a fool, and fit for thy master. *Exit.*

FLAMINIUS May these add to the number that may
scald thee.
Let molten coin be thy damnation,
Thou disease of a friend, and not himself.
Has friendship such a faint and milky heart
It turns in less than two nights? O you gods!
I feel my master's passion. This slave
Unto his honor has my lord's meat in him;
Why should it thrive and turn to nutriment
When he is turned to poison?
O may diseases only work upon't,
And when he's sick to death, let not that part of
nature
Which my lord paid for be of any power
To expel sickness, but prolong his hour. *Exit.*

46 **solidares** (perhaps Shakespeare was referring to the Roman "solidus," which was used in England for a shilling) 46 **wink** shut your eyes 48 **differ** change 49 **And we alive that lived** i.e., the world changes so swiftly, it is hard to believe that the same people are still alive 53 **these** (the rejected coins) 53 **scald** i.e., in hell 54 **thy damnation** the torment you will suffer in hell (perhaps a reference to the pouring of molten gold down the throat of Marcus Crassus by the Parthians, thought of as a punishment in hell for avarice) 57 **turns** curdles 58 **passion** anger, suffering (trisyllabic) 58–59 **slave/Unto his honor** (ironical: "this man who claims to be so devoted to honor") 59 **meat** food (in general, in contradistinction to "drink") 63 **that part of nature** i.e., that part of his body nourished by Timon's food 65 **but prolong his hour** i.e., may he have a lingering death

[Scene II. *A public place.*]

Enter Lucius, with three Strangers.

LUCIUS Who, the Lord Timon? He is my very good friend and an honorable gentleman.

FIRST STRANGER We know him for no less, though we are but strangers to him. But I can tell you one thing, my lord, and which I hear from common rumors: now Lord Timon's happy hours are done and past, and his estate shrinks from him.

LUCIUS Fie, no, do not believe it; he cannot want for money.

SECOND STRANGER But believe you this, my lord, that not long ago, one of his men was with the Lord Lucullus to borrow so many talents, nay urged extremely for't, and showed what necessity belonged to't, and yet was denied.

LUCIUS How?

SECOND STRANGER I tell you, denied, my lord.

LUCIUS What a strange case was that! Now before the gods I am ashamed on't. Denied that honorable man? There was very little honor showed in't. For my own part, I must needs confess, I have received some small kindnesses from him, as money, plate, jewels, and suchlike trifles, nothing comparing to his; yet had he mistook him and sent to me, I should ne'er have denied his occasion so many talents.

III.ii.s.d. **Strangers** foreigners, non-Athenians 12 **so many talents** (an indefinite number probably intended to be replaced, in revision, by a definite number) 21 **plate** utensils for domestic use, especially of gold or silver 23 **his** i.e., Lucullus' 23 **mistook him** made a mistake 24 **occasion** need

SERVILIUS See, by good hap, yonder's my lord; I have sweat to see his honor. My honored lord.

LUCIUS Servilius? You are kindly met, sir. Fare thee well; commend me to thy honorable virtuous lord, my very exquisite friend.

SERVILIUS May it please your honor, my lord hath sent——

LUCIUS Ha? What has he sent? I am so much endeared to that lord; he's ever sending. How shall I thank him, think'st thou? And what has he sent now?

SERVILIUS Has only sent his present occasion now, my lord, requesting your lordship to supply his instant use with so many talents.

LUCIUS I know his lordship is but merry with me,
He cannot want fifty five hundred talents.

SERVILIUS But in the meantime he wants less, my lord.
If his occasion were not virtuous,
I should not urge it half so faithfully.

LUCIUS Dost thou speak seriously, Servilius?

SERVILIUS Upon my soul 'tis true, sir.

LUCIUS What a wicked beast was I to disfurnish myself against such a good time, when I might ha' shown myself honorable! How unluckily it happ'ned that I should purchase the day before for a little part, and undo a great deal of honor! Servilius, now before the gods I am not able to do—the more beast, I say! I was sending to use

33–34 **endeared** indebted 41 **want** (1) be without, lack (2) need, desire 41 **fifty five hundred talents** a huge sum 47–48 **disfurnish myself against** to allow myself to be unprovided for 50–51 **for a little part** for a little business transaction (deliberately vague) 51 **undo a great deal of honor** i.e., lose the anticipated honor of lending to Timon

Lord Timon myself, these gentlemen can witness; but I would not for the wealth of Athens I had done't now. Commend me bountifully to his good lordship, and I hope his honor will conceive the fairest of me, because I have no power to be kind. And tell him this from me, I count it one of my greatest afflictions, say, that I cannot pleasure such an honorable gentleman. Good Servilius, will you befriend me so far as to use mine own words to him?

SERVILIUS Yes, sir, I shall.

LUCIUS I'll look you out a good turn, Servilius.
Exit Servilius.
True, as you said, Timon is shrunk indeed,
And he that's once denied will hardly speed. *Exit.*

FIRST STRANGER Do you observe this, Hostilius?

SECOND STRANGER Ay, too well.

FIRST STRANGER Why this is the world's soul, and just of the same piece
Is every flatterer's sport. Who can call him his friend
That dips in the same dish? For in my knowing
Timon has been this lord's father,
And kept his credit with his purse;
Supported his estate; nay, Timon's money
Has paid his men their wages. He ne'er drinks
But Timon's silver treads upon his lip,
And yet—O see the monstrousness of man
When he looks out in an ungrateful shape—
He does deny him, in respect of his,
What charitable men afford to beggars.

THIRD STRANGER Religion groans at it.

57–58 **conceive the fairest** think the best 67 **speed** be successful, prosper 69 **piece** sort, kind 70 **sport** mockery, diversion (as Lucius has just made sport of Timon) 73 **kept his** sustained Lucius' 73 **his** i.e., Timon's 76 **treads** presses 78 **shape** form 79 **in respect of his** in relation to what Lucius is worth

FIRST STRANGER For mine own part,
I never tasted Timon in my life,
Nor came any of his bounties over me
To mark me for his friend. Yet I protest,
For his right noble mind, illustrious virtue,
And honorable carriage,
Had his necessity made use of me,
I would have put my wealth into donation,
And the best half should have returned to him,
So much I love his heart. But I perceive
Men must learn now with pity to dispense,
For policy sits above conscience. *Exeunt.*

[Scene III. *Sempronius' house.*]

Enter a Third Servant [*of Timon*] *with Sempronius, another of Timon's friends.*

SEMPRONIUS Must he needs trouble me in't—humh!—
'bove all others?
He might have tried Lord Lucius or Lucullus,
And now Ventidius is wealthy too,
Whom he redeemed from prison. All these
Owes their estates unto him.

THIRD SERVANT My lord,
They have all been touched and found base metal,
For they have all denied him.

SEMPRONIUS How? Have they denied him?
Has Ventidius and Lucullus denied him,
And does he send to me? Three? Humh!

82 **tasted** experienced the qualities of 85 **right** very 86 **carriage** moral conduct 88 **put my wealth into donation** i.e., treated my fortune as a gift from Timon 89 **returned** been given back 92 **policy** cunning III.iii.6 **touched** tested (by being rubbed on a touchstone; unlike base metals, gold and silver produced the proper colored streak)

It shows but little love or judgment in him.
Must I be his last refuge? His friends, like physicians,
Thrive, give him over. Must I take th' cure upon me?
Has much disgraced me in't; I'm angry at him
That might have known my place. I see no sense for't,
But his occasions might have wooed me first;
For, in my conscience, I was the first man
That e'er received gift from him.
And does he think so backwardly of me now
That I'll requite it last? No.
So it may prove an argument of laughter
To th' rest, and I 'mongst lords be thought a fool.
I'd rather than the worth of thrice the sum,
Had sent to me first, but for my mind's sake;
I'd such a courage to do him good. But now return,
And with their faint reply this answer join:
Who bates mine honor shall not know my coin.

Exit.

THIRD SERVANT Excellent. Your lordship's a goodly villain. The devil knew not what he did when he made man politic; he crossed himself by't: and I cannot think but in the end the villainies of man will set him clear. How fairly this lord strives to appear foul! Takes virtuous copies to be wicked. Like those that under hot ardent zeal

12 **Thrive, give him over** i.e., prosper on his money while they are giving him up for dead (?) 14 **my place** i.e., before Lucullus, Lucius, and Ventidius 15 **occasions** needs 18 **backwardly** (1) poorly (2) near the end, late 20 **argument** occasion, subject 23 **Had** i.e., he had (perhaps "H'ad"?) 23 **but for my mind's sake** if only to express my good will towards him 24 **courage** desire 26 **bates** abates, undervalues 29 **politic** cunning 29 **he crossed himself by't** i.e., the devil thwarted his own purposes by making man his rival in shrewdness and guile 31 **will set him clear** will make the devil appear innocent (when compared with the "villainies of man") 31 **How fairly** with what a beautiful appearance 32 **foul** ugly 32–33 **Takes virtuous copies to be wicked** i.e., models himself on exemplars of virtue to serve as disguise for his wickedness 33 **those** i.e., religious fanatics (perhaps "zeal" suggests an allusion to Puritans)

would set whole realms on fire, of such a nature is his politic love.

This was my lord's best hope; now all are fled
Save only the gods. Now his friends are dead,
Doors that were ne'er acquainted with their wards
Many a bounteous year, must be employed
Now to guard sure their master.
And this is all a liberal course allows;
Who cannot keep his wealth must keep his house.
Exit.

[Scene IV. *Timon's house.*]

Enter Varro's [two Servants], meeting others. All [the Servants of] Timon's creditors to wait for his coming out. Then enter [the Servant of] Lucius; [then Titus] and Hortensius.

VARRO'S FIRST SERVANT Well met; good morrow, Titus and Hortensius.

TITUS The like to you, kind Varro.

HORTENSIUS Lucius!
What, do we meet together?

LUCIUS' SERVANT Ay, and I think
One business does command us all;
For mine is money.

TITUS So is theirs and ours.

Enter Philotus.

LUCIUS' SERVANT And, sir, Philotus' too!

PHILOTUS Good day at once.

38 **wards** locks 40 **sure** securely 41 **liberal** generous 42 **keep his house** remain at home (for fear of being arrested for debt) III.iv.6 **at once** to you all

LUCIUS' SERVANT Welcome, good brother. What do you think the hour?

PHILOTUS Laboring for nine.

LUCIUS' SERVANT So much?

PHILOTUS Is not my lord seen yet?

LUCIUS' SERVANT Not yet.

PHILOTUS I wonder on't; he was wont to shine at seven.

LUCIUS' SERVANT Ay, but the days are waxed shorter with him.
You must consider that a prodigal course
Is like the sun's,
But not like his recoverable, I fear.
'Tis deepest winter in Lord Timon's purse;
That is, one may reach deep enough and yet
Find little.

PHILOTUS I am of your fear for that.

TITUS I'll show you how t' observe a strange event.
Your lord sends now for money?

HORTENSIUS Most true, he does.

TITUS And he wears jewels now of Timon's gift,
For which I wait for money.

HORTENSIUS It is against my heart.

LUCIUS' SERVANT Mark how strange it shows,
Timon in this should pay more than he owes;
And e'en as if your lord should wear rich jewels
And send for money for 'em.

HORTENSIUS I'm weary of this charge, the gods can witness.

11 **waxed** grown 12–14 **prodigal course . . . recoverable** i.e., the prodigal, like the sun, declines, but cannot renew himself every day 18 **observe** observe and interpret 22 **against my heart** contrary to my natural feeling 23 **should pay more than he owes** i.e., he has given the gifts, and now he is also asked for the money for them 26 **charge** task

I know my lord hath spent of Timon's wealth,
And now ingratitude makes it worse than stealth.

VARRO'S FIRST SERVANT Yes, mine's three thousand crowns. What's yours?

LUCIUS' SERVANT Five thousand mine.

VARRO'S FIRST SERVANT 'Tis much deep, and it should seem by th' sum
Your master's confidence was above mine,
Else surely his had equaled.

Enter Flaminius.

TITUS One of Lord Timon's men.

LUCIUS' SERVANT Flaminius? Sir, a word. Pray is my lord ready to come forth?

FLAMINIUS No, indeed he is not.

TITUS We attend his lordship; pray signify so much.

FLAMINIUS I need not tell him that; he knows you are too diligent. [*Exit.*]

Enter [Flavius, the] Steward, in a cloak, muffled.

LUCIUS' SERVANT Ha! Is not that his steward muffled so?
He goes away in a cloud. Call him, call him.

TITUS Do you hear, sir?

VARRO'S SECOND SERVANT By your leave, sir.

FLAVIUS What do ye ask of me, my friend?

TITUS We wait for certain money here, sir.

FLAVIUS Ay,
If money were as certain as your waiting,

28 **stealth** stealing 32 **confidence** trust 32 **mine** i.e., my master's 40 s.d. **muffled** wrapped up, especially about the face 42 **in a cloud** (1) in a state of gloominess and concern (2) covered with a cloud because he is muffled

'Twere sure enough.
Why then preferred you not your sums and bills
When your false masters ate of my lord's meat?
Then they could smile, and fawn upon his debts,
And take down th' int'rest into their glutt'nous maws.
You do yourselves but wrong to stir me up;
Let me pass quietly.
Believe't, my lord and I have made an end;
I have no more to reckon, he to spend.

LUCIUS' SERVANT Ay, but this answer will not serve.

FLAVIUS If 'twill not serve, 'tis not so base as you,
For you serve knaves [*Exit.*]

VARRO'S FIRST SERVANT How? What does his cashiered worship mutter?

VARRO'S SECOND SERVANT No matter what; he's poor, and that's revenge enough. Who can speak broader than he that has no house to put his head in? Such may rail against great buildings.

Enter Servilius.

TITUS O here's Servilius. Now we shall know some answer.

SERVILIUS If I might beseech you, gentlemen, to repair some other hour, I should derive much from't. For take't of my soul, my lord leans wondrously to discontent. His comfortable temper has forsook him, he's much out of health, and keeps his chamber.

LUCIUS' SERVANT Many do keep their chambers are not sick;

49 **preferred** proffered, presented 51 **fawn upon** seek favor by servility (used especially of dogs) 52 **th' int'rest** i.e., what they ate was equivalent to the interest due on the money owed them by Timon 56 **reckon** keep account of 60 **cashiered** dismissed from employment 63 **broader** more critically 67–68 **repair** come 69 **tak't of my soul** take it from my heart (i.e., sincerely) 70 **comfortable** cheerful

And if it be so far beyond his health,
Methinks he should the sooner pay his debts,
And make a clear way to the gods.

SERVILIUS Good gods!

TITUS We cannot take this for answer, sir.

FLAMINIUS (*Within*) Servilius, help! My lord, my lord!

Enter Timon in a rage.

TIMON What, are my doors opposed against my passage?
Have I been ever free, and must my house
Be my retentive enemy? My jail?
The place which I have feasted, does it now,
Like all mankind, show me an iron heart?

LUCIUS' SERVANT Put in now, Titus.

TITUS My lord, here is my bill.

LUCIUS' SERVANT Here's mine.

HORTENSIUS And mine, my lord.

BOTH VARRO'S SERVANTS And ours, my lord.

PHILOTUS All our bills.

TIMON Knock me down with 'em, cleave me to the girdle.

LUCIUS' SERVANT Alas, my lord——

TIMON Cut my heart in sums.

TITUS Mine, fifty talents.

76 **clear** (1) free from debt (2) innocent, unstained (because he has paid his debts) (3) untrammeled, without the obstacle of debts 80 **free** (1) generous (2) unrestrained 81 **retentive** confining 82 **The place which I have feasted** i.e., the house itself in which I have given feasts 84 **Put in** i.e., put in your claim for money 90 **Knock . . . girdle** (Timon chooses to understand "bills" not as "accounts of money due," but as "weapons"—a bill had a long wooden handle with a blade or ax-shaped head at one end, and it was capable of cutting a man through to the belt) 92 **in sums** into sums of money

TIMON Tell out my blood.

LUCIUS' SERVANT Five thousand crowns, my lord.

TIMON Five thousand drops pays that. What yours? And yours?

VARRO'S FIRST SERVANT My lord—

VARRO'S SECOND SERVANT My lord—

TIMON Tear me, take me, and the gods fall upon you.
Exit Timon.

HORTENSIUS Faith, I perceive our masters may throw their caps at their money; these debts may well be called desperate ones, for a madman owes 'em.
Exeunt.

Enter Timon [*and Flavius*].

TIMON They have e'en put my breath from me, the slaves.
Creditors? Devils!

FLAVIUS My dear lord——

TIMON What if it should be so?

FLAVIUS My lord——

TIMON I'll have it so. My steward!

FLAVIUS Here, my lord.

TIMON So fitly? Go, bid all my friends again,
Lucius, Lucullus, and Sempronius—all.
I'll once more feast the rascals.

FLAVIUS O my lord,
You only speak from your distracted soul;
There's not so much left to furnish out
A moderate table.

94 **Tell out** count out 100–01 **may throw . . . money** may give up their money for lost 102 **desperate** beyond hope of recovery (cf. "sperate," recoverable) 103 **put my breath from me** put me out of breath 110 **fitly** conveniently 110 **bid** invite

TIMON Be it not in thy care.
Go, I charge thee, invite them all, let in the tide
Of knaves once more; my cook and I'll provide.
Exeunt.

[Scene V. *The Senate House.*]

Enter three Senators at one door, Alcibiades meeting them with Attendants.

FIRST SENATOR My lord, you have my voice to't. The fault's
Bloody; 'tis necessary he should die.
Nothing emboldens sin so much as mercy.

SECOND SENATOR Most true; the law shall bruise 'em.

ALCIBIADES Honor, health, and compassion to the senate.

FIRST SENATOR Now, captain?

ALCIBIADES I am an humble suitor to your virtues;
For pity is the virtue of the law,
And none but tyrants use it cruelly.
It pleases time and fortune to lie heavy
Upon a friend of mine, who in hot blood
Hath stepped into the law; which is past depth
To those that, without heed, do plunge into't.
He is a man, setting his fate aside,
Of comely virtues;
Nor did he soil the fact with cowardice
(An honor in him which buys out his fault),

115 **Be it not in thy care** i.e., let the feast be my concern III.v.1 **voice** vote 4 **bruise 'em** crush them (possibly sinners or wrongdoers in general?) 8 **virtue** characteristic excellence 12 **stepped into the law** done something to bring him within the jurisdiction of the law 12 **past depth** beyond any measurable depth 14 **his fate** i.e., this one fateful action of his 16 **soil the fact** sully the deed 17 **buys out** redeems

But with a noble fury and fair spirit,
Seeing his reputation touched to death,
He did oppose his foe;
And with such sober and unnoted passion
He did behove his anger, ere 'twas spent,
As if he had but proved an argument.

FIRST SENATOR You undergo too strict a paradox,
Striving to make an ugly deed look fair.
Your words have took such pains as if they labored
To bring manslaughter into form, and set
Quarreling upon the head of valor, which indeed
Is valor misbegot, and came into the world
When sects and factions were newly born.
He's truly valiant that can wisely suffer
The worst that man can breathe,
And make his wrongs his outsides,
To wear them like his raiment, carelessly,
And ne'er prefer his injuries to his heart,
To bring it into danger.
If wrongs be evils and enforce us kill,
What folly 'tis to hazard life for ill.

ALCIBIADES My lord——

FIRST SENATOR You cannot make gross sins look clear.
To revenge is no valor, but to bear.

ALCIBIADES My lords, then, under favor, pardon me,
If I speak like a captain.
Why do fond men expose themselves to battle,
And not endure all threats? Sleep upon't,

18 **fair** excellent 21 **unnoted** not notable, i.e., calm 22 **behove** control 23 **argument** i.e., a *point d'honneur* rather than a personal passion 24 **undergo too strict a paradox** i.e., attempt to argue a position that is excessively paradoxical 27 **form** i.e., a legal and acceptable form 30 **factions** (trisyllabic) 32 **breathe** utter 33 **outsides** mere externals 35 **prefer** present 39 **clear** innocent 40 **bear** tolerate (our wrongs) 41 **under favor** by your leave (a formula of politeness) 43 **fond** foolish

And let the foes quietly cut their throats
Without repugnancy? If there be
Such valor in the bearing, what make we
Abroad? Why then, women are more valiant
That stay at home, if bearing carry it,
And the ass more captain than the lion, the fellow
Loaden with irons wiser than the judge,
If wisdom be in suffering. O my lords,
As you are great, be pitifully good.
Who cannot condemn rashness in cold blood?
To kill, I grant, is sin's extremest gust,
But in defense, by mercy, 'tis most just.
To be in anger is impiety;
But who is man that is not angry?
Weigh but the crime with this.

SECOND SENATOR You breathe in vain.

ALCIBIADES In vain? His service done
At Lacedaemon and Byzantium
Were a sufficient briber for his life.

FIRST SENATOR What's that?

ALCIBIADES Why say, my lords, h'as done fair service,
And slain in fight many of your enemies.
How full of valor did he bear himself
In the last conflict, and made plenteous wounds!

SECOND SENATOR He has made too much plenty with 'em.
He's a sworn rioter; he has a sin that often
Drowns him and takes his valor prisoner.
If there were no foes, that were enough
To overcome him. In that beastly fury
He has been known to commit outrages,

46 **repugnancy** resistance, fighting back 48 **Abroad** i.e., away from home, at battle 49 **bearing** (1) enduring of wrongs (2) childbearing (3) bearing of men in sexual intercourse 49 **carry it** win the day 53 **be pitifully good** i.e., be good in showing pity 55 **gust** (1) taste, relish (2) strong wind or storm 56 **by mercy** in a merciful interpretation 63 **say** let us say, let us admit 68 **rioter** debauchee 68 **sin** i.e., drunkenness

And cherish factions. 'Tis inferred to us
His days are foul and his drink dangerous.

FIRST SENATOR He dies.

ALCIBIADES Hard fate. He might have died in war.
My lords, if not for any parts in him—
Though his right arm might purchase his own time,
And be in debt to none—yet, more to move you,
Take my deserts to his, and join 'em both.
And for I know your reverend ages love
Security, I'll pawn my victories, all
My honor to you, upon his good returns.
If by this crime he owes the law his life,
Why, let the war receive't in valiant gore,
For law is strict, and war is nothing more.

FIRST SENATOR We are for law. He dies. Urge it no more,
On height of our displeasure. Friend or brother,
He forfeits his own blood that spills another.

ALCIBIADES Must it be so? It must not be.
My lords, I do beseech you know me.

SECOND SENATOR How?

ALCIBIADES Call me to your remembrances.

THIRD SENATOR What?

ALCIBIADES I cannot think but your age has forgot me;
It could not else be I should prove so base
To sue and be denied such common grace.
My wounds ache at you.

FIRST SENATOR Do you dare our anger?
'Tis in few words, but spacious in effect:
We banish thee for ever.

73 **cherish factions** foster dissension 73 **inferred** reported 76 **parts** good qualities 77 **his own time** i.e., his proper time to die 81 **Security** (1) safety, freedom from care or apprehension (2) collateral for a debt 82 **good returns** profit on an investment 92 **your age** i.e., you, because of your age 94 **To sue** to beg

ALCIBIADES Banish me?
Banish your dotage, banish usury,
That makes the senate ugly.

FIRST SENATOR If after two days' shine Athens contain thee,
Attend our weightier judgment. And, not to swell our spirit,
He shall be executed presently.
Exeunt [Senators].

ALCIBIADES Now the gods keep you old enough, that you may live
Only in bone, that none may look on you.
I'm worse than mad. I have kept back their foes,
While they have told their money, and let out
Their coin upon large interest, I myself
Rich only in large hurts. All those, for this?
Is this the balsam that the usuring Senate
Pours into captains' wounds? Banishment!
It comes not ill. I hate not to be banished;
It is a cause worthy my spleen and fury,
That I may strike at Athens. I'll cheer up
My discontented troops and lay for hearts.
'Tis honor with most lands to be at odds;
Soldiers should brook as little wrongs as gods.
Exit.

101 **Attend our weightier judgment** expect a more severe sentence from us 101 **not to swell our spirit** not to allow our anger any further scope 102 **presently** at once 104 **Only in bone** i.e., be mere hideous skeletons 106 **told** counted 109 **balsam** balm 112 **spleen** malice, passionate hatred 114 **lay for hearts** i.e., try to win their hearts to my cause (or, possibly, try to win the hearts of new followers) 116 **brook** endure

[Scene VI. *A banqueting hall in Timon's house.*

Music. Tables set out, Servants attending.] *Enter divers Friends* [*of Timon*] *at several doors.*

FIRST LORD The good time of day to you, sir.

SECOND LORD I also wish it to you. I think this honorable lord did but try us this other day.

FIRST LORD Upon that were my thoughts tiring when we encount'red. I hope it is not so low with him as he made it seem in the trial of his several friends.

SECOND LORD It should not be, by the persuasion of his new feasting.

FIRST LORD I should think so. He hath sent me an earnest inviting, which many my near occasions did urge me to put off; but he hath conjured me beyond them, and I must needs appear.

SECOND LORD In like manner was I in debt to my importunate business, but he would not hear my excuse. I am sorry, when he sent to borrow of me, that my provision was out.

FIRST LORD I am sick of that grief too, as I understand how all things go.

SECOND LORD Every man here's so. What would he have borrowed of you?

III.vi.4 **tiring** feeding (especially, to tear flesh in feeding as does a bird of prey) 7 **by the persuasion of** on the evidence of 10 **many my near occasions** my many pressing social obligations 16 **provision** supply (of money) 17–18 **as I . . . go** i.e., on the evidence of his "new feasting," things seem to be picking up again with Timon

FIRST LORD A thousand pieces.

SECOND LORD A thousand pieces?

FIRST LORD What of you?

SECOND LORD He sent to me, sir——

Enter Timon and Attendants.

Here he comes.

TIMON With all my heart, gentlemen both; and how fare you?

FIRST LORD Ever at the best, hearing well of your lordship.

SECOND LORD The swallow follows not summer more willing than we your lordship.

TIMON [*Aside*] Nor more willingly leaves winter, such summer birds are men.—Gentlemen, our dinner will not recompense this long stay. Feast your ears with the music awhile, if they will fare so harshly o' th' trumpet's sound; we shall to't presently.

FIRST LORD I hope it remains not unkindly with your lordship that I returned you an empty messenger.

TIMON O sir, let it not trouble you.

SECOND LORD My noble lord——

TIMON Ah my good friend, what cheer?

SECOND LORD My most honorable lord, I am e'en sick of shame that when your lordship this other day sent to me, I was so unfortunate a beggar.

TIMON Think not on't, sir.

SECOND LORD If you had sent but two hours before—

21 **pieces** gold coins worth about a pound (but probably used vaguely) 29 **swallow** (cf. the proverb: "Swallows, like false friends, fly away upon the approach of winter") 34 **fare so harshly** feed on such rough food 35 **we shall to't presently** we shall sit down to eat immediately

TIMON Let it not cumber your better remembrance.

The banquet brought in.

Come, bring in all together.

SECOND LORD All covered dishes.

FIRST LORD Royal cheer, I warrant you.

THIRD LORD Doubt not that, if money and the season can yield it.

FIRST LORD How do you? What's the news?

THIRD LORD Alcibiades is banished. Hear you of it?

FIRST AND SECOND LORDS Alcibiades banished?

THIRD LORD 'Tis so, be sure of it.

FIRST LORD How? How?

SECOND LORD I pray you upon what?

TIMON My worthy friends, will you draw near?

THIRD LORD I'll tell you more anon. Here's a noble feast toward.

SECOND LORD This is the old man still.

THIRD LORD Will't hold? Will't hold?

SECOND LORD It does; but time will—and so—

THIRD LORD I do conceive.

TIMON Each man to his stool, with that spur as he would to the lip of his mistress. Your diet shall be in all places alike. Make not a city feast of it, to let

46 **cumber your better remembrance** burden your good memory 48 **covered dishes** (signifies food of high quality) 49 **Royal cheer** i.e., food fit for a king 57 **upon what** for what cause 59 **anon** soon 60 **toward** forthcoming 61 **still** ever, without change 62 **Will't hold** will it last 63 **time will** (presumably a platitude such as "time will alter all things") 64 **conceive** understand 65 **spur** spurring, speed 66 **diet** food 67 **in all places alike** the same at all places of the table (i.e., no need for seating according to rank) 67 **city feast** a formal London banquet (London is the "City")

the meat cool ere we can agree upon the first place. Sit, sit. The gods require our thanks.

You great benefactors, sprinkle our society with thankfulness. For your own gifts, make yourselves praised. But reserve still to give, lest your deities be despised. Lend to each man enough that one need not lend to another; for were your godheads to borrow of men, men would forsake the gods. Make the meat be beloved more than the man that gives it. Let no assembly of twenty be without a score of villains. If there sit twelve women at the table, let a dozen of them be as they are. The rest of your fees, O gods—the senators of Athens, together with the common leg of people—what is amiss in them, you gods, make suitable for destruction. For these my present friends, as they are to me nothing, so in nothing bless them, and to nothing are they welcome.

Uncover, dogs, and lap.

[*The dishes are uncovered and seen to be full of water.*]

SOME SPEAK What does his lordship mean?

SOME OTHER I know not.

TIMON May you a better feast never behold,
You knot of mouth-friends. Smoke and lukewarm water
Is your perfection. This is Timon's last,
Who, stuck and spangled with your flatteries,
Washes it off and sprinkles in your faces
Your reeking villainy. [*Throws the water in their faces.*]
Live loathed and long,

72 **reserve** i.e., keep something in reserve 80 **fees** property, possessions 81 **leg** limb (as a literal part of the body politic) 90 **knot of mouth-friends** pack of (1) friends merely in speech (2) friends won through feeding, "trencher-friends" 90 **Smoke** (1) insubstantiality (2) mere talk 91 **perfection** highest excellence (?) perfect likeness of you (?) 92 **stuck and spangled** bespattered and tricked out (as if with spangles) 94 **reeking** giving off smoke or fumes, stinking

Most smiling, smooth, detested parasites,
Courteous destroyers, affable wolves, meek bears,
You fools of fortune, trencher-friends, time's flies,
Cap-and-knee slaves, vapors, and minute-jacks.
Of man and beast the infinite malady
Crust you quite o'er. What, dost thou go?
Soft, take thy physic first; thou too, and thou.
Stay, I will lend thee money, borrow none.
[*Drives them out.*]
What? All in motion? Henceforth be no feast,
Whereat a villain's not a welcome guest.
Burn house, sink Athens, henceforth hated be
Of Timon man and all humanity. *Exit.*

Enter the Senators, with other Lords.

FIRST LORD How now, my lords?

SECOND LORD Know you the quality of Lord Timon's fury?

THIRD LORD Push, did you see my cap?

FOURTH LORD I have lost my gown.

FIRST LORD He's but a mad lord, and naught but humors sways him. He gave me a jewel th' other day, and now he has beat it out of my hat. Did you see my jewel?

THIRD LORD Did you see my cap?

SECOND LORD Here 'tis.

FOURTH LORD Here lies my gown.

FIRST LORD Let's make no stay.

95 **smooth** flattering 97–98 **You fools ... minute-jacks** you dupes of fortune, friends won by feeding, insects that appear only in fair weather, servile slaves always kneeling or removing caps in deference, insubstantial creatures, and figures who strike the bell of a clock (i.e., opportunistic persons) 99 **infinite** unlimited 101 **physic** medicine 102 **borrow** i.e., borrow none from others (?) I will borrow none (?) 106 **Of** by 110 **Push** (an effeminate expression of impatience) 113 **humors** whims, caprices

SECOND LORD Lord Timon's mad.

THIRD LORD I feel't upon my bones.

FOURTH LORD One day he gives us diamonds, next day stones.

Exeunt the Senators [*and others*].

[ACT IV

Scene I. *Outside the walls of Athens.*]

Enter Timon.

TIMON Let me look back upon thee. O thou wall
That girdles in those wolves, dive in the earth,
And fence not Athens. Matrons, turn incontinent;
Obedience fail in children. Slaves and fools,
Pluck the grave wrinkled senate from the bench,
And minister in their steads. To general filths
Convert o' th' instant green virginity;
Do't in your parents' eyes. Bankrupts, hold fast
Rather than render back; out with your knives,
And cut your trusters' throats. Bound servants,
steal;
Large-handed robbers your grave masters are,
And pill by law. Maid, to thy master's bed,
Thy mistress is o' th' brothel. Son of sixteen,
Pluck the lined crutch from thy old limping sire,
With it beat out his brains. Piety, and fear,

IV.i.6 **minister** govern 6 **filths** harlots (or, more generally, immoral acts or corruption) 7 **green** young, inexperienced 9 **render back** repay debts 10 **Bound** under obligation to serve for a stated period 11 **Large-handed** rapacious (usually means "generous") 12 **pill** steal 14 **lined** padded

Religion to the gods, peace, justice, truth,
Domestic awe, night-rest, and neighborhood,
Instruction, manners, mysteries, and trades,
Degrees, observances, customs, and laws,
Decline to your confounding contraries,
And let confusion live. Plagues incident to men,
Your potent and infectious fevers heap
On Athens ripe for stroke. Thou cold sciatica,
Cripple our senators, that their limbs may halt
As lamely as their manners. Lust and liberty
Creep in the minds and marrows of our youth,
That 'gainst the stream of virtue they may strive,
And drown themselves in riot. Itches, blains,
Sow all th' Athenian bosoms, and their crop
Be general leprosy. Breath infect breath,
That their society, as their friendship, may
Be merely poison. Nothing I'll bear from thee
But nakedness, thou detestable town;
Take thou that too, with multiplying bans.
Timon will to the woods, where he shall find
Th' unkindest beast more kinder than mankind.
The gods confound—hear me, you good gods all—
Th' Athenians both within and out that wall.
And grant, as Timon grows, his hate may grow
To the whole race of mankind, high and low.
Amen. *Exit.*

16 **Religion to** religious concern for 17 **Domestic awe** the respect appropriate to domestic relations (to parents, home, etc.) 17 **neighborhood** neighborliness 18 **mysteries** crafts, callings 19 **Degrees** social classes 20 **confounding contraries** opposites which destroy each other and so bring on general chaos 21 **confusion** ruin 21 **incident to** natural to 24 **halt** limp 25 **liberty** licentiousness 28 **blains** blisters 32 **merely** utterly 33 **detestable** (primary accent on first syllable) 34 **multiplying bans** ever-increasing curses (?) multiple curses (?) 36 **more kinder** (1) more generous, gracious (2) more natural, closer to the moral law of nature

[Scene II. *Athens. Timon's house.*]

Enter [Flavius, the] Steward, with two or three Servants.

FIRST SERVANT Hear you, master steward, where's our master?
Are we undone, cast off, nothing remaining?

FLAVIUS Alack, my fellows, what should I say to you?
Let me be recorded by the righteous gods,
I am as poor as you.

FIRST SERVANT Such a house broke?
So noble a master fall'n, all gone, and not
One friend to take his fortune by the arm,
And go along with him?

SECOND SERVANT As we do turn our backs
From our companion thrown into his grave,
So his familiars to his buried fortunes
Slink all away, leave their false vows with him,
Like empty purses picked; and his poor self,
A dedicated beggar to the air,
With his disease of all-shunned poverty,
Walks like contempt alone.

Enter other Servants.

More of our fellows.

FLAVIUS All broken implements of a ruined house.

THIRD SERVANT Yet do our hearts wear Timon's livery,

IV.ii.4 **Let me be recorded** let it be recorded of me 7 **his fortune** i.e., Timon in his ill fortune 10 **his familiars to his buried fortunes** those who were the familiar friends of his now buried fortunes (also suggests "familiar spirit," a personal servant from the spirit world) 13 **A dedicated beggar to the air** a beggar vowed or doomed to wander about in the open air

That see I by our faces; we are fellows still,
Serving alike in sorrow. Leaked is our bark,
And we poor mates stand on the dying deck,
Hearing the surges threat. We must all part
Into this sea of air.

FLAVIUS Good fellows all,
The latest of my wealth I'll share amongst you.
Wherever we shall meet, for Timon's sake,
Let's yet be fellows. Let's shake our heads and say,
As 'twere a knell unto our master's fortunes,
"We have seen better days." Let each take some.
[*Gives money.*]
Nay, put out all your hands. Not one word more;
Thus part we rich in sorrow, parting poor.
Embrace, and part several ways.
O the fierce wretchedness that glory brings us!
Who would not wish to be from wealth exempt,
Since riches point to misery and contempt?
Who would be so mocked with glory, or to live
But in a dream of friendship,
To have his pomp and all what state compounds
But only painted, like his varnished friends?
Poor honest lord, brought low by his own heart,
Undone by goodness. Strange, unusual blood,
When man's worst sin is, he does too much good.
Who then dares to be half so kind again?
For bounty, that makes gods, do still mar men.
My dearest lord, blessed to be most accursed,
Rich only to be wretched, thy great fortunes
Are made thy chief afflictions. Alas, kind lord,
He's flung in rage from this ingrateful seat
Of monstrous friends;

18 **fellows** fellow servants 22 **this sea of air** i.e., the open air, which is as comfortless to us as is the sea to sailors on a sinking ship 23 **latest** last 32 **point to** lead to 33 **to live** i.e., who would wish to live 35 **all what state compounds** all that worldly splendor is composed of 36 **painted** illusory 36 **varnished** fair-seeming 38 **blood** disposition 40 **half so kind** i.e., as Timon was, who came to grief because of it 42 **blessed to be** i.e., blessed with wealth only to be 45 **seat** residence

Nor has he with him to supply his life,
Or that which can command it.
I'll follow and inquire him out.
I'll ever serve his mind with my best will;
Whilst I have gold, I'll be his steward still. *Exit.*

[Scene III. *Before Timon's cave.*]

Enter Timon in the woods.

TIMON O blessèd breeding sun, draw from the earth
Rotten humidity; below thy sister's orb
Infect the air. Twinned brothers of one womb,
Whose procreation, residence, and birth,
Scarce is dividant—touch them with several fortunes,
The greater scorns the lesser. Not nature,
To whom all sores lay siege, can bear great fortune
But by contempt of nature.
Raise me this beggar, and deny't that lord,
The senators shall bear contempt hereditary,
The beggar native honor.
It is the pasture lards the brother's sides,
The want that makes him lean. Who dares? Who dares

47 **to supply his life** i.e., he has no food and drink 48 **that** i.e., money IV.iii.2 **Rotten humidity** humidity that causes things to rot 2 **below thy sister's orb** beneath the moon (i.e., in the middle air between earth and moon) 5 **dividant** divisible, separable 5 **touch** test 5 **several** different 6–8 **Not nature . . . nature** i.e., human nature, which is subjected to all sorts of miseries, when it encounters good fortune rejects its own natural affection and despises mankind 9 **deny't** i.e., deny to raise 10 **hereditary** i.e., as if they were born that way and not simply victims of fortune's caprices 11 **native** i.e., as if he were born with it 12–13 **It is . . . lean** i.e., the "twinned brothers" (line 3) are distinguished by their gifts of fortune; the rich pasture, and not any intrinsic worth, makes one brother fat and the other lean

In purity of manhood stand upright
And say, this man's a flatterer? If one be,
So are they all, for every grise of fortune
Is smoothed by that below. The learned pate
Ducks to the golden fool. All's obliquy;
There's nothing level in our cursèd natures
But direct villainy. Therefore be abhorred
All feasts, societies, and throngs of men.
His semblable, yea himself, Timon disdains;
Destruction fang mankind. Earth, yield me roots.
[*Digs.*]
Who seeks for better of thee, sauce his palate
With thy most operant poison. What is here?
Gold? Yellow, glittering, precious gold?
No, gods, I am no idle votarist.
Roots, you clear heavens! Thus much of this will make
Black, white; foul, fair; wrong, right;
Base, noble; old, young; coward, valiant.
Ha, you gods! Why this? What this, you gods? Why this
Will lug your priests and servants from your sides;
Pluck stout men's pillows from below their heads.
This yellow slave
Will knit and break religions, bless th' accursed,
Make the hoar leprosy adored, place thieves,
And give them title, knee, and approbation
With senators on the bench. This is it
That makes the wappened widow wed again;
She, whom the spital-house and ulcerous sores

16 **grise** step 17 **smoothed** flattered, facilitated by flattery 17 **pate** head 18 **Ducks to the golden fool** inclines in deference to the rich fool 18 **obliquy** obliquity, moral crookedness 22 **semblable** anything like himself 23 **fang** (1) seize, as with fangs (2) provide with fangs 24 **sauce** season 25 **operant** potent 27 **no idle votarist** i.e., I have not sworn my vow in an idle or trifling way 28 **clear** pure 33 **Pluck . . . heads** i.e., kill even strong men by sudden suffocation 36 **hoar** white 36 **place** elevate to a place or office of dignity 39 **wappened** sexually exhausted 40 **spital-house** hospital (especially for the lower classes and sufferers from loathsome diseases) 40 **ulcerous sores** i.e., those afflicted with ulcerous sores

Would cast the gorge at, this embalms and spices
To th' April day again. Come, damnèd earth,
Thou common whore of mankind, that puts odds
Among the rout of nations, I will make thee
Do thy right nature.

March afar off.

Ha? A drum? Th' art quick,
But yet I'll bury thee. Thou't go, strong thief,
When gouty keepers of thee cannot stand.
Nay, stay thou out for earnest. [*Keeps some gold.*]

Enter Alcibiades, with drum and fife, in warlike manner; and Phrynia and Timandra.

ALCIBIADES What art thou there? Speak.

TIMON A beast as thou art. The canker gnaw thy heart
For showing me again the eyes of man.

ALCIBIADES What is thy name? Is man so hateful to thee
That art thyself a man?

TIMON I am Misanthropos and hate mankind.
For thy part, I do wish thou wert a dog,
That I might love thee something.

ALCIBIADES I know thee well,
But in thy fortunes am unlearnèd and strange.

TIMON I know thee too, and more than that I know thee
I not desire to know. Follow thy drum,
With man's blood paint the ground gules, gules.

41 **cast the gorge** vomit 41–42 **embalms and spices/To th' April day** i.e., preserves, perfumes, and generally revivifies to a springlike and youthful amorousness 43–44 **puts odds/Among the rout of nations** sets the disorderly mob of nations at strife with each other 45 **Do thy right nature** i.e., cause strife and dissension 45 **quick** (1) alive (2) speedily had and lost 46 **go** walk, move 48 **for earnest** as an installment 50 **canker** (1) ulcerous sore (2) canker-worm 54 **Misanthropos** the man-hater 56 **something** somewhat 57 **strange** ignorant 60 **gules** red (the heraldic term)

Religious canons, civil laws are cruel;
Then what should war be? This fell whore of thine
Hath in her more destruction than thy sword,
For all her cherubin look.

PHRYNIA Thy lips rot off.

TIMON I will not kiss thee; then the rot returns
To thine own lips again.

ALCIBIADES How came the noble Timon to this change?

TIMON As the moon does, by wanting light to give.
But then renew I could not like the moon;
There were no suns to borrow of.

ALCIBIADES Noble Timon, what friendship may I do thee?

TIMON None, but to maintain my opinion.

ALCIBIADES What is it, Timon?

TIMON Promise me friendship, but perform none.
If thou wilt not promise, the gods plague thee,
For thou art a man. If thou dost perform,
Confound thee, for thou art a man.

ALCIBIADES I have heard in some sort of thy miseries.

TIMON Thou saw'st them when I had prosperity.

ALCIBIADES I see them now; then was a blessed time.

TIMON As thine is now, held with a brace of harlots.

TIMANDRA Is this th' Athenian minion, whom the world
Voiced so regardfully?

62 **fell** destructive 65 **the rot returns** (based on a prevalent belief that by transmitting a venereal infection to another, one loses it himself) 68 **wanting** lacking 69 **renew** (1) to become new (2) to extend a loan (as in the next line) 72 **maintain my opinion** i.e., be a misanthropist, too 81 **brace** (usually used for a pair of dogs on a leash) 82 **minion** favorite, darling 83 **Voiced so regardfully** spoke of with so much regard

TIMON Art thou Timandra?

TIMANDRA Yes.

TIMON Be a whore still; they love thee not that use
thee.
Give them diseases, leaving with thee their lust.
Make use of thy salt hours. Season the slaves
For tubs and baths; bring down rose-cheeked
youth
To the tub-fast and the diet.

TIMANDRA Hang thee, monster!

ALCIBIADES Pardon him, sweet Timandra, for his wits
Are drowned and lost in his calamities.
I have but little gold of late, brave Timon,
The want whereof doth daily make revolt
In my penurious band. I have heard, and grieved,
How cursèd Athens, mindless of thy worth,
Forgetting thy great deeds, when neighbor states,
But for thy sword and fortune, trod upon them—

TIMON I prithee beat thy drum and get thee gone.

ALCIBIADES I am thy friend and pity thee, dear Timon.

TIMON How dost thou pity him whom thou dost
trouble?
I had rather be alone.

ALCIBIADES Why fare thee well.
Here is some gold for thee.

TIMON Keep it, I cannot eat it.

ALCIBIADES When I have laid proud Athens on a
heap——

85 **leaving** i.e., while they leave 86 **salt** lustful, salacious 86 **Season** spice 87 **tubs and baths** sweating-tubs and hot baths (used to treat venereal disease) 88 **tub-fast and the diet** (fasting and special diet were treatments for venereal disease) 91 **brave** excellent 93 **penurious** needy 96 **trod** i.e., would have trodden 97 **beat thy drum** i.e., let thy drummer give the signal for departure

TIMON War'st thou 'gainst Athens?

ALCIBIADES Ay, Timon, and have cause.

TIMON The gods confound them all in thy conquest,
And thee after when thou hast conquerèd.

ALCIBIADES Why me, Timon?

TIMON That by killing of villains
Thou wast born to conquer my country.
Put up thy gold. Go on, here's gold, go on.
Be as a planetary plague, when Jove
Will o'er some high-viced city hang his poison
In the sick air. Let not thy sword skip one.
Pity not honored age for his white beard:
He is an usurer. Strike me the counterfeit matron:
It is her habit only that is honest,
Herself's a bawd. Let not the virgin's cheek
Make soft thy trenchant sword: for those milk paps,
That through the window-bars bore at men's eyes,
Are not within the leaf of pity writ,
But set them down horrible traitors. Spare not the babe
Whose dimpled smiles from fools exhaust their mercy:
Think it a bastard, whom the oracle
Hath doubtfully pronounced thy throat shall cut,
And mince it sans remorse. Swear against objects.
Put armor on thine ears and on thine eyes,
Whose proof nor yells of mothers, maids, nor babes,

104 **in thy conquest** i.e., in your victory over them 108 **Put up** put away 109 **planetary plague** plague caused by the planets 114 **habit** dress 114 **honest** chaste 116 **trenchant** cutting 117 **window-bars** lattice work of a window (?) open-work squares of the bodice of a woman's frock (?) 118 **within the leaf of pity writ** i.e., written down on the page with the names of those who are to be pitied and spared 120 **exhaust** draw out, elicit 122 **doubtfully** ambiguously 123 **mince it sans remorse** cut it up without pity 123 **objects** objections, accusations of cruelty 125 **proof** high quality (of armor), impenetrability

Nor sight of priests in holy vestments bleeding,
Shall pierce a jot. There's gold to pay thy soldiers.
Make large confusion; and, thy fury spent,
Confounded be thyself. Speak not, begone.

ALCIBIADES Hast thou gold yet, I'll take the gold thou givest me,
Not all thy counsel.

TIMON Dost thou or dost thou not, heaven's curse upon thee.

PHRYNIA AND TIMANDRA Give us some gold, good Timon; hast thou more?

TIMON Enough to make a whore forswear her trade,
And to make whores, a bawd. Hold up, you sluts,
Your aprons mountant. You are not oathable,
Although I know you'll swear, terribly swear
Into strong shudders and to heavenly agues
Th' immortal gods that hear you. Spare your oaths;
I'll trust to your conditions. Be whores still,
And he whose pious breath seeks to convert you,
Be strong in whore, allure him, burn him up;
Let your close fire predominate his smoke,
And be no turncoats. Yet may your pains six months
Be quite contrary. And thatch
Your poor thin roofs with burdens of the dead—
Some that were hanged, no matter.
Wear them, betray with them; whore still;

128 **confusion** destruction 130 **Hast** i.e., if you have 135 **And to make whores, a bawd** i.e., and enough to make a bawd give up her trade of making whores (or, perhaps, enough to make a whore set herself up as a bawd, making whores instead of being one) 136 **aprons mountant** rising aprons (a mock heraldic phrase with sexual overtones) 136 **oathable** capable of being placed under oath 140 **conditions** dispositions 140 **still** always 143 **Let . . . smoke** i.e., let the hidden fire of your sexuality or disease dominate over the smoke of idle words of he who "seeks to convert you" 144–45 **Yet . . . contrary** i.e., may you spend six months of the year in being whores and the other six in repairing the physical damage occasioned by your debaucheries (?) 145–46 **And thatch . . . dead** i.e., wear wigs (or possibly false pubes) made from loads of hair taken from the dead (venereal disease was thought to cause loss of hair)

Paint till a horse may mire upon your face.
A pox of wrinkles!

PHRYNIA AND TIMANDRA Well, more gold. What then?
Believe't that we'll do anything for gold.

TIMON Consumptions sow
In hollow bones of man; strike their sharp shins,
And mar men's spurring. Crack the lawyer's voice,
That he may never more false title plead,
Nor sound his quillets shrilly. Hoar the flamen,
That scolds against the quality of flesh
And not believes himself. Down with the nose,
Down with it flat, take the bridge quite away
Of him, that his particular to foresee,
Smells from the general weal. Make curled-pate ruffians bald,
And let the unscarred braggarts of the war
Derive some pain from you. Plague all,
That your activity may defeat and quell
The source of all erection. There's more gold.
Do you damn others, and let this damn you,
And ditches grave you all.

PHRYNIA AND TIMANDRA More counsel with more money, bounteous Timon.

TIMON More whore, more mischief first; I have given you earnest.

149 **mire** sink into the mire or mud (because of the thickness of cosmetics) 150 **A pox of wrinkles** i.e., a pox on wrinkles, away with wrinkles (since they can be covered with cosmetics) 152 **Consumptions** wasting diseases (here venereal disease) 153 **hollow . . . sharp** i.e., the disease will make the bones hollow and the shins painful 156 **quillets** subtle verbal distinctions 156 **Hoar the flamen** whiten the priest with disease, or cause his hair to turn white (possible pun on "whore") 157 **quality of flesh** the nature of the flesh, sexual pleasure 158 **Down with the nose** (an effect of syphilis) 160–61 **his particular . . . weal** i.e., to provide for his private advantage or profit, he abandons the proper scent that contributes to the public good or welfare 165 **The source of all erection** i.e., sexuality itself 167 **grave** be a grave for, bury 169 **earnest** a part payment to seal a bargain

ALCIBIADES Strike up the drum towards Athens. Farewell, Timon.
If I thrive well, I'll visit thee again.

TIMON If I hope well, I'll never see thee more.

ALCIBIADES I never did thee harm.

TIMON Yes, thou spok'st well of me.

ALCIBIADES Call'st thou that harm?

TIMON Men daily find it. Get thee away, and take
Thy beagles with thee.

ALCIBIADES We but offend him. Strike!
[*Drum beats.*] *Exeunt* [*Alcibiades, Phrynia, and Timandra*].

TIMON That nature, being sick of man's unkindness,
Should yet be hungry! Common mother, thou,
[*Digging*]
Whose womb unmeasurable and infinite breast
Teems and feeds all; whose selfsame mettle,
Whereof thy proud child, arrogant man, is puffed,
Engenders the black toad and adder blue,
The gilded newt and eyeless venomed worm,
With all th' abhorrèd births below crisp heaven
Whereon Hyperion's quick'ning fire doth shine;
Yield him, who all the human sons do hate,
From forth thy plenteous bosom, one poor root.
Ensear thy fertile and conceptious womb;
Let it no more bring out ingrateful man.
Go great with tigers, dragons, wolves, and bears,
Teem with new monsters, whom thy upward face
Hath to the marbled mansion all above

172 **If I hope well** if my hopes are realized 177 **of** as a result of 180 **Teems** brings forth 180 **mettle** (1) substance (2) vigorous spirit 181 **puffed** puffed up with pride 184 **crisp** with curled clouds (?) shining, clear (?) 185 **Hyperion's quick'ning fire** (the sun was thought to have the power of generating some of the lower forms of insect life) 188 **Ensear** dry up 188 **conceptious** conceiving, prolific 190 **great** pregnant 192 **above** in heaven

Never presented. O, a root, dear thanks!
Dry up thy marrows, vines and plough-torn leas,
Whereof ingrateful man, with liquorish draughts
And morsels unctious, greases his pure mind,
That from it all consideration slips——

Enter Apemantus.

More man? Plague, plague!

APEMANTUS I was directed hither. Men report
Thou dost affect my manners, and dost use them.

TIMON 'Tis then because thou dost not keep a dog
Whom I would imitate. Consumption catch thee.

APEMANTUS This is in thee a nature but infected,
A poor unmanly melancholy sprung
From change of future. Why this spade? This
place?
This slave-like habit and these looks of care?
Thy flatterers yet wear silk, drink wine, lie soft,
Hug their diseased perfumes, and have forgot
That ever Timon was. Shame not these woods
By putting on the cunning of a carper.
Be thou a flatterer now, and seek to thrive
By that which has undone thee. Hinge thy knee,
And let his very breath whom thou'lt observe
Blow off thy cap; praise his most vicious strain
And call it excellent. Thou wast told thus.

194 **marrows** (the type of a rich food, not a necessity of life, produced by the "vines" and "leas") 196 **unctious** (an obsolete variant form of "unctuous") 197 **consideration** ability to consider 200 **affect** imitate 202 **Consumption** any wasting disease 203 **infected** (1) affected, factitious (2) caught like an infection from your changed circumstances 205 **change of future** i.e., change in your material prospects 206 **habit** dress, garb 208 **diseased perfumes** diseased and perfumed mistresses 210 **By ... carper** i.e., by pretending to the profession of a cynic or railer (which any fool can do) 213–14 **let his ... cap** kneel so obsequiously close to the person you are paying court to that his breath may blow off your cap 214 **strain** quality 215 **Thou wast told thus** i.e., in your prosperity others spoke to you in this manner

Thou gav'st thine ears, like tapsters that bade welcome,
To knaves and all approachers. 'Tis most just
That thou turn rascal; hadst thou wealth again,
Rascals should have't. Do not assume my likeness.

TIMON Were I like thee, I'd throw away myself.

APEMANTUS Thou hast cast away thyself, being like thyself:
A madman so long, now a fool. What, think'st
That the bleak air, thy boisterous chamberlain,
Will put thy shirt on warm? Will these moist trees,
That have outlived the eagle, page thy heels
And skip when thou point'st out? Will the cold brook,
Candied with ice, caudle thy morning taste
To cure thy o'er-night's surfeit? Call the creatures
Whose naked natures live in all the spite
Of wreakful heaven, whose bare unhousèd trunks,
To the conflicting elements exposed,
Answer mere nature. Bid them flatter thee.
O thou shalt find——

TIMON A fool of thee. Depart.

APEMANTUS I love thee better now than e'er I did.

TIMON I hate thee worse.

APEMANTUS Why?

TIMON Thou flatter'st misery.

APEMANTUS I flatter not, but say thou art a caitiff.

216 **tapsters** (tavern-keepers or bartenders are proverbial for their indiscriminate hospitality) 223 **chamberlain** one who waits on a king or lord in his bedchamber 224 **moist** damp 226 **point'st out** indicate your desires 227 **Candied** congealed, encrusted 227 **caudle** offer a caudle (a warm, spiced, mildly alcoholic drink given to the sick) 228 **o'er-night's surfeit** previous night's indulgence in drink 230 **wreakful** vengeful 232 **Answer mere nature** correspond to or reflect nature in its barest and most rigorous form 236 **caitiff** wretch

TIMON Why dost thou seek me out?

APEMANTUS To vex thee.

TIMON Always a villain's office or a fool's.
Dost please thyself in't?

APEMANTUS Ay.

TIMON What, a knave too?

APEMANTUS If thou didst put this sour cold habit on
To castigate thy pride, 'twere well; but thou
Dost it enforcedly. Thou'dst courtier be again
Wert thou not beggar. Willing misery
Outlives incertain pomp, is crowned before.
The one is filling still, never complete;
The other, at high wish. Best state, contentless,
Hath a distracted and most wretched being,
Worse than the worst, content.
Thou shouldst desire to die, being miserable.

TIMON Not by his breath that is more miserable.
Thou art a slave, whom Fortune's tender arm
With favor never clasped, but bred a dog.
Hadst thou, like us, from our first swath proceeded
The sweet degrees that this brief world affords
To such as may the passive drudges of it
Freely command, thou wouldst have plunged thyself
In general riot, melted down thy youth
In different beds of lust, and never learned

238 **office** duty 240 **habit** (1) garment (2) outward manner, bearing 242 **enforcedly** i.e., as if you were being forced to do it 243 **Willing misery** voluntary poverty 244 **is crowned before** comes earlier to the fulfillment of its desires and wishes 245 **The one is filling still** i.e., pomp, like a leaky vessel, can never be filled (or fulfilled) 246 **The other, at high wish** i.e., "willing misery," because it wishes little, can easily arrive at the height of its wishes 246–48 **Best state . . . content** i.e., a man in even the best material condition, if he is without content or happiness, is confused and wretched, worse than a man in the poorest condition who is contented 250 **breath** voice 253 **swath** swaddling clothes 253–54 **proceeded/The sweet degrees** advanced from one stage to the next above it (in sense of academic "degrees") 255 **passive drudges** submissive menial servants 257 **riot** debauchery

The icy precepts of respect, but followed
The sug'red game before thee. But myself—
Who had the world as my confectionary,
The mouths, the tongues, the eyes, and hearts of men
At duty, more than I could frame employment;
That numberless upon me stuck, as leaves
Do on the oak, have with one winter's brush
Fell from their boughs, and left me open, bare
For every storm that blows—I to bear this,
That never knew but better, is some burden.
Thy nature did commence in sufferance, time
Hath made thee hard in't. Why shouldst thou hate men?
They never flattered thee. What hast thou given?
If thou wilt curse, thy father, that poor rogue,
Must be thy subject; who in spite put stuff
To some she-beggar and compounded thee
Poor rogue hereditary. Hence, begone.
If thou hadst not been born the worst of men,
Thou hadst been a knave and flatterer.

APEMANTUS Art thou proud yet?

TIMON Ay, that I am not thee.

APEMANTUS I, that I was
No prodigal.

TIMON I, that I am one now.
Were all the wealth I have shut up in thee,
I'd give thee leave to hang it. Get thee gone.
That the whole life of Athens were in this!
Thus would I eat it. [*Eats a root.*]

259 **icy precepts of respect** i.e., the chilling rules of reason which constitute proper social conduct 260 **sug'red game** outwardly sweet quarry (probably whores) 261 **confectionary** a place where sweetmeats or candy are made 263 **frame employment** invent work for 265 **winter's brush** i.e., brush of a wintry wind 266 **Fell** fallen 269 **sufferance** suffering 273–74 **put stuff/To** i.e., made pregnant (contemptuous) 276 **worst** i.e., in social and financial position 282 **That** i.e., would that

APEMANTUS Here, I will mend thy feast. [*Offers him food.*]

TIMON First mend my company, take away thyself.

APEMANTUS So I shall mend mine own, by th' lack of thine.

TIMON 'Tis not well mended so, it is but botched;
If not, I would it were.

APEMANTUS What wouldst thou have to Athens?

TIMON Thee thither in a whirlwind. If thou wilt,
Tell them there I have gold; look, so I have.

APEMANTUS Here is no use for gold.

TIMON The best and truest;
For here it sleeps and does no hirèd harm.

APEMANTUS Where liest a nights, Timon?

TIMON Under that's above me.
Where feed'st thou a days, Apemantus?

APEMANTUS Where my stomach finds meat, or rather where I eat it.

TIMON Would poison were obedient and knew my mind!

APEMANTUS Where wouldst thou send it?

TIMON To sauce thy dishes.

APEMANTUS The middle of humanity thou never knewest, but the extremity of both ends. When thou wast in thy gilt and thy perfume, they mocked thee for too much curiosity; in thy rags thou know'st none, but art despised for the contrary. There's a medlar for thee; eat it.

283 **mend** improve 286 **botched** clumsily repaired (because Apemantus is still present—with himself) 288 **to** in 293 **that's above me** i.e., that which is above me, the sky 304 **curiosity** carefulness, fastidiousness 306 **medlar** a fruit like a small brown-skinned apple, not ready to be eaten until in the early stages of decay

TIMON On what I hate I feed not.

APEMANTUS Dost hate a medlar?

TIMON Ay, though it look like thee.

APEMANTUS And th'hadst hated meddlers sooner, thou shouldst have loved thyself better now. What man didst thou ever know unthrift that was beloved after his means?

TIMON Who, without those means thou talk'st of, didst thou ever know beloved?

APEMANTUS Myself.

TIMON I understand thee; thou hadst some means to keep a dog.

APEMANTUS What things in the world canst thou nearest compare to thy flatterers?

TIMON Women nearest, but men—men are the things themselves. What wouldst thou do with the world, Apemantus, if it lay in thy power?

APEMANTUS Give it the beasts, to be rid of the men.

TIMON Wouldst thou have thyself fall in the confusion of men, and remain a beast with the beasts?

APEMANTUS Ay, Timon.

TIMON A beastly ambition, which the gods grant thee t' attain to. If thou wert the lion, the fox would beguile thee. If thou wert the lamb, the fox would eat thee. If thou wert the fox, the lion would suspect thee, when peradventure thou wert accused by the ass. If thou wert the ass, thy

308 **hate** ("eat" and "hate" were pronounced alike in Elizabethan English) 310 **And** if 310 **meddlers** (1) the fruit (2) busybodies, intriguers (3) those who overindulge in sexual intercourse 312 **unthrift** prodigal, spendthrift 313 **after** in accordance with (i.e., the true love for an "unthrift" is not in proportion with his bounty) 318 **a dog** i.e., you had just enough to keep a dog so that something might love you 325–26 **the confusion of men** i.e., the original Fall in the Garden of Eden 330 **beguile** trick 332 **peradventure** perchance

dullness would torment thee, and still thou liv'dst but as a breakfast to the wolf. If thou wert the wolf, thy greediness would afflict thee, and oft thou shouldst hazard thy life for thy dinner. Wert thou the unicorn, pride and wrath would confound thee, and make thine own self the conquest of thy fury. Wert thou a bear, thou wouldst be killed by the horse. Wert thou a horse, thou wouldst be seized by the leopard. Wert thou a leopard, thou wert german to the lion, and the spots of thy kindred were jurors on thy life. All thy safety were remotion, and thy defense absence. What beast couldst thou be that were not subject to a beast? And what a beast art thou already, that seest not thy loss in transformation!

APEMANTUS If thou couldst please me with speaking to me, thou mightst have hit upon it here. The commonwealth of Athens is become a forest of beasts.

TIMON How has the ass broke the wall, that thou art out of the city?

APEMANTUS Yonder comes a poet and a painter. The plague of company light upon thee! I will fear to catch it, and give way. When I know not what else to do, I'll see thee again.

TIMON When there is nothing living but thee, thou shalt be welcome. I had rather be a beggar's dog than Apemantus.

APEMANTUS Thou art the cap of all the fools alive.

338 **unicorn** (an untamable beast, who, in his fury to attack the treed lion, runs his horn into the tree and puts himself at the mercy of the lion) 338 **confound** destroy 343 **german** akin 343 **spots** (1) markings (2) moral stains, vices 344 **jurors** witnesses (especially false ones) 345 **remotion** removal of yourself (to a distance), remoteness 348 **in transformation** i.e., in seeking to be transformed into a beast 355 **a poet and a painter** (they do not actually enter until the beginning of Act V) 357 **give way** retire 362 **cap** chief, summit

TIMON Would thou wert clean enough to spit upon.

APEMANTUS A plague on thee, thou art too bad to curse.

TIMON All villains that do stand by thee are pure.

APEMANTUS There is no leprosy but what thou speak'st.

TIMON If I name thee.
I'll beat thee, but I should infect my hands.

APEMANTUS I would my tongue could rot them off.

TIMON Away, thou issue of a mangy dog.
Choler does kill me that thou art alive;
I swound to see thee.

APEMANTUS Would thou wouldst burst.

TIMON Away, thou tedious rogue, I am sorry I shall lose a stone by thee. [*Throws a stone at him.*]

APEMANTUS Beast!

TIMON Slave!

APEMANTUS Toad!

TIMON Rogue, rogue, rogue!
I am sick of this false world, and will love naught
But even the mere necessities upon't.
Then, Timon, presently prepare thy grave.
Lie where the light foam of the sea may beat
Thy gravestone daily. Make thine epitaph,
That death in me at others' lives may laugh.
[*To the gold*] O thou sweet king-killer, and dear divorce
'Twixt natural son and sire, thou bright defiler
Of Hymen's purest bed, thou valiant Mars,

365 **that do stand by thee** compared to you 371 **Choler** anger 372 **swound** swoon 381 **But even ... upon't** i.e., except the bare necessities of life 382 **presently** immediately 385 **in me** by my example 387 **natural** son by birth (does not mean "illegitimate") 382 **Hymen** Greek god of marriage

Thou ever young, fresh, loved, and delicate wooer,
Whose blush doth thaw the consecrated snow
That lies on Dian's lap. Thou visible god,
That sold'rest close impossibilities
And mak'st them kiss; that speak'st with every tongue
To every purpose. O thou touch of hearts,
Think thy slave man rebels, and by thy virtue
Set them into confounding odds, that beasts
May have the world in empire.

APEMANTUS Would 'twere so,
But not till I am dead. I'll say th'hast gold.
Thou wilt be thronged to shortly.

TIMON Thronged to?

APEMANTUS Ay.

TIMON Thy back, I prithee.

APEMANTUS Live, and love thy misery.

TIMON Long live so, and so die. I am quit.

Enter the Banditti.

APEMANTUS Moe things like men! Eat, Timon, and abhor them. *Exit Apemantus.*

FIRST BANDIT Where should he have this gold? It is some poor fragment, some slender ort of his remainder. The mere want of gold, and the falling-from of his friends, drove him into this melancholy.

SECOND BANDIT It is noised he hath a mass of treasure.

THIRD BANDIT Let us make the assay upon him. If

390 **blush** glow 391 **Dian** Diana, the virgin huntress, Greek goddess of chastity 392 **sold'rest close impossibilities** joins closely together things thought to be irreconcilable 394 **touch** touchstone 396 **into confounding odds** at ruinous strife 401 **quit** rid (of Apemantus) 404 **ort** leftover bit 405 **mere** sheer 405–06 **falling-from** falling-off 408 **noised** rumored 410 **make the assay** put it to the test

he care not for't, he will supply us easily; if he covetously reserve it, how shall's get it?

SECOND BANDIT True, for he bears it not about him; 'tis hid.

FIRST BANDIT Is not this he?

ALL Where?

SECOND BANDIT 'Tis his description.

THIRD BANDIT He? I know him.

ALL Save thee, Timon.

TIMON Now, thieves?

ALL Soldiers, not thieves.

TIMON Both too, and women's sons.

ALL We are not thieves, but men that much do want.

TIMON Your greatest want is, you want much of meat.
Why should you want? Behold, the earth hath roots;
Within this mile break forth a hundred springs;
The oaks bear mast, the briers scarlet hips;
The bounteous huswife nature on each bush
Lays her full mess before you. Want? Why want?

FIRST BANDIT We cannot live on grass, on berries, water,
As beasts and birds and fishes.

TIMON Nor on the beasts themselves, the birds and fishes;
You must eat men. Yet thanks I must you con
That you are thieves professed, that you work not
In holier shapes; for there is boundless theft

419 **Save thee** God save thee (a conventional salutation) 422 **want** need, lack 423 **you want much of meat** you desire (or lack) a good deal of food (i.e., if you didn't eat so much your wants would be smaller) 426 **mast** acorns (generally fed to swine) 426 **hips** fruit of the rose 427 **huswife** housewife 428 **mess** meal 432 **con** offer

In limited professions. Rascal thieves,
Here's gold. Go, suck the subtle blood o' th' grape,
Till the high fever seethe your blood to froth,
And so 'scape hanging. Trust not the physician;
His antidotes are poison, and he slays
Moe than you rob. Take wealth and lives together,
Do, villain, do, since you protest to do't.
Like workmen, I'll example you with thievery:
The sun's a thief, and with his great attraction
Robs the vast sea. The moon's an arrant thief,
And her pale fire she snatches from the sun.
The sea's a thief, whose liquid surge resolves
The moon into salt tears. The earth's a thief,
That feeds and breeds by a composture stol'n
From gen'ral excrement. Each thing's a thief.
The laws, your curb and whip, in their rough power
Has unchecked theft. Love not yourselves; away,
Rob one another. There's more gold; cut throats,
All that you meet are thieves. To Athens go,
Break open shops; nothing can you steal
But thieves do lose it. Steal less for this I give you,
And gold confound you howsoe'er. Amen.

THIRD BANDIT Has almost charmed me from my profession by persuading me to it.

FIRST BANDIT 'Tis in the malice of mankind that he thus advises us, not to have us thrive in our mystery.

435 **limited** limited in numbers, restricted (as a guild) 436 **subtle** treacherous 437 **high fever** i.e., of drunkenness 440 **Moe** more 441 **protest** profess 442 **Like ... thievery** i.e., as one instructs workmen by practical example, so I will give you some precedents for your line of work, thievery 443 **attraction** drawing power 446–47 **whose ... tears** (the idea is that the sea's tides are stolen from the moon's precipitation) 448 **composture** compost, manure 455 **Steal less for this I give you** i.e., even if you steal less because of the gold I am giving you 456 **howsoe'er** nevertheless 459 **in the malice of mankind** i.e., because of the malice Timon bears to all mankind 461 **mystery** trade, profession

SECOND BANDIT I'll believe him as an enemy, and give over my trade.

FIRST BANDIT Let us first see peace in Athens; there is no time so miserable but a man may be true.

Exit Thieves.

Enter [Flavius,] the Steward to Timon.

FLAVIUS O you gods!
Is yond despised and ruinous man my lord?
Full of decay and failing? O monument
And wonder of good deeds evilly bestowed!
What an alteration of honor has desp'rate want
made!
What vilder thing upon the earth than friends,
Who can bring noblest minds to basest ends!
How rarely does it meet with this time's guise,
When man was wished to love his enemies!
Grant I may ever love, and rather woo
Those that would mischief me than those that do.
Has caught me in his eye; I will present
My honest grief unto him, and as my lord
Still serve him with my life. My dearest master.

TIMON Away! What art thou?

FLAVIUS Have you forgot me, sir?

TIMON Why dost ask that? I have forgot all men.
Then, if thou grunt'st th'art a man,
I have forgot thee.

462 **I'll believe him as an enemy** i.e., since he is an enemy, I'll do the opposite of what he advises 463 **give over** give up 464–65 **there is . . . true** i.e., you can become an honest man any time you choose (therefore, why do it now?) 467 **ruinous** ruined 468–69 **monument/And wonder** i.e., wonderful monument (memorial or tombstone) 470 **alteration of honor** change (for the worse) in honor 471 **vilder** viler 473 **How . . . guise** i.e., how excellently does Timon's example fit in with the moral tone of these times (spoken ironically) 474 **wished** desired (by God) 476 **Those . . . do** i.e., I will love those enemies who are direct and open in their desire to harm me better than those who harm me under the guise of friendship 482 **grunt'st** i.e., even your claim to be a man is delivered in an animal grunt (since all men are bestial)

FLAVIUS An honest poor servant of yours.

TIMON Then I know thee not.
I never had honest man about me, I; all
I kept were knaves, to serve in meat to villains.

FLAVIUS The gods are witness,
Nev'r did poor steward wear a truer grief
For his undone lord than mine eyes for you.

TIMON What, dost thou weep? Come nearer. Then
I love thee
Because thou art a woman, and disclaim'st
Flinty mankind, whose eyes do never give
But thorough lust and laughter. Pity's sleeping.
Strange times, that weep with laughing, not with
weeping!

FLAVIUS I beg of you to know me, good my lord,
T' accept my grief, and whilst this poor wealth lasts,
To entertain me as your steward still.

TIMON Had I a steward
So true, so just, and now so comfortable?
It almost turns my dangerous nature mild.
Let me behold thy face. Surely, this man
Was born of woman.
Forgive my general and exceptless rashness,
You perpetual-sober gods. I do proclaim
One honest man. Mistake me not, but one.
No more I pray—and he's a steward.
How fain would I have hated all mankind,
And thou redeem'st thyself. But all save thee
I fell with curses.
Methinks thou art more honest now than wise;
For, by oppressing and betraying me,

487 **knaves** (1) servants (2) villains 493 **Flinty** hardhearted 493 **give** weep 494 **But thorough** except through 498 **entertain** receive into service 500 **comfortable** comforting 504 **exceptless** making no exceptions 510 **fell** cause to fall, strike down 512 **oppressing** distressing

Thou might'st have sooner got another service.
For many so arrive at second masters
Upon their first lord's neck. But tell me true—
For I must ever doubt, though ne'er so sure—
Is not thy kindness subtle, covetous,
A usuring kindness, as rich men deal gifts,
Expecting in return twenty for one?

FLAVIUS No, my most worthy master, in whose breast
Doubt and suspect, alas, are placed too late.
You should have feared false times when you did
feast.
Suspect still comes where an estate is least.
That which I show, heaven knows, is merely love,
Duty and zeal to your unmatchèd mind,
Care of your food and living; and believe it,
My most honored lord,
For any benefit that points to me,
Either in hope or present, I'd exchange
For this one wish, that you had power and wealth
To requite me by making rich yourself.

TIMON Look thee, 'tis so. Thou singly honest man,
Here, take. The gods out of my misery
Has sent thee treasure. Go, live rich and happy,
But thus conditioned: thou shalt build from men;
Hate all, curse all, show charity to none,
But let the famished flesh slide from the bone
Ere thou relieve the beggar. Give to dogs
What thou deniest to men. Let prisons swallow 'em,
Debts wither 'em to nothing; be men like blasted
woods,
And may diseases lick up their false bloods.
And so farewell, and thrive.

513 **service** position as a servant 515 **Upon their first lord's neck** i.e., by treading down their first master and mounting on his neck (or shoulders) 516 **doubt** suspect, fear 518 **deal** distribute 521 **suspect** suspicion 523 **still** always 524 **merely** entirely 528 **points** might accrue 532 **singly** (1) uniquely (2) truly 535 **But thus conditioned** with this condition 535 **from** away from 540 **blasted** blighted

FLAVIUS O let me stay and comfort you, my master.

TIMON If thou hat'st curses
Stay not; fly, whilst thou art blessed and free.
Ne'er see thou man, and let me ne'er see thee.
Exit [*Flavius; and exit Timon into his cave*].

[ACT V

Scene I. *Before Timon's cave.*]

Enter Poet and Painter; [*Timon listens from his cave, unseen*].

PAINTER As I took note of the place, it cannot be far where he abides.

POET What's to be thought of him? Does the rumor hold for true that he's so full of gold?

PAINTER Certain. Alcibiades reports it. Phrynia and Timandra had gold of him. He likewise enriched poor straggling soldiers with great quantity. 'Tis said he gave unto his steward a mighty sum.

POET Then this breaking of his has been but a try for his friends?

PAINTER Nothing else. You shall see him a palm in Athens again, and flourish with the highest. Therefore 'tis not amiss we tender our loves to him in this supposed distress of his. It will show honestly in us, and is very likely to load our purposes with what they travail for, if it be a just and true report that goes of his having.

V.i.7 **soldiers** i.e., the banditti, who claimed to be soldiers 9 **breaking** going bankrupt 9 **try** test 11 **palm** (cf. Psalm 92:11 "The righteous shall flourish like the palm-tree") 13 **tender** offer 14 **honestly** honorably 16 **travail** (1) labor (2) travel 17 **having** wealth

POET What have you now to present unto him?

PAINTER Nothing at this time but my visitation; only I will promise him an excellent piece.

POET I must serve him so too, tell him of an intent that's coming toward him.

PAINTER Good as the best. Promising is the very air o' th' time; it opens the eyes of expectation. Performance is ever the duller for his act, and but in the plainer and simpler kind of people, the deed of saying is quite out of use. To promise is most courtly and fashionable; performance is a kind of will or testament, which argues a great sickness in his judgment that makes it.

Enter Timon from his cave.

TIMON [*Aside*] Excellent workman, thou canst not paint a man so bad as is thyself.

POET I am thinking what I shall say I have provided for him. It must be a personating of himself; a satire against the softness of prosperity, with a discovery of the infinite flatteries that follow youth and opulency.

TIMON [*Aside*] Must thou needs stand for a villain in thine own work? Wilt thou whip thine own faults in other men? Do so, I have gold for thee.

POET Nay, let's seek him.
Then do we sin against our own estate,
When we may profit meet, and come too late.

PAINTER True.
When the day serves, before black-cornered night,

25 **his act** its act, its having been put into action 26–27 **the deed of saying** i.e., the doing of what a person says he will do 34 **personating of himself** representation of Timon and his situation 35 **softness** weakness, flabbiness 36 **discovery** revelation (a theatrical term) 38 **stand for** serve as a model for 42 **estate** fortune, material possessions 45 **black-cornered night** i.e., night which creates dark corners and is obscure like them

Find what thou want'st by free and offered light.
Come.

TIMON [*Aside*] I'll meet you at the turn.
What a god's gold, that he is worshiped
In a baser temple than where swine feed!
'Tis thou that rig'st the bark and plough'st the
foam,
Settlest admirèd reverence in a slave.
To thee be worshiped and thy saints for aye;
Be crowned with plagues that thee alone obey.
Fit I meet them. [*Comes forward.*]

POET Hail, worthy Timon.

PAINTER Our late noble master.

TIMON Have I once lived to see two honest men?

POET Sir,
Having often of your open bounty tasted,
Hearing you were retired, your friends fall'n off,
Whose thankless natures, O abhorrèd spirits,
Not all the whips of heaven are large enough—
What, to you,
Whose star-like nobleness gave life and influence
To their whole being! I am rapt, and cannot cover
The monstrous bulk of this ingratitude
With any size of words.

TIMON Let it go;
Naked, men may see't the better.
You that are honest, by being what you are,
Make them best seen and known.

PAINTER He and myself

48 **I'll meet you at the turn** i.e., I will match your tricks with better ones of my own 50 **baser temple** i.e., the human body 52 **Settlest admirèd reverence** establishes a wondering awe (of his master) 53 **for aye** forever 54 **Be** i.e., may they be 57 **once** indeed (an intensive) 60 **retired** withdrawn 64 **influence** i.e., astrological influence 65 **rapt** carried away with emotion 67 **size** (1) magnitude (2) starch-like glue used on cloth, especially before painting on it 70 **them** i.e., the thankless natures of his fair-weather friends

Have traveled in the great show'r of your gifts,
And sweetly felt it.

TIMON Ay, you are honest men.

PAINTER We are hither come to offer you our service.

TIMON Most honest men. Why, how shall I requite you?
Can you eat roots and drink cold water? No?

BOTH What we can do, we'll do to do you service.

TIMON Y'are honest men. Y'have heard that I have gold,
I am sure you have. Speak truth, y'are honest men.

PAINTER So it is said, my noble lord, but therefore
Came not my friend nor I.

TIMON Good honest men. Thou draw'st a counterfeit
Best in all Athens. Th'art indeed the best;
Thou counterfeit'st most lively.

PAINTER So-so, my lord.

TIMON E'en so, sir, as I say. And for thy fiction,
Why thy verse swells with stuff so fine and smooth
That thou art even natural in thine art.
But for all this, my honest-natured friends,
I must needs say you have a little fault;
Marry, 'tis not monstrous in you, neither wish I
You take much pains to mend.

BOTH Beseech your honor
To make it known to us.

TIMON You'll take it ill.

BOTH Most thankfully, my lord.

81 **counterfeit** (1) representation, picture (2) false representation 83 **most lively** in a most lifelike manner 84 **fiction** imaginative feigning 85 **smooth** polished (with implication of flattery) 86 **thou . . . art** (1) your writings represent a triumph of nature over art; your art conceals itself (2) you show your evil natural self in your artful dissimulation 89 **Marry** indeed

TIMON Will you indeed?

BOTH Doubt it not, worthy lord.

TIMON There's never a one of you but trusts a knave
That mightily deceives you.

BOTH Do we, my lord?

TIMON Ay, and you hear him cog, see him dissemble,
Know his gross patchery, love him, feed him,
Keep in your bosom, yet remain assured
That he's a made-up villain.

PAINTER I know none such, my lord.

POET Nor I.

TIMON Look you, I love you well; I'll give you gold:
Rid me these villains from your companies.
Hang them, or stab them, drown them in a draught,
Confound them by some course, and come to me,
I'll give you gold enough.

BOTH Name them, my lord, let's know them.

TIMON You that way, and you this; but two in company.
Each man apart, all single and alone,
Yet an arch-villain keeps him company.
[*To one*] If where thou art, two villains shall not be,
Come not near him. [*To the other*] If thou wouldst not reside
But where one villain is, then him abandon.
Hence, pack, there's gold; you came for gold, ye slaves.
[*To one*] You have work for me, there's payment. Hence!

96 **cog** cheat 97 **patchery** roguery 98 **Keep** i.e., let him dwell 99 **made-up** complete 103 **draught** privy, sink 104 **Confound** destroy 107 **but two in company** i.e., wherever either of them is, there is both a poet (or painter) and a villain 112 **But** except 113 **pack** be off

[*To the other*] You are an alchemist, make gold
of that.
Out, rascal dogs!
[*Beats them out, then retires into his cave.*]

Enter [Flavius, the] Steward, and two Senators.

FLAVIUS It is vain that you would speak with Timon,
For he is set so only to himself
That nothing but himself, which looks like man,
Is friendly with him.

FIRST SENATOR Bring us to his cave.
It is our part and promise to th' Athenians
To speak with Timon.

SECOND SENATOR At all times alike
Men are not still the same; 'twas time and griefs
That framed him thus. Time with his fairer hand
Offering the fortunes of his former days,
The former man may make him. Bring us to him,
And chance it as it may.

FLAVIUS Here is his cave.
Peace and content be here. Lord Timon! Timon!
Look out, and speak to friends. Th' Athenians
By two of their most reverend senate greet thee.
Speak to them, noble Timon.

Enter Timon out of his cave.

TIMON Thou sun that comforts, burn! Speak and be
hanged.
For each true word a blister, and each false
Be as a cauterizing to the root o' th' tongue,
Consuming it with speaking.

FIRST SENATOR Worthy Timon——

TIMON Of none but such as you, and you of Timon.

118 **is set so only to himself** is so completely preoccupied with himself 121 **our part and promise** the role we promised to play 127 **chance it** may it turn out 133 **For each true word a blister** (an ironic reversal of the proverbial belief that a lie causes a blister on the tongue)

FIRST SENATOR The senators of Athens greet thee,
Timon.

TIMON I thank them, and would send them back the
plague,
Could I but catch it for them.

FIRST SENATOR O forget
What we are sorry for ourselves in thee.
The senators, with one consent of love,
Entreat thee back to Athens, who have thought
On special dignities, which vacant lie
For thy best use and wearing.

SECOND SENATOR They confess
Toward thee forgetfulness too general gross;
Which now the public body, which doth seldom
Play the recanter, feeling in itself
A lack of Timon's aid, hath sense withal
Of it own fall, restraining aid to Timon;
And send forth us to make their sorrowed render,
Together with a recompense more fruitful
Than their offense can weigh down by the dram—
Ay, even such heaps and sums of love and wealth
As shall to thee blot out what wrongs were theirs,
And write in thee the figures of their love,
Ever to read them thine.

TIMON You witch me in it;
Surprise me to the very brink of tears.

140 **in thee** i.e., in the wrongs we have caused you 141 **consent of love** harmonious voice of affection 144 **For thy best use and wearing** i.e., only you are suited to fill these dignities with the proper distinction 145 **general** universally 146 **the public body** the senate as representative of the body politic 148 **withal** at the same time 149 **it own fall** its own fall from grace 149 **restraining** keeping back 150 **sorrowed render** sorrowful rendering of an account 151 **fruitful** abundant 152 **weigh down by the dram** i.e., balance in weight even if measured to the last tiny unit 155 **figures** (1) written characters (2) numerals (as in counting money) (3) images, representations 156 **them** i.e., the Athenians as represented in the "figures of their love" 156 **witch** bewitch

Lend me a fool's heart and a woman's eyes,
And I'll beweep these comforts, worthy senators.

FIRST SENATOR Therefore so please thee to return with
us,
And of our Athens, thine and ours, to take
The captainship, thou shalt be met with thanks,
Allowed with absolute power, and thy good name
Live with authority. So soon we shall drive back
Of Alcibiades th' approaches wild,
Who like a boar too savage doth root up
His country's peace.

SECOND SENATOR And shakes his threat'ning sword
Against the walls of Athens.

FIRST SENATOR Therefore, Timon——

TIMON Well, sir, I will; therefore I will, sir, thus:
If Alcibiades kill my countrymen,
Let Alcibiades know this of Timon,
That Timon cares not. But if he sack fair Athens,
And take our goodly agèd men by th' beards,
Giving our holy virgins to the stain
Of contumelious, beastly, mad-brained war,
Then let him know, and tell him Timon speaks it,
In pity of our agèd and our youth,
I cannot choose but tell him that I care not,
And let him take't at worst. For their knives care not
While you have throats to answer. For myself,
There's not a whittle in th' unruly camp
But I do prize it at my love before
The reverend'st throat in Athens. So I leave you

159 **comforts** pleasures 163 **Allowed** endowed 175 **contumelious** insolent 179 **take't at worst** put the worst interpretation he wishes on it 180 **throats to answer** i.e., throats to be cut by the knives of Alcibiades' soldiers (and voices to protest for yourselves) 181 **whittle** small knife 181 **th' unruly camp** (1) the party of those revolting against Athens (2) the disorderly, turbulent army (of Alcibiades) 182 **prize it at my love** value it in my esteem

To the protection of the prosperous gods,
As thieves to keepers.

FLAVIUS Stay not, all's in vain.

TIMON Why I was writing of my epitaph;
It will be seen tomorrow. My long sickness
Of health and living now begins to mend,
And nothing brings me all things. Go, live still;
Be Alcibiades your plague, you his,
And last so long enough.

FIRST SENATOR We speak in vain.

TIMON But yet I love my country, and am not
One that rejoices in the common wrack,
As common bruit doth put it.

FIRST SENATOR That's well spoke.

TIMON Commend me to my loving countrymen.

FIRST SENATOR These words become your lips as they pass thorough them.

SECOND SENATOR And enter in our ears like great triumphers
In their applauding gates.

TIMON Commend me to them,
And tell them that to ease them of their griefs,
Their fears of hostile strokes, their aches, losses,
Their pangs of love, with other incident throes
That nature's fragile vessel doth sustain
In life's uncertain voyage, I will some kindness do them;
I'll teach them to prevent wild Alcibiades' wrath.

184 **prosperous** propitious 185 **As thieves to keepers** i.e., as I would leave thieves to the protection of their jailers 189 **nothing** nothingness, oblivion 191 **last** endure 193 **wrack** destruction 194 **bruit** rumor 196 **become** befit 197 **triumphers** triumphant marchers 198 **applauding gates** i.e., city gates thronged with those applauding the triumph 200 **aches** (two syllables, pronounced "aitches") 201 **incident throes** agonies likely to occur 204 **prevent** anticipate (but First Senator interprets "to keep from occurring")

FIRST SENATOR I like this well; he will return again.

TIMON I have a tree which grows here in my close,
That mine own use invites me to cut down,
And shortly must I fell it. Tell my friends,
Tell Athens, in the sequence of degree,
From high to low throughout, that whoso please
To stop affliction, let him take his haste;
Come hither ere my tree hath felt the ax,
And hang himself. I pray you do my greeting.

FLAVIUS Trouble him no further; thus you still shall find him.

TIMON Come not to me again, but say to Athens,
Timon hath made his everlasting mansion
Upon the beachèd verge of the salt flood,
Who once a day with his embossèd froth
The turbulent surge shall cover. Thither come,
And let my gravestone be your oracle.
Lips, let four words go by and language end.
What is amiss, plague and infection mend.
Graves only be men's works and death their gain.
Sun, hide thy beams; Timon hath done his reign.
Exit Timon.

FIRST SENATOR His discontents are unremovably
Coupled to nature.

SECOND SENATOR Our hope in him is dead. Let us return,

206 **close** enclosure 209 **sequence of degree** proper order of the social hierarchy 214 **still** always 217 **beachèd verge of the salt flood** edge of the sea that forms a beach 218 **Who** i.e., "the beachèd verge" 218 **embossèd** covered with foam (usually from the mouth of a hunted animal) 220 **be your oracle** i.e., be consulted by you as if it were an oracle (a place where divine pronouncements are made, or the god making such pronouncements) 221 **let four words go by and language end** i.e., speak only a few more words ("four" is used indefinitely) and then not speak any further 226 **Coupled to nature** a part of his nature

And strain what other means is left unto us
In our dear peril.

FIRST SENATOR It requires swift foot. *Exeunt.*

[Scene II. *Before the walls of Athens.*]

Enter two other Senators with a Messenger.

THIRD SENATOR Thou hast painfully discovered. Are his files
As full as thy report?

MESSENGER I have spoke the least.
Besides, his expedition promises
Present approach.

FOURTH SENATOR We stand much hazard if they bring not Timon.

MESSENGER I met a courier, one mine ancient friend,
Whom though in general part we were opposed,
Yet our old love made a particular force,
And made us speak like friends. This man was riding
From Alcibiades to Timon's cave
With letters of entreaty, which imported
His fellowship i' th' cause against your city,
In part for his sake moved.

228 **strain** exert to the utmost 229 **dear** grievous, dire V.ii.1 **Thou hast painfully discovered** (1) your revelation was painful to us (2) you have made your revelation in painstaking detail 1 **files** ranks 2 **spoke the least** reported the minimum 3 **expedition** speed 4 **Present** immediate 6 **ancient** former 7 **in general part** i.e., in matters of general or public interest 8 **particular** personal 11 **imported** bore as their message (with additional suggestion of "importuned" or urged) 13 **moved** instigated

Enter the other Senators [from Timon].

THIRD SENATOR Here come our brothers.

FIRST SENATOR No talk of Timon, nothing of him expect.
The enemy's drum is heard, and fearful scouring
Doth choke the air with dust. In, and prepare.
Ours is the fall, I fear, our foes the snare. *Exeunt.*

[Scene III. *Before Timon's cave.*]

Enter a Soldier in the woods, seeking Timon.

SOLDIER By all description this should be the place.
Who's here? Speak, ho! No answer? What is this?
"Timon is dead, who hath outstretched his span.
Some beast read this; there does not live a man."
Dead, sure, and this his grave. What's on this tomb
I cannot read. The character I'll take with wax;
Our captain hath in every figure skill,
An aged interpreter, though young in days.
Before proud Athens he's set down by this,
Whose fall the mark of his ambition is. *Exit.*

14 **No talk** i.e., let us not talk 15 **scouring** scurrying about (in preparation for battle) 17 **our foes the snare** i.e., our foes are the snare or trap which will cause the downfall of Athens V.iii.2 **What is this** (presumably the Soldier finds an inscription or trial epitaph composed by Timon in English, which the Soldier can read, whereas the epitaph on Timon's tomb is in Latin, which the Soldier cannot read) 3 **outstretched his span** lived beyond his allotted or desired life span 4 **there does not live a man** i.e., all men left alive are merely beasts 6 **The character I'll take with wax** I will take a wax impression of the letters 7 **figure** written character 8 **aged** experienced 9 **set down** i.e., in a siege 10 **mark** goal

[Scene IV. *Before the walls of Athens.*]

Trumpets sound. Enter Alcibiades with his powers before Athens.

ALCIBIADES Sound to this coward and lascivious town
Our terrible approach. *Sounds a parley.*

The Senators appear upon the walls.

Till now you have gone on, and filled the time
With all licentious measure, making your wills
The scope of justice. Till now, myself and such
As slept within the shadow of your power,
Have wandered with our traversed arms and breathed
Our sufferance vainly. Now the time is flush,
When crouching marrow in the bearer strong
Cries, of itself, "No more." Now breathless wrong
Shall sit and pant in your great chairs of ease,
And pursy insolence shall break his wind
With fear and horrid flight.

FIRST SENATOR Noble and young,
When thy first griefs were but a mere conceit,

V.iv.2 **terrible** terrifying 2 s.d. **Sounds a parley** i.e., by a special signal on drum or trumpet, Alcibiades calls for a conference with the enemy to try to make peace 2 s.d. **upon the walls** i.e., upon the upper stage 4 **With all licentious measure** with all kinds of unbridled conduct 5 **scope** extent 6 **slept** (1) were asleep, inactive (2) lived 7 **traversed** folded across (in resignation) 7–8 **breathed/Our sufferance vainly** spoke in vain about our sufferings 8 **flush** ripe 9 **When ... strong** i.e., when the resolute man's courage is aroused 10 **breathless wrong** wrongdoers breathless through fear 11 **great chairs of ease** comfortably upholstered chairs of state 12 **pursy** short-winded 13 **horrid** horrible 14 **griefs** grievances 14 **conceit** idea

Ere thou hadst power or we had cause of fear,
We sent to thee to give thy rages balm,
To wipe out our ingratitude with loves
Above their quantity.

SECOND SENATOR So did we woo
Transformèd Timon to our city's love
By humble message and by promised means.
We were not all unkind, nor all deserve
The common stroke of war.

FIRST SENATOR These walls of ours
Were not erected by their hands from whom
You have received your grief; nor are they such
That these great tow'rs, trophies, and schools
should fall
For private faults in them.

SECOND SENATOR Nor are they living
Who were the motives that you first went out
Shame that they wanted, cunning in excess
Hath broke their hearts. March, noble lord,
Into our city with thy banners spread.
By decimation and a tithèd death,
If thy revenges hunger for that food
Which nature loathes, take thou the destined tenth,
And by the hazard of the spotted die,
Let die the spotted.

FIRST SENATOR All have not offended.
For those that were, it is not square to take

18 **their** (the antecedent is either "griefs" or "rages" or both) 20 **means** conditions of peace (or possibly "riches") 25 **trophies, and schools** monuments, and public buildings 27 **motives that you first went out** instigators or movers of your original banishment 28–29 **Shame . . . hearts** i.e., their hearts were broken with remorse for two common moral failings: lack of a sense of disgrace for their wrongdoing and excess of crafty deceit 31 **decimation and a tithèd death** the killing of one person in ten 34 **by the hazard of the spotted die** by chance, as in dice ("die" is the singular of "dice") 35 **spotted** (1) guilty (2) those selected by the "spots" on the dice 36 **square** honest

On those that are, revenge. Crimes, like lands,
Are not inherited. Then, dear countryman,
Bring in thy ranks, but leave without thy rage.
Spare thy Athenian cradle and those kin
Which in the bluster of thy wrath must fall
With those that have offended. Like a shepherd,
Approach the fold and cull th' infected forth,
But kill not all together.

SECOND SENATOR What thou wilt,
Thou rather shalt enforce it with thy smile
Than hew to't with thy sword.

FIRST SENATOR Set but thy foot
Against our rampired gates, and they shall ope,
So thou wilt send thy gentle heart before
To say thou't enter friendly.

SECOND SENATOR Throw thy glove,
Or any token of thine honor else,
That thou wilt use the wars as thy redress
And not as our confusion. All thy powers
Shall make their harbor in our town till we
Have sealed thy full desire.

ALCIBIADES Then there's my glove.
Descend and open your unchargèd ports.
Those enemies of Timon's and mine own
Whom you yourselves shall set out for reproof,
Fall, and no more. And to atone your fears
With my more noble meaning, not a man
Shall pass his quarter, or offend the stream
Of regular justice in your city's bounds,

39 **without** outside 41 **bluster** tempest 43 **fold** enclosure for sheep or the flock itself 46 **hew to't** cut thy way to it 47 **rampired** fortified 48 **So** provided that 52 **confusion** destruction 52 **powers** armed forces 53 **make their harbor** be billeted 54 **sealed** solemnly ratified (by fulfilling) 55 **unchargèd ports** unassailed gates 57 **reproof** shame 58 **atone** appease 59 **meaning** intention 60 **quarter** billet (?) area of duty (?)

But shall be remedied to your public laws
At heaviest answer.

BOTH SENATORS 'Tis most nobly spoken.

ALCIBIADES Descend, and keep your words.
[*The Senators descend, and open the gates.*]

Enter a Soldier.

SOLDIER My noble general, Timon is dead,
Entombed upon the very hem o' th' sea,
And on his gravestone this insculpture which
With wax I brought away, whose soft impression
Interprets for my poor ignorance.

Alcibiades reads the epitaph.

ALCIBIADES "Here lies a wretched corse, of wretched soul bereft.
Seek not my name. A plague consume you, wicked caitiffs left.
Here lie I, Timon, who alive all living men did hate.
Pass by and curse thy fill, but pass, and stay not here thy gait."
These well express in thee thy latter spirits.
Though thou abhorr'dst in us our human griefs,
Scorn'dst our brains' flow, and those our droplets which
From niggard nature fall; yet rich conceit
Taught thee to make vast Neptune weep for aye
On thy low grave, on faults forgiven. Dead
Is noble Timon, of whose memory
Hereafter more. Bring me into your city,

62 **remedied** turned over for remedy 63 **At heaviest answer** for the maximum punishment 66 **hem** edge (the "beachèd verge" of V.i.217) 67 **insculpture** inscription 69 **Interprets** acts as an interpreter 69 s.d. **epitaph** (there are two epitaphs here, both from North's *Plutarch*, and it seems very likely that one of them—probably the first—was intended to be omitted) 70 **corse** corpse 71 **caitiffs** wretches 74 **latter** later, more recent 76 **brains' flow** tears 77 **niggard** stingy 77 **rich conceit** fanciful imagination 78 **for aye** forever

And I will use the olive with my sword,
Make war breed peace, make peace stint war, make each
Prescribe to other, as each other's leech.
Let our drums strike. *Exeunt.*

FINIS

82 **use the olive with my sword** i.e., combine the olive branch of peace with the sword of war, show mercy even though I enter your city as a conqueror 83 **stint** cause to stop 84 **leech** physician

Textual Note

Our sole authority for the text of *Timon of Athens* is the First Folio of Shakespeare, published in 1623. It may only be the result of a lucky accident that the play was printed at all, since *Troilus and Cressida* was intended to follow *Romeo and Juliet* in the section of Tragedies, and three pages of *Troilus* were actually set up and printed. But difficulties over the copyright of *Troilus* probably forced Jaggard to stop work on it. He allowed a sufficient number of blank pages for it, and then went on to set up and print *Julius Caesar*. Contrary to Jaggard's expectations, the difficulties with *Troilus* were not quickly resolved. Something had to fill the space left for *Troilus*, and *Timon* was decided on. It is a relatively short play, so that it only partially fills the allotted pages. Signature ii is omitted and there is an awkward gap between pages 98 and 109 (beginning of *Julius Caesar*), despite the blown-up and elaborately decorated list of actors' names that has a page to itself at the end of *Timon*.

Whether *Timon* would have been printed at all if the difficulties with *Troilus* had not occurred is a teasing question, but the condition of its text strongly confirms its role as an afterthought or stopgap. *Timon* is full of the kind of inconsistencies and roughnesses that suggest a play that has not received any final revision. There is no record of a performance of the play during Shakespeare's lifetime, and the possibility seems unlikely. It is obviously not the sort of play that a business-minded publisher would be eager to include in an expensive and speculative venture like the Shakespeare Folio. The text of *Timon* was set up either directly from Shakespeare's "foul papers" (rough draft), or from a transcript of them made by a scribe.

The state of the text has an important bearing on the editing of the play. If *Timon* is indeed a play that has not received that final revision and polishing necessary to put it into actable (or printable) form, it is not the job of a modern editor to undertake this task for Shakespeare. It is not up to a modern editor, for example, to make the lines scan by piecing them out differently (a formidable task here), or to distribute specific roles to the First, Second, Third, and Fourth Lords, or to make other changes of an essentially "improving" nature. I assume that the present-day reader would like to have the play in a modernized form, but as close as possible to the way Shakespeare left it. I have therefore made very few changes in the Folio text, even at the expense of leaving loose ends or inconsistencies. (It would be wonderfully satisfying to know whom Alcibiades is pleading for in Act III, Scene v.)

Two matters of special interest are related to the nature of the text: lineation and stage directions. In the text of *Timon* there is either serious mislineation (the printing of blank verse lines in some other form, either broken in two or run together as prose), or a failure in a number of places to write regular, five-beat, iambic lines. That is, either the compositor took wide liberties with the metrics, or the author himself made errors or allowed himself a great deal of freedom. Considering the unrevised state of the text, one is forced to conclude that the printed version is probably an accurate rendering of the copy. "Mislineation" is, therefore, a misleading term. I have generally followed the lineation of the Folio, except where lines are obviously broken into two to fill up the "cast off" space (that is, the amount of space estimated to be needed for a certain quantity of copy), or run together as prose where not enough space was allowed. The Folio lineation usually makes for good speech rhythm, with important pauses at the ends of lines. To run these lines through the blank verse meat grinder would distort their quality as dramatic speech.

How one treats the Folio stage directions of *Timon* also depends upon one's attitude to the text. The indications of action in this play are of the permissive and literary sort characteristic of an author's manuscript. For example, the final part of the stage direction that opens Act I, Scene ii, reads: "*Then comes dropping after all, Apemantus, discontentedly, like himself.*" This is a descriptive stage direction, which would have been put into a more practical form in a promptbook prepared by the stage manager. To change this direction to "*Then enter Apemantus, alone and at a distance*" (as Sisson does in his fine text) is to throw away a significant Shakespearean line for the sake of some imagined modern production. In an unrevised play such as *Timon* there is a special sanction for retaining the obviously authorial stage directions of the Folio, which bring us closer to the original manuscript of the play than do the colorless, clarified directions of a modern editor. I have also avoided one other type of correction in the stage directions. When it is not clear who is being addressed, I have not seen fit to supply a name. In Act V, Scene i, for example, Timon is upbraiding Poet and Painter in turn, but the text never specifies which one. I have simply indicated *To one* and *To the other*, although in a production it would obviously have to be either to Poet or Painter. Perhaps these two characters are meant to have a Rosencrantz and Guildenstern interchangeability.

In the present text spelling has been modernized, except that certain older forms have been retained when they are essentially different from their modern counterparts, for example, "vild" (for "vile"), "huswife" (for "housewife"), "a th'" (for "o' th'"). The punctuation has been modernized within limits, but I have generally been wary of introducing changes where the Folio pointing makes good sense. Even editors scrupulous about the language of the Folio seem not to feel bound by the punctuation. Capitalization has been modernized, and contractions not affecting pronunciation have been eliminated (especially in the verb forms). For stylistic reasons, I have omitted many traditional exclamation marks. The speech prefixes have been expanded and somewhat clarified. The list of actors' names is taken from the Folio, where it is printed (with one name given twice, and with the names in a slightly different order) at the end of the play.

Typographical errors have been corrected, and some stage directions have been slightly moved. Many traditional stage directions, not in the Folio, have been supplied in square brackets. The traditional act and scene divisions and scene locations have been indicated for convenience, but the reader should recall that the action of the play was continuous and the scenes often unlocalized. The Folio indicates only "Actus Primus, Scœna Prima."

Other departures from the Folio are listed below. The reading of the present text is given first, in bold, and then the reading of the Folio (F) in roman.

I.i.s.d. **Enter Poet, Painter, Jeweler, Merchant** [F adds "and Mercer"] 21 **gum, which oozes** Gowne, which vses 87 **hands** hand 87 **slip** sit 166 **satiety** saciety 215 **cost** cast 280 **Come** Comes 289 **I'll keep you company** [in F part of speech of Second Lord]

I.ii.29 **ever** verie 115 s.d. **Sound tucket** [F follows this with another s.d., "Enter the Maskers of Amazons, with Lutes in their hands, dauncing and playing," incorrectly anticipating the entry at line 132; the necessary part of this s.d. is therefore added to that of line 132] 127 **Th'ear** There 132 **First Lord** First Lord Luc. 154 **First Lady** I Lord

II.ii.4 **resumes** resume 43 **of broken** of debt, broken 80 **mistress'** Masters 110 **mistress'** Masters 138 **proposed** propose 195 **Flaminius** Flauius 195 s.d. **Enter Flaminius, Servilius, and Third Servant** Enter three Seruants

III.i.s.d. **with** with a

III.iii.21 **and I** and

III.iv.s.d. **two Servants** man 50 **ate** eate 87 **Hortensius** 1. Var. 111 **Sempronius—all** Sempronius Vllorxa

III.v.17 **An** And 67 **'em** him

III.vi.92 **with your** you with 116–17 [speech prefixes reversed]

IV.i.13 **Son** Some 21 **let** yet

IV.iii.12 **pasture** Pastour 13 **lean** leaue 88 **tub-fast** fubfast 117 **window-bars** window Barne 122 **thy** the 157 **scolds** scold'st 255 **drudges** drugges 256 **command** command'st 272 **rogue** ragge 284 **my** thy 402 **them** then 501 **mild** wilde 518 **A usuring kindness, as** If not a Vsuring kindnesse, and as

V.i.5–6 **Phrynia and Timandra** Phrinica and Timandylo 72 **men** man 116 s.d. **Beats . . . cave** Exeunt 127 **chance** chanc'd 134 **cauterizing** Cantherizing 148 **sense** since 183 **reverend'st** reuerends

V.iv.55 **Descend** Defend 64 s.d. **Soldier** Messenger

WILLIAM SHAKESPEARE

THE TRAGEDY OF CORIOLANUS

Edited by Reuben Brower

[*Dramatis Personae*

CAIUS MARCIUS, afterwards Caius Marcius Coriolanus
TITUS LARTIUS, COMINIUS — generals against the Volscians
MENENIUS AGRIPPA, friend to Coriolanus
SICINIUS VELUTUS, JUNIUS BRUTUS — tribunes of the people
YOUNG MARCIUS, son to Coriolanus
A ROMAN HERALD
A ROMAN, named Nicanor
TULLUS AUFIDIUS, general of the Volscians
LIEUTENANT TO AUFIDIUS
CONSPIRATORS WITH AUFIDIUS
A VOLSCIAN, named Adrian
A CITIZEN OF ANTIUM
TWO VOLSCIAN GUARDS
VOLUMNIA, mother to Coriolanus
VIRGILIA, wife to Coriolanus
VALERIA, friend to Virgilia
GENTLEWOMAN ATTENDING ON VIRGILIA
USHER ATTENDING ON VALERIA
ROMAN AND VOLSCIAN SENATORS, PATRICIANS, AEDILES, LICTORS, SOLDIERS, CITIZENS, MESSENGERS, SERVANTS TO AUFIDIUS, AND OTHER ATTENDANTS

Scene: Rome and the neighborhood; Corioli and the neighborhood; Antium]

THE TRAGEDY OF CORIOLANUS

ACT I

Scene I. [*Rome. A street.*]

Enter a company of mutinous Citizens, with staves, clubs, and other weapons.

FIRST CITIZEN Before we proceed any further, hear me speak.

ALL Speak, speak.

FIRST CITIZEN You are all resolved rather to die than to famish?

ALL Resolved, resolved.

FIRST CITIZEN First you know, Caius Marcius is chief enemy to the people.

ALL We know't, we know't.

FIRST CITIZEN Let us kill him, and we'll have corn at our own price. Is't a verdict?

ALL No more talking on't; let it be done. Away, away!

A footnote is keyed to the text by line number. Text references are printed in **boldface** type; the annotation follows in roman type. I.i.10 **corn** grain (wheat, barley, etc., not Indian corn)

SECOND CITIZEN One word, good citizens.

FIRST CITIZEN We are accounted poor citizens, the patricians good. What authority surfeits on would relieve us. If they would yield us but the superfluity while it were wholesome, we might guess they relieved us humanely; but they think we are too dear; the leanness that afflicts us, the object of our misery, is as an inventory to particularize their abundance; our sufferance is a gain to them. Let us revenge this with our pikes ere we become rakes. For the gods know I speak this in hunger for bread, not in thirst for revenge.

SECOND CITIZEN Would you proceed especially against Caius Marcius?

FIRST CITIZEN Against him first: he's a very dog to the commonalty.

SECOND CITIZEN Consider you what services he has done for his country?

FIRST CITIZEN Very well, and could be content to give him good report for't, but that he pays himself with being proud.

SECOND CITIZEN Nay, but speak not maliciously.

FIRST CITIZEN I say unto you, what he hath done famously he did it to that end; though soft-conscienced men can be content to say it was for his country, he did it to please his mother and to be partly proud, which he is, even to the altitude of his virtue.

SECOND CITIZEN What he cannot help in his nature you account a vice in him. You must in no way say he is covetous.

16 **good** well-off 18 **guess** think 20 **dear** expensive 20 **object** sight 21–22 **inventory to particularize their abundance** list in which to read a detailed account of their wealth as compared with our poverty 23 **pikes** pitchforks 24 **rakes** cf. "lean as a rake" 29 **commonalty** common people 39–40 **to be partly proud** in part from pride 41 **virtue** valor (Latin sense)

FIRST CITIZEN If I must not, I need not be barren of accusations. He hath faults (with surplus) to tire in repetition. (*Shouts within.*) What shouts are these? The other side o' th' city is risen. Why stay we prating here? To th' Capitol!

ALL Come, come.

FIRST CITIZEN Soft, who comes here?

Enter Menenius Agrippa

SECOND CITIZEN Worthy Menenius Agrippa, one that hath always loved the people.

FIRST CITIZEN He's one honest enough; would all the rest were so!

MENENIUS What work's, my countrymen, in hand?
Where go you
With bats and clubs? The matter? Speak, I pray you.

FIRST CITIZEN Our business is not unknown to th' Senate; they have had inkling this fortnight what we intend to do, which now we'll show 'em in deeds. They say poor suitors have strong breaths; they shall know we have strong arms too.

MENENIUS Why, masters, my good friends, mine
honest neighbors,
Will you undo yourselves?

FIRST CITIZEN We cannot, sir; we are undone already.

MENENIUS I tell you, friends, most charitable care
Have the patricians of you. For your wants,
Your suffering in this dearth, you may as well
Strike at the heaven with your staves as lift them
Against the Roman state, whose course will on
The way it takes, cracking ten thousand curbs
Of more strong link asunder than can ever

49 **Capitol** Capitoline Hill, on which the Temple of Jupiter stood (here and often, for the Senate House nearby) 51 **Soft** stop (an interjection) 68 **dearth** famine 71 **curbs** restraints

Appear in your impediment. For the dearth,
The gods, not the patricians, make it, and
Your knees to them (not arms) must help. Alack,
You are transported by calamity
Thither where more attends you; and you slander
The helms o' th' state, who care for you like fathers,
When you curse them as enemies.

FIRST CITIZEN Care for us! True, indeed! They ne'er cared for us yet. Suffer us to famish, and their storehouses crammed with grain; make edicts for usury, to support usurers; repeal daily any wholesome act established against the rich, and provide more piercing statutes daily to chain up and restrain the poor. If the wars eat us not up, they will; and there's all the love they bear us.

MENENIUS Either you must
Confess yourselves wondrous malicious,
Or be accused of folly. I shall tell you
A pretty tale; it may be you have heard it;
But since it serves my purpose, I will venture
To stale't a little more.

FIRST CITIZEN Well, I'll hear it, sir. Yet you must not think to fob off our disgrace with a tale. But, and't please you, deliver.

MENENIUS There was a time when all the body's members
Rebelled against the Belly; thus accused it:
That only like a gulf it did remain
I' th' midst o' th' body, idle and unactive,
Still cupboarding the viand, never bearing
Like labor with the rest; where th' other instruments

73 **in your impediment** in any hindrance you make 76 **transported** carried out of your minds 78 **helms** helmsmen 93 **stale't** make it stale 95 **fob off** set aside with a trick 95 **disgrace** misfortune 96 **and't** if it 99 **gulf** whirlpool 101 **viand** food 102 **instruments** organs

Did see and hear, devise, instruct, walk, feel,
And, mutually participate, did minister
Unto the appetite and affection common
Of the whole body. The Belly answered——

FIRST CITIZEN Well, sir, what answer made the Belly?

MENENIUS Sir, I shall tell you. With a kind of smile,
Which ne'er came from the lungs, but even thus—
For, look you, I may make the Belly smile
As well as speak—it tauntingly replied
To th' discontented members, the mutinous parts
That envied his receipt; even so most fitly
As you malign our senators for that
They are not such as you.

FIRST CITIZEN Your Belly's answer—What?
The kingly crownèd head, the vigilant eye,
The counselor heart, the arm our soldier,
Our steed the leg, the tongue our trumpeter,
With other muniments and petty helps
In this our fabric, if that they—

MENENIUS What then?
'Fore me, this fellow speaks! What then? What then?

FIRST CITIZEN Should by the cormorant Belly be restrained,
Who is the sink o' th' body——

MENENIUS Well, what then?

FIRST CITIZEN The former agents, if they did complain,
What could the Belly answer?

MENENIUS I will tell you;
If you'll bestow a small (of what you have little)
Patience awhile, you'st hear the Belly's answer.

FIRST CITIZEN Y'are long about it.

104 **mutually participate** taking part in common 105 **affection** inclination 133 **his receipt** what he received 119 **muniments** furnishings (fortifications) 121 **'Fore me** by my soul 123 **sink** sewer 127 **you'st** you'll (for "you shalt") 128 **Y'are** you're

MENENIUS Note me this, good friend;
Your most grave Belly was deliberate,
Not rash like his accusers, and thus answered:
"True is it, my incorporate friends," quoth he,
"That I receive the general food at first,
Which you do live upon; and fit it is,
Because I am the storehouse and the shop
Of the whole body. But, if you do remember,
I send it through the rivers of your blood,
Even to the court, the heart, to th' seat o' th' brain;
And, through the cranks and offices of man,
The strongest nerves and small inferior veins
From me receive that natural competency
Whereby they live; and though that all at once"—
You, my good friends, this says the Belly, mark me—

FIRST CITIZEN Ay, sir; well, well.

MENENIUS "Though all at once cannot
See what I do deliver out to each,
Yet I can make my audit up, that all
From me do back receive the flour of all,
And leave me but the bran." What say you to't?

FIRST CITIZEN It was an answer. How apply you this?

MENENIUS The senators of Rome are this good Belly,
And you the mutinous members. For examine
Their counsels and their cares, disgest things rightly
Touching the weal o' th' common, you shall find
No public benefit which you receive
But it proceeds or comes from them to you,
And no way from yourselves. What do you think,
You, the great toe of this assembly?

129 **Your most grave Belly** this most grave belly we speak of 134 **Shop** factory 138 **cranks** winding paths 138 **offices** parts of a house where household work is done, e.g., kitchen 139 **nerves** tendons 140 **natural competency** supply adequate to their nature 151 **disgest** digest 152 **weal o' th' common** welfare of the people

FIRST CITIZEN I the great toe! Why the great toe?

MENENIUS For that, being one o' th' lowest, basest, poorest,
Of this most wise rebellion, thou goest foremost.
Thou rascal, that are worst in blood to run,
Lead'st first to win some vantage.
But make you ready your stiff bats and clubs;
Rome and her rats are at the point of battle;
The one side must have bale.

Enter Caius Marcius.

Hail, noble Marcius!

MARCIUS Thanks. What's the matter, you dissentious rogues
That, rubbing the poor itch of your opinion,
Make yourselves scabs?

FIRST CITIZEN We have ever your good word.

MARCIUS He that will give good words to thee will flatter
Beneath abhorring. What would you have, you curs,
That like nor peace nor war? The one affrights you,
The other makes you proud. He that trusts to you,
Where he should find you lions, finds you hares;
Where foxes, geese. You are no surer, no,
Than is the coal of fire upon the ice,
Or hailstone in the sun. Your virtue is
To make him worthy whose offense subdues him
And curse that justice did it. Who deserves greatness
Deserves your hate; and your affections are
A sick man's appetite, who desires most that
Which would increase his evil. He that depends
Upon your favors swims with fins of lead

160 **rascal** a lean deer, or a hound 160 **blood** condition 161 **vantage** advantage 162 **stiff** stout 164 **bale** harm 167 **Make yourselves scabs** make scabs for yourselves (also, "make yourselves into loathsome fellows") 176 **subdues him** lays him low 177 **that justice did it** the justice that punished him 178 **affections** desires

And hews down oaks with rushes. Hang ye! Trust ye?
With every minute you do change a mind,
And call him noble that was now your hate,
Him vile that was your garland. What's the matter
That in these several places of the city
You cry against the noble Senate, who
(Under the gods) keep you in awe, which else
Would feed on one another? What's their seeking?

MENENIUS For corn at their own rates, whereof they say
The city is well stored.

MARCIUS Hang 'em! They say!
They'll sit by th' fire, and presume to know
What's done i' th' Capitol: who's like to rise,
Who thrives and who declines; side factions and give out
Conjectural marriages, making parties strong,
And feebling such as stand not in their liking
Below their cobbled shoes. They say there's grain enough!
Would the nobility lay aside their ruth,
And let me use my sword, I'd make a quarry
With thousands of these quartered slaves, as high
As I could pick my lance.

MENENIUS Nay, these are almost thoroughly persuaded;
For though abundantly they lack discretion,
Yet are they passing cowardly. But, I beseech you,
What says the other troop?

MARCIUS They are dissolved. Hang 'em!
They said they were an-hungry; sighed forth proverbs——

194 **side factions** take sides (form parties) 196 **feebling** weakening (bringing down) 198 **ruth** compassion 199 **quarry** heap of dead (usually of game animals) 204 **passing** exceedingly 206 **an-hungry** hungry 206 **sighed forth proverbs** (implying that they talk like rustics)

That hunger broke stone walls, that dogs must eat,
That meat was made for mouths, that the gods sent not
Corn for the rich men only. With these shreds
They vented their complainings, which being answered,
And a petition granted them, a strange one,
To break the heart of generosity
And make bold power look pale, they threw their caps
As they would hang them on the horns o' th' moon,
Shouting their emulation.

MENENIUS What is granted them?

MARCIUS Five tribunes to defend their vulgar wisdoms,
Of their own choice. One's Junius Brutus—
Sicinius Velutus, and—I know not. 'Sdeath!
The rabble should have first unroofed the city,
Ere so prevailed with me; it will in time
Win upon power and throw forth greater themes
For insurrection's arguing.

MENENIUS This is strange.

MARCIUS Go, get you home, you fragments!

Enter a Messenger, hastily.

MESSENGER Where's Caius Marcius?

MARCIUS Here: what's the matter?

MESSENGER The news is, sir, the Volsces are in arms.

MARCIUS I am glad on't: then we shall ha' means to vent
Our musty superfluity. See, our best elders.

212 **break the heart of generosity** give the deathblow to the nobility 215 **Shouting their emulation** expressing envious joy 216 **vulgar** common, plebeian 221 **Win upon power** get the better of authority 222 **For insurrection's arguing** for rebels to debate in action (abstract for concrete, as often in *Coriolanus*) 226 **vent** get rid of

Enter Sicinius Velutus, Junius Brutus, Cominius, Titus Lartius, with other Senators.

FIRST SENATOR Marcius, 'tis true that you have lately told us;
The Volsces are in arms.

MARCIUS They have a leader,
Tullus Aufidius, that will put you to't.
I sin in envying his nobility;
And were I anything but what I am,
I would wish me only he.

COMINIUS You have fought together.

MARCIUS Were half to half the world by th' ears, and he
Upon my party, I'd revolt, to make
Only my wars with him. He is a lion
That I am proud to hunt.

FIRST SENATOR Then, worthy Marcius,
Attend upon Cominius to these wars.

COMINIUS It is your former promise.

MARCIUS Sir, it is,
And I am constant. Titus Lartius, thou
Shalt see me once more strike at Tullus' face.
What, art thou stiff? Stand'st out?

TITUS No, Caius Marcius;
I'll lean upon one crutch and fight with t'other
Ere stay behind this business.

MENENIUS O, true-bred!

FIRST SENATOR Your company to th' Capitol; where I know
Our greatest friends attend us.

TITUS [*To Cominius*] Lead you on.

230 **put you to't** test you severely 240 **constant** faithful 242 **stiff** obstinate, set (on not fighting) 242 **Stand'st out** you're staying out of it?

[*To Marcius*] Follow Cominius; we must follow you;
Right worthy you priority.

COMINIUS Noble Marcius!

FIRST SENATOR [*To the Citizens*] Hence to your homes; begone!

MARCIUS Nay, let them follow.
The Volsces have much corn; take these rats thither
To gnaw their garners. Worshipful mutineers,
Your valor puts well forth. Pray, follow. *Exeunt.*

Citizens steal away. Manet Sicinius and Brutus.

SICINIUS Was ever man so proud as is this Marcius?

BRUTUS He has no equal.

SICINIUS When we were chosen tribunes for the people—

BRUTUS Marked you his lip and eyes?

SICINIUS Nay, but his taunts.

BRUTUS Being moved, he will not spare to gird the gods.

SICINIUS Bemock the modest moon.

BRUTUS The present wars devour him; he is grown
Too proud to be so valiant.

SICINIUS Such a nature,
Tickled with good success, disdains the shadow
Which he treads on at noon. But I do wonder
His insolence can brook to be commanded
Under Cominius.

248 **Right worthy you priority** you well deserve first place 252 **puts well forth** gives fair promise (literally, buds) 252 s.d. **Manet** remains (Latin; although the subject is plural, this form, the third person singular, commonly appears in Elizabeth stage directions) 257 **gird** taunt 259–60 **grown/Too proud to be so valiant** i.e., such pride is not permissible in one so warlike (because dangerous) 261 **success** outcome

BRUTUS Fame, at the which he aims,
In whom already he's well graced, can not
Better be held, nor more attained, than by
A place below the first. For what miscarries
Shall be the general's fault, though he perform
To th' utmost of a man; and giddy censure
Will then cry out of Marcius "O, if he
Had borne the business!"

SICINIUS Besides, if things go well,
Opinion, that so sticks on Marcius, shall
Of his demerits rob Cominius.

BRUTUS Come:
Half all Cominius' honors are to Marcius,
Though Marcius earned them not; and all his faults
To Marcius shall be honors, though indeed
In aught he merit not.

SICINIUS Let's hence, and hear
How the dispatch is made; and in what fashion,
More than his singularity, he goes
Upon this present action.

BRUTUS Let's along. *Exeunt.*

[Scene II. *Corioli. The Senate House.*]

Enter Tullus Aufidius, with Senators of Corioles.

FIRST SENATOR So, your opinion is, Aufidius,
That they of Rome are ent'red in our counsels,
And know how we proceed.

AUFIDIUS Is it not yours?

273 **demerits** deserts 278 **dispatch** execution of the business 279 **More than his singularity** apart from his usual peculiarity of manner I.ii.2 **ent'red in** initiated into (familiar with)

What ever have been thought on in this state
That could be brought to bodily act ere Rome
Had circumvention? 'Tis not four days gone
Since I heard thence—these are the words—I think
I have the letter here. Yes, here it is:
"They have pressed a power, but it is not known
Whether for east or west. The dearth is great;
The people mutinous; and it is rumored,
Cominius, Marcius your old enemy
(Who is of Rome worse hated than of you),
And Titus Lartius, a most valiant Roman,
These three lead on this preparation
Whither 'tis bent—most likely 'tis for you.
Consider of it."

FIRST SENATOR Our army's in the field.
We never yet made doubt but Rome was ready
To answer us.

AUFIDIUS Nor did you think it folly
To keep your great pretenses veiled till when
They needs must show themselves; which in the
hatching,
It seemed, appeared to Rome. By the discovery
We shall be short'ned in our aim, which was
To take in many towns ere almost Rome
Should know we were afoot.

SECOND SENATOR Noble Aufidius,
Take your commission; hie you to your bands:
Let us alone to guard Corioles.
If they set down before's, for the remove
Bring up your army; but I think you'll find
They've not prepared for us.

AUFIDIUS O, doubt not that;
I speak from certainties. Nay, more,

4 **What** (plural, i.e., "counsels," line 2) 6 **circumvention** means to circumvent 9 **pressed a power** collected troops 15 **preparation** force that has been prepared 20 **great pretenses** main intentions (cf. "grand design") 24 **take in** capture 28 **set down before's** lay siege to us 28 **remove** raising of the siege

Some parcels of their power are forth already,
And only hitherward. I leave your honors.
If we and Caius Marcius chance to meet,
'Tis sworn between us we shall ever strike
Till one can do no more.

ALL The gods assist you!

AUFIDIUS And keep your honors safe!

FIRST SENATOR Farewell.

SECOND SENATOR Farewell.

ALL Farewell. *Exeunt omnes.*

[Scene III. *Rome. A room in Marcius' house.*]

Enter Volumnia and Virgilia, mother and wife to Marcius. They set them down on two low stools, and sew.

VOLUMNIA I pray you, daughter, sing, or express yourself in a more comfortable sort. If my son were my husband, I should freelier rejoice in that absence wherein he won honor than in the embracements of his bed where he would show most love. When yet he was but tender-bodied, and the only son of my womb; when youth with comeliness plucked all gaze his way; when, for a day of kings' entreaties, a mother should not sell him an hour from her beholding; I, considering how honor would become such a person—that it was no better than picture-like to hang by th' wall, if renown made it not stir—was pleased to let him seek

32 parcels portions **33 hitherward** i.e., to attack Rome **38 s.d. omnes** all (Latin) I.iii.2 **Comfortable** cheerful **8 plucked all gaze** drew the eyes of all **11 person** handsome figure

danger where he was like to find fame. To a cruel war I sent him, from whence he returned, his brows bound with oak. I tell thee, daughter, I sprang not more in joy at first hearing he was a man-child than now in first seeing he had proved himself a man.

VIRGILIA But had he died in the business, madam, how then?

VOLUMNIA Then his good report should have been my son; I therein would have found issue. Hear me profess sincerely: had I a dozen sons, each in my love alike, and none less dear than thine and my good Marcius, I had rather had eleven die nobly for their country than one voluptuously surfeit out of action.

Enter a Gentlewoman.

GENTLEWOMAN Madam, the Lady Valeria is come to visit you.

VIRGILIA Beseech you give me leave to retire myself.

VOLUMNIA Indeed, you shall not.
Methinks I hear hither your husband's drum;
See him pluck Aufidius down by th' hair;
As children from a bear, the Volsces shunning him.
Methinks I see him stamp thus, and call thus:
"Come on, you cowards, you were got in fear,
Though you were born in Rome." His bloody brow
With his mailed hand then wiping, forth he goes,
Like to a harvest-man that's tasked to mow
Or all or lose his hire.

VIRGILIA His bloody brow? O Jupiter, no blood!

VOLUMNIA Away, you fool! It more becomes a man
Than gilt his trophy. The breasts of Hecuba,
When she did suckle Hector, looked not lovelier
Than Hector's forehead when it spit forth blood

16 **oak** ("garland" of honor for saving a fellow Roman in battle) 23 **profess** declare 30 **Beseech** I beg 36 **got** begotten 40 **Or** either 43 **trophy** monument 43 **Hecuba** (Queen of Troy and mother of Hector, who defended the city from the Greeks)

At Grecian sword, contemning. Tell Valeria
We are fit to bid her welcome. *Exit Gentlewoman.*

VIRGILIA Heavens bless my lord from fell Aufidius!

VOLUMNIA He'll beat Aufidius' head below his knee,
And tread upon his neck.

Enter Valeria with an Usher and a Gentlewoman.

VALERIA My ladies both, good day to you.

VOLUMNIA Sweet madam!

VIRGILIA I am glad to see your ladyship.

VALERIA How do you both? You are manifest housekeepers. What are you sewing here? A fine spot, in good faith. How does your little son?

VIRGILIA I thank your ladyship; well, good madam.

VOLUMNIA He had rather see the swords and hear a drum than look upon his schoolmaster.

VALERIA O' my word, the father's son! I'll swear 'tis a very pretty boy. O' my troth, I looked upon him o' Wednesday half an hour together; has such a confirmed countenance! I saw him run after a gilded butterfly; and when he caught it, he let it go again; and after it again; and over and over he comes, and up again; catched it again; or whether his fall enraged him, or how 'twas, he did so set his teeth, and tear it. O, I warrant, how he mammocked it!

VOLUMNIA One on's father's moods.

VALERIA Indeed, la, 'tis a noble child.

VIRGILIA A crack, madam.

46 **contemning** in scorn 47 **fit** ready 48 **bless** guard 48 **fell** savage 50 s.d. **Usher** servant accompanying a lady 54–55 **manifest housekeepers** clearly stay-at-homes 55 **spot** pattern in embroidery 63 **confirmed** determined 68–69 **mammocked** tore to pieces 70 **on's** of his 72 **crack** rascal

VALERIA Come, lay aside your stitchery; I must have you play the idle huswife with me this afternoon.

VIRGILIA No, good madam; I will not out of doors.

VALERIA Not out of doors!

VOLUMNIA She shall, she shall.

VIRGILIA Indeed, no, by your patience; I'll not over the threshold till my lord return from the wars.

VALERIA Fie, you confine yourself most unreasonably; come, you must go visit the good lady that lies in.

VIRGILIA I will wish her speedy strength, and visit her with my prayers; but I cannot go thither.

VOLUMNIA Why I pray you?

VIRGILIA 'Tis not to save labor, nor that I want love.

VALERIA You would be another Penelope; yet, they say, all the yarn she spun in Ulysses' absence did but fill Ithaca full of moths. Come; I would your cambric were sensible as your finger, that you might leave pricking it for pity.Come, you shall go with us.

VIRGILIA No, good madam, pardon me; indeed, I will not forth.

VALERIA In truth, la, go with me, and I'll tell you excellent news of your husband.

VIRGILIA O, good madam, there can be none yet.

VALERIA Verily, I do not jest with you; there came news from him last night.

VIRGILIA Indeed, madam?

VALERIA In earnest, it's true; I heard a senator speak it. Thus it is: the Volsces have an army forth;

78 **patience** leave 85 **want** am lacking in 86 **Penelope** (Ulysses' faithful wife, who by using her weaving as an excuse, postponed her answer to offers of marriage) 88 **Ithaca** (Ulysses' home city) 89 **sensible** sensitive

against whom Cominius the general is gone, with one part of our Roman power. Your lord and Titus Lartius are set down before their city Corioles; they nothing doubt prevailing, and to make it brief wars. This is true, on mine honor; and so, I pray, go with us.

VIRGILIA Give me excuse, good madam; I will obey you in everything hereafter.

VOLUMNIA Let her alone, lady; as she is now, she will but disease our better mirth.

VALERIA In troth, I think she would. Fare you well, then. Come, good sweet lady. Prithee, Virgilia, turn thy solemness out o'door, and go along with us.

VIRGILIA No, at a word, madam; indeed, I must not. I wish you much mirth.

VALERIA Well then, farewell.

Exeunt Ladies.

[Scene IV. *Before Corioli.*]

Enter Marcius, Titus Lartius, with drum and colors, with Captains and Soldiers, as before the city Corioles. To them a Messenger.

MARCIUS Yonder comes news: a wager they have met.

LARTIUS My horse to yours, no.

MARCIUS 'Tis done.

LARTIUS Agreed.

MARCIUS Say, has our general met the enemy?

111 **disease our better mirth** spoil our fun, which would be better (without her) 115 **at a word** to put it briefly

MESSENGER They lie in view, but have not spoke as yet.

LARTIUS So, the good horse is mine.

MARCIUS I'll buy him of you.

LARTIUS No, I'll nor sell nor give him; lend you him I will
For half a hundred years. Summon the town.

MARCIUS How far off lie these armies?

MESSENGER Within this mile and half.

MARCIUS Then shall we hear their 'larum, and they ours.
Now, Mars, I prithee, make us quick in work,
That we with smoking swords may march from hence
To help our fielded friends! Come, blow thy blast.

They sound a parley. Enter two Senators with others, on the walls of Corioles.

Tullus Aufidius, is he within your walls?

FIRST SENATOR No, nor a man that fears you less than he;
That's lesser than a little. (*Drum afar off.*) Hark, our drums
Are bringing forth our youth. We'll break our walls
Rather than they shall pound us up. Our gates,
Which yet seem shut, we have but pinned with rushes;
They'll open of themselves. (*Alarum far off.*) Hark you, far off!
There is Aufidius. List what work he makes
Amongst your cloven army.

MARCIUS O, they are at it!

I.iv.4 spoke engaged **9 'larum** alarum, call to arms **11 smoking** reeking (with blood) **12 fielded** in the field of battle **17 pound us up** shut us in (cf. "dog pound") **21 Cloven** divided

LARTIUS Their noise be our instruction. Ladders, ho!

Enter the Army of the Volsces.

MARCIUS They fear us not, but issue forth their city.
Now put your shields before your hearts, and fight
With hearts more proof than shields. Advance,
brave Titus.
They do disdain us much beyond our thoughts,
Which makes me sweat with wrath. Come on, my
fellows.
He that retires, I'll take him for a Volsce,
And he shall feel mine edge.

Alarum. The Romans are beat back to their trenches. Enter Marcius, cursing.

MARCIUS All the contagion of the south light on you,
You shames of Rome! You herd of—boils and
plagues
Plaster you o'er, that you may be abhorred
Farther than seen, and one infect another
Against the wind a mile! You souls of geese
That bear the shapes of men, how have you run
From slaves that apes would beat! Pluto and hell!
All hurt behind, backs red, and faces pale
With flight and agued fear! Mend and charge
home,
Or, by the fires of heaven, I'll leave the foe,
And make my wars on you. Look to't. Come on;
If you'll stand fast, we'll beat them to their wives,
As they us to our trenches. Follow's.

22 **be our instruction** be a lesson to us 25 **proof** tested (and so impenetrable) 30 **South** south wind (pestilential) 34 **Against the wind a mile** i.e., the infection carrying a mile in the face of a contrary wind 38 **agued** i.e., shaking as if from an ague-fit (*Ague* = malarial fever) 38 **Mend** do better (pun on the hygienic sense) 38 **Home** i.e., into the heart of the enemy's forces 42 **Follow's** follow us, i.e., follow me (the Folio gives "trenches followes." The adopted reading makes sense out of the Folio reading, but it is ugly and anticlimactic. Perhaps "followes" is a misplaced stage direction)

Another alarum; and Marcius follows them to [the] gates and is shut in.

So, now the gates are ope. Now prove good
  seconds!
'Tis for the followers Fortune widens them,
Not for the fliers. Mark me, and do the like.
Enters the gates.

FIRST SOLDIER Foolhardiness; not I.

SECOND SOLDIER Nor I.

FIRST SOLDIER See, they have shut him in.
Alarum continues.

ALL To th' pot, I warrant him.

Enter Titus Lartius.

LARTIUS What is become of Marcius?

ALL Slain, sir, doubtless.

FIRST SOLDIER Following the fliers at the very heels,
With them he enters; who, upon the sudden,
Clapped to their gates. He is himself alone,
To answer all the city.

LARTIUS O noble fellow!
Who sensibly outdares his senseless sword,
And when it bows stand'st up! Thou art left,
  Marcius!
A carbuncle entire, as big as thou art,
Were not so rich a jewel. Thou wast a soldier
Even to Cato's wish, not fierce and terrible
Only in strokes; but with thy grim looks and
The thunder-like percussion of thy sounds
Thou mad'st thine enemies shake, as if the world
Were feverous and did tremble.

42 s.d. **is shut in** i.e., at the end of this speech Marcius enters the gates and is shut in 43 **seconds** helpers 44 **followers** pursuers 48 **to th' pot** to destruction (cf. "gone to pot") 54 **sensibly** though subject to feeling 56 **A carbuncle** a red precious stone 58 **Cato** (the Censor, stern upholder of old Roman virtues).

Enter Marcius, bleeding, assaulted by the enemy.

FIRST SOLDIER Look, sir.

LARTIUS O, 'tis Marcius!
Let's fetch him off, or make remain alike.

They fight, and all enter the city.

[Scene V. *Within Corioli.*]

Enter certain Romans, with spoils.

FIRST ROMAN This will I carry to Rome.

SECOND ROMAN And I this.

THIRD ROMAN A murrain on't! I took this for silver.

Exeunt.

Alarum continues still afar off.

Enter Marcius and Titus Lartius with a Trumpet.

MARCIUS See here these movers that do prize their hours
At a cracked drachma! Cushions, leaden spoons,
Irons of a doit, doublets that hangmen would
Bury with those that wore them, these base slaves,
Ere yet the fight be done, pack up. Down with them!
And hark, what noise the general makes! To him!
There is the man of my soul's hate, Aufidius,
Piercing our Romans. Then, valiant Titus, take
Convenient numbers to make good the city;

63 **make remain alike** stay like him (*remain*, a noun, means "a stay") I.v.3 **murrain on't** plague on it 3 s.d. **Trumpet** trumpeter 4 **movers** active fellows (ironical) 5 **drachma** Greek coin 6 **of a doit** worth a doit (coin of little value) 12 **make good** make sure of

Whilst I, with those that have the spirit, will haste
To help Cominius.

LARTIUS Worthy sir, thou bleed'st;
Thy exercise hath been too violent
For a second course of fight.

MARCIUS Sir, praise me not;
My work hath yet not warmed me. Fare you well.
The blood I drop is rather physical
Than dangerous to me. To Aufidius thus
I will appear, and fight.

LARTIUS Now the fair goddess, Fortune,
Fall deep in love with thee; and her great charms
Misguide thy opposers' swords! Bold gentleman,
Prosperity be thy page!

MARCIUS Thy friend no less
Than those she placeth highest! So farewell.

LARTIUS Thou worthiest Marcius!
[*Exit Marcius.*]
Go, sound thy trumpet in the marketplace;
Call thither all the officers o' th' town,
Where they shall know our mind. Away! *Exeunt.*

[Scene VI. *Near the camp of Cominius.*]

Enter Cominius, as it were in retire, with soldiers.

COMINIUS Breathe you, my friends; well fought; we
are come off
Like Romans, neither foolish in our stands
Nor cowardly in retire. Believe me, sirs,
We shall be charged again. Whiles we have struck,

16 **course** bout 18 **physical** beneficial 23 **page** attendant I.vi.1 **Breathe** rest 1 **are come off** leave the field 3 **retire** retreat

By interims and conveying gusts we have heard
The charges of our friends. The Roman gods,
Lead their successes as we wish our own,
That both our powers, with smiling fronts encount'ring,
May give you thankful sacrifice!

Enter a Messenger.

Thy news?

MESSENGER The citizens of Corioles have issued,
And given to Lartius and to Marcius battle.
I saw our party to their trenches driven,
And then I came away.

COMINIUS Though thou speakest truth,
Methinks thou speak'st not well. How long is't since?

MESSENGER Above an hour, my lord.

COMINIUS 'Tis not a mile; briefly we heard their drums.
How couldst thou in a mile confound an hour,
And bring thy news so late?

MESSENGER Spies of the Volsces
Held me in chase, that I was forced to wheel
Three or four miles about; else had I, sir,
Half an hour since brought my report.

Enter Marcius.

COMINIUS Who's yonder
That does appear as he were flayed? O gods!
He has the stamp of Marcius, and I have
Before-time seen him thus.

MARCIUS Come I too late?

5 **By interims and conveying gusts** at intervals, by gusts of wind carrying (the sound) 7 **successes** outcomes 8 **fronts** first lines (also, "faces") 16 **briefly** a short time ago 17 **confound** waste 23 **stamp** characteristic features (metaphor from coining)

COMINIUS The shepherd knows not thunder from a tabor
More than I know the sound of Marcius' tongue
From every meaner man.

MARCIUS Come I too late?

COMINIUS Ay, if you come not in the blood of others,
But mantled in your own.

MARCIUS O, let me clip ye
In arms as sound as when I wooed; in heart
As merry as when our nuptial day was done,
And tapers burned to bedward!

COMINIUS Flower of warriors!
How is't with Titus Lartius?

MARCIUS As with a man busied about decrees:
Condemning some to death and some to exile;
Ransoming him, or pitying, threat'ning th' other;
Holding Corioles in the name of Rome,
Even like a fawning greyhound in the leash,
To let him slip at will.

COMINIUS Where is that slave
Which told me they had beat you to your trenches?
Where is he? Call him hither.

MARCIUS Let him alone;
He did inform the truth. But for our gentlemen,
The common file—a plague! tribunes for them!—
The mouse ne'er shunned the cat as they did budge
From rascals worse than they.

COMINIUS But how prevailed you?

MARCIUS Will the time serve to tell? I do not think.
Where is the enemy? Are you lords o' th' field?
If not, why cease you till you are so?

COMINIUS Marcius,

25 **tabor** small drum 29 **clip** embrace 32 **burned to bedward** burned low, announcing the time for bed 39 **let him slip** unleash him 42 **inform** report 42 **gentlemen** (ironically) 43 **common file** i.e., the plebeian soldiers

We have at disadvantage fought and did
Retire to win our purpose.

MARCIUS How lies their battle? Know you on which side
They have placed their men of trust?

COMINIUS As I guess, Marcius,
Their bands i' th' vaward are the Antiates,
Of their best trust; o'er them Aufidius,
Their very heart of hope.

MARCIUS I do beseech you,
By all the battles wherein we have fought,
By th' blood we have shed together, by th' vows
We have made to endure friends, that you directly
Set me against Aufidius and his Antiates;
And that you not delay the present, but,
Filling the air with swords advanced and darts,
We prove this very hour.

COMINIUS Though I could wish
You were conducted to a gentle bath,
And balms applied to you, yet dare I never
Deny your asking. Take your choice of those
That best can aid your action.

MARCIUS Those are they
That most are willing. If any such be here—
As it were sin to doubt—that love this painting
Wherein you see me smeared; if any fear
Lesser his person than an ill report;
If any think brave death outweighs bad life,
And that his country's dearer than himself;
Let him alone, or so many so minded,
Wave thus, to express his disposition,
And follow Marcius.

They all shout, and wave their swords; take him up in their arms, and cast up their caps.

53 **vaward** vanguard, advance troops 60 **delay the present** put off the present occasion 62 **prove** make trial of 69–70 **fear/Lesser his person** fear less for his body 74 **disposition** inclination

O me alone! Make you a sword of me?
If these shows be not outward, which of you
But is four Volsces? None of you but is
Able to bear against the great Aufidius
A shield as hard as his. A certain number,
Though thanks to all, must I select from all. The rest
Shall bear the business in some other fight,
As cause will be obeyed. Please you to march;
And four shall quickly draw out my command,
Which men are best inclined.

COMINIUS March on, my fellows:
Make good this ostentation, and you shall
Divide in all with us. *Exeunt.*

[Scene VII. *The gates of Corioli.*]

Titus Lartius, having set a guard upon Corioles, going with drum and trumpet toward Cominius and Caius Marcius, enters with a Lieutenant, other Soldiers, and a Scout.

LARTIUS So, let the ports be guarded; keep your duties
As I have set them down. If I do send, dispatch
Those centuries to our aid; the rest will serve
For a short holding. If we lose the field,
We cannot keep the town.

LIEUTENANT Fear not our care, sir.

LARTIUS Hence, and shut your gates upon's.
Our guider, come; to th' Roman camp conduct us.
Exit [with the rest].

83 **cause will be obeyed** occasion shall demand 86 **ostentation** display
I.vii.1 **ports** gates 3 **centuries** companies (smallest units of Roman legion)

[Scene VIII. *A field of battle.*]

Alarum as in battle. Enter Marcius and Aufidius, at several doors.

MARCIUS I'll fight with none but thee, for I do hate thee
Worse than a promise-breaker.

AUFIDIUS We hate alike:
Not Afric owns a serpent I abhor
More than thy fame and envy. Fix thy foot.

MARCIUS Let the first budger die the other's slave,
And the gods doom him after!

AUFIDIUS If I fly, Marcius,
Holloa me like a hare.

MARCIUS Within these hours, Tullus,
Alone I fought in your Corioles walls,
And made what work I pleased. 'Tis not my blood
Wherein thou seest me masked. For thy revenge
Wrench up thy power to th' highest.

AUFIDIUS Wert thou the Hector
That was the whip of your bragged progeny,
Thou shouldst not scape me here.

Here they fight, and certain Volsces come in the aid of Aufidius. Marcius fights till they be driven in breathless.

Officious, and not valiant, you have shamed me
In your condemnèd seconds.

I.viii.s.d. **at several doors** from different entrances 3 **Afric** Africa 5 **budger** one who moves 7 **Holloa** shout "halloo" after (in hunting) 12 **whip of your bragged progeny** the whip used by your boasted ancestors, the Trojans, against the Greeks 15 **In your condemnèd seconds** by your damnable help (cf. I.iv.43)

[Scene IX. *The Roman camp.*]

Flourish. Alarum. A retreat is sounded. Enter at one door, Cominius with the Romans; at another door, Marcius, with his arm in a scarf.

COMINIUS If I should tell thee o'er this thy day's work,
Thou't not believe thy deeds. But I'll report it
Where senators shall mingle tears with smiles;
Where great patricians shall attend, and shrug,
I' th' end admire; where ladies shall be frighted,
And, gladly quaked, hear more; where the dull tribunes,
That with the fusty plebeians hate thine honors,
Shall say against their hearts "We thank the gods
Our Rome hath such a soldier."
Yet cam'st thou to a morsel of this feast,
Having fully dined before.

Enter Titus [Lartius], with his power, from the pursuit.

LARTIUS O general,
Here is the steed, we the caparison!
Hadst thou beheld—

MARCIUS Pray now, no more. My mother,
Who has a charter to extol her blood,
When she does praise me grieves me. I have done
As you have done, that's what I can; induced
As you have been, that's for my country.

I.ix.2 **Thou't** thou wouldst 4 **shrug** i.e., in disbelief 6 **quaked** made to shake 7 **fusty** moldy 10 **cam'st thou to a morsel of this feast** (refers to Marcius' coming to support Cominius in the latter part of the battle just ended) 12 **caparison** the (mere) trappings 14 **charter** privilege granted her

He that has but effected his good will
Hath overta'en mine act.

COMINIUS You shall not be
The grave of your deserving; Rome must know
The value of her own. 'Twere a concealment
Worse than a theft, no less than a traducement,
To hide your doings; and to silence that
Which, to the spire and top of praises vouched,
Would seem but modest. Therefore, I beseech you,
In sign of what you are, not to reward
What you have done, before our army hear me.

MARCIUS I have some wounds upon me, and they smart
To hear themselves remembʼred.

COMINIUS Should they not,
Well might they fester 'gainst ingratitude,
And tent themselves with death. Of all the horses—
Whereof we have ta'en good, and good store—of all
The treasure in this field achieved and city,
We render you the tenth; to be ta'en forth
Before the common distribution at
Your only choice.

MARCIUS I thank you, general;
But cannot make my heart consent to take
A bribe to pay my sword. I do refuse it,
And stand upon my common part with those
That have beheld the doing.

A long flourish. They all cry "Marcius! Marcius!" cast up their caps and lances. Cominius and Lartius stand bare.

18 **good will** firm intention 19 **overta'en** surpassed 22 **traducement** slander 24 **To the spire and top of praises vouched** though attested in the highest terms of praise 30 **'gainst** against, in the face of 31 **tent themselves** be cleansed (refers to cleaning a wound with a linen roll, a "tent") 31 **death** (the "tent" being "death," the wounds would prove fatal) 32 **good store** plenty

MARCIUS May these same instruments, which you profane,
Never sound more! When drums and trumpets shall
I' th' field prove flatterers, let courts and cities be
Made all of false-faced soothing!
When steel grows soft as the parasite's silk,
Let him be made a coverture for th' wars!
No more, I say! For that I have not washed
My nose that bled, or foiled some debile wretch,
Which without note here's many else have done,
You shout me forth
In acclamations hyperbolical;
As if I loved my little should be dieted
In praises sauced with lies.

COMINIUS Too modest are you;
More cruel to your good report than grateful
To us that give you truly. By your patience,
If 'gainst yourself you be incensed, we'll put you
(Like one that means his proper harm) in manacles,
Then reason safely with you. Therefore, be it known,
As to us, to all the world, that Caius Marcius
Wears this war's garland: in token of the which,
My noble steed, known to the camp, I give him,
With all his trim belonging; and from this time,
For what he did before Corioles, call him,
With all th' applause and clamor of the host,
Caius Marcius Coriolanus.
Bear th' addition nobly ever!

Flourish. Trumpets sound, and drums.

OMNES Caius Marcius Coriolanus!

CORIOLANUS I will go wash:
And when my face is fair, you shall perceive
Whether I blush, or no. Howbeit, I thank you.

44 soothing flattery **46 coverture** clothing **47 For that** because **48 foiled** defeated **48 debile** weak **52–53 dieted/In** fed by **55 give** report **57 proper** own **62 his trim belonging** the equipment that goes with it **66 addition** title **67 Omnes** all (Latin)

I mean to stride your steed, and at all times
To undercrest your good addition
To th' fairness of my power.

COMINIUS So, to our tent;
Where, ere we do repose us, we will write
To Rome of our success. You, Titus Lartius,
Must to Corioles back; send us to Rome
The best, with whom we may articulate
For their own good and ours.

LARTIUS I shall, my lord.

CORIOLANUS The gods begin to mock me. I, that now
Refused most princely gifts, am bound to beg
Of my lord general.

COMINIUS Take't; 'tis yours. What is't?

CORIOLANUS I sometime lay here in Corioles
At a poor man's house; he used me kindly.
He cried to me; I saw him prisoner;
But then Aufidius was within my view,
And wrath o'erwhelmed my pity. I request you
To give my poor host freedom.

COMINIUS O, well begged!
Were he the butcher of my son, he should
Be free as is the wind. Deliver him, Titus.

LARTIUS Marcius, his name?

CORIOLANUS By Jupiter, forgot!
I am weary; yea, my memory is tired.
Have we no wine here?

COMINIUS Go we to our tent.
The blood upon your visage dries; 'tis time
It should be looked to. Come. *Exeunt.*

72 **undercrest your good addition** support the fine title you give (a "crest" in heraldry is a figure above a shield; the suggested image is of a shield with a man on horseback [line 71], beneath a crest [the "addition"]) 73 **To th' fairness** to the exact measure 77 **best** chief men 77 **articulate** make terms

[Scene X. *The camp of the Volsces.*]

A flourish. Cornets. Enter Tullus Aufidius, bloody, with two or three soldiers.

AUFIDIUS The town is ta'en!

FIRST SOLDIER 'Twill be delivered back on good condition.

AUFIDIUS Condition!
I would I were a Roman; for I cannot,
Being a Volsce, be that I am. Condition!
What good condition can a treaty find
I' th' part that is at mercy? Five times, Marcius,
I have fought with thee; so often hast thou beat me;
And wouldst do so, I think, should we encounter
As often as we eat. By th' elements,
If e'er again I meet him beard to beard,
He's mine or I am his. Mine emulation
Hath not that honor in't it had; for where
I thought to crush him in an equal force,
True sword to sword, I'll potch at him some way,
Or wrath or craft may get him.

FIRST SOLDIER He's the devil.

AUFIDIUS Bolder, though not so subtle. My valor's poisoned
With only suff'ring stain by him; for him
Shall fly out of itself. Nor sleep nor sanctuary,
Being naked, sick, nor fane nor Capitol,
The prayers of priests nor times of sacrifice,

I.x.2 **condition** terms 6 **condition** (with pun on sense of "quality") 7 **I' th' part that is at mercy** on the side that is vanquished (at the mercy of the victor) 15 **potch** poke (thrust, in fencing) 18 **stain** darkening 19 **fly out of itself** go out of its natural course 20 **naked** unarmed 20 **fane** shrine

Embarquements all of fury, shall lift up
Their rotten privilege and custom 'gainst
My hate to Marcius. Where I find him, were it
At home, upon my brother's guard, even there,
Against the hospitable canon, would I
Wash my fierce hand in's heart. Go you to th' city;
Learn how 'tis held, and what they are that must
Be hostages for Rome.

FIRST SOLDIER Will not you go?

AUFIDIUS I am attended at the cypress grove. I pray
you—
'Tis south the city mills—bring me word thither
How the world goes, that to the pace of it
I may spur on my journey.

FIRST SOLDIER I shall, sir. [*Exeunt.*]

22 **Embarquements** restraints 25 **upon my brother's guard** with my brother on guard (over him) 26 **hospitable canon** law of hospitality 30 **attended** awaited

[ACT II

Scene I. *Rome. A public place.*]

Enter Menenius, with the two Tribunes of the people, Sicinius, and Brutus.

MENENIUS The augurer tells me we shall have news tonight.

BRUTUS Good or bad?

MENENIUS Not according to the prayer of the people, for they love not Marcius.

SICINIUS Nature teaches beasts to know their friends.

MENENIUS Pray you, who does the wolf love?

SICINIUS The lamb.

MENENIUS Ay, to devour him, as the hungry plebeians would the noble Marcius.

BRUTUS He's a lamb indeed, that baas like a bear.

MENENIUS He's a bear indeed, that lives like a lamb. You two are old men: tell me one thing that I shall ask you.

BOTH Well, sir.

MENENIUS In what enormity is Marcius poor in, that you two have not in abundance?

II.i.1 **augurer** (more correctly "augur," Roman official who foretold the future) 16 **enormity** fault

BRUTUS He's poor in no one fault, but stored with all.

SICINIUS Especially in pride.

BRUTUS And topping all others in boasting.

MENENIUS This is strange now. Do you two know how you are censured here in the city—I mean of us o' th' right-hand file? Do you?

BOTH Why, how are we censured?

MENENIUS Because you talk of pride now—will you not be angry?

BOTH Well, well, sir, well.

MENENIUS Why 'tis no great matter; for a very little thief of occasion will rob you of a great deal of patience. Give your dispositions the reins, and be angry at your pleasures; at the least, if you take it as a pleasure to you in being so. You blame Marcius for being proud?

BRUTUS We do it not alone, sir.

MENENIUS I know you can do very little alone; for your helps are many, or else your actions would grow wondrous single: your abilities are too infantlike for doing much alone. You talk of pride: O that you could turn your eyes toward the napes of your necks, and make but an interior survey of your good selves! O that you could!

BOTH What then, sir?

MENENIUS Why, then you should discover a brace of unmeriting, proud, violent, testy magistrates (alias fools) as any in Rome.

SICINIUS Menenius, you are known well enough too.

21–22 **how you are censured** the opinion held of you 23 **o' th' right-hand file** of the upper classes, patricians 28–29 **a very little thief of occasion** i.e., a very little occasion is a thief who 37 **single** weak, slight 44 **testy** snappish 46 **known well enough** i.e., notorious

MENENIUS I am known to be a humorous patrician, and one that loves a cup of hot wine with not a drop of allaying Tiber in't; said to be something imperfect in favoring the first complaint, hasty and tinderlike upon too trivial motion; one that converses more with the buttock of the night than with the forehead of the morning. What I think I utter, and spend my malice in my breath. Meeting two such wealsmen as you are—I cannot call you Lycurguses—if the drink you give me touch my palate adversely, I make a crooked face at it. I cannot say your worships have delivered the matter well, when I find the ass in compound with the major part of your syllables; and though I must be content to bear with those that say you are reverend grave men, yet they lie deadly that tell you you have good faces. If you see this in the map of my microcosm, follows it that I am known well enough too? What harm can your bisson conspectuities glean out of this character, if I be known well enough too?

BRUTUS Come, sir, come, we know you well enough.

MENENIUS You know neither me, yourselves, nor any thing. You are ambitious for poor knaves' caps and legs. You wear out a good wholesome forenoon in hearing a cause between an orange-wife and a forset-seller, and then rejourn the controversy of threepence to a second day of audience. When you are hearing a matter between party and party, if you chance to be pinched with the colic, you make

47 **humorous** whimsical 49 **allaying** diluting 49–50 **something imperfect in favoring the first complaint** somewhat at fault in siding with the party who first puts his case 51 **motion** impulse 51–52 **Converses** associates 55 **wealsmen** statesmen 56 **Lycurgus** (a Greek lawgiver) 59–60 **ass in compound with the major part of your syllables** (pun on over-use of "as-es" in legal expressions, e.g., "whereas") 64 **map** i.e., face 64 **microcosm** little world, i.e., body 66 **bisson conspectuities** blind visual powers 70–71 **caps and legs** salutes and bows 72 **cause** case 73 **forset-seller** seller of taps for wine kegs 73 **rejourn** adjourn

faces like mummers, set up the bloody flag against all patience, and, in roaring for a chamber pot, dismiss the controversy bleeding, the more entangled by your hearing. All the peace you make in their cause is calling both the parties knaves. You are a pair of strange ones.

BRUTUS Come, come, you are well understood to be a perfecter giber for the table than a necessary bencher in the Capitol.

MENENIUS Our very priests must become mockers, if they shall encounter such ridiculous subjects as you are. When you speak best unto the purpose, it is not worth the wagging of your beards; and your beards deserve not so honorable a grave as to stuff a botcher's cushion or to be entombed in an ass's packsaddle. Yet you must be saying Marcius is proud; who, in a cheap estimation, is worth all your predecessors since Deucalion; though peradventure some of the best of 'em were hereditary hangmen. Good-e'en to your worships. More of your conversation would infect my brain, being the herdsmen of the beastly plebeians. I will be bold to take my leave of you.

Brutus and Sicinius [*step*] *aside.*

Enter Volumnia, Virgilia, and Valeria.

How now, my as fair as noble ladies—and the moon, were she earthly, no nobler—whither do you follow your eyes so fast?

VOLUMNIA Honorable Menenius, my boy Marcius approaches; for the love of Juno, let's go.

MENENIUS Ha? Marcius coming home?

77 **mummers** Christmas masquers, who act impromptu plays 77 **bloody flag** war flag 84 **giber** joker 84–85 **necessary bencher in the Capitol** indispensable judge in the Senate (cf. "the bench" for "court") 91 **botcher** mender of old clothes 94 **Deucalion** (the Noah of Greek myth) 97 **conversation** cf. lines 51–52

VOLUMNIA Ay, worthy Menenius; and with most prosperous approbation.

MENENIUS Take my cap, Jupiter, and I thank thee. Hoo! Marcius coming home!

TWO LADIES Nay, 'tis true.

VOLUMNIA Look, here's a letter from him; the state hath another, his wife another; and, I think, there's one at home for you.

MENENIUS I will make my very house reel tonight. A letter for me?

VIRGILIA Yes, certain, there's a letter for you; I saw't.

MENENIUS A letter for me? It gives me an estate of seven years' health; in which time I will make a lip at the physician. The most sovereign prescription in Galen is but empiricutic, and, to this preservative, of no better report than a horse-drench. Is he not wounded? He was wont to come home wounded.

VIRGILIA O, no, no, no.

VOLUMNIA O, he is wounded; I thank the gods for't.

MENENIUS So do I too, if it be not too much. Brings 'a victory in his pocket? The wounds become him.

VOLUMNIA On's brows, Menenius. He comes the third time home with the oaken garland.

MENENIUS Has he disciplined Aufidius soundly?

VOLUMNIA Titus Lartius writes they fought together, but Aufidius got off.

MENENIUS And 'twas time for him too, I'll warrant him that. And he had stayed by him, I would

106–07 **with most prosperous approbation** with signs of the greatest success 108 **Jupiter** (god of the sky and upper air) 117 **estate** state (fortune?) 118–19 **make a lip** make a face 120 **Galen** Greek physician 120 **empiricutic** quackish 121 **report** reputation 121 **horse-drench** drink of horse-medicine 127 **'a** he 134 **And** if

not have been so fidiused for all the chests in Corioles, and the gold that's in them. Is the Senate possessed of this?

VOLUMNIA Good ladies, let's go. Yes, yes, yes. The Senate has letters from the General, wherein he gives my son the whole name of the war. He hath in this action outdone his former deeds doubly.

VALERIA In troth, there's wondrous things spoke of him.

MENENIUS Wondrous! Ay, I warrant you, and not without his true purchasing.

VIRGILIA The gods grant them true!

VOLUMNIA True? Pow waw!

MENENIUS True! I'll be sworn they are true. Where is he wounded?—[*To the Tribunes*] God save your good worships! Marcius is coming home. He has more cause to be proud.—Where is he wounded?

VOLUMNIA I' th' shoulder and i' th' left arm. There will be large cicatrices to show the people, when he shall stand for his place. He received in the repulse of Tarquin seven hurts i' th' body.

MENENIUS One i' th' neck, and two i' th' thigh—there's nine that I know.

VOLUMNIA He had before this last expedition twenty-five wounds upon him.

MENENIUS Now it's twenty-seven: every gash was an enemy's grave. (*A shout and flourish.*) Hark! the trumpets.

VOLUMNIA These are the ushers of Marcius. Before

135 **fidiused** "Aufidius-ed" (cf. line 130 "disciplined Aufidius soundly") 137 **possessed** duly informed 140 **name of** credit for 145 **true purchasing** really earning (the praise) 147 **Pow waw** (a Volumnian "pooh-pooh") 153 **cicatrices** scars (Latin) 154 **place** i.e., the consulship

him he carries noise, and behind him he leaves tears.
Death, that dark spirit, in's nervy arm doth lie,
Which, being advanced, declines, and then men die.

A sennet. Trumpets sound. Enter Cominius the general and Titus Lartius; between them, Coriolanus, crowned with an oaken garland; with Captains and Soldiers, and a Herald.

HERALD Know, Rome, that all alone Marcius did fight
Within Corioles gates, where he hath won,
With fame, a name to Caius Marcius; these
In honor follows Coriolanus.
Welcome to Rome, renownèd Coriolanus!
Sound. Flourish.

ALL Welcome to Rome, renownèd Coriolanus!

CORIOLANUS No more of this, it does offend my heart;
Pray now, no more.

COMINIUS Look, sir, your mother!

CORIOLANUS O,
You have, I know, petitioned all the gods
For my prosperity! *Kneels.*

VOLUMNIA Nay, my good soldier, up;
My gentle Marcius, worthy Caius, and
By deed-achieving honor newly named—
What is it?—Coriolanus must I call thee?—
But, O, thy wife!

CORIOLANUS My gracious silence, hail!
Wouldst thou have laughed had I come coffined home,
That weep'st to see me triumph? Ah, my dear,
Such eyes the widows in Corioles wear,
And mothers that lack sons.

166 **nervy** sinewy 167 s.d. **sennet** (set of notes for trumpet or cornet to herald an important person, differing from a "flourish" or "fanfare"; cf. s.d. line 161) 179 **deed-achieving** achieved by deeds (cf. "the deeds of Coriolanus," II.ii.83)

MENENIUS Now, the gods crown thee!

CORIOLANUS And live you yet? [*To Valeria*] O my sweet lady, pardon.

VOLUMNIA I know not where to turn. O, welcome home!
And welcome, General: and y'are welcome all.

MENENIUS A hundred thousand welcomes. I could weep,
And I could laugh, I am light and heavy. Welcome!
A curse begin at very root on's heart
That is not glad to see thee! You are three
That Rome should dote on. Yet, by the faith of men,
We have some old crab-trees here at home that will not
Be grafted to your relish. Yet welcome, warriors.
We call a nettle but a nettle, and
The faults of fools but folly.

COMINIUS Ever right.

CORIOLANUS Menenius, ever, ever.

HERALD Give way there, and go on.

CORIOLANUS [*To Volumnia and Virgilia*] Your hand, and yours!
Ere in our own house I do shade my head,
The good patricians must be visited;
From whom I have received not only greetings,
But with them change of honors.

VOLUMNIA I have lived
To see inherited my very wishes
And the buildings of my fancy. Only
There's one thing wanting, which I doubt not but
Our Rome will cast upon thee.

190 **light and heavy** both merry and sad 195 **grafted** i.e., improved
204 **change of honors** fresh honors 205 **inherited** in my possession

CORIOLANUS Know, good mother,
I had rather be their servant in my way
Than sway with them in theirs.

COMINIUS On, to the Capitol!

Flourish. Cornets. Exeunt in state, as before. Brutus and Sicinius [*come forward*].

BRUTUS All tongues speak of him, and the blearèd sights
Are spectacled to see him. Your prattling nurse
Into a rapture lets her baby cry
While she chats him; the kitchen malkin pins
Her richest lockram 'bout her reechy neck,
Clamb'ring the walls to eye him. Stalls, bulks, windows,
Are smothered up, leads filled and ridges horsed
With variable complexions, all agreeing
In earnestness to see him. Seld-shown flamens
Do press among the popular throngs, and puff
To win a vulgar station. Our veiled dames
Commit the war of white and damask in
Their nicely gawded cheeks to th' wanton spoil
Of Phoebus' burning kisses. Such a pother,
As if that whatsoever god who leads him
Were slyly crept into his human powers,
And gave him graceful posture.

SICINIUS On the sudden,
I warrant him consul.

BRUTUS Then our office may,
During his power, go sleep.

SICINIUS He cannot temp'rately transport his honors

213 **rapture** fit 214 **chats** gossips about 214 **malkin** slut 215 **lockram** coarse linen 215 **reechy** dirty 216 **bulks** stalls (stands for goods to be sold) 217 **leads** roofs (leaded) 217 **horsed** "ridden" by viewers 218 **variable complexions** different physical types 219 **Seld-shown flamens** priests rarely seen in public (each flamen was in charge of the cult of a particular deity) 221 **vulgar station** place with the common people 223 **gawded** adorned 224 **Phoebus** sun-god 224 **pother** commotion

From where he should begin and end, but will
Lose those he hath won.

BRUTUS In that there's comfort.

SICINIUS Doubt not
The commoners, for whom we stand, but they
Upon their ancient malice will forget
With the least cause these his new honors; which
That he will give them make I as little question
As he is proud to do't.

BRUTUS I heard him swear,
Were he to stand for consul, never would he
Appear i' th' marketplace, nor on him put
The napless vesture of humility;
Nor, showing, as the manner is, his wounds
To th' people, beg their stinking breaths.

SICINIUS 'Tis right.

BRUTUS It was his word. O, he would miss it rather
Than carry it but by the suit of the gentry to him
And the desire of the nobles.

SICINIUS I wish no better
Than have him hold that purpose and to put it
In execution.

BRUTUS 'Tis most like he will.

SICINIUS It shall be to him then as our good wills:
A sure destruction.

BRUTUS So it must fall out
To him or our authorities. For an end,
We must suggest the people in what hatred
He still hath held them; that to's power he would
Have made them mules, silenced their pleaders and

231 **and end** i.e., to where he should end 234 **Upon** on account of 235 **which** i.e., "cause" 237 **As** as that 240 **napless** threadbare 244 **carry** win 248 **as our good wills** as we strongly desire 250 **For an end** to force the issue (?) finally (?) 251 **suggest** insinuate into the minds of 252 **still** ever

Dispropertied their freedoms; holding them,
In human action and capacity,
Of no more soul nor fitness for the world
Than camels in their war, who have their provand
Only for bearing burdens, and sore blows
For sinking under them.

SICINIUS This, as you say, suggested
At some time when his soaring insolence
Shall touch the people—which time shall not want,
If he be put upon't, and that's as easy
As to set dogs on sheep—will be his fire
To kindle their dry stubble; and their blaze
Shall darken him forever.

Enter a Messenger.

BRUTUS What's the matter?

MESSENGER You are sent for to the Capitol. 'Tis thought
That Marcius shall be consul.
I have seen the dumb men throng to see him and
The blind to hear him speak. Matrons flung gloves,
Ladies and maids their scarfs and handkerchers,
Upon him as he passed; the nobles bended,
As to Jove's statue, and the commons made
A shower and thunder with their caps and shouts.
I never saw the like.

BRUTUS Let's to the Capitol,
And carry with us ears and eyes for th' time,
But hearts for the event.

SICINIUS Have with you. *Exeunt.*

254 **Dispropertied** dispossessed them of 257 **provand** provisions 261 **want** be lacking 262 **put upon't** provoked to it 276 **event** outcome 276 **Have with you** coming with you!

[Scene II. *Rome. The Senate House.*]

Enter two Officers, to lay cushions, as it were, in the Capitol.

FIRST OFFICER Come, come, they are almost here. How many stand for consulships?

SECOND OFFICER Three, they say; but 'tis thought of everyone Coriolanus will carry it.

FIRST OFFICER That's a brave fellow; but he's vengeance proud, and loves not the common people.

SECOND OFFICER Faith, there hath been many great men that have flattered the people, who ne'er loved them; and there be many that they have loved, they know not wherefore; so that, if they love they know not why, they hate upon no better a ground. Therefore, for Coriolanus neither to care whether they love or hate him manifests the true knowledge he has in their disposition, and out of his noble carelessness lets them plainly see't.

FIRST OFFICER If he did not care whether he had their love or no, he waved indifferently 'twixt doing them neither good nor harm. But he seeks their hate with greater devotion than they can render it him, and leaves nothing undone that may fully discover him their opposite. Now, to seem to affect the malice and displeasure of the people is as bad as that which he dislikes, to flatter them for their love.

II.ii.s.d. **cushions** i.e., seats for dignitaries 5–6 **vengeance** frightfully (cf. "with a vengeance" 14 **in their disposition** of their mood 17 **waved** would waver 20–21 **discover** show 21 **opposite** opponent 21 **affect** aim at 22 **malice** ill will

SECOND OFFICER He hath deserved worthily of his country; and his ascent is not by such easy degrees as those who, having been supple and courteous to the people, bonneted, without any further deed to have them at all into their estimation and report. But he hath so planted his honors in their eyes and his actions in their hearts that for their tongues to be silent and not confess so much were a kind of ingrateful injury; to report otherwise were a malice that, giving itself the lie, would pluck reproof and rebuke from every ear that heard it.

FIRST OFFICER No more of him; he's a worthy man. Make way, they are coming.

A sennet. Enter the Patricians and the Tribunes of the People, Lictors before them; Coriolanus, Menenius, Cominius the Consul. Sicinius and Brutus take their places by themselves. Coriolanus stands.

MENENIUS Having determined of the Volsces, and
To send for Titus Lartius, it remains,
As the main point of this our after-meeting,
To gratify his noble service that
Hath thus stood for his country. Therefore, please you
Most reverend and grave elders, to desire
The present consul and last general
In our well-found successes, to report
A little of that worthy work performed
By Caius Marcius Coriolanus; whom
We met here both to thank and to remember
With honors like himself.

FIRST SENATOR Speak, good Cominius:

28 **bonneted** took off their caps (in flattery) 29–30 **to have them at all into their estimation and report** to get themselves at all into, win their way into, their esteem 34 **malice** act of ill will 37 s.d. **Lictors** (attendants who preceded Roman officials to announce their approach) 38 **determined of** decided concerning 41 **gratify** reward 42 **stood for** defended 44 **last** late 45 **well-found** fortunately met with 48 **remember** distinguish

Leave nothing out for length, and make us think
Rather our state's defective for requital
Than we to stretch it out. [*To the Tribunes*] Masters o' th' people,
We do request your kindest ears; and, after,
Your loving motion toward the common body,
To yield what passes here.

SICINIUS We are convented
Upon a pleasing treaty, and have hearts
Inclinable to honor and advance
The theme of our assembly.

BRUTUS Which the rather
We shall be blessed to do, if he remember
A kinder value of the people than
He hath hereto prized them at.

MENENIUS That's off, that's off;
I would you rather had been silent. Please you
To hear Cominius speak?

BRUTUS Most willingly.
But yet my caution was more pertinent
Than the rebuke you gave it.

MENENIUS He loves your people;
But tie him not to be their bedfellow.
Worthy Cominius, speak.

Coriolanus rises and offers to go away.

Nay, keep your place.

FIRST SENATOR Sit, Coriolanus; never shame to hear
What you have nobly done.

CORIOLANUS Your honors' pardon:
I had rather have my wounds to heal again
Than hear say how I got them.

51–52 **our state's . . . out** our government (the Senate) is lacking in the resources for reward rather than we in our effort to extend it 54 **motion toward the common body** influence with the common people 55 **yield** approve 55 **convented** convened 56 **treaty** proposal for discussion 58 **rather** sooner 59 **blessed** happy 60 **value** estimate 61 **off** not to the point

BRUTUS Sir, I hope
My words disbenched you not.

CORIOLANUS No, sir. Yet oft,
When blows have made me stay, I fled from words.
You soothed not, therefore hurt not; but your people,
I love them as they weigh——

MENENIUS Pray now, sit down.

CORIOLANUS I had rather have one scratch my head i' th' sun
When the alarum were struck than idly sit
To hear my nothings monstered. *Exit Coriolanus.*

MENENIUS Masters of the people,
Your multiplying spawn how can he flatter—
That's thousand to one good one—when you now see
He had rather venture all his limbs for honor
Than one on's ears to hear it? Proceed, Cominius.

COMINIUS I shall lack voice: the deeds of Coriolanus
Should not be uttered feebly. It is held
That valor is the chiefest virtue and
Most dignifies the haver. If it be,
The man I speak of cannot in the world
Be singly counterpoised. At sixteen years,
When Tarquin made a head for Rome, he fought
Beyond the mark of others. Our then dictator,
Whom with all praise I point at, saw him fight,
When with his Amazonian chin he drove
The bristled lips before him. He bestrid
An o'erpressed Roman, and i' th' consul's view
Slew three opposers; Tarquin's self he met,

72 **disbenched** unseated 74 **soothed** flattered 78 **monstered** turned into marvels 82 **Than one on's ears** than venture one of his ears 85 **virtue** (cf. Latin *virtus*, manly strength) 88 **singly counterpoised** matched in value (literally, in weight) by one man 89 **Tarquin** (early king of Rome, expelled from the city) 89 **made a head for** raised a force against 92 **Amazonian** i.e., beardless

And struck him on his knee. In that day's feats,
When he might act the woman in the scene,
He proved best man i' th' field, and for his meed
Was brow-bound with the oak. His pupil age
Man-ent'red thus, he waxèd like a sea;
And, in the brunt of seventeen battles since,
He lurched all swords of the garland. For this last,
Before and in Corioles, let me say,
I cannot speak him home. He stopped the fliers,
And by his rare example made the coward
Turn terror into sport; as weeds before
A vessel under sail, so men obeyed
And fell below his stem. His sword, death's stamp,
Where it did mark, it took; from face to foot
He was a thing of blood, whose every motion
Was timed with dying cries. Alone he ent'red
The mortal gate of th' city, which he painted
With shunless destiny; aidless came off,
And with a sudden reinforcement struck
Corioles like a planet. Now all's his,
When by and by the din of war 'gan pierce
His ready sense, then straight his doubled spirit
Requick'ned what in flesh was fatigate,
And to the battle came he; where he did
Run reeking o'er the lives of men, as if
'Twere a perpetual spoil; and till we called
Both field and city ours, he never stood
To ease his breast with panting.

MENENIUS Worthy man!

96 **on his knee** to his knees 97 **in the scene** on that stage 98 **meed** reward 99 **His pupil age** the years when he was learning (the art of war) 100 **Man-ent'red** having been initiated into manhood 102 **lurched** robbed 104 **speak him home** find words to match his merit 108 **stem** bow 108 **stamp** a die for stamping a coin or medal 109 **took** made its mark; killed (perhaps also, "infected fatally," cf. "struck," line 114) 112–13 **painted/With shunless destiny** smeared with blood of dying men, who could not shun their fate 114–15 **struck/Corioles like a planet** (planets supposedly had power to "strike," i.e., infect with disease) 116 **'gan** began to 117 **ready** responsive 117 **doubled** renewed 118 **fatigate** fatigued 121 **spoil** slaughter

FIRST SENATOR He cannot but with measure fit the honors
Which we devise him.

COMINIUS Our spoils he kicked at,
And looked upon things precious as they were
The common muck of the world. He covets less
Than misery itself would give, rewards
His deeds with doing them, and is content
To spend the time to end it.

MENENIUS He's right noble.
Let him be called for.

FIRST SENATOR Call Coriolanus.

OFFICER He doth appear.

Enter Coriolanus.

MENENIUS The Senate, Coriolanus, are well pleased
To make thee consul.

CORIOLANUS I do owe them still
My life and services.

MENENIUS It then remains
That you do speak to the people.

CORIOLANUS I do beseech you
Let me o'erleap that custom, for I cannot
Put on the gown, stand naked, and entreat them,
For my wounds' sake, to give their suffrage. Please you
That I may pass this doing.

SICINIUS Sir, the people
Must have their voices; neither will they bate
One jot of ceremony.

124 **with measure fit** measure up to; or, "bear with self-control" (?) 128 **misery** poverty 130 **To spend the time to end it** to kill it in action ("to live it up in action") 134 **still** always 138 **gown** "vesture of humility" (cf. II.i.240) 138 **naked** i.e., "without any coat underneath" (North) 140 **pass** pass over 141 **voices** votes 141 **bate** deduct

MENENIUS Put them not to't.
Pray you, go fit you to the custom, and
Take to you, as your predecessors have,
Your honor with your form.

CORIOLANUS It is a part
That I shall blush in acting, and might well
Be taken from the people.

BRUTUS. [TO SICINIUS] Mark you that.

CORIOLANUS To brag unto them, "Thus I did, and thus!"
Show them th' unaching scars which I should hide,
As if I had received them for the hire
Of their breath only!

MENENIUS Do not stand upon't.
We recommend to you, tribunes of the people,
Our purpose to them; and to our noble consul
Wish we all joy and honor.

SENATORS To Coriolanus come all joy and honor!

Flourish cornets. Then exeunt. Manet Sicinius and Brutus.

BRUTUS You see how he intends to use the people.

SICINIUS May they perceive's intent! He will require them,
As if he did contemn what he requested
Should be in them to give.

BRUTUS Come, we'll inform them
Of our proceedings here. On th' marketplace,
I know, they do attend us. [*Exeunt.*]

142 **Put them not to't** don't test them (by omitting any part of the ceremony) 145 **Your honor with your form** the honor with the ceremony it imposes on you 151 **stand upon't** make an issue of it 153 **purpose** proposal 157 **require** ask

[Scene III. *Rome. The Forum.*]

Enter seven or eight Citizens.

FIRST CITIZEN Once if he do require our voices, we ought not to deny him

SECOND CITIZEN We may, sir, if we will.

THIRD CITIZEN We have power in ourselves to do it, but it is a power that we have no power to do; for if he show us his wounds and tell us his deeds, we are to put our tongues into those wounds and speak for them; so, if he tell us his noble deeds, we must also tell him our noble acceptance of them. Ingratitude is monstrous; and for the multitude to be ingrateful, were to make a monster of the multitude; of the which we being members, should bring ourselves to be monstrous members.

FIRST CITIZEN And to make us no better thought of, a little help will serve; for once we stood up about the corn, he himself stuck not to call us the many-headed multitude.

THIRD CITIZEN We have been called so of many; not that our heads are some brown, some black, some abram, some bald, but that our wits are so diversely colored. And truly I think, if all our wits were to issue out of one skull, they would fly east, west, north, south, and their consent of one direct way should be at once to all the points o' th' compass.

SECOND CITIZEN Think you so? Which way do you judge my wit would fly?

II.iii.1 Once if he if he once **15 once we stood up** when we took a stand **20 abram** auburn **23 consent of** agreement on

THIRD CITIZEN Nay, your wit will not so soon out as another man's will; 'tis strongly wedged up in a blockhead; but if it were at liberty, 'twould, sure, southward.

SECOND CITIZEN Why that way?

THIRD CITIZEN To lose itself in a fog; where being three parts melted away with rotten dews, the fourth would return for conscience sake, to help to get thee a wife.

SECOND CITIZEN You are never without your tricks. You may, you may.

THIRD CITIZEN Are you all resolved to give your voices? But that's no matter, the greater part carries it. I say, if he would incline to the people, there was never a worthier man.

Enter Coriolanus in a gown of humility, with Menenius.

Here he comes, and in the gown of humility. Mark his behavior. We are not to stay all together, but to come by him where he stands, by ones, by twos, and by threes. He's to make his requests by particulars; wherein every one of us has a single honor, in giving him our own voices with our own tongues. Therefore follow me, and I'll direct you how you shall go by him.

ALL Content, content. [*Exeunt Citizens.*]

MENENIUS O sir, you are not right. Have you not known
The worthiest men have done't?

CORIOLANUS What must I say?—
"I pray, sir"—Plague upon't! I cannot bring
My tongue to such a pace. "Look, sir, my wounds!

34 **rotten** unhealthy 35–36 **for conscience . . . wife** i.e., because of the bastards he had fathered (?) 38 **You may, you may** cf. "O.K., O.K." 40 **greater part** majority 46–47 **by particulars** to each in turn

I got them in my country's service, when
Some certain of your brethren roared and ran
From th' noise of our own drums."

MENENIUS O me, the gods!
You must not speak of that. You must desire them
To think upon you.

CORIOLANUS Think upon me! Hang 'em!
I would they would forget me, like the virtues
Which our divines lose by 'em.

MENENIUS You'll mar all.
I'll leave you. Pray you, speak to 'em, I pray you,
In wholesome manner. *Exit.*

Enter three of the Citizens.

CORIOLANUS Bid them wash their faces,
And keep their teeth clean. So, here comes a brace.
You know the cause, sir, of my standing here.

THIRD CITIZEN We do, sir; tell us what hath brought you to't.

CORIOLANUS Mine own desert.

SECOND CITIZEN Your own desert?

CORIOLANUS Ay, not mine own desire.

THIRD CITIZEN How not your own desire?

CORIOLANUS No, sir, 'twas never my desire yet to trouble the poor with begging.

THIRD CITIZEN You must think, if we give you anything, we hope to gain by you.

CORIOLANUS Well then, I pray, your price o' th' consulship?

FIRST CITIZEN The price is, to ask it kindly.

60 think upon think well of **62 lose by 'em** waste on them in preaching ("pearls before swine") **64 wholesome** reasonable **65 brace** pair (of dogs)

CORIOLANUS Kindly sir, I pray let me ha't. I have wounds to show you, which shall be yours in private. Your good voice, sir; what say you?

SECOND CITIZEN You shall ha't, worthy sir.

CORIOLANUS A match, sir. There's in all two worthy voices begged. I have your alms. Adieu.

THIRD CITIZEN But this is something odd.

SECOND CITIZEN And 'twere to give again—but 'tis no matter. *Exeunt.*

Enter two other Citizens.

CORIOLANUS Pray you now, if it may stand with the tune of your voices that I may be consul, I have here the customary gown.

FIRST CITIZEN You have deserved nobly of your country, and you have not deserved nobly.

CORIOLANUS Your enigma?

FIRST CITIZEN You have been a scourge to her enemies, you have been a rod to her friends. You have not indeed loved the common people.

CORIOLANUS You should account me the more virtuous, that I have not been common in my love. I will, sir, flatter my sworn brother, the people, to earn a dearer estimation of them; 'tis a condition they account gentle; and since the wisdom of their choice is rather to have my hat than my heart, I will practice the insinuating nod, and be off to them most counterfeitly; that is, sir, I will counterfeit the bewitchment of some popular man, and give it bountiful to the desirers. Therefore, beseech you I may be consul.

84 **A match** agreed 86 **something** somewhat 89 **stand** agree 101 **dearer estimation of** higher valuation from 101 **condition** quality 104 **be off** take my hat off 106 **popular man** ("friend of the people")

SECOND CITIZEN We hope to find you our friend; and therefore give you our voices heartily.

FIRST CITIZEN You have received many wounds for your country.

CORIOLANUS I will not seal your knowledge with showing them. I will make much of your voices and so trouble you no farther.

BOTH The gods give you joy, sir, heartily! [*Exeunt.*]

CORIOLANUS Most sweet voices!
Better it is to die, better to starve,
Than crave the hire which first we do deserve.
Why in this woolvish toge should I stand here,
To beg of Hob and Dick that does appear
Their needless vouches? Custom calls me to't.
What custom wills, in all things should we do't,
The dust on antique time would lie unswept,
And mountainous error be too highly heaped
For truth to o'erpeer. Rather than fool it so,
Let the high office and the honor go
To one that would do thus. I am half through:
The one part suffered, the other will I do.

Enter three Citizens more.

Here come moe voices.
Your voices! For your voices I have fought;
Watched for your voices; for your voices bear
Of wounds two dozen odd; battles thrice six
I have seen, and heard of; for your voices have
Done many things, some less, some more. Your voices!
Indeed, I would be consul.

113 **seal** make authentic (legal sense) 120 **in this woolvish toge** i.e., disguising myself (a backhand reference to "wolf in sheep's clothing"; note that Coriolanus "lives like a lamb," according to II.i.12) 121 **Hob** (nickname of "Robert"; a country fellow) 121 **that does appear** i.e., as they come, one by one 122 **vouches** confirmations 126 **o'erpeer** rise above 130 **moe** more 132 **Watched** kept watch

FIRST CITIZEN He has done nobly, and cannot go without any honest man's voice.

SECOND CITIZEN Therefore let him be consul. The gods give him joy, and make him good friend to the people!

ALL Amen, amen. God save thee, noble consul!
[*Exeunt Citizens.*]

CORIOLANUS Worthy voices!

Enter Menenius, with Brutus and Sicinius.

MENENIUS You have stood your limitation; and the tribunes
Endue you with the people's voice. Remains
That in th' official marks invested you
Anon do meet the Senate.

CORIOLANUS Is this done?

SICINIUS The custom of request you have discharged:
The people do admit you, and are summoned
To meet anon upon your approbation.

CORIOLANUS Where? At the Senate House?

SICINIUS There, Coriolanus.

CORIOLANUS May I change these garments?

SICINIUS You may, sir.

CORIOLANUS That I'll straight do, and, knowing myself again,
Repair to th' Senate House.

MENENIUS I'll keep you company. Will you along?

BRUTUS We stay here for the people.

SICINIUS Fare you well.
Exeunt Coriolanus and Menenius.

144 **limitation** time set for requesting votes 146 **Marks** insignia 150 **anon upon your approbation** at once to confirm your appointment (as consul) 154 **Repair** return 155 **along** come too

He has it now; and, by his looks, methinks
'Tis warm at's heart.

BRUTUS With a proud heart he wore
His humble weeds. Will you dismiss the people?

Enter the Plebeians.

SICINIUS How now, my masters, have you chose this man?

FIRST CITIZEN He has our voices, sir.

BRUTUS We pray the gods he may deserve your loves.

SECOND CITIZEN Amen, sir. To my poor unworthy notice,
He mocked us when he begged our voices.

THIRD CITIZEN Certainly;
He flouted us downright.

FIRST CITIZEN No, 'tis his kind of speech—he did not mock us.

SECOND CITIZEN Not one amongst us, save yourself, but says
He used us scornfully. He should have showed us
His marks of merit, wounds received for's country.

SICINIUS Why, so he did, I am sure.

ALL No, no; no man saw 'em.

THIRD CITIZEN He said he had wounds which he could show in private;
And with his hat, thus waving it in scorn,
"I would be consul," says he. "Agèd custom,
But by your voices, will not so permit me;
Your voices therefore." When we granted that,
Here was "I thank you for your voices. Thank you,
Your most sweet voices. Now you have left your voices,

157 **it** (the emotion that "warms his heart," either the satisfaction of success, or the irritation of offended pride; cf. "his fire," II.i.263) 158 **at's** at his 160 **my masters** gentlemen

I have no further with you." Was not this mockery?

SICINIUS Why either were you ignorant to see't,
Or, seeing it, of such childish friendliness
To yield your voices?

BRUTUS Could you not have told him
As you were lessoned: when he had no power,
But was a petty servant to the state,
He was your enemy, ever spake against
Your liberties and the charters that you bear
I' th' body of the weal; and now, arriving
A place of potency and sway o' th' state,
If he should still malignantly remain
Fast foe to th' plebeii, your voices might
Be curses to yourselves? You should have said
That as his worthy deeds did claim no less
Than what he stood for, so his gracious nature
Would think upon you for your voices, and
Translate his malice towards you into love,
Standing your friendly lord.

SICINIUS Thus to have said,
As you were fore-advised, had touched his spirit
And tried his inclination; from him plucked
Either his gracious promise, which you might,
As cause had called you up, have held him to;
Or else it would have galled his surly nature,
Which easily endures not article
Tying him to aught. So, putting him to rage,
You should have ta'en th' advantage of his choler,
And passed him unelected.

BRUTUS Did you perceive
He did solicit you in free contempt

179 **no further** no more to do 180 **ignorant** too dull 182 **yield** give 183 **lessoned** instructed 186 **charters** privileges 187 **weal** commonwealth 188 **A place** (direct object of "arriving," i.e., "reaching") 188 **potency and sway o' th' state** power in managing the state 190 **plebeii** (Latin for "plebeians") 193 **what he stood for** the office he ran for 194 **think upon you** think well of you 195 **Translate** transform 197 **touched** tested 200 **As cause had called you up** as an occasion (emergency) would have roused you 202 **article** condition 204 **choler** anger 206 **free** open

When he did need your loves; and do you think
That his contempt shall not be bruising to you
When he hath power to crush? Why, had your bodies
No heart among you? Or had you tongues to cry
Against the rectorship of judgment?

SICINIUS Have you
Ere now denied the asker, and now again,
Of him that did not ask but mock, bestow
Your sued-for tongues?

THIRD CITIZEN He's not confirmed; we may deny him yet.

SECOND CITIZEN And will deny him.
I'll have five hundred voices of that sound.

FIRST CITIZEN I twice five hundred, and their friends to piece 'em.

BRUTUS Get you hence instantly, and tell those friends
They have chose a consul that will from them take
Their liberties, make them of no more voice
Than dogs that are as often beat for barking
As therefor kept to do so.

SICINIUS Let them assemble;
And, on a safer judgment, all revoke
Your ignorant election. Enforce his pride
And his old hate unto you; besides, forget not
With what contempt he wore the humble weed,
How in his suit he scorned you; but your loves,
Thinking upon his services, took from you
Th' apprehension of his present portance,
Which most gibingly, ungravely, he did fashion
After the inveterate hate he bears you.

BRUTUS Lay

210 **heart** spirit 210 **cry** give your voices 211 **rectorship** rule 213 **Of** on 218 **piece 'em** add to them (cf. "piece out") 223 **therefore** for that reason 224 **safer** sounder 225 **ignorant election** choice made in ignorance 225 **Enforce** urge, insist on 230 **apprehension** perception 230 **portance** bearing

A fault on us, your tribunes, that we labored,
No impediment between, but that you must
Cast your election on him.

SICINIUS Say you chose him
More after our commandment than as guided
By your own true affections; and that your minds,
Preoccupied with what you rather must do
Than what you should, made you against the grain
To voice him consul. Lay the fault on us.

BRUTUS Ay, spare us not. Say we read lectures to you,
How youngly he began to serve his country,
How long continued; and what stock he springs of,
The noble house o' th' Marcians, from whence came
That Ancus Marcius, Numa's daughter's son,
Who after great Hostilius here was king;
Of the same house Publius and Quintus were,
That our best water brought by conduits hither;
[And Censorinus that was so surnamed]
And nobly namèd so, twice being censor,
Was his great ancestor.

SICINIUS One thus descended,
That hath beside well in his person wrought
To be set high in place, we did commend
To your remembrances: but you have found,
Scaling his present bearing with his past,
That he's your fixèd enemy, and revoke
Your sudden approbation.

BRUTUS Say you ne'er had done't
(Harp on that still) but by our putting on;
And presently, when you have drawn your number,
Repair to th' Capitol.

234 **No impediment between** putting no obstacle in your way (i.e., we have made the way free for you to choose him) 236 **after** following 237 **Affections** desires 240 **voice him consul** make him consul by your votes 245 **Numa** (second king of Rome) 249 **And ... surnamed** (see Textual note, p. 769) 255 **Scaling** weighing 257 **sudden** hasty 258 **putting on** urging 259 **drawn your number** gathered your crowd (of supporters)

CITIZENS We will so. Almost all
Repent in their election. *Exeunt Plebeians.*

BRUTUS Let them go on;
This mutiny were better put in hazard
Than stay, past doubt, for greater.
If, as his nature is, he fall in rage
With their refusal, both observe and answer
The vantage of his anger.

SICINIUS To th' Capitol, come.
We will be there before the stream o' th' people;
And this shall seem, as partly 'tis, their own,
Which we have goaded onward. *Exeunt.*

262 **This ... hazard** i.e., it would be better to run the risk of this minor disorder 265–66 **answer/The vantage of his anger** take advantage of the opportunity his anger affords

ACT III

[Scene I. *Rome. A street.*]

Cornets. Enter Coriolanus, Menenius, all the Gentry, Cominius, Titus Lartius, and other Senators.

CORIOLANUS Tullus Aufidius then had made new head?

LARTIUS He had, my lord; and that it was which caused
Our swifter composition.

CORIOLANUS So then the Volsces stand but as at first;
Ready, when time shall prompt them, to make road
Upon's again.

COMINIUS They are worn, Lord Consul, so
That we shall hardly in our ages see
Their banners wave again.

CORIOLANUS Saw you Aufidius?

LARTIUS On safeguard he came to me; and did curse
Against the Volsces, for they had so vilely
Yielded the town. He is retired to Antium.

CORIOLANUS Spoke he of me?

LARTIUS He did, my lord.

CORIOLANUS How? What?

III.i.1 **made new head** raised a new force 3 **swifter composition** coming to terms sooner 5–6 **make road/Upon's** invade us 6 **worn** worn out 7 **ages** lifetime 9 **On safeguard** under safe-conduct

LARTIUS How often he had met you, sword to sword;
That of all things upon the earth he hated
Your person most; that he would pawn his fortunes
To hopeless restitution, so he might
Be called your vanquisher.

CORIOLANUS At Antium lives he?

LARTIUS At Antium.

CORIOLANUS I wish I had a cause to seek him there,
To oppose his hatred fully. Welcome home.

Enter Sicinius and Brutus.

Behold, these are the tribunes of the people,
The tongues o' th' common mouth. I do despise them;
For they do prank them in authority,
Against all noble sufferance.

SICINIUS Pass no further.

CORIOLANUS Ha? What is that?

BRUTUS It will be dangerous to go on—no further.

CORIOLANUS What makes this change?

MENENIUS The matter?

COMINIUS Hath he not passed the noble and the common?

BRUTUS Cominius, no.

CORIOLANUS Have I had children's voices?

FIRST SENATOR Tribunes, give way; he shall to th' marketplace.

BRUTUS The people are incensed against him.

16 **To hopeless restitution** without hope of their being redeemed 23 **prank them** dress themselves up 24 **Against all noble sufferance** so that no noble can endure it 29 **the noble and the common** the patricians and the plebeians

SICINIUS Stop,
Or all will fall in broil.

CORIOLANUS Are these your herd?
Must these have voices, that can yield them now,
And straight disclaim their tongues? What are your offices?
You being their mouths, why rule you not their teeth?
Have you not set them on?

MENENIUS Be calm, be calm.

CORIOLANUS It is a purposed thing, and grows by plot,
To curb the will of the nobility.
Suffer't, and live with such as cannot rule,
Nor ever will be ruled.

BRUTUS Call't not a plot.
The people cry you mocked them; and of late,
When corn was given them gratis, you repined,
Scandaled the suppliants for the people, called them
Time-pleasers, flatterers, foes to nobleness.

CORIOLANUS Why, this was known before.

BRUTUS Not to them all.

CORIOLANUS Have you informed them sithence?

BRUTUS How! I inform them!

CORIOLANUS You are like to do such business.

BRUTUS Not unlike
Each way to better yours.

CORIOLANUS Why then should I be consul? By yond clouds,

33 **in broil** into a riot 34 **now** at one time 35 **disclaim** disown 38 **purposed thing** premeditated affair 43 **repined** regretted it 44 **Scandaled** slandered 47 **informed** instructed 47 **sithence** since 48–49 **Not unlike/ Each way to better yours** likely in every way to do your business better

Let me deserve so ill as you, and make me
Your fellow tribune.

SICINIUS You show too much of that
For which the people stir. If you will pass
To where you are bound, you must inquire your way,
Which you are out of, with a gentler spirit,
Or never be so noble as a consul,
Nor yoke with him for tribune.

MENENIUS Let's be calm.

COMINIUS The people are abused; set on. This palt'ring
Becomes not Rome; nor has Coriolanus
Deserved this so dishonored rub, laid falsely
I' th' plain way of his merit.

CORIOLANUS Tell me of corn!
This was my speech, and I will speak't again——

MENENIUS Not now, not now.

FIRST SENATOR Not in this heat, sir, now.

CORIOLANUS Now, as I live, I will.
My nobler friends, I crave their pardons.
For the mutable, rank-scented meiny, let them
Regard me as I do not flatter, and
Therein behold themselves. I say again,
In soothing them, we nourish 'gainst our Senate
The cockle of rebellion, insolence, sedition,
Which we ourselves have ploughed for, sowed, and scattered,
By mingling them with us, the honored number;
Who lack not virtue, no, nor power, but that
Which they have given to beggars.

MENENIUS Well, no more.

53 **stir** are rebelling 55 **are out of** are straying from 57 **for** as 58 **abused** deceived 58 **set on** incited 58 **palt'ring** cheating 60 **rub** hindrance (in bowling on the green, any roughness of ground) 60 **falsely** treacherously 66 **meiny** crowd 70 **cockle** weed

FIRST SENATOR No more words, we beseech you.

CORIOLANUS How! No more!
As for my country I have shed my blood,
Not fearing outward force, so shall my lungs
Coin words till their decay against those measles,
Which we disdain should tetter us, yet sought
The very way to catch them.

BRUTUS You speak o' th' people,
As if you were a god, to punish, not
A man of their infirmity.

SICINIUS 'Twere well
We let the people know't.

MENENIUS What, what? His choler?

CORIOLANUS Choler?
Were I as patient as the midnight sleep,
By Jove, 'twould be my mind!

SICINIUS It is a mind
That shall remain a poison where it is,
Not poison any further.

CORIOLANUS Shall remain!
Hear you this Triton of the minnows? Mark you
His absolute "shall"?

CORIOLANUS 'Twas from the canon.

CORIOLANUS "Shall"!
O good but most unwise patricians! Why,
You grave but reckless senators, have you thus
Given Hydra here to choose an officer,
That with his peremptory "shall," being but
The horn and noise o' th' monster's, wants not spirit
To say he'll turn your current in a ditch,

78 **decay** death 78 **measles** (the disease; and "foul wretches," from *mesel*, "leper") 79 **tetter** infect with leprous eruption 82 **of their infirmity** having the same weaknesses as they 89 **Triton** sea-god, trumpeter of Neptune (cf. "horn," line 95) 90 **from the canon** against the law 93 **Given Hydra here** permitted this many-headed beast 96 **in** (aside) into

And make your channel his? If he have power,
Then vail your ignorance; if none, awake
Your dangerous lenity. If you are learned,
Be not as common fools; if you are not,
Let them have cushions by you. You are plebeians,
If they be senators; and they are no less,
When, both your voices blended, the great'st taste
Most palates theirs. They choose their magistrate;
And such a one as he, who puts his "shall,"
His popular "shall," against a graver bench
Than ever frowned in Greece. By Jove himself,
It makes the consuls base; and my soul aches
To know, when two authorities are up,
Neither supreme, how soon confusion
May enter 'twixt the gap of both and take
The one by th' other.

COMINIUS Well, on to th' marketplace.

CORIOLANUS Whoever gave that counsel to give forth
The corn o' th' storehouse gratis, as 'twas used
Sometime in Greece—

MENENIUS Well, well, no more of that.

CORIOLANUS Though there the people had more absolute pow'r,
I say they nourished disobedience, fed
The ruin of the state.

BRUTUS Why shall the people give
One that speaks thus their voice?

CORIOLANUS I'll give my reasons,
More worthier than their voices. They know the corn

98 **vail your ignorance** let your ignorance (that gave the power) bow (to him) 99 **learned** wise 101 **cushions** (symbol of senatorial rank; cf. II.ii.s.d.) 102 **no less** i.e., no less than senators 103–04 **the great'st taste/ Most palates theirs** the dominant flavor tastes most of them (they have the most votes) 106 **bench** court 109 **up** active 110 **confusion** violent disorder (in a revolution) 111–12 **take/The one by th' other** seize and overthrow one by means of the other

Was not our recompense, resting well assured
They ne'er did service for't. Being pressed to th' war,
Even when the navel of the state was touched,
They would not thread the gates; this kind of
service
Did not deserve corn gratis. Being i' th' war,
Their mutinies and revolts, wherein they showed
Most valor, spoke not for them. Th' accusation
Which they have often made against the Senate,
All cause unborn, could never be the native
Of our so frank donation. Well, what then?
How shall this bosom multiplied digest
The Senate's courtesy? Let deeds express
What's like to be their words: "We did request it;
We are the greater poll, and in true fear
They gave us our demands." Thus we debase
The nature of our seats, and make the rabble
Call our cares fears; which will in time
Break ope the locks o' th' Senate and bring in
The crows to peck the eagles.

MENENIUS Come, enough.

BRUTUS Enough, with over measure.

CORIOLANUS No, take more.
What may be sworn by, both divine and human,
Seal what I end withal! This double worship,
Where one part does disdain with cause, the other
Insult without all reason; where gentry, title,
wisdom,
Cannot conclude but by the yea and no

121 **recompense** reward for past services 122 **pressed to** conscripted for 123 **navel** center (cf. Menenius' fable, I.i) 124 **thread** pass through 129 **All cause unborn** with no cause in existence 129 **native** original, parent (i.e., their accusation not the origin of our gift) 130 **frank** unsolicited 131 **bosom multiplied** many-bosomed beast ("Hydra," line 93) 131 **digest** (1) digest (2) understand ("bosom" can mean both "cavity of the stomach" and "heart," i.e., "mind") 134 **poll** number 137 **cares** (concern for the state) 142 **withal** with 144 **without** beyond 144 **gentry** gentle birth 145 **conclude** decide

Of general ignorance—it must omit
Real necessities, and give way the while
To unstable slightness. Purpose so barred, it
follows
Nothing is done to purpose. Therefore, beseech
you—
You that will be less fearful than discreet;
That love the fundamental part of state
More than you doubt the change on't; that prefer
A noble life before a long, and wish
To jump a body with a dangerous physic
That's sure of death without it—at once pluck out
The multitudinous tongue; let them not lick
The sweet which is their poison. Your dishonor
Mangles true judgment, and bereaves the state
Of that integrity which should become't;
Not having the power to do the good it would,
For th' ill which doth control't.

BRUTUS 'Has said enough.

SICINIUS Has spoken like a traitor and shall answer
As traitors do.

CORIOLANUS Thou wretch, despite o'erwhelm thee!
What should the people do with these bald tribunes,
On whom depending, their obedience fails
To th' greater bench? In a rebellion,
When what's not meet, but what must be, was law,
Then were they chosen; in a better hour

146 **omit** overlook 148 **unstable slightness** unsteady trifling 148 **Purpose so barred** when the intention (of charting a policy in advance) is so thwarted 150 **less fearful than discreet** i.e., more prudent than fearful 151 **fundamental part of state** basic constitution of the government 152 **doubt** fear 154 **jump** risk harming 154 **physic** medicine, treatment 156 **multitudinous tongue** (the voice of the "Hydra," the tribuneship) 159 **integrity** wholeness 161 **control't** overpower it 162 **answer** i.e., in court, be brought to trial; cf. lines 176, 323 164 **bald** trivial (pun) 166 **th' greater bench** i.e., the senate

Let what is meet be said it must be meet,
And throw their power i' th' dust.

BRUTUS Manifest treason!

SICINIUS This a consul? No.

BRUTUS The aediles, ho!

Enter an Aedile.

Let him be apprehended.

SICINIUS Go, call the people, [*exit Aedile*] in whose name myself
Attach thee as a traitorous innovator,
A foe to th' public weal. Obey, I charge thee,
And follow to thine answer.

CORIOLANUS Hence, old goat!

ALL [PATRICIANS] We'll surety him.

COMINIUS Aged sir, hands off.

CORIOLANUS Hence, rotten thing, or I shall shake thy bones
Out of thy garments.

SICINIUS Help, ye citizens!

Enter a rabble of Plebeians, with the Aediles.

MENENIUS On both sides more respect.

SICINIUS Here's he that would take from you all your power.

BRUTUS Seize him, aediles!

ALL [CITIZENS] Down with him, down with him!

SECOND SENATOR Weapons, weapons, weapons!

They all bustle about Coriolanus.

169 **it must be meet** that it *must* be fitting 172 **aediles** officers attached to the tribunes 174 **Attach** arrest 176 **answer** (legal term for "meeting a charge") 176 **goat** (the tribunes are evidently bearded; cf. II.i.89) 177 **surety** stand surety for

[ALL] Tribunes!—Patricians!—Citizens!—What, ho!—
Sicinius!—Brutus!—Coriolanus!—Citizens!—
Peace, peace, peace!—Stay! Hold! Peace!

MENENIUS What is about to be? I am out of breath.
Confusion's near. I cannot speak. You, tribunes
To th' people! Coriolanus, patience!
Speak, good Sicinius.

SICINIUS Hear me, people; peace!

ALL [CITIZENS] Let's hear our tribune. Peace!—Speak, speak, speak.

SICINIUS You are at point to lose your liberties:
Marcius would have all from you; Marcius,
Whom late you have named for consul.

MENENIUS Fie, fie, fie!
This is the way to kindle, not to quench.

FIRST SENATOR To unbuild the city, and to lay all flat.

SICINIUS What is the city but the people?

ALL [CITIZENS] True,
The people are the city.

BRUTUS By the consent of all, we were established
The people's magistrates.

ALL [CITIZENS] You so remain.

MENENIUS And so are like to do.

COMINIUS That is the way to lay the city flat,
To bring the roof to the foundation,
And bury all which yet distinctly ranges,
In heaps and piles of ruin.

SICINIUS This deserves death.

189 **Confusion** ruin (resulting from civil disorder, cf. line 110) 193 **at point to lose** on point of losing 205 **distinctly ranges** extends in separate orderly rows (of buildings)

BRUTUS Or let us stand to our authority,
Or let us lose it. We do here pronounce,
Upon the part o' th' people, in whose power
We were elected theirs, Marcius is worthy
Of present death.

SICINIUS Therefore lay hold of him;
Bear him to th' rock Tarpeian, and from thence
Into destruction cast him.

BRUTUS Aediles, seize him!

ALL [CITIZENS] Yield, Marcius, yield!

MENENIUS Hear me one word;
Beseech you, tribunes, hear me but a word.

AEDILES Peace, peace!

MENENIUS [*To Brutus*] Be that you seem, truly your country's friend,
And temp'rately proceed to what you would
Thus violently redress.

BRUTUS Sir, those cold ways,
That seem like prudent helps, are very poisonous
Where the disease is violent. Lay hands upon him,
And bear him to the rock.

Coriolanus draws his sword.

CORIOLANUS No, I'll die here.
There's some among you have beheld me fighting;
Come, try upon yourselves what you have seen me.

MENENIUS Down with that sword! Tribunes, withdraw awhile.

BRUTUS Lay hands upon him.

MENENIUS Help Marcius, help,
You that be noble; help him, young and old!

207 **Or** either 207 **stand to** stand by 209 **in** by 210 **theirs** i.e., their representatives 212 **rock Tarpeian** (from which criminals were thrown)

ALL [CITIZENS] Down with him, down with him!

In this mutiny, the Tribunes, the Aediles, and the people are beat in.

MENENIUS Go, get you to your house; begone, away!
All will be naught else.

SECOND SENATOR Get you gone.

CORIOLANUS Stand fast;
We have as many friends as enemies.

MENENIUS Shall it be put to that?

FIRST SENATOR The gods forbid!
I prithee, noble friend, home to thy house;
Leave us to cure this cause.

MENENIUS For 'tis a sore upon us
You cannot tent yourself. Begone, beseech you.

COMINIUS Come, sir, along with us.

CORIOLANUS I would they were barbarians, as they are,
Though in Rome littered; not Romans, as they are not,
Though calved i' th' porch o' th' Capitol.

MENENIUS Begone.
Put not your worthy rage into your tongue:
One time will owe another.

CORIOLANUS On fair ground
I could beat forty of them.

MENENIUS I could myself
Take up a brace o' th' best of them; yea, the two tribunes.

228 s.d. **mutiny** riot 229 **naught** ruined 232 **put to that** driven to that extremity 234 **cause** dispute 235 **tent** treat (cf. I.ix.31) 239 **porch o' th' Capitol** (portico of the temple of Jupiter on the Capitoline Hill) 240 **worthy** justifiable (?) noble (?) 241 **One time will owe another** one time (the present, when the people are in revolt) will be compensated by another (when the people are checked) 243 **Take up a brace** take on a couple ("brace" often of dogs)

COMINIUS But now 'tis odds beyond arithmetic;
And manhood is called foolery when it stands
Against a falling fabric. Will you hence
Before the tag return? Whose rage doth rend
Like interrupted waters, and o'erbear
What they are used to bear.

MENENIUS Pray you, begone.
I'll try whether my old wit be in request
With those that have but little. This must be
patched
With cloth of any color.

COMINIUS Nay, come away.
Exeunt Coriolanus and Cominius.

PATRICIAN This man has marred his fortune.

MENENIUS His nature is too noble for the world:
He would not flatter Neptune for his trident,
Or Jove for's power to thunder. His heart's his
mouth:
What his breast forges, that his tongue must vent;
And, being angry, does forget that ever
He heard the name of death. *A noise within.*
Here's goodly work!

PATRICIAN I would they were abed!

MENENIUS I would they were in Tiber! What the
vengeance!
Could he not speak 'em fair?

Enter Brutus and Sicinius, with the rabble again.

SICINIUS Where is this viper
That would depopulate the city and
Be every man himself?

MENENIUS You worthy tribunes——

244 **beyond arithmetic** beyond number 246 **fabric** building 247 **tag** riffraff ("tag and rag") 248 **o'erbear** overcome 261 **What the vengeance** (an emphatic "What!"; cf. "What the devil!") 262 **speak 'em fair** talk civilly to them (and so flatter)

SICINIUS He shall be thrown down the Tarpeian rock
With rigorous hands. He hath resisted law,
And therefore law shall scorn him further trial
Than the severity of the public power,
Which he so sets at nought.

FIRST CITIZEN He shall well know
The noble tribunes are the people's mouths,
And we their hands.

ALL [CITIZENS] He shall, sure on't.

MENENIUS Sir, sir——

SICINIUS Peace!

MENENIUS Do not cry havoc, where you should but hunt
With modest warrant.

SICINIUS Sir, how comes't that you
Have holp to make this rescue?

MENENIUS Hear me speak:
As I do know the consul's worthiness,
So can I name his faults.

SICINIUS Consul! What consul?

MENENIUS The consul Coriolanus.

BRUTUS He consul!

ALL [CITIZENS] No, no, no, no, no.

MENENIUS If, by the tribunes' leave, and yours, good people,
I may be heard, I would crave a word or two;
The which shall turn you to no further harm
Than so much loss of time.

SICINIUS Speak briefly then;
For we are peremptory to dispatch

268 **the public power** i.e., the power derived from the people 273 **cry havoc** call for general slaughter ("total war") 274 **With modest warrant** with moderate justification 275 **holp** helped 284 **peremptory** resolved

This viperous traitor. To eject him hence
Were but our danger, and to keep him here
Our certain death. Therefore it is decreed
He dies tonight.

MENENIUS Now the good gods forbid
That our renownèd Rome, whose gratitude
Towards her deservèd children is enrolled
In Jove's own book, like an unnatural dam
Should now eat up her own!

SICINIUS He's a disease that must be cut away.

MENENIUS O, he's a limb that has but a disease;
Mortal, to cut it off; to cure it, easy.
What has he done to Rome that's worthy death?
Killing our enemies, the blood he hath lost—
Which I dare vouch is more than that he hath
By many an ounce—he dropped it for his country;
And what is left, to lose it by his country
Were to us all that do't and suffer it
A brand to th' end o' th' world.

SICINIUS This is clean kam.

BRUTUS Merely awry. When he did love his country,
It honored him.

MENENIUS The service of the foot
Being once gangrened, is not then respected
For what before it was.

BRUTUS We'll hear no more.
Pursue him to his house and pluck him thence,
Lest his infection, being of catching nature,
Spread further.

MENENIUS One word more, one word!
This tiger-footed rage, when it shall find
The harm of unscanned swiftness, will, too late,

286 **but our danger** only the risk we now run 290 **deservèd** deserving 295 **Mortal** deadly 302 **brand** mark of disgrace 302 **clean kam** completely wrong (literally *kam* = crooked) 303 **Merely** absolutely 307 **pluck** take 311 **unscanned** thoughtless

Tie leaden pounds to's heels. Proceed by process;
Lest parties (as he is beloved) break out,
And sack great Rome with Romans.

BRUTUS If it were so—

SICINIUS What do ye talk?
Have we not had a taste of his obedience?
Our aediles smote? Ourselves resisted? Come!

MENENIUS Consider this: he has been bred i' th' wars
Since 'a could draw a sword, and is ill schooled
In bolted language; meal and bran together
He throws without distinction. Give me leave,
I'll go to him, and undertake to bring him
Where he shall answer, by a lawful form,
In peace, to his utmost peril.

FIRST SENATOR Noble tribunes,
It is the humane way. The other course
Will prove too bloody, and the end of it
Unknown to the beginning.

SICINIUS Noble Menenius,
Be you then as the people's officer.
Masters, lay down your weapons.

BRUTUS Go not home.

SICINIUS Meet on the marketplace. We'll attend you there,
Where, if you bring not Marcius, we'll proceed
In our first way.

MENENIUS I'll bring him to you.
[*To the Senators*] Let me desire your company. He must come,
Or what is worst will follow.

SENATORS Pray you, let's to him.
Exeunt omnes.

312 **pounds** pound-weights 312 **to's** to his 312 **process** due process of law 315 **What** why 320 **bolted** refined (literally, sifted) 323 **answer, by a lawful form** meet the charges according to the forms of law 324 **to his utmost peril** at the risk of the severest penalty 334 s.d. **omnes** all (Latin)

[Scene II. *Rome. The house of Coriolanus.*]

Enter Coriolanus with Nobles.

CORIOLANUS Let them pull all about mine ears; present me
Death on the wheel or at wild horses' heels;
Or pile ten hills on the Tarpeian rock,
That the precipitation might down stretch
Below the beam of sight; yet will I still
Be thus to them.

A NOBLE You do the nobler.

CORIOLANUS I muse my mother
Does not approve me further, who was wont
To call them woolen vassals, things created
To buy and sell with groats; to show bare heads
In congregations, to yawn, be still and wonder,
When one but of my ordinance stood up
To speak of peace or war.

Enter Volumnia.

I talk of you:
Why did you wish me milder—Would you have me
False to my nature? Rather say I play
The man I am.

VOLUMNIA O, sir, sir, sir,
I would have had you put your power well on,
Before you had worn it out.

III.ii.2 **the wheel** (by being bound to a wheel and beaten to death; an Elizabethan, not Roman, penalty) 4 **precipitation** steepness 5 **Below the beam of sight** i.e., beyond the range of sight (*beam* = a ray passing from the object to the eye) 7 **muse** wonder 9 **woolen vassals** i.e., rough-dressed members of the lowest class 10 **groats** four-penny coins 12 **ordinance** rank

CORIOLANUS Let go.

VOLUMNIA You might have been enough the man you are,
With striving less to be so. Lesser had been
The thwartings of your dispositions, if
You had not showed them how ye were disposed
Ere they lacked power to cross you.

CORIOLANUS Let them hang.

VOLUMNIA Ay, and burn too.

Enter Menenius with the Senators.

MENENIUS Come, come, you have been too rough, something too rough;
You must return and mend it.

SENATOR There's no remedy,
Unless, by not so doing, our good city
Cleave in the midst and perish.

VOLUMNIA Pray be counseled;
I have a heart as little apt as yours,
But yet a brain that leads my use of anger
To better vantage.

MENENIUS Well said, noble woman!
Before he should thus stoop to th' herd, but that
The violent fit o' th' time craves it as physic
For the whole state, I would put mine armor on,
Which I can scarcely bear.

CORIOLANUS What must I do?

MENENIUS Return to th' tribunes.

CORIOLANUS Well, what then? What then?

MENENIUS Repent what you have spoke.

18 **Let go** enough of that 21 **dispositions** inclinations 25 **something** somewhat 26–28 **There's ... midst** there's no help for it; (you must compromise;) else, because of your failure to do so, our good city may be split in two 29 **apt** compliant 33 **physic** medical treatment

CORIOLANUS For them! I cannot do it to the gods;
Must I then do't to them?

VOLUMNIA You are too absolute;
Though therein you can never be too noble
But when extremities speak. I have heard you say,
Honor and policy, like unsevered friends,
I' th' war do grow together. Grant that, and tell me
In peace what each of them by th' other lose
That they combine not there.

CORIOLANUS Tush, tush!

MENENIUS A good demand.

VOLUMNIA If it be honor in your wars to seem
The same you are not, which for your best ends
You adopt your policy, how is it less or worse
That it shall hold companionship in peace
With honor as in war; since that to both
It stands in like request?

CORIOLANUS Why force you this?

VOLUMNIA Because that now it lies you on to speak
To th' people, not by your own instruction,
Nor by th' matter which your heart prompts you,
But with such words that are but roted in
Your tongue, though but bastards and syllables
Of no allowance to your bosom's truth.
Now, this no more dishonors you at all
Than to take in a town with gentle words,
Which else would put you to your fortune and
The hazard of much blood.
I would dissemble with my nature, where
My fortunes and my friends at stake required

41 **when extremities speak** when the most critical situations demand. 42 **unsevered** inseparable 48 **adopt** adopt as 49 **it** (pretense, "to seem/The same you are not") 51 **stands in like request** is equally in demand 51 **force** urge 52 **it lies you on** it is your duty 55 **roted** learned by rote 56–57 **but . . . truth** only false expressions of your heart's true understanding wholly unacceptable to it 59 **take in** capture 60 **put you to your fortune** force you to take your chances (in war)

I should do so in honor. I am in this
Your wife, your son, these senators, the nobles;
And you will rather show our general louts
How you can frown than spend a fawn upon 'em
For the inheritance of their loves and safeguard
Of what that want might ruin.

MENENIUS Noble lady!
Come, go with us; speak fair; you may salve so,
Not what is dangerous present, but the loss
Of what is past.

VOLUMNIA I prithee now, my son,
Go to them with this bonnet in thy hand;
And thus far having stretched it (here be with them),
Thy knee bussing the stones (for in such business
Action is eloquence, and the eyes of th' ignorant
More learnèd than the ears), waving thy head,
Which often thus correcting thy stout heart,
Now humble as the ripest mulberry
That will not hold the handling; or say to them,
Thou art their soldier, and being bred in broils
Hast not the soft way which, thou dost confess,
Were fit for thee to use, as they to claim,
In asking their good loves; but thou wilt frame
Thyself, forsooth, hereafter theirs, so far
As thou hast power and person.

MENENIUS This but done,
Even as she speaks, why, their hearts were yours;
For they have pardons, being asked, as free
As words to little purpose.

64 **in honor** in honor bound (*not* Coriolanus' understanding of "Honor") 64 **I am in this** I speak in this for (implying also, "I stand in place of") 66 **general** common 68 **inheritance** possession 69 **that want** (of their loves) 74–80 (the text may be corrupt) 75 **bussing** kissing (touching) 77 **waving** bowing up and down 78 **Which** (subject of "correcting" in a nominative absolute; the sentence is urgent; the syntax, sketchy) 78 **stout** proud 80 **or** (marks the turn from "action" to "eloquence," line 76) 85 **forsooth** in truth 88 **free** liberal (to grant)

VOLUMNIA Prithee now,
Go, and be ruled; although I know thou hadst rather
Follow thine enemy in a fiery gulf
Than flatter him in a bower.

Enter Cominius.

Here is Cominius.

COMINIUS I have been i' th' marketplace; and, sir, 'tis fit
You make strong party, or defend yourself
By calmness or by absence. All's in anger.

MENENIUS Only fair speech.

COMINIUS I think 'twill serve, if he
Can thereto frame his spirit.

VOLUMNIA He must, and will.
Prithee now, say you will, and go about it.

CORIOLANUS Must I go show them my unbarbed sconce? Must I
With my base tongue give to my noble heart
A lie that it must bear? Well, I will do't.
Yet, were there but this single plot to lose,
This mold of Marcius, they to dust should grind it,
And throw't against the wind. To th' marketplace!
You have put me now to such a part which never
I shall discharge to th' life.

COMINIUS Come, come, we'll prompt you.

VOLUMNIA I prithee now, sweet son, as thou has said
My praises made thee first a soldier, so,
To have my praise for this, perform a part
Thou hast not done before.

CORIOLANUS Well, I must do't.

91 **in a fiery gulf** into an abyss of flame 92 **bower** ladies' chamber 93 **marketplace** i.e., Forum of ancient Rome 94 **make strong party** maintain your side strongly 99 **unbarbed sconce** unarmed head ("sconce" often used in comic contexts) 102 **plot** (of earth) 103 **mold** (both "frame" and "earth"; cf. V.iii.22) 105 **part** (in a play) 106 **discharge** perform

Away, my disposition, and possess me
Some harlot's spirit! My throat of war be turned,
Which quired with my drum, into a pipe
Small as an eunuch or the virgin voice
That babies lulls asleep! The smiles of knaves
Tent in my cheeks, and schoolboys' tears take up
The glasses of my sight! A beggar's tongue
Make motion through my lips, and my armed knees,
Who bowed but in my stirrup, bend like his
That hath received an alms! I will not do't;
Lest I surcease to honor mine own truth,
And by my body's action teach my mind
A most inherent baseness.

VOLUMNIA At thy choice then.
To beg of thee, it is my more dishonor
Than thou of them. Come all to ruin! Let
Thy mother rather feel they pride than fear
Thy dangerous stoutness, for I mock at death
With as big heart as thou. Do as thou list.
Thy valiantness was mine, thou suck'st it from me,
But owe thy pride thyself.

CORIOLANUS Pray, be content:
Mother, I am going to the marketplace;
Chide me no more. I'll mountebank their loves,
Cog their hearts from them, and come home beloved
Of all the trades in Rome. Look, I am going.
Commend me to my wife. I'll return consul;
Or never trust to what my tongue can do
I' th' way of flattery further.

112 **harlot** rascal (used of both sexes) 113 **quired** sang harmoniously 113 **pipe** i.e., voice 116 **take up** possess 117 **The glasses of my sight** my eyeballs 121 **surcease** cease 123 **inherent** firmly settled 126–27 **feel . . . stoutness** suffer the effects of thy pride, but not fear the danger of it (*stoutness* = obstinacy, as in North, nearly equal to "pride"; cf. line 78) 127 **thou list** you please 130 **owe** own, have 132 **mountebank** win their loves by tricky actions (cf. a "mountebank," a quack doctor, who puts on an act to sell his wares) 133 **Cog** cheat

VOLUMNIA Do your will. *Exit Volumnia.*

COMINIUS Away, the tribunes do attend you. Arm yourself
To answer mildly; for they are prepared
With accusations, as I hear, more strong
Than are upon you yet.

CORIOLANUS The word is "mildly." Pray you, let us go.
Let them accuse me by invention, I
Will answer in mine honor.

MENENIUS Ay, but mildly.

CORIOLANUS Well, mildly be it then—mildly. *Exeunt.*

[Scene III. *Rome. The Forum.*]

Enter Sicinius and Brutus.

BRUTUS In this point charge him home, that he affects
Tyrannical power. If he evade us there,
Enforce him with his envy to the people,
And that the spoil got on the Antiates
Was ne'er distributed.

Enter an Aedile.

What, will he come?

AEDILE He's coming.

BRUTUS How accompanied?

142 word password **143 accuse me by invention** invent accusations against me **144 in** in a way consistent with **III.iii.1 charge him home** press your accusations against him to the limit **1 affects** aims at **3 Enforce him** press him hard **3 envy** ill-will **4 got on** won from

AEDILE With old Menenius and those senators
That always favored him.

SICINIUS Have you a catalog
Of all the voices that we have procured,
Set down by th' poll?

AEDILE I have; 'tis ready.

SICINIUS Have you collected them by tribes?

AEDILE I have.

SICINIUS Assemble presently the people hither:
And when they hear me say "It shall be so
I' th' right and strength o' th' commons," be it either
For death, for fine, or banishment, then let them,
If I say "Fine," cry "Fine!"—if "Death," cry "Death!"
Insisting on the old prerogative
And power i' th' truth o' th' cause.

AEDILE I shall inform them.

BRUTUS And when such time they have begun to cry,
Let them not cease, but with a din confused
Enforce the present execution
Of what we chance to sentence.

AEDILE Very well.

SICINIUS Make them be strong, and ready for this hint,
When we shall hap to give't them.

BRUTUS Go about it. [*Exit Aedile.*]
Put him to choler straight. He hath been used
Ever to conquer and to have his worth

10 **by th' poll** by counting heads 12 **presently** at once (cf. line 21) 18 **i' th' truth o' th' cause** resting in the justice of the case 19 **when such time** at such time when 21 **Enforce** press for 23 **hint** opportunity 25 **Put him to** drive him to 26 **his worth** his pennyworth, i.e., his fill

Of contradiction. Being once chafed, he cannot
Be reined again to temperance; then he speaks
What's in his heart, and that is there which looks
With us to break his neck.

Enter Coriolanus, Menenius, and Cominius, with others.

SICINIUS Well, here he comes.

MENENIUS Calmly, I do beseech you.

CORIOLANUS Ay, as an ostler, that for th' poorest piece
Will bear the knave by th' volume. Th' honored gods
Keep Rome in safety, and the chairs of justice
Supplied with worthy men! Plant love among's!
Throng our large temples with the shows of peace,
And not our streets with war!

FIRST SENATOR Amen, amen.

MENENIUS A noble wish.

Enter the Aedile, with the Plebeians.

SICINIUS Draw near, ye people.

AEDILE List to your tribunes. Audience! peace, I say!

CORIOLANUS First, hear me speak.

BOTH TRIBUNES Well, say. Peace, ho!

CORIOLANUS Shall I be charged no further than this present?
Must all determine here?

SICINIUS I do demand,
If you submit you to the people's voices,
Allow their officers, and are content

29–30 **looks/With us** promises in harmony with our intent 32 **piece** coin 33 **bear the knave by th' volume** endure being called knave enough times to fill a book 40 **Audience** give ear 42 **this present** this immediate occasion 43 **determine** reach a conclusion 43 **demand** ask 45 **Allow** acknowledge

To suffer lawful censure for such faults
As shall be proved upon you.

CORIOLANUS I am content.

MENENIUS Lo, citizens, he says he is content.
The warlike service he has done, consider; think
Upon the wounds his body bears, which show
Like graves i' th' holy churchyard.

CORIOLANUS Scratches with briers,
Scars to move laughter only.

MENENIUS Consider further,
That when he speaks not like a citizen,
You find him like a soldier. Do not take
His rougher accents for malicious sounds,
But, as I say, such as become a soldier
Rather than envy you.

COMINIUS Well, well, no more.

CORIOLANUS What is the matter
That, being passed for consul with full voice,
I am so dishonored that the very hour
You take it off again?

SICINIUS Answer to us.

CORIOLANUS Say, then. 'Tis true, I ought so.

SICINIUS We charge you, that you have contrived to take
From Rome all seasoned office, and to wind
Yourself into a power tyrannical,
For which you are a traitor to the people.

CORIOLANUS How! Traitor!

MENENIUS Nay, temperately! Your promise.

54 **like a soldier** 57 **envy** express malice towards 64 **seasoned** established (or "moderate," "well moderated") 64–65 **wind/Yourself into** make your way by indirect and crooked means

CORIOLANUS The fires i' th' lowest hell fold in the people!
Call me their traitor, thou injurious tribune!
Within thine eyes sat twenty thousand deaths,
In thy hands clutched as many millions, in
Thy lying tongue both numbers, I would say
"Thou liest" unto thee with a voice as free
As I do pray the gods.

SICINIUS Mark you this, people?

ALL [CITIZENS] To th' rock, to th' rock with him!

SICINIUS Peace!
We need not put new matter to his charge.
What you have seen him do and heard him speak,
Beating your officers, cursing yourselves,
Opposing laws with strokes, and here defying
Those whose great power must try him—even this,
So criminal and in such capital kind,
Deserves th' extremest death.

BRUTUS But since he hath
Served well for Rome——

CORIOLANUS What do you prate of service?

BRUTUS I talk of that that know it.

CORIOLANUS You!

MENENIUS Is this the promise that you made your mother?

COMINIUS Know, I pray you——

CORIOLANUS I'll know no further.
Let them pronounce the steep Tarpeian death,
Vagabond exile, flaying, pent to linger
But with a grain a day, I would not buy
Their mercy at the price of one fair word,

69 injurious insulting **70 Within** if within **73 free** unrestrained **81 capital** (defined by line 82) **88 steep Tarpeian death** cf. line 103 **89 pent** i.e., "Let them pronounce" the sentence of being "pent," imprisoned

Nor check my courage for what they can give,
To have't with saying "Good morrow."

SICINIUS For that he has
(As much as in him lies) from time to time
Envied against the people, seeking means
To pluck away their power, as now at last
Given hostile strokes, and that not in the presence
Of dreaded justice, but on the ministers
That do distribute it—in the name o' th' people,
And in the power of us the tribunes, we,
Even from this instant, banish him our city,
In peril of precipitation
From off the rock Tarpeian, never more
To enter our Rome gates. I' th' people's name,
I say it shall be so.

ALL [CITIZENS] It shall be so, it shall be so! Let him away!
He's banished, and it shall be so.

COMINIUS Hear me, my masters and my common friends——

SICINIUS He's sentenced; no more hearing.

COMINIUS Let me speak.
I have been consul, and can show for Rome
Her enemies' marks upon me. I do love
My country's good with a respect more tender,
More holy and profound, than mine own life,
My dear wife's estimate, her womb's increase
And treasure of my loins; then if I would
Speak that—

SICINIUS We know your drift. Speak what?

BRUTUS There's no more to be said, but he is banished
As enemy to the people and his country.
It shall be so.

92 **courage** spirit 94 **as in him lies** as lies in his power 95 **Envied against** shown malice towards 96 **as now** with respect to this occasion (or, "now," "as" being redundant) 97 **not** not only 114 **estimate** worth

ALL [CITIZENS] It shall be so, it shall be so.

CORIOLANUS You common cry of curs, whose breath
I hate
As reek o' th' rotten fens, whose loves I prize
As the dead carcasses of unburied men
That do corrupt my air, I banish you.
And here remain with your uncertainty!
Let every feeble rumor shake your hearts!
Your enemies, with nodding of their plumes,
Fan you into despair! Have the power still
To banish your defenders, till at length
Your ignorance (which finds not till it feels,
Making but reservation of yourselves,
Still your own foes) deliver you as most
Abated captives to some nation
That won you without blows! Despising
For you the city, thus I turn my back.
There is a world elsewhere.

Exeunt Coriolanus, Cominius, [Menenius,] with the other Senators.

AEDILE The people's enemy is gone, is gone!

ALL [CITIZENS] Our enemy is banished, he is gone!
Hoo—oo!

They all shout, and throw up their caps.

SICINIUS Go see him out at gates, and follow him,
As he hath followed you, with all despite;
Give him deserved vexation. Let a guard
Attend us through the city.

ALL [CITIZENS] Come, come, let's see him out at gates;
come!
The gods preserve our noble tribunes! Come.

Exeunt.

120 **cry** pack 121 **reek** mist 129 **finds not till it feels** does not understand until it suffers the consequences 130 **Making . . . yourselves** saving only yourselves 131 **Still** ever 132 **Abated** beaten down 139 **despite** contempt 140 **Give him deserved vexation** torment him as he deserves

ACT IV

[Scene I. *Rome. Before a gate of the city.*]

Enter Coriolanus, Volumnia, Virgilia, Menenius, Cominius, with the young Nobility of Rome.

CORIOLANUS Come, leave your tears; a brief farewell. The beast
With many heads butts me away. Nay, mother,
Where is your ancient courage? You were used
To say extremities was the trier of spirits;
That common chances common men could bear;
That when the sea was calm all boats alike
Showed mastership in floating; fortune's blows
When most struck home, being gentle wounded craves
A noble cunning. You were used to load me
With precepts that would make invincible
The heart that conned them.

VIRGILIA O heavens! O heavens!

CORIOLANUS Nay, I prithee, woman—

IV.i.4 **extremities was** (plural subject permissible in Elizabethan usage) 7 **fortune's blows** (supply introductory "that") 7–9 **fortune's ... cunning** (when fortune's blows strike hardest, to act the gentleman though wounded demands a noble use of intelligence) 11 **conned** studied

VOLUMNIA Now the red pestilence strike all trades in Rome,
And occupations perish!

CORIOLANUS What, what, what!
I shall be loved when I am lacked. Nay, mother,
Resume that spirit when you were wont to say,
If you had been the wife of Hercules,
Six of his labors you'd have done, and saved
Your husband so much sweat. Cominius,
Droop not; adieu. Farewell, my wife, my mother.
I'll do well yet. Thou old and true Menenius,
Thy tears are salter than a younger man's,
And venomous to thine eyes. My sometime general,
I have seen thee stern, and thou hast oft beheld
Heart-hard'ning spectacles; tell these sad women
'Tis fond to wail inevitable strokes,
As 'tis to laugh at 'em. My mother, you wot well
My hazards still have been your solace, and
Believe't not lightly—though I go alone,
Like to a lonely dragon, that his fen
Makes feared and talked of more than seen—your son
Will or exceed the common or be caught
With cautelous baits and practice.

VOLUMNIA My first son,
Whither wilt thou go? Take good Cominius
With thee awhile. Determine on some course
More than a wild exposture to each chance
That starts i' th' way before thee.

CORIOLANUS O the gods!

COMINIUS I'll follow thee a month, devise with thee
Where thou shalt rest, that thou mayst hear of us

23 **sometime** former 26 **fond** foolish 27 **wot** know 28 **solace** interest
32 **or exceed the common** either surpass the usual achievements of men
33 **cautelous** crafty 33 **practice** treachery 36 **exposture** exposure

And we of thee. So, if the time thrust forth
A cause for thy repeal, we shall not send
O'er the vast world to seek a single man,
And lose advantage, which doth ever cool
I' th' absence of the needer.

CORIOLANUS Fare ye well!
Thou hast years upon thee; and thou art too full
Of the wars' surfeits to go rove with one
That's yet unbruised. Bring me but out at gate.
Come, my sweet wife, my dearest mother, and
My friends of noble touch; when I am forth,
Bid me farewell, and smile. I pray you, come.
While I remain above the ground you shall
Hear from me still, and never of me aught
But what is like me formerly.

MENENIUS That's worthily
As any ear can hear. Come, let's not weep.
If I could shake off but one seven years
From these old arms and legs, by the good gods,
I'd with thee every foot.

CORIOLANUS Give me thy hand.
Come. *Exeunt.*

[Scene II. *Rome. Near the gate.*]

Enter the two Tribunes, Sicinius and Brutus, with the Aedile.

SICINIUS Bid them all home; he's gone, and we'll no further.

41 **repeal** recall 43 **advantage** the opportune moment 44 **needer** (of "advantage") 47 **Bring** conduct 49 **noble touch** tested nobility (cf. "touchstone") 57 **I'd** I would (go) IV.ii.1 **them all** (the plebeians)

The nobility are vexed, whom we see have sided
In his behalf.

BRUTUS Now we have shown our power,
Let us seem humbler after it is done
Than when it was a-doing.

SICINIUS Bid them home.
Say their great enemy is gone, and they
Stand in their ancient strength.

BRUTUS Dismiss them home. [*Exit Aedile.*]
Here comes his mother.

Enter Volumnia, Virgilia, and Menenius.

SICINIUS Let's not meet her.

BRUTUS Why?

SICINIUS They say she's mad.

BRUTUS They have ta'en note of us. Keep on your way.

VOLUMNIA O, y'are well met. Th' hoarded plague o' th' gods
Requite your love!

MENENIUS Peace, peace, be not so loud.

VOLUMNIA If that I could for weeping, you should hear—
Nay, and you shall hear some. [*To Brutus*] Will you be gone?

VIRGILIA. [*To Sicinius*] You shall stay too. I would I had the power
To say so to my husband.

SICINIUS Are you mankind?

VOLUMNIA Ay, fool; is that a shame? Note but this, fool.
Was not a man my father? Hadst thou foxship

11 **hoarded** stored up (for punishment) 16 **mankind** mad, of manlike violence (Sicinius' meaning; but Volumnia takes it in the sense of "human") 18 **foxship** cunning

To banish him that struck more blows for Rome
Than thou hast spoken words?

SICINIUS O blessed heavens!

VOLUMNIA Moe noble blows than ever thou wise words;
And for Rome's good. I'll tell thee what—yet go!
Nay, but thou shalt stay too. I would my son
Were in Arabia, and thy tribe before him,
His good sword in his hand.

SICINIUS What then?

VIRGILIA What then!
He'd make an end of thy posterity.

VOLUMNIA Bastards and all.
Good man, the wounds that he does bear for Rome!

MENENIUS Come, come, peace.

SICINIUS I would he had continued to his country
As he began, and not unknit himself
The noble knot he made.

BRUTUS I would he had.

VOLUMNIA "I would he had!" 'Twas you incensed the rabble;
Cats, that can judge as fitly of his worth
As I can of those mysteries which heaven
Will not have earth to know.

BRUTUS Pray, let's go.

VOLUMNIA Now, pray, sir, get you gone;
You have done a brave deed. Ere you go, hear this:
As far as doth the Capitol exceed
The meanest house in Rome, so far my son—
This lady's husband here, this, do you see?
Whom you have banished—does exceed you all.

BRUTUS Well, well, we'll leave you.

21 **Moe** more 24 **Arabia** a desert (outside Roman law and order) 32 **noble knot he made** (bond to Rome made by his heroic deeds)

SICINIUS Why stay we to be baited
With one that wants her wits? *Exit Tribunes.*

VOLUMNIA Take my prayers with you.
I would the gods had nothing else to do
But to confirm my curses! Could I meet 'em
But once a day, it would unclog my heart
Of what lies heavy to't.

MENENIUS You have told them home,
And by my troth you have cause. You'll sup with me?

VOLUMNIA Anger's my meat; I sup upon myself,
And so shall starve with feeding. Come, let's go.
Leave this faint puling, and lament as I do,
In anger, Juno-like. Come, come, come.
Exeunt [Volumnia and Virgilia].

MENENIUS Fie, fie, fie! *Exit.*

[Scene III. *Between Rome and Antium.*]

Enter a Roman and a Volsce.

ROMAN I know you well, sir, and you know me: your name, I think, is Adrian.

VOLSCE It is so, sir. Truly, I have forgot you.

ROMAN I am a Roman; and my services are, as you are, against 'em. Know you me yet?

VOLSCE Nicanor? No!

ROMAN The same, sir.

VOLSCE You had more beard when I last saw you; but

44 With by 48 told them home ("hit them where it hurts") 52 puling whining IV.iii.5 'em the Romans

your favor is well appeared by your tongue. What's the news in Rome? I have a note from the Volscian state to find you out there. You have well saved me a day's journey.

ROMAN There hath been in Rome strange insurrections; the people against the senators, patricians, and nobles.

VOLSCE Hath been! Is it ended then? Our state thinks not so; they are in a most warlike preparation, and hope to come upon them in the heat of their division.

ROMAN The main blaze of it is past, but a small thing would make it flame again; for the nobles receive so to heart the banishment of that worthy Coriolanus, that they are in a ripe aptness to take all power from the people and to pluck from them their tribunes forever. This lies glowing, I can tell you, and is almost mature for the violent breaking out.

VOLSCE Coriolanus banished!

ROMAN Banished, sir.

VOLSCE You will be welcome with this intelligence, Nicanor.

ROMAN The day serves well for them now. I have heard it said the fittest time to corrupt a man's wife is when she's fall'n out with her husband. Your noble Tullus Aufidius will appear well in these wars, his great opposer, Coriolanus, being now in no request of his country.

VOLSCE He cannot choose. I am most fortunate thus accidentally to encounter you. You have ended my business, and I will merrily accompany you home.

9 **favor** face 9 **appeared** made to appear 10 **a note** instructions 21 **receive** take 32 **them** (the Volscians) 36–37 **in no request of** in no demand by 38 **cannot choose** (but appear well)

ROMAN I shall, between this and supper, tell you most strange things from Rome, all tending to the good of their adversaries. Have you an army ready, say you?

VOLSCE A most royal one; the centurions and their charges, distinctly billeted, already in th' entertainment, and to be on foot at an hour's warning.

ROMAN I am joyful to hear of their readiness, and am the man, I think, that shall set them in present action. So, sir, heartily well met, and most glad of your company.

VOLSCE You take my part from me, sir. I have the most cause to be glad of yours.

ROMAN Well, let us go together. *Exeunt.*

[Scene IV. *Antium. Before Aufidius' house.*]

Enter Coriolanus in mean apparel, disguised and muffled.

CORIOLANUS A goodly city is this Antium. City,
'Tis I that made thy widows: many an heir
Of these fair edifices 'fore my wars
Have I heard groan and drop. Then know me not,
Lest that thy wives with spits and boys with stones
In puny battle slay me.

Enter a Citizen.

Save you, sir.

41 **this** this time 45 **centurions** commanders of smallest unit (century) of a Roman legion 46 **charges** men under them 46 **distinctly billeted** separately enrolled 46–47 **in th' entertainment** in service (maintained by the army) IV.iv.3 **'fore my wars** before my attacks 6 **Save you** God save you

CITIZEN And you.

CORIOLANUS Direct me, if it be your will,
Where great Aufidius lies. Is he in Antium?

CITIZEN He is, and feasts the nobles of the state
At his house this night.

CORIOLANUS Which is his house, beseech you?

CITIZEN This here before you.

CORIOLANUS Thank you, sir: farewell.
Exit Citizen.
O world, thy slippery turns! Friends now fast sworn,
Whose double bosoms seems to wear one heart,
Whose hours, whose bed, whose meal and exercise
Are still together, who twin, as 'twere, in love
Unseparable, shall within this hour,
On a dissension of a doit, break out
To bitterest enmity. So fellest foes,
Whose passions and whose plots have broke their sleep
To take the one the other, by some chance,
Some trick not worth an egg, shall grow dear friends
And interjoin their issues. So with me:
My birthplace hate I, and my love's upon
This enemy town. I'll enter. If he slay me,
He does fair justice; if he give me way,
I'll do his country service. *Exit.*

8 **lies** lives 13 **seems** (perhaps an old plural in -s) 17 **of a doit** worth a doit (coin of little value; cf. I.v.6) 18 **fellest** fiercest 21 **trick** trifle 22 **interjoin their issues** let their children intermarry; become close partners in action ("issues" in sense of "deeds"?)

[Scene V. *Antium. A hall in Aufidius' house.*]

Music plays. Enter a Servingman.

FIRST SERVINGMAN Wine, wine, wine! What service is here! I think our fellows are asleep. [*Exit.*]

Enter another Servingman.

SECOND SERVINGMAN Where's Cotus? My master calls for him. Cotus! *Exit.*

Enter Coriolanus.

CORIOLANUS A goodly house. The feast smells well, but I
Appear not like a guest.

Enter the First Servingman.

FIRST SERVINGMAN What would you have, friend? Whence are you? Here's no place for you: pray go to the door! *Exit.*

CORIOLANUS I have deserved no better entertainment,
In being Coriolanus.

Enter Second Servingman.

SECOND SERVINGMAN Whence are you, sir? Has the porter his eyes in his head that he gives entrance to such companions? Pray get you out.

CORIOLANUS Away!

SECOND SERVINGMAN "Away!" Get you away.

CORIOLANUS Now thou'rt troublesome.

IV.v.9 **to the door** out of doors 14 **companions** fellows (in bad sense)

SECOND SERVINGMAN Are you so brave? I'll have you talked with anon.

Enter Third Servingman; the first meets him.

THIRD SERVINGMAN What fellow's this?

FIRST SERVINGMAN A strange one as ever I looked on! I cannot get him out o' th' house. Prithee call my master to him.

THIRD SERVINGMAN What have you to do here, fellow? Pray you avoid the house.

CORIOLANUS Let me but stand; I will not hurt your hearth.

THIRD SERVINGMAN What are you?

CORIOLANUS A gentleman.

THIRD SERVINGMAN A marv'lous poor one.

CORIOLANUS True, so I am.

THIRD SERVINGMAN Pray you, poor gentleman, take up some other station; here's no place for you. Pray you avoid. Come.

CORIOLANUS Follow your function, go and batten on cold bits.

Pushes him away from him.

THIRD SERVINGMAN What, you will not? Prithee, tell my master what a strange guest he has here.

SECOND SERVINGMAN And I shall.

Exit Second Servingman.

THIRD SERVINGMAN Where dwell'st thou?

CORIOLANUS Under the canopy.

THIRD SERVINGMAN Under the canopy!

CORIOLANUS Ay.

18 **brave** impudent 19 **anon** soon 25 **avoid** leave 30 **marv'lous** strangely 35 **Follow your function** do your regular work 35 **batten** grow fat 41 **canopy** sky (cf. "canopy" over a throne)

THIRD SERVINGMAN Where's that?

CORIOLANUS I' th' city of kites and crows.

THIRD SERVINGMAN I' th' city of kites and crows! What an ass it is! Then thou dwell'st with daws too?

CORIOLANUS No, I serve not thy master.

THIRD SERVINGMAN How, sir! Do you meddle with my master?

CORIOLANUS Ay; 'tis an honester service than to meddle with thy mistress. Thou prat'st, and prat'st; serve with thy trencher. Hence!

Beats him away.

Enter Aufidius with the [*Second*] *Servingman.*

AUFIDIUS Where is this fellow?

SECOND SERVINGMAN Here, sir. I'd have beaten him like a dog, but for disturbing the lords within.

AUFIDIUS Whence com'st thou? What wouldst thou?
Thy name?
Why speak'st not? Speak, man. What's thy name?

CORIOLANUS [*Unmuffling*] If, Tullus,
Not yet thou know'st me, and, seeing me, dost not
Think me for the man I am, necessity
Commands me name myself.

AUFIDIUS What is thy name?

CORIOLANUS A name unmusical to the Volscians' ears,
And harsh in sound to thine.

AUFIDIUS Say, what's thy name?
Thou hast a grim appearance, and thy face
Bears a command in't. Though thy tackle's torn,
Thou show'st a noble vessel. What's thy name?

47 **daws** (foolish birds) 53 **trencher** wooden plate 60 **Think me** i.e., take me 65 **a command** i.e., a look of authority 66 **show'st** appear'st

CORIOLANUS Prepare thy brow to frown. Know'st thou
me yet?

AUFIDIUS I know thee not. Thy name!

CORIOLANUS My name is Caius Marcius, who hath done
To thee particularly, and to all the Volsces,
Great hurt and mischief; thereto witness may
My surname, Coriolanus. The painful service,
The extreme dangers, and the drops of blood
Shed for my thankless country, are requited
But with that surname—a good memory
And witness of the malice and displeasure
Which thou shouldst bear me. Only that name
remains.
The cruelty and envy of the people,
Permitted by our dastard nobles, who
Have all forsook me, hath devoured the rest;
And suffered me by th' voice of slaves to be
Whooped out of Rome. Now, this extremity
Hath brought me to thy hearth; not out of hope
(Mistake me not) to save my life; for if
I had feared death, of all the men i' th' world
I would have 'voided thee; but in mere spite,
To be full quit of those my banishers,
Stand I before thee here. Then if thou hast
A heart of wreak in thee, that wilt revenge
Thine own particular wrongs and stop those maims
Of shame seen through thy country, speed thee
straight
And make my misery serve thy turn. So use it
That my revengeful services may prove
As benefits to thee; for I will fight
Against my cank'red country with the spleen
Of all the under fiends. But if so be

71 **mischief** serious harm 72 **painful** laborious 75 **memory** memorial 78 **envy** ill-will 87 **full quit of** fully revenged on (cf. "quits with") 89 **heart of wreak** vengeful heart 90–91 **maims/Of shame** shameful wounds (e.g., the Roman occupation of Corioli) 95 **cank'red** corrupted (by ingratitude and envy) 95 **spleen** rage 96 **under fiends** devils in hell

Thou dar'st not this and that to prove more fortunes
Thou'rt tired, then, in a word, I also am
Longer to live most weary, and present
My throat to thee and to thy ancient malice;
Which not to cut would show thee but a fool,
Since I have ever followed thee with hate,
Drawn tuns of blood out of thy country's breast,
And cannot live but to thy shame, unless
It be to do thee service.

AUFIDIUS O Marcius, Marcius!
Each work thou hast spoke hath weeded from my heart
A root of ancient envy. If Jupiter
Should from yond cloud speak divine things,
And say " 'Tis true," I'd not believe them more
Than thee, all noble Marcius. Let me twine
Mine arms about that body, where against
My grainèd ash an hundred times hath broke
And scarred the moon with splinters. Here I clip
The anvil of my sword, and do contest
As hotly and as nobly with thy love
As ever in ambitious strength I did
Contend against thy valor. Know thou first,
I loved the maid I married; never man
Sighed truer breath. But that I see thee here,
Thou noble thing, more dances my rapt heart
Than when I first my wedded mistress saw
Bestride my threshold. Why, thou Mars, I tell thee,
We have a power on foot, and I had purpose
Once more to hew thy target from thy brawn,
Or lose mine arm for't. Thou hast beat me out
Twelve several times, and I have nightly since
Dreamt of encounters 'twixt thyself and me.
We have been down together in my sleep,

97 **prove more fortunes** try the chances of fortune further 103 **tuns** casks 112 **grainèd ash** spear of ash, the grain showing 113 **clip** embrace 119 **that** because 120 **rapt** enraptured 123 **power on foot** force in the field 124 **target** shield 124 **brawn** brawny arm 125 **out** completely

Unbuckling helms, fisting each other's throat,
And waked half dead with nothing. Worthy
Marcius,
Had we no other quarrel else to Rome but that
Thou art thence banished, we would muster all
From twelve to seventy, and pouring war
Into the bowels of ungrateful Rome,
Like a bold flood o'erbeat. O, come, go in,
And take our friendly senators by th' hands,
Who now are here, taking their leaves of me
Who am prepared against your territories,
Though not for Rome itself.

CORIOLANUS You bless me, gods!

AUFIDIUS Therefore, most absolute sir, if thou wilt
have
The leading of thine own revenges, take
Th' one half of my commission, and set down—
As best thou art experienced, since thou know'st
Thy country's strength and weakness—thine own
ways,
Whether to knock against the gates of Rome,
Or rudely visit them in parts remote
To fright them ere destroy. But come in.
Let me commend thee first to those that shall
Say yea to thy desires. A thousand welcomes!
And more a friend than e'er an enemy;
Yet, Marcius, that was much. Your hand:
most welcome! *Exeunt.*

Enter two of the Servingmen.

FIRST SERVINGMAN Here's a strange alteration!

SECOND SERVINGMAN By my hand, I had thought to have strucken him with a cudgel; and yet my mind gave me his clothes made a false report of him.

130 **waked** (I have) awakened 135 **o'erbeat** surge over (the land) 140 **absolute** perfect 142 **my commission** the forces under me 142 **set down** determine 151 s.d **Enter** (perhaps they come forward from backstage, since neither has been assigned an "*Exit*") 154–55 **my mind gave me** I had an idea

FIRST SERVINGMAN What an arm he has! He turned me about with his finger and his thumb, as one would set up a top.

SECOND SERVINGMAN Nay, I knew by his face that there was something in him; he had, sir, a kind of face, methought—I cannot tell how to term it.

FIRST SERVINGMAN He had so, looking as it were—would I were hanged, but I thought there was more in him than I could think.

SECOND SERVINGMAN So did I, I'll be sworn. He is simply the rarest man i' th' world.

FIRST SERVINGMAN I think he is; but a greater soldier than he, you wot one.

SECOND SERVINGMAN Who, my master?

FIRST SERVINGMAN Nay, it's no matter for that.

SECOND SERVINGMAN Worth six on him.

FIRST SERVINGMAN Nay, not so neither. But I take him to be the greater soldier.

SECOND SERVINGMAN Faith, look you, one cannot tell how to say that. For the defense of a town our general is excellent.

FIRST SERVINGMAN Ay, and for an assault too.

Enter the Third Servingman.

THIRD SERVINGMAN O slaves, I can tell you news—news, you rascals!

BOTH [FIRST AND SECOND SERVINGMEN] What, what, what? Let's partake.

THIRD SERVINGMAN I would not be a Roman, of all nations; I had as lief be a condemned man.

168–77 (the *First Servingman* is cautiously and cunningly vague in his references to the "greater soldier") 168 wot know 183 lief willingly

BOTH Wherefore? Wherefore?

THIRD SERVINGMAN Why here's he that was wont to thwack our general—Caius Marcius.

FIRST SERVINGMAN Why do you say "thwack our general"?

THIRD SERVINGMAN I do not say "thwack our general," but he was always good enough for him.

SECOND SERVINGMAN Come, we are fellows and friends. He was ever too hard for him; I have heard him say so himself.

FIRST SERVINGMAN He was too hard for him directly, to say the troth on't. Before Corioles he scotched him and notched him like a carbonado.

SECOND SERVINGMAN And he had been cannibally given, he might have boiled and eaten him too.

FIRST SERVINGMAN But more of thy news?

THIRD SERVINGMAN Why, he is so made on here within as if he were son and heir to Mars; set at upper end o' th' table; no question asked him by any of the senators but they stand bald before him. Our general himself makes a mistress of him; sanctifies himself with's hand, and turns up the white o' th' eye to his discourse. But the bottom of the news is, our general is cut i' th' middle and but one half of what he was yesterday, for the other has half by the entreaty and grant of the whole table. He'll go, he says, and sowl the porter of Rome gates by th' ears. He will mow all down before him, and leave his passage polled.

191 **fellows** comrades 194 **directly** plainly 195 **scotched** slashed 196 **carbonado** meat scored with knife, for broiling 200 **so made on** made so much of 203 **bald** bareheaded 205 **sanctifies himself with's hand** touches his hand as if it were a holy relic 205–06 **turns up the white o' th' eye** (in pious wonder) 206 **bottom** last (jokingly for "the climax") 209–10 **has . . . table** i.e., has half because all at the table beg him to take it, and give it to him 210 **sowl** drag 212 **polled** cleared (used of cutting hair)

SECOND SERVINGMAN And he's as like to do't as any man I can imagine.

THIRD SERVINGMAN Do't! He will do't; for look you, sir, he has as many friends as enemies; which friends, sir, as it were, durst not (look you, sir) show themselves (as we term it) his friends whilst he's in directitude.

FIRST SERVINGMAN Directitude! What's that?

THIRD SERVINGMAN But when they shall see, sir, his crest up again and the man in blood, they will out of their burrows (like conies after rain) and revel all with him.

FIRST SERVINGMAN But when goes this forward?

THIRD SERVINGMAN Tomorrow, today, presently. You shall have the drum struck up this afternoon. 'Tis as it were a parcel of their feast, and to be executed ere they wipe their lips.

SECOND SERVINGMAN Why, then we shall have a stirring world again. This peace is nothing but to rust iron, increase tailors, and breed ballad-makers.

FIRST SERVINGMAN Let me have war, say I; it exceeds peace as far as day does night; it's sprightly walking, audible, and full of vent. Peace is a very apoplexy, lethargy; mulled, deaf, sleepy, insensible; a getter of more bastard children than war's a destroyer of men.

SECOND SERVINGMAN 'Tis so; and as wars in some sort may be said to be a ravisher, so it cannot be denied but peace is a great maker of cuckolds.

FIRST SERVINGMAN Ay, and it makes men hate one another.

219 **directitude** (comic mistake for "discredit"?) 222 **crest up** (like an animal aroused) 222 **in blood** in top condition 223 **conies** rabbits 226 **presently** now 228 **parcel** part 235 **audible** of good hearing 235 **full of vent** with plenty of outlets for energy (?: cf. I.i.226) 236 **mulled** dulled (like wine sweetened and heated)

THIRD SERVINGMAN Reason: because they then less need one another. The wars for my money. I hope to see Romans as cheap as Volscians. They are rising, they are rising.

BOTH [FIRST AND SECOND SERVINGMEN] In, in, in, in!
Exeunt.

[Scene VI. *Rome. A public place.*]

Enter the two Tribunes, Sicinius and Brutus.

SICINIUS We hear not of him, neither need we fear him;
His remedies are tame. The present peace
And quietness of the people, which before
Were in wild hurry, here do make his friends
Blush that the world goes well; who rather had,
Though they themselves did suffer by't, behold
Dissentious numbers pest'ring streets than see
Our tradesmen singing in their shops, and going
About their functions friendly.

BRUTUS We stood to't in good time.

Enter Menenius.

Is this Menenius?

SICINIUS 'Tis he, 'tis he. O, he is grown most kind
Of late. Hail, sir!

MENENIUS Hail to you both!

SICINIUS Your Coriolanus is not much missed

247 **rising** getting up from table IV.vi.2 **His remedies are tame** his attempts to "cure" the state are (now) harmless (cf. "dangerous physic," III.i.154) 4 **hurry** commotion 7 **pest'ring** filling with disturbance 10 **stood to't** made an issue of it

But with his friends. The commonwealth doth stand,
And so would do, were he more angry at it.

MENENIUS All's well; and might have been much better, if
He could have temporized.

SICINIUS Where is he, hear you?

MENENIUS Nay, I hear nothing. His mother and his wife
Hear nothing from him.

Enter three or four Citizens.

ALL [CITIZENS] The gods preserve you both!

SICINIUS Good-e'en, our neighbors.

BRUTUS Good-e'en to you all, good-e'en to you all.

FIRST CITIZEN Ourselves, our wives, and children, on our knees,
Are bound to pray for you both.

SICINIUS Live, and thrive!

BRUTUS Farewell, kind neighbors. We wished Coriolanus
Had loved you as we did.

ALL [CITIZENS] Now the gods keep you!

BOTH TRIBUNES Farewell, farewell.

Exeunt Citizens.

SICINIUS This is a happier and more comely time
Than when these fellows ran about the streets
Crying confusion.

BRUTUS Caius Marcius was
A worthy officer i' th' war, but insolent,
O'ercome with pride, ambitious past all thinking,
Self-loving——

20 **Good-e'en** good evening 27 **comely** respectable 29 **Crying confusion** calling for disorder

SICINIUS And affecting one sole throne,
Without assistance.

MENENIUS I think not so.

SICINIUS We should by this, to all our lamentation,
If he had gone forth consul, found it so.

BRUTUS The gods have well prevented it, and Rome
Sits safe and still without him.

Enter an Aedile.

AEDILE Worthy tribunes,
There is a slave, whom we have put in prison,
Reports the Volsces with two several powers
Are ent'red in the Roman territories,
And with the deepest malice of the war
Destroy what lies before 'em.

MENENIUS 'Tis Aufidius,
Who, hearing of our Marcius' banishment,
Thrusts forth his horns again into the world,
Which were inshelled when Marcius stood for Rome,
And durst not once peep out.

SICINIUS Come, what talk you
Of Marcius?

BRUTUS Go see this rumorer whipped. It cannot be
The Volsces dare break with us.

MENENIUS Cannot be!
We have record that very well it can;
And three examples of the like hath been
Within my age. But reason with the fellow,
Before you punish him, where he heard this,
Lest you shall chance to whip your information
And beat the messenger who bids beware
Of what is to be dreaded.

32 **affecting** aiming at 33 **Without assistance** not sharing his powers with others 35 **found** have found 39 **several powers** separate forces 44 **horns** (like a snail) 52 **reason with** talk with

SICINIUS Tell not me:
I know this cannot be.

BRUTUS Not possible.

Enter a Messenger.

MESSENGER The nobles in great earnestness are going
All to the Senate House. Some news is coming
That turns their countenances.

SICINIUS 'Tis this slave—
Go whip him 'fore the people's eyes—his raising,
Nothing but his report.

MESSENGER Yes, worthy sir,
The slave's report is seconded; and more,
More fearful, is delivered.

SICINIUS What more fearful?

MESSENGER It is spoke freely out of many mouths,
How probable I do not know, that Marcius,
Joined with Aufidius, leads a power 'gainst Rome,
And vows revenge as spacious as between
The young'st and oldest thing.

SICINIUS This is most likely!

BRUTUS Raised only that the weaker sort may wish
Good Marcius home again.

SICINIUS The very trick on't.

MENENIUS This is unlikely:
He and Aufidius can no more atone
Than violent'st contrariety.

Enter [a second] Messenger.

SECOND MESSENGER You are sent for to the Senate.
A fearful army, led by Caius Marcius

60 **turns** changes 61 **his raising** his starting (i.e., the rumor; note comma and the following explanatory phrase) 63 **seconded** confirmed (by further reports) 68–69 **as spacious . . . thing** covering the span between youngest and oldest, i.e., the whole population 73 **atone** be reconciled

Associated with Aufidius, rages
Upon our territories, and have already
O'erborne their way, consumed with fire, and took
What lay before them.

Enter Cominius.

COMINIUS O, you have made good work!

MENENIUS What news? What news?

COMINIUS You have holp to ravish your own daughters and
To melt the city leads upon your pates,
To see your wives dishonored to your noses——

MENENIUS What's the news? What's the news?

COMINIUS Your temples burnèd in their cement, and
Your franchises, whereon you stood, confined
Into an auger's bore.

MENENIUS Pray now, your news?—
You have made fair work, I fear me.—Pray, your news?—
If Marcius should be joined wi' th' Volscians—

COMINIUS If!
He is their god; he leads them like a thing
Made by some other deity than Nature,
That shapes man better; and they follow him
Against us brats with no less confidence
Than boys pursuing summer butterflies,
Or butchers killing flies.

MENENIUS You have made good work,
You and your apron-men; you that stood so much
Upon the voice of occupation and
The breath of garlic-eaters!

COMINIUS He'll shake
Your Rome about your ears.

79 **O'erborne their way** (like a stream) overflowed everything in their way 83 **leads** roofs 84 **to** before 87 **franchises, whereon you stood** rights on which you insisted 97 **apron-men** artisans 98 **occupation** manual workers

MENENIUS As Hercules
Did shake down mellow fruit. You have made fair work!

BRUTUS But is this true, sir?

COMINIUS Ay; and you'll look pale
Before you find it other. All the regions
Do smilingly revolt, and who resists
Are mocked for valiant ignorance,
And perish constant fools. Who is't can blame him?
Your enemies and his find something in him.

MENENIUS We are all undone, unless
The noble man have mercy.

COMINIUS Who shall ask it?
The tribunes cannot do't for shame; the people
Deserve such pity of him as the wolf
Does of the shepherds. For his best friends, if they
Should say "Be good to Rome," they charged him even
As those should do that had deserved his hate,
And therein showed like enemies.

MENENIUS 'Tis true:
If he were putting to my house the brand
That should consume it, I have not the face
To say "Beseech you, cease." You have made fair hands,
You and your crafts! You have crafted fair!

COMINIUS You have brought
A trembling upon Rome, such as was never
S' incapable of help.

TRIBUNES Say not we brought it.

106 **constant** loyal 113 **charged** would attack, urge (both senses relevant) 115 **showed** would show 118 **made fair hands** handled matters finely 119 **crafted fair** plied your trade (of cunning) beautifully 121 **S' incapable** so unsusceptible

MENENIUS How! Was't we? We loved him, but, like beasts
And cowardly nobles, gave way unto your clusters,
Who did hoot him out o' th' city.

COMINIUS But I fear
They'll roar him in again. Tullus Aufidius,
The second name of men, obeys his points
As if he were his officer. Desperation
Is all the policy, strength, and defense,
That Rome can make against them.

Enter a troop of Citizens.

MENENIUS Here come the clusters.
And is Aufidius with him? You are they
That made the air unwholesome when you cast
Your stinking greasy caps in hooting at
Coriolanus' exile. Now he's coming,
And not a hair upon a soldier's head
Which will not prove a whip. As many coxcombs
As you threw caps up will he tumble down,
And pay you for your voices. 'Tis no matter;
If he could burn us all into one coal,
We have deserved it.

OMNES Faith, we hear fearful news.

FIRST CITIZEN For mine own part,
When I said banish him, I said 'twas pity.

SECOND CITIZEN And so did I.

THIRD CITIZEN And so did I; and, to say the truth, so did very many of us. That we did, we did for the best; and though we willingly consented to his banishment, yet it was against our will.

COMINIUS Y'are goodly things, you voices!

123 **clusters** crowds 126 **second name of men** second in renown (to Coriolanus) 126 **points** directions (?) 135 **coxcombs** fools' heads (cf. costume of a fool) 137 **voices** votes 138 **coal** piece of burned fuel (cf. charcoal)

MENENIUS You have made
Good work, you and your cry! Shall's to the
Capitol?

COMINIUS O, ay, what else? *Exeunt both.*

SICINIUS Go masters, get you home; be not dismayed;
These are a side that would be glad to have
This true which they so seem to fear. Go home,
And show no sign of fear.

FIRST CITIZEN The gods be good to us! Come, masters, let's home. I ever said we were i' th' wrong when we banished him.

SECOND CITIZEN So did we all. But come, let's home.
Exit Citizens.

BRUTUS I do not like this news.

SICINIUS Nor I.

BRUTUS Let's to the Capitol. Would half my wealth
Would buy this for a lie!

SICINIUS Pray, let's go.
Exeunt Tribunes.

[Scene VII. *A camp not far from Rome.*]

Enter Aufidius with his Lieutenant.

AUFIDIUS Do they still fly to th' Roman?

LIEUTENANT I do not know what witchcraft's in him,
but
Your soldiers use him as the grace 'fore meat,
Their talk at table and their thanks at end;
And you are dark'ned in this action sir,
Even by your own.

148 **cry** pack 148 **Shall's** shall us (we) 151 **side** faction IV.vii.5 **dark'ned** put in the shade 6 **your own** your own men

AUFIDIUS I cannot help it now,
Unless by using means I lame the foot
Of our design. He bears himself more proudlier,
Even to my person, than I thought he would
When first I did embrace him; yet his nature
In that's no changeling, and I must excuse
What cannot be amended.

LIEUTENANT Yet I wish, sir—
I mean for your particular—you had not
Joined in commission with him, but either
Have borne the action of yourself, or else
To him had left it solely.

AUFIDIUS I understand thee well; and be thou sure,
When he shall come to his account, he knows not
What I can urge against him. Although it seems,
And so he thinks, and is no less apparent
To th' vulgar eye, that he bears all things fairly,
And shows good husbandry for the Volscian state,
Fights dragon-like, and does achieve as soon
As draw his sword. Yet he hath left undone
That which shall break his neck or hazard mine,
Whene'er we come to our account.

LIEUTENANT Sir, I beseech you, think you he'll carry
Rome?

AUFIDIUS All places yields to him ere he sits down,
And the nobility of Rome are his;
The senators and patricians love him too.
The tribunes are no soldiers, and their people
Will be as rash in the repeal, as hasty
To expel him thence. I think he'll be to Rome
As is the osprey to the fish, who takes it
By sovereignty of nature. First he was
A noble servant to them, but he could not

7 **using means** taking steps 11 **no changeling** i.e., he is the self-same man 13 **your particular** your own sake 14 **Joined in commission** shared the command 22 **husbandry** management 28 **sits down** lays siege 34 **osprey** fish hawk 35 **By sovereignty of nature** (refers to the osprey's supposed power of subduing its prey before touching it)

Carry his honors even. Whether 'twas pride,
Which out of daily fortune ever taints
The happy man; whether defect of judgment,
To fail in the disposing of those chances
Which he was lord of; or whether nature,
Not to be other than one thing, not moving
From th' casque to th' cushion, but commanding peace
Even with the same austerity and garb
As he controlled the war; but one of these—
As he hath spices of them all—not all,
For I dare so far free him—made him feared,
So hated, and so banished. But he has a merit
To choke it in the utt'rance. So our virtues
Lie in th' interpretation of the time;
And power, unto itself most commendable,
Hath not a tomb so evident as a chair
T' extol what it hath done.
One fire drives out one fire; one nail, one nail;
Rights by rights founder, strengths by strengths do fail.
Come, let's away. When, Caius, Rome is thine,
Thou art poor'st of all; then shortly art thou mine.
Exeunt.

37 **even** (and keep his balance) 38 **daily fortune ever taints** success coming day after day always infects 39 **happy** lucky 43 **casque** helmet, i.e., military life 43 **cushion** i.e., position of authority in civil life; cf. III.i.101 46 **spices** flavors, i.e., traces 48–49 **a merit/To choke it in the utt'rance** a merit that is nullified in the very act of being expressed (because of faults inseparable from the particular virtues being praised) 50 **the time** the age (our contemporaries) 52 **chair** (of the speaker who praises the achievements made possible by "power," line 51; probably with reference to the Roman rostrum, or speakers' platform) 54–55 **One fire . . . fail** (examples of the self-destructive process described in lines 48–53)

ACT V

[Scene I. *Rome. A public place.*]

Enter Menenius, Cominius, Sicinius, Brutus, the two Tribunes, with others.

MENENIUS No, I'll not go. You hear what he hath said
Which was sometime his general, who loved him
In a most dear particular. He called me father;
But what o' that? Go you that banished him,
A mile before his tent fall down, and knee
The way into his mercy. Nay, if he coyed
To hear Cominius speak, I'll keep at home.

COMINIUS He would not seem to know me.

MENENIUS Do you hear?

COMINIUS Yet one time he did call me by my name.
I urged our old acquaintance, and the drops
That we have bled together. Coriolanus
He would not answer to; forbad all names;
He was a kind of nothing, titleless,
Till he had forged himself a name o' th' fire
Of burning Rome.

V.i.2 **sometime** formerly 3 **a most dear particular** a most precious intimacy 5–6 **knee/The way** make your way on your knees 6 **coyed** showed reluctance

MENENIUS Why, so! You have made good work!
A pair of tribunes that have wracked fair Rome
To make coals cheap! A noble memory!

COMINIUS I minded him how royal 'twas to pardon
When it was less expected; he replied,
It was a bare petition of a state
To one whom they had punished.

MENENIUS Very well.
Could he say less?

COMINIUS I offered to awaken his regard
For's private friends. His answer to me was,
He could not stay to pick them in a pile
Of noisome musty chaff. He said 'twas folly,
For one poor grain or two, to leave unburnt
And still to nose th' offense.

MENENIUS For one poor grain or two!
I am one of those; his mother, wife, his child,
And this brave fellow too, we are the grains;
You are the musty chaff, and you are smelt
Above the moon. We must be burnt for you.

SICINIUS Nay, pray, be patient; if you refuse your aid
In this so never-needed help, yet do not
Upbraid's with our distress. But, sure, if you
Would be your country's pleader, your good tongue,
More than the instant army we can make,
Might stop our countryman.

MENENIUS No, I'll not meddle.

SICINIUS Pray you, go to him.

MENENIUS What should I do?

BRUTUS Only make trial what your love can do
For Rome, towards Marcius.

16 **wracked** ruined 17 **coals** charcoal 18 **minded** reminded 20 **bare** mere 23 **offered** tried 28 **nose th' offense** smell the offensive stuff 34 **so never-needed** never so needed (as now) 37 **the instant army we can make** the army we can raise at this time 41 **towards** in relation to

MENENIUS Well, and say that Marcius
Return me, as Cominius is returned,
Unheard—what then?
But as a discontented friend, grief-shot
With his unkindness? Say't be so?

SICINIUS Yet your good will
Must have that thanks from Rome after the measure
As you intended well.

MENENIUS I'll undertake't:
I think he'll hear me. Yet to bite his lip
And hum at good Cominius much unhearts me.
He was not taken well; he had not dined.
The veins unfilled, our blood is cold, and then
We pout upon the morning, are unapt
To give or to forgive; but when we have stuffed
These pipes and these conveyances of our blood
With wine and feeding, we have suppler souls
Than in our priestlike fasts. Therefore I'll watch him
Till he be dieted to my request,
And then I'll set upon him.

BRUTUS You know the very road into his kindness,
And cannot lose your way.

MENENIUS Good faith, I'll prove him,
Speed how it will. I shall ere long have knowledge
Of my success. *Exit.*

COMINIUS He'll never hear him.

SICINIUS Not?

COMINIUS I tell you he does sit in gold, his eye
Red as 'twould burn Rome, and his injury
The jailer to his pity. I kneeled before him;

44 **grief-shot** struck by grief 46–47 **after the measure/As you intended well** in proportion to your good intentions 49 **unhearts** discourages 50 **taken well** approached at a good time 54 **conveyances** channels 57 **dieted to** prepared for by feeding 60 **prove** make trial of 61 **Speed** turn out 64 **injury** sense of the wrong done to him

'Twas very faintly he said "Rise"; dismissed me
Thus with his speechless hand. What he would do
He sent in writing after me, what he would not,
Bound with an oath to yield to his conditions;
So that all hope is vain,
Unless his noble mother and his wife,
Who (as I hear) mean to solicit him
For mercy to his country. Therefore, let's hence,
And with our fair entreaties haste them on.
Exeunt.

[Scene II. *Entrance of the Volscian camp before Rome.*]

Enter Menenius to the Watch on Guard.

FIRST WATCH Stay. Whence are you?

SECOND WATCH Stand, and go back.

MENENIUS You guard like men, 'tis well; but, by your leave,
I am an officer of state, and come
To speak with Coriolanus.

FIRST WATCH From whence?

MENENIUS From Rome.

FIRST WATCH You may not pass, you must return: our general
Will no more hear from thence.

67–69 **What . . . yield** i.e., he sent a written message saying what he would do and what he would not, all this (the statement of terms) being bound with an oath that we should yield (text probably corrupt) 70 **vain** (because the conditions are ruinous) 71 **Unless** except for (or perhaps "solicit him," line 72, is to be understood: "unless his noble mother and his wife solicit him")

SECOND WATCH You'll see your Rome embraced with fire, before
You'll speak with Coriolanus.

MENENIUS Good my friends,
If you have heard your general talk of Rome
And of his friends there, it is lots to blanks
My name hath touched your ears: it is Menenius.

FIRST WATCH Be it so; go back. The virtue of your name
Is not here passable.

MENENIUS I tell thee, fellow,
Thy general is my lover. I have been
The book of his good acts whence men have read
His fame unparalleled—haply amplified;
For I have ever verified my friends
(Of whom he's chief) with all the size that verity
Would without lapsing suffer. Nay, sometimes,
Like to a bowl upon a subtle ground,
I have tumbled past the throw, and in his praise
Have almost stamped the leasing. Therefore, fellow,
I must have leave to pass.

FIRST WATCH Faith, sir, if you had told as many lies in his behalf as you have uttered words in your own, you should not pass here; no, though it were as virtuous to lie as to live chastely. Therefore go back.

MENENIUS Prithee, fellow, remember my name is Menenius, always factionary on the party of your general.

V.ii.10 **lots to blanks** (more than an even chance; "lots" refers to tickets in a lottery taking prizes; "blanks," to those not taking prizes) 13 **passable** current (of money, but with a pun on "password") 17 **verified** testified to the merit of 19 **lapsing** slipping (into error) 20 **subtle** deceptive 21 **tumbled past the throw** rolled beyond the proper distance 22 **stamped** given currency to (cf. "stamp" a coin) 22 **leasing** falsehood 30 **factionary** an active worker

SECOND WATCH Howsoever you have been his liar, as you say you have, I am one that, telling true under him, must say you cannot pass. Therefore go back.

MENENIUS Has he dined, canst thou tell? For I would not speak with him till after dinner.

FIRST WATCH You are a Roman, are you?

MENENIUS I am, as thy general is.

FIRST WATCH Then you should hate Rome, as he does. Can you, when you have pushed out your gates the very defender of them, and in a violent popular ignorance given your enemy your shield, think to front his revenges with the easy groans of old women, the virginal palms of your daughters, or with the palsied intercession of such a decayed dotant as you seem to be? Can you think to blow out the intended fire your city is ready to flame in, with such weak breath as this? No, you are deceived; therefore, back to Rome, and prepare for your execution. You are condemned; our general has sworn you out of reprieve and pardon.

MENENIUS Sirrah, if thy captain knew I were here, he would use me with estimation.

FIRST WATCH Come, my captain knows you not.

MENENIUS I mean, thy general.

FIRST WATCH My general cares not for you. Back, I say; go, lest I let forth your half-pint of blood. Back—that's the utmost of your having. Back.

MENENIUS Nay, but, fellow, fellow——

Enter Coriolanus with Aufidius.

CORIOLANUS What's the matter?

MENENIUS Now, you companion, I'll say an errand

43 **front** face 46 **dotant** dotard 53 **estimation** esteem 58 **of your having** you can get 61 **companion** fellow 61 **say an errand** give a message

for you; you shall know now that I am in estimation; you shall perceive that a Jack guardant cannot office me from my son Coriolanus. Guess but by my entertainment with him if thou stand'st not i' th' state of hanging, or of some death more long in spectatorship and crueller in suffering; behold now presently, and swoon for what's to come upon thee. [*To Coriolanus*] The glorious gods sit in hourly synod about thy particular prosperity, and love thee no worse than thy old father Menenius does! O my son, my son! Thou art preparing fire for us; look thee, here's water to quench it. I was hardly moved to come to thee; but being assured none but myself could move thee, I have been blown out of your gates with sighs; and conjure thee to pardon Rome and thy petitionary countrymen. The good gods assuage thy wrath, and turn the dregs of it upon this varlet here; this, who, like a block, hath denied my access to thee.

CORIOLANUS Away!

MENENIUS How! Away!

CORIOLANUS Wife, mother, child, I know not. My affairs
Are servanted to others. Though I owe
My revenge properly, my remission lies
In Volscian breasts. That we have been familiar,
Ingrate forgetfulness shall poison rather
Than pity note how much. Therefore be gone.
Mine ears against your suits are stronger than
Your gates against my force. Yet, for I loved thee,
Take this along; I writ it for thy sake,

63 **Jack guardant** wretch of a sentry 64 **office me** use his office to keep me 65 **entertainment** reception 74 **hardly** with difficulty 76 **your** (of Rome) 77 **petitionary** who are asking for mercy 80 **block** blockhead 84 **servanted** subject (servant-like) 84–85 **I owe/My revenge properly** my revenge belongs to me alone 85 **remission** power to pardon 86 **That we have been familiar** our intimacy in the past 87 **Ingrate forgetfulness** my ungrateful forgetfulness 88 **how much** (how much "we have been familiar," how great the intimacy was) 90 **for** because

And would have sent it. Another word, Menenius,
I will not hear thee speak. This man, Aufidius,
Was my beloved in Rome; yet thou behold'st.

AUFIDIUS You keep a constant temper.

Exeunt [*Coriolanus and Aufidius*].
Manet the Guard and Menenius.

FIRST WATCH Now, sir, is your name Menenius?

SECOND WATCH 'Tis a spell, you see, of much power. You know the way home again.

FIRST WATCH Do you hear how we are shent for keeping your greatness back?

SECOND WATCH What cause, do you think, I have to swoon?

MENENIUS I neither care for th' world nor your general. For such things as you, I can scarce think there's any, y'are so slight. He that hath a will to die by himself fears it not from another. Let your general do his worst. For you, be that you are, long; and your misery increase with your age! I say to you, as I was said to, Away! *Exit.*

FIRST WATCH A noble fellow, I warrant him.

SECOND WATCH The worthy fellow is our general. He's the rock, the oak not to be wind-shaken.

Exit Watch.

95 **constant** loyal, true 99 **shent** scolded 106 **by himself** by his own hand

[Scene III. *The tent of Coriolanus.*]

Enter Coriolanus and Aufidius [*with others*].

CORIOLANUS We will before the walls of Rome tomorrow
Set down our host. My partner in this action,
You must report to th' Volscian lords how plainly
I have borne this business.

AUFIDIUS Only their ends
You have respected; stopped your ears against
The general suit of Rome; never admitted
A private whisper—no, not with such friends
That thought them sure of you.

CORIOLANUS This last old man,
Whom with a cracked heart I have sent to Rome,
Loved me above the measure of a father,
Nay, godded me indeed. Their latest refuge
Was to send him; for whose old love I have
(Though I showed sourly to him) once more offered
The first conditions, which they did refuse
And cannot now accept; to grace him only
That thought he could do more, a very little
I have yielded to. Fresh embassies and suits,
Nor from the state nor private friends, hereafter
Will I lend ear to. (*Shout within.*) Ha! What shout is this?
Shall I be tempted to infringe my vow
In the same time 'tis made? I will not.

V.iii.2 **Set down** i.e., in a siege 3 **plainly** openly 4 **borne** conducted 11 **godded me** made me a god 11 **latest refuge** last resource 13 **showed** appeared 15 **grace** honor 18 **Nor** neither

Enter Virgilia, Volumnia, Valeria, young Marcius, with Attendants.

My wife comes foremost; then the honored mold
Wherein this trunk was framed, and in her hand
The grandchild to her blood. But out, affection!
All bond and privilege of nature, break!
Let it be virtuous to be obstinate.
What is that curtsy worth? Or those doves' eyes,
Which can make gods forsworn? I melt, and am not
Of stronger earth than others. My mother bows,
As if Olympus to a molehill should
In supplication nod; and my young boy
Hath an aspect of intercession which
Great Nature cries "Deny not." Let the Volsces
Plough Rome, and harrow Italy! I'll never
Be such a gosling to obey instinct, but stand
As if a man were author of himself
And knew no other kin.

VIRGILIA My lord and husband!

CORIOLANUS These eyes are not the same I wore in Rome.

VIRGILIA The sorrow that delivers us thus changed
Makes you think so.

CORIOLANUS Like a dull actor now,
I have forgot my part and I am out,
Even to a full disgrace.—Best of my flesh,
Forgive my tyranny; but do not say,
For that, "Forgive our Romans." O, a kiss
Long as my exile, sweet as my revenge!
Now, by the jealous queen of heaven, that kiss
I carried from thee, dear, and my true lip
Hath virgined it e'er since. You gods! I prate,
And the most noble mother of the world

22 **mold** form (also "earth") 23 **trunk** body 28–29 **not/Of stronger earth** cf. "our common clay" 30 **Olympus** a mountain, home of the Greek gods 35 **to** as to 39 **delivers** presents 41 **out** speechless ("stuck") 43 **tyranny** cruelty 46 **queen of heaven** Juno, guardian of marriage 48 **prate** babble

Leave unsaluted. Sink, my knee, i' th' earth; [*Kneels.*]
Of thy deep duty more impression show
Than that of common sons.

VOLUMNIA O, stand up blest!
Whilst with no softer cushion than the flint
I kneel before thee, and unproperly
Show duty, as mistaken all this while
Between the child and parent. [*Kneels.*]

CORIOLANUS What's this?
Your knees to me? To your corrected son?
Then let the pebbles on the hungry beach
Fillip the stars! Then let the mutinous winds
Strike the proud cedars 'gainst the fiery sun,
Murd'ring impossibility, to make
What cannot be, slight work.

VOLUMNIA Thou art my warrior;
I holp to frame thee. Do you know this lady?

CORIOLANUS The noble sister of Publicola,
The moon of Rome, chaste as the icicle
That's curdied by the frost from purest snow
And hangs on Dian's temple—dear Valeria!

VOLUMNIA This is a poor epitome of yours,
Which by th' interpretation of full time
May show like all yourself.

CORIOLANUS The god of soldiers,
With the consent of supreme Jove, inform
Thy thoughts with nobleness, that thou mayst
prove
To shame unvulnerable, and stick i' th' wars

51 **duty** reverence 51 **impression** i.e., "i' th' earth" 54 **unproperly** (defined by lines 55–56: in a way that does not belong to me, as though I had always misunderstood the relation between child and parent) 57 **corrected** who is corrected (by your kneeling) 58 **hungry** barren 59 **Fillip** strike 66 **curdied** congealed 68 **epitome** brief but comprehensive version of a larger work 68 **of yours** belonging to you, of you 69 **time** ("time" is compared to a commentator on a text) 70 **show** appear 70 **god of soldiers** Mars, Coriolanus' special divinity 71 **inform** imbue (give an inner form or character to) 73 **stick** stand out

Like a great sea-mark, standing every flaw,
And saving those that eye thee!

VOLUMNIA Your knee, sirrah.

CORIOLANUS That's my brave boy!

VOLUMNIA Even he, your wife, this lady, and myself
Are suitors to you.

CORIOLANUS I beseech you, peace!
Or, if you'd ask, remember this before:
The thing I have forsworn to grant may never
Be held by you denials. Do not bid me
Dismiss my soldiers, or capitulate
Again with Rome's mechanics. Tell me not
Wherein I seem unnatural. Desire not
T' allay my rages and revenges with
Your colder reasons.

VOLUMNIA O, no more, no more!
You have said you will not grant us anything;
For we have nothing else to ask but that
Which you deny already. Yet we will ask,
That, if you fail in our request, the blame
May hang upon your hardness. Therefore hear us.

CORIOLANUS Aufidius, and you Volsces, mark; for we'll
Hear nought from Rome in private. Your request?

VOLUMNIA Should we be silent and not speak, our raiment
And state of bodies would bewray what life
We have led since thy exile. Think with thyself
How more unfortunate than all living women
Are we come hither; since that thy sight, which should

74 **a great sea-mark** some prominent object that guides mariners (cf. "land-mark," the common modern term) 74 **flaw** gust of wind 75 **sirrah** sir (affectionately) 80 **forsworn** sworn not to 81 **denials** i.e., refusals to all of you (therefore, plural) 82 **capitulate** arrange terms 83 **mechanics** manual laborers 90 **fall in** fail to grant 95 **bewray** reveal

Make our eyes flow with joy, hearts dance with comforts,
Constrains them weep and shake with fear and sorrow,
Making the mother, wife, and child, to see
The son, the husband, and the father, tearing
His country's bowels out. And to poor we
Thine enmity's most capital: thou barr'st us
Our prayers to the gods, which is a comfort
That all but we enjoy. For how can we,
Alas, how can we for our country pray,
Whereto we are bound, together with thy victory,
Whereto we are bound? Alack, or we must lose
The country, our dear nurse, or else thy person,
Our comfort in the country. We must find
An evident calamity, though we had
Our wish, which side should win; for either thou
Must as a foreign recreant be led
With manacles through our streets, or else
Triumphantly tread on thy country's ruin,
And bear the palm for having bravely shed
Thy wife and children's blood. For myself, son,
I purpose not to wait on fortune till
These wars determine. If I can not persuade thee
Rather to show a noble grace to both parts
Than seek the end of one, thou shalt no sooner
March to assault thy country than to tread
(Trust to't, thou shalt not) on thy mother's womb
That brought thee to this world.

VIRGILIA. Ay, and mine,
That brought you forth this boy, to keep your name
Living to time.

BOY 'A shall not tread on me;
I'll run away till I am bigger, but then I'll fight.

103 **we** (for "us") 104 **capital** deadly 109 **or** either 112 **evident** certain 114 **recreant** traitor 120 **determine** come to an end 121 **grace** consideration, favor 121 **parts** sides (parties) 126–27 **keep your name/ Living to time** perpetuate your name (keep living as long as time lasts) 127 **'A** he

CORIOLANUS Not of a woman's tenderness to be,
Requires nor child nor woman's face to see.
I have sat too long.

VOLUMNIA Nay, go not from us thus.
[*Rises.*]
If it were so that our request did tend
To save the Romans, thereby to destroy
The Volsces whom you serve, you might condemn us,
As poisonous of your honor. No, our suit
Is that you reconcile them; while the Volsces
May say "This mercy we have showed," the Romans,
"This we received"; and each in either side
Give the all-hail to thee, and cry "Be blest
For making up this peace!" Thou know'st, great son,
The end of war's uncertain; but this certain,
That, if thou conquer Rome, the benefit
Which thou shalt thereby reap is such a name
Whose repetition will be dogged with curses,
Whose chronicle thus writ, "The man was noble,
But with his last attempt he wiped it out,
Destroyed his country, and his name remains
To th' ensuing age abhorred." Speak to me, son.
Thou hast affected the fine strains of honor,
To imitate the graces of the gods,
To tear with thunder the wide cheeks o' th' air,
And yet to charge thy sulphur with a bolt
That should but rive an oak. Why dost not speak?
Think'st thou it honorable for a noble man
Still to remember wrongs? Daughter, speak you:
He cares not for your weeping. Speak thou, boy:
Perhaps thy childishness will move him more

145 **writ** will be written 146 **attempt** undertaking 146 **it** (his nobility) 149 **affected the fine strains** aimed at the refinements 150 **graces of the gods** (qualities that give the gods splendor and power; illustrated with irony, lines 151–53) 152 **charge** load (make heavy, or "load," as of a gun) 152 **sulphur** lightning

Than can our reasons. There's no man in the world
More bound to's mother, yet here he lets me prate
Like one i' th' stocks. Thou hast never in thy life
Showed thy dear mother any courtesy,
When she (poor hen) fond of no second brood,
Has clocked thee to the wars, and safely home
Loaden with honor. Say my request's unjust,
And spurn me back. But if it be not so,
Thou art not honest, and the gods will plague thee,
That thou restrain'st from me the duty which
To a mother's part belongs. He turns away.
Down, ladies! Let us shame him with our knees.
To his surname Coriolanus 'longs more pride
Than pity to our prayers. Down! An end;
This is the last. So we will home to Rome,
And die among our neighbors. Nay, behold's!
This boy, that cannot tell what he would have,
But kneels and holds up hands for fellowship,
Does reason our petition with more strength
Than thou hast to deny't. Come, let us go.
This fellow had a Volscian to his mother;
His wife is in Corioles, and his child
Like him by chance. Yet give us our dispatch.
I am hushed until our city be a-fire,
And then I'll speak a little.

Holds her by the hand, silent.

CORIOLANUS O mother, mother!
What have you done? Behold, the heavens do ope,
The gods look down, and this unnatural scene
They laugh at. O my mother, mother! O!
You have won a happy victory to Rome;
But, for your son—believe it, O, believe it!—
Most dangerously you have with him prevailed,
If not most mortal to him. But let it come.
Aufidius, though I cannot make true wars,
I'll frame convenient peace. Now, good Aufidius,

162 **fond of** eager for 163 **clocked** clucked 164 **Loaden** laden 166 **honest** honorable 173 **behold's** behold us 176 **reason** plead for 180 **dispatch** dismissal 189 **mortal to** with deadly results for 191 **convenient** fitting

Were you in my stead, would you have heard
A mother less? Or granted less, Aufidius?

AUFIDIUS I was moved withal.

CORIOLANUS I dare be sworn you were!
And, sir, it is no little thing to make
Mine eyes to sweat compassion. But, good sir,
What peace you'll make, advise me. For my part,
I'll not to Rome, I'll back with you; and pray you
Stand to me in this cause. O mother! Wife!

AUFIDIUS [*Aside*] I am glad thou hast set thy mercy and thy honor
At difference in thee. Out of that I'll work
Myself a former fortune.

CORIOLANUS [*To Volumnia and Virgilia*] Ay, by and by;
But we will drink together; and you shall bear
A better witness back than words, which we
On like conditions will have countersealed.
Come, enter with us. Ladies, you deserve
To have a temple built you. All the swords
In Italy, and her confederate arms,
Could not have made this peace. *Exeunt.*

[Scene IV. *Rome. A public place.*]

Enter Menenius and Sicinius.

MENENIUS See you yond coign o' th' Capitol, yond cornerstone?

194 **withal** by it (thereby) 199 **Stand to** stand by 201–02 **work/Myself a former fortune** regain my former position and power 204 **which** i.e., the written document 207 **temple** (of the Fortune of Women; see Plutarch, p. 246) 208 **confederate arms** allied powers. V.iv.1 **coign** corner

SICINIUS Why, what of that?

MENENIUS If it be possible for you to displace it with your little finger, there is some hope the ladies of Rome, especially his mother, may prevail with him. But I say there is no hope in't; our throats are sentenced, and stay upon execution.

SICINIUS Is't possible that so short a time can alter the condition of a man?

MENENIUS There is differency between a grub and a butterfly; yet your butterfly was a grub. This Marcius is grown from man to dragon: he has wings; he's more than a creeping thing.

SICINIUS He loved his mother dearly.

MENENIUS So did he me; and he no more remembers his mother now than an eight-year-old horse. The tartness of his face sours ripe grapes. When he walks, he moves like an engine and the ground shrinks before his treading. He is able to pierce a corslet with his eye, talks like a knell, and his hum is a battery. He sits in his state as a thing made for Alexander. What he bids be done is finished with his bidding. He wants nothing of a god but eternity and a heaven to throne in.

SICINIUS Yes, mercy, if you report him truly.

MENENIUS I paint him in the character. Mark what mercy his mother shall bring from him . There is no more mercy in him than there is milk in a male tiger; that shall our poor city find. And all this is 'long of you.

SICINIUS The gods be good unto us!

MENENIUS No, in such a case the gods will not be

8 **stay upon** wait for 19 **engine** machine of war 21 **corslet** body armor 21–22 **his hum** i.e., his saying "Hum!" 22 **battery** beating of drums for an attack 22 **state** chair of state 22–23 **thing made for Alexander** image of Alexander the Great 31 **'long of** along of, because of

good unto us. When we banished him, we respected not them; and, he returning to break our necks, they respect not us.

Enter a Messenger.

MESSENGER Sir, if you'd save your life, fly to your house.
The plebeians have got your fellow-tribune,
And hale him up and down; all swearing if
The Roman ladies bring not comfort home
They'll give him death by inches.

Enter another Messenger.

SICINIUS What's the news?

SECOND MESSENGER Good news, good news! The ladies have prevailed,
The Volscians are dislodged, and Marcius gone.
A merrier day did never yet greet Rome,
No, not th' expulsion of the Tarquins.

SICINIUS Friend,
Art thou certain this is true? Is't most certain?

SECOND MESSENGER As certain as I know the sun is fire.
Where have you lurked, that you make doubt of it?
Ne'er through an arch so hurried the blown tide,
As the recomforted through th' gates. Why, hark you!

Trumpets, hautboys; drums beat; all together.

The trumpets, sackbuts, psalteries, and fifes,
Tabors and cymbals, and the shouting Romans,
Make the sun dance. Hark you! (*A shout within.*)

MENENIUS This is good news.
I will go meet the ladies. This Volumnia
Is worth of consuls, senators, patricians,

39 **hale** haul 43 **are dislodged** have broken up camp 48 **lurked** been hiding 49 **blown** swollen (by wind) 50 s.d. **hautboy** (original of the modern oboe) 51 **sackbuts** trombones 51 **psalteries** harp-like stringed instruments 52 **Tabors** small drums

A city full; of tribunes such as you,
A sea and land full. You have prayed well today.
This morning for ten thousand of your throats
I'd not have given a doit. Hark, how they joy!

Sound still with the shouts.

SICINIUS First, the gods bless you for your tidings; next,
Accept my thankfulness.

SECOND MESSENGER Sir, we have all
Great cause to give great thanks.

SICINIUS They are near the city!

SECOND MESSENGER Almost at point to enter.

SICINIUS We'll meet them,
And help the joy. *Exeunt.*

[Scene V. *Rome. Near the gate.*]

Enter two Senators, with Ladies, passing over the Stage, with other Lords.

FIRST SENATOR Behold our patroness, the life of Rome!
Call all your tribes together, praise the gods,
And make triumphant fires; strew flowers before them.
Unshout the noise that banished Marcius,
Repeal him with the welcome of his mother.
Cry "Welcome, ladies, welcome!"

ALL Welcome, ladies,
Welcome!

A flourish with drums and trumpets.

V.v.5 **Repeal** recall

[Scene VI. *Corioli. A public place.*]

Enter Tullus Aufidius, with Attendants.

AUFIDIUS Go tell the lords o' th' city I am here.
Deliver them this paper. Having read it,
Bid them repair to th' marketplace, where I,
Even in theirs and in the commons' ears,
Will vouch the truth of it. Him I accuse
The city ports by this hath entered, and
Intends t' appear before the people, hoping
To purge himself with words. Dispatch.
[*Exeunt Attendants.*]

Enter three or four Conspirators of Aufidius' faction.

Most welcome!

FIRST CONSPIRATOR How is it with our general?

AUFIDIUS Even so
As with a man by his own alms empoisoned,
And with his charity slain.

SECOND CONSPIRATOR Most noble sir,
If you do hold the same intent wherein
You wished us parties, we'll deliver you
Of your great danger.

AUFIDIUS Sir, I cannot tell;
We must proceed as we do find the people.

THIRD CONSPIRATOR The people will remain uncertain whilst
'Twixt you there's difference; but the fall of either
Makes the survivor heir of all.

V.vi.5 **Him** he whom 6 **ports** gates 11 **empoisoned** destroyed 12 **with** by 14 **parties** partisans

AUFIDIUS I know it,
And my pretext to strike at him admits
A good construction. I raised him, and I pawned
Mine honor for his truth; who being so heightened,
He watered his new plants with dews of flattery,
Seducing so my friends; and, to this end,
He bowed his nature, never known before
But to be rough, unswayable, and free.

THIRD CONSPIRATOR Sir, his stoutness
When he did stand for consul, which he lost
By lack of stooping——

AUFIDIUS That I would have spoke of.
Being banished for't, he came unto my hearth,
Presented to my knife his throat. I took him,
Made him joint-servant with me; gave him way
In all his own desires; nay, let him choose
Out of my files, his projects to accomplish,
My best and freshest men; served his designments
In mine own person; holp to reap the fame
Which he did end all his; and took some pride
To do myself this wrong; till at the last
I seemed his follower, not partner; and
He waged me with his countenance, as if
I had been mercenary.

FIRST CONSPIRATOR So he did, my lord.
The army marveled at it; and, in the last,
When he had carried Rome and that we looked
For no less spoil than glory——

AUFIDIUS There was it;
For which my sinews shall be stretched upon him.
At a few drops of women's rheum, which are

21 **pawned** staked 22 **truth** loyalty 27 **stoutness** proud obstinacy 32 **joint-servant with me** sharer of my service (to the state) 32 **gave him way** humored him 34 **files** ranks 35 **designments** designs 37 **end** get in (of crops) 40 **waged me with his countenance** for wages gave me patronizing looks 41 **mercenary** serving for pay 42 **in the last** in the last place, finally 43 **carried** won 44 **There was it** that was the crucial thing 45 **sinews** i.e., strength 45 **upon** against 46 **At** at the price of 46 **rheum** tears

As cheap as lies, he sold the blood and labor
Of our great action. Therefore shall he die,
And I'll renew me in his fall. But hark!

Drums and trumpets sounds, with great shouts of the people.

FIRST CONSPIRATOR Your native town you entered like a post,
And had no welcomes home; but he returns,
Splitting the air with noise.

SECOND CONSPIRATOR And patient fools,
Whose children he hath slain, their base throats tear
With giving him glory.

THIRD CONSPIRATOR Therefore, at your vantage,
Ere he express himself or move the people
With what he would say, let him feel your sword,
Which we will second. When he lies along,
After your way his tale pronounced shall bury
His reasons with his body.

AUFIDIUS Say no more:
Here come the lords.

Enter the Lords of the city.

ALL LORDS You are most welcome home.

AUFIDIUS I have not deserved it.
But, worthy lords, have you with heed perused
What I have written to you?

ALL [LORDS] We have.

FIRST LORD And grieve to hear't.
What faults he made before the last, I think
Might have found easy fines; but there to end
Where he was to begin, and give away

50 **post** messenger 54 **at your vantage** at a moment opportune for you 57 **second** support (with our swords) 57 **along** stretched at full length 58 **After your way his tale pronounced** his story told in your version 65 **fines** penalties

The benefit of our levies, answering us
With our own charge, making a treaty where
There was a yielding—this admits no excuse.

AUFIDIUS He approaches. You shall hear him.

Enter Coriolanus, marching with drum and colors, the commoners being with him.

CORIOLANUS Hail, lords! I am returned your soldier;
No more infected with my country's love
Than when I parted hence, but still subsisting
Under your great command. You are to know
That prosperously I have attempted, and
With bloody passage led your wars even to
The gates of Rome. Our spoils we have brought home
Doth more than counterpoise a full third part
The charges of the action. We have made peace
With no less honor to the Antiates
Than shame to th' Romans; and we here deliver,
Subscribed by th' consuls and patricians,
Together with the seal o' th' senate, what
We have compounded on.

AUFIDIUS Read it not, noble lords;
But tell the traitor in the highest degree
He hath abused your powers.

CORIOLANUS Traitor! How now!

AUFIDIUS Ay, traitor, Marcius!

CORIOLANUS Marcius!

AUFIDIUS Ay, Marcius, Caius Marcius! Dost thou think
I'll grace thee with that robbery, thy stol'n name
Coriolanus, in Corioles?

67 **our levies** the armies we raised 67–68 **answering us/With our own charge** paying us (only) with our own expenditure 73 **parted** departed 73 **subsisting** remaining 76 **passage** action 78–79 **more ... charges** exceed the costs by a whole third (cf. line 68) 82 **Subscribed** signed 84 **compounded** agreed 89 **grace** honor

You lords and heads o' th' state, perfidiously
He has betrayed your business and given up,
For certain drops of salt, your city Rome,
I say "your city," to his wife and mother;
Breaking his oath and resolution, like
A twist of rotten silk; never admitting
Counsel o' th' war; but at his nurse's tears
He whined and roared away your victory;
That pages blushed at him, and men of heart
Looked wond'ring each at others.

CORIOLANUS Hear'st thou, Mars?

AUFIDIUS Name not the god, thou boy of tears!

CORIOLANUS Ha!

AUFIDIUS No more.

CORIOLANUS Measureless liar, thou hast made my heart
Too great for what contains it. "Boy"! O slave!
Pardon me, lords, 'tis the first time that ever
I was forced to scold. Your judgments, my grave lords,
Must give this cur the lie; and his own notion—
Who wears my stripes impressed upon him, that
Must bear my beating to his grave—shall join
To thrust the lie unto him.

FIRST LORD Peace, both, and hear me speak.

CORIOLANUS Cut me to pieces, Volsces, men and lads,
Stain all your edges on me. "Boy"! False hound!
If you have writ your annals true, 'tis there,
That, like an eagle in a dovecote, I
Fluttered your Volscians in Corioles.
Alone I did it. "Boy"?

AUFIDIUS Why, noble lords,

96 twist thread (made of more than one strand) **99 That** so that **99 of heart** of spirit **107 notion** understanding **114 there** (written) there

Will you be put in mind of his blind fortune,
Which was your shame, by this unholy braggart,
'Fore your own eyes and ears?

ALL CONSPIRATORS Let him die for't.

ALL PEOPLE Tear him to pieces!—Do it presently!—
He killed my son!—My daughter!—He killed my cousin Marcius!—He killed my father!

SECOND LORD Peace, ho! no outrage, peace!
The man is noble, and his fame folds in
This orb o' th' earth. His last offenses to us
Shall have judicious hearing. Stand, Aufidius,
And trouble not the peace.

CORIOLANUS O that I had him,
With six Aufidiuses or more—his tribe,
To use my lawful sword!

AUFIDIUS Insolent villain!

ALL CONSPIRATORS Kill, kill, kill, kill, kill him!

Draw the Conspirators and kills Marcius, who falls. Aufidius stands on him.

LORDS Hold, hold, hold, hold!

AUFIDIUS My noble masters, hear me speak.

FIRST LORD O Tullus!

SECOND LORD Thou hast done a deed whereat valor will weep.

THIRD LORD Tread not upon him. Masters all, be quiet;
Put up your swords.

AUFIDIUS My lords, when you shall know—as in this rage
Provoked by him, you cannot—the great danger
Which this man's life did owe you, you'll rejoice

118 **blind fortune** mere good luck (Fortune is a blind goddess) 121 **presently** at once 125 **folds in** embraces 127 **judicious** judicial 127 **Stand** stop 138 **did owe you** held in payment for you

That he is thus cut off. Please it your honors
To call me to your senate, I'll deliver
Myself your loyal servant, or endure
Your heaviest censure.

FIRST LORD Bear from hence his body,
And mourn you for him. Let him be regarded
As the most noble corse that ever herald
Did follow to his urn.

SECOND LORD His own impatience
Takes from Aufidius a great part of blame.
Let's make the best of it.

AUFIDIUS My rage is gone,
And I am struck with sorrow. Take him up.
Help, three o' th' chiefest soldiers; I'll be one.
Beat thou the drum, that it speak mournfully;
Trail your steel pikes. Though in this city he
Hath widowed and unchilded many a one,
Which to this hour bewail the injury,
Yet he shall have a noble memory.
Assist.

Exeunt bearing the body of Marcius.
A dead march sounded.

FINIS

140 deliver prove **142 censure** sentence **144 corse** corpse **154 memory** memorial

Textual Note

The text of *Coriolanus* has survived only in the First Folio (1623), on which the present edition is based. There are no records of performances earlier than 1623, but there is a mocking imitation of the curious phrase, "lurched all swords of the garland" (II.ii.102), in Ben Jonson's *Epicoene, or The Silent Woman* (1609). It is therefore almost certain that the play was written and performed not later than 1609. The use in Menenius' fable of the body and its members of expressions from William Camden's *Remains* of 1605 and the probable allusion to the Midlands revolt of 1607, point to a date of 1607 or later. There is also the possible reference to the Great Frost of 1607–08 in the phrase "the coal of fire upon the ice" (I.i.174). It seems safe to assume that *Coriolanus* was written after *Antony and Cleopatra*, somewhere between 1607 and 1609.

The Folio text of *Coriolanus* might be described, like that of *The Tempest*, as a distinguished one; it was prepared with great care and is especially remarkable for its elaborate stage directions. W. W. Greg's assertion that the text was printed from the author's manuscript is now widely accepted. The stage directions, presumably Shakespeare's own, are those of a man of the theater who has his eye on the stage and the actors. For example: "*Enter Marcius and Aufidius, at several doors*" (I.viii); "*They all bustle about Coriolanus*" (III.i.184); and the most telling gesture of the play, "*Holds her by the hand, silent*" (V.iii.182).

But though the text brings us so close to the practicing hand of the poet-playwright, it was edited and printed by mortal men. It has a fairly high number of errors, and emendations have been found necessary in at least twenty to twenty-five places. One line has been omitted (II.iii.249), and in two passages the style is so cryptic as to seem almost surely corrupt (III.ii.74–80; V.i.67–69). The most disturbing defect of the Folio text of *Coriolanus* is the widespread mislineation. There are many lines that are either too short or too long, as measured by the usual blank-verse norm, and it is often very hard to determine where the line division should occur. Most of these abnormalities, it has been pointed out, come in short speeches, or at the end or beginning of speeches in rapid dialogue. There are a relatively few instances in which speeches are assigned to seemingly inappropriate speakers. There are also variations in the names of speakers, most of them of little significance, and usually in names of minor persons. The town that gives the hero his honorific title is usually called "Corioles," though "Coriolus" and "Corialus" also occur. There is considerable uncertainty as to how both "Corioles" and "Coriolanus" are to be accented. The common reader, like the learned editor, is free to follow his rhythmic sense in particular lines: "Corīoles" or "Coriōles"? "Coriolānus" (the usual pronunciation) or "Corīolanus"?

The present edition follows the Folio text closely, but spelling and punctuation are modernized, abbreviations are amplified, names of speakers regularized, and some stage directions are moved slightly. The act divisions (translated from Latin) are those of the Folio; no scenes, except the first, are indicated in the Folio text. All other scene divisions printed here (in square brackets) are those of the Globe edition. The list of readings given in the following table includes only those words in the Folio that have been omitted or emended. The reading adopted in this edition is printed in bold, followed by the original reading in roman.

I.i.7 **Marcius** Martius (throughout the play) 16 **on** one 28 **First Citizen** All 35 **Second Citizen** All 58 **First Citizen** 2 Cit. (throughout the rest of Scene i) 93 **stale't** scale't 111 **tauntingly** taintingly 215 **Shouting** Shooting 219 **unroofed** vnroo'st 227 s.d. **Junius** Annius 240 **Lartius** Lucius

I.ii. s.d. **Corioles** Coriolus 4 **on** one 30 **They've** Th'haue

I.iii.39 **that's** that 46 **sword, contemning. Tell** sword. Contenning, tell 85 **Virgilia** Vlug. 87 **yarn** yearne 88 **Ithaca** Athica 102 **whom** who

TEXTUAL NOTE

I.iv. s.d., 12s.d. **Corioles** Corialus 31 **herd of—boils** Heard of Byles 42 **trenches. Follow's** Trenches followes 45 s.d. **Enters the gates** Enter the Gati 57 **Were** Weare 58 **Cato's** Calues

I.vi.21 **Who's** Whose 22 **flayed** Flead 53 **Antiates** Antients 70 **Lesser** Lessen

I.viii.7 **Holloa** hollow

I.ix.46 **coverture** Ouerture 50 **shout** shoot 65 **Caius Marcius** Marcus Caius (in this order throughout)

I.x.30 **cypress** Cyprus

II.i.24 **how are** ho ware 58 **cannot** can 63 **you you** you 66 **bisson** beesome 171 **Coriolanus** Martius Caius Coriolanus 184 **wear** were 186 **Coriolanus** Com. 192 **you** yon 210 s.d. **Brutus** Enter Brutus 219 **flamens** Plamins 240 **napless** Naples 261 **touch** teach

II.ii.26 **ascent** assent 51 **state's** states 82 **one on's** on ones 92 **chin** Shinne 93 **bristled** brizled

II.iii.29 **wedged** wadg'd 44 **all together** altogether 71 **Ay, not** I, but 119 **hire** higher 120 **toge** tongue 249 **And Censorinus that was so surnamed** [F omits. This line, invented by N. Delius in his edition of 1872, is indebted to Plutarch. 260 **Citizens** All

III.i.33 **herd** Heard 48 **Coriolanus** Com. 91 **good** God! 92 **reckless** wreaklesse 126 **Their** There 143 **Where one** Whereon 185 **All** [F has no speech prefix here, but gives "All" before line 187] 214 **All [Citizens]** All Ple. 228 **him!** him. Exeunt. 229 **your** our 230 **Coriolanus** Com. 236 **Cominius** Corio. 237 **Coriolanus** Mene. [speech assigned to Menenius through line 241] 239 **Menenius** [see preceding note] 286 **our** one 322 **bring him** bring him in peace

III.ii.21 **thwartings** things 32 **herd** heart 55 **roted** roated 115 **lulls** lull

III.iii.32 **for th'** fourth 36 **Throng** Through 55 **accents** Actions 89 **flaying** Fleaing 99 **do** doth 110 **for** from 135 s.d. **The other Senators** Cumalijs

IV.i.24 **thee** the 34 **Whither wilt** Whether will

IV.iii.35 **will** well

IV.iv.23 **hate** haue

IV.v.3 **master** M. 82 **Whooped** Hoop'd 98 **Thou'rt** Th'art 113 **clip** cleep 183 **lief** liue 236 **sleepy** sleepe

IV.vi.4 **do** do we 34 **lamentation** Lamention 90 **wi'** th'

IV.vii.34 **osprey** Aspray 37 **'twas** 'was 39 **defect** detect 49 **virtues** Vertue 55 **founder** fouler

V.i.16 **wracked fair** Wrack'd for
with 138 **one** oue

TEXTUAL NOTE

V.ii.s.d. **on** or 16 **haply** happely 61 **errand** arrant 64–65 **but by me** but my 102 **swoon** swoond

V.iii.48 **prate** pray 63 **holp** hope 104 **enmity's** enmities 141 **war's** Warres 149 **fine** fiue 152 **charge** change 169 **him with** him with him with 192 **stead** steed

V.iv.50 s.d. **all together** altogether

V.v.4 **Unshout** Vnshoot

V.vi.116 **Fluttered** Flatter'd 131 s.d. **the Conspirators** both the Conspirators

ABOUT THE INTRODUCER

TONY TANNER is Professor of English and American Literature in Cambridge University, and Fellow of King's College. Previous publications include *The Reign of Wonder*, *City of Words*, *Adultery and the Novel*, and *Venice Desired*. He has also published studies of Jane Austen, Henry James, Saul Bellow and Thomas Pynchon.